HEROES
of
Conscience:
A Biographical Dictionary

HEROES
of
Conscience:
A Biographical Dictionary

Kathlyn Gay
Martin K. Gay

ABC-CLIO

Library of Congress Cataloging-in-Publication Data

Gay, Kathlyn.
    Heroes of conscience : a biographical dictionary / Kathlyn Gay,
    Martin K. Gay.
        p. cm.
    Includes bibliographical references and index.
        1. Heroes—Biography—Dictionaries.   I. Gay, Martin, 1950– .
    II. Title.
CT120.G36 1996   920.02—dc20 96-26370

ISBN 0-87436-874-X

02 01 00 99 98 97 96   10 9 8 7 6 5 4 3 2 1

Photographs were provided by the following sources: AP/Wide World, p. 90; The Bettmann Archive, pp. 330, 339; CorbisBettmann, pp. 54, 67, 71, 77, 207, 262, 302; Library of Congress, pp. 111, 349; The Nobel Foundation, p. 6; Reuters/Bettmann, p. 311; Reuters/CorbisBettmann, pp. 13, 19, 101, 150, 188, 243, 399, 421; *Rocky Mountain News*/Dennis Weiser, p. 429; Rykodisc USA, p. 435; Sophia Smith Collection, Smith College (Northampton, MA), p. 317; UPI/Bettmann, pp. 153, 304, 327, 343, 356, 362, 365; UPI/CorbisBettmann, pp. 3, 28, 42, 79, 94, 108, 116, 123, 133, 137, 143, 172, 195, 213, 216, 224, 239, 258, 271, 277, 289, 292, 373, 383, 389, 406, 418; *Washington Post*, reprinted by permission of the D.C. Public Library, p. 64.

ABC-CLIO, Inc.
130 Cremona Drive, P.O. Box 1911
Santa Barbara, California 93116-1911

This book is printed on acid-free paper ∞ .
Manufactured in the United States of America

CONTENTS

ACKNOWLEDGMENTS

We sincerely appreciate the help of several writers/researchers who contributed biographical sketches for this compilation. Special thanks Douglas Gay, Kiki Klassen, and Mark Stucky for their efforts. Thank you also Amy Catala for her editorial assistance and guidance.

INTRODUCTION

A hero or heroine in legend and mythology is usually a person of great courage, someone noted for bold exploits and sometimes godlike qualities. In daily life, heroic people are also known for their daring acts and special achievements. Firefighters, police officers, and emergency workers are just a few of those who risk their own safety to protect the health and lives of others. Since its founding in 1904, the Carnegie Hero Fund Commission, established by industrialist Andrew Carnegie, has honored nearly 8,000 such individuals in the United States and Canada; their heroic efforts have ranged from administering cardiopulmonary resuscitation after an accidental electrocution to saving people bent on suicide.

During wartime, some military personnel become heroes and are singled out for their bravery. Retired Colonel Wesley L. Fox of the U.S. Marine Corps is just one of numerous examples. In 1969, he was awarded the Congressional Medal of Honor—the highest military honor in the United States—for his service "above and beyond the call of duty" in Vietnam. Fox's company was attacked by a well-concealed enemy force, and Fox (a captain at the time) was wounded in the initial strike, as were all but the executive officer in his command group. Under intense enemy fire, Fox led his company in an assault against the "hostile emplacements." When his executive officer was killed, Fox

reorganized the company and directed the fire of his men as they hurled grenades against the enemy and drove the hostile forces into retreat. Wounded again in the final assault, Captain Fox refused medical attention, established a defensive posture, and supervised the preparation of casualties for medical evacuation. His indomitable courage, inspiring initiative, and unwavering devotion to duty in the face of grave personal danger inspired his Marines to such aggressive actions that they overcame all enemy resistance and destroyed a large bunker complex (Citation for the Medal of Honor, Captain Wesley L. Fox, U.S. Marine Corps).

Nonmilitary individuals and those who do not have high-risk careers also act others' behalf and may be recognized by such organizations as the Giraffe Project. Headquartered on Whidbey Island just off the Olympic Peninsula in Washington State, the Giraffe Project attempts to motivate people "to stick their necks out for the common good." According to its newsletter, the organization finds and commends 'Giraffes,' people who are already sticking their necks out. Supporters of the project are urged to spot such people and report sightings to the Project. Each quarter a volunteer jury decides who will receive the Giraffe commendations. They focus on the personal risks nominees faced . . . [which] can be social, financial or physical, and can range from risking the loss of peer approval to risking physical harm."

HEROES OF CONSCIENCE

The people "nominated" for this book also were willing to "stick their necks out for the common good," but they fit one more criterion as well. They were motivated by ethical, religious, or moral convictions. In other words, conscience played a major role in their actions. Some of the individuals included were national or community leaders and were expected to work for the general welfare, but they went well beyond their established duties and responsibilities.

The biographical sketches of these heroes and heroines of conscience are not meant to be comprehensive. Rather, they represent a broad spectrum of individuals from diverse nations and varied walks of life, economic backgrounds, religious persuasions, and causes. The individuals included in this book have lived and worked in the period ranging from the late 1800s to the last decade of the 1900s.

In spite of threats to their lives, some were (or still are) actively involved in efforts to save their fellow citizens from government persecution and repression. Others have drawn attention to corporate actions that harm a community or individuals; or they have opposed violations of basic human rights and civil liberties, such as religious freedom; or they have refused to serve in the military based on their religious or ethical opposition to armed conflict.

For the most part, the heroic individuals described in these pages acted without violence, but quite often violence was committed against them. Some were martyred because of their convictions, or they were forced to serve long prison terms and survived brutal, unspeakable tortures.

In other instances, people of conscience suffered economic losses, discrimination, social isolation, or loss of status. A few of these people became heroes or heroines almost by accident—they were in situations in which they felt compelled to act because of a long-standing conviction about "doing the right thing."

WORLD PEACE ACTIVISTS

Some heroes of conscience are dedicated to global causes, such as world peace. They may be committed pacifists, who believe that armed conflict is morally wrong and participate in a variety of protest activities, some of them sponsored by groups such as Project Ploughshares, founded in 1976 by Canadians Murray Thomson and Ernie Regehr. Now an activity of the Canadian Council of Churches, Project Ploughshares is based on the biblical injunction to beat swords into plows, which the organization describes as a "vision" to transform "the material and human wealth consumed by military preparations into resources for human development." In the United States, Daniel and Philip Berrigan are two well-known participants in such activities, and their biographical sketches are included in this book.

There are countless others who challenge the military and generally work to provide an alternative to militarism. In 1968, an antiwar group called the Honeywell Project was formed to pressure the Minneapolis-based Honeywell company to stop producing nuclear weapons. Over the years, many Honeywell

oject participants were threatened or physically attacked. Some were arrested
d jailed. Founder Marvin Davidov and his longtime friend Daniel Ellsberg,
e former U.S. Defense Department employee who leaked the Pentagon Papers
the press, have frequently been imprisoned for their protests.

Within the worldwide pacifist movement are conscientious objectors who, by
tue of their stand against military service, may pay the ultimate price—dying
the cause. That was particularly true, although not readily apparent, during
orld War II. On 8 May 1995, when people worldwide marked the fiftieth an-
versary of the end of the war in Europe, the Brussels-based European Bureau
Conscientious Objection announced that it wanted to commemorate not only
ose soldiers who defeated the German military but also "those whose resis-
nce to the Nazi regime was expressed in nonviolent ways." Those resisters in-
ded "100,000 Austrian and German soldiers who decided to refuse military
vice or to desert their army. Among these, 50,000 were sentenced to death by
litary courts, and at least 20,000 were executed." The conscientious objectors
re the "forgotten" people of World War II and "died for their conviction and
maintenance of human values," the bureau stated (European Bureau for
nscientious Objection 1995).

HUMAN RIGHTS ACTIVISTS

Heroes of conscience also are those who have a
commitment to justice and the basic human
rights spelled out during the 1950s by the
ited Nations General Assembly in its Universal Declaration of Human Rights
e the appendix for the complete text), which states in part:

All human beings are born free and equal in dignity and rights. They are
endowed with reason and conscience and should act toward one another
in a spirit of brotherhood.

Everyone is entitled to all the rights and freedoms set forth in this
Declaration, without distinction of any kind, such as race, colour, sex, language, religion, political or other opinion, national or social origin, property, birth or other status. . . .

Everyone has the right to life, liberty and security of person.

No one shall be held in slavery or servitude; slavery and the slave trade
shall be prohibited in all their forms.

No one shall be subjected to torture or to cruel, inhuman or degrading
treatment or punishment.

Everyone has the right to recognition everywhere as a person under the
law.

All are equal before the law and are entitled without any discrimination
to equal protection of the law. . . .

No one shall be subjected to arbitrary arrest, detention or exile.

Everyone is entitled in full equality to a fair and public hearing by an independent and impartial tribunal, in the determination of his rights and
obligations and of any criminal charge against him.

Everyone charged with a penal offence has the right to be presumed in-

nocent until proven guilty according to law in a public trial at which he has had all the guarantees necessary for his defence. . . .

No one shall be subjected to arbitrary interference with his privacy, family, home or correspondence, nor to attacks upon his honor and reputation. Everyone has the right to the protection of the law against such interference or attacks.

More than 150 governments pledged to respect the rights spelled out in the international document and to promote these rights in their own nations and throughout the world. In reality, however, the promise is unfulfilled in many nations. In half the world's countries, people do not have freedom of speech and seldom get fair trials, if any trial at all. Furthermore, the governments of at least one-third of the nations routinely torture people, according to Amnesty International (AI), a politically independent organization that works to free prisoners of conscience—people who are imprisoned solely for their beliefs, race, or national origin.

Many individuals who work for basic human rights have never been incarcerated but are well known for their contributions in science, politics, law, education, religion, or some other field. The sketches of these heroes of conscience focus on their moral convictions and efforts for justice in repressive situations.

Heroes in this category also include activists who sacrificed much for the U.S. civil rights movement. Physical violence against civil rights demonstrators and workers was common during the 1960s. Those martyred for the cause include familiar names such as Martin Luther King, Jr., James Meredith, Medgar Evers, and civil rights workers James Chaney, Andrew Goodman, and Michael Schwerner. Chaney, a black Mississippian, and New Yorkers Goodman and Schwerner were part of a group participating in "Freedom Summer," an effort to register black voters in the South. The three young men were brutally murdered, and Americans who previously had paid little attention to civil rights activists began to react. As one New York columnist wrote in 1989 on the twenty-fifth anniversary of the murders:

It takes the death of whites, the injury of whites, the pain and suffering of whites before America acknowledges a problem and seeks a solution. . . . Nationality, the fact that blacks are American citizens, does not outweigh the fact that we are black American citizens. While I understand the feeling of group identity, too often it goes too far when it comes to how we feel toward other human beings.

Had Goodman and Schwerner not been white, it would have been just another trio of blacks added to the long line of those murdered in the South, which is why the civil rights movement needed people like Goodman and Schwerner. The civil rights movement needed whites who were willing to take the blows and the bullets, whites who were willing to lose their lives.

. . . I admire the courage of Goodman and Schwerner who went South to join hands with Chaney and others like him who were struggling to be free. It took guts . . . to give up everything they had to help those who did

not even look like them. It took a certain amount of faith and idealism to view their fate as inextricably intertwined with their darker countrymen. They moved beyond the rhetoric and came to Mississippi . . . truly believing that no one was free until all were free. . . .

They died, like so many in the struggle for civil and human rights . . . so that others might live in dignity as human beings (Harris 1989).

OTHER HEROIC INDIVIDUALS

Certainly it takes "guts" to engage in civil and human rights activities, particularly when oppression of minorities is the rule in a nation or hen people live under dictatorships, but other activists face dangers as well. nose working for political and labor reform, improvements in public health, environmental protection, and equitable educational opportunities may be hassed, ostracized, or forced to flee their homelands because of their moral ands.

During the early decades of the 1900s, labor organizers in the United States, r example, frequently had to put their health or lives on the line to change orking conditions and improve employees' wages. At that time, it was common for manufacturers to hire gangs who used vicious tactics against strikers to eak up unions.

Labor organizer Kenny Malone helped form a union at a General Motors M) plant in Flint, Michigan, when thousands of workers were laid off during e Great Depression of the 1930s. There was no government organization to lp and seldom any group in the private sector to turn to. As Malone stated, "It as simply this, no work, no eat, and a lot of us didn't eat. I well remember the ss coming to me and saying, 'Ken, production has been cut two-thirds and we e going to lay off a large number of men and here is the way we are going to it. The next two weeks, we are going to watch all the men and see who runs e most production and we are going to keep the men who run the most. . . .' e all speeded up, so instead of 70 percent being laid off it was 90 percent. After e layoff came we worked about two days a week but in those two days we did out four days work." During that time, about 1 million cars were produced d, according to Malone, "about half" of that production "was taken out of our des." Workers were driven "almost beyond endurance. The soft or weaker es fell at their machines and were carried out to be fired later if they got well" he Searchlight, 20 January 1944).

In Malone's view, there was no alternative except to strike. He helped stage hat became known as the Great Flint Sit-Down Strike of 1936–1937. With demination, toughness, and a sense of commitment, Malone and other labor ders at GM gained benefits for their working-class "brothers and sisters."

In some instances, activists sacrifice their time and a great deal of their own oney to protect their communities. Rex Dagi of Papua New Guinea is one such rson. He is a member of the Yonggom tribe and lives downstream from the ant Ok Tedi gold and copper mine, which releases all its mine tailings and her waste materials directly into the local river system. Not yet 30 years old,

Rex owns a small construction company that subcontracts jobs from the mine. At the risk of losing those contracts, he has challenged the mining operations, spending thousands of dollars of his own money to travel around the world to gain support and organize resistance to the mine. He has also filed a $6 billion lawsuit against the Ok Tedi mine, hoping that the lawsuit will discourage other multinational companies from damaging the environment. Most important, he wants to prevent the kind of violence that occurred on the island of Bougainville (also in Papua New Guinea), where villagers protested two decades of environmental destruction caused by the Panguna copper mine.

Wherever they live and work, whether little known or famous, heroes of conscience frequently share a common motivation: they hope to right injustices in their own communities or nations or throughout the world. Hundreds of other individuals could have been included in this book, but perhaps the representative sketches that follow will spark interest in further research on people who work for the common good as well as inspire a personal commitment to make the world a better, safer, and more humane place in which to live.

A

ABERNATHY, *RALPH*

(1926–1990)

Usually overshadowed by the charismatic nature and legendary status of MARTIN LUTHER KING, JR., the Reverend Ralph David Abernathy cofounded the movement for African American civil rights in the 1950s. Although Abernathy eventually died from natural causes and not as the result of an assassin's bullet, it is also true that he and his family—his wife Juanita and their three children, one of whom became a state senator—lived in peril most of their lives because of Abernathy's courageous stand against inequality.

On his birth certificate, Abernathy's name is David, but a sister began calling him Ralph David for an admired teacher, and Abernathy used that name throughout most of his adult years. Born in the small town of Linden, Alabama,

Abernathy was the tenth of 12 children of Louiverny Valentine Abernathy and William L. Abernathy, who died when Ralph was 16.

In 1944, Abernathy was drafted and joined an all-black unit under the direction of white officers, a common occurrence at the time. Near the end of World War II, he became a sergeant, and he and his platoon were sent to Europe as replacements for soldiers due to come home. Even though he later advocated nonviolence, he felt that it was his duty to serve and to obey authority.

Abernathy was discharged in 1945 and enrolled at Alabama State College in Montgomery, where his ability to lead was proved. He became student body and class president and organized successful student protests against the bad food served in the dining hall and the poor living conditions for men, who were housed in barracks. Eventually the school was forced to make improvements. While at Alabama State, he decided to pursue a career in the ministry and accepted a part-time pastorship in a small Baptist church in nearby Demopolis. In 1950, he became a full-time minister at the First Baptist Church in Montgomery, and in 1952, he married Juanita Odessa Jones. The couple's first child, Ralph David, Jr., died shortly after birth, but eventually they had three other children.

Abernathy attended graduate school at Atlanta University, where he first met Martin Luther King, Jr., who was preaching at nearby Ebenezer Baptist Church. But the link between the Reverends Abernathy and King was not firmly established until 1954, when King accepted a pastorship in Montgomery. Not satisfied to simply preach to their black congregations, the two men came together to take a proactive stance against the then customary and often legal practices of segregation of and discrimination against nonwhite peoples. Their first action in the

emerging civil rights movement was the organization of the Montgomery, Al-abama, bus boycott, initiated by ROSA PARKS, which lasted 13 months.

The effectiveness of the boycott as a direct but nonviolent strategy to bring about a change in the Montgomery segregation statutes led to future actions by Abernathy and King. Assertive demonstration, marked by a willingness to ac-cept abuse without responding in kind, was the modus operandi of the South-ern Christian Leadership Conference (SCLC), which these men founded in 1957. That same year, Abernathy's Montgomery home was bombed (the year before, King's home had been bombed), and Abernathy's church plus three other churches were also blasted.

Nevertheless, with King as the president and Abernathy in the administrative position of secretary-treasurer, the SCLC continued to grow and became the most important civil rights group in the United States up until the late 1960s. Abernathy was in the front row of marchers when the SCLC demonstrated against the segregation of restaurants and stores in Birmingham in 1963, and he was there later that same year during the Selma voter registration drive, when the police moved to break up the demonstration. The threat of violence did little to deter any of the SCLC members from pursuing their goal of establishing legal equality in the United States. Reverend Abernathy placed his people's needs be-fore his own safety, and the innumerable threats, taunts, attacks, and firebombs aimed at him and his family had very little effect. In the end, the main goals of the SCLC were accomplished, and discrimination based on color was declared illegal (although it certainly has not been eliminated) when President Lyndon Johnson signed the Civil Rights Act of 1964.

In 1968, King turned the SCLC's energy toward the problem of poverty, but his efforts where dramatically silenced on 4 April of that year, when a gunman shot him down in Memphis, Tennessee. Abernathy became the president of the organization and stepped up to lead the Poor People's Campaign, which in-cluded a mass demonstration in Washington, D.C., that summer. Thousands of followers of all races constructed a makeshift tent city in a park near the halls of Congress. Abernathy used this site as his base to lobby the legislators to address the issue of the nation's poor. He was eventually arrested for failing to vacate the park.

To this day, little legislation has been passed that directly speaks to the needs of the underclass, but this is not because Abernathy was shy about speaking up for his constituents. He continued his efforts as the head of the SCLC, as pastor of his church, and as one of the most venerable civil rights fighters of the century.

In 1989, Abernathy's autobiography *And the Walls Came Tumbling Down* stirred nationwide controversy, and Abernathy was ostracized by many black leaders. In the book, he claimed that King had had liaisons with two women the night before he was shot, and the next morning he struck or shoved a third woman who was angry because King had spurned her. Abernathy wrote that King often used him to straighten out quarrels growing out of King's extramar-ital affairs. Although King's womanizing was apparently common knowledge, numerous prominent blacks snubbed Abernathy, and some have yet to forgive

him for airing stories about King and giving them credence because of his long-time and close connections with the slain leader.

When Abernathy died of cardiac arrest in April 1990, however, he was praised as "one of the legendary giants of the civil rights movement." Others called him an "ordinary man who did extraordinary things." His epitaph said it simply: "I tried."

References

Abernathy, Ralph David. 1989. *And the Walls Came Tumbling Down: An Autobiography*. New York: Harper & Row.

Browne, Ray B., ed. 1990. *Contemporary Heroes and Heroines*. Detroit, MI: Gale Research.

Freeman, Orville. 1968. *Letter to Dr. Ralph Abernathy on the Poor People's Campaign*. Washington, DC: U.S. Department of Agriculture, 14 June.

ADDAMS, JANE

(1860–1935)

A social reformer inspired by the works of early Christians, Jane Addams gained fame as the founder of Hull House, a settlement house in Chicago, Illinois, that served the city's poorest residents. In spite of the poor health that plagued her throughout most of her life and the public criticism that labeled her a radical, she also spent many years working for pacifist programs and for women's rights.

The youngest child of Sarah and John Addams, Jane was born in Cedarville, Illinois, where her father was a founding father of the city. John's business skills and leadership capabilities made the Addamses the wealthiest and most prominent family in the small town. When Jane was only two years old, her mother died after a fall. By all accounts, her father and later her stepmother raised her with love and gave her all the advantages their position would afford. This did not mean that young Addams had an easy life, however. She was often ill. Her spine was deformed by tuberculosis, and back problems plagued her in later years.

When John Addams married the widow Anna Haldeman, she brought her two sons to join Addams and her four older siblings. George Haldeman was about Addams's age, and the two became fast companions. As they grew, George was always there to encourage his stepsister to strive for her goals. Because of this encouragement, as well as the quiet support of her father—who was one of the few intellectual elite who understood that education was just as

important for girls as it was for boys—Addams early on fancied a vocation in the sciences or even medicine. That goal was not to be attained, however.

Addams wanted to attend the newly opened Smith College in the East, because it emulated the rigorous instruction common to men's institutions such as Yale and Harvard, but her father insisted on a school closer to home. Rockford Seminary was his choice, and that is where Addams went as part of the class of 1881. By all accounts, she was an average student who began to rebel, like many of her classmates, against the strict religious doctrine and conservative control that was at the center of this Presbyterian finishing academy. She was criticized by the headmistress, for instance, when she and some other writers on the college magazine began to use that forum to address societal "reform" issues that were the hot topics of the day. These years in college were instrumental in her development of a new outlook regarding the role of women in society. Like many women of her generation, who were among the first allowed to attend institutions of higher learning, she came to realize that there could be more to life than purity, domesticity, and submission.

The world at the end of the 1800s was undergoing massive changes. None of these was more important, nor more disconcerting to families, than the notion that women could take an active role in society. Addams wanted to take her place in the world and do something that would have meaning beyond maintaining a home and raising children. She intended to go to Smith after completing the Rockford curriculum, but soon after returning home between school terms, she once again became ill. She complained of backaches and a loss of energy. Each day was filled with depression and despair. Many historians suggest that this illness was a result of reconnecting with the family and being allowed the luxury of pampering and dependency. At school, none of the symptoms was evident when she was supported by a community of women dedicated to attaining independence. The condition persisted for months, forcing her to cancel her plans to begin studying at Smith. After her father died unexpectedly, Addams accepted her stepmother's offer to travel with her to Philadelphia so that she could attend the only women's medical school in the country. But before long, the depression and melancholy returned, and Addams was forced to abandon her dream. She decided to travel to Europe for a change of scenery in the hope of overcoming the condition.

While in Europe, Addams toured the English slums, where she saw the exploitation of workers and the most negative results of industrialization. When

she returned to her midwestern home, her family expected her to take on the role of the "kindly aunt" who would tend to the sick nieces and nephews and oversee the family's affairs, but her friend Ellen Starr intervened.

Starr and Addams had met in college their first year, and then Starr had gone to Chicago to teach school. The two had stayed in close contact through letters, and Addams had expressed her concern for the victims of the industrial revolution, the poorest residents of the city. She wanted to do something about the dreadful conditions in which they were forced to live. When it became apparent that Addams's family was going to detour her once more from a path of active participation in the world, Starr insisted that she move to Chicago so that they could work on their "scheme." To her great credit, acting against strong family ties and pressure to remain in a life of privilege, Addams made the trip to Chicago, where, in her words:

> I gradually became convinced that it would be a good thing to rent a house in a part of the city where many primitive and actual needs are found, in which young women who had been given over too exclusively to study might restore a balance of activity along traditional lines and learn of life from life itself (Sawaya 1994).

Within a few months, using contacts through her church and her position, she raised enough money to establish her "settlement," or sanctuary. Called Hull House, it was opened in 1889 and was located in the slums of Chicago, where

> representatives of nineteen different nationalities swarmed in the ward . . . [and] swarmed in foulness. The streets were covered inches deep with packed and dirty refuse over broken pavements; the miry alleys smelled like sewers, and the sewers themselves were in hundreds of instances unconnected with the houses or tenements; the stables, of which there were many, were inexpressibly foul; Greeks slaughtered sheep in basements, Italian women and children sorted rags collected from the city dump, in courtyards thick with babies and vermin; bakers made bread in dirty holes under sidewalks, and distributed it to their immigrant neighbors (Linn 1968, 168).

Hull House took its name from the Hull mansion where the organization was established, and Addams quickly went to work to provide welfare services for the needy population. Her inspiration came from "reading of the life of the early Christians" and their humanitarian works (Bush 1993). Programs were created to help feed, house, and tend the sick and impoverished among the working class and newly arrived immigrants. Hull House also commissioned one of the earliest surveys that resulted in a mapping of the slums of Chicago. The result was publicity for Addams's work and a consciousness-raising for the affluent in the city.

Eventually, using only private funds, Hull House would become a complex of 13 buildings offering services that included nursery care, physical education,

recreational activities for children and adults, arts-and-crafts workshops, adult education courses, a music school, theater arts workshops and presentations, and a social service center. Addams helped initiate the settlement house movement, which was to flourish during the great social upheaval in the late nineteenth and early twentieth centuries. Yet for all her positive influence, Addams was frequently branded a radical and was attacked for being a peril to society.

She wrote four books during the first decade of the 1900s; the best known was *Twenty Years at Hull House*, published in 1910. Seven more books followed in later years. Addams was also deeply involved in the suffrage movement and campaigns to bring about child-labor laws. In addition, she became known as one of the most effective peace advocates in the world, for which she received the Nobel Peace Prize in 1931.

Her efforts for peace began in the late 1890s, long before the United States entered World War I. Although she protested the horrors of war and the lives lost, she also decried the fact that war prevents mutual understanding between peoples. She often lectured at college campuses on the topic of peace and helped organize the Woman's Peace Party, becoming its first chairwoman in 1915. She also presided over the first congress of women, which formed the basis for what later became known as the Women's International League for Peace and Freedom. Women from a number of nations gathered in the Netherlands to protest war and discuss ways of making war impossible in the future. When the United States declared war in 1917, Addams was vilified in the press and elsewhere— often called a traitor—for her outspoken pacifism. Even her social work suffered, as many who had formerly sought her advice refused to contact her.

During the 1920s, Addams traveled throughout the United States soliciting funds for German mothers and children who had suffered during the fighting. The attacks against her became increasingly abusive, and she was denounced as a communist by those who believed that there was a huge communist conspiracy operating in the United States. Still, she had her defenders, and many of her friends urged her to file lawsuits to stop the slander against her. "In 1927, they gave her a huge testimonial dinner in Chicago to try to counteract the adverse publicity she was receiving. . . . From all around the country the great and the unknown praised her patriotism" (Davis 1973, 268). But the adverse publicity took its toll; her popularity declined, as did her income from public appearances, which were often canceled.

In spite of the unjustified attacks, Addams continued to write, lecture, and present her views not only on pacifism but also on the improvement of economic and social conditions. She was a role model for thousands of women during her lifetime and even after her death in 1935. During the 1960s and 1970s, when urban reform and the peace movement gained public attention, Addams's achievements were highly praised once more.

References

Addams, Jane. 1990. *Twenty Years at Hull House*. Urbana: University of Illinois Press.

Bush, Malcolm. 1993. "Jane Addams: No Easy Heroine." *Free Inquiry*, fall.

Davis, Allen Freeman. 1973. *American Heroine: The Life and Legend of Jane Addams*. New York: Oxford University Press.

Linn, James Weber. 1968. *Jane Addams: A Biography*. New York: Greenwood Press.

Sawaya, Francesca. 1994. "Domesticity, Cultivation, and Vocation in Jane Addams and Sarah Orne Jewett." *Nineteenth-Century Literature*, March.

Tims, Margaret. 1961. *Jane Addams of Hull House, 1860–1935*. New York: Macmillan.

ALI, MUHAMMAD

(1942–)

He was named Cassius Marcellus Clay at birth, a name handed down from his grandfather, but Clay renounced the name in later years because of its slave origins. He became known for his great boxing skills and also for his refusal to serve in the military. More important to him, he once said, was being "a fighter who stayed with his people . . . and didn't sell his people and forget them. I've seen too many blacks become successful then look down on their own and leave them. This spirit of sticking with my black brothers and sisters was always in me. They are forever first with me" (McCallum 1975, 72).

Growing up in Louisville, Kentucky, Clay had a reputation as a loud-mouthed braggart and goof-off. He did little schoolwork. Instead, he studied how to gain attention for himself. At the age of 12, he discovered the venue that would gain him celebrity status. That was when he met Joe Martin, a boxing coach who trained youngsters and then put them on television to display their skills in the ring. Young Clay, insufferably vain already, became almost unbearable when his hard work led to a broadcast victory. True to a style that he would perfect in the ensuing years, Clay predicted his victory to anyone who would listen.

The young fighter developed his ring skills during high school, and he won the national Golden Gloves and Amateur Athletic Union titles for his weight class in 1959. This qualified him for the Rome Olympics the following year, and he came back from that event with the gold medal. At this point, Clay was already calling himself "The Greatest," which became his trademark, along with his famed rhyme "fly like a butterfly, sting like a bee."

Turning professional immediately after his return from the Olympics, the accomplished boxer quickly impressed many in the fight game. His flamboyant and boastful manner made him many enemies, however. Mainstream America expected black people to stay in the background. Even famous black athletes and entertainers were expected to "appreciate" their position and maintain the facade that all was well with the world, in spite of the fact that they were still denied basic human rights by the very people who paid to see them perform. Clay's outrageous behavior and his impossible statements created an image that white Americans loved to hate. It is likely, however, that this self-promotion genius was the first true superstar.

Clay's antics in and out of the ring brought larger crowds to the fights than ever before. People who had never followed the sport now watched to see if the "Louisville Lip" would finally get beaten. At the age of 22, Clay challenged Sonny Liston for the heavyweight championship, demanding and receiving a purse of half a million dollars. The fight itself brought in more money than any in history to that point, but it almost did not take place.

Unbeknownst to the public, Clay had been undergoing a personal spiritual transformation for years. Although he played to the crowd in public, the private man was studying religion with representatives of the Nation of Islam. He was friendly with Malcolm X, and he studied the writings of Elijah Muhammad. Three days before the big championship fight with Liston, news stories connected Clay to the Black Muslims. This group was almost universally feared by the white population, who considered the Black Muslims "racist" because they advocated self-reliance and did not favor integration into the majority white society. When the promoter heard of Clay's affiliation, he threatened to cancel the fight unless the boxer renounced Islam.

Clay refused to do so, and the promoter carried out his threat, which meant that Clay might never have the chance to fight Sonny Liston again. But the strength of Clay's convictions and his faith were much stronger than the need for money or fame. He was ready to give up everything to do what he believed was right for him, regardless of the consequences. After many tense hours, the promoter finally gave in, and the fight proceeded. History records that Clay went on to humiliate the champ in six rounds, and the next day he stunned the world by telling the press that he was now to be known as Cassius X, the Islamic heavyweight champion of the world. A month later, the champion again changed his name to Muhammad Ali. About that time he also married Sonji Roi, a Chicago model, whom he later divorced because she would not abide by Muslim customs.

There were calls to strip Ali of his title, and he was forced to fight a rematch with Liston. That fight lasted less than three minutes. He had to fight Floyd

Patterson, who was going to win the title back for "real" Americans. On 22 November 1965, Ali pummeled Patterson for 12 rounds. Like it or not, the country would have to accept the unhumbled Ali as the champion of the world.

In one of the most famous incidents of a famed life, Ali refused to be inducted into the Army when he was drafted on 28 April 1967. He was initially given a deferment because he could not pass the intelligence test (Ali had never learned to read well), but the government lowered the standards, and he was declared A-1 without ever taking a test or being officially notified. Since the Nation of Islam was not recognized as a religion by the U.S. government, that group's doctrine against the making of war was not recognized as a valid basis for Ali's claim of conscientious objector status. Even though the government promised Ali that he would not have to go to the front but could tour as part of a boxing exhibition, his loyalty to his faith and the Nation of Islam precluded him from joining the service. He understood the consequences, and as he told it later:

> When I was asked to stand up and be sworn into the service, I thought about all the black people who'd been here for 400 years—all the lynching, raping and killing they'd suffered—and there was an Army fellow my age acting like God and telling me to go to Viet Nam and fight Asians who'd never called me Nigger, had never lynched me, had never put dogs on me—and outside I had millions of black people waiting to see what I was going to do. . . . I couldn't take that step because I knew the war was wrong, it was against my religious beliefs, and I was willing to go to jail for those beliefs (McCallum 1975, 73).

Ali was convicted of draft evasion and faced a five-year prison sentence. His lawyers appealed the conviction, but almost every state in the union suspended his license to box. The sanctioning organizations stripped him of his titles, and he lost all his money. He was even shot at and threatened for being that "draft-dodging nigger." For three and one-half years, Ali made speeches and worked against oppression wherever he saw it, and public sentiment about the Vietnam War began to shift. Increasingly, Americans objected to U.S. involvement in Vietnam. The Supreme Court overturned Ali's draft evasion conviction in 1971, and he was finally able to resume his career in the ring.

His fights are the stuff of sports legend, of course. But more important to his many fans—ordinary folks of all colors and every nationalilty—is the legendary manner in which this singular individual was willing to sacrifice it all to live the way he believed. Ali announced his retirement from the ring in 1979, but a year later he fought Larry Holmes, who captured the heavyweight title. Ali fought and lost one more match in 1981 before he was finally finished with boxing. A few years later he was diagnosed with Parkinson's syndrome, but that did not stop his efforts to help oppressed people around the globe. He traveled the world, promoting peace. In 1990, on his own initiative he visited Iraq and met with dictator Saddam Hussein, returning to the United States with 15 American hostages. One hostage, Harry Brill-Edwards, said on his return home, "I've always known that Muhammad Ali was a super sportsman; but during those

hours that we were together, inside that enormous body, I saw an angel" (Schuyler 1992). When he is not traveling for charitable causes, Ali spends his time in Berrien Springs, Michigan, where he and his fourth wife, Lonnie, have a large farm.

References

Edwards, Audrey, and Gary Wohl. 1977. *Muhammad Ali: The People's Champ*. Toronto, Canada: Little, Brown.

Hano, Arnold. 1977. *Muhammad Ali the Champion*. New York: G. P. Putnam's Sons.

Hauser, Thomas. 1991. *Muhammad Ali: His Life and Times*. New York: Simon & Schuster.

McCallum, John D. 1975. *The Encyclopedia of World Boxing Champions*. Radnor, PA: Chilton Book Company.

Mailer, Norman. 1975. *The Fight*. Boston: Little, Brown.

Pacheco, Ferdie. 1992. *Muhammad Ali: A View from the Corner*. New York: Birch Lane Press, Carol Publishing Group.

Schuyler, Ed, Jr. 1992. "Muhammad Ali Turns 50." *South Bend Tribune*, 12 January.

AQUINO, CORAZON

(1933–)

On 25 February 1986, Corazon Aquino, a quiet housewife and mother of five, took the oath of office and became the president of the Philippines. She had never pursued this high office, and no one would ever have predicted this outcome for her, but tragic events, combined with her sense of duty, belief in working for the betterment of her people, and love of country, allowed her to make the dangerous decision to accept this leadership role. Her "People Power" revolution, which had begun when she stepped into the political arena and announced for the presidency less than three months before, peacefully displaced one of the most powerful and entrenched dictators in the world: Ferdinand Marcos.

Aquino was born Maria Corazon Cojuangco in Tarlac Province, the Philippines, to a wealthy sugar-producing family with a long tradition of political involvement. The men in each of the last three generations had served in national office, and the Cojuangcos were well connected. Young Aquino was exposed to this political environment, but her training and education, like that of most well-to-do girls, were centered on homemaking skills, art, foreign languages, and the like. The expectation was for her to be a homemaker and mother.

In 1946, just after the liberation of the islands by the U.S. Army, the 13-year-old, her parents, and seven siblings sailed to the United States. Aquino attended

private schools in Philadelphia and New York, finally graduating from a Catholic women's college in 1953 with a concentration in French. Although she was a good student, her shyness and self-effacing manner precluded her from seeking any school government offices, club positions, or recognition of any type. She rarely thought about how she would use her degree after graduation.

Aquino decided to enter law school when she returned to the Philippines but dropped the effort after one year to marry the charismatic Benigno Aquino, Jr. Ninoy, as he was called by family and supporters, was a 21-year-old reporter, the son of another of the Philippines most important political dynasties. His father had been a senator and a member of the president's cabinet, and it did not take long for him to throw his own hat in the ring. At the age of 22 he ran for mayor of his hometown. Aquino, tending to their first child, accompanied her husband as he made speeches and met the people. She would smile and wave, but she stayed in the background.

Ninoy was eventually elected senator, and Aquino continued to support his efforts by keeping the family together and maintaining the household. She would defer to her husband in all matters when others were in the house (a common occurrence, as Benigno was the ultimate social and political animal), never speaking her mind when others were around. But the election of Ferdinand Marcos in 1965 as president set events in motion that would change Aquino's quiet life forever.

To solidify his power and quash his enemies, Marcos modified the constitution and declared martial law. Free from legal restraints, he then began a 20-year process of siphoning his country's assets into his own bank accounts and real estate holdings throughout the world. By the time he was forced from office, his net worth was close to $3 billion. Marcos's erosion of the democratic process brought some vocal opposition from Benigno Aquino and other senators, but the president's power was well established by 1972. He had Ninoy, a potential rival in future elections, arrested on bogus charges that included murder and subversion.

Aquino spent seven years in prison as a result of Marcos's effort to silence his strong critical voice. During the first trying weeks of her husband's confinement,

Aquino did what she could to comfort her family and to learn where they had taken him. She soon discovered that her so-called friends would not even recognize her anymore. Everyone was afraid of the dictator's wrath, so she had to go on alone.

Bolstered by prayer and her undying faith, Aquino traveled for a month and a half throughout the countryside, going from prison to prison seeking information about Ninoy. She finally found him and arranged to visit on a regular basis. She even made certain that the children could spend special days in the cell with their father so that the family would survive. But more important to the future of the country, she and Ninoy began to discuss politics.

The couple made a decision to carry on the work of the opposition from Benigno's prison cell. It was decided that Aquino would take Ninoy's message to the streets through press conferences and speeches. Although nervous and uncertain in the beginning, Aquino became more comfortable as her own passions for the cause began to develop over the five years of this effort. She eventually campaigned for her husband when Marcos decided to open the senate race to the opposition parties. He lost, as did all those not favored by the president. In that election, Marcos's wife Imelda won 21 different positions.

Thanks to pressure from U.S. government officials, whom Marcos wanted to keep happy, the Aquino family was allowed to move to Boston, where Ninoy underwent a heart bypass operation. They stayed there for three years in relative safety and happiness, but by 1983, Benigno knew that he must go back to his country to lead the opposition in preparation for the assembly elections of 1984. He expected to be arrested immediately upon arrival, so the plan was for Aquino to bring the family two weeks later. Ninoy's plane touched down in Manila on 21 August 1983, and 20,000 people were waiting to cheer their leader. As Benigno Aquino walked out the door, a shot rang out, and he was dead.

The political fallout from the assassination was devastating for the Marcos regime, which became increasingly isolated. Demonstrations, strikes, and protests affected the economy as well as the government's standing throughout the world. The United States backed away from Marcos when it became clear that he was losing control of the country. The day after Marcos's judges acquitted the men accused of murdering Benigno Aquino, Corazon declared that she would be a candidate in the upcoming election for the presidency. "I am just one of the thousands and millions of victims of the Marcos regime," she said. "I am not the victim who has suffered the most, but perhaps the victim who is the best known. I look around me and I see a nation that is sinking deeper and deeper into despair. I sense a growing feeling of helplessness and a creeping belief that no matter what abuse may be thrown in our faces, we are powerless to do anything about it" (Nadel 1987, 59).

Working tirelessly with a new sense of purpose and trust in her own instincts, Aquino did what her husband had been unable to accomplish in his many years as a political leader: she brought the opposition factions together under her personal campaign to defeat Marcos. The whirlwind campaign of the people held that coalition together until election day, when millions of Filipinos went to the polls.

An independent commission found widespread fraud on the part of the Marcos forces, and an independent count showed that Aquino had been chosen by the people. Marcos refused to step down, and each candidate declared victory. Aquino did not back down, and her supporters followed her lead. When tanks were sent to crush the army forces loyal to Aquino, her people knelt down in front of the tanks as a human blockade and refused to move. The tanks turned back. U.S. President Ronald Reagan was able to pressure Marcos to leave, and President Aquino began her tenure.

References

Aquino, Corazon Cojuangco. 1986–1989. *Speeches of President Corazon C. Aquino*. Manila: Republic of the Philippines.

Crisostomo, Isabelo T. 1987. *Cory: Profile of a President*. Boston: Branden Publishing Company.

Gullas, Cecilia K. 1987. *Corazon Aquino: The Miracle of a President*. New York: Cultural House.

Komisar, Lucy. 1987, *Corazon Aquino: The Story of a Revolution*. New York: G. Braziller.

Nadel, Laurie. 1987. *Corazon Aquino: Journey to Power*. New York: Julian Messner.

Scariano, Margaret. 1987. *The Picture Life of Corazon Aquino*. New York: Franklin Watts.

Siegel, Beatrice. 1988. *Cory: Corazon Aquino and the Philippines*. New York: Dutton.

ASHE, ARTHUR

(1943–1993)

He was the first black tennis player to win the U.S. Open and Wimbledon championships in 1968 and 1975, respectively, which would have been enough to ensure lasting fame long after his death. However, Arthur Ashe was also a noted civil rights activist, and in 1992, he became a spokesman for victims of AIDS, after announcing in his open and honest manner that he had

contracted HIV (the virus producing AIDS) from a blood transfusion. Instead of bowing to defeat, he used his position as a famous athlete to try to "destigmatize" AIDS and to fight for those who suffer from the disease. As a 1992 article in *Sports Illustrated* magazine pointed out:

> Racism has tried his soul, disease has attacked his heart, and now another malady, AIDS, is assailing his body—and his dignity. But Ashe . . . the most prominent black tennis player in history and one of the most respected athletes of our time, perseveres when battling ills, whether medical or societal (Jenkins 1992).

The oldest of two sons born to Arthur Sr. and Mattie (Cunningham) of Richmond, Virginia, Ashe lost his mother when he was six years old, and his father raised both him and his brother, Johnnie, to be disciplined youngsters. The senior Ashe taught his boys to help others and to honor the family's good name.

Ashe grew up in a segregated part of Richmond, close to the only tennis courts that blacks were allowed to use. After Ashe turned ten years old, Dr. Robert Walter Johnson, Jr., of Lynchburg, Virginia, became his tennis mentor during the summers. Johnson shaped much of Ashe's talent in the early years and taught him to be calm and focused during a match. Ashe also developed his own practice ethic. It was common for him to take 3,000 serves and returns on a daily basis, which left him little time for any other type of recreation or a social life.

Despite objections from his father that there were no blacks in professional tennis at that time, Ashe was determined to make it his life—even though he was banned from participation in an all-white tennis tournament in 1955 at the age of 12. He became a tennis prodigy and won a scholarship to the University of California, Los Angeles, where he earned a degree in business and also laid the foundation for his tennis career.

Early on, Ashe played in white country clubs and had to watch his decorum—"stay in his place" and not appear too "uppity" for a black man—which was part of the southern way of life. By the 1960s, however, he had broken the color barrier to become one of the top-ranked players in the world, capping it off with the U.S. Open championship in 1968 and the Australian Open in 1970.

In 1973, he was invited to play in the South African Open tennis tournament. Ashe felt that accepting the invitation might help ease racial tensions in the apartheid nation. Unfortunately, his stand seemed to cause more resentment than anything else.

In 1975, he won at Wimbledon. Later that year he helped found the Association of Tennis Professionals (the players' union). Two years later, he married Jeanne Moutoussamy, a photographer, and their daughter, Camera, was born in 1986.

Ashe suffered a heart attack in 1979 at the age of 36, which effectively ended his playing career, but that did not deter his activities on behalf of others. Within a year, he was the national campaign chairman of the American Heart Association. He also got involved in many other causes, raising millions of dollars for a

variety of organizations, including the United Negro College Fund and the Safe Passage Foundation, which operates tennis centers in four inner cities. He established the African American Athletic Association, which counsels high school athletes in New York City, and he was a member of a think tank called TransAfrica, focusing on the effects of U.S. foreign policy on the Caribbean and Africa.

In 1983, Ashe taught a course called the Black Athlete in Contemporary Society at Miami's Florida Memorial College, but when he went to the library to locate resource material on successful black athletes of the past, there was little to be found. The stories of black athletes in the United States "had never been collected, organized, analyzed and interpreted," Ashe explained (Reed 1989). After five years of research, using primary sources such as black newspapers and conducting interviews with black families, Ashe's three-volume work *A Hard Road to Glory* was published in 1988. Ashe said at the time that he hoped to accomplish two things with the publication:

> [First,] to see the so-called history of American sports rewritten. If you're going to talk about the history of basketball, you're going to have to include black teams like the Harlem Globetrotters. Second, I'd like to see a fuller appreciation of the contribution of certain black athletes to black American history.
>
> Heavyweight champions Jack Johnson and Joe Louis were, in their prime, the most famous black persons on earth, and their success stories should be recorded alongside those of politicians and civil rights leaders (Reed 1989).

While Ashe was researching his historical work, he was also an instruction editor at *Tennis* magazine, wrote a sports column for the *Washington Post*, and did commentary for ABC and HBO Sports. During this time, he still had his eye on the political situation in South Africa, and in 1983, he and Harry Belafonte organized Artists and Athletes against Apartheid. In 1985, Ashe took part in an antiapartheid demonstration outside the South African embassy in Washington, D.C. During a protest demonstration in behalf of Haitian political refugees, he was arrested and suffered another mild heart attack. Under his doctor's orders, he was forced to forgo any further protest activities.

Because of numbness in his hand, Ashe underwent exploratory brain surgery in 1988, and doctors found an abscess caused by an infection called toxoplasmosis. This led to the discovery that Ashe had contracted the AIDS virus, which was traced to tainted blood from a transfusion during earlier bypass surgery (at a time when there was no routine blood screening). For several years, Ashe kept the details of his condition private, telling only family and close friends. However, when *USA Today* learned in 1992 that Ashe had AIDS, the newspaper informed him that it would break the story without his permission, which Ashe said made him "feel violated." He would have had to lie about his health to maintain his privacy, so he went public on his own. When asked why he did not deny his illness, he reportedly replied: "Because you can never tell just one lie.

There's always another" (Jenkins 1992). He determined at that time to make the best of the situation and to help educate the public about AIDS.

After his announcement, Ashe continued to keep up a hectic schedule, not only playing golf and tennis but also writing a book (*Days of Grace*, published posthumously) and working with disadvantaged youngsters. He gave speeches, raised funds, and established foundations for AIDS victims. In 1992, *Sports Illustrated* announced that it had named Ashe Sportsman of the Year, not because of his bravery as an AIDS victim, but because of his philanthropy, civility, and the moral way he conducted his life.

Ashe gave his last speech at an AIDS forum just a few days before the disease killed him. On the day he died of pneumonia, he was scheduled to give another speech but was forced to send a tape instead, saying that he was too weak to attend. Ashe was eulogized by numerous Americans from varied walks of life and was, in the words of President Bill Clinton, "a true American hero and a great example to us all."

References

Ashe, Arthur. 1993. *Days of Grace*. New York: Alfred A. Knopf.

Huzinec, Mary, Maria Speidel, Rochelle Jones, and Sarah Skolnik. 1993. "Man of Grace and Glory." *People Weekly*, 22 February.

Jenkins, Sally. 1992. "Another Battle Joined." *Sports Illustrated*, 20 April.

Moore, Kenny. 1992. "The Eternal Example." *Sports Illustrated*, 21 December.

Reed, Susan. 1989. "Arthur Ashe Remembers the Forgotten Men of Sport—America's Early Black Athletes" (interview). *People Weekly*, 6 March.

AUNG SAN SUU KYI

(1945–)

In July 1995, news stories announced the release of Nobel Peace Prize winner Aung San Suu Kyi from a six-year detention under house arrest. She had been held without trial in Yangon, Myanmar (formerly Rangoon, Burma—the military government changed the name in 1989). Aung San Suu Kyi had been arrested in July 1989 while leading a nonviolent movement to create a democratic

government and resisting a junta, which had seized power in 1988 after killing hundreds if not thousands of pro-democracy demonstrators. In the May 1989 elections, the National League for Democracy, which Aung San Suu Kyi led, won 392 of 495 seats in the parliament, but the junta refused to honor the election results. The military jailed or killed many opponents or forced them into hiding or exile.

Aung San Suu Kyi's father was General Aung San, who led the movement for Burma's independence from Great Britain, but she never knew him. He was assassinated by pro-government forces in 1947, when she was two years old. Although she spent most of her life outside Burma, she was inspired and influenced by her father's role as "the architect of modern Burma," according to Aung San Suu Kyi's husband, Michael Aris, an Oxford University professor (Chandler 1991). Educated in Burma and India, where her mother was ambassador from 1960 to 1967, Aung San Suu Kyi graduated from Oxford and worked at the United Nations in New York. She married Aris in 1972; the couple's sons, Alexander and Kim, were in British schools when their mother was arrested.

Although she had no political ambitions, Aung San Suu Kyi knew that she might be expected to take a leadership role because she was the daughter of a national hero. She did not anticipate, however, what happened when she returned to Burma in 1988 to care for her dying mother. At the time, a major antigovernment movement was under way—"a large, leaderless political rebellion," as Aris called it—and Aung San Suu Kyi was asked to speak before huge crowds. She quickly emerged as the leader of the movement, which formed the National League for Democracy. Although her life was endangered, she condemned the government for human rights abuses and economic policies that were destroying the country.

Aung San Suu Kyi was a major threat to the military junta, and General Saw Maung, who had seized power, ordered soldiers to crush the protesters and to

silence Aung San Suu Kyi by arresting her and holding her virtually incommunicado in the family home on University Avenue in Rangoon. She was accused of inspiring hatred of the military and of violating a 1975 law aimed at those accused of subversive acts against the state. The law originally permitted detention without charge or trial for a maximum of three years, with renewal every six months, but it was amended in 1991 to allow detention for five years, with renewal required annually. The junta announced that Aung San Suu Kyi would be released if she agreed to voluntary exile abroad, but she refused to accept such conditions and insisted that she would leave the country only if she received assurances that she would be able to return safely.

In December 1989, Aris was allowed to visit his wife, who was in the midst of a hunger strike, demanding to be imprisoned with her supporters—duly elected members of parliament who were jailed so that they could not take office. She feared that these pro-democracy prisoners would be tortured. When she was assured that they would not be mistreated, she ended the strike after 12 days. However, she remained under house arrest in almost complete isolation, with armed guards in her home. She was permitted occasional visits from immediate family members.

When she was awarded the 1991 Nobel Peace Prize for her leadership "of a democratic opposition which employs nonviolent means to resist a regime characterized by brutality," the Nobel Committee noted that "Suu Kyi's struggle is one of the most extraordinary examples of civil courage in Asia in recent decades. She has become an important symbol in the struggle against oppression." Aung San Suu Kyi was unable to attend ceremonies in Washington, D.C., to accept the award, but her son, Alexander, delivered a speech on her behalf.

From the time of Aung San Suu Kyi's detention in 1989, Amnesty International campaigned for her release, as did many other human rights organizations such as Free Burma and the Burma Peace Foundation, as well as leaders of Western governments, including the United States, Britain, Australia, and the Philippines. In 1993, the United Nations Human Rights Commission issued a report on human rights abuses and the brutal regime of Burma's State Law and Order Restoration Council (SLORC), which has tortured, executed, and unfairly imprisoned thousands. According to the report, "serious repression and an atmosphere of pervasive fear" exist throughout the country, and political opponents, ethnic minorities, and others are detained under slavelike conditions. The report called for international human rights monitors to be sent to Burma's border region with Bangladesh to check on abuses in the repatriation of more than 250,000 Burmese Muslims.

In February 1994, the junta rulers allowed Aung San Suu Kyi to receive three outside visitors for the first time: U.S. Congressman Bill Richardson, a UN representative, and a reporter for the *New York Times*. There was no indication that the military would free her, and Richardson left with the impression that she would be detained indefinitely. In late 1994, the UN General Assembly passed a resolution encouraging the government of Burma to begin "a substantive political dialogue with Aung San Suu Kyi and other political leaders, including

representatives from ethnic groups, as the best means of promoting national reconciliation and the full and early restoration of democracy."

The SLORC Aung San freed Aung San Suu Kyi unconditionally on 10 July 1995, surprising many political analysts and human rights groups. Although leaders such as U.S. President Bill Clinton, Philippines President CORAZON AQUINO, and South Africa's DESMOND TUTU hailed Aung San Suu Kyi's release, numerous political dissidents are still in Burmese prisons, and the military is not expected to voluntarily give up power. In fact, some reports indicate that there are even tighter restrictions on Burmese citizens, including oppressive curfews, police inspections of personal property, and nightly searches of people's homes for "subversives." In addition, many Burmese villagers are still forced, as they have been for years, to serve as unpaid laborers for the military, building roads, cleaning lakes, gardening, or doing whatever else the soldiers demand.

After her release, Aung San Suu Kyi issued a statement declaring her continuing commitment to achieving stability and reconciliation in her country through dialogue. As she noted,

> dialogue has been undoubtedly the key to a happy resolution of long-festering problems. Once bitter enemies in South Africa are now working together for the betterment of their peoples. Why can't we look forward to a similar process? We have to choose between dialogue or utter devastation. I would like to believe that the human instinct for survival alone, if nothing else, would eventually lead all of us to prefer dialogue. . . .
>
> Extreme viewpoints are not confined to any particular group, and it is the responsibility of the leaders to control such elements as threaten the spirit of conciliation. There is more in common between the authorities and we of the democratic forces than existed between the black and white people of South Africa.

Aung San Suu Kyi urged "authorities to release those of us who still remain in prison. I am happy to be able to say that in spite of all that they have undergone, the forces of democracy in Burma remain strong and dedicated. I on my part bear no resentment towards anybody for anything that happened during the last six years." She ended her statement by expressing "sincere thanks to people all over the world and especially to my countrymen who have done so much to strengthen my resolve and to effect my release" (Hutcheon 1995).

Since her release, Aung San Suu Kyi's "resolve" has included a number of speeches in support of democracy and civil rights in Burma. One was a video-taped address smuggled out of Burma and presented on 31 August at the Non-Government Organisation Forum held near the site of the 1995 UN International Women's Conference in Beijing, China. Aung San Suu Kyi did not attend the conference, fearing that military rulers would not permit her to return to Burma. In her speech, she declared, "It is not the prerogative of men alone to bring light to this world. Women, with their capacity for compassion and self-sacrifice, their courage and perseverance, have done much to dissipate the darkness of intolerance and hate." She urged governments to spend "less on the war toys of grown

men and much more on the urgent needs of humanity as a whole." She insisted that "women have a most valuable contribution to make in situations of conflict by leading the way to solutions based on dialogue rather than on viciousness or violence" and concluded that "the education and empowerment of women throughout the world cannot fail to result in a more caring, tolerant, just and peaceful life for all" (Free Burma 1995).

References

Associated Press. 1991. "Burma Denounces Pleas on Suu Kyi." *Boston Globe*, 27 December.

———. 1993. "Burma Extends Opposition Leader's House Arrest." *Boston Globe*, 21 July, National/Foreign section.

"Burma's Captives." 1994. Editorial. *Boston Globe*, 18 July.

"Burma's Long Walk to Freedom." 1995. Editorial. *Boston Globe*, 11 July.

Chandler, David L. 1991. "Nobel Goes to Burmese Dissident." *Boston Globe*, 15 October, National/Foreign section.

Free Burma. 1995. "Daw Aung San Suu Kyi's Address at Beijing Forum." Electronic conference on EcoNet, 31 August.

Hutcheon, Stephen. 1995. "The World Can Learn from Us, Says Suu Kyi." *Sydney Morning Herald*, 1 September.

B

BAKER, *ELLA*

(1903–1986)

During the civil rights movement of the 1950s and 1960s, Ella Baker was seldom in the spotlight, but she was, as she often called herself, "a facilitator," working behind the scenes "to make things happen." She helped establish the Southern Christian Leadership Conference (SCLC) and the Student Nonviolent Coordinating Committee (SNCC), which together led efforts to end segregation in the United States. In short, she was an effective and energetic organizer who did not seek recognition but made it clear that even though women were seldom in the forefront making speeches or leading marches for the civil rights movement, they did not have to be subordinate. She worked for decades for a cause that was more important to her than her personal health—she suffered from intense asthma attacks most of her life—and she was frequently in danger when she and others in the movement were involved in direct-action tactics.

Ella Jo Baker was born in Norfolk, Virginia, and grew up in a small North Carolina town. Some writers have credited her "steely will" to her family heritage. As Paula Giddings wrote: "Her grandparents were former slaves, and her grandmother had once refused to marry a light-skinned man of her master's choice, preferring a less refined man of darker hue. As a consequence her grandmother, a house slave, was banished to the life of a field hand" (Giddings 1984, 268).

Although Baker wanted to be a missionary, she could not afford to pursue her dream. After graduating from Shaw University in Raleigh, North Carolina, as class valedictorian, she moved to New York City in 1927, just as the economic depression was beginning to take its toll. During the 1930s, she identified and worked with the unemployed and with community groups that were attempting to help the poverty stricken. She joined forces with George Schuyler, a *Pittsburgh Courier* reporter, to form the Young Negro Cooperative League, which promoted consumer co-ops.

During World War II, Baker began working with and for the National Association for the Advancement of Colored People (NAACP), eventually becoming the national field secretary. She organized NAACP branches throughout the South, traveling thousands of miles and making hundreds of speeches. After she became director of the New York branch, she helped end de facto segregation in the New York public schools. Baker later resigned from her national position because she believed that organizations should be run from the grassroots up rather than following charismatic leaders at the top. However, she remained active with the New York branch of the NAACP and continued her work for school desegregation and integration of housing.

Baker went to Alabama in the mid-1950s to advise organizers of the Montgomery bus boycott, but after the successful boycott, the desegregation movement almost died for lack of plans or initiative to continue the fight. Baker met

with MARTIN LUTHER KING, JR., to find out why there was no organization in place to capitalize on the bus boycott. According to Baker, King's "rationale was that after a big demonstration, there was a natural letdown and a need for people to sort of catch their breath" (Giddings 1984, 268). Baker adamantly disagreed, and in 1957, she set out to establish headquarters for the SCLC in Atlanta. Although King led the SCLC, Baker prompted the organization to expand and helped create affiliates to fight all types of racial discrimination.

By the 1960s, students in southern black colleges, joined by some white youths from the North, were staging sit-ins at segregated restaurants. Baker urged the SCLC to support the burgeoning movement, which she believed came about because of youthful enthusiasm and their "need for action," as well as "dissatisfaction among the young with the older leadership" (Williams 1987, 136). Baker convinced the SCLC to sponsor a conference at Shaw University in Raleigh to help provide leadership and direction to the student movement. Between 200 and 300 students attended the meeting on 15 April 1960, and with Baker as its founder, the SNCC was born. A month later, Baker wrote that "the Student Leadership Conference made it crystal clear that current sit-ins and other demonstrations are concerned with something much bigger than a hamburger . . . students, North and South, are seeking to rid America of the scourge of racial segregation and discrimination—not only at lunch counters, but in every aspect of life" (Williams 1987, 137).

SCLC leaders attempted to bring the SNCC under their wing, but Baker insisted that students had a right to decide how they would be organized, and the SNCC became an independent organization. According to James Forman, a civil rights activist with the SNCC, the SCLC leaders "may never have forgiven Miss Baker for her act of defiance. Throughout the years that followed they consistently made unkind remarks about Miss Baker and her influence in SNCC. What they did not understand, perhaps, is that her position simply reflected the students' attitudes. Many . . . were extremely critical of the adult civil rights organizations existing at that time" (Forman 1985, 217).

Whatever the criticism from and conflict with other civil rights efforts, Baker continued her work with students, helping as the SNCC sponsored a variety of boycotts of businesses and organized students for voter registration drives. The SNCC became an aggressive civil rights organization, guiding later struggles over the war in Vietnam and the women's movement. According to Forman: "Throughout the decade of the sixties, many people helped to ignite or were touched by the creative fire of SNCC," but seldom did people understand that "the generating force" was Baker, whom Forman described as someone with "an endless faith in people and their power to change their status in life" (Forman 1985, 215).

Although she was often in the background during the turbulent period from the mid-1950s through the 1960s, Baker received more widespread recognition when she became the subject of a 1983 public television documentary called *Fundi: The Story of Ella Baker*. In Swahili, *fundi* means "one who hands down a craft from one generation to the next." She was also profiled in the acclaimed 1987 television documentary *Eyes on the Prize*.

References

Forman, James. 1985. *The Making of Black Revolutionaries.* Washington, DC: Open Hand Publishers.

Giddings, Paula. 1984. *When and Where I Enter: The Impact of Black Women on Race and Sex in America.* New York: William Morrow.

Lerner, Gerda. 1973. *Black Women in White America: A Documentary History.* New York: Vintage Books.

Smith, Jessie Carney. 1992. *Notable Black American Women.* Detroit, MI: Gale Research.

Wiley, Jean. 1990. "On the Front Lines." *Essence*, February.

Williams, Juan. 1987. *Eyes on the Prize: America's Civil Rights Years, 1954–1965* (companion volume to the PBS television series). New York: Viking Penguin.

BALCH, EMILY GREENE

(1867–1961)

She called herself "a citizen of the world" and declared that she was "at home wherever there are people," but during World War I, many Americans decided that they were not "at home" with Emily Greene Balch. Because of her pacifist stand and opposition to the war, she was often publicly ridiculed and abused, and in 1918, at the age of 51, Professor Balch's contract to teach at Wellseley College was not renewed. After 20 years of teaching, she was faced with a decision: how to proceed with her life. She chose to embark on a third career (the first had been social work) that spanned four decades, dedicating her energies and considerable time to world peace efforts, for which she was recognized with the Nobel Peace Prize in 1946.

Balch was born just after the Civil War in Jamaica Plains, a small village near Boston, Massachusetts. She was one of six children in a "proper" Bostonian family, with household servants, nurses, and a hired man. Her father, Francis Balch, was an attorney. He was "identified with the best of New England life" and was

described as a selfless person, "gentle, modest, affectionate, sympathetic," but with "an iron will when it came to what he believed to be his duty" (Randall 1964, 33). He is credited with having a great influence on Balch's life, particularly in his sense of tolerance, love of reading and education, and advocacy for justice. Her mother, Ellen, who died when Balch was 17, was an avid storyteller and helped instill in Balch a love for literature and poetry.

The Balch family was not rigid in its religious beliefs, and none of the children went to Sunday school. Their parents "felt that the atmosphere of Sunday schools as they knew them was conducive to irreverence by making children too glib," Balch wrote. "Instead we attended the Bible class of a much loved and re-

spected neighbor [who had studied at Harvard]. She gave us a fairly adult instruction in Bible history interpreted in a liberal and scientific spirit" (Randall 1964, 47–48). Early in her childhood, Balch vowed to herself that she would be of service in the world and would try to be as selfless as her father. She eventually joined the Quakers.

Balch's early education was at private schools, and at 13, she entered a girls' school, Miss Ireland's, in Boston. In 1886, a time when women were just beginning to be encouraged to go to college, Balch enrolled in Bryn Mawr, a Quaker school for women founded the year before. She graduated three years later and was awarded a fellowship to study political economy and French literature in France. Along with an American friend, Balch lived with a French family in Paris during her year of study. When she returned to the United States, she realized that she had gained only book knowledge, "completely second hand and unreal. I came home determined to see something of things for myself," she wrote (Randall 1964, 80–81).

During the next two years, Balch was an apprentice in the fledgling field of social work, which was being undertaken by the Boston Children's Aid Society. She worked in a home for poor and neglected children and delinquents. In 1892, she attended the Summer School of Applied Ethics at Plymouth, Massachusetts, where she met a number of stimulating lecturers, among them JANE ADDAMS of Hull House fame, who later became a close associate. The summer gathering focused on the settlement movement and social democracy through humanitarian efforts. That same year, Balch, with a group from the summer school, opened Denison House, a settlement in the South Cove district of Boston. At Denison, Balch was exposed to the realities of the labor movement and the struggle for decent wages and working conditions through trade unionism. She organized numerous women from affluent homes to work for labor reforms.

Within two years, Balch decided to give up social work for teaching at the college level, because she felt that she "could awaken the desire of women students to work for social betterment." She explained in later years, "The time I had put in active social work was of enormous value to me and colored and widened my

teaching and gave it most of what value it may have had" (Randall 1964, 86). She continued her own education at Harvard Annex (now Radcliffe) and the University of Chicago and spent a year studying in Berlin, Germany. While in Europe, she attended the 1896 International Social Workers' and Trade Union Congress in London and saw firsthand the deplorable conditions of workers and the degrading poverty of the slums.

In 1897, Balch began her teaching career in economics at Wellseley, which was among the first colleges to offer studies in socialism and the labor movement. Later, at the request of college trustees, she established a course in sociology, stressing social responsibility and direct action.

When war broke out in Europe in 1914, Balch joined several groups working for peace and became part of the Woman's Peace Party, cofounded in 1915 by Jane Addams and Carrie Chapman Catt, leader of the U.S. suffrage movement. The congress met at The Hague in the Netherlands. Balch's peace efforts cost her her job, but she was a devoted pacifist, advocating a league of nations, opposing military conscription, and pressing for a just peace. After the United States declared war on Germany in 1918, many well-known pacifists renounced their antiwar stance, but opponents such as Balch—who joined one of the first religious pacifist groups, called the Fellowship of Reconciliation—marched, wrote letters, and lectured on behalf of peace. She also spoke out against war profiteering and in favor of workers' rights. All this was in direct opposition to U.S. mainstream opinion, since the majority of Americans believed that views of social justice were akin to communist ideas in Russia.

After the armistice was signed in 1919, Balch joined the second women's peace congress at Zurich, Switzerland, and was elected to serve as international secretary-treasurer of what then became the Women's International League for Peace and Freedom, or the WIL. The international office was established at Geneva, and Balch worked for the organization for the next 30 years, traveling frequently to garner support for the league's causes. During World War II, she reluctantly approved of the U.S. efforts against Hitler. One biographer wrote that this appeared to be a "triumph of her realistic intellect over her moral conscience" but that it was probably "something else—the inability of even her fine-tempered and fertile mind to see how to implement that deeper and more enduring deliverance of experience, reflection and moral insight that we call 'conscience'" (Randall 1964, 348). Although Balch remained a Quaker and a pacifist for the rest of her life, she continued to struggle with the concept of a so-called righteous war and to work for the means to create a more rational and peaceful world.

References

Balch, Emily Greene. 1972. *Beyond Nationalism: The Social Thought of Emily Greene Balch*. New York: Twayne Publishers.

Randall, Mercedes M. 1964. *Improper Bostonian: Emily Greene Balch*. New York: Twayne Publishers.

BARNARD, *CATHERINE ANN*

(1875–1930)

Known as the "Good Angel of Oklahoma," Kate Barnard dedicated her life to seeing that the needs of the poor, the young, and the unrepresented were heard in the legislative houses of her state. Speaking out in a world dominated by men and their conflicting priorities in the first decades of the twentieth century took its toll on the physical and mental health of this diminutive leader of the child-labor movement in the United States. Ultimately, she was forced into seclusion and likely an early demise.

Her proclivity for helping others developed from her experiences in early life, as she too survived trying times. Her mother died when she was just two years old, and her father (to whom she dedicated her life) found it necessary to board her with strangers for extended periods. The family business had seen terrible reversals, throwing them into grinding poverty, and John Barnard left to homestead land in the Oklahoma Territory. Barnard took refuge in religious services and the company of the congregation, where she probably learned the value of sacrificing oneself for the needs of others.

When she was 16, Barnard's father sent for her. He needed her to live on the land he was homesteading to meet the legal requirements for validating his claim, while he went on to work in Oklahoma City. Barnard stayed there for two years in virtual isolation until she was able to follow her father and attend teacher training classes in the big city. She eventually became a secretary and found employment in the territorial capital of Guthrie, where she worked in the legislative assembly. This entry into the political arena proved to be a turning point in her career.

Barnard was chosen to serve as the Oklahoma Territory's representative at the 1904 World's Fair, and there she was exposed to the new thinking of the Age of Reform. Activists were working to improve the conditions of the homeless, workers, and other poor and powerless people. Barnard embraced the ideals of the reform leaders with all her heart. She researched and reported on conditions in the slums of St. Louis and Chicago and started writing articles warning of what could happen in Oklahoma City. No sooner did she return to her own neighborhood than she began to see the effects of poverty firsthand. All around her home, the area was fast becoming a slum.

Using her home as the base for her outreach, Barnard began soliciting donations to help her neighbors and the rest of the city's poor. She was very successful and expanded her efforts by breathing new life into the city's longtime charity organization (and precursor to the United Fund), the United Provident Association. She also used her knowledge and contacts in the political realm to bring attention to the problems of poverty and actually helped establish a union

for unskilled workers. She used the union to support candidates who were sympathetic to her cause. When it came time to establish a state constitution for Oklahoma, she led a coalition of farm and labor interests that helped ensure that there were child-labor and workplace rights statements in that document.

The territorial vote that created the state of Oklahoma also saw the election of the first woman to a state office. Barnard became the commissioner for charities and corrections. Initiating a new process for government that she dubbed "scientific statecraft," Commissioner Barnard invited top experts in such fields as mental health, juvenile justice, prison reform, and child labor to the capital to present their particular expertise to the legislators. With this exposure and doses of rousing oratory, the public became aware that there were problems with the status quo. After two years of intense lobbying, Barnard's efforts resulted in legislation with the strongest language up to that time for protecting the rights of children in the workplace.

With similar passion, Barnard took on juvenile detention, prisons, and the conditions that caused people to turn to crime. She was one of the first to see the connection between poverty and lawlessness, and her reform efforts always included a skills training component so that people could earn a decent wage. She also worked to improve mental health programs and working conditions in various industries, and even to protect clean sources of drinking water.

One of her pet concerns, however, was the plight of Native American youngsters who had been left orphaned and without homes. These children were being exploited by "foster parents" who sometimes had as many as 50 children in their charge. More often than not, the guardians had no idea where these children were. Once they got the orphans to sign over coal and oil rights that they had inherited from their parents, the children were no longer of value. Barnard's office aggressively prosecuted the guardians, and eventually, over 1,300 orphans had money returned to them. Meanwhile, Barnard was making powerful enemies of both political parties. These guardianships were common spoils for men who supported judges and legislators running for election. The commissioner was hurting a lot of the players in the good-old-boys' network. They did not like it, and the public had little concern about orphaned Indian children.

Unable to abolish the office of charities and corrections, the legislature gutted the funding. Barnard was no longer able to operate at full capacity because of money problems, but her mental health was of even more concern. Stress had affected her several times in previous years, and she had always blamed her inability to continue her work on various physical diseases. She spent many months in a sanitarium in 1911 and 1912, but April of 1913 was the worst. A total breakdown was under way because of the orphan advocacy issue, and she wisely chose not to run for a third term as commissioner.

Not finished yet, she organized the People's Lobby to help candidates who would continue to support her reforms, and she made one more attempt to publicize the problems of the Oklahoma tribes. When her last effort fell on deaf ears in the legislature, Barnard's spirit was finally broken. For the remaining 15 years of her life, she led a sad and tragic existence as a reclusive and bitter woman who blamed others for her ills and bad fortune. Although she was unable to see the

progress she had helped manifest, history has recorded her singular spirit and will to help the helpless.

References

Copeland, Edith. 1971. *Notable American Women*. Vol. 1. New York: Belknap Press.

Peavy, Linda, and Ursula Smith. 1983. *Women Who Changed Things*. New York: Charles Scribner's Sons.

Truman, Margaret. 1976. *Women of Courage*. New York: William Morrow.

BARNETT, IDA B. WELLS

(1862–1930)

Ida Barnett is best known for her fiery journalism and her crusade against white mob violence that led to barbarous lynchings of blacks in the late 1800s. Her work continued into the first two decades of the 1900s with her struggle for racial justice and her tireless efforts for women's suffrage, black voter registration, and integrated school systems.

Born into slavery just six months before the Emancipation Proclamation was signed, Ida Bell Wells was the eldest of eight children of James Wells and Elizabeth Bell Wells. Her parents, who were slaves, were "married as such" and then "were married again after freedom came" (Wells 1970, 7). The family lived in Holly Springs, Mississippi, where her father was a carpenter and her mother was a cook. Wells was unsure where or when she started school, but she noted that her earliest recollections were "reading the newspaper to my father and an admiring group of his friends" (Wells 1970, 9). She attended a freedmen's high school called Shaw University, later renamed Rust College.

Both her parents and her youngest brother died in 1878 during a yellow fever epidemic, and at the age of 16, Wells assumed responsibility for her younger siblings. A family friend stayed with the children while she went to work as a teacher. After one term, she moved with her two youngest sisters to Memphis to live with an aunt, her father's sister, and to find a better-paying teaching position. The rest of the family stayed with her mother's sister.

While in Memphis, Wells studied for a state examination to qualify for a teaching position in the city and taught in a rural school in nearby Woodstock. She traveled to the school and back by train, and during one of those trips, she publicly protested one of the many injustices blacks faced in the segregated South. She got on the train in Memphis and sat down in the ladies' coach, but the conductor would not take her first-class ticket, telling her that she had to move to a smoker car. There were no separate cars for blacks and whites at that time, but this was one way to segregate. When Wells refused to leave the ladies' car, the conductor tried to pull her out of her seat, and as Wells recalled:

> The moment he caught hold of my arm I fastened my teeth in the back of his hand. I had braced my feet against the seat in front and was holding to the back, and as he had already been badly bitten he didn't try it again by himself. He went forward and got the baggage-man and another man to help him and of course they succeeded in dragging me out. They were en- couraged . . . by the . . . [whites] in the car; some of them even stood on the seats so that they could get a good view . . . applauding the conductor for his brave stand (Wells 1970, 19).

Rather than being forced into the smoker, she got off the train and returned to Memphis, where she promptly filed a lawsuit against the railroad. After months of delay, the court awarded her damages, which the *Memphis Appeal* recorded on 25 December 1884 with these headlines: "A Darky Damsel Obtains a Verdict for Damages against the Chesapeake & Ohio Railroad—What It Cost To Put a Col- ored School Teacher in a Smoking Car—Verdict for $500."

Throughout the late 1800s, Wells continued to teach and to further her own education. She also began to write articles for the black press and gained a rep- utation as a fearless journalist for her angry editorials against the wholesale lynchings of black men. Because lynchings were conducted without any proven charges against blacks and were tolerated by most whites, Wells believed that there was no choice but armed resistance and called for blacks to rise up and fight with whatever weapons were available. Her writings brought her national attention, particularly after she moved to Chicago and wrote for the first black newspaper in the city, the *Chicago Conservator*, founded by attorney Ferdinand L. Barnett, whom she married in 1895.

The couple continued the crusade for equal justice under the law for blacks, and in 1909, Ida Wells Barnett helped convene a national conference in New York City to deal with racial violence. The National Association for the Advancement of Colored People (NAACP) was born from that conference, and Barnett helped found the NAACP's publication *Crisis*.

Some of Barnett's other accomplishments included efforts on behalf of a Chicago settlement house established by the Negro Fellowship League in 1910 and longtime efforts for voting rights. In 1913, she founded the first black suf- frage organization—the Alpha Suffrage Club of Chicago—and was active in Chicago politics and civic affairs until her death in 1930. Since then she has been honored in numerous ways. In 1950, for example, she was named one of the 25

outstanding women in Chicago's history and was commemorated in 1990 by the U.S. Postal Service with a postage stamp.

References

Smith, Jessie Carney. 1992. *Notable Black American Women*. Detroit, MI: Gale Research.

Thompson, Mildred I. 1990. *Ida B. Wells-Barnett: An Exploratory Study of an American Black Woman, 1893–1930*. Brooklyn, NY: Carlson Publishing.

Wells, Ida B. 1970. *Crusade for Justice: The Autobiography of Ida B. Wells*. Edited by Alfreda M. Duster. Chicago: University of Chicago Press.

BARTON, CLARA

(1821–1912)

Known as the "Angel of the Battlefield," Clarissa Harlowe Barton was heroine to Civil War soldiers fighting for the Union. Much later she became even more famous as founder of the American Red Cross.

Raised in Cambridge, Massachusetts, Barton was shy when she was young and would often hide behind her mother's skirt when they went to town or to church. This trait concerned her affluent parents to such a degree that they sent her away to boarding school when she was just nine years old. Young Barton was unhappy at the school and lost weight, so her parents quickly allowed her to return home.

A year later, Barton began her first experience as a caregiver. Her favorite brother, David, fell from the roof of a barn he was helping to raise on their parents' property. Initially shaking off the effects of the fall and continuing the work, the boy eventually suffered severe headaches and fevers. Doctors prescribed a common treatment of the day: bleeding to reduce the blood pressure. Barton stayed by her brother's bedside to administer medicines, handle the leeches used for bleeding, and generally comfort the boy, who was not expected to recover. His illness continued for two years until new physicians were called in, who stopped the bloodletting. Within three weeks, David showed signs of

improvement, and he soon recovered full health, thanks in good measure to the dedication and substantial sacrifice of his sister.

Barton's hypersensitivity and shyness continued to concern her parents, who sought advice from members of the intellectual community who frequented their home. One of these visitors, phrenologist Lorenzo Fowler, suggested that Barton take on the responsibility of teaching others in order to break free from her self-doubt. The study of the skull has now fallen into disrepute, but Barton was inspired by Fowler's work, and she spent much time throughout her long life studying the workings of the mind.

At the age of 17, Barton received her teaching license and taught for over a decade. After a sabbatical to take further training in New York, she resumed her teaching career at a Bordentown, New Jersey, school. There she discovered that even though laws mandating free public education were on the books, many of the city's youth spent their days in the streets, unable to afford a seat in one of the private schools. With the support of the local board, Barton opened the first "pauper school" in Bordentown in 1852, with herself as the only, unpaid, staff person. By the end of the first year, 600 students were attending classes there, and the board decided to hire a male headmaster. The headmaster made the 32-year-old Barton's life miserable at the institution she had created. He found ways to undermine her authority at every turn, and Barton could do little to fight back. She avoided a complete mental collapse but lost her voice due to the stress. She was forced to resign in 1854.

While recovering her health at her sister's place in Washington, D.C., Barton was able to make important contacts in the government. She was one of the first women to be hired to do sensitive work in the Patent Office, copying secret documents. Once again, she received a good measure of abuse for daring to be of the "wrong" gender. President Franklin Pierce's representatives attempted to get all the female clerks fired; failing that, they pressed to have the women do their work outside of the regular office space. Fortunately, her boss was more enlightened, and he protected Barton's position, but he could not always protect her from the tobacco-spitting attacks of her coworkers.

When the Civil War started, Washington was immediately affected. Wounded troops were cared for in various government buildings. Men from the 6th Massachusetts were bedded down in the Senate chambers. Barton gathered soap, clothes, and food and rushed to the Capitol building to tend to the men, who were in immediate need of supplies, food, and medical attention. She was cheered for her efforts, but she knew that there was much more to be done. Soldiers often died from lack of immediate care.

Barton began a letter-writing campaign to the people of Massachusetts and to all her political contacts. The result was an outpouring of supplies that eventually had to be stored in a warehouse. She was even more concerned that the army was ill prepared to respond to the medical needs of the wounded. She knew that if she could provide care early—on the battlefield—more of the men would live. She also knew that women would not be welcome anywhere near the fighting. However, she persistently lobbied the surgeon general, and he eventually granted her request to follow the Massachusetts Regiment. Her first

test was at Cedar Mountain, Virginia, where she drove a wagon to aid battlefield surgeon James Dunn, the man who gave her the title "Angel of the Battlefield."

Two weeks later, she received permission for three more women to join her at the second battle of Bull Run, and their sacrifice is now legendary. Barton was at countless battles and saw horror after horror. With little regard for her own safety or comfort, she sometimes worked 48 hours nonstop, making certain that her soldier patients received the care they deserved. When there was insufficient funding to keep up her work, she used her own money.

At the end of the war, she helped find the bodies of missing Union soldiers so that the men's families could have peace of mind. She was also instrumental in seeing to it that Andersonville Prison was turned into a national cemetery. To pay for her efforts, she undertook an extensive lecture tour between 1866 and 1868, but the stress of this activity brought back a familiar malady: once again she lost her voice. She traveled to Europe to recuperate but soon found herself working with the Red Cross nursing the wounded in the Franco-Prussian War. Her activity with the Red Cross was to have a lasting effect. She admired how the organization was able to respond to the needs of those without hope. When she returned to the United States, she brought with her an authorization to establish the American branch of that body. After lobbying her political contacts, including President James Garfield, she gained enough support to open the first office of the American National Red Cross Society in 1881.

For the next 23 years, she established the tone and the framework for this volunteer agency. She organized responses to natural disasters and demonstrated how peacetime preparedness was as important as tending to the wounded in battle. At the end of the Spanish-American War in 1898, the 77-year-old Barton was on the first relief ship as it steamed into Havana harbor.

In her later years, she continued to organize relief efforts in the United States after floods and other disasters. When she officially retired, she wrote several books; *The Story of the Red Cross* was published in 1907. Her charitable work continued until her death in 1912.

References

Bains, Rae. 1982. *Clara Barton, Angel of the Battlefield.* Mahwah, NJ: Troll Associates.

Barton, Clara. 1907. *The Story of My Childhood.* New York: Baker & Taylor.

Barton, William Eleazar. 1969. *The Life of Clara Barton, Founder of the American Red Cross.* New York: AMS Press.

Boylston, Helen Dore. 1955. *Clara Barton, Founder of the American Red Cross.* New York: Random House.

Hamilton, Leni. 1988. *Clara Barton.* New York: Chelsea House.

Ross, Ishbel. 1956. *Angel of the Battlefield: The Life of Clara Barton.* New York: Harper & Brothers.

BELL, DERRICK

(1931–)

Whenever he is asked why he challenges authority, Derrick Bell recounts the story of his mother, who dared to stand up to her landlord during the Great Depression. As Bell wrote:

> My family lived in the Hill, the mainly black area of Pittsburgh, Pennsylvania. I was six or seven years old, but I remember my mother, Ada Childress Bell, taking my brother, Charles, and me with her to the rent office. My mother, standing in front of the barred teller's window, taking cash from her purse, waved it in front of the clerk. "This is the rent money. I have it—and you will get it when you fix the back steps so that my children won't fall and hurt themselves." Then, we left the office (Bell 1994, 11).

The landlord fixed the steps, but the confrontation had been a risky undertaking. Had the landlord evicted the family, they would have been homeless.

Bell's father, Derrick Bell, Sr., worked as a laborer and did not have steady employment. Still, Bell's father was the sole wage earner for his family and took pride in the fact that his wife could stay home to care for their children and home. When Bell was a teenager, his father was able to start his own trash-hauling business and obtain middle-class status, enabling his parents to pay for a college education for Bell, his brother, and two sisters.

Bell spent two years in the military and then enrolled at the University of Pittsburgh Law School in 1954. He planned to pursue civil rights law, although a black federal judge, William H. Hastie, discouraged him from doing so, reasoning that with the landmark U.S. Supreme Court decision striking down school segregation, there would be little need for civil rights lawyers. Bell soon discovered, however, that precious little real racial reform took place in the latter part of the 1950s.

When he took his first job as a lawyer with the U.S. Department of Justice, Bell was asked to give up his membership in the National Association for the Advancement of Colored People (NAACP). Belonging to the group was considered a conflict of interest. Bell refused and resigned his position. In 1959, he accepted a job as the executive director of an NAACP branch in Pittsburgh and organized groups to attempt to desegregate public places.

From 1960 to 1966, Bell was on the staff of the NAACP Legal Defense Fund in New York City. During this time, he married, and the couple had three children. Bell credits his wife Jewel with being his "fiercely loyal companion" during his protests. She died of cancer in 1990, and Bell remarried in 1992.

In 1966, Bell became deputy director of civil rights with what was then the U.S. Department of Health, Education, and Welfare. He found, however, that the

department took little action to force schools and other facilities to desegregate or to abide by the 1964 Civil Rights Act banning discrimination in employment.

After submitting a number of applications for teaching positions, Bell joined the faculty of Harvard Law School in 1969. He described the appointment as "pioneering," since he was the first full-time black law teacher in Harvard's history. He understood that the offer had been prompted by the civil rights movement of the 1960s and by the fact that many top all-white law schools were being pressured to hire black faculty members. When he accepted the position, Bell stated that he "did not wish to be a token black and expected that the school would actively seek and hire other minority lawyers for the faculty" (Bell 1994, 34).

After 20 years, little progress was made in this regard. Bell was given tenure, and although Harvard hired several white women and black men as professors, the law school had no black woman in a tenured or tenure-track position. The school lagged behind many other law schools in diversifying its traditionally white male faculty. In 1990, Bell announced that he would stop teaching at Harvard and, in protest, take a leave without pay. He later accepted a position at New York University as a visiting professor. In 1992, he refused to return to Harvard after a two-year leave and filed a discrimination complaint against the law school, charging that the school obtained its faculty "through an insider-based network of colleagues at a few elitist institutions." He also charged that the practice of citing faculty candidates' lack of merit was "a smokescreen for . . . nepotism . . . a way of continuing a racist, sexist, homophobic tradition with words whose viciousness is cloaked by what appears to be an insistence on excellence" (Jordan 1992).

To date, it appears that Bell's protest did little to change practices at Harvard Law School, but as he told his students in 1992, "my protest leave was undertaken less to change the school than to influence students through example as well as through exhortations of perhaps the most important lesson my life experience has taught: commitment to change must be combined with readiness to confront authority . . . because your faith in what you believe is right must be a living, working faith, a faith that draws you away from comfort and security and toward risk, when necessary, through confrontation" (Bell 1994, 162–163).

References

Bell, Derrick. 1994. *Confronting Authority: Reflections of an Ardent Protester*. Boston: Beacon Press.

Daly, Christopher B. 1992. "Black Law Professor Fights Harvard." *Washington Post*, 2 July.

Jordan, Mary. 1992. "Black Harvard Law Professor Files Discrimination Complaint against School." *Washington Post*, 3 March.

BENARIO, OLGA

(1908–1942)

"I have struggled for the just and the good, for the betterment of the world. I promise you now, as I say farewell, that until the last instant I will give you no reason to be ashamed of me." Those were some of the parting words of Olga Benario, written in her last letter to her lover, communist guerrilla leader Luís Carlos Prestes, and their daughter Anita. Benario wrote her letter the day before Nazis sent her to the gas chamber at Bernburg in February 1942. She had been turned over to the Nazis as a "gift" to Adolf Hitler by the fascist regime of Brazil.

Little in Benario's background suggested that while she was still a teenager she would be considered one of the most remarkable communist activists of the twentieth century. She was born in Munich into a middle-class Jewish family. Although her mother, Eugenie, was considered an elegant high-society lady, her father, Leo, was a lawyer and Social Democrat with liberal leanings. Benario was influenced a great deal by her father, who often accepted working-class clients, providing free services for those who could not afford his fees. She frequently read the cases of people who had claims against their employers and saw for herself the poverty and injustice that she had only known superficially from books (Morais 1990). She attributed her later conversion to communism to her father's work rather than to any reading of Marxist theory. At the time—the early 1920s—the class struggle in Germany was acute, with many working people nearly destitute and the middle class rapidly eroding.

For Benario, communism was the solution to the deteriorating economic situation, and a few months before she turned 15, she joined the Communist Youth, which had been banned and had gone underground. She became an integral part of the most militant faction, the Schwabing Group, taking on such tasks as blanketing Munich and suburban areas with communist posters, which could have resulted in her arrest.

In late 1923, Benario met Professor Otto Braun, seven years her senior and a revolutionary. He responded to her eager requests for theoretical background on communism by directing her to various Marxist journals published in Berlin. The two soon fell in love, and Benario began urging that they go to Berlin and become part of the Communist Youth movement there. Although her parents certainly did not approve of her decision, she left her comfortable home and moved with her partner to a tiny apartment in Berlin, taking on a new identity as Frieda Wolf Behrendt, wife of Arthur Behrendt, the alias of Braun, who continued his illegal and clandestine work as a communist organizer.

The couple never married, because Benario associated the idea of marriage with what she considered the worst of bourgeois deformities—the economic dependence of women, obligatory love, forced intimacy. When people asked

why she and Braun—apparently very happy together—did not get married, Benario had a ready answer: "That's exactly why we won't marry—because we're happy, because we love each other. I will never allow myself to become another person's property" (Morais 1990, 23).

Benario had no tolerance for promiscuity, however, and thought that women who boasted of numerous bed partners were nothing more than prostitutes. She argued that Lenin would disapprove of such behavior.

In Berlin, Benario dedicated herself to numerous Communist Youth activities, from printing and distributing pamphlets to organizing worker demonstrations and strikes. In addition, to provide income, she held a job as a typist for the Soviet Trade Bureau. By 1926, she directed the propaganda and agitation activities of the Communist Youth, who often were harassed by the growing number of young Nazis.

Even though the Communist Party was legal, both Braun and Benario were arrested for their activities in 1927, accused of high treason. She was released after spending two months in Moabit Prison, but he was held, and his trial was set for May 1928. In March, however, with the help of Communist Party leaders, Benario led a daring raid on the prison and freed Braun, with no deaths or injuries. The two escaped to Moscow, where they became leaders in the international communist movement.

Benario's total dedication to communism eventually caused a rift in her relationship with Braun, who was sent by the party to China. During this time, Benario met Luís Carlos Prestes, who was living in Moscow but preparing to return to Brazil. In the late 1920s, Prestes had gained fame in Brazil as a "Knight of Hope," a revolutionary general who had led an uprising to depose the repressive government of Artur da Silva Bernardes, which had restricted all democratic freedoms in the country. After more than two years of battles, however, Prestes knew that his army could not change Brazil's oligarchy by deposing a dictator. In spite of being undefeated, he voluntarily laid down his arms and led more than 600 men into exile in Bolivia. In 1931, believing that only a popular uprising could save Brazil, he accepted an invitation by the Communist Party to move to the Soviet Union.

When Benario met Prestes, he was scheduled to return to his homeland, where he hoped to mount a communist revolution. Benario was assigned to be his bodyguard. Using aliases, they traveled as a married couple across Europe and North and South America before reaching Brazil. The planned uprising failed, however, and both Prestes and Benario, who was now pregnant, were imprisoned.

In prison, Benario was threatened with torture and was constantly interrogated, but at first she was not physically harmed because of the "reverential awe of policemen at all levels for Luís Carlos Prestes . . . [and] the woman they believed was his wife" (Morais 1990, 142). She was jailed with other revolutionary women and quickly became a leader, teaching classes on Marxist theory. When she was about four months pregnant, Benario learned that she would be deported to Nazi Germany, her worst fear. Yet there had been no request for extradition. Officials of the fascist government simply wanted to send Hitler a Jewish

communist. For several months, numerous attempts were made inside and outside the prison to save Benario from deportation—prisoners even staged a rebellion, which was put down with a promise by Brazilian officials to take Benario to a hospital. Instead, however, she was put on a ship headed for Nazi Germany. Although no charges were ever filed against her, she knew that she would be kept in prison simply because she was a Jew and a communist.

In spite of terrible conditions in Berlin's women's prison, where Benario was held, her baby, Anita, was born healthy, and Benario was told that her daughter could stay with her as long as she could nurse her. Meantime, Prestes's mother, dona Leocádia, had begun a campaign to gain the release of Olga and Anita, mobilizing support all across Europe. Benario's own family had disowned her. None of these efforts brought freedom for Benario, and after 14 months, Anita was taken from her and, fortunately, turned over to her paternal grandmother. Benario was devastated, and her fate was sealed. She was sent to the infamous Ravensbruck concentration camp, where she was interrogated for hours, placed in solitary confinement in an underground cell with slime-covered walls, and brutally whipped until she was nearly unconscious—all to try to break her activism among the prisoners. She remained defiant until the day she died in the Bernburg gas chambers. Her name and legend survive in the more than 90 buildings in Germany that were named for her.

Reference
Morais, Fernando. 1990. *Olga*. Translated by Ellen Watson. New York: Grove Weidenfeld.

BERRIGAN, *DANIEL,* AND BERRIGAN, *PHILIP*

(1921–) and (1924–)

Both Father Daniel Berrigan, a Jesuit priest, and former priest Philip Berrigan are known for their activism and civil disobedience, which began with protests against the Vietnam War during the 1960s. They have continued their peace activism ever since. In fact, Philip Berrigan has frequently called himself "a criminal for peace."

Born in Minnesota, the Berrigan brothers grew up in poverty. Even though their father, Thomas Berrigan, possessed many skills, he often worked at

Father Philip Berrigan (left) and his brother Father Daniel Berrigan (right) watch two baskets of draft board records burn 17 May 1968. The brothers, along with seven other demonstrators, burned close to 600 draft cards in Catonsville, Maryland, in protest of the Vietnam War.

jobs that went nowhere. Still, he somehow managed to feed, clothe, and house his wife and their family of six boys through various odd jobs, while their mother washed the clothes (sometimes in nearby streams), prepared meals, shopped, mended, and cared for children: in short, leading the life of a frontier woman.

The Berrigans were reared in the folklore atmosphere of the American West, where the men defended "their women," subdued brute creatures, walked tall, drank deep, and shot from the hip. Men were a law unto themselves, not to be provoked. Daniel Berrigan, an author and poet with numerous books to his credit, described his father as tyrannical, ruthless, violent in his moods, and impossible to please, expecting precise obedience to his demands. Thomas Berrigan also preached to his children that their disobedience would be punished by the wrath of God.

In contrast, the Berrigans' mother was instrumental in establishing a nonviolent, nonconfrontational way for them to endure. Daniel Berrigan followed the example of his mother and escaped his father's violence by avoiding him whenever possible.

In 1927, the family moved to New York State; their father was homesick for the Tipperary Irish, a farm clan outside of Syracuse. Daniel Berrigan's education progressed from Catholic elementary and secondary schools to Jesuit school, an order that requires strict obedience to church doctrine. Upon leaving Jesuit school in 1952, Daniel Berrigan was ordained a priest. Philip Berrigan was educated in a similar manner and also became a Jesuit priest. After leaving the priesthood, he married Elizabeth McAlister, a former nun. The couple has three children, the last born in 1981, and all have been activists in the peace movement.

During the 1960s, the Berrigans were outspoken critics of the Vietnam War. They came into national prominence in 1968 when they, along with seven others, went to Catonsville, Maryland. The group, which later became known as the Catonsville Nine, burned some 600 draft cards in a parking lot. The Catonsville event marked a turning point in the growing antiwar movement, which up to that time had been less confrontational—more in the nature of carrying protest signs. Now, civil disobedience was being encouraged by the antiwar leadership. Because of their actions, Daniel and Philip were imprisoned for two years. After Daniel served his term, he went underground for many months to avoid the Federal Bureau of Investigation. As he recalled in 1993, "It allowed me to focus on the important things" (Lockwood 1993, 14).

Both Philip and Daniel Berrigan belong to a group called Ploughshares, which believes in the biblical injunction to beat swords (in this case, nuclear missiles) into plows. Their first action took place in 1980 in King of Prussia, Pennsylvania, where they damaged two unarmed warheads at a General Electric nuclear facility. Since that first action, there have been dozens of others, with a lot of court and prison time being logged as a result.

Daniel Berrigan is also active in Kairos, an ecumenical group based in New York City. The group meets every two weeks to pray together and plan events, such as a march to the Riverside Research Corporation, where engineers and scientists conduct top-secret war research for the federal government. As Berrigan

points out, while one scenario is unfolding inside the building, "another scenario, a far different one, is playing at their doors; it is by now familiar . . . we sit, we pray and sing . . . and are hauled away by the police" (Wackerman 1995).

When asked why he was still so committed to activism when so many from the civil rights and antiwar movements of the 1960s and 1970s have faded from the scene, his response was: "American culture doesn't provide enough to draw on to keep going, for many obvious reasons. It is so instantaneous and destructive. You have to have something older and more tested. Something clearer." In short, he believes that there has to be faith and commitment, which also explains his lifestyle today. He writes poetry, lectures, and teaches college courses, but his primary work is as a volunteer with the dying at St Vincent's, a New York City AIDS hospice. "I've been a volunteer at St. Vincent eight years now. I'm assigned the dying who have special needs—usually two, no more than three people at a time. I stay in touch with them as long as they live and then I often attend the funeral. I try to encourage loved ones to join a grieving group for a year or so after the death. That is all a part of it, of course" (Wackerman 1995).

In spite of his diverse activities, Daniel Berrigan does not divide them into categories. All his work shares a "common thread . . . not to be obsessed with results or proving anything to yourself or justifying yourself . . . but to try to be a Christian in the real world" (Wackerman 1995).

Philip Berrigan and Elizabeth McAlister have also continued their activism, taking part in numerous confrontational antiwar protests. The two agreed early in their marriage that because one parent always had to be with the children, they would not take part in actions that would bring them simultaneous jail terms. In 1983, Elizabeth McAlister received a prison sentence for her role in hammering a B-52 bomber at Griffis Air Force Base in New York, but Philip Berrigan was not involved in that demonstration. His activism, however, has resulted in more than 100 arrests and a total of nearly seven years in jail. One of the most recent demonstrations took place in December 1993, when Philip Berrigan and three others staged a protest against weapons of war by scaling the barbedwire fence around the Seymour Johnson Air Force Base at Goldsboro, North Carolina, hammering the nose of an F-15E jet, splattering it with vials of their own blood, and then raising their fingers in peace gestures as they waited for security forces. The four were tried in 1994, and Berrigan was sentenced to an eightmonth prison term.

In recent years, Philip Berrigan has also been asked why he continues with efforts that have gained little attention since the end of the Cold War and the end of the threat of nuclear attack by the former Soviet Union. To Berrigan and other peace activists, the answer is simple: they are bearing witness to their beliefs. Even though they seldom receive much publicity for their actions, they continue to act out of a sense of faith, responsibility, and conscience, believing that, in the long run, their efforts may bring about social change. They draw their strength from biblical teachings and such models of nonviolence as GANDHI, MARTIN LUTHER KING, JR., and, most recently, NELSON MANDELA. Why would a person in his seventies continue such activism when younger people might be willing to step into his shoes? In Philip Berrigan's words: "If I made the choice to eliminate

myself because of my age, or because I'm getting feeble or anything like that, or because I'm getting in my dotage, well, that's strictly subjective, and it might not be true or just or faithful to do that" (McNulty 1994).

References

Berrigan, Daniel. 1973. *Prison Poems*. Greensboro, NC: Unicorn Press.

———. 1987. *To Dwell in Peace*. New York: Harper & Row.

Buckley, Stephen. 1992. "Berrigan Released while Appealing Contempt Term." *Washington Post*, 28 March.

Lockwood, Lee. 1993. "Still Radical after All These Years." *Mother Jones*, September/October.

McNulty, Timothy. 1994. "Jail Time Still Doesn't Deter Philip Berrigan." *Chicago Tribune*, 20 June.

May, Eric Charles. 1990. "19 Arrested Protesting Gulf Action." *Washington Post*, 31 December.

Reuters. 1990. "Activists Dump Dye in White House Fountain." *Los Angeles Times*, 31 December.

Smith, Gary. 1988. "Peace Warriors." *Washington Post Magazine*, 5 June, W22.

Wackerman, Daniel T. 1995. "Mind's Eye" (interview). *America*, 18 March.

BETHUNE, MARY McLEOD

(1875–1955)

Until their emancipation after the Civil War, Mary McLeod's parents, Sam and Patsy McLeod, were slaves, as were most of her 16 brothers and sisters. Despite numerous setbacks, society's discrimination against blacks, and Ku Klux Klan threats, McLeod became a major activist for women's rights, a prominent educator, and an influential government official.

Born in Sumter County, South Carolina, McLeod grew up on a farm, which the family was able to acquire after gaining freedom from slavery. Her family recognized her leadership abilities and encouraged her to get an education and to

practice her Christian beliefs. "When a white playmate snatched a book away and told her that because Blacks could not read, the book was not for her, Mary McLeod Bethune was filled with her life's central mission: education" ("Portraits of Leadership" 1994).

McLeod attended a small black religious school near her home and earned a scholarship to attend a Presbyterian school for black girls in Concord, North Carolina, where both black and white teachers provided role models. She wanted to be a missionary, and after graduating in 1894, she attended what later became known as the Moody Bible Institute in Chicago to train for an assignment in Africa. She was told, however, that African Americans were not placed in such positions—one of her greatest disappointments.

The discrimination did not stop her, and she decided to teach black students, which was almost the only profession open to black women at that time. She taught first at the Haines Institute in Augusta, Georgia, where she met Lucy Craft Laney, principal and founder of the school. Laney became McLeod's model, inspiring her to dedicate her life to helping others. Then she accepted a teaching position in Sumter, South Carolina, at the Kendall Institute. There she met her future husband, Albertus Bethune. They married in 1898 and for a time lived in Savannah, where their only child was born in 1899.

Bethune did not adapt well to domesticity and wanted to pursue her goal of educating black children, believing that this was the best way to overcome discriminatory practices. In 1900, after the family had moved to Palatka, Florida, she established a Presbyterian school for girls. Albertus did not share his wife's missionary zeal, and after about eight years, they separated, although they remained married until his death in 1918.

With little money, hardly any supplies, but a strong faith in God (which she often stressed and maintained throughout her life), Bethune went on to found the Daytona Educational and Industrial Institute in Daytona, Florida, in 1904. The school grew from its facilities in a rented house, where she taught five little girls and her own five-year-old son, to a thriving institution with an enrollment of 300 in 1922. Supported by black and white leaders in Daytona, the school eventually offered secondary education and a teacher training program for young women. In addition, the school conducted numerous outreach programs such as summer camps and schools, grew food products for sale, and held worship services. According to one biographical account, the school was a success because Bethune was an "incomparable" role model.

With her extremely dark skin, flat nose, and full lips, which clashed sharply with America's idea of physical attractiveness and which both blacks and whites deemed liabilities to leadership in middle class black America, Bethune transcended the restricted sphere that society usually assigned to one of her color and, for that matter one of her gender. Her sense of an unfettered self was so great that she defied Jim Crow customs and ordinances, most notably in her insistence on desegregated seating at the Daytona Institute. And despite Ku Klux Klan threats, she and her entire faculty and staff voted in 1920 and afterwards (Smith 1992, 88).

Bethune eventually merged the Daytona Institute with the Cookman Institute of Jacksonville, and in 1929, it became the coeducational Bethune-Cookman College. She served as its president until 1942.

During the 1920s, Bethune also worked for the advancement of black women through the Southeastern Association of Colored Women and then the National Association of Colored Women (NACW), serving as president of NACW from 1924 to 1928. In 1935, she established the National Council of Negro Women, an organization that helped link black female leaders to federal government officials; she headed that organization for 14 years. In 1936, President Franklin D. Roosevelt appointed her director of the Division of Negro Affairs of the National Youth Administration, a federal agency assisting young people during the Great Depression and throughout World War II. She was the first African American woman to head a federal office.

Because of her many contacts with officials in the Roosevelt administration, Bethune was able to present the needs of black Americans and state the case for equal rights, recommending federal government responses. However, being in government and in the good graces of the president and Eleanor Roosevelt, who considered Bethune a friend, did not prevent prejudicial acts and statements. Bethune often used humor to deal with bigotry. In one instance, "she was leaving the White House and a southern politician said 'Auntie, what are you doing here?' and she replied, 'Which one of my sister's children are you?'" (Height and Trescott 1994).

Outside of government she also worked for civil rights, marching and speaking out whenever she could. She continued her efforts for civil rights and her unrelenting struggle for educational opportunities for blacks until she died in 1955, just before her eightieth birthday.

References

Height, Dorothy I., and Jacqueline Trescott. 1994. "Remembering Mary McLeod Bethune." *Essence*, February.

Holt, Rackham. 1964. *Mary McLeod Bethune: A Biography*. Garden City, NY: Doubleday.

Peare, Owen. 1951. *Mary McLeod Bethune*. New York: Vanguard Press.

"Portraits of Leadership: Great African Americans in the Struggle for Freedom." 1994. *Black Collegian*, January/February.

Sicherman, Barbara, and Carol Hurd Green, eds. 1980. *Notable American Women: The Modern Period*. Cambridge, MA: Belknap Press.

Smith, Jessie Carney. 1992. *Notable Black American Women*. Detroit, MI: Gale Research.

BIEHL, *AMY ELIZABETH*

(1967–1993)

I n August 1993, Amy Biehl, an American Fulbright scholar from Newport Beach, California, was murdered by a militant black gang in the South African township of Guguletu. The African National Congress (ANC) denounced the murder "as racism in its crudest form" and said that the organization was "deeply shocked and angered that such acts should take place at a time when all should be united in their efforts to achieve peace and racial tolerance in our country" ("Two in South Africa Charged in Killing" 1993). The killers, who were members of the black militant Pan-Africanist Students Organization, apparently took the dictum of the antiwhite slogan "one settler, one bullet" seriously. The nation had been divided for decades by laws designed to separate people of color from whites. From the mid-1980s, political violence had increased, and tension was especially high in 1993, because the country was preparing for a national election in which blacks would be allowed to vote for the first time.

Biehl, one of four children of Peter and Linda Biehl, attended Stanford University and was an idealistic scholar and athlete—a marathon runner. She had planned to study medicine but decided instead to devote her life to the fight for human rights. She often spoke out about the apartheid system in South Africa, and when she graduated from Stanford, she wore a "Free Mandela" (referring to then-jailed South African activist NELSON MANDELA) sign on her mortarboard. After graduation, she took a job in Washington, D.C., with the National Democratic Institute for International Affairs, working as a program assistant from 1990 to 1992 and traveling to various African countries to conduct voter education programs. One of her college friends, a lawyer in Palo Alto, California, reported that Biehl

> told of a mock election during a program in South Africa when people cried as they dropped their ballots in the box. They had never voted before.
>
> In her work and in her friendships, Amy listened to people. She stopped cold and focused intently on their desires, their pain. To the people she tried to help politically, that quality made her a figure of respect (Soosai-pillai 1993).

In 1993, Biehl went to South Africa on a Fulbright research fellowship to study at the black University of the Western Cape, where she concentrated on women's issues. She also worked as a researcher for a member of the ANC and its women's league and took part in efforts to eliminate apartheid and make liberty a reality. She was "committed to bring justice, to work for peace," said the minister who conducted her funeral, adding that "Amy was not naive—she knew precisely what could have happened to her." But the minister insisted that Biehl would not have harbored any hatred toward her killers (Dizon 1993).

Vusi Shangase, chairman of the California chapter of the ANC, called Biehl a "hero" and noted that "our job is to make sure that her spirit is picked up by some other younger people to help our people in South Africa head toward democracy" (Dizon 1993).

At the time of her death, Biehl had just completed her ten-month study tour. She was murdered two days before her scheduled flight home as she was driving several colleagues to the township of Guguletu. She was the only white person in the car, and when she pulled off the road, a gang of about 30 youths started throwing stones and bricks, smashing the windshield. In spite of her friends' pleas that Biehl was a comrade, several in the mob dragged Biehl from the car and beat and stabbed her to death while others chanted antiwhite slogans. Several people were arrested the next day, but for a time it seemed that they would not be brought before a judge (there are no jury trials in South Africa), because witnesses were intimidated by threats of violence. However, three men were convicted of murder on the basis of their own confessions and the testimony of witnesses who eventually came forward; in mid-1995, a fourth man was also convicted.

Peter and Linda Biehl harbor no bitterness, even though Linda and her oldest daughter, both of whom attended the trial in Cape Town, South Africa, were harassed and taunted by militant blacks outside the courthouse. According to news reports, militants tried to make the trial a political circus, demonstrating daily and making fun of the grisly accounts of Biehl's murder. On numerous occasions, the Biehls have expressed their sympathy for the families of the murderers, calling the whole situation a terrible tragedy for all and expressing the hope that the killers would not be sentenced to death, since that penalty would not bring their daughter back.

To commemorate their daughter's work, the Biehls have set up a scholarship fund in her name at Stanford University to finance studies for a South African student. They have also established the Amy Biehl Foundation, which will distribute grants for grassroots efforts, such as food programs for the poor and work for the disenfranchised. Biehl's father noted that "everything [Amy] did was from the ground up," so each member of the family "is highly committed to seeing that her work is continued" and that the ideals she stood for are promoted (Scheibal 1995).

References

Dizon, Lily. 1993. "Hosannas for Slain Activist." *Los Angeles Times*, 4 September.

Scheibal, Steve. 1995. "Foundation To Continue Work of Amy Biehl." *Los Angeles Times*, 19 March.

Soosaipillai, Miruni. 1993. "Dear Amy . . . My Unstoppable Friend, Slain in South Africa." *Washington Post*, 5 September.

"Two in South Africa Charged in Killing." 1993. *Washington Post*, 27 August.

BIKO, STEVEN

(1946–1977)

In 1968, the major leaders of the antiapartheid movement in racist South Africa had been effectively silenced. Robert Sobukwe of the Pan-Africanist Conference and NELSON MANDELA of the African National Congress had been jailed for their activities in support of overthrowing the Afrikaner nationalist government. Others had been forced underground due to a government crackdown on all black political groups. For several years, a leadership vacuum had existed within the black community, but a new movement was beginning to emerge. Called the Black Consciousness Movement, its self-effacing leader was Steven Biko.

Biko was born in 1946, a Bantu of King William's Town, South Africa. Raised by his mother after his father's death when Biko was four, the boy was a good student and a standout among his peers in many ways. Even those who were twice his age would comment about his presence and the charisma that prompted them to defer to his insights and opinions. Like many truly great personalities, Biko never sought notoriety or fame. He spoke the truth as he saw it with a total lack of animosity toward others, including those who sought to maintain the status quo of the immoral society they had created. Even though they imprisoned, beat, and hobbled him whenever they could, Biko always differentiated between the people and the evil acts they committed. He had a remarkable ability to win the respect of those who were his enemy.

At the end of the 1960s, Biko was attending the University of Natal Medical School, but he could not maintain his grades. Studying had become impossible, as political activities were taking up more and more of his time. He and a small group of followers had begun to articulate the ideas of black consciousness. After 300 years of being defined by the white imperialist culture that had come to dominate their homeland, these students were beginning to express their own view of the world. Biko, as the leading spokesperson for these students, put it this way at the end of an essay on black consciousness.

> We are aware that the white man is sitting at our table. We know he has no right to be there; we want to remove him from our table, strip the table of all the trappings put on it by him, decorate it in true African style, settle down and then ask him to join us on our terms if he wishes (Woods 1987, 60).

Some in the liberal white community accused Biko of being a black racist, and government officials portrayed him as a white hater, but Biko was neither. He was totally convinced, however, that his people's struggle for freedom would progress only when they had thrown off both the yoke of the white liberals' guilt

and the government's laws. His South African Students Organization (SASO) was unabashedly open regarding the need to establish a unique black voice and a strong black movement to break the back of white domination and exploitation.

Biko was arrested several times for his activities in support of the SASO, and government agents threatened and intimidated him in attempts to end his leadership role. Even beatings had no effect on this man, who was fearless in the face of the ultimate threat: death. "You are either alive and proud or you are dead," he related in an interview just before his life ended, "and when you are dead, you can't care anyway" (Woods 1987, ix).

By the early 1970s, the government's fear of Biko and the black consciousness movement led them to officially "ban" the charismatic leader. Banning was a legal action, but it was done without the benefit of a trial. It required the accused person to stay within the geographic confines of his home area, forbade him to publish or be quoted, and allowed him to speak to no more than one other person at a time. In addition, he was under constant surveillance by the police. The authorities could, and did, enter any place where Biko was for the express purpose of monitoring the terms of the banishment. If they decided that the conditions were not being met, he was subject to immediate arrest.

Biko took great pleasure in defying the order, and with the help of his network, he maintained his contacts throughout the country—even going many miles from his home in King William's Town to speak to throngs of people. On 18 August 1977, the police stopped him and a friend at a security checkpoint in Eastern Cape Province. In violation of his banning order, Biko was arrested and taken to Port Elizabeth for "interrogation." The police at that station had a reputation for violence, but none of Biko's friends really had any fear about his safety. After all, he was too important a political figure and too well known internationally for the authorities to do something foolish while he was in their custody.

Unfortunately, the authorities were more foolish and more savage than anyone had feared. On 6 September, Biko was taken into Room 619 wearing handcuffs and leg irons. There, he was chained to a grill and underwent 22 hours of interrogation. Throughout that period he was tortured and beaten, and at least one of the blows struck his head. The helpless man fell unconscious and later lapsed into a coma. On 12 September he was pronounced dead.

Initially, the chief magistrate blamed the death on Biko himself: he starved to death refusing to eat. But as the facts began to emerge, no one could deny that Biko's death was the result of a violent act. An official inquest said as much but failed to indict anyone. In the long history of the South African government's immoral treatment of its disenfranchised majority, this was the death of just one more "black bugger."

The importance of Biko's life becomes more obvious with the passing of time. His martyrdom put into perspective for many whites, in and out of South Africa, the truly horrendous nature of apartheid. In a very real sense, his passing was one of the last big steps in the eventual dismantling of that system.

Reference
Woods, Donald. 1987. *Biko*. New York: Henry Holt.

BOJAXHIA, *AGNES GONXHA*

See *TERESA, MOTHER*

BONHOEFFER, *DIETRICH*

(1906–1945)

He was a theologian, a German Lutheran pastor, and a pacifist who believed in the biblical commandment not to kill. During World War II, however, the evil of Adolf Hitler forced Dietrich Bonhoeffer to question whether there was ever a time when killing was right to save humanity. It is an ethical dilemma that many people of conscience have faced over the ages, and Bonhoeffer had to weigh his religious convictions against the need to act against Hitler's atrocities. He found that he had to "sin boldly," as Luther advised, in order to take moral action, and he died as a result.

The son of a well-known neurologist, Bonhoeffer was reared as a traditional Lutheran and was taught that the religious and political worlds should be separate. After completing his theological studies at the age of 20, he pastored various churches in Europe and also taught theology, but he became uncomfortable with established religion and believed that faith was of the spirit.

In the early 1930s, he became increasingly concerned about Hitler's rise to power. Days after Hitler's election, Bonhoeffer, in a radio broadcast, warned listeners about leaders who become idols and dictators. In 1933, Bonhoeffer and Martin Niemoller organized the Confessing Church—called a "religionless Christianity"—which declared that a church is a church only when it works in behalf of others. Bonhoeffer believed that Christians should put themselves on the line—be martyrs, if necessary. He rejected the kind of piety displayed by Christians who could stand by while Jews were persecuted.

Bonhoeffer led the Confessing Church, which became the strongest resistance movement against National Socialism in Germany, until it was banned in 1935. When World War II began, Bonhoeffer's life was in danger, and American friends helped him escape to New York City. He was offered a position at Union Theological Seminary, but after a month of torturous self-examination, he decided to return to Germany. In a letter to theologian Reinhold Niebuhr, he wrote:

> Christians in Germany will face the terrible alternative of either willing the defeat of their nation in order that Christian civilization may survive, or willing the victory of their nation and thereby destroying our civilization.

I know which of these alternatives I must choose; but I cannot make this choice in security (Broadway 1995).

Bonhoeffer joined the underground in Germany, which eventually saved more than 1,000 Jews from the Nazis. As he pointed out in a letter to his family and members of the German Resistance movement:

We have for once learned to see the great events of world history from below, from the perspective of the outcast, the suspects, the maltreated, the powerless, the oppressed, the reviled—in short, from the perspective of those who suffer (Reardon 1990).

He joined a conspiracy to assassinate Hitler, but the plan failed. In 1943, the Nazis arrested Bonhoeffer, and he was held for a year in Flossenburg prison as officials gathered evidence to convict him of treason. During that time, Bonhoeffer wrote letters to friends and family members and to Maria von Wedemeyer, to whom he was engaged. Compilations of these letters have been published in book form. In 1945, Bonhoeffer was hanged along with five others implicated in the assassination conspiracy.

References

Barnett, Victoria. 1993. *For the Soul of the People*. New York: Oxford University Press.

Bethge, Eberhard, Renate Bethge, and Christian Gremmels. 1987. *Dietrich Bonhoeffer: A Life in Pictures*. Philadelphia, PA: Augsburg Fortress.

Bonhoeffer, Dietrich. 1995. *Love Letters from Cell 92*. Nashville, TN: Abingdon Press.

Bosanquet, Mary. 1968. *The Life and Death of Dietrich Bonhoeffer*. New York: Harper & Row.

Broadway, Bill. 1995. "The Theology and Martyrdom of Dietrich Bonhoeffer." *Washington Post*, 8 April.

Kelly, Geffrey B., and F. Burton Nelson, eds. 1990. *A Testament to Freedom: The Essential Writings of Dietrich Bonhoeffer*. San Francisco: Harper San Francisco.

Rasmussen, Larry, and Renate Bethge. 1989. *Dietrich Bonhoeffer: His Significance for North Americans*. Philadelphia, PA: Augsburg Fortress.

Reardon, Patrick T. 1990. "Protestant Pastor Bonhoeffer's Life Has Tough Message for All." *Chicago Tribune*, 24 November.

Robertson, Edwin. 1988. *Shame and Sacrifice: The Life and Martyrdom of Dietrich Bonhoeffer*. New York: Macmillan.

Wind, Renate. 1992. *Dietrich Bonhoeffer: A Spoke in the Wheel*. Grand Rapids, MI: William B. Eerdmans.

BRANDEIS, *LOUIS D.*

(1856–1941)

He was known as the "people's counsel," and early in his life, Louis Brandeis became a leader in the labor movement to improve working conditions in the United States. He fought powerful interests—against monopolies and big business—and was labeled a radical, but for most of his life, much of it spent as a justice of the U.S. Supreme Court, he endeavored to bring about social reforms.

Brandeis was born in Louisville, Kentucky, to Adolph and Frederika Brandeis, who had emigrated from Bohemia to find a freer life in the United States. A cultured and fairly prosperous family, the Brandeises went back to Europe for a visit in 1873, and Louis attended German schools for two years. In 1875, the family returned to the United States, and Brandeis enrolled in Harvard Law School, where he excelled. He practiced law for a year in St. Louis, Missouri, but in 1879, he established a partnership with former classmate Samuel D. Warren in Boston, Massachusetts. Warren & Brandeis drew clients from among well-established corporations and businesses, and the firm flourished.

Brandeis married Alice Goldmark in 1891, and the couple had two daughters. Although the family was wealthy, they lived frugally, and both Louis and Alice devoted much of their time and money to social and political causes. One of the first major reform efforts Brandeis undertook as a lawyer was a revision of the Massachusetts liquor control laws; his goal was to make the laws more reasonable and thus less likely to be circumvented by liquor dealers who bribed state legislators to prevent strict controls. About this time, Brandeis also initiated the practice of working *pro bono publico*—for the good of the public—which he had vowed to do early in his life. As he explained: "Some men buy diamonds and rare works of art. . . . My luxury is to invest my surplus effort, beyond that required for the proper support of my family, to the pleasure of taking up a problem and solving or helping to solve it for the people without receiving any compensation" (Urofsky 1981, 16). In short, he gained satisfaction and happiness from serving and adamantly believed that one of the major obligations of any lawyer was to seek justice for all.

During the late 1800s and early 1900s, the industrial revolution was under way, and giant companies began to dominate U.S. politics and economy. Brandeis became involved in numerous trials and public hearings dealing with such issues

as the minimum wage, regulation of the workday, protection for strikers, and antimerger legislation to prevent huge corporations from controlling an industry.

Before the United States became involved in World War I, Brandeis was active in Zionism, the effort to establish a free and democratic Palestinian homeland for Jews. He became a leader of the Zionist movement in the United States and advocated self-help programs, not just philanthropic efforts, for people in Palestine.

In 1916, President Woodrow Wilson nominated Brandeis to be an associate justice of the U.S. Supreme Court. Up to that time, the Senate had routinely approved presidential nominations, but the Brandeis nomination stirred a heated debate that lasted for four months. Supporters praised his liberal views and efforts to establish humane laws. Opponents were critical of Brandeis's activism for social and economic reforms, and some launched anti-Semitic attacks, repeating an old stereotype and the outright fabrication that wealthy Jews were trying to take over the world. The debate was a trying ordeal for Brandeis and his family, but he refused to respond personally to any pro or con arguments. His nomination was confirmed, and he served on the high court until 1939, when he retired due to heart problems. His health deteriorated, and he died of a heart attack in 1941.

References

Auerbach, Jerold S. 1990. *Rabbis and Lawyers: The Journey from Torah to Constitution*. Bloomington: Indiana University Press.

Lerner, Max. 1994. *Nine Scorpions in a Bottle: Great Judges, Great Cases of the Supreme Court*. New York: Arcade Publishing.

Strum, Philippa. 1993. *Brandeis: Beyond Progressivism*. Lawrence: University Press of Kansas.

Urofsky, Melvin I. 1981. *Louis D. Brandeis and the Progressive Tradition*. Boston: Little, Brown.

BRANDT, WILLY

(1913–1992)

In 1970, *Time* magazine named Willy Brandt man of the year and described one of the German chancellor's most memorable moments—when he fell to his knees "on a freezing December day in Warsaw in 1970, before Poland's memorial to victims of World War II . . . making an act of atonement for his country's wrongs, a gesture that electrified the world" (Jackson 1992). The next year, Brandt was awarded the Nobel Peace Prize.

The son of a young, unmarried salesgirl in Lübeck, Brandt was named Herbert Ernst Karl Frahm at birth. When he was about four or five years old, he and his mother lived with his widowed grandfather, whom he called Papa. Later, when his grandfather remarried, he went to live with the couple; his mother worked nearby and visited several times a week. His grandfather, a factory worker and truck driver, was an ardent socialist and had a great influence on his grandson. In Brandt's words: "To Grandfather socialism was more than a political program; it was rather a kind of religion. It would make all men brothers, eliminate all injustice from the world, even the money would disappear" (Brandt 1960, 32–33). Among young Frahm's heroes were leaders of the Social Democratic Party, and while he was still a teenager, Frahm wrote for its newspaper.

His mother married while he was in high school, and she and her husband joined the Social Democratic Party, as did Frahm in 1930. Three years later, Adolf Hitler, whose Nazi Party had gained power, outlawed workers' parties. Thus, to escape the police, Frahm had to conceal his identity, calling himself Willy Brandt. In 1933, Brandt attended a national convention of the "illegal" Social Democratic Party in Dresden, where

> incredulously and with mounting exasperation we listened to the first reports about the persecution of the Jews. The humiliations and beatings were nothing in comparison with the horrors of the following years, but already appalling in their malice and senseless brutality. Active opponents of Hitler fell as victims of their resistance like soldiers on the battlefield. But here were human beings, the majority of whom had not even taken part in the political struggle, and they were now persecuted and tortured only because they were born as Jews (Brandt 1960, 59).

Back in Lübeck, Brandt was warned that he would soon be arrested, and he escaped on a fishing boat to Norway, where he was befriended by Norwegian trade unionists. Writing in 1990, historian Arthur M. Schlesinger, Jr., noted:

Today . . . it is hard to remember to what a low point the prestige of democracy had fallen half a century ago, how desperate the situation was for brave men who had fled dictatorships in their native lands to continue the fight from abroad. Many in the West, highminded people as well as scoundrels, felt there was no point to resistance. They saw totalitarianism . . . as the wave of the future (Schlesinger 1990).

In Norway, Brandt found work as a journalist in Oslo. He mastered the Norwegian language, completed his education, and became actively involved with the Labor Party's Youth Federation. During his years in Norway, Brandt and other party members tried to help their comrades in Germany, collecting funds, smuggling newspapers and pamphlets into Berlin, and attempting to aid those arrested by the Nazis. Although he was stripped of his German citizenship, he was active in the German underground.

In 1940, the Nazis invaded Norway, and because of Brandt's militant anti-Nazism, he was forced to flee again. He escaped to Sweden, leaving his wife, Carlota, who was pregnant, in the care of friends. In Sweden, he continued his activism against the Nazis and occasionally saw Carlota and his daughter, Ninja, but the marriage did not survive the long separations, and the two eventually divorced in 1944.

After the war, Brandt returned to Germany, where Berlin was divided among the four powers—the United States, the Soviet Union, Great Britain, and France—into occupaiton zones. In 1948, the Soviets began a blockade of Berlin, hoping to starve Western-occupied Berlin into capitulating and becoming part of Russian-controlled Berlin. The blockade lasted until 1949, but an airlift of supplies by the Americans and the British helped westerners hold their ground. At the beginning of 1948, Brandt also remarried. While the daily privations caused by the blockade were at their worst, his wife, Ruth, a Norwegian refugee, gave birth to the couple's first son, Peter. Their second son, Lars, was born in 1951.

After the Soviets ended the blockade, the three western zones in Germany formed the Federal Republic of Germany, or West Germany, and the Soviets formed the German Democratic Republic, or East Germany. At the same time, two sections of the capital were formed: West Berlin and East Berlin. During this time, Brandt's citizenship was restored, and he became an aide to the mayor of West Berlin, Ernst Reuter. He also began to reject the socialist dogma that called for state ownership of resources, and he vigorously supported the Social Democrats' move toward a democratic system with freedom of choice, a mixed economy, and social welfare programs.

Brandt became mayor of West Berlin in 1957, and in 1961 and 1965, he ran as the Social Democratic Party's candidate for chancellor of West Germany, losing both elections. During the campaigns, Brandt was sometimes called a traitor for leaving Germany during the war, and there were numerous smear tactics regarding his humble origins. The 1965 defeat prompted Brandt to leave public life for a time, but, in 1966, the Christian Democrats and Social Democrats formed a coalition, and Brandt later became vice-chancellor and foreign minister. He won election as chancellor in 1969.

Meantime, in 1961, the Soviets had built a wall dividing East and West Berlin, and Brandt became convinced that the United States had abandoned West Germany. Thus, as chancellor, he tried to improve relations with the USSR, abandoning German claims to land lost to Poland and the USSR and recognizing the new borders established at the end of World War II. He did not believe that communism and democracy had anything in common, however. Instead he was convinced that tensions between East and West Berlin had to be eased to aid the cause of peace.

Brandt was criticized in the United States for his *Ostpolitik*, or Eastern policy, but according to historian Arthur Schlesinger, "It hastened the demoralization of the Communist empire and invigorated the forces of reason and reform within the Soviet Union and Eastern Europe" (Schlesinger 1990). In addition, West Germans were able to travel to the East to visit friends and relatives, and eventually both East and West became part of the United Nations. All these efforts led the Nobel committee to award Brandt the Peace Prize in 1971.

Because one of Brandt's aides was arrested in 1974 and charged with spying for East Germany, Brandt "resigned under pressure, a decision he later regretted." He wrote that he should have demanded "a stop to all the nonsense" (Jackson 1992). His successors continued with his *Ostpolitik*, and the Berlin Wall fell in 1989. Brandt did not retire after his resignation. Instead, he continued as president of the Socialist International until his death in 1992.

References

Brandt, Willy. 1976. *People and Politics: The Years 1960–1973*. Translated by Maxwell Brownjohn. Boston: Little, Brown.

———. 1992. *My Life in Politics*. New York: Viking Press. Brandt, Willy, as told to Leo Lania. 1960. *My Road to Berlin*. Garden City, NY: Doubleday.

Jackson, James O. 1992. "A Bold Peacemaker: Willy Brandt: 1913–1992." *Time*, 19 October.

Schlesinger, Arthur M., Jr. 1990. "The Difference Willy Brandt Has Made." *New Leader*, 29 October.

BROWN, *OLYMPIA*

(1835–1926)

Olympia Brown was 85 years old when she and millions of other American women cast their first ballots ever in 1920. Brown had spent nearly her entire life in the effort to win equality for women and had worked with such well-known suffrage leaders as Susan B. Anthony and Elizabeth Cady Stanton, both of whom died before realizing their goal. Brown's contributions to the fight for women's rights have usually been overlooked in historical accounts of the suffrage movement, but she was at the forefront of women's struggles for equality and justice. She also was the first woman in the United States to achieve full ministerial standing recognized by a religious denomination. That and other achievements came only after overcoming numerous obstacles and discriminatory practices against women that were common in the nineteenth and early twentieth centuries. She persevered because of a sense of idealism and her desire to seek justice for all women.

Brown was the first of four children of Asa and Lephia Brown, who settled in what was then the territory of Michigan on a farm near the village of Schoolcraft, where Lephia's sister Pamela and her husband Thomas Nathan lived. The Nathans were abolitionists and operated an Underground Railroad, helping nearly 1,500 ex-slaves escape to Canada. Brown learned early in her childhood about the dangers of fighting against slavery and for justice and equality. She often listened to the stories of ex-slaves, and according to her biographer, "she never forgot her astonishment when she first learned that many people regarded Negroes as inferior simply because of the color of their skin" (Coté 1988, 10).

Much of Brown's early education took place at home with her mother, who believed fervently in the equality of the sexes and instilled that principle in her children when they were small. She was their sole teacher for several years before a school was established in the area. Besides teaching them to read, write, spell, and do arithmetic, she read poetry to them and taught them some of the basic Universalist tenets—that salvation is extended to all human beings; that God is kind and loving, not angry and vengeful; and that there is no such place as hell. This affected Brown's life deeply, and when she went away to school, she had to cope with the tactics of zealous evangelists who preached hellfire-and-brimstone sermons and stressed the sinful nature of all human beings (Coté 1988, 11).

When Brown was 14 years old, she and her sister Oella left the farm to attend a school in town (after overcoming objections from their father, who thought that it was unnecessary for girls to get a secondary education). Later, both Olympia and Oella wanted to further their education, and with the persuasive help of their mother, they entered Mount Holyoke Female Seminary at South Hadley, Massachusetts. The boarding school required strict adherence to rules of

behavior—a far cry from the freedom they had enjoyed on the farm. The course of study was also rigid, and after a year of frustration, Brown refused to return to the seminary or to attend any other religious school. This time with her father's support, she enrolled in 1861 at Antioch College in Ohio. The Civil War had just begun, but the battles were far from the campus. Many students, however, spoke out against slavery and demanded freedom and liberty for all. "Olympia, thinking that their speeches included . . . women, too, complimented the speakers on their progressive attitude. The young men, however, were appalled at the idea of freedom and liberty for *women*" (Coté 1988, 55). Brown also found that the school rarely prepared women for a career other than teaching. While attending Antioch, she arranged to have Antoinette Brown (unrelated to Olympia), a Congregational minister, appear as a guest lecturer and role model. Although Antoinette Brown's ordination was not recognized by the church, she had a profound influence on Brown, who decided that she wanted to be a minister and was faced with the task of finding a theology school that would accept her. At the age of 26, she enrolled at St. Lawrence Theological School at Canton, New York, and in June 1863, after much opposition from the school and the Northern Universalist Association, she was ordained a minister.

Brown accepted pastorships in several small churches before going to Weymouth Landing, south of Boston, where she served for five years. Her installation at the church in Weymouth Landing created much attention, since she was the first woman in the United States to become an ordained minister. There were still numerous discriminatory practices against women to be overcome, however.

From the late 1860s through the early 1900s, Brown not only delivered sermons but also traveled extensively, lectured at meetings and rallies, and wrote articles advocating equality for women and women's suffrage. She presented one of her speeches appealing for suffrage before a U.S. congressional committee, but the congressmen were not persuaded by her words.

In 1873, Brown married John Henry Willis, a newspaper publisher and printer who was committed to suffrage and strongly supported his wife's work. Contrary to well-entrenched custom, Brown did not take her husband's name and for the rest of her life was known as Reverend Olympia Brown. The couple had two children.

In 1878, Brown and her family moved to Racine, Wisconsin, where she became minister of the Church of the Good Shepherd, and served for nine years. Her father died in 1887, and that year she decided to give up the ministry for a new career—campaigning for women's right to vote. For the next 15 years she canvassed the Midwest, lecturing on women's suffrage. After her husband died in 1893, her campaigning activities came to a halt for a time. She devoted her efforts to her husband's newspaper and to the care of her invalid mother, who died seven years later.

Once again, Brown took up her suffrage work, continuing her campaigning into the new century, when she was in her seventies and eighties. She tirelessly confronted hostile men and women who opposed enfranchisement. After World War I ended in 1918, Brown attended a rally in Washington, D.C., protesting

President Woodrow Wilson's lack of support for the proposed Nineteenth Amendment granting women's suffrage. Wilson had gone to France to sign the peace agreement, and the Washington protest group gathered to burn Wilson's papers and speeches. Reverend Brown, 84 and quite frail, was asked to speak. She told the crowd: "America has fought for France and the common cause of liberty. I have fought for liberty for seventy years, and I protest against the President's leaving our country with this old fight here unwon" (Coté 1988, 164).

The Nineteenth Amendment was finally ratified in 1919, and Brown cast her first ballot the next year. That was not the end of her activism, however. For the last six years of her life, she agitated for peace and military reform, joining the Women's International League for Peace and Freedom, the League of Nations, and the American Civil Liberties Union. As her biographer stated: "Today Olympia Brown would be in the vanguard of those women working for equal rights" (Coté 1988, 177).

Reference
Coté, Charlotte. 1988. *Olympia Brown: The Battle for Equality*. Racine, WI: Mother Courage Press.

BRUNDTLAND, *GRO HARLEM*

(1939–)

A practicing physician and the prime minister of Norway, Gro Harlem Brundtland is known worldwide as a successful environmental activist and women's rights leader. Since the 1970s, she has led a movement in Norway that has almost eliminated the so-called glass ceiling that prevents women from reaching the highest administrative positions in business and government. From 1974 to 1979, Brundtland was Norway's environment minister and became head of the country's Labor Party and Norway's prime minister for nine months after Prime Minister Odvar Nordli resigned for health reasons in 1981. She served her second term as prime minister from 1986 to 1989. Although she was reelected to a third term, she resigned in the fall of 1992 for "personal reasons"—one of her four children had committed suicide. In 1993, she again won reelection.

It was no easy task for Brundtland to rise in political stature and power. Because of her gender, few in Norway expected her to succeed during her first term as prime minister, but she was reelected. Since then, partly because of

Brundtland's advocacy for women and the appointment of many women to governmental office, gender is no longer much of an issue in Norwegian politics.

Born in Oslo, Norway, Brundtland was educated at the university there and at Harvard in the United States. While she was growing up, her father—a doctor and Laborite defense minister—encouraged political conversations and debates at the dinner table. As a youngster, she was also encouraged to play football, chop wood, and do other activities that traditionally were relegated to male family members. Early on, Brundtland decided to become a physician and also marry and have a family. She married Arne Olav Brundtland in 1960, and they had their first child while Gro was still in medical school. After her husband finished his education, he became the primary parent while she became involved in politics as an outspoken pro-choice advocate. Gro and Arne, a conservative columnist, have politically opposite views, but the two apparently do not allow politics to create divisions in their personal lives.

Since she first held political office, Brundtland's medical career has been surpassed by politics, but she has been active in numerous health care organizations and does not hesitate to practice her profession when needed. Once while on a flight during an election campaign, she treated a press photographer who became extremely ill (and later had to undergo surgery for gallstones). According to a *Time* magazine report:

> Dr. Gro Harlem Brundtland dropped her paperwork, moved to the back of the plane, and for the next 45 minutes tended the victim. She swaddled him in blankets on the floor of the narrow aisle, administering oxygen, monitoring his pulse, ordering the pilots to radio Oslo for an ambulance. When another photographer tried to shoot the scene, her aides waved him off. This was not a photo op (Gibbs 1989).

As a social democrat, Brundtland sees "a very close connection between being a doctor and being a politician." In her view, "The doctor first tries to prevent illness, then tries to treat it if it comes. It's exactly the same as what you try to do as a politician, but with regard to society." She also believes that people who "are born strong with parents who give [them] the best" have a special responsibility to help those who do not get the same kind of privileged start in life (Gibbs 1989).

In 1983, Brundtland chaired the United Nations World Commission on Environment and Development, made up of 22 policymakers and scientists from 22 countries. Over the next few years, they developed proposals for action to deal with crucial environmental and development problems worldwide. The commission's report, titled "Our Common Future" but commonly known as the Brundtland Report, was published in 1987, and many of the ideas in the report were central to the 1992 Earth Summit held in Rio de Janeiro, Brazil. Since its publication, "Our Common Future" has spurred an international movement for sustainable development—that is, global economic policies based on the concept of meeting people's basic needs without jeopardizing the environment and nurturing and sustaining the earth's natural resources. According to one analysis, those policies

have matured under the firm but caring guidance of Brundtland, who comes from a culture that has self-consciously defined a special relationship with nature. Norwegians are fervent lovers of the outdoors. From early childhood until old age they are found walking and skiing on their rugged country's abundant mountain slopes. Little wonder that Norway has served as the primary seedbed for "deep ecology," a philosophy that recognizes the integrity of nature as a supreme good ("The Road from Rio" 1993).

In a 1993 interview, Brundtland noted that developing countries need help from industrialized nations to eliminate such global environmental problems as destruction of the ozone layer, acid rain, and the emission of gases that contribute to the greenhouse effect. The top priority in her view, however, is alleviating poverty. "Only by educating people and giving them a fair chance to break out of poverty can we hope to find a sustainable relationship between population and resources. Otherwise, we will be forced, by default, to continue overusing natural resources" ("The Road from Rio" 1993).

Although she has served four terms, Brundtland's social-democratic form of government has been roundly criticized by conservatives, who complain about high taxes to support government programs that provide generous benefits for qualified recipients from the cradle to the grave. Conservatives are also critical of generous Norwegian aid to foreign countries, which Brundtland champions. In spite of threats to her political power, Brundtland does not pander to those who oppose her views. No matter what the costs—personal or political—she has steadfastly maintained that "without education and without health, people have no human rights and there can be no development. All these concepts are interrelated to the extent that they are rooted in human values and rights" ("Gro Harlem Brundtland" 1990).

References

Gibbs, Nancy. 1989. "Norway's Radical Daughter: Gro Harlem Brundtland. . . ." *Time*, 25 September.

"Gro Harlem Brundtland" (interview). 1990. *UNESCO Courier*, September.

"Growing with Brundtland." 1993. *Economist*, 4 September.

"The Road from Rio." 1993. *Technology Review*, April.

Uglow, Jennifer S., comp. and ed. 1989. *The Continuum Dictionary of Women's Biography*. New York: Continuum.

BUCK, *PEARL S.*

(1892–1973)

Pearl Buck wrote in her autobiography:

When I remember the fateful morning of March 27, 1927, I see it as a scene, as though I had nothing to do with it. A little group of white people stands, uncertain and alone, on the early green lawn of a grey brick house, three men, two women, three small children. The wind blows damp and chill over the compound wall. The sky is dark with clouds. They hold their coats about them, shivering, and they stare at each other.

"Where can we hide?" This is what they are whispering (Buck 1960, 236).

Packs of armed rebels and thieves, calling themselves "communists," were rampaging throughout the countryside burning the homes and businesses of foreigners, who were the target of their aggression. Buck knew that if her family was

discovered there at her home in Nanking, the revolutionaries would show them no mercy. They had been hearing many reports of murdered whites for days. Now, apparently, the day of reckoning had arrived.

Pearl Sydenstricker, born in Hillsboro, West Virginia, some 35 years before, had much sympathy for the Chinese people. In many ways, she understood the hate these marauders had for her and for all foreigners. Besides the fear for her family's safety that was overwhelming her on the lawn that morning, she must have felt a deep sadness. China was her land too. Brought there as a baby by her Christian missionary parents, who settled near Shanghai, Sydenstricker spoke and understood Chinese, preferred the local food and customs, and spent much of her time with native Chinese. Being born white was purely an accident of birth, she believed, but she had come to understand the difference.

As an eight-year-old during the Boxer Rebellion, she had heard the hateful remarks of former playmates directed at her because she was white. Europeans were killing the Chinese who dared to revolt against their pervasive influence, and some American soldiers had harmed people close to the Sydenstricker's mission. Sydenstricker and her mother had had to flee the area until the revolt was suppressed, and when they returned months later, she experienced the feeling of being "foreign" for the first time. The prejudice that went both ways, East and West, was something she would work against for the rest of her life.

Sydenstricker went back to the United States to earn her degree from Randolph-Macon College in Lynchburg, Virginia, but she felt very out of place there. When her mother became ill in 1914, she willingly returned to China to care for her and to teach at the University of Nanking. In 1917, she met and married Lossing Buck, an American agriculture researcher, and they moved to the rural north.

After struggling through trials that included the death of her mother and the birth and care of a mentally retarded daughter, Buck began what would be an extremely successful writing career. The sale of a short story, "A Chinese Woman Speaks," to *Asia Magazine* encouraged her to find as much time as possible to write, between child care, housework, cooking, and caring for her husband.

The theme of her work was the heroic nature of the lives of the people she had come to know in China: authentic and honest rural folk with a deep understanding of the land and their place in it. She hoped that when her countrymen across the Pacific Ocean read about her adopted land, true understanding might be possible. That hope was almost extinguished when the communists threatened her home.

She stood there on the lawn, wondering what to do, where to go. Then, through the gate came old

> Mrs. Lu, who lives in a cluster of little mud houses just over the wall in a pocket of an alley off the street that runs in front of the house. She comes hobbling toward us on her badly bound feet, her loose trousers hanging over her ankles. Her hair is uncombed as usual, rusty brown locks hanging down her cheeks, and her kind stupid face is all concern and alarm and love.
>
> "Wise Mother," she gasps, "you and your family, come and hide in my little half-room. Nobody will look for you there" (Buck 1960, 237–238).

Buck and her family hid in Mrs. Lu's house for days; then they made their way to Japan. Eventually they could return to their home, but life in China was changing. The communists continued to threaten the government, and no one was safe. She decided to take her daughter out of the country and return to the United States. There she settled down once more to concentrate on her writing and produced *The Good Earth*. In 1932, she was awarded the Pulitzer Prize for this work.

For the rest of her life, she continued to write books, publishing more than 100. Her work drew on her experiences, such as *Sons*, published in 1932, and *A House Divided*, published in 1935. Two biographies, one about her mother and the other about her father, were published in 1936. She also wrote several children's books and books about American life under the pen name John Sedges. Because of her success as a writer, she was in a financial position to further her humanitarian goals. She established organizations and gave millions of dollars to promote understanding and provide aid for people in need. Many of her efforts focused on aid for orphaned Asian children and retarded youngsters.

References
Buck, Pearl S. 1960. *My Several Worlds*. New York: Pocket Books.

Buck, Pearl S., with Theodore F. Harris. 1966. *For Spacious Skies: Journey in Dialogue*. New York: John Day.

Harris, Theodore. 1969. *Pearl S. Buck: A Biography*. New York: John Day.

Lipscomb, Elizabeth Johnsonton, ed. 1994. *The Several Worlds of Pearl S. Buck: Essays Presented at a Centennial Symposium, Randolph-Macon Woman's College, March 26–28, 1992*. Westport, CT: Greenwood Press.

Sterling, Nora B. 1983. *Pearl Buck, a Woman in Conflict*. Piscataway, NJ: New Century Publishers.

BUNCHE, RALPH J.

(1904–1971)

R alph Bunche was the first black American to become a high-ranking official in the U.S. State Department and the first to win a Nobel Peace Prize, but he was also known as a teacher and scholar and as a diplomat and peace negotiator during his years with the United Nations. Bunche spent most of his life working against racial and religious bigotry and as a peace activist.

Bunche was born in Detroit, Michigan, where his parents, Olive Agnes and Fred Bunche, lived with Olive's family, the Johnsons. Bunche's father was a baker and, like most black men of the time, had little or no opportunity to attain any kind of high-paying job. Lucy Johnson, Bunche's grandmother, had been widowed at an early age but had reared and educated five children. The Bunche-Johnson household was poor, but Nana, as Bunche called his grandmother, constantly reminded everyone that they were "rich in character, spirit and decency." Nana undoubtedly was head of the household; she was "strong in character and spirit and deeply religious . . . fiercely proud of her origin and her race, and everyone in our clan got the race-pride message early," Bunche noted (Haskins 1974, 11). Throughout his life, Bunche credited Nana and his mother with nurturing positive feelings about himself and stressing education as a means to get ahead in life.

In 1915, when Bunche's mother became ill with rheumatic fever (for which there was no quick cure at the time), the family moved to Albuquerque, New Mexico, so that she could be in a warmer climate. Although the family had

experienced discrimination in Detroit, it had been nothing like the overt racial prejudice they were subjected to in Albuquerque, which was segregated. There were separate sections for whites and nonwhites on streetcars, in theaters, and in other public facilities. Blacks were denied access to public pools and were forced to attend segregated schools. On numerous occasions, Bunche and others in his family were the objects of racial prejudice, but he followed the guidance of his grandmother and mother, both of whom refused to be put down and taught him to harbor no bitterness.

Whatever the obstacles, Bunche excelled in high school and at the University of California, Los Angeles—in both academics and athletics—and went on to earn a Ph.D. in political science at Howard University. He met Ruth Harris, a

teacher taking graduate courses at Howard, in 1929, and they were married the following year. They eventually had three children.

During the 1930s, Bunche headed the political science department at Howard University, where he worked with Gunnar Myrdal on portions of *An American Dilemma: The Negro Problem and Modern Democracy*, a groundbreaking study on race relations in the United States. He wrote numerous other works and spoke often about the struggles of black Americans against racial discrimination, about the lack of job opportunities, and about the need for blacks to obtain full citizenship rights. "In a world where democracy is gravely besieged, the United States must consider seriously the implications of its own failure to extend the democratic process in full to some thirteen million of its citizens whose present status tends to make a mockery of the Constitution," he wrote in 1941 (Urquhart 1993, 98).

Yet "Bunche believed at this time that it was a mistake to assume that [black] problems were basically racial in nature. Most of these problems, he felt, stemmed from the wider failure to improve the standard of living of the working classes," wrote biographer Brian Urquhart (1993, 98). Because of Bunche's view that most struggles in the world were actually class wars between the haves and the have-nots, he was often labeled a communist.

After the United States entered World War II, Bunche was appointed to the U.S. Office of Strategic Services (OSS), which later became the Central Intelligence Agency. While with the OSS, Bunche consistently urged U.S. officials to educate white Americans and Europeans about blacks' contributions to the war effort. Following the war, Bunche helped draft the charter for the United Nations and became part of the UN staff in 1946. The following year, he was appointed to the Palestine Commission, which struggled to find a way to divide Palestine, a former British territory, which had been turned over to the UN. In a decision that still creates heated and bitter controversy today, the UN set aside a portion of the land for the new Jewish state of Israel, a second portion as an Arab state, and a third international partition in Jerusalem. In 1948, Bunche became chief mediator in the Palestine conflict; during the 1950s and 1960s, as a

UN undersecretary, he directed peacekeeping forces. Bunche was undersecretary-general of the UN from 1967 to 1971.

Although Bunche received much international acclaim for his work with the United Nations, he had to face not only discriminatory practices in the United States but also charges that he was a communist. Even after he won the Nobel Peace Prize in 1950, he was called before the loyalty board set up by U.S. Senator Joseph McCarthy. The senator summoned numerous prominent Americans to hearings at which they were required to defend their loyalty to the United States and swear that they had no communist affiliations. Many lives were ruined by insinuations and unfounded charges aired at the McCarthy hearings, but even though Bunche was maligned, he was vindicated when no evidence could be found linking him to communist activities.

Dedicated to peace efforts around the world, Bunche continued his work with the United Nations even when a diabetic condition began to wreak havoc on his physical health. He was hospitalized frequently because of various stress ailments, and eventually his kidneys failed, requiring dialysis. Family and friends finally convinced Bunche that he should retire in June 1971, but his health continued to deteriorate, and six months later, on 9 December, he died.

References

Haskins, Jim. 1974. *Ralph Bunche: A Most Reluctant Hero*. New York: Hawthorn Books.

Urquhart, Brian. 1993. *Ralph Bunche: An American Life*. New York: W. W. Norton.

C

CARSON, RACHEL

(1907–1964)

*S*ilent Spring, Rachel Carson's book warning society that the heavy use of pesticides could bring about a "silent spring" by destroying animals, fish, plants, and birds, has almost completely eclipsed the woman herself. Published in 1962 and translated widely, Carson's book exposed loopholes in legislation, uncovered information showing the dangers of pesticides, and demanded the right of the individual to live in a safe environment. Carson argued that nothing exists alone in nature and that science and technology must reflect a reverence for life.

In *Silent Spring*, Carson was one of the first to challenge science, industry, agriculture, and government to turn from their destructive technologies. Carson concluded that this is

an era dominated by industry, in which the right to make money, at whatever cost to others, is seldom challenged. . . . We shall have no relief from this poisoning of the environment until our officials have the courage and integrity to declare that public welfare is more important than dollars, and to enforce this point of view in the face of all pressures and all protests, even from the public itself (Brodeur 1993).

Needless to say, her words made enemies. Because *Silent Spring* was serialized in the *New Yorker* before it was published as a book, some offended parties

tried to stop the book's publication or minimize its effect. Velsicol Corporation of Chicago, claiming that the book contained inaccurate statements about its product chlordane, threatened a lawsuit if the book was published. When the publishers verified the author's conclusions, Velsicol backed down. Monsanto Chemical Company had a parody written called *The Desolate Year*, which attempted to discredit Carson by using absurdities to exaggerate the dangers of living in a world without pesticides.

Many companies just let the National Agricultural Chemicals Association respond to Carson's criticism. It began by printing *Fact and Fancy*, a publication that quoted from Carson's book without crediting it and refuted her statements. The association allocated a quarter of a million dollars to improve the industry's image after *Silent Spring* was published.

Although attacks against Carson and her book in such publications as *Chemical and Engineering News*, *American Agriculturalist*, and *County Agent and Vo-Ag Teacher* were to be expected, it was more surprising that the nutrition and medical industries aligned themselves against her. The Nutrition Foundation, Inc. of

New York City worked with the Manufacturing Chemicals Association to print and distribute a selection of the most negative reviews of *Silent Spring*. The reviews included one by Frederick T. Stare of the School of Public Health, Harvard University, in which he called the book "baloney" (Brooks 1972, 297). Although many physicians wrote to Carson supporting her views, the American Medical Association, in the *AMA News*, referred readers away from Carson's publication and toward the National Agricultural Chemicals Association for information.

Carson avoided the controversy her work had inspired. Aside from one televised appearance on a CBS report, "The Silent Spring of Rachel Carson," she let the book speak for itself.

Carson grew up wanting to be a writer. Her first story was published in a children's magazine before she was 10. At 17, Carson told a friend that in college, her major would be literature, not boys. In her second year at Pennsylvania College for Women (now Chatham College), however, Carson took a biology course that led her away from literature to the natural sciences. Her professor, Mary Skinker, was a passionate teacher. Carson changed her major to biology, then did her graduate work at Johns Hopkins University. Carson worked for 14 years for the federal government's Fish and Wildlife Service as a marine biologist before embarking on *Silent Spring*. By then, she had written other books—*The Sea around Us*, *The Edge of the Sea*, and *Under the Sea Wind*—all of which inspire a deeper love and respect for the sea.

Carson was deeply influenced by her mother, Maria Carson, who would carry insects and spiders out of the house instead of killing them. In Rachel Carson's own words, "Her love of life and of all living things was her outstanding quality. . . . More than anyone else I know, she embodied Albert Schweitzer's 'reverence for life.' And while gentle and compassionate, she could fight fiercely against anything she believed wrong" (Hynes 1989, 55). The two women lived together for almost 50 years, raising Rachel's nieces and, later, the son of one niece.

With her closest friend, Dorothy Freeman, Carson shared her love of the sea. They spent summers at their Maine cottages, picnicking, basking in the natural world, reading to each other, and talking about Carson's work.

Silent Spring was begun in response to a letter Carson received from a stranger who was concerned about her bird sanctuary. Olga Owens Huckins wrote to Carson after planes flew over the sanctuary to spray for mosquitoes but killed other insects, grasshoppers, bees, and songbirds as well. Huckins's home state of Massachusetts had proposed more extensive spraying, which alarmed her. In response to Huckins's letter, Carson went to the *New Yorker* and offered to write an article on pesticides.

The effects of Carson's writings were far-reaching. *Silent Spring* led to the establishment of the U.S. Environmental Protection Agency and the Environmental Defense Fund, and it has been a major factor in the current environmental movement's demand for reform. In addition, based on Carson's premise of citizens' right to a safe environment, the Environmental Defense Fund launched a courtroom battle—the first of its kind—against the pesticide DDT. In 1972, the Environmental Protection Agency banned the use of DDT.

Carson received many awards for her work, among them the Albert Schweitzer Medal of the Animal Welfare League, Conservationist of the Year from the National Wildlife Federation, the Audubon Medal (she was the first female recipient), and the Cullum Medal of the American Geographical Society. The honor that meant the most to Carson, however, was her election to the American Academy of Arts and Letters. The academy's citation read,

> A scientist in the grand literary style of Galileo and Buffon, she had used her scientific knowledge and moral feeling to deepen our consciousness of living nature and to alert us to the calamitous possibility that our short-sighted technological conquests might destroy the very sources of our being (Hynes 1989, 41).

Carson died of cancer at the age of 56, just two years after *Silent Spring* was published.

References

Brodeur, Paul. 1993. "Legacy." *New Yorker*, 7 June.

Brooks, Paul. 1972. *The House of Life: Rachel Carson at Work*. Boston: Houghton Mifflin.

Easterbrook, Gregg. 1994. "Averting a Death Foretold." *Newsweek*, 28 November.

Hynes, H. Patricia. 1989. *The Recurring Silent Spring*. New York: Pergamon Press.

Manning, Anita. 1995. "Rachel Carson's Letters Speak Volumes of Love and Nature." *USA Today*, 22 March.

CARTER, JIMMY

(1924–)

From 1977 to 1980, James Earl Carter, Jr., better known as Jimmy Carter, was the thirty-ninth president of the United States. Since then, however, he has received more acclaim as a diplomat and humanitarian than he did as president.

Born into the Baptist church and proclaiming to be a born-again Christian, Carter is deeply and openly spiritual. His multitude of good works is motivated, he explained, by his faith:

My faith goes beyond theology and religion and requires considerable work and effort. My faith demands—this is not optional—my faith *demands* that I do whatever I can, wherever I can, whenever I can, for as long as I can with whatever I have to try to make a difference (Wooten 1995, 28).

Carter grew up in the small town of Plains, Georgia. As a young man, he attended the Georgia Institute of Technology and the U.S. Naval Academy. He married Rosalynn Smith and served in the navy as an engineer, working with nuclear-powered submarines. After the death of his father, he resigned his commission in 1953 to manage his family's peanut-farming business.

Gradually, he became involved in civic affairs on a local, regional, and state basis. He was elected to the Georgia state senate in 1962 and was elected governor in 1970. While governor, Carter tackled unpopular causes, such as opening up the government to minorities, improving the prison system, and streamlining the bureaucracy in state agencies.

In 1976, he won the Democratic presidential nomination. His opponent in the election was former Vice-President Gerald Ford, who had become president following the resignation of Richard Nixon. After the Watergate scandal, the American people wanted a change, and they wanted a government that they could trust again. "Washington 'outsider' Carter ran on a populist platform that blended conservative language and liberal goals," including a slogan of "I will never lie to you" (Straub 1992, 114). Carter narrowly won the election with 48 percent of the total vote. As president, he placed global justice and humanitarianism above national self-interest. His strong commitment to human rights was applauded by many but was also criticized by others at home and abroad.

After tensions over the Panama Canal worsened, with the Panamanians demanding the end of U.S. control over the waterway, Carter concluded that the goodwill of Latin American countries was more valuable than control over the canal. The original Panama Canal treaty, signed in 1903 under questionable circumstances, gave very favorable terms to the United States at the expense of Panama. Carter "was convinced that we needed to correct an injustice. Our failure to take action after years of promises under five previous Presidents had created something of a diplomatic cancer, which was poisoning our relations with Panama" (Carter 1982, 155). In 1977, he negotiated a controversial treaty to give ownership of the canal to the Panamanians in 1999.

In 1979, disturbed by the slow progress of peace talks in the Middle East, Carter invited Israeli prime minister Menachem Begin and Egyptian president ANWAR SADAT to join him at the presidential retreat in Camp David, Maryland. The three men worked in isolation for nearly two weeks and broke the deadlock. After more months spent negotiating details, Begin and Sadat signed a peace treaty, called the Camp David Accord, between Israel and Egypt.

In spite of this breakthrough, Carter faced a number of more obstinate crises at home and abroad. The United States suffered increases in oil prices, inflation, interest rates, and unemployment. When the Soviet Union invaded Afghanistan in 1979, Carter responded with nonmilitary sanctions by banning new sales of high-tech goods to the Soviets, curtailing their fishing rights in U.S. waters,

cutting grain sales to them, and boycotting Moscow's Summer Olympics. These actions seemed to have little impact on the Soviets but had adverse effects on American farmers and businesses.

The worst crisis, however, developed in Iran. In 1979, Muslim fundamentalists took over Iran and drove out the shah (the former Iranian ruler and ally of the United States). The shah's family lived temporarily in Morocco, the Bahamas, and then Mexico. When the shah became ill with cancer and required treatment that was available only in the United States, Carter, in a humanitarian gesture, agreed to allow them entrance. Outraged Iranian student extremists responded by storming the U.S. embassy in Teheran and taking 52 U.S. citizens as hostages.

At first, Carter worked through an Algerian mediator to secure the hostages' freedom, but progress stalled. Months passed, and Americans, infuriated by the sight of militant Iranians parading blindfolded hostages and burning U.S. flags, grew impatient with Carter to do *something*. With diplomacy seemingly stalemated, Carter finally authorized a secret military rescue mission that failed disastrously when a helicopter crashed into a cargo plane, killing eight marines.

In the 1980 presidential election, voters, tired of domestic economic woes and the Iranian debacle, overwhelmingly elected Ronald Reagan. As the defeated Carter completed the last months of his term, negotiations with the Iranians finally produced results. As perhaps a final insult to Carter, the Iranians released the hostages minutes after Reagan was sworn into office. Feeling hurt and rejected by the American people they had pledged to serve, the Carters quietly returned to Plains to find even more problems. The peanut warehouse was deeply in debt, and they faced uncertainty about what to do with the rest of their lives.

After that dismal time, Carter experienced a resurgence in popularity. In 1982, he joined Habitat for Humanity, regularly participating in the building of houses for low-income families across the country. In 1986, the Carter Presidential Center opened. Determined that it would be more than a monument to a presidency, Carter envisioned the center as an institution performing vital public service. Since opening, the center has become a locus of research and social activism for many problems facing the world.

Carter has begun a new informal career as an international citizen-diplomat-activist, mediating world conflicts and refereeing elections in emerging democracies. In spite of criticisms of his being a loose cannon rolling about the decks of official foreign policy, he has found a unique niche due to "the authority of his former office and the credibility gained by years of global good works outside official channels" (Wooten 1995, 42). His successes result from the international community's accepting him as an honest broker who is willing to go the extra mile for peace.

In 1990, he monitored the delicate election in Nicaragua. When the Sandinista leader, Daniel Ortega Saavedra, lost, Carter appealed to him personally to refrain from overturning the results. He said to Ortega, "Daniel, I've also been in politics, and I've won elections and I've lost elections and I can assure you that losing is not the end of the world" (Wooten 1995, 33).

In 1994, he helped end the tense standoff over North Korea's nuclear weapons program. Later that year in Haiti, he helped restore President Aristide to power and avoid bloody resistance to an American invasion.

Although the voters in the 1980 election apparently decided that Carter had failed as president, "people engaged in reassessing the Carter presidency have maintained that anyone entering the White House in 1977 would have faced a herculean task." Carter's humanitarian efforts since leaving office "have led a number of commentators to suggest that if Carter was not the country's best president, he has been its best ex-president" (Kaufman 1993, 1–2).

References

Carter, Jimmy. 1982. *Keeping Faith: Memoirs of a President.* New York: Bantam Books.

Kaufman, Burton I. 1993. *The Presidency of James Earl Carter, Jr.* Lawrence: University Press of Kansas.

Straub, Deborah Gillan, ed. 1992. "Jimmy and Rosalynn Carter." *Contemporary Heroes and Heroines, Book II.* Detroit, MI: Gale Research.

Wooten, Jim. 1995. "Meddler, Moralist or Peacemaker?" *New York Times Magazine,* 29 January.

CARVER, GEORGE WASHINGTON

(1864?–1943)

The words on George Washington Carver's headstone read: "He could have added fortune to fame, but caring for neither, he found happiness and honor in being helpful to the world."

Carver was born around 1864 or 1865 to a young slave woman owned by Moses and Susan Carver of Missouri. The sickly boy was soon orphaned when a raiding party from Arkansas kidnapped his mother and himself. The Carvers sent out a search party that returned with the boy, but his mother was never found. For the next 11 years, the Carvers raised George and his brother in their home. To her credit, Susan Carver taught George all she could with the resources at hand, but the local school would not allow nonwhites to attend class.

Botanist George Washington Carver instructs a student at the Tuskegee Institute in this undated photograph. Active in his community, Carver taught black farmers ways to maximize crop productivity through crop rotation, organic fertilizers, and the planting of crops that replenished the soil, such as peanuts and sweet potatoes.

Carver had an overriding passion to learn about life. He was especially interested in plants and knowing what made them grow. He had already earned a reputation as a "plant doctor" because of his uncanny ability to grow flowers in a little garden patch that he tended every day, but he needed the opportunity to learn more. The Carvers wished George well when he left to go live with a black family some eight miles away in Neosha, Missouri, where there was a nearby school he could attend.

Within a year, he had picked up all that the small school could offer, and he once more struck out on his own. Wandering for ten years doing odd jobs and continuing to study nature on his own prepared him to enter an institute of higher education. In 1885, he was accepted, via the mail, at Kansas Highland College. Unfortunately, Carver was unceremoniously turned away when he showed up at those gates of learning. Even though he was qualified academically, the school decided that he was the wrong color.

He was in Iowa in 1890, working as a laundryman, when he decided to try to enter college again. With the encouragement of several white families who had befriended him in the town of Winterset, Carver became the only African American student at Simpson College. There he studied painting and art, but a favorite teacher encouraged him to turn his attention to botany when she took note

that almost all his paintings were of plants in intricate detail. Carver agreed that the study of plants was probably what God had intended for him. Always a religious person, he had been searching for years for a way to please his lord and to help his people. He decided to dedicate himself to finding ways to improve the lot of all black Americans through botany. Iowa State was the place he needed to go to achieve that end.

Life for the only student of color at that school was a challenge. Carver was taunted with racial slurs and nasty insults, and he became very discouraged. Soon, however, Carver's appealing manner and obvious intelligence won him acceptance on campus. He was called "Doctor" for his superior ability with plants, and after graduation, he was asked to stay on to teach while he worked on a master's degree. His work at Iowa became well known, and he was eventually offered many positions in agricultural departments across the United States. When an offer came from Booker T. Washington of the Tuskegee Institute, he did not hesitate to accept.

It was an underfunded and understaffed facility that Carver found when he arrived at the all-black institution in the heart of the South. It was here, however, that he could have the greatest impact on the lives of the poor ex-slaves who were living all around him. Unschooled in the latest techniques for getting the best out of the land, most were earning bare subsistence livings by continuing to grow cotton on already depleted soil. Carver was one of the first to promulgate the idea that the earth's ecosystems must be considered as interrelated, and he began to demonstrate how crop productivity could be improved by paying attention to this concept. He advocated crop rotation, organic fertilizers, and the planting of crops that replenished the soil, such as peanuts and sweet potatoes.

His work with the peanut is now legendary. In his laboratory, he created hundreds of products from that one plant. Shampoo, glycerin, paints, wood stains, hen food, vinegar, laxatives, and gasoline are just a few of the remarkably diverse uses he found for the legume. If that is all he accomplished, he would still be famous. Carver did more, though. He reached out to his community to teach the poor black farmers how to incorporate what he was learning into the management of their struggling farm businesses. He also lived as an example of tolerance and love for his fellow humans. Although he suffered from the prejudice that is still common in the lives of nonwhite Americans, he urged his students to get beyond the hate and to do what they could to improve their lot instead. In fact, he lived by the Golden Rule and once said that he believed that "real Christian people speak the same language. They do unto others as they would have them do unto them. The texture of the hair, nationality, and pigment of the skin has absolutely nothing to do with it" (McMurry 1981, 274). Many of his white students commented that because of him they understood that humankind was only one race.

References

Carver, George Washington, and Gary R. Kremer. 1987. *George Washington Carver in His Own Words.* Columbia: University of Missouri Press.

Holt, Rackham. 1944. *George Washington Carver: An American Biography*. Garden City, NY: Doubleday, Doran and Company.

McMurry, Linda O. 1981. *George Washington Carver, Scientist and Symbol*. New York: Oxford University Press.

Rogers, Teresa. 1992. *George Washington Carver: Nature's Trailblazer*. Frederick, MD: Twenty-First Century Books.

CHAVEZ, CESAR

(1927–1993)

I n the six days before his death at the age of 66, Cesar (Estrada) Chavez had consumed nothing but a few glasses of water. This was not unusual for the dedicated labor organizer and spiritual leader of millions of Chicanos in the United States. Fasting had become one of Chavez's rituals as he prepared to perform important duties as president of the United Farm Workers of America

(UFW), which he cofounded in 1966. This final duty was one of the most critical faced by the UFW, and Chavez was willing to die for the cause—one he had worked for most of his life.

Chavez was born on his parents' ranch outside of Yuma, Arizona, where he spent his first ten years. When the sheriff kicked his family off their land during the Great Depression, they joined many other poor first- and second-generation Mexican Americans and other migrants in the fields of California. Because he spent many hours in the field, Chavez received only a seventh-grade education. Working all day as a farm laborer brought the reward of a one-dollar bill. Sometimes the contractor would leave with the picked fruit or vegetables without paying his workers even that pittance. And as Chavez was soon to discover, there was little or no recourse for his people in a culture that held "his kind" to be "inferior" to the white mainstream.

The farmworkers had no power. Laws and the police worked in concert with the growers to break any attempt by the laborers to organize. This was first obvious to Chavez when he returned from duty in World War II and started picking grapes in the Delano, California, vineyards. The workers were soon striking for union recognition. After 17 Immigration Service raids on the migrant camps, the strike was broken. Another aborted strike action several years later convinced Chavez that organization and dedication were key to establishing rights for his people. He joined the Community Services Organization (CSO) in 1951 as an organizer in northern California and became its director in 1958. He resigned four years later to spend more time on his main area of concern: migrant labor.

The National Farm Worker's Association (NFWA), the result of Chavez's organizing effort, had its first convention in Fresno in 1962. By 1966, Chavez and his wife Helen created the United Farm Workers Organizing Committee (UFWOC) by merging the NFWA with the AFL-CIO's Agricultural Workers Organizing Committee. In 1972, the AFL-CIO granted a full charter to Chavez's group, and its name changed to the United Farm Workers of America. Little of this progress would have been accomplished without the sacrifice of Chavez.

The first proactive action under his direction was the strike against California grape growers in 1965. The goal was to win recognition of the NFWA as a bargaining body for the farmworkers. The growers had never been forced to sign an agreement protecting the rights of migrant laborers, whom they had exploited for many years. Growers did not intend to give in without a fight. Chavez upped the stakes by calling for a national boycott against Schenley Industries, a major grape producer, and the press began to take notice. Popular sentiment supported the Chavez efforts.

Some growers yielded to the pressure and signed contracts with the NFWA, but others banded together to bring lawsuits, harass pickets, and actually change labels to circumvent the boycott. Many of the workers were furious and frustrated after years of trying to establish a base of power. Violent confrontations became more common, and events seemed to be getting out of control. Chavez told a reporter, "I thought I had to bring the Movement to a halt, to do something that would force them and me to deal with the whole question of violence and ourselves. We had to stop long enough to take account of what we were doing. . . . So I stopped eating" (Rodriquez 1991, 18–19).

Twenty-five days later, the fast was broken at a mass in Delano attended by 4,000 supporters, including presidential candidate Robert F. Kennedy, who broke bread with the activist that day. The nonviolent nature and the spiritual connection of Chavez's work were forged on this occasion, and the power began to flow to *La Causa*, the farmworkers' struggle. Two years later, growers and the union settled this strike, but Chavez found it necessary to return to the fast as a spiritual aid as well as a political tactic.

In 1972, he fasted for 24 days to protest antiunion legislation passed by Arizona lawmakers. In his most famous fast in 1988, he went without food for 36 days to publicize the continuing injustice done to grape pickers and the dangers of chemicals sprayed on the fruit. In the mass that ended that debilitating and dangerous fast, Chavez was helped to the podium by two of his eight children.

He was passed a piece of the *semita* by Ethel Kennedy, as Edward James Olmos, Martin Sheen, and other celebrities and dignitaries looked on. Chavez gave a wooden cross to JESSE JACKSON, who vowed to the thousands in the audience that he would take up the fast for three days to support the sacrifice of Chavez. Doctors were concerned that Chavez was doing permanent damage to his body by denying himself food, and they discovered that he had liver damage from this last fast. Chavez would not heed their advice to end his efforts, and in the end, the damage done by the fasts may indeed have contributed to his early demise (his parents both lived a century).

During his final fast in 1993, Chavez prepared for a lawsuit that threatened to destroy the UFW. Bruce Church, Inc. (BCI) was suing the organization for $2.9 million in connection with a UFW lettuce boycott that the large Arizona-based grower claimed had harmed its sales. Loss of this suit would mean the end of the UFW. The pressures of testifying at that trial were enormous. After the second grueling day on the witness stand, Chavez went to bed, and his heart stopped beating sometime that night. He was mourned by people from all walks of life. Yet as many who eulogized him noted, Chavez's contributions would live on. In the 30 years of his personal struggle for farmworkers' rights, Chavez helped improve the lives of hundreds of thousands of people who now have a voice in their destiny. Chavez was awarded the Medal of Freedom posthumously in 1994.

References

Browne, Ray B., ed. 1990. *Contemporary Heroes and Heroines*. Detroit, MI: Gale Research.

Levy, Jacque E. 1975. *Cesar Chavez*. New York: W. W. Norton.

Rodriquez, Consuelo. 1991. *Cesar Chavez*. New York: Chelsea House.

Taylor, Ronald. 1975. *Chavez and the Farm Workers*. Boston: Beacon Press.

CHESTNUT, J. L., JR.

(1930–)

Since the late 1950s, J. L. Chestnut, Jr., has been a leader in the black community in Selma, Alabama, his hometown. While growing up in Alabama's rural black belt—named for the dark, rich soil—where cotton was king and large southern plantations flourished, Chestnut learned early the injustice of white supremacy. Once he watched white police beat a black bootlegger because he refused to give them kickbacks. He also learned how the black leaders were chosen in the community (by white men) and understood that the power of money and landownership were out of his reach if he stayed in Alabama.

As a youngster, his main ambition was to become a jazz musician and a professional gambler. Although he eventually became a lawyer and a civil rights leader, Chestnut maintained that the methods he used to fight segregation stemmed from the card table, where he discovered that it was easier to beat someone who expected to lose than a person who was determined to win.

Segregation was part of Chestnut's life during childhood. He grew up at a time when blacks in Alabama and other parts of the South had virtually no legal rights. Many were subjected to violence, and the perpetrators were seldom brought to justice because of discrimination by the police, the courts, and the state.

Chestnut's quest for justice blossomed as a college student. Because of his parents' sacrifices, he was able to attend two southern black colleges and later, in 1953, went to Howard University Law School in Washington. There he was able to observe the legal team of the National Association for the Advancement of Colored People (NAACP) prepare its arguments for a landmark case before the U.S. Supreme Court, *Brown v. Board of Education of Topeka*, in which the Court ruled that schools must be desegregated.

In 1958, Chestnut moved back to Selma, accompanied by his wife Vivian and their two children, who had been born while he was in law school. He become the first black lawyer in town and, over the next three decades, became embroiled in every major legal battle and political and social movement challenging white control, including the Selma-to-Montgomery civil rights march. He fought for civil rights legislation, working with MARTIN LUTHER KING, JR., JESSE JACKSON, and other black leaders.

Although marches and protests in Selma helped gain passage of the 1965 Voting Rights Act, it took longer for the locals in Selma to accept the reality, which Chestnut found discouraging. In fact, his frustration led him to excessive drinking, taking a toll on his family and his legal practice. He reformed himself, however, and went on to become a major force in white-dominated courtrooms.

One of the turning points in his life was an incident he witnessed during the 1960s, when John Lewis, president of the Student Nonviolent Coordinating

Committee, confronted Sheriff Jim Clark, who came to national attention for his brutality against blacks attempting to register to vote. Lewis planned to lead about 20 civil rights marchers into the Dallas County (Alabama) courthouse, but Sheriff Clark, backed by deputies and state troopers who lined the street on each side, blocked the marchers' way. Clark demanded that Lewis turn around, but as Chestnut recalled, Lewis would not be deterred, and said:

> "The courthouse is a public place and we have a right to go inside. We will not be turned around."
>
> A moment passed. "Did you hear what I said?" Clark demanded. "Turn around and go back." He got right up in John's face and glared at him, eyeball to eyeball. He was gripping his billy club, one hand at each end, twisting hard. The tension was almost unbearable.
>
> "Did you hear what *I* said?" John replied. "We are *not* going back." He stood his ground, staring directly at Clark with his usual impassive all business expression.

After several minutes, "Clark blinked and walked away." Chestnut was "stunned," and from that moment on he realized that what seemed to be an awesome power of numbers and weapons could be overcome. "That gave me a whole new lease on life," he wrote. "The white South did not own this whole ballpark to do with as it pleased. I saw a future with more possibility than I'd ever imagined. . . . Fears that had followed me almost from day one of my life were just gone" (Chestnut 1990, 214–215).

Over the years, Chestnut has had good reason to leave Selma and enjoy an affluent lifestyle, but he has opted to forgo luxuries and work for racial justice. In addition, even though he has been distrustful of whites, he has not given up on them. During the height of the civil rights movement, he maintained a friendship with Judge James Hare, a segregationist and the force behind Sheriff Clark. Even as Chestnut represented the NAACP and civil rights demonstrators, he and Hare remained friends. Steve Suitts, executive director of the Southern Regional Council, attributed this contradiction to Chestnut's "generous human spirit," combined with "a stubborn Southern love of one's own. This quality, virtually rooted in the character of many older blacks in the South's Black Belt, helped to give both black and white Southerners their long-overdue freedom from segregation, and it is the elemental force that may someday free Selma and the Black Belt from the burdens of the tormented past" (Suitts 1990).

References
Chestnut, J. L., Jr. 1990. *Black in Selma: The Uncommon Life of J. L. Chestnut*. New York: Farrar, Straus & Giroux.
Suitts, Steve. 1990. "Liberating Selma." *Philadelphia Inquirer*, 29 July, Features View.

CLAY, CASSIUS

See *ALI, MUHAMMAD*

CLEGG, JOHNNY

(1953–)

A former anthropology professor and South African musician and composer, Johnny Clegg wrote songs during the 1970s and 1980s protesting the apartheid government that had established laws to separate the ruling white minority from the black majority. As a white man, he crossed the color barrier on countless occasions when it was especially dangerous to do so, because as he said during a 1993 tour in the United States, "We dreamed of making the world a better place" (Lewis 1993).

The life-threatening dangers were always there. In fact, attacks on activists were common in the decades before apartheid was outlawed in South Africa, and incidents escalated in the late 1980s. In 1989, one of Clegg's good friends, David Webster, was assassinated in Johannesburg because of his political activism against apartheid. Clegg had met Webster at the University of the Witwatersrand, where Webster was an anthropology professor; he had encouraged Clegg to earn his degree in the field. Webster was killed while walking home, shot by a white gunman riding in a car with two other whites. A colleague of Webster's noted that the assassination had "all the hallmarks of a professional, well-informed hit squad" (Kraft 1989).

Clegg was born in England to a woman of Lithuanian Jewish heritage who had been born in Zimbabwe, Africa. His father left before Clegg was a year old, and his mother remarried a journalist who was fascinated with Africa. The family moved to Africa, first to Zimbabwe, then to Zambia, and finally to South Africa. Clegg once told a *Los Angeles Times* reporter that his varied cultural background made him "a patchwork." As the reporter noted: "By the time Clegg was twelve years old, he had attended six different schools (some biracial, some white-only) in three different countries and shared his stepfather's love for African culture" (Hochman 1990).

In South Africa, Clegg's musical interests were shaped during his early teen years, initiated by a routine trip to the store to get a loaf of bread for his mom. On that trip, Clegg spotted a black man playing a guitar under the street lamp outside the store. The music reminded him of the Celtic music he had been

exposed to as a young boy in England. He asked the black man to teach him how to play in his style, and the man consented.

The next day, while his mother was at work, Clegg went to the apartment building where the musician, a Zulu warrior named Charlie Mzila, worked as a janitor. The superintendent, an Afrikaner, asked what the boy was doing on the property. When Clegg stated his reason, he was ordered home, but Clegg defied the order and found a way to sneak into Mzila's room, where Mzila played and sang songs in Zulu about his lifestyle. To young Clegg, the songs seemed to be of another place and time. "And yet they were discussing something about the world. There was a secret locked in there. And then I knew that I had to know the secret" (Love 1993, 463).

For three months, Mzila taught Clegg about the dances and language of the Zulus and took him to the strictly segregated migrant hostels, gambling dens, and township bars. One day, the white superintendent caught the teenager in Mzila's apartment and grabbed Clegg by the shirt to force him out. Mzila did the unthinkable by turning his fists on a white man, risking the loss of his job and arrest. This act had a profound effect on Clegg. He recalled: "All I'd wanted to do was play music. And yet I was terribly moved. Because this was the first time anyone older than me had stood up for me. Just to be with me" (Love 1993, 464).

Things came to a head for Johnny Clegg during a police raid on the migrants' hostel. The police were looking for stolen goods and workers without passports. When they found Clegg among the black population, they were incensed. The police turned Clegg over to his mother, Muriel Pienaar, with instructions to keep her son out of the housing projects—it was illegal for him to be there. They also told Pienaar that her son was crazy. Even his grandmother thought that he was crazy, wondering what kind of white boy would be hanging around his *schwartzer* friends.

The "problem"—Clegg's challenge of apartheid laws—became more pronounced the older he got: the authorities began to view him as a troublemaker. After being arrested over a dozen times for political agitation, he was faced with deportation to England, since he held a British passport. To avoid deportation he was forced to carry paperwork from the South African Folk Music Association, stating that his work was purely apolitical.

Although Clegg lived a segregated lifestyle by day, at night he rejected that lifestyle at every turn. Dubbed the "White Zulu" for his crossover musical style—a fusion of Western pop and Zulu street music—he formed a band in 1979 called Juluka (meaning "sweat" in Zulu), the first racially mixed band in South Africa. The band stayed together until 1985, when the members went their separate ways. Clegg later formed another racially mixed band called Savuka (meaning "we have arisen") in the late 1980s. About this time, he was married in a Zulu ceremony, and he and his wife, Jenny, a former dancer, have a son, Jesse. The family lives in Johannesburg.

Clegg's music and band have been tremendously popular in South Africa, and they have produced a number of albums. The group had to start touring overseas because they could not sustain themselves financially in their homeland, where only a relatively small number can afford cassettes and compact

discs. In addition, there are few venues for concerts. In Europe, Clegg is a widely respected performer, but he has not gained that status in the United States. Nevertheless, he continues because he feels that music is still the one universal language. His songs continue to present political messages, frequently challenging those who would deny equality to others.

References

Freeman, Patricia. 1988. "Black and White and Heard All Over, Johnny Clegg and Savuka Cross South Africa's Color Barriers." *People Weekly*, 24 October.

Hochman, Steve. 1990. "South Africa's Clegg Has a Song of Change." *Los Angeles Times*, 23 May.

Kraft, Scott. 1989. "Slain Apartheid Foe Mourned in Protest March." *Los Angeles Times*, 7 May.

Lewis, Randy. 1993. "Clegg Faces Up to the Pain of Life." *Los Angeles Times*, 12 August.

Love, Robert, ed. 1993. *The Best of Rolling Stone: 25 Years of Journalism on the Edge*. New York: Doubleday.

CLEMENTE, ROBERTO WALKER

(1934–1972)

Although most people think of Roberto Clemente as a baseball hero, he was also a man with a personal mission to serve others. He was killed when his plane went down while on a mercy mission to deliver supplies to earthquake victims in Nicaragua.

Roberto Walker was born in Carolina, Puerto Rico, to Melchor and Luisa Clemente. Melchor managed a sugarmill, and Luisa was a laundress for the mill owner. Although poor, the Clementes were a charitable and loving family and often helped those less fortunate than themselves. Roberto, the youngest son among six children, learned these values early in life, and he also decided early on that he would be a baseball player. By the time he was 18 years old, he had honed his baseball skills so well that at local tryouts in Puerto Rico, scouts were eager to sign him up for minor league teams. He started his baseball career in

1954 with the Dodgers' farm team, but by the end of the season, the Pittsburgh Pirates had signed him as their right fielder.

With the team for 18 years, Clemente created a reputation as one of the outstanding baseball players of all time. He had an extremely good throwing arm and was known for his speed around the bases. He not only won batting titles but was a 12-time All-Star team member and received the National League's Most Valuable Player award, plus the award for outstanding player in the World Series. In short, he was a superstar and certainly a hero to millions of Latinos. His outstanding success came in spite of widespread stereotypes about Latino players and discriminatory practices regarding product endorsements—people of color were seldom if ever offered lucrative contracts to promote goods or services.

Clemente was outspoken about the way mainstream America depicted people of color, once saying, "My greatest satisfaction comes from helping to erase the old opinion about Latin Americans and blacks. People never questioned our ability, but they considered us inferior to their station of life. Simply because many of us were poor we were thought to be low-class. Even our integrity was questioned" (Feldman 1993). For his entire baseball career, Clemente was committed to helping his people and was a strong advocate for Latino rights. He also supported and helped new Latino players who joined the Pittsburgh team. During off-seasons, he traveled throughout Puerto Rico, holding sports clinics for young Puerto Ricans. He stressed the importance of playing sports, being a good citizen, and having respect for parents.

Since Clemente's death on New Year's Eve 1972, his wife, Vera, and their sons have devoted much of their time to the Roberto Clemente Sports City in Carolina. The complex is designed to help kids stay out of trouble by taking part in athletics and cultural activities.

References

Collier, Gene. 1992. "Pride and Petulance." *Sporting News*, 28 December.

Feldman, Jay. 1993. "Roberto Clemente Went To Bat for All Latino Ballplayers." *Smithsonian*, September.

Musick, Phil. 1974. *Who Was Roberto: A Biography of Roberto Clemente*. New York: Doubleday.

National Baseball Hall of Fame Staff and Gerald Astor. 1990. *The Baseball Hall of Fame Fiftieth Anniversary Book*. Englewood Cliffs, NJ: Prentice-Hall.

O'Brien, Jim. 1994. *Remember Roberto: Clemente Recalled by Teammates, Friends and Fans*. Pittsburgh, PA: J. P. O'Brien.

Sanz, Cynthia. 1994. "A League of His Own: Roberto Clemente Jr. Builds on His Father's Legacy with an Ambitious Inner-City Baseball Program." *People Weekly*, 6 June.

Wulf, Steve. 1994. "Roberto Clemente." *Sports Illustrated*, 19 September.

COCCIA, *CAROL*

(1939–)

"I'm just a mom, just a housewife, not the kind of person to get involved in controversy," she says about herself, but for more than two decades, Carol Coccia of Taylor, Michigan, has consistently championed the rights of minority children and worked to end racism in the U.S. child-care system, which includes state social service departments and other agencies responsible for children placed in foster and adoptive homes.

Born in the Detroit, Michigan, area, Coccia determined early in her life that she wanted to be a foster mom. While growing up, she enjoyed being around foster children who lived in a relative's home. Several years after she married Dan Coccia, she read an article in the magazine section of the *Detroit News* that stressed the need for foster families to care for young children. The Coccias inquired about becoming foster parents, and they easily qualified for a state license to do so in 1966. Over the next 20 years, the couple (who are white) cared for more than two dozen foster children—many of them minorities and most of them under the age of five.

Beginning in the 1970s, however, state agency staff became increasingly reluctant to place children with foster or adoptive parents who were not of the same color or ethnic background as the children needing care. This reluctance came about because of a 1972 policy statement by the National Association of Black Social Workers (NABSW) that expressed "vehement opposition" to placing black children and black-white biracial children with white adoptive parents. In 1985, the NABSW president told a U.S. Senate committee that black social workers "view the placement of black children in white homes as a hostile act against our community. It is a blatant form of race and cultural genocide." The NABSW declared that black homes were available for children, but white social workers made unfair, stereotyped judgments about the quality of those homes.

Color-matching policies can have negative impacts on children, however. They may be forced to stay in institutional settings for longer than necessary because same-color parents cannot be found, or they may be moved constantly from one home to another—in some cases, youngsters are moved five to eight times as attempts are made to find parents with matching skin color. The policies also violate Title VI of the Civil Rights Act of 1964, which states that it is unlawful for any agency that receives federal funds to discriminate on the basis of race, color, or national origin.

In 1981, when Coccia was informed by Michigan's child-care services that she would be recommended to provide foster care only for white children, Coccia had to take action according to her conscience, even though, as she put it, "I'm a quiet type person." She was warned by family and friends that if she "made

waves," she might lose her foster-care license and might even face violence. She sought the advice of a respected acquaintance, who told her: "Protests aren't my style either, but sometimes we have to stand up. If we don't, we'll embarrass the Lord." So Coccia decided that she would stand up for minority children who needed care in a loving home.

With the aid of a few other concerned foster-care parents and the Michigan Department of Civil Rights, she formed a group called the Committee To End Racism in Michigan's Child Care System. The group picketed the state's Department of Social Services and publicized the committee's efforts through a newsletter, interviews with newspaper reporters, appearances on TV shows, and presentations at a variety of regional and national foster and adoptive parent groups. Coccia often made the presentations, which occasionally met with heated backlash and hassles from black social workers and a few parents.

In 1985, at Coccia's request, the American Civil Liberties Union (ACLU) filed a lawsuit on behalf of the committee and two Michigan foster parents whose foster child was removed from their home because of nonmatching skin color. The case was settled in March 1986 with a consent decree that, among other provisions, states that even though color and ethnic matching of children is the first preference, a child cannot be removed from a home solely on the ground that the foster child and foster parent are of different races.

The case brought national attention to the Michigan committee, but even earlier the group had heard from foster and adoptive parents across the United States who shared similar concerns about racist policies regarding child care. As a result, in 1984, the National Coalition To End Racism in America's Child Care System (NCERACCS) was formed, with Coccia as president. Through NCERACCS, Coccia has helped families in many other states, from New York to Washington, file civil rights complaints regarding the discriminatory placement of foster and adoptive children. Coccia as well as other members of the group continue to face some opposition from various African American, Native American, and Hispanic groups, but along with being an advocate for foster children of all backgrounds, Coccia speaks out frequently on the unfair treatment of minority parents, who are often prejudged by white social workers. Foster children may be removed from minority homes for minor conflicts that occur in day-to-day living in most families. In spite of her quiet, unassuming manner and the time and energy demands of such advocacy, Coccia plans to continue her "work of conscience," because "I don't want to embarrass the Lord."

References

The Children's Voice. 1984–1995. Bimonthly newsletter of the National Coalition To End Racism in America's Child Care System.

Coccia, Carol. 1995. Personal correspondence, March.

Gay, Kathlyn. 1987. *The Rainbow Effect: Interracial Families*. New York: Franklin Watts.

CORBETT, JIM

(1933–)

In late 1985, Jim Corbett, a Quaker; Reverend John Fife, pastor of the Southside Presbyterian Church in Tucson; and 14 others were indicted in Arizona federal court on charges of conspiracy and transporting and harboring illegal aliens, a felony. Eleven of the sixteen, including Corbett, went to trial in 1986, and in his opening statement, Special Assistant U.S. Attorney Donald Reno, Jr., charged that four of the defendants—Corbett, Fife, a church employee, and a Catholic nun—were "generals" or "chief executive officers" in an "Underground Railroad" that smuggled aliens from Mexico into Arizona and on to other states (Becklund 1985). All the defendants countered that they were acting out of hu-

manitarian and religious concern and that the federal government was actually breaking its own laws and international agreements by refusing to grant refugee status to people who were fleeing political repression and, in some cases, torture or certain death in El Salvador and other Central American countries.

Corbett and Fife are cofounders of the sanctuary movement, which began in the United States in the early 1980s, when clergy and laypeople in various parts of the country, particularly in Arizona, openly defied immigration laws and began to provide safe haven for Salvadoran and Guatemalan refugees who otherwise would have been deported by the U.S. Immigration and Naturalization Service (INS). They were prompted by the widely publicized deaths of 29 Salvadoran refugees who had been abandoned by "coyotes" (smugglers promising to bring people into the United States in exchange for high fees) in the Arizona desert in 1980.

Corbett's controversial work on behalf of the sanctuary movement evolved from his passion for justice, which he developed early in his life. He was born in Casper, Wyoming, to Gladys and Raymond Corbett, who taught Jim and his older sister to be self-reliant by taking them every summer to the nearby Shoshone Indian Reservation or the Teton Mountains, where they lived in a tent and caught fish and gathered wild plants for food. During his teenage years, Corbett was greatly influenced by his father, a teacher and state legislator, who exhibited a social conscience and often stood up for the rights of others. His mother once said that his father taught him "to be honest and stand up for what he thought was right" (Davidson 1988, 54).

Majoring in philosophy, Corbett earned a degree at Colgate University in Hamilton, New York, and then went to Harvard on a fellowship, completing a

master's degree in one year. He decided not to teach philosophy and married a woman from Casper. The couple had three children, but the marriage ended in divorce after a few years.

Not long afterward, Corbett became a member of the Religious Society of Friends, or Quakers, who believe in living their moral convictions and bringing about political change through acts of conscience. He also continued his education in the field of library science at the University of Southern California, where he met Pat Collins, whom he married in 1963. They moved to Arizona, and Corbett accepted a position as head librarian and philosophy instructor at a junior college, but his job was terminated after he opposed bans on various reading materials and paintings for an art exhibit.

The couple returned to California about the time many Americans were protesting the Vietnam War. For a time, Corbett worked for the Fellowship of Reconciliation, a Christian protest group working for world peace, and later took part in antiwar rallies in Tucson, Arizona.

Corbett became involved in efforts to help Salvadoran refugees somewhat by accident. A friend had picked up a hitchhiker, a Salvadoran refugee who was later imprisoned. The friend asked Corbett for help because of his ability to speak Spanish. Corbett visited the Salvadoran in jail and posted bond for him and some other refugees. He and his wife began to visit imprisoned Salvadorans on a regular basis and learned about the violence they had witnessed or endured in their homeland. Most refugees also faced extreme difficulty in filing the necessary papers for political asylum. In fact, Corbett soon learned that the INS deliberately prevented Salvadorans from getting legal aid, and between mid-1980 and mid-1981, more than 10,000 of the 13,000 Salvadorans caught in the United States by the INS had been sent back to their homeland (voluminous evidence proved these charges much later during court cases). As Ann Crittenden, a reporter for *Newsweek* and the *New York Times* wrote:

> The prisoners had no access to lawyers and were being told to sign papers, printed in English, stating that they agreed to return voluntarily to El Salvador. If they balked at signing, they were reminded that they faced months in detention and would probably be deported back to El Salvador in the end anyway. Once they did sign, they were put on buses to Los Angeles and from there flown to San Salvador (Crittenden 1988, 43).

In mid-1981, Corbett took part in a two-week effort by about two dozen people to bail out 150 refugees from a deplorable detention center in El Centro, California. The temperature at the compound, which was surrounded by electrified fences, reached 110 to 120 degrees, and prisoners were forced to remain outdoors all day, with little if any shade. Corbett and the group had to obtain a federal court order and raise almost $200,000 so that the Salvadorans could go free on bond. That experience spurred Corbett's resolve to help refugees avoid capture and imprisonment by smuggling them into the United States.

Over the next few years, Corbett and Reverend Fife, whose church was declared a sanctuary in March 1982, sheltered hundreds of refugees. The sanctuary

movement spread, and by the end of 1984, "every major Protestant denomination (with the exception of the National Association of Evangelicals) had endorsed the movement, and, although the nation's Catholic bishops refrained from making any statement as a group, individual bishops continued to lend their support" (Davidson 1988, 84–85). However, there were also arrests of sanctuary members in 1984, and the federal government sent spies to infiltrate the movement.

In 1985, 16 members were arrested and indicted, but only 11 stood trial. The trial lasted for six months, but all attempts by defense lawyers to submit evidence on the defendants' motivations and international law were denied. Eight defendants were convicted of conspiracy to smuggle and transport illegal aliens from Central America into the United States. Corbett and two others were acquitted of all charges. The judge placed the convicted members on probation, which they appealed. In 1989, a federal court in San Francisco upheld the convictions. In the words of Judge Cynthia Holcomb Hall, who wrote for the court, "The government's interest in controlling immigration outweighs their purported religious interest, and an exemption for that reason would be unfeasible" (Chiang 1989).

In spite of all the legal battles, the sanctuary movement has continued to operate and has been strongly supported by churches throughout the United States. Although Corbett tried to find his own sanctuary out of the limelight on his Arizona ranch, he is still actively involved in peace and justice movements and environmental protection efforts.

References

Becklund, Laurie. 1985. "Sanctuary Movement Leaders Assailed." *Los Angeles Times*, 16 November, sec. 1.

Chiang, Harriet. 1989. "Verdicts Upheld in Sanctuary Smuggling Case." *San Francisco Chronicle*, 31 March, A6.

Collins, Sheila D. 1986. "The New Underground Railroad." *Monthly Review*, May.

Crittenden, Ann. 1988. *Sanctuary: A Story of American Conscience and the Law in Collision*. New York: Weidenfeld & Nicolson.

Davidson, Miriam. 1988. *Convictions of the Heart: Jim Corbett and the Sanctuary Movement*. Tucson: University of Arizona Press.

"Deporting Dissent." 1986. *Nation*, 19 April.

Spilken, Aron. 1983. *Escape*. New York: New American Library.

CORRIGAN, *MAIREAD,*
AND WILLIAMS, *BETTY*

(1944–) and (1943–)

Their names became linked in the 1970s as the two women, Mairead Corrigan and Betty Williams, began a heroic campaign to protest the violence in Northern Ireland. Their efforts were recognized with the Nobel Peace Prize in 1977.

Both women were born in Belfast some 20 years after the partitioning of the island that created their nation of Northern Ireland. Corrigan was raised in a Catholic family with close ties to the church but with little sympathy for the Republican struggle to reunite the "northern counties" with Ireland. Williams's family was a mixture of religious heritages (Protestant, Catholic, and Jewish), but she attended Catholic schools. Nothing in their first 30 years was out of the norm. Like most people in Belfast, they had to stay out of the path of stray bullets in the violence-ridden city, but otherwise, they led quiet lives of tolerance and Christian goodwill toward all their neighbors. For the most part, they managed to avoid the strife that was all around them—until the event that brought them together in 1976.

On 10 August of that year, Williams witnessed a horrible accident. A car operated by the Irish Republican Army (IRA) went out of control and struck a mother and her three children as they were walking along the street. The young ones were killed. Their mother, who survived, was the sister of Corrigan. Williams was so incensed that she initiated a petition drive against the violence, going door to door and collecting nearly 6,000 signatures in a few days. For her part, Corrigan took to the television to speak out against the IRA. The two women got together and formed an organization, the Community of Peace People, that would finally take some action to end the horrid conditions that put everyone at risk.

The Community of Peace People organized a march the next month that had 30,000 women carrying placards for peace in the streets of Belfast. They continued to organize marches on a regular basis, and more and more people were inspired to walk to show their support for the pacification process. The women had their enemies in both factions, however. Catholic Republicans were certain that the women's actions were supporting the Protestants, and the Protestant extremists decided that the women were working with the IRA. Thugs threatened both women and actually beat them, but Corrigan and Williams were determined.

The two women continued their efforts to speak out for peace all over the world, and in 1977, they were awarded the Noble Peace Prize for those efforts.

Leaders of the Community of Peace People organization in Northern Ireland, Betty Williams (far left) and Mairead Corrigan (far right), at a rally in 1976

Williams has since left the Peace People, but Corrigan Maguire is still quite active. Recently, she was encouraged by the conciliatory actions of the British government and the pledge by the IRA to put away their weapons. But in a 1994 interview, she made it clear that government action alone would not solve the problems of her people:

> The Community of the Peace People believes that the missing link in the peace process is the right of the Northern Irish people themselves to define what they want and how they want to achieve it. When the Peace People started in 1976, our main message was that violence is not working, be it paramilitary or state violence. Nonviolence is the only way forward. Second, we said that only if the two traditions in the North of Ireland work together as the Northern Irish people can they solve their problem. In 1976 that was considered too idealistic. People said, "You can't change identity." We were greatly encouraged by the Downing Street Declaration in December, in which the British and Irish governments stated that the right to self-determination of the Northern Irish people was central to the building of constitutional stability in Northern Ireland. It set out principles with which the majority of British and Irish people can agree. But the peace process is really up to the people; we are the only ones who can deliver real constitutional stability (Schroeder 1994).

References:

Deutsch, Richard. 1977. *Mairead Corrigan, Betty Williams*. Woodbury, NY: Barron's.

Schroeder, Steven. 1994. "Toward a Higher Identity: An Interview with Mairead Corrigan Maguire." *Christian Century*, 20 April.

COUGHLIN, PAULA

(1961–)

People have stopped her on the street to tell her how much they appreciate her stand against sexual harassment, but more often she has been subjected to charges that she betrayed the U.S. military with her accusations against navy and marine officers. Paula Coughlin's ordeal in a sexual harassment case became national news in 1992, projecting her into the limelight and jeopardizing her career.

The daughter of a naval aviator, Coughlin believed throughout her growing-up years that a naval career was honorable and heroic. She joined the navy in 1984 and was commissioned through the navy's ROTC program at Old Dominion University in Norfolk, Virginia. She became a helicopter pilot and admiral's aide and planned to continue in a career she loved. All that changed in Las Vegas, Nevada, when she attended the 1991 Tailhook convention (named after the hook on navy jets that catches on cables when the aircraft lands on a carrier). Traditionally, the convention brings retired and active-duty navy and marine officers together for professional seminars, golf outings, and evening parties. More than 5,000 officers attended the weekend convention, and of the officers present, only about 4 percent were women.

Coughlin attended what she thought was a cocktail party in one of the hospitality suites of the Hilton Hotel. When she walked down a hall toward one of the suites, she had no clue as to what would happen next. About two dozen pilots were lined up along the hall, and one yelled "Admiral's aide!" apparently setting the stage for an attack. Coughlin was grabbed by the buttocks so forcefully that she was lifted off the floor. She angrily confronted the pilot who had assaulted her, but others joined in the attack, grabbing her breasts and reaching

under her skirt to pull at her underpants. Although she appealed to a friend for help, he turned his back; no one came to her aid, and she was forced through another gauntlet. She was finally able to kick, claw, and bite her way free.

Coughlin was not the only officer who was abused. Dozens of female guests were assaulted, and some feared that they would be gang-raped. The next day, Coughlin reported the attack to her immediate superior; over the next few weeks, several other women also went to navy officials with reports of assaults. Months passed, and no action was taken. Coughlin received no support from the navy brass and was subjected to the hostile attitudes of male officers and further sexual harassment by one official assigned to investigate the Tailhook incident.

The navy released a report of its investigation in April 1992, but only two suspects were identified. It was clear to some members of the U.S. Congress and to much of the public that the navy was covering up the entire sordid mess. By June 1992, Coughlin—encouraged by her mother, Rena, who had spent 27 years associated with the navy as a career officer's wife—decided to speak to the press about the cover-up and the abuse of women that had gone unpunished. As Coughlin explained during a 1992 CNN news interview:

> The honorable thing, in my mind, is to come forward. . . . I think at all levels, in and out of the Navy, civilian and military, that there's not a clear understanding of the terrible side effects of sexual harassment, sexual assault. And I think that's why I kind of needed to come forward and put a face to this terrible incident. And it's not a glamorous thing to come forward with a very humiliating and degrading experience, but if somebody can understand what I suffered and appreciate why it shouldn't happen again, then it's worth it, then that's part of the evolution. . . . I'd like to think that some good's coming out of it, that women understand and men understand that abuse is a terrible thing in the workplace, out of the workplace, military or civilian.

The public scandal that followed Coughlin's revelations forced the immediate resignation of the secretary of the navy. The Office of the Inspector General of the U.S. Department of Defense reviewed the navy's investigation of "Tailhook 91," as it was called, and in its first report in 1992 stated that a failure of leadership had "created an atmosphere in which the assaults and other misconduct took place." A second report on Tailhook 91 released in April 1993 concluded that a total of 83 women had been assaulted. The report included graphic descriptions and photographs documenting the lewd and drunken behavior of male officers.

By the end of 1993, one admiral had been reduced in rank, and two others had been censured for failing to intervene to stop the Tailhook orgy. Thirty other admirals and about fifty junior officers were sent letters of caution about conduct unbecoming an officer, but there were no courts-martial, and no one was sued for sexual harassment.

Meantime, Coughlin was subjected to continued harassment. In February 1994, she submitted her letter of resignation to the secretary of the navy,

explaining that the Tailhook assault and "the covert attacks on me that followed have stripped me of my ability to serve." Rena Coughlin said that her daughter, who was normally outgoing and physically fit, became an introvert and was at times suicidal. Since her resignation, Coughlin has suffered post-traumatic stress disorder and deep depression, which was confirmed by psychiatrists on both sides of the court battle in which she sued the Las Vegas Hilton for lack of adequate security during the convention. Her commanding officer also testified that Lieutenant Coughlin had been a superb officer but had changed and seemed to lack confidence as a result of the convention. A jury awarded her punitive and compensatory damages. Coughlin told news reporters that she thought that justice had been served but was unsure of her future and hoped "to slip into obscurity."

References

"Billing the Victim." 1994. *Time*, 2 May.

Boo, Katherine. 1992. "Universal Soldier: What Paula Coughlin Can Teach American Women." *Washington Monthly*, September.

CNN News transcript of "Newsmaker Sunday." 1992. Remarks by Navy Lt. Paula Coughlin, 28 June.

Gay, Kathlyn. 1995b. *Rights and Respect: What You Need To Know about Gender Bias and Sexual Harassment*. Brookfield, CT: Millbrook Press.

Waller, Douglas. 1994. "Tailhook's 'Lightning Rod.'" *Newsweek*, 28 February.

D

DALAI LAMA

(1935–)

In 1989, the Dalai Lama (Tenzin Gyatso) of Tibet, the religious leader of Tibetan Buddhism, received the Nobel Peace Prize. Practicing a reverence for all living things, he is considered one of the world's leading advocates for the resolution of international problems through peaceful means. Upon receiving the award, he said that he hoped that the prize would

> provide courage to the six million people of Tibet. For some forty years now Tibetans have been undergoing the most painful period of our long history. During this time, over a million of our people perished and more than six thousand monasteries—the seat of our peaceful culture—were destroyed. . . . Yet our people's determination and commitment to spiritual values and the practice of non-violence remain unshaken (Mathews 1989).

To Tibetans, the Dalai Lama is the living incarnation of Buddha, the absolute spiritual and temporal leader of Tibet. However, he has described himself as a "simple monk" and has often said that the idea of god-king is "a misconception. This is a translation from the Chinese, in which Dalai Lama means the living

Buddha. In Tibetan it means the king of dharma, king of truth, of teaching. I am an ordained monk. Nobody can change that as long as I keep these precepts as a monk. But the title, the Dalai Lama, can belong to others" (Nickson 1988). The incarnation of the Dalai Lama is believed to pass from one previous lama, or teacher, to another, and he is sought and identified through a traditional and exotic (to the Western mind) set of practices.

Tibet, now under Chinese rule, was a free and sovereign country when the fourteenth Dalai Lama was born in the village of Pari Takstar. For two years after the death of the thirteenth Dalai Lama, there had been a search for his reincarnation in a newborn boy whose identity would be determined by Tibetan oracles and numerous omens and tests of possible candidates, including a youngster's ability to select the actual possessions of the former Dalai Lama from a group of similar objects, such as walking sticks and drums. When Tenzin Gyatso was two years old, monks went to the farming village in the mountains of eastern Tibet and, unbeknownst to his parents, identified the child as the fourteenth Dalai Lama. They escorted him to a monastery, where he stayed for more than a year until he was able to go to Lhasa, the capital of the mountain kingdom.

Near the end of the summer of 1939, the young Dalai Lama was taken by *trel-jam* (a sedan-chair carried by mules) on a three-month journey to Lhasa, where he was ceremoniously installed as the god-king in 1940. He was reared by monks in the palaces of Potala and Norbulingka and schooled in much the same way as boys in British boarding school. However, there were no other students except for his older brother, Lobsang Samten. His parents and other siblings, known as the royal family, lived within the walls of the palace but were separated from the area reserved for His Holiness and attendants. Formal school consisted primarily of religious studies and the basics of reading and writing. He also learned to meditate, an essential part of Buddhist practices, taught himself English from books in palace libraries, and educated himself about world geography with numerous maps and atlases. In addition, he developed what appeared to be a natural mechanical ability, learning by trial and error how to repair watches, for example, and to refurbish old English and American cars that had been in storage for years on the palace grounds.

In 1950, when the Dalai Lama was 15, China invaded Tibet, and the small, poorly equipped Tibetan army could do little to defend the kingdom. Tibet called for help from world powers, but no government responded; neither did the United Nations. Since Tibet stood alone, the Dalai Lama's advisers urged him to leave the capital; they feared for his life and believed that as long as the Dalai Lama lived, so would a free Tibet—at least in Tibetan minds and spirits. The Dalai Lama left for Yatung, where he could quickly flee into Sikkim; he also moved some of the vast Tibetan treasure that had accumulated over the centuries. Although the gold and silver was part of his personal treasure, he held it in trust for the people of Tibet, realizing the funds might be needed for the continuing struggle against the Chinese outside Tibet.

The Dalai Lama hoped to live peacefully with the Chinese and to avoid bloodshed. He eventually returned to the capital, and whenever possible over the next few years, he tried to cool down potentially explosive situations between Tibetan and Chinese officials and to ward off possible uprisings among Tibetans. There were occasional armed conflicts as the Chinese communist rulers, in spite of a Seventeen Point Agreement to aid Tibetans, carried out their plan to destroy Tibetan culture by a variety of "reeducation" and repressive activities.

In 1959, the situation became intolerable to Tibetans, and there were cries for independence. The Dalai Lama hoped to meet with the Chinese military to bring about some type of accommodation, but Tibetans protested such a visit. There was an armed revolt in the city, which was put down by the Chinese military and brought more repression. In March, the Chinese shelled the Norbulingka palace and other buildings. As the situation became even more volatile, the Dalai Lama and his attendants were forced to flee, traveling for two weeks over the mountains on foot and on horseback through snow, sleet, and rain, to India.

India granted the Dalai Lama asylum and took in thousands of Tibetan refugees that streamed into the country. Within the year, the government helped the Dalai Lama set up headquarters for a government in exile in the mountain community of Dharamsala, which quickly became a Tibetan "colony" of sorts.

The funds (US$1.5 million) that the Dalai Lama had managed to salvage in 1950 were put in a trust and have been used over the years to aid refugees and establish self-help projects. About 100,000 Tibetan refugees now live in India, not only in Dharamsala but also in other communities throughout the country.

Since China's occupation of Tibet, more than 6,000 buildings—monastaries, temples, and other historic structures—have been destroyed and their contents looted. Thousands of Tibetans, including monks and nuns, have been jailed and tortured, and an estimated 1.2 million Tibetans have died because of China's occupation. In addition, many thousands of Chinese have moved into Tibet, making Tibetans a minority in the cities and fertile valleys. Many militant Tibetan exiles have continued to call for armed force against the Chinese, but the Dalai Lama has insisted on a nonviolent struggle to free Tibet and has spent much of his time traveling to Western countries in an attempt to press his case for Tibetan freedom, which the Chinese have consistently and vehemently denounced as interference in their domestic affairs. In fact, few Western leaders have met with the Dalai Lama until recent years—President George Bush's private meeting with him in 1991 was the first ever by a U.S. president.

After the Dalai Lama was awarded the Nobel Peace Prize, a *New Republic* article pointed out that the world might finally "focus some attention on one of the cruelest and most neglected stories of the 20th century"—the Chinese occupation and crimes in Tibet, "which have been documented and confirmed by human rights groups such as Asia Watch and Amnesty International, the Dalai Lama's government-in-exile in India, and several committees of the U.S. Senate and House of Representatives." Those crimes were also documented in a 1984 book by John Avedon (*In Exile from the Land of Snows*) that showed how the Chinese military "routinely practiced the most sickening kinds of torture upon Tibetans, including disembowelment, mutilations, and blindings, and gang rapes of Tibetan women"(Moynihan 1989).

In exile, the Dalai Lama has sent several envoys to China to attempt real dialogue and to propose a five-point peace plan for Tibet, which includes making Tibet a demilitarized zone between India and China. The plan also called on the Chinese to permit self-government in Tibet except for foreign affairs and defense, to respect human rights of the Tibetans, and to ban the production of nuclear weapons and the dumping of nuclear waste in Tibet.

Little has changed over the years, but the Dalai Lama has not given up hope or his cause, and he has consistently worked for nonviolent solutions for Tibetan problems.

In 1990, while he was visiting both the United States and Canada, a journalist for *Maclean's* asked if he thought that violence was justifiable under some circumstances. The Dalai Lama's response:

In one in a thousand cases, violence is justifiable. In this century, I believe that there may be some justification for the Second World War to check Nazi atrocities. War is like a very strong drug: the side effect is immense (Bilski 1990).

The Dalai Lama has continued to emphasize his nonviolent approach to obtaining self-rule for Tibetans, seeking international support to bring about meaningful negotiations with China. At the same time, militant Tibetans keep urging armed action against the Chinese, but the Dalai Lama has not deviated from his view that a peaceful approach is necessary. As he has often stated, "as long as I lead our freedom struggle, there will be no deviation from the path of non-violence."

References

Bilski, Andrew. 1990. "A God-King in Exile." *Maclean's*, 15 October.

Dalai Lama. 1977. *My Land and My People*. New York: Potala Corporation.

———. 1995. "The Dalai Lama on Compassion." Electronic posting from an article in *Asian Age*, 1 January.

Mathews, Jay. 1989. "The Dalai Lama's Call for Kindness." *Washington Post*, 6 October.

Moffett, George. 1995. "Tibet's 'God-King' Tours US in Stoic Quest for Self-Rule." *Christian Science Monitor*, 13 September.

Moynihan, Marua. 1989. "Tibet's Agony: Nobel Prize, Ignoble Story." *New Republic*, 20 November.

Nickson, Liz. 1988. "The Dalai Lama." *Life*, June.

Rosellini, Lynn. 1990. "The Days of a Holy Man." *U.S. News & World Report*, 29 October.

Strauss, Valerie. 1992. "'A Simple Buddhist Monk.'" *Washington Post*, 30 April.

DARROW, CLARENCE

(1857–1938)

C larence Darrow is remembered today for taking the argument of creation versus evolution into the courtroom. He went up against William Jennings Bryan to defend a young physics teacher, John T. Scopes, who had defied a Tennessee law banning the teaching of evolution. The American Civil

Liberties Union offered to come to Scopes's defense, but Darrow convinced the ACLU to let him act as counsel. The case generated worldwide attention.

"From the start, the trial was influenced by the presence of the two rival celebrities. Just as Bryan was popular because he was a man of God, so Darrow was disliked as the Devil" (Tierney 1979, 362). The trial became a passionate confrontation between two men who had had years to develop their dislike of each other. In the first place, their arguments stemmed from totally different points of view. Darrow was a lifelong agnostic, and Bryan was devoutly religious. During the trial, they went well beyond creationism versus evolution to debate in eloquent and dramatic fashion whether there was a God and whether the Bible contained literal truths.

Although Darrow was believed to have won the argument, he changed his client's plea to guilty near the end of the trial to protect Scopes from a retrial. The case then went to the Supreme Court of Tennessee, where it was dismissed. The court later repealed the law against teaching evolution.

The passion that Darrow displayed in the courtroom was part of his nature. "Not only did he not believe in dispassionate advocacy; he was incapable of it. Once possessed by an emotion, he could not rid himself of it; there was an obsessive aspect to his make-up that would not let him rest after his feelings had been engaged" (Tierney 1979, 30).

Before the Scopes trial, one of Darrow's most famous cases was that of Nathan Leopold and Richard Loeb. The two young men were not yet 20 when they murdered a 14-year-old boy. The public was horrified by the calculation of the two, who had killed for the thrill alone. The boys had never been mistreated; they had, in fact, been given every advantage. When Darrow helped the boys escape the death penalty, the public was outraged.

Darrow's view of the criminal mind had been shaped by a pamphlet written by John Peter Altgeld. In the pamphlet, Altgeld rejected the prevailing attitude that crime was due to a criminal's innate sinfulness. Instead, he argued, personality and environment had an effect on criminal behavior. When Altgeld became more involved in politics and was appointed a judge, he and Darrow met and developed a lifelong friendship.

Darrow had also been profoundly influenced by his parents, who inspired in their seven children a disregard for popular opinion. His father, Amirus, was a Democrat, an abolitionist, and a dreamer. In short, he was the opposite of his neighbors, yet he turned this into strength, courageously living his beliefs and standing firm despite their unpopularity. This was the kind of strength Darrow would need to practice law in a way that was consistent with his own beliefs.

Both Darrow's father and mother loved to read and taught their children to be critical thinkers. Amirus had attended seminary, but lost his faith upon graduation. He turned to cabinetmaking and eventually coffin making to help support his large family. Darrow's mother, Emily, was an advocate of women's rights and kept up her knowledge of current events. He was 14 when she died. He later wrote: "I know she had a long illness, and for months calmly looked forward to a swift and certain death. She had no religious beliefs . . . she faced the future without hope or fear. . . . I still remember the blank despair that settled

over the home when we realized that her tireless energy and devoted love were lost forever" (Darrow 1932, 27).

The fifth child, Darrow learned debate from two of his older siblings, Edward and Mary, who took him on Friday nights to a literary society. Even as a small child, Darrow thrilled to the lectures and debates.

He completed one year at Allegheny College, his father's alma mater. Then he taught for three years, until his family convinced him to enroll at the University of Michigan. Amirus, Edward, and Mary believed that he would make a good lawyer, and they offered to pay for his education. Darrow completed one year there before becoming a lawyer's apprentice.

His legal career, which began in small Ohio towns, did not really take off until he moved to Chicago, where he practiced law for the city's legal department and with the Chicago and North Western Railway Company, before concentrating on labor cases. He became involved in trying to free eight anarchists who had been charged with killing eleven people in a bombing at a workers' rally. Three of the men's sentences were commuted to life, and the other five were hanged. Darrow, who was deeply opposed to capital punishment, became active in the Amnesty Association, an organization that worked to obtain pardons for convicted criminals whose death sentences had not yet been carried out.

For 17 years, Darrow took cases defending unions and fighting for workers' right to strike. His last labor case was defending brothers Joseph and James McNamara, socialists who had been accused of dynamiting the *Los Angeles Times* building and killing 21 people. Although strongly opposed to the use of violence to settle labor disputes, Darrow agreed to defend the McNamaras but persuaded them to plead guilty, thus avoiding the death penalty for his clients. The deal outraged labor leaders, who thought that the McNamaras were innocent. The plea bargain also ruined the socialist candidate's chances in an upcoming Los Angeles election. Practically on the eve of that election came accusations that Darrow, through an intermediary on his staff, had attempted to bribe a juror into voting for the McNamaras' acquittal. Tried twice on bribery charges and found not guilty both times, Darrow—penniless and with his reputation in shambles—returned to Chicago and never again argued another labor case.

Back in Chicago, Darrow rebuilt his private practice. Until the end of World War I, he defended people who refused to serve in the military or who were communists or socialists. Then he focused on criminal law. In the 1920s, the Leopold and Loeb trial and the Scopes trial brought Darrow back into the public eye. In another famous case, Darrow successfully defended members of a black American family accused of murdering a member of the Ku Klux Klan. The man had been part of a mob trying to drive the family from their home. Darrow retired in 1929 but came back in 1932 for one last case of murder in self-defense.

Darrow "carved his own niche in history, a voice for the inarticulate, the oppressed, the poor." He was "a figure of genuine intellectual importance and an artist with words. . . . When he was down, in 1912, he told the court: 'I am pretty near done anyhow. If they had taken me twenty years ago, it might have been worth their while, but there are younger men than I . . . who will do this work when I am gone.' He was wrong; nobody took his place" (Tierney 1979, 439).

References
Darrow, Clarence. 1932. *The Story of My Life*. New York: Charles Scribner's Sons.
Straub, Deborah Gillan, ed. 1992. *Contemporary Heroes and Heroines, Book II*. Detroit, MI: Gale Research.
Tierney, Kevin. 1979. *Darrow: A Biography*. New York: Thomas Y. Crowell.

DAY, DOROTHY

(1897–1980)

"Once you're touched by Dorothy Day you've altered your whole life. She's always looking over your shoulder," recalled an elderly man who met Day in 1934 and was reminiscing while preparations were under way for a sixtieth anniversary celebration of Maryhouse, a Catholic Worker hospitality house in New York City (McCarthy 1993). Hospitality houses for the homeless and unemployed are part of the international Catholic Worker movement—Christian social activism—cofounded by Day in the 1930s. There was little in her early life that suggested that she would be one of the most influential laypersons in U.S. Catholicism, yet she showed by personal example and conviction of conscience how a person can bring about a society where it is easier to be good through nonviolent actions.

Born in Brooklyn, New York, Day was the third of five children of John and Grace (Satterlee) Day. The Days moved their family to Oakland, California, but after the San Francisco earthquake of 1906 resulted in a three-day fire that razed the central city, the family moved to Chicago. After attending high school in Chicago, Day received a scholarship in 1914 to the University of Illinois, where she joined the Socialist Party. Although she seldom went to socialist meetings, she was greatly influenced by writers who raised her awareness of the poor and stressed the need for social reforms. She noted that although she "was free to go to college," she was also

mindful of girls working in stores and factories through their youth and afterward married to men who were slaves in those same factories. The

Marxist slogan "Workers of the world, unite, you have nothing to lose but your chains" seemed a most stirring battle cry, a clarion call that made me feel one with the masses, apart from the bourgeoisie, the smug, the satisfied (Ellsberg 1988, 14).

Day intended to be a writer and left school in 1916 to go to New York City to pursue her career. In New York, she became a reporter for *The Call*, a socialist newspaper, and also joined the Industrial Workers of the World (IWW), a union

that hoped to form one large labor organization that would help terminate capitalism. She later worked for *The Liberator* and *The Masses*, two other communist publications, and wrote articles not only about the labor movement but also about women's suffrage, birth control, and other women's rights issues.

Day joined the suffragist movement for a time and, along with other protesters, attempted to picket the White House. The pickets were arrested and jailed for 30 days in a brutal penitentiary known as Occoquan. In 1918, Day felt compelled to live with the poor and moved to a New York tenement, working as a nurse trainee at King's County Hospital in Brooklyn. Then, after more than a year, she left, traveling to Europe and then back to the United States. She continued her journalism, and in 1924, her autobiographical novel *The Eleventh Virgin* was published. Although she called the book "very bad," proceeds from movie rights allowed her to buy a small home on Staten Island.

In 1925, Day and anarchist Forster Batterham "entered into a common-law marriage," as she described it. Batterham was "an Englishman by descent, and a biologist. . . . His enthusiasms were such that I could not help but be fascinated by the new world of nature he opened up to me," Day wrote (Ellsberg 1988, 22–23). Their daughter, Tamar Theresa, was born in 1927. The relationship between Day and Batterham faltered, however, primarily because Day had been developing strong Christian convictions, in spite of years of doubts about religious beliefs. She began going to mass on a regular basis and found "delight in prayer." As she became more absorbed in the supernatural, Batterham rebelled.

We both suffered in body as well as in soul and mind. He would not talk about the faith and relapsed into complete silence if I tried to bring up the subject. The point of my bringing it up was that I could not become a Catholic and continue living with him, because he was averse to any ceremony before officials of either Church or State. He was an anarchist and an atheist, and he did not intend to be a liar or a hypocrite. He was a creature of utter sincerity, and however illogical and bad-tempered about it all, I loved him. It was killing me to think of leaving him (Ellsberg 1988, 22–23).

Day joined the Roman Catholic Church in late 1927, which led to the breakup of her common-law marriage. It also brought criticism from many of her former communist and anarchist associates. However, she was still against capitalism and imperialism and criticized the church for its alignment with the wealthy and powerful. Her conversion to Catholicism stemmed from a belief that the "Church was Christ made visible."

For a time, Day worked for the Catholic publication *Commonweal*, but in 1932, she met a French priest and Catholic reformer, Peter Maruin, who had developed a philosophy that combined the ideals of communism and Catholicism. Maruin and Day shared common concerns about social justice and serving victims of poverty. Together they launched the Catholic Worker movement and, in 1933, established a newspaper by the same name to spread information about their purpose: to establish communal farming and hospitality houses for the urban poor. Circulation of the *Catholic Worker* that year was 100,000; by 1936, it reached 150,000.

In 1934, to help victims of the Great Depression, the cofounders of the movement established St. Joseph's House of Hospitality in New York City. Within ten years, there were at least 30 more hospitality houses across the United States, and farm communes also developed. "A genuine lay movement had come alive, a movement based on religious principles, Catholic social teaching, personal moral responsibility, a decentralized society, the dignity of labor, nonviolence, works of mercy and voluntary poverty" (McCarthy 1993). Day herself vowed to live a life of poverty and continually spoke out against materialism in whatever form it took. "To live with the poor, to forgo luxury and privilege, to feed some people, to 'visit the prisoner' by going to jail . . . Dorothy's life was made up of such small things, chosen deliberately and repeated daily" (Ellsberg 1988, xxiv). She spent many of her days in the New York hospitality house and worked to restore dignity and self-respect to the poor, homeless, and unwanted.

Because of her outspoken opposition to the capitalist system; her longtime advocacy of economic, social, and political reform; and her stand against nuclear weapons and the Vietnam War, she was often under surveillance by the FBI. She continued her activities undaunted and was even somewhat scornful of the federal authorities. Throughout the decades—for more than 50 years—she continued to write, publishing numerous articles and six nonfiction books, including *From Union Square to Rome* (1938), *House of Hospitality* (1939), and her autobiography *The Long Loneliness* (1952).

Day's last years were spent at Maryhouse, which had become a shelter for homeless women. She continued to write for the *Catholic Worker* whenever she could, and near the end of her life she was given a great deal of media attention, but she remained as many remembered her—a kind of saint. An editorial in *The Progressive*, for example, noted that "Dorothy Day deserved to be called a saint," but it was not a "sentiment she would have appreciated." Nevertheless, Day "devoted her life to achieving a peaceful and just world. She didn't embrace peace and justice as a goal or a cause or a vocation: she lived peace and justice, and she brooked no compromise" (Knoll 1994).

References

Ellsberg, Robert, ed. 1988. *By Little and by Little: The Selected Writings of Dorothy Day.* New York: Alfred A. Knopf.

Knoll, Erwin. 1994. "'Put Away Your Flags.'" *Progressive*, April.

McCarthy, Tim. 1993. "Light of Day Shines Yet at Catholic Worker." *National Catholic Reporter*, 21 May.

DEBS, EUGENE VICTOR

(1855–1926)

A colorful leader and spokesman for the labor movement and socialism, Eugene Debs spent his adult life trying to better working conditions for railroad and other industrial employees and espousing his views on socialism. Because of his efforts, he was convicted of conspiracy to interfere with interstate commerce and jailed in 1894, and because of his stand against World War I, he was convicted of violating the Espionage Law of 1918. At that time, he declared to the jury:

> I am prepared for the sentence. . . . Years ago I recognized my kinship with all living beings, and I made up my mind that I was not one bit better than the meanest of earth. I said then, and I say now, that while there is a lawyer class, I am in it; while there is a criminal element, I am of it; while there is a soul in prison, I am not free (Debs 1948, 437).

Debs was the third of six children born to Marguerite Bettrich Debs and Jean Daniel Debs, who emigrated from Europe in 1849 and settled in Terre Haute, Indiana, where Daniel eventually established a grocery store. Debs attended elementary and high school but dropped out due to boredom when he was 14 years old. Always eager to learn, however, he continued his education under his father's excellent tutelage, studying French and German classics. He also went hunting with his father and quickly learned the names of wild plants and animals.

His religious education was limited to one visit to St. Joseph's Cathedral, where, he recalled, "the priest delivered an address on Hell." The sermon was filled with threats of terrible horrors that would be visited on "all who did not accept the interpretation of Christianity as given by the priest." Debs left "with a rich and royal hatred of the priest as a person, and a loathing for the church as an institution" (Ginger 1949, 10). He vowed never to return because he believed that the church should preach Christ's love rather than fear of retribution.

During the 1870s, Debs worked for the Terre Haute and Indianapolis Railway as a fireman, but at his mother's urging he left the dangerous job and became a billing clerk for a wholesale grocer. He maintained his ties with the railroad,

however, by joining the Brotherhood of Locomotive Firemen and, at the age of 20, was elected secretary of the local lodge.

In 1885, he married Kate Metzel. Their marriage was childless, and his wife spent many lonely days while her husband worked for the union or was on the political trail. Debs got into politics in the latter part of the decade, winning the office of city clerk, then a term as a state legislator. Rather than run for reelection, he became assistant editor and eventually editor of the *Locomotive Firemen's Magazine*. Through the 1880s, he was actively involved not only with the magazine but also in organizing the American Railway Union (ARU), which began in 1893 and quickly grew from a few thousand to tens of thousands of members by 1894. That same year, the union was almost destroyed by the notorious Pullman strike, brought about by drastic wage cuts, layoffs, and poor working conditions suffered by employees of the Pullman Palace Car Company. Although Debs was against a strike, he supported ARU members when they voted to boycott trains with Pullman cars attached, stopping rail traffic between Chicago and points west. Federal courts brought an injunction to stop the strike, but Debs ignored it and was arrested and indicted for conspiracy to interfere with interstate commerce. President Grover Cleveland sent federal troops to Illinois to smash the strike.

Criminal charges were dropped against Debs, but he served six months in jail for contempt of court, an imprisonment that changed his life. He began to ponder the significance of the failed strike and determined that the class struggle between big business and labor could be resolved only through socialism. When he was released from jail, he delivered a speech on personal liberty and how powerful corporations were threatening the liberties of American workers.

By the end of the nineteenth century, Debs had transformed what was left of the ARU into a socialist political party, which in 1900 became the Socialist Party of America. He spent the last 25 years of his life speaking and writing about his socialist views and the labor movement and became a perennial Socialist Party candidate for president.

Before the United States entered World War I, Debs delivered numerous anti-war speeches in which he castigated the "master class" for advocating a war in

which the "subject class" had to do battle. In a speech in Canton, Ohio, he declared:

> The master class has had all to gain and nothing to lose, while the subject class has had nothing to gain and all to lose—including their lives. . . . [T]he working class who fight all the battles, the working class who make the supreme sacrifices, the working class who freely shed their blood and furnish the corpses, have never yet had a voice in either declaring war or making peace. It is the ruling class that invariably does both (Debs 1948, 425).

Because of his outspoken opposition to World War I, Debs was arrested and convicted under the Espionage Act of 1918; on 12 September 1918, he was sentenced to ten years in prison. During his imprisonment, he ran for president in the 1920 election and received nearly 1 million votes. Debs was pardoned by President William Harding in 1921 and released on Christmas Day. Upon his release, he continued his support for socialist and labor causes and wrote *Walls and Bars,* dealing with prison conditions and the need for reforms, even though his health was declining. When he died of a heart attack in October 1926, he was mourned by hundreds of thousands, including the wealthy and famous as well as the common folks he championed.

References
Currie, Harold W. 1976. *Eugene V. Debs*. Boston: Twayne Publishers.
Debs, Eugene. 1948. *Writings and Speeches of Eugene V. Debs*. New York: Hermitage Press.
Ginger, Ray. 1949. *The Bending Cross: A Biography of Eugene Victor Debs*. New Brunswick, NJ: Rutgers University Press.
Whitman, Alden, ed. 1985. *American Reformers*. New York: H. W. Wilson.

DEES, MORRIS

(1936–)

Cofounder and chief trial counselor of the Southern Poverty Law Center in Montgomery, Alabama, Morris Dees is considered one of the most effective civil rights lawyers in U.S. history and could easily make an exceptionally good living as a trial lawyer in private practice. In spite of harassment and death threats from the Ku Klux Klan, neo-Nazis, and other hate groups and arson attacks on his home and office, he has chosen to pursue a career fighting for the oppressed and has become a hero to many.

Dees was born in rural Mount Meigs, Alabama, where his parents were tenant farmers, working on cotton plantations and eventually buying their own land to grow cotton. During his early childhood, he worked in the fields with black farmhands and played with their children. From his parents he learned to respect people whatever their racial or economic background, but he seldom questioned southern segregation and the constant denigration, exploitation, and abuse of people of color.

Dees dreamed of becoming a Baptist preacher, and he also wanted to be a farmer like his father. His father encouraged him to study law. While still a senior in high school, however, he eloped with Beverly Crum, a teenager whose parents were in the military and who longed for a stable life on the farm that Dees still hoped to buy one day. Although Dees's father was angry that his son had eloped, he continued to encourage him to go to law school. In 1955, Morris and Beverly Dees went to Tuscaloosa, where he enrolled in the University of Alabama. It was during that year that he heard about the kidnapping, beating, and murder of a young black teenager—14-year-old Emmett Till—by two white men. The story enraged much of the nation, and Dees said that it "touched me so deeply that for the first time I seriously examined the Southern way of life" (Dees and Fiffer 1991, 76). The following year, he again had occasion to question the effects of white-supremacy beliefs. In 1956, under a federal court order, Autherine Lucy, a black student, entered the University of Alabama, and Dees watched from the student union building as

> a mob of ten thousand angry whites, including scores of Klansmen who screamed "Nigger, go home" . . . threw bricks and bottles at her car. . . . [T]his was the first time I had ever seen Klansmen in action, the first time I had ever seen a mob. As it surged, retreated, and surged again like some monster, I felt frightened and disgusted. . . . I found myself . . . trying to put some distance between me and them. I felt sick to my stomach. In Autherine Lucy's face, I saw the faces of many of the black people I had known in [Mount Meigs]. . . . [A]ll my sympathy for the underdog came out at that moment (Dees and Fiffer 1991, 77).

Dees's empathy heightened in 1963 when white supremacists bombed a black Baptist church in Birmingham, killing four little girls in Sunday school. Dees tried to get members of his all-white church to help out fellow Baptists, but the congregation walked out on him. Years later, he realized that this was the beginning of a great change in his life—he would commit himself to civil rights and justice.

Although he completed law school, Dees did not devote his time to practicing law. Instead, he and a partner continued to expand a mail-order and publishing business they had started in college. Dees also became involved in various civil rights activities, such as supporting the Voting Rights Act of 1965, which did not sit well with many whites in Montgomery; they ostracized his family.

During the late 1960s, Morris and Beverly divorced. He later married Maureene Buck, who had worked for his company; their blended family consisted of Dees's two sons and Buck's son and daughter. Two years after their marriage, another daughter was born. At the time Dees remarried, he also sold his business and began to take on a series of lawsuits challenging segregation and discrimination.

In 1969, Dees and a partner from New York City, Joe Levine, Jr., established a law firm in Montgomery that in 1971 became the nonprofit Southern Poverty Law Center (SPLC)—a legal and educational foundation specializing in "socially significant cases," as Dees described them. "Our primary goal was to fight the effects of poverty with innovative lawsuits and education programs . . . [targeting] customs, practices, and laws that were used to keep low-income blacks and whites powerless" (Dees and Fiffer 1991, 132). Initially, pro bono cases were supported by paying clients, but thousands of supporters across the United States now contribute to the cause, which includes the Klanwatch project, a system to monitor Ku Klux Klan activities and to sue Klan groups and members who violate others' civil rights.

Since the early 1970s, Dees and the SPLC have won numerous cases that have helped protect the rights of minorities and the powerless. Among them were cases that resulted in the integration of the Montgomery YMCA and the Alabama state troopers and that established the right of blacks to serve as jurors. One widely publicized case in 1981 won protection for Vietnamese fishermen in Galveston Bay, Texas; a Klan group had harassed the fishermen, burning two Vietnamese boats and threatening the fishermen's lives. Another successful case in 1987 was against members of the United Klans of America (UKA) who had selected a black man (Michael Donald) at random for lynching; the result was a guilty verdict, life sentences for two of the Klan, and a death sentence for a third, plus a $7 million settlement, which bankrupted the UKA. In 1990, Dees and the SPLC brought a civil suit against Tom Metzger and his White Aryan Resistance group for inciting three skinheads in Portland, Oregon, to beat to death a young Ethiopian college student, Mulegeta Seraw. A jury found them guilty on all counts and awarded the Mulegeta family $10 million in punitive damages. Nevertheless, Metzger and his group vowed to continue their activities, as have other hate groups.

Dees, along with the SPLC, continues to bring lawsuits and, through a teaching tolerance project, tries to educate young people "before the Metzgers of the world turn them into caldrons of seething bigotry," as Dees put it. He believes that "America can be a great nation and live up to its ideals of social, racial, and economic justice. No goal is more important to our survival as a free society" (Dees and Fiffer 1993, 280).

References
Dees, Morris, and Steve Fiffer. 1991. *A Season for Justice: The Life and Times of Civil Rights Lawyer Morris Dees*. New York: Macmillan.
————. 1993. *Hate on Trial: The Case against America's Most Dangerous Neo-Nazi*. New York: Villard Books/ Random House.

DELLINGER, DAVID

(1915–)

C alled "one of the bravest nonviolent revolutionaries of the twentieth century," David Dellinger, by most standards, was born with a silver spoon in his mouth. His parents were from well-to-do and respected families, and they made their home in what was considered by some the "Center of Modern Enlightenment," Boston, Massachusetts. His mother especially could trace her ancestry to that line of all important and "correct" families who had settled in New England and who could be considered New World royalty. His grandmother was a leader of the Daughters of the American Revolution. While it is true that his paternal pre–Revolutionary War roots were traceable to a less important clan in poor, rural North Carolina, his father had done well by attending Yale and working at the Massachusetts Constitutional Convention after becoming a lawyer. He was a player in Boston political circles, and he numbered President Calvin Coolidge among his friends.

Dellinger respected his father's ability to get along with everyone with whom he had contact, and he considered him to be one of the most loving persons he knew. Eventually, however, he came to oppose his father's more conservative

views of life, especially the intolerance he showed for members of other groups in society such as anarchists, atheists, and labor leaders. While still a child, Dellinger was deeply affected by the trial and execution of Italian-born anarchists Nicola Sacco, a shoemaker, and Bartolomeo Vanzetti, a fish peddler. Many believe the two men were wrongly convicted of a murder because of their ancestry and political beliefs, and there were numerous demonstrations and some violent confrontations at the time of their execution in 1920.

When the two anarchists were arrested, Dellinger was only 5 years old, but by the time of their deaths he was 12 and had come to see them as victims of a repressive government and bigoted social structure. He learned that his father had spoken intimately with the governor and could have requested mercy for the men. Because his father declined to do so, Dellinger became increasingly disillusioned about people of high social class—including his father—who would not speak out for justice. When he entered Yale University at the age of 17, Dellinger recalled that he went "without a lot of questions about its class composition, even though that concern had led me to refuse to spend a year at an exclusive prep school between high school and college" (Dellinger 1993, 17).

At Yale, Dellinger became a political activist, fighting for causes such as efforts to start a union to improve conditions for nonacademic employees of the university. When he showed interest in helping with this project, the dean pulled him aside to explain that he should not get involved because the communists would try to recruit him at one of the organizing meetings. He decided to take part regardless and discovered that it was the Christian radicals who were leading the effort. He was influenced by their strong love ethic and their commitment to nonviolent action, which seemed to match the objectives and teachings of MO-HANDAS GANDHI, the Indian leader who was very much in the news during this time and who Dellinger had come to admire.

In an effort to further his own practical education about what life was like for those not born into advantage, the young collegian would often dress in his poorest clothes and take to the streets near the university. It was the height of the Depression, and he wanted to discover firsthand what it was like to be homeless, hungry, and desperate. He was often befriended by people who were learning to survive on nothing. These were not slackers and drunks, as he had been told by his peers, but ordinary citizens caught in the wake of changes in what Dellinger concluded was an inhumane capitalist system. He often stood in bread lines, spent nights in shelters, rode the freight trains, and visited "hobo" villages in his quest to understand what was happening to people.

His commitment ". . . to live in accord with . . . feelings of human solidarity and love, rather than by the selfish competitiveness that is enshrined in the present society" was set. That society, as one might expect, often found Dellinger's approach to life counter to established goals.

The first time Dellinger personally experienced the consequences of this conflict was in 1940 when he was arrested for refusing to register for the draft. This incident is a good example of how the activist used his own life as a model for action that others would only talk about. As a divinity student, he was exempt from the draft but still required by law to register. He was promised the directorship of the conscientious objector camp if he would follow that legally acceptable path. He determined, however, that to do so was to work in complicity with a system that had little moral accountability. He was sentenced to a year and a day for breaking the law. While in solitary confinement in the Danbury prison he came close to death, but was empowered with a courage to act that would serve him unfalteringly in the years to come.

Dellinger married soon after his release and eventually had five children with his wife, but he did not settle into a typical American lifestyle. He helped start the People's Peace Now Committee in 1943, which led to a protest demonstration in the nation's capital against the continued bombing in Germany. He was arrested weeks later when the federal government cited him for refusing to take his Selective Service physical. He received a two-year sentence at the Lewisburg maximum-security prison. A lifelong pattern of antiwar protest was set.

Through his writings, his organizing, and his personal leadership, Dellinger has been a model of moral and ethical activism. He was on the front lines of the struggle for racial equality and justice in the northern urban centers, prisons, and in the South during the dangerous days of the freedom marches. His commitment to nonviolence and pacificsm made him a leader of the antiwar movement that peaked with the protest against government conduct during the Vietnam War.

On 18 August 1968, Dellinger addressed 50,000 peace demonstrators who were in Chicago to protest the war, gathering outside the hotel where the National Democratic Convention was held. As police moved in to disperse the crowd, Dellinger told them, "The whole world is watching!" Thousands picked up the phrase, chanting it in a warning to Chicago police who closed in with clubs raised. The "police riot" that followed was seen by millions of Americans on the evening news, and the federal government used this violence as a pretense to arrest the top leadership of the antiwar movement. Bobby Seale, Tom Hayden, Rennie Davis, Abbie Hoffman, Jerry Rubin, Lee Weiner, John Froines, and David Dellinger were charged with conspiracy and crossing state lines to incite a riot.

The trial of the Chicago Eight (later called the Chicago Seven when Bobby Seale's case was severed from the original defendants) became a media circus and a legal fiasco under the authority of Judge Julius Hoffman. After more than four months, Dellinger and four of his codefendants were convicted of crossing state lines to incite a riot. Additionally, he was sentenced to two years, five months, and sixteen days in jail for contempt of court charges. Seizing the opportunity to turn the spotlight on the government, Dellinger had refused to be silent about his views of social justice and the manner in which the society had abused its citizens. Eventually, all of the convictions were overturned, and he was freed to continue his lifelong work for peace, justice, and social equality in a

world governed by love and understanding. He has also written six books, among them *Revolutionary Non-Violence, More Power than We Know: The People's Movement toward Democracy*, and *Vietnam Revisited: Covert Action to Invasion to Reconstruction*.

References:

Dellinger, David. 1993. *From Yale to Jail: The Life of a Moral Dissenter*. New York: Pantheon Books.

Farber, David. 1988. *Chicago '68*. Chicago: University of Chicago Press.

DOUGLASS, *RAMONA*

(1949–)

President of the San Francisco–based National Association of Multiethnic Americans, Ramona Douglass has spent a good portion of her adult life working for equity and justice for people of every faith, hue, or lifestyle. As a woman of mixed-race ancestry, she has known the stings of being labeled and stereotyped by people of many different racial groups.

The daughter of Howard William Douglass (of African American and Native American ancestry) and Lena Verona Douglass (of Italian ancestry), Ramona was born in the Bronx, New York, and is the elder of two children. She was educated in southeastern Queens, New York, in a neighborhood that she called "a real rainbow of ethnicities, races, and cultures." The rainbow mix did not shield her from discriminatory incidents, however, and she learned to stand up for her rights. During her combined third-fourth–grade year, she wrote a play about a cowgirl who had fallen in love with a Native American man. Her class was supposed to produce the play, but the teacher was convinced that the play had been written by an adult, and because the main character's name was Jewish, the teacher thought that the play carried an anti-Semitic message. As Douglass pointed out: "I never realized that Lerner was a Jewish name and had picked it only because a friend of the family was named Gerta Lerner and I admired her because she was a civil rights activist." The play was finally produced the

following school year due to the outspoken efforts of Douglass's honor class teacher, an African American woman who recognized that the play was about an independent woman who was not afraid to make decisions that were unpopular but true to her own heart and spirit. That has been Douglass's theme through her life.

Graduating from high school in 1966 as a member of the National Honor Society, she entered the Colorado School of Mines in Golden, Colorado, at age 16. She was the first woman of color enrolled at the school, a highly conservative institution. Douglass recalled that on the day that MARTIN LUTHER KING, JR., was killed,

> there was a big beer bash held in celebration of his death by the campus fraternities. A fellow New Yorker, who happened to be Jewish (which was also frowned upon in this uptight campus) heard a rumor that some frat members thought it would be fun to harass the "half-breed." Apparently, that was me, so this fellow New Yorker came to get me, escorted me to the Memorial Service held in Dr. King's honor in Denver. The next morning my ignorant mathematics professor ridiculed me in class, asking me what was so special about the previous day—was I sick or something? I calmly told him and the snickering fellow students in my class that a great man had died and I had chosen to pay my personal respects to his memory rather than attend class (Douglass 1995).

Douglass has continued to stand up for her beliefs and ideals, in spite of financial risks and public disapproval. One of the most important influences in her life was a lifetime family friend and mentor, the late Ruth V. Washington, the first woman of color (of mixed ancestry, but identified as black) to graduate from New York University's School of Law in 1947. Washington was appointed by President George Bush in 1989 to be the U.S ambassador to Gambia, but she was killed in an auto accident four days before she was to leave the United States to assume her new post. Douglass noted that Washington "embodied for me all that a woman could be without dependence on a man for her survival or sense of self-worth. She had integrity in her personal life and in her politics. I patterned my personal ethics and dreams for a successful career on her example and wisdom" (Douglass 1995).

Part of the civil rights movement in the United States since the early 1970s, Douglass joined the Biracial Family Network (BFN) of Chicago in 1985 with the understanding that she would be a persistent voice for multiracial people throughout the nation. She served on BFN's board for seven years and was its president for a year.

Now a senior sales manager with a medical manufacturing company, Douglass has given freely of her leisure time and has diligently worked to raise public awareness of race and ethnicity issues. She has consistently spoken out about the right of self-identification for people of multiracial ancestry. Her views have often met with heated debate, insults, and sometimes threats of violence from those who believe that a person must choose only one racial or ethnic category

with which to identify, based primarily on a person's appearance and the perception and classification system of others.

A founding member of the National Alliance against Racist and Political Repression and more recently a founding member of the Association of Multiethnic Americans, for which she has served as president and vice-president, Douglass has lectured often at universities and colleges on the topic of multiracial identity. In June 1993, she presented her personal testimony at a congressional hearing regarding consideration of a multiracial category on U.S. Census Bureau forms.

References

Douglass, Ramona. 1995. Personal correspondence with Kathlyn Gay, 8 June.

Gay, Kathlyn. 1995a. *I Am Who I Am: Speaking Out about Multiracial Identity.* New York: Franklin Watts.

Hearst, Margo Ruark, ed. 1993. *Interracial Identity: Celebration, Conflict, or Choice?* Chicago: Biracial Family Network.

Katz, William Loren. 1986. *Black Indians: A Hidden Heritage.* New York: Atheneum.

"The New Face of America." 1993. *Time,* fall (special issue).

No Collective, ed. 1992. *Voices of Identity, Rage and Deliverance: An Anthology of Writings by People of Mixed Descent.* Oakland, CA: No Press.

Root, Maria P. P., ed. 1992. *Racially Mixed People in America.* Newbury Park, CA: Sage Publications.

E

EINSTEIN, ALBERT

(1879–1955)

Although famous for his revolutionary work in physics, Albert Einstein also championed ethics and humanitarianism. His deep fusion of science and spirituality induced his statement: "Science without religion is lame, religion without science is blind" (Einstein 1954, 46).

Einstein was born in Ulm, Germany, to a nonobservant Jewish family. The Einsteins finally left the harsh school and business climate in Germany and moved in 1895 to Milan, Italy, where Albert started becoming a "citizen of the world." From 1896 to 1900, Einstein studied math and physics at the Polytechnic Academy in Zurich, Switzerland. He graduated as a secondary school teacher of mathematics and physics and taught in Winterthur Technical School. A year

later, he became a patent examiner at the Swiss Patent Office in Bern. While there, Einstein wrote an astonishing range of papers on theoretical physics in his spare time. With these works he earned a doctorate and attained an appointment as associate professor of physics at the University of Zurich.

Einstein returned to Germany in April 1914 to become director of the Kaiser Wilhelm Institute for Physics in Berlin. The following July, World War I began, and Einstein became deeply distressed by how quickly his fellow scientists supported Germany's aggression, especially in their work to develop weapon systems of mass destruction. In response to this fervent nationalism and militarism, Einstein worked for internationalism and pacifism. Because of the risk, however, Einstein's public views were not as radical as his private views (such as hoping for the defeat of Germany).

Nevertheless, Einstein's unpopular causes "were enough to make his name disliked by German nationalists while he remained obscure, and detested once he became famous. As a result, his scientific fame became inextricably entangled with political controversies," according to biographer Ronald W. Clark (1971, 217).

Although his work on the photoelectric effect and relativity revolutionized views on space, time, energy, matter, and gravity, Einstein and his theories were largely unknown outside of scientific and academic circles until 1919. Then, when his prediction that the sun's gravity would warp space and bend the path of light from distant stars was finally confirmed during a solar eclipse, Einstein received international fame. To some Germans, Einstein's "success was deeply offensive, uniting in one man all that they detested—the success of an intellectual left-wing pacifist Jew" (Clark 1971, 251). A number of anti-Semitic physicists, led by Philipp Lenard, savagely attacked Einstein's theory of relativity. This outbreak of anti-Semitism increased Einstein's interest in Zionism, the

preservation of Jewish culture, and the establishment of a Jewish homeland in what is now the nation of Israel.

After the war, Einstein worked for reconciliation between Germany and other countries, even serving as an unofficial ambassador in his lecture travels abroad. In 1931, while he was a visiting professor at Oxford University in England, he discussed pacifism as much as physics. He authorized the establishment of the Einstein War Resisters' International Fund. The fund attempted to bring massive public pressure to bear on the World Disarmament Conference, but when the talks foundered, Einstein was bitterly disappointed.

During the rise of fascism in Germany, Adolf Hitler branded Einstein a Jew with a price on his head. Einstein escaped to the United States and settled in Princeton, New Jersey, at the Institute for Advanced Study of Princeton University. While at Princeton, he reluctantly abandoned his pacifism because of the growing threat of Nazism. In 1939, news came that Germany had achieved a successful atomic chain reaction in a laboratory. Other news indicated that Hitler was racing to harness the destructive force of nuclear energy. Einstein and other American physicists were afraid that German work on an atomic bomb might succeed and bring catastrophe to other nations. Persuaded by his colleagues, Einstein signed a historic letter on 2 August 1939, advising President Franklin Roosevelt of the possibilities of an atomic bomb.

Einstein became a U.S. citizen in 1940. He helped build the foundation for the Manhattan Project, which produced the first atomic bomb, but he was not told any details of the project. Because of his pacifist background, he was considered a security risk. A personal acquaintance, Peter Bucky, said:

> One of the greatest ironies of history centers on the fact that one of the gentlest of men, Albert Einstein, was instrumental in the development of the greatest destructive force ever unleashed upon mankind: the atomic bomb. Indeed, the irony is doubly curious when we reflect upon the fact that he was one of the most visible and well-known pacifists of all time (Bucky 1992, 66).

In 1945, when Einstein heard the news of Hiroshima's destruction, he was deeply saddened. History later revealed that Hitler's atomic bomb project had been a failure rather than a real threat—partly through mismanagement and partly because of the German physicists' distaste for the job. In hindsight, Einstein later said to LINUS PAULING about the matter, "I may have made one great mistake in my life when I signed the letter to President Roosevelt" (Bucky 1992, 74). After the war, Einstein reverted to pacifism, stating:

> the murder of men is repulsive to me. And let me state unequivocally that I see absolutely no difference whether one commits a murder in civilian life or during the war. My attitude of pacifism, thus, did not stem from any intellectual theory but was based on my antipathy to every kind of cruelty and hatred. . . . [War] is the real evil of humanity which we must all realize and fight to erase with all of our energies" (Bucky 1992, 75).

For several years after World War II, Einstein was a leading figure in the movement for a world government, to "be founded by the United States, the Soviet Union, and Great Britain, the only three powers with great military strength. . . . The power of this world government would be over all military matters" (Einstein 1954, 118–119). Fearing the spread of nuclear weapons, Einstein dreamed of this "supranational security system" keeping the peace on the planet (Einstein 1954, 130). On 12 February 1950, he appeared on national television and warned against the dangers of an arms race between the United States and the Soviet Union. However, politicians again rejected Einstein's ideals.

Einstein always played down his Jewishness because he felt a common bond with all of humanity and even the cosmos. Yet because of Jewish suffering before and during World War II, he supported the Zionist movement. As a result of his efforts, in 1948 and again in 1952, he was asked to become president of the state of Israel, but he declined both times.

In the early 1950s, he objected to the political witch-hunt led by Senator Joseph McCarthy. "The McCarthyite assault on civil liberties evoked, for Einstein and most refugees from fascism, visions of the rise of Nazism twenty years earlier. Just as Communists, socialists, and Jews had been the Nazi scapegoats, Communists, liberals, and intellectuals were now pictured as enemies of American freedom" (Sayer 1985, 269). Einstein called for Ghandi-like noncooperation with the House Committee on Un-American Activities. This created a furor that divided even those who were against McCarthy. Some thought that Einstein's stance was courageous; others thought that he was wrong to advocate disrespect for the law. Einstein's controversial stance became one of the factors in McCarthyism's eventual downfall.

When Einstein died in his sleep after a long illness, he left a remarkable legacy. His physics—after physicists listened—united space and time. His philosophy—had politicians listened—might have united the people of the world.

References

Bucky, Peter A. 1992. *The Private Albert Einstein*. Kansas City, KS: Andrews & McMeel.

Clark, Ronald W. 1971. *Einstein: The Life and Times*. New York: World Publishing.

Einstein, Albert. 1954. *Ideas and Opinions*. New York: Bonanza Books.

Hoffman, Banesh. 1972. *Albert Einstein: Creator and Rebel*. New York: New American Library.

Sayer, Jamie. 1985. *Einstein in America*. New York: Crown Publishers.

EVERS, MEDGAR

(1925–1963)

I n 1954, Medgar Evers accepted one of the most dangerous jobs in the South: first field secretary in Mississippi for the National Association for the Advancement of Colored People (NAACP). His assignment was to register blacks to vote, encourage boycotts of white businesses practicing discrimination, and make sure that incidents of violence and racism against blacks received ample media coverage. The group most actively fighting racial equality was the Citizen's Council, which Evers referred to as the "up-town Ku Klux Klan" (Vollers 1995, 57). He said that the group sought to keep blacks subservient by maintaining segregated schools, preventing blacks from voting, and keeping blacks economically dependent on whites. The council seemed to set no limits on accomplishing its goals: members of the council cut the credit of black businessmen and home owners, engaged in beatings and drive-by shootings, committed murders, and rigged court cases.

By 1955, when Reverend George Lee was murdered for refusing to take his name off the voting rolls, most blacks in Mississippi knew that there was a death list, and that Evers's name was on that list. A television appearance in May 1963 increased the danger to his life by making him more recognizable to the people of Mississippi. The mayor of Jackson, Allen Thompson, had gone on television and declared that racial harmony reigned in his city; blacks enjoyed 24-hour police protection, were respected, and made a decent living. Thompson blamed outsiders for coming in and stirring up trouble in Mississippi. Evers knew that this was untrue and demanded that the television station give him a chance to speak as a native Mississippian.

According to author Maryanne Vollers, many people helped prepare the speech, but "it was pure Medgar: reasonable, forceful, and relentlessly logical." This probably

rattled white Mississippians, most of whom knew blacks only as farmhands and domestic workers. Here was a well-spoken, smart black man, a college graduate with a Yankee accent. And in the state where it was still the custom for a black to step off the sidewalk to let a white pass, here was a Negro talking back to the mayor of the capital city. Disputing him. . . .

Medgar Evers may have lacked the fire and poetry of Martin Luther King, but rarely has a better case been made for desegregation. King appealed to the heart; Evers went for the mind and soul. He knew how to appeal to the sympathy of whites, and he knew he needed to win at least some of them to his cause. By his own example he could show whites that a black man could be reasonable, and educated, and well spoken. To a

white supremacist, Medgar Evers, at that moment, must have seemed like the most dangerous man in Mississippi (Vollers 1995, 107–108).

Less than a month later, Evers was murdered, shot in his driveway. Ironically, it was the same day, 11 June 1963, that President John F. Kennedy gave his speech outlining a new civil rights bill, describing race relations as having reached a moral crisis and calling for changes in each American's daily life.

Medgar Wiley Evers had grown up with the powerful example of his father, James Evers, who was more financially independent than most southern blacks, who were often sharecroppers. James, like his father, owned his land, where his milk cows, chickens, and crops kept his family from going hungry. He worked in the lumberyard or on the railroad to earn a living. James Evers's mind was as independent as his economic condition. He would not get off the sidewalk to let a white man pass, and he railed against his children ever accepting charity.

James Evers' wife, Jessie, had divorced her first husband, with whom she had had three children. She then had four more, and Medgar was their second youngest. He was closest to his brother Charles, who also grew up to be a civil rights activist. When the two were eight and eleven years old, they heard Theodore Bilbo speak to a white audience. The topic was how to treat blacks, and the two boys were the only blacks there. In his presentation, Bilbo referred to the two boys, saying that if whites were not careful, they would live to see the day when blacks were elected to political positions in Washington. Charles said later that the speech inspired him.

While in high school, Evers was able to escape the restrictive South in the summers. He worked in Chicago, enjoying the freedom he experienced there. He volunteered for service in World War II and was stationed in a segregated battalion in France. When he returned, he attended Alcorn College in Mississippi and majored in business administration. He was active in student affairs, editing the school newspaper, participating in sports, and singing in the school choir. At college, Evers met Myrlie, and the two were married while they were both students. Together they had three children.

After his graduation, Evers was recruited by Dr. T. R. M. Howard to work for Magnolia Mutual Life Insurance Company. Howard was a successful black businessman and community leader in Mound Bayou, Mississippi, the only town in the state founded, settled, and governed by blacks. Howard had started a leadership council for black businessmen, and the council had encouraged the first economic boycott of white businesses. He became Evers's mentor.

Selling insurance brought Evers in contact with the poor black farmers of Mississippi. He empathized with their suffering and was prompted to help change the way black people had to live. In 1953, Evers volunteered to be the first black to try to enroll at the University of Mississippi. When he was rejected, he turned his efforts at reform in other directions. The following year, he accepted the position with the NAACP.

In addition to Howard, Evers cited Jomo Kenyatta as a main influence in his life. To protest British rule in Kenya, Kenyatta and his Mau Mau followers killed

dozens of white farmers in the African highlands. Although Evers had considered starting a Mississippi Mau Mau, he turned against violence: "It didn't take much reading of the Bible to convince me that two wrongs would not make the situation any different, and that I couldn't hate the white man and at the same time hope to convert him" (Vollers 1995, 72). Evers's mother also deplored violence and certainly had an influence on him.

Evers's murderer, Byron De La Beckwith, was twice acquitted by all-white juries. Finally in 1994, due primarily to the persistence of Evers's wife, Myrlie Evers-Williams, who had remarried, Beckwith was convicted of murdering Evers.

When asked what she thought Medgar would be doing today if he had lived, Evers-Williams replied, "He'd be an elected official of the state of Mississippi. He used to say, 'The day will come when enough of our people are voting and we will have elected officials and I plan to be one.' I'm so proud that Mississippi has the largest number of African-American elected officials in the country. That's a tribute to Medgar and all the others" (Dreifus 1994).

References

Browne, Ray B., ed. 1990. *Contemporary Heroes and Heroines*. Detroit, MI: Gale Research.

Dreifus, Claudia. 1994. "The Widow Gets Her Verdict." *New York Times Magazine*, 27 November.

Vollers, Maryanne. 1995. *Ghosts of Mississippi: The Murder of Medgar Evers, the Trials of Byron De La Beckwith, and the Haunting of the New South*. Boston: Little, Brown.

F

FLOOD, CURT

(1938–)

During the 1960s, Curt Flood was a baseball legend, known as one of the sport's greatest stars. Among his St. Louis Cardinals teammates were three other black players who later became famous: Bill White, now president of the National League, and Hall-of-Famers Lou Brock and Bob Gibson. Flood, however, sacrificed his career and was ostracized by players and managers alike when he fought for the right of all ballplayers to negotiate the terms of their employment. Because of Flood's actions, baseball players today earn an average of $1.5 million a year, compared with $24,000 a year when Flood was in the major leagues.

Flood was born on 18 January 1938 in Houston, Texas, the youngest of six children. When he was two years old, the family moved to Oakland, California, where jobs were supposed to be more plentiful, but his parents "held not fewer than four underpaid jobs at a time" to provide for the family's basic needs (Flood 1970, 19). When he was nine years old, Flood began playing midget baseball, which was sponsored by the local police, and continued his interest into high school. In high school, he also began developing his artistic talents.

During the 1950s, Flood played with minor leagues in the South, and like other black ballplayers, he was forced to use segregated public accommodations such as hotels and restaurants. His food was delivered to the back door of restaurants while his white teammates ate inside. While playing in the minors, Flood recalled how some whites harassed him during games, loudly cursing or yelling "black bastard," "nigger," "eight-ball," "jigaboo," and similar insults at him.

Flood joined the St. Louis Cardinals as an outfielder in 1957. In 1969, he was a Gold Glove winner and was offered a salary of $90,000 when the Cardinals traded him to the Philadelphia Phillies, but he refused to go. At the time, agreements between players and ball club owners contained a reserve clause that bound a player to his team for an indefinite period—until the team traded or released him. If a player refused to accept the trade or salary offered by the team that held his contract, he could not play for another team, even if that team offered a more lucrative contract. Sports writers quickly criticized Flood's actions, predicting that if Flood was allowed to ignore the reserve clause, there would be chaos in baseball. It would create an imbalance in competition, with rich clubs getting richer and poor clubs going bankrupt because they could not afford to pay the high salaries that the players would demand.

Flood did not play for a year after refusing to be traded, and during that time he wrote to the commissioner of baseball, stating his position: "After 12 years in the major leagues, I do not feel that I am a piece of property to be bought and sold irrespective of my wishes. I believe that any system that produces that result violates my basic right as a citizen and is inconsistent with the laws of the United States" (Whiteside 1994).

Flood brought a lawsuit in a New York federal court, challenging baseball's exemption from antitrust laws that, in effect, gave team owners control over players. Flood sought the right to play for the team of his choice and the right of all players to sell their talents and labor in a free market. The court ruled in favor of baseball club owners, so Flood appealed his case to the U.S. Court of Appeals, which upheld the lower court's ruling on 7 April 1971. Then, represented by former U.S. Supreme Court Justice Arthur Goldberg, Flood appealed to the U.S. Supreme Court. In a five-to-three vote, the Court ruled against Flood, upholding professional baseball's reserve clause. In short, the courts held that the basic agreement between players and owners was protected from any type of litigation because of baseball's exemption from antitrust laws.

During the long months of legal proceedings, Flood was ostracized by team owners and abandoned by players—they did not support Flood, even though most knew that they would benefit from his efforts. As Flood recalled in 1994: "It was sad that none of the players came to my trial. They felt guilt by association would be harmful to them. Some of my dear friends, who under any other circumstances would have been behind me, just decided not to come. They were intimidated" (Whiteside 1994).

Although Flood lost his lawsuits, he paved the way for others to find loopholes in the reserve clause. A federal arbitrator, Peter Seitz, ruled that the reserve clause was a violation of the collective bargaining agreement and therefore was not exempt from antitrust laws. The clause, Seitz declared, must be subject to negotiation. After that ruling, a new basic agreement was drawn up, granting players free agency after six years. The reserve clause was finally abolished in 1975.

While Flood's legal battles were under way, he was traded once more to the Washington Senators, and he played 13 games during the 1971 season. After that, he left professional baseball and spent most of the 1970s in Europe, where he became known as an accomplished painter. Back in the United States in the 1980s, he supervised the Parks and Recreation Department of Oakland, California, and set up the Curt Flood Youth Organization in Oakland. He also worked for the Oakland A's in public relations. In the early 1990s, he became part of the management team for the new United Baseball League, an alternative to the other two major leagues. Flood reported that in the new league, players would be part of the decision-making process and enjoy profit-sharing, which had never been done before. He noted in 1994 that he felt "good about management offering opportunities for minorities. This will be high on my list of things to accomplish." He pointed out that his presence as a black man would call attention to the fact that major league baseball has largely ignored hiring minorities at its highest levels:

> Up until now, no one has addressed the great dearth of African-Americans that have the wherewithal to be owners. We plan to do that. We're not talking about giving a preference to teams that have minority owners. You can't do that. We're talking about consideration. Up until now, minorities have not even been considered as owners of team (Whiteside 1994).

References

Dell'Apa, Frank. 1994. "Flood Recalls His Break-through." *Boston Globe*, 7 August, Sports section.

Flood, Curt. 1970. *The Way It Is*. New York: Trident Press.

Whiteside, Larry. 1994. "Flood's Gates Opened It Up." *Boston Globe*, 8 November, Sports section.

Will, George F. 1993. "A Baseball Lesson in Freedom." *Washington Post*, 21 November.

FONDA, JANE

(1937–)

J ane Fonda gained international fame as an actress, then as a left-wing political firebrand, and most recently as an aerobics guru, living many contrasts and contradictions. She was the scantily clad sex symbol who later championed feminism, the Miss Army Recruiting of 1962 whose 1972 radio broadcasts from North Vietnam gave her the derisive nickname "Hanoi Jane," the chain-smoking bulimic who became a leading fitness expert, and the outspoken anticapitalist who grew rich through her film roles and eventually married a business tycoon.

Daughter of actor Henry Fonda, Jane worked as a model and stage actress before making her 1960 debut in the first of over 40 films. She earned early crit-

ical praise as an actress. She was devoutly apolitical until she moved to France and began mingling with a number of socialists and pacifists.

In 1963, she journeyed to Moscow with her future husband, film director Roger Vadim, on a pilgrimage to his father's birthplace. Discovering that Russians were similar to people everywhere else stunned her. "All my life I'd been brought up to believe the Russians were some alien, hostile people sitting over there just waiting to swallow up America. Nothing could be further from the truth." She claimed to have had her "eyes opened" to American "propaganda" (Anderson 1990, 121).

In 1965, while still living in France, she married Vadim, whose biggest international film success was the 1968 camp space fantasy *Barbarella*. Fonda, in the starring role, reached her peak as a sex symbol, but it also became a turning point in her life. In opposition to the sexual exploitation she had experienced in making movies, she became more conscious of her rights as a woman and embraced the feminist philosophy.

In 1968, politics became inescapable. In France, a student revolt and national strike rocked Paris for several weeks. Then Fonda watched TV coverage of the bloody clash between antiwar demonstrators and police outside the Democratic National Convention in Chicago, Illinois.

Feeling confused and philosophically empty, she traveled through India and Nepal seeking enlightenment. The poverty and human misery she witnessed there appalled her. Instead of finding the path to inner peace, she became convinced that the solution was to turn outward, not inward.

As she moved away from her sex-symbol status to more serious films, Fonda also changed politically. Describing herself as a "revolutionary woman," she spent much of 1970 touring the United States, speaking against the war, and supporting the Black Panthers and Native American militants. Everything Fonda did in her life she pursued with passionate intensity. Swayed by radical left-wing rhetoric, she expressed strong feelings about issues—even though she often lacked understanding of the issues' complexities. Her national exposure made her an instant spokesperson, but her superficial knowledge sometimes caused more harm than good. Native American leaders believed that the public relations Fonda was enthusiastically providing them was largely negative, and they pleaded with her in 1970 to limit her support to the background.

Because of her activism, Fonda was on the Nixon administration's "enemies" list. The FBI placed her under close surveillance and labeled her file "Jane Fonda: Anarchist."

In 1971, Fonda and other actors toured military service centers and other such venues in the United States and the Far East. Their satirical antiwar revue "FTA" (Free the Army) was designed as an alternative to Bob Hope's official shows.

Fonda provoked a cyclone of controversy in 1972 by visiting North Vietnam. She made several broadcasts over Radio Hanoi, urging American soldiers to disobey their orders and stop bombing North Vietnam. She called those contributing to the bombing "war criminals" (Anderson 1990, 9). Her support of North Vietnam made her a lightning rod for American rage. She was reviled as "Hanoi Jane" and as a traitor. The Maryland and Colorado legislatures introduced resolutions censuring her, and several members of Congress urged that she be tried for treason. "What is a traitor?" Fonda responded to reporters. "I cried every day I was in Vietnam. The bombs are falling on Vietnam, but it is an American tragedy. . . . I believe the people in this country who are speaking out are the real patriots" (Anderson 1990, 257).

She had few film offers during the mid-1970s. In 1973, three years after divorcing Vadim, she married Tom Hayden, who was a founder of the Students for a Democratic Society and a "Chicago Seven" radical. Fonda helped bankroll Hayden's various campaigns for elected political office. Together they founded the Campaign for Economic Democracy, an egalitarian grassroots organization devoted to such issues as rent control, protection of the rights of farmworkers and secretaries, the development of solar energy, and an end to nuclear power.

In 1977, Fonda began making a comeback in films, becoming one of Hollywood's most sought-after actresses. She and producer Bruce Gilbert also formed their own production company, IPC (the initials of her antiwar organization, the

Indochina Peace Campaign). The company's purpose was to make entertaining and commercially successful "message" movies. Fonda starred in a number of IPC's prosperous films, such as *Coming Home*, *The China Syndrome*, *The Electric Horseman*, and *Nine to Five*. In each film, Fonda played a character who experiences a personal or political transformation. These films managed to examine important topics, such as the impact of war, nuclear power, and corporate corruption, in compelling and entertaining ways.

Even though her political rhetoric became less inflammatory and more reasonable as she grew older, the old nickname "Hanoi Jane" would haunt her for many years. Sporadically, she would encounter protesters demonstrating about her Vietnam-era politics. In 1988, the controversy flared up anew when the small, blue-collar town of Waterbury, Connecticut, the shooting location for her movie *Stanley and Iris*, nearly banned her from the city.

In a subsequent interview with Barbara Walters, Jane said to Vietnam veterans angered by her old Hanoi radio broadcasts: "I owe them an apology. My intentions were never to hurt them or make their situation worse. It was the contrary. I was trying to help end the killing, end the war, but there were times when I was thoughtless and careless about it" (Anderson 1990, 11).

When Fonda wanted to invest in a business other than filmmaking, she started a workout studio in Beverly Hills. Its success led to a chain of other studios, books, and videos. In 1991, two years after divorcing Hayden, she married cable-TV mogul Ted Turner. Although her political activism is now substantially more subdued than during the turbulent times a quarter century ago, she still takes interest in political and environmental concerns.

References

Anderson, Christopher. 1990. *Citizen Jane: The Turbulent Life of Jane Fonda*. New York: Henry Holt.

Bibb, Porter. 1993. *It Ain't as Easy as It Looks: Ted Turner's Amazing Story*. New York: Crown Publishers.

Davidson, Bill. 1990. *Jane Fonda: An Intimate Biography*. New York: Dutton.

FORD, BETTY

(1918–)

She seemed to have a perfect life as first lady of the United States, married to a man she loved and mother of four wonderful children. Then in the mid-1970s, she underwent surgery for breast cancer and frankly discussed her mastectomy in public, which was hardly ever done at that time. Her revelation helped raise awareness of the disease and the need for examinations and early treatment of breast cancer. A few years later, in the late 1970s, she revealed her addiction to alcohol and pain medications, risking public censure in the hope that she would be able to help others seek treatment for the disease of alcoholism.

Born in Chicago on 18 April 1918, Elizabeth Ann Bloomer was reared with two older brothers in Grand Rapids, Michigan, by her parents, Hortense and William Bloomer. Her father, a traveling salesman, died of carbon monoxide poisoning when she was 16. After graduating from high school, she went to the Bennington School of Dance in Vermont for two summers to train for a dancing career. Then it was on to New York City for a brief stint with a Martha Graham auxiliary dance group. She returned to Michigan and married, but was divorced five years later. In 1947, Betty met Gerald Ford, a World War II veteran, lawyer, and well-known former high school football star. The two were married the following year, in the midst of his campaign for election to the U.S. House of Representatives. He won the election and later became vice-president of the United States, serving with President Richard Nixon.

When Gerald Ford became president of the United States after Nixon resigned from office, little was known about his wife's use of painkillers or her drinking habits. She had taken medication for years—to dispel the pain of arthritis, to sleep, and to relax. Then she took other pills to counteract the side effects of the medication. As many people do, she drank alcoholic beverages socially but also to relieve "feelings of inadequacy," as she put it. She explained, "I was a controlled drinker, no binges. When I went to parties I was on my best behavior. I drank, but never too much. I always knew there would be more available at home" (Ford with Chase 1978, 289, 291–292). Her drinking became a matter of major concern to her family, who intervened to convince her to get treatment.

As many drug-dependent people are aware, Ford's decision to write and speak about her disease of alcoholism was much more difficult than discussing cancer. Although she was widely praised for her lack of fear and her frankness and honesty, she pointed out that she didn't deserve accolades. "I've been both afraid and embarrassed. I've gone through every possible emotion, suffered every possible mood, loneliness, depression, anger, discouragement." When she sought treatment, she found that "in the end . . . you have to take the responsibility [for healing and recovery]. . . . Blaming other people for your condition is a total waste of time" (Ford with Chase 1978, 289, 291–292).

First Lady Betty Ford greets the supporters at her arrival in Dayton, Ohio, in 1976. Praised for publicly discussing her battle with alcoholism, Ford founded the Betty Ford Center for alcohol and drug treatment in 1982.

In recovery, Ford began to set in motion her plan to establish the Betty Ford Center for alcohol and drug treatment. The center, which is part of the Eisenhower Medical Center in Rancho Mirage, California, opened in 1982 with a dedication ceremony that included the famed Serenity Prayer, written by Protestant theologian Reinhold Niebuhr: "God grant me the Serenity to accept the things I cannot change; Courage to change the things I can; and Wisdom to know the difference." In a book about her addiction and recovery and the operation of the treatment center, Ford explained that she has given away the proceeds from her writing and speaking to help support not only her center but also other treatment facilities. She concluded her book with words of gratitude for her own recovery, because it gave her the ability "to help some other people come forward and address their own addictions . . . one day at a time" (Ford with Chase 1987, 217).

References
Ford, Betty, with Chris Chase. 1978. *The Times of My Life.* New York: Harper & Row.
———. 1987. *A Glad Awakening.* Garden City, NY: Doubleday.

FOSSEY, _DIAN_

(1932–1985)

A zoologist known for her field studies of the rare mountain gorilla, Dian Fossey was murdered because of her incessant work to preserve this endangered species.

From early childhood, Fossey loved animals and dreamed of going to Africa to observe various species in the wild. She wanted to enter veterinary school, but her grades were too low, so she became an occupational therapist instead. Fossey's love of animals persisted, however, as did her desire to see Africa. In 1963, she took out a loan, quit her job, and visited anthropologist Dr. Louis Leakey in Tanzania. She also saw the mountain gorillas in Zaire.

Even though she had no formal training in zoology, Fossey was determined to study the gorillas. After returning home, she began preparations by having surgery to remove her healthy appendix. Leakey had declared that anyone serious about African research should do so—he later admitted that he was just testing Fossey's determination.

In 1966, funded by the Wilkie Brothers' Foundation and the National Geographic Society, she returned to Africa to carry on a long-term study of the mountain gorillas. After a year in Zaire, Fossey was arrested, beaten, and raped during a military uprising. She escaped from Zaire and would have risked death if she had tried to return, but she refused to give up. She went to neighboring Rwanda and established the Karisoke Research Center inside Volcano National Park on the Virunga volcano range. There, at an altitude of 10,000 feet and far from civilization, she was scientific director from 1967 to 1980. With little outside assistance, living in solitude and enduring enormous discomfort and hardship, she observed the gorillas in their natural habitat.

In spite of their "King Kong" image, Fossey discovered gorillas to be "gentle giants," dangerous only when threatened or approached without warning. They also exhibited surprising degrees of altruism, intelligence, and family bonding. In contrast to their huge physiques, their habitat was limited to a few volcanic peaks in the central African countries of Zaire, Uganda, and Rwanda.

Mountain gorillas neared extinction largely because poachers roamed the national park hunting for game, and traps meant for other animals often wounded gorillas. These animals were also intentionally hunted, since the heads and hands of gorillas brought large payments on the black market. Baby gorillas were captured for zoos, and capturing a single baby gorilla sometimes entailed killing the highly protective family.

The Rwandans' ever-increasing need for land also presented a complex conservation problem. Rwanda was the most densely populated African country, and the government reduced the size of the park by over 4,000 acres to

accommodate its people. Fossey said that this encroachment alone accounted for a 60 percent drop in the gorilla population.

From 1960 to 1980, the gorilla population in Rwanda dwindled by half, to an estimated 242 animals. The mountain gorilla, not recognized as a distinct species until 1902, "might possibly be doomed to extinction in the same century in which it had been discovered," Fossey lamented (Fossey 1983, xviii).

As a practicing scientist, her job description was only to record her observations, but she was determined to preserve the gorillas—at any cost. She fought to protect the gorillas from poachers and bring their plight to international attention. International concern helped fund antipoaching patrols and needed equipment.

Between 1970 and her death, Fossey divided her time among Rwanda, Britain, and the United States. She received a doctorate in zoology from Cambridge and taught as a visiting associate professor at Cornell. In 1983, she completed *Gorillas in the Mist*, bringing the plight of the gorilla to a large audience. The book chronicled her observations of three generations of mountain gorillas and urged the preservation of this endangered species.

Fossey's obsession to preserve the gorillas from extinction had a dark side. Her fiery temper and brash methods made her enemies. Besides poachers, her perceived foes included cattle herders, park officials, trophy hunters, those hired to capture gorillas for foreign zoos, and even some conservationists, other researchers, and members of her own staff. Some natives believed her to be a witch—a belief she sometimes used to her advantage. At times she shot at people, kidnapped their children, confiscated and destroyed their property, whipped them, smeared them with ape dung, and sent them to jail.

One night in 1985, she was brutally murdered in her camp, but many people were not surprised. Fossey "understood the risks of the life she had chosen. . . . Clearly, had it not been for her gorillas, she wouldn't have tempted fate. . . . Fossey had died for her gorillas" (Hayes 1990, 34). Fossey was buried in the mountain graveyard beside her favorite gorilla, Digit, killed earlier by poachers.

The Rwandan government later charged Wayne McGuire, Fossey's assistant, and Emmanuel Rwelekana, her tracker, with the crime. Rwelekana died in prison, allegedly by hanging himself, and McGuire fled the country. Many believe that Rwelekana and McGuire were both innocent scapegoats. Poachers or even a political conspiracy were the likely culprits.

After her death, the Dian Fossey Gorilla Fund continued to document the gorillas' lives. The $1 million annual budget was raised from private contributions and charitable donations from around the world. Fossey's legacy was saving the mountain gorillas from extinction and obtaining intimate knowledge about them.

Some of the gorillas Fossey studied became part of the 1988 movie *Gorillas in the Mist*, a dramatization of Fossey's life and work. The popular movie revealed Fossey's legacy to an audience of millions.

During the savage 1994 Rwandan civil war, many naturalists feared that the gorillas might also be decimated. Fortunately, the population of about 600 gorillas emerged virtually unscathed from the conflict. Nevertheless, leftover land

mines planted in the park and other postwar problems in the devastated country will continue to threaten the precarious existence of the largest wild relative of humanity.

References

Fossey, Dian. 1983. *Gorillas in the Mist*. Boston: Houghton Mifflin.

Gordon, Nicholas. 1993. *Murders in the Mist: Who Killed Dian Fossey*. London: Hodder and Stoughton.

Hayes, Harold T. P. 1990. *The Dark Romance of Dian Fossey*. New York: Simon & Schuster.

Mowat, Farley. 1987. *Woman in the Mists: The Story of Dian Fossey and the Mountain Gorillas of Africa*. New York: Warner Books.

Reed, Susan. 1995. "Survivors in the Mist: Threats to Last Surviving Mountain Gorillas in Rwanda." *People Weekly*, 6 March.

Wallace, Bruce. 1995. "High above It All: How War Brought Peace to Rwanda's Gorillas." *Maclean's*, 6 February.

FOX, MATTHEW

(1940–)

Matthew Fox's radical ideas on feminism, sexuality, and God as Mother troubled his superiors in the Catholic Church, but it was not until his book *Original Blessing* was published that the Dominican priest found himself in real trouble. In his book, Fox attacks the traditional views of the human as sinner, passion as curse, and God's role as redemptive. Instead, Fox celebrates the blessing of passion and the divinity of the human being. Publicly, Fox has criticized the Catholic Church for maintaining its patriarchal stance, for not adopting an inclusive atmosphere for homosexuals, for its obsession with sexuality as sin, and for its mandated celibacy for the men and women who give their lives in service to the church.

What made it difficult for the church hierarchy to respond to Fox is that his work is well grounded in the church's own mystics: Thomas Aquinas, Hildegard

of Bingen, and Meister Eckhart. Although one review of his work commended Fox for his creativity, Cardinal Joseph Ratzinger continued to press the Vatican to bar Fox from publishing. In 1988, the Vatican took disciplinary action, silencing Fox for one year. During that year, he was not allowed to preach, speak, or publish, but the year off did not have the desired effect. When it was over, Fox resumed his active schedule of writing, teaching, speaking, and serving as the head of his Institute in Culture and Creation Spirituality at Oakland's Holy Names College. The institute includes on its faculty a Jewish Sufi, a Yoruba priestess, a Zen master, and—the most insufferable for Cardinal Ratzinger and the Vatican—Starhawk, who practices wicca, a form of witchcraft.

The response to Fox by former and current Catholics has run the gamut from sending him death threats to seeing him as the new political leader for a Catholicism free of Rome's influence. Catholics United for the Faith wrote to Cardinal Ratzinger demanding that he review Fox's work; they organized protests outside his lectures and sent him death threats in the mail. In 1993, Fox was dismissed by the Dominican order, thus ending his ability to dialogue with the Catholic Church from the inside. He was charged with cavorting with witches, among other things.

Fox's quest for spiritual awakening began in his childhood. Young Timothy, as Fox was christened, suffered from polio at the age of 11. He lost the use of his legs for months and spent a year recovering in the hospital. During that time, a Dominican priest visited him regularly, nourishing the boy's intellectual and philosophical curiosity. When he emerged from the hospital, his family noticed a new purpose in him—his decision to become a priest. He joined the Dominicans at the age of 19 and was renamed Matthew.

In his studies with the Dominicans, Fox was attracted to the joyous side of his faith. Aquinas's view of philosophy as arising from wonder struck a chord in him. When his exploring led him to the dark side of Catholicism, Fox voiced his understanding. After reading a text on celibacy by an Italian cardinal that discussed whether celibates should be allowed to wash their genitals, Fox threw out the book and wrote his conclusion: "I am an American and not an Italian. . . . My questions are different" (Wright 1993, 221).

In May 1967, after Fox took his vows and graduated from the Aquinas Institute, he went to Paris to continue his studies. There he met a priest, M. D. Chenu, who embodied the mystic and the prophet, a combination that Fox felt was essential. Chenu had been silenced by the church for 12 years for his involvement in protesting the conditions of Parisian workers in the 1940s. Later, the Vatican appointed Chenu to the Second Vatican Council. Chenu became Fox's mentor, teaching him about creation theology and showing him that there was room in the Catholic Church for diversity.

When he completed his studies, Fox was offered a teaching position at the Aquinas Institute. Although his views led to popularity with the students, they threatened the faculty. When an election was held for a vice-prior, Fox won a large majority of the student vote; the faculty, however, overruled the vote. As news spread, a number of students were so upset that they left the order. Fox finished out his year of teaching and then moved to Chicago.

The next year, a disheartened Fox struggled with whether he should stay in the Dominican order. He finally decided to stay and began to receive offers to teach and conduct a study of how spirituality is taught in the United States. After critiquing how theology is taught and detailing his own model, Fox was offered the opportunity to put his ideas into practice at Mundelein College in Chicago. The result was the Institute in Culture and Creation Spirituality; the institute was based in Chicago for eight years and then moved to California.

Fox will, no doubt, continue to write, teach, and speak publicly. Some wonder whether his being part of the Catholic Church and struggling against it has been essential to both his popularity and his controversialism. Within the Catholic Church, Fox was an unusual priest. His inclusion said to many people: If the church has room for him, then certainly it has room for me too. Outside the Catholic Church, he may be seen as simply another New Age guru. It is still too soon to predict.

References

Spayde, Jon. 1995. "100 Visionaries." *Utne Reader*, January-February.

Wright, Lawrence. 1993. *Saints and Sinners*. New York: Alfred A. Knopf.

FOX, TERRY

(1958–1981)

At the age of 21, Terry Fox embarked on a nearly impossible endeavor: he set out to run across Canada in an effort to raise money for cancer research. It was a noble task, made more so by the fact that he had lost his right leg to cancer. The farther he ran, the more media coverage he got, until all of Canada began to watch the progress of this persistent young man. Almost in spite of themselves, Canadians began to consider Fox a hero, a rare honor in Canadian society.

Sheila Fox, a Canadian Cancer Society representative (not related to Terry), said it best, "They say the United States is built on a history of heroes while Canada has none to look up to. But when I looked down the street today and saw Terry, I said, 'There's a hero'" (Gerard 1980).

Twenty-two-year-old Terry Fox, who lost his right leg to cancer in 1977, runs outside Sudbury, Ontario, just before reaching the halfway mark in his cross-Canada run on 8 August 1980.

Terry Fox began his Marathon of Hope at St. John's, Newfoundland, on 12 April 1980 with no fanfare. He dipped his foot into the ocean and set off down the road. The Canadian Cancer Society, although it thought that Fox's idea was a good one, had offered him no financial support. Instead, Fox had to come up with his own sponsors, who donated supplies, equipment, and a van.

Fox's plan had been to run 26 miles—the length of a marathon—every day until he crossed the country and returned to his native British Columbia. His best friend, Doug Alward, drove the van and marked out each mile for Fox. As Fox covered more ground, the Canadian Cancer Society helped publicize his efforts. All along the way, people would run out to shake his hand, offer words of encouragement or appreciation, hand him a few dollars, or run part of the way with him. Once, a motorcycle gang surrounded him and handed him their donations. By the time Fox arrived in Toronto, a crowd of 10,000 had gathered to cheer his efforts.

Fox exerted enormous effort each day. Eric Fryer, who had also lost his right leg to cancer, understood that effort—perhaps more than anyone. Fryer played the part of Fox in "The Terry Fox Story," a 1982 movie that closely followed the truths of the man and his marathon. Fryer said:

The most painful part about learning to run is, surprisingly, [using] the good leg. It takes an awkward swing of the hips to get the stiff leg to swing

around, and the only way to do this without stopping is to take an extra hop on your real leg after each stride. The constant strain on that leg after a short distance is more painful than the pressure of the sensitive stump. I really don't know how Terry did it. I worked up to one mile. That was my limit (McQuilken 1983).

Fox's limit was reached after running 3,339 miles. When he collapsed in northern Ontario on the Thunder Bay bypass, Canada held its breath. The diagnosis was grim. Fox's cancer had traveled to his lungs. The young man who had inspired Canadians was forced to return to British Columbia for treatment.

In the hospital, Fox promised that he would not give up, that he would continue to fight. "If I did die of cancer, I don't want people to forget and say, 'It was a great thing, but now it's over.' I just wish people would remember that anything's possible if you try," he said (McQuilken 1983).

Fox did not have long to live. Before he died in June 1981, he had raised $24 million for cancer research and received Canada's highest civilian award, the Companion of the Order of Canada.

Fox's participation in sports before he lost his leg prepared him for the rigors of training for his run. In high school and university, he had competed in track, soccer, and basketball. In 1976, after suffering pain in his knee, he was diagnosed with cancer and his leg was amputated. His chemotherapy treatments finally ended in 1979, the same year he began training for the cross-country marathon. He ran a quarter of a mile the first day, gradually working up to 11 miles a day. He kept adding mileage, gradually making 20 miles a day. He said:

At times I had shin splints, bone bruises, and swelling in my foot. I lost toenails, I had chafing and sometimes my stump was bleeding. I went through bad weather and snow, and every day I completed the mileage; I didn't miss a day. I knew then that if I could do it in training, I could do it when it counted (Browne 1990, 145).

The idea for the run came from an article that his high school basketball coach gave him about an amputee, Dick Traum, who had run the New York City Marathon. Although Fox had learned to play basketball in a wheelchair, Traum's example made Fox realize that he could run again. He thought that if he ran across Canada, he might be able to raise $1 million for cancer research. Fox's motivation was, at various times, attributed to rage, obsession, pride, altruism, even insanity.

If the public was curious about Fox's motivations when he started his run, they no longer cared why by the time the marathon ended. The country was in awe that Fox had even attempted it. He had made an unforgettable effort. At the end of "The Terry Fox Story," Bill Vigors, the public relations director of the Canadian Cancer Society, noted this about Fox:

He was so simple and honest. If you want to run across Canada, you just go out and do it. You say 'I'm going to do it.' There's no trick, no magic.

But he was embarrassed when people started calling him a hero for doing what he loved. He said he felt like he was Dorothy in the *Wizard of Oz* having one big adventure, going places he'd never gone, seeing things he'd never seen. He hurt all the time, but it didn't matter. He could quit anytime, but he didn't.

Fox's efforts to raise money for cancer research did not die with him. In 1981, the Canadian Cancer Society began an annual ten-kilometer walk/run in memory of Terry Fox. By 1988, the Terry Fox Foundation was formed to manage fundraising efforts. According to Ray Ryan, chief financial officer of the foundation, Fox and his story are responsible for having raised a total of $149 million for cancer research to date.

References
Browne, Ray B., ed. 1990. *Contemporary Heroes and Heroines*. Detroit, MI: Gale Research.
Gerard, Warren. 1980. "The Agony and Ecstasy of Terry Fox." *Maclean's*, 15 September.
McQuilken, Robert. 1983. "Making a Legend Indelible." *Runner's World*, April.
Thomas, R. L., dir. 1982. "The Terry Fox Story." Home Box Office.

G

GANDHI, *INDIRA*

(1917–1984)

S he was stoned, jailed, and reviled by her enemies, but she was also admired, honored, and revered by her supporters in India and around the world. Indira Gandhi has been called a mother figure, charming, and dedicated; she has also been derided as arrogant, dominating, and ruthless. Gandhi was a controversial ruler—elected in 1966 to govern the world's most populous country, swept out of power in 1977, returned to office again in 1980, and assassinated in 1984 by her own bodyguards. To many of her loyal admirers, however, she is remembered as a woman of great courage who was devoted to making sure that India survived as an independent, democratic nation.

Born in Allahabad in northern India, Indira Priyadarshini was the only child of Jawaharlal and Kamala Nehru, both of the highest-ranking Brahman caste of Hindus, who were originally priests and intellectuals. Another child, a son, was born six years later, but the boy died not long after birth. Her father would eventually become the first prime minister of independent India, but prior to that time he was often jailed—as was her beloved grandfather, her mother, and other women in the family—for their involvement with the nationalist movement espoused by MOHANDAS GANDHI (no relation to Indira).

The Nehrus lived in the 42-room mansion called Anand Bhawan, home of Jawaharlal's father, Motilal, a successful lawyer. When the family first accepted the precepts of the Mahatma and his *satyagraha*—nonviolent civil disobedience to protest British rule—in 1919, they gave up many of their luxuries to live in an austere fashion. Anand Bhawan became a center for the nationalist struggle, and visitors came constantly, as did the police, who confiscated many of the Nehrus' personal belongings as payment for fines imposed by the courts because of the family's civil disobedience.

Due to his political activities and subsequent imprisonment, Indira's father was often absent from the household. Her mother had tuberculosis and was frequently bedridden or confined to a sanitarium. Her childhood, therefore, "had tremendous highs and lows, depending on the time the adults in the household had at their disposal. Sometimes she was petted and spoiled, at other times she was neglected," wrote her friend and biographer (Jayakar 1992, 14).

Indira's education was also irregular. She was in and out of several schools, primarily because her father objected to her enrollment in British government institutions. For a time, she was tutored at home, and during her teenage years, she attended an academy run by a poet-philosopher. After her mother's death in 1936, she went to England and enrolled in the London School of Economics, where Feroze Gandhi from Allahabad was also a student. Indira knew Feroze because he had been involved in the nationalist movement, and the two went on to Oxford, where Feroze courted her. They returned to India in 1941 and were married in 1942, in spite of family and widespread public criticism because the two did not share the same social status and were of different religions—Feroze was a Parsi, and Indira was Hindu.

Indian prime minister Indira Gandhi dedicates India's first SOS Children's Village near Badarpur, India, on 2 February 1970.

Not long after her marriage, Indira Gandhi, who had hoped to withdraw from politics and live with her husband in solitude, was forced into the public arena. Demonstrations calling for Indian independence were on the rise, but the British were involved in World War II and responded to Indian demands with more repressive measures. Jawaharlal Nehru, the Mahatma, and other members of the Congress Party who struggled against the British were arrested, and the Gandhis were left to carry on the cause. They too ran into trouble with the police when Indira addressed a crowd at a public meeting in December 1942:

> A police sergeant menacingly pointed a revolver at her, whereupon Feroze—who had been watching the scene from a discreet distance—rushed to his wife's rescue. Husband and wife were taken into custody and driven to Naini Prison. All her life Indira had watched her parents and aunts and family friends going to jail, and now she, too, was part of the tradition (Gupte 1992, 207).

The Gandhis were freed some nine months later and settled down for a time at the Nehru mansion. Then they moved to Bombay, where their first son, Rajiv, was born in 1944. A second son, Sanjay, was born in 1946. Meantime, World War II was coming to a close, and the Mahatma and Nehru were released from prison. The British granted India its independence in 1947, and Nehru became the nation's first prime minister. His daughter acted as the official hostess and was his confidante, often traveling with him to other countries and throughout India. During the 1950s, she also became a member of the Congress Party and in 1959 was unanimously elected president of the Indian National Congress.

Her political activities and her duties on her father's behalf strained her marriage, which began to disintegrate during the 1950s. Although they never divorced, the couple were seldom together publicly. Feroze, however, was a highly public figure and was elected to Parliament for two terms. While still in office, he suffered a heart attack and died in 1960.

Four years later, Prime Minister Nehru died, and "the question of succession came up immediately. . . . The 'Syndicate'—a loose body of Congressmen made up of all shades of opinion, from all parts of the country, and critical of Nehru during his last days—chose [Bahadur] Shastri as the next Prime Minister. As a gesture of courtesy, he met Indira and offered her the prime ministership. She refused without reflection" (Jayakar 1992, 121–122). Gandhi believed that she would have been destroyed by the opposition had she accepted the prime ministership. Instead, she presided over the Ministry of Information and Broadcasting. When Shastri died in 1966, she was elected leader of Congress and became prime minister—a major accomplishment, considering the male-dominated culture in India.

From then on, Prime Minister Gandhi's political life was a series of triumphs and defeats. Among her accomplishments was a green revolution that helped India overcome terrible food shortages and feed itself. She also led the country in a successful war against Pakistan in 1971 to recognize Bangladesh (formerly East Pakistan) as an independent nation. Economic and social problems persisted,

however, and Gandhi's enemies used numerous tactics to force her to resign. According to a number of journalists and biographers, Gandhi became almost paranoid about people who might betray her and dismissed anyone who criticized her. She also countered her opposition by assuming more and more power for herself, and in 1975, she declared a state of emergency. Hundreds of opposition leaders were arrested, labor strikes were crushed, and the media were censored.

By 1977, the Congress Party was defeated, and Gandhi was out of office. She was reelected prime minister in 1980, but she continued to have many bitter critics. She was gunned down in 1984 by Sikh extremists who were angry about the government's takeover of a holy temple where Sikh terrorists, who wanted a separate state, had fortified themselves.

Throughout the years after her death, Gandhi and her government have been criticized extensively, but Indian-born journalist and columnist Pranay Gupte noted in his biography:

> Perhaps Indira Gandhi's greatness lay not so much in what she did but in what she wanted for her country. She was confident that India would make it. And that confidence resonated through the system and across the land—at least during the early years of Indira's stewardship. . . . Measured by statistical yardsticks, India's record during the Indira era may not have been great. . . . Yet Indira Gandhi always maintained that these were the foundation years—and that the fruits of her enterprise and that of ordinary Indians would grow once the tree of nationhood was firmly rooted (Gupte 1992, 39).

References
Gupte, Pranay. 1992. *Mother India: A Political Biography of Indira Gandhi*. New York: Charles Scribner's Sons.
Jayakar, Pupul. 1992. *Indira Gandhi: An Intimate Biography*. New York: Pantheon Books.
Malhotra, Inder. 1989. *Indira Gandhi: A Personal and Political Biography*. Boston: Northeastern University Press.
Moraes, Dom. 1980. *Indira Gandhi*. Boston: Little, Brown.

GANDHI, *MOHANDAS KARAMCHAND*

(1869–1948)

Presidents, kings, religious leaders, and hundreds of thousands of ordinary citizens paid tribute to the Mahatma (meaning Great Soul) after he was shot and killed. Many people worldwide believed "that when Gandhi fell by the assassin's three bullets the conscience of mankind had been left without a spokesman. . . . No one who survived him had faced mighty adversaries at home and abroad with the weapons of kindness, honesty, humility, and nonviolence, and, with these alone, won so many victories," wrote one biographer (Fischer 1954, 8).

Born in Porbandar, a town in what was then a semi-independent state on the seacoast in western India, Mohandas was the youngest of four children of

Karamchand Gandhi and his fourth wife, Putlibai. In his autobiography, Gandhi described his father as "a lover of his clan, truthful, brave, and generous, but short-tempered," a man "who had no education save that of experience"; he had little religious training but rather a "religious culture" that came from frequent visits to Hindu temples. Gandhi's memory of his mother was "that of saintliness." She was a devoutly religious adherent of Jainism, a Hindu sect based on the concepts of nonviolence, vegetarianism, and caring for the poor (Gandhi 1957, 3–4).

Gandhi's well-to-do family was of the commercial caste known as the Bania. The ancient Indian caste system (probably originating 3,500 years ago) was rigidly in force, dividing people socially and economically and creating a group at the bottom known as pariahs—the "untouchables" or outcasts of society. Gandhi's efforts later in life contributed to the passage of laws that banned untouchability.

When he was 13 years old, his parents, in traditional fashion, arranged for his marriage to Kasturbai, a girl of the same age. Eventually the couple had four children. After his marriage, Gandhi completed high school and followed another custom—tutoring his wife, who had had no formal schooling. When he graduated, he went to England in 1888 to study law, leaving his wife and a son behind. He ignored caste leaders who declared him an outcaste because they believed that he would compromise his religion by eating meat and drinking alcohol, which were forbidden.

Gandhi earned his law degree in 1891 and returned to India to practice in Bombay. His practice was not successful, and in 1893, he accepted an offer to work as a legal adviser for a large trading firm with offices in South Africa, which was then under British control. His wife and children joined him in 1896.

Not long after his arrival in South Africa, Gandhi faced discrimination and abuse from whites because of his skin color, and he quickly learned that other Indians suffered ill treatment as well. For two decades—until 1914—Gandhi worked for Indian rights in South Africa, publishing a newspaper, promoting civil disobedience, and organizing strikes among mine workers. Because of his activism against the British, he was arrested often, but he also sided with the British when he felt that this was the right thing to do—for example, working for the ambulance corps during the Boer War (1899–1902) when Dutch farmers in South Africa fought the British. "I felt that, if I demanded rights as a British citizen, it was also my duty, as such, to participate in the defence of the British Empire. I held then that India could achieve her complete emancipation only within and through the British Empire" (Gandhi 1957, 214).

Gandhi's experiences in South Africa shaped his philosophy of life, his spiritual vision, and his quest for truth based on *ahimsa*, or nonviolence, and the principles of *satyagraha*, meaning truth-force or love-force—a characteristic of the soul, thus known as soul-force. Biographer Fischer explained, "Satyagraha is peaceful. If words fail to convince the adversary, perhaps purity, humility, and honesty will. The opponent must be . . . weaned, not crushed; converted, not annihilated. . . . Satyagraha is just the opposite of the policy of an eye-for-an-eye-for-an-eye which ends in making everybody blind" (Fischer 1954, 77). Based on this philosophy, Gandhi lived and dressed simply, followed a vegetarian diet, and removed himself as much as possible from the materialistic way of life. He believed that "modern civilization" was a threat to

> man's true nature by inculcating false wants generated by the capacity for excessive consumption; and furthermore, through the unequal distribution of wealth and the factory system of production, inevitably led to competition and violence between man and his fellows. It was truly the reign of the devil and unrighteousness, as opposed to the reign of truth and morality: it had the West in its grip and through Western influence threatened to strangle the life out of India (Brown 1989, 88).

In 1914, just as World War I began, Gandhi and his family returned to India by way of England. When he again settled in his homeland in January 1915, he felt that India should uphold Britain in the war and recruited for the British Army, in spite of his principles of nonviolence and protests from friends and villagers. He reasoned that India enjoyed the protection of England and should support the Empire. He also hoped that India would eventually enjoy a partnership with Britain such as that of Australia, Canada, and New Zealand.

Nevertheless, Gandhi soon became the leader of the Indian nationalist movement and got involved in organizing labor. When the British passed the Rowlatt Act in 1919 to deal with perceived conspiracies against the government, the law suspended safeguards for individual liberties and provided for quick trials and punishments with no appeals. Gandhi's response was to lead a nationwide *hartal*, or suspension of economic activity, to demonstrate against British authorities. This idea "united vast multitudes in common action; it gave the people a sense

of power. They loved Gandhi for it. The hartal paralyzed economic life; the dead cities and towns were tangible proof that Indians could be effective" (Fischer 1954, 177).

The British retaliated. In one incident in the Punjab, between 10,000 and 20,000 people had gathered inside a walled garden to celebrate the Hindu New Year's Day in the holy city of Amristar, and British troops were sent to disperse the crowd. There was only one way out of the garden, and people were unable to leave quickly and in an orderly fashion. The troops fired on the crowd, killing nearly 400 people. Following the Amristar Massacre, as it became known, Gandhi became even more determined to lead a nonviolent campaign for national status. He soon launched the Indian National Congress, based on noncooperation with the British.

Living with his followers in ashrams—communal groups following common spiritual principles—Gandhi dedicated his life and work to Indian independence from the British. He also concentrated on the social problem of untouchability. Even though he had often spoken out against rejection of a whole group of people, he became even more opposed to the practice during the 1920s as he traveled widely through India and saw the grinding poverty and terrible degradation it caused. One of his strategies to end the outcaste status was personal example, eating with untouchables and treating them as equals with other ashram members. He also denounced the other inequities in the caste system and the subordination of women. When advocating any social or political reforms, he exhorted his followers to practice nonviolent civil disobedience.

One of the best-known acts of civil disobedience was a protest in 1930 against the Salt Acts, which made it illegal to possess salt that had not been purchased from the government. Gandhi led a 200-mile march to the sea, where he and his followers evaporated sea water to make salt. The British reacted with brutal repression, and Gandhi was arrested and jailed—as he often was in the years that followed.

Whether in or out of jail, Gandhi continued his nonviolent disobedience campaigns during World War II, and he often fasted to call attention to British injustices and reprisals. Great Britain finally granted India independence in 1947 but partitioned the land into two nations—Pakistan, a predominantly Muslim state, and India, with its Hindu majority—which was not what Gandhi had envisaged. He adamantly opposed partition and consistently advocated peaceful coexistence of all peoples, regardless of religious or political affiliations.

As Hindus and Muslims went to their respective new nations, riots broke out, and hundreds of thousands were killed or injured. To restore peace between religious groups, Gandhi began a fast on 13 January 1948; it ended five days later when religious leaders agreed to stop fighting. Just twelve days later, he was shot by a Hindu fanatic who feared Gandhi's advocacy of a single nation and tolerance of all people. Gandhi died on 30 January.

References
Ashe, Geoffrey. 1968. *Gandhi*. New York: Stein & Day.

Brown, Judith M. 1989. *Gandhi: Prisoner of Hope*. New Haven, CT: Yale University Press.

Fischer, Louis. 1950. *The Life of Mahatma Gandhi*. New York: Harper & Brothers.

———. 1954. *Gandhi: His Life and Message for the World*. New York: Signet Key Books.

Gandhi, Mohandas K. 1957. *An Autobiography: The Story of My Experiments with Truth*. Translated by Mahadev Desai. Boston: Beacon Press.

Green, Martin. 1993. *Gandhi: Voice of a New Age Revolution*. New York: Continuum.

Green, Martin, ed. 1987. *Gandhi in India: In His Own Words*. London: University Press of New England.

Rolland, Romain. 1924. *Mahatma Gandhi: The Man Who Became One with the Universal Being*. New York: Century.

GOLD, LOU

(1938–)

He has been called the "Hermit of Bald Mountain" and the "Johnny Appleseed of Environmentalism" for his staunch opposition to logging in what remains of the old-growth trees in southern Oregon's Siskiyou National Forest. Lou Gold hardly expected to be an environmental activist. A native of Chicago, Illinois, he had established a successful university career, teaching political science at Oberlin College in Ohio and at the University of Illinois. He left academic life during the 1960s, became part of the counterculture for a time, and then headed for the West Coast in 1983, looking for experiences that might bring wholeness to his life. "I wanted to touch fundamental ground," he recalled (Gold 1990).

After he settled in Oregon, Gold learned of the U.S. Forest Service's plans to build a logging road into Bald Mountain, an area now known as the North Kalmiopsis Wilderness and a place Gold considered a sanctuary. To Gold and environmentalists in the area, the logging road meant that the Forest Service planned to harvest ancient trees and replace them with a managed forest—in effect, a tree farm rather like the vast Midwest cornfields. In protest, Gold joined

an environmental group blocking a bulldozer working on the road construction. He and other protesters were arrested for their efforts, spent a night in jail, and were ordered to stay out of the forest.

Gold—with hiking supplies and food provided by volunteers in Takilma, Oregon—returned to the mountain to clean up trash. Alone, he set up camp on the crest of Bald Mountain, a barren site as bald as "Friar Tuck's head." From the spot—about 30 feet in diameter—he could "see the great expanse of the untouched North Kalmiopsis. . . . It is a holy place: good for seeing the four directions, for touching the four winds, for sleeping under the stars, and for talking to God" (Dietrich 1992, 269). He decided to maintain a vigil and become a self-appointed caretaker of the mountain.

After two weeks, Gold ran out of supplies and planned a trek back down the mountain, but a hiker came by, listened to Gold's story about his vigil, and encouraged Gold to stay. The hiker offered to bring food. Over the next six weeks, other backpackers as well as friends brought up food, clean clothes, and mail. Gold stayed for 56 days, declaring that he "had found a power spot. . . . And so I committed my life to this place" (Dietrich 1992, 271).

When Gold left the mountain, he was arrested for violating the terms of his probation and spent another five days in jail, although the judge dropped remaining prohibitions against visiting the mountain. Ever since, Gold has returned to the mountaintop each summer, where he watches for signs of further U.S. Forest Service incursions into the wilderness. Each evening in camp, he conducts a medicine-wheel ritual and prayer service, patterned after Native American teachings, to save the forest, and most visitors to the campsite take part in the ceremony.

Gold's brand of activism stems from a belief that individuals should take a stand. In his words:

> As an Oregonian I have taken my stand on Bald Mountain, but wherever you live, these lands belong to you as a citizen and a taxpayer. As a part owner, you have a right and perhaps an obligation to make your voice heard in the debate over how our national lands should be managed (Gold 1990).

Gold knows that few would camp atop a mountain to defend a cherished— even holy—place. He spends the winter months presenting a slide show and lecture called "Lessons from the Ancient Forest: Earth Wisdom and Political Activism," which covers Gold's summer experiences in an area that he calls the most biologically diverse place on the West Coast between Mexico and Canada. He is paid only with donations, which he uses to finance his summer vigils. His main purpose is to urge people to preserve northwestern forests from logging and to make sure that campers treat forest areas with respect.

In 1987, Gold was driven off the mountain by a forest fire and then became embroiled in a bitter controversy with the Forest Service about building a road for salvage logging—to retrieve dead trees. Gold and other concerned citizens argued during Forest Service hearings that the trees should be allowed to

decompose and new growth to return naturally. In the end, the Forest Service won, building 20 miles of new roads and logging 9,000 acres of the burned area.

Gold has not given up. He continues his prayerful vigils, in spite of the fact that timber sales from national forestlands go on. One of his most recent efforts, which is supported by two environmental groups, Siskiyou Regional Education Project and Headwaters, is to save trees in an area called Sugarloaf, which has never been logged. During the late 1980s, timber in the area was sold to Boise Cascade for $2.3 million, and the plan was to clear-cut the area. According to new Forest Service rules initiated by the Clinton administration, old commitments must be honored, but logging is allowed only to salvage dead trees or to improve the health of the forest. Opponents of the logging argue that the Forest Service has misrepresented the planned timber cuts by saying that dense stands of young trees will be cut when, in fact, most of the timber will be from larger trees, many of which are decades old. Still, some changes have occurred in planned logging operations. Trees are now individually marked for cutting, some are saved for endangered species such as the spotted owl, and the U.S. Forest Service requires Boise Cascade to use helicopters rather than build roads to haul out timber. Nevertheless, the fights goes on. Some ecologists claim that logging large trees will leave great gaps in the forest, which allows wind to sweep through and dry out trees and the ground, increasing the danger of fire.

At times, Gold's long summer vigils seem to have failed, but he has no intention of turning his back on his cause. To explain, he described an analogous situation: "Suppose you have a grandmother who is terminally ill. Do you abandon her? No, you care for her. Not because you can change the situation, but because it is the good and honorable thing to do" (Dietrich 1992, 274).

References

Associated Press. 1992. "Bald Mountain Activist Won't Be Ousted." *Oregonian*, 31 July.

Barnard, Jeff. 1994. "Forest Activist Battles To Save the Biggest Trees." *Seattle Times*, 6 November.

Dietrich, William. 1992. *The Final Forest: The Battle for the Last Great Trees of the Pacific Northwest*. New York: Simon & Schuster.

Durbin, Kathie. 1990. "Lou Gold." *Oregonian*, 20 September.

Gold, Lou. 1990. "A Call from the Forest." *Orion*, winter.

Watkins, T. H. 1990. "The Laughing Prophet of Bald Mountain." *Orion*, winter.

GOLDMAN, EMMA

(1869–1940)

In the U.S. sensationalist press of the early 1900s, Emma Goldman was labeled "Red Emma" and portrayed as the most dangerous woman in the country, a charge that was never proved. A spellbinding speaker and a passionate and prolific writer, Goldman became an enemy of the U.S. government and the monopolistic business interests that held sway over it by ceaselessly exposing the state's exploitation of its citizens. Her philosophy of anarchism grew from the harsh discrimination that all Jews experienced in her native czarist Russia. Later, she developed her views in the United States under the tutelage of Johann Most and other radicals of the European émigré workers' movement. That philosophy coalesced into an activist cause with the execution of the men convicted of inciting the Haymarket riot in 1886. Goldman and many others believed that the men had been tried and convicted in a kangaroo court to deter the efforts of other social protesters, and when she heard of their execution, she became physically ill and fainted. Years later, she wrote in her autobiography,

> I woke as from a long illness, but free from the numbness and depression of those harrowing weeks of waiting, ending with the final shock. I had a distinct sensation that something new and wonderful had been born in my soul. A great ideal, a burning faith, a determination to dedicate myself to my martyred comrades, to make their cause my own (Goldman 1970, 10).

She held true to that goal for almost 50 years, lecturing throughout the world, writing books, and publishing her magazine, *Mother Earth*. Because of her speeches and writings, she was constantly hounded, harassed, and arrested by the police—agents of the state that she could not abide. In her view, people were meant to live free and unfettered by governments that could impel them to wage war, work under inhuman conditions, or ignore their natural proclivities to pursue truth and beauty. Goldman subscribed to the theories of Michael Bakunin and other anarchist writers who saw the industrial-based economy and the modern state as the successor to the czars, kings, and despots who kept the common people in Europe in a perpetual condition of slavery. For her, the ancient community of individuals and families who gathered to meet their own needs was the appropriate structure of human existence. As she wrote:

> Human society then was not a State but an association; a voluntary association for mutual protection and benefit. . . . Political government and the State were a much later development, growing out of the desire of the

stronger to take advantage of the weaker, of the few against the many (Schulman 1972, 89–90).

Goldman believed that it was her mission to help her fellow humans throw off the yoke of oppressive government—any form of government or oppression. Early in her career as an activist, she helped her lover Alexander Berkman in the botched assassination attempt on industrialist Henry Clay Frick, whom they blamed for oppressing workers. Afterward, she repudiated violence as a means to achieve her ends, and her words became her weapons. Her controversial statements attacking social institutions were reported by newspapers in every city where she appeared, and the popular media vilified and demonized her for her outspoken attacks against injustice. Goldman became the most highly visible anarchist in the United States.

On 6 September 1901, newspapers all over the country carried banner headlines reporting that President McKinley had been shot. Accompanying stories related how the accused assassin, Leon Czolgosz, had been inspired to act after hearing a speech by Goldman days before. Arrested later in Chicago, she was held in jail for 15 days, where the police questioned her intensely for hours at a stretch. She even lost a tooth when one of the men smashed her in the mouth with his fist. Although Goldman had been introduced to Czolgosz by an associate, there was no evidence that she had collaborated with him. The chief of police was convinced of her innocence, and he ordered her released. The publicity, however, forever linked the assassination to anarchism and Goldman.

Wherever she appeared on her speaking tours throughout the nation, Goldman was in danger from individuals or crowds of vigilantes who blamed her for the death of the president. In one instance, a crowd captured her manager, Ben Reitman, tarred and feathered him, and drove him out of town. The police did little to protect her. Quite often they would attempt to ban her appearances on the pretense that she was out to provoke violence, lawlessness, and revolution. She "welcomed the difficulties. They helped to rekindle my fighting spirit and to convince me that those in power never learn to what extent persecution is the leaven of revolutionary zeal" (Goldman 1970, 331).

Goldman was arrested numerous times for defying police orders, which she believed violated her right to free speech as guaranteed by the U.S. Constitution. However, she found many ways to circumvent the obstacles and to speak out for workers' rights, birth control, open education, and women's rights. She also opposed U.S. involvement in World War I and the draft that was eventually instituted to fight it.

In June 1917, the U.S. government seized an opportunity to finally silence Goldman, arresting her and Alexander Berkman for conspiring to oppose the draft. The marshal who came to her offices had no warrant and no legal authority to confiscate papers that were taken from her, which was typical of the authorities' dealings with Goldman. Bail was set at a very high $25,000, and she was not allowed to convert her liberty bonds or to have her friends' real estate put up as collateral to meet the cash requirement. In short order, Goldman was convicted without evidence and sentenced to prison, but the government went

one giant step further. It had been investigating her U.S. citizenship, which was based on a marriage to a naturalized citizen in Rochester, New York, years before. The immigration department voided her ex-husband's legal status, and that made her an illegal alien too. She could now be charged under the recently passed Anarchist Exclusion Act, which barred known alien anarchists from entry into the United States and sanctioned the deportation of those already in the country. The U.S. government deported Goldman, Berkman, and 247 aliens that it had labeled anarchists.

Goldman understood during her deportation trial that the state controlled her destiny, and she decided to use the opportunity to make a final point to the United States. Acting as her own lawyer, she told the jury, "whatever your decision, the struggle must go on. We are but the atoms in the incessant human struggle towards the light that shines in the darkness—the Ideal of economic, political and spiritual liberation of mankind" (Shulman 1972, 327).

For the next 21 years, Goldman lived in Russia, England, France, and Spain, never ceasing to write and speak out for the anarchist ideals that were her reason for living. Although the United States got rid of the gadfly, the issues Goldman raised during her lifetime of activism are still very much with us today. Reproductive rights, women's roles, conscription, working conditions, the class struggle, and free speech are still debated because Goldman and a few other brave souls had the courage to question, in public, the role of government in the individual's life. In an essay written toward the end of her life, "Was My Life Worth Living," she puts her efforts into perspective:

> I think my life and my work have been successful. What is generally regarded as success—acquisition of wealth, the capture of power or social prestige—I consider the most dismal failures. I hold when it is said of a man that he has arrived, it means that he is finished—his development has stopped at that point. I have always striven to remain in a state of flux and continued growth, and not to petrify in a niche of self-satisfaction (Shulman 1972, 397).

References

Chalberg, John. 1991. *Emma Goldman: American Individualist*. New York: HarperCollins.

Drinnon, Richard. 1961. *Rebel in Paradise: A Biography of Emma Goldman*. Chicago: University of Chicago Press.

Falk, Candace. 1990. *Love, Anarchy, and Emma Goldman*. New Brunswick, NJ: Rutgers University Press.

Gay, Martin, and Kathlyn Gay. 1996. *The Importance of Emma Goldman*. San Diego, CA: Lucent Books.

Goldman, Emma. 1969. *Anarchism and Other Essays*. 1910. Reprint, New York: Dover.

———. 1970. *Living My Life*. 1931. Reprint, New York: Dover.

Shulman, Alix. 1972. *Red Emma Speaks: Selected Writings and Speeches by Emma Goldman*. New York: Random House.

Solomon, Martha. 1987. *Emma Goldman*. Boston: Twayne, Macmillan.

GREEN, SADIE

(1955–)

In 1994, Sadie Green was one of 11 women honored by Resourceful Women, a nonprofit educational organization in San Francisco, California, which awarded each honoree $12,500—$5,000 for personal use and $7,500 for their designated organization. They were singled out for their efforts to bring about social change in rural areas, helping women overcome poverty, sexism, poor health, racism, and violent assaults. Green's resourcefulness has included work with homeless women through the Women's Transitional Housing Coalition in Duluth, Minnesota, and efforts on behalf of Aurora: A Northland Lesbian Center. Her accomplishments for low-income women and children are so numerous that as one board member for Aurora put it, "they could not be fitted on two pages."

Considering Green's brutally abusive childhood, her humanitarian efforts and her very survival are truly major feats. Green was born in a rural area near Brainerd, Minnesota. She is one of nine children in a family that, as Green describes it,

> was desperately poor, hardworking, proud, and violent, steeped in the disdain of "phony highbrow types." No one ever went to college. Six brothers and two sisters still live within miles of the old farmhouse.
>
> I grew up just off a county road, where red sumac and beer cans lined the ditches; where old stoves and rusty bedsprings fell down steep ravines to clear creekbeds below; where country men in beatup trucks stopped for any traveler in trouble, drove them 40 miles out of their way if needed, then came home to beat their kids before bedtime (Green, "Essay on Class").

In an essay for a writing course, Green describes herself as a "white working class rural lesbian . . . able-bodied, average-sized, with a birth defect—cleft

palate—in the middle of my face." In her teenage years, the defect was corrected with seven operations. But in her early years, Green's mother believed the birth defect was the mark of the devil's hoof and continually tried to banish Satan by heaping abuse upon her daughter. In one instance, as Green recorded in an unpublished fictional account of her life, she recalled one particularly brutal punishment for just being alive: her mother forced her inside a large barrel that was then turned upside down and left out in the summer heat. Telling her story through a character named Eva in an unpublished book, *Evalina: Years in Hiding,* she wrote:

> . . . early mornings were not so bad beneath the barrel, even nights weren't horrible. It was the muggy heat of early afternoon heating the barrel hot enough to fry an egg on top that made it hellish.
>
> Pulling up handfuls of dirt with both her hands, she dug underneath the barrel edge and put her mouth close to the ground to breathe in air. Everything within her being reduced down to a single struggle—a fight to breathe in cool fresh air. The barrel grew too hot to touch. This meant she huddled in a ball on arms and knees and stayed alert so not to accidentally fall against the side. Sweat ran down her forehead, dripped off her eyelashes and made salty water on her tongue.
>
> This barrel treatment went on day after day . . . but the day it finally ended was when Eva managed an escape. When the family trailed off to the swimming hole one hot late afternoon, Eva . . . took her clothes off and layered them as thick as possible between her bare back and the barrel roof. Then she stood on hands and feet with her knees bent and pushed up with her legs . . . [trying repeatedly] until finally she rolled the barrel off . . . quickly put her clothes back on, ran over the road, across the ditch and up the hill to Granma's house (Green, *Evalina: Years in Hiding*).

Green's mother routinely beat and tortured her daughter for at least 14 years. Although she attended a one-room school for a time, Green was isolated during much of her early years. About the only place she was allowed to stay in the home was on a porch packed with junk and old magazines, which she read repeatedly. At the age of 12, she was forced to live outside year-round, wrapping herself in overcoats to protect herself from winter weather and sleeping in abandoned farmyard cars. She had to steal food in order to stay alive, sneaking into the basement of her parents' home to eat from jars of old, moldy canned fruit or to grab a loaf of bread from the freezer.

Finally, Green's grandmother, who had known for years about the abuse but did not want to interfere, called in authorities who found her parents guilty of "technical neglect." In 1970, she was admitted to the child psychiatry division of a hospital for a six-month period and was for the first time able to speak about her experiences. She was then placed with what she called a "do-goody foster family—well-intentioned but condescending." Through all of her struggles, Sadie managed to read every book she could get her hands on (Green, "Essay on Class").

For most of her adult years Green has lived at the poverty level and has been fiercely independent. At one time, she lived in a former chicken coop in extremely primitive conditions. On a voluntary basis for several years, she facilitated a creative writing class at a shelter for battered women. For two years she produced a two-hour Minneapolis radio program for a women's radio collective that produced women's music, history, and interview shows, featuring women who were least likely to have access to the media, such as welfare women and Native American activist women.

Since the late 1980s, Green has worked for the Women's Transitional Housing Coalition, an organization serving women who have experienced poverty, battering, jail, chemical dependency, and single parenting. The program's stated purpose is to help women set goals in education, job searching and training, and independence, and at the same time provide transitional housing for up to two years. Women and children live in a two-building apartment complex with a total of 22 family and efficiency units, sharing their common experiences and providing mutual support and social contact. Green has been a maintenance worker for the apartment buildings, painting, plastering, sanding floors, and doing plumbing, heating, and electrical work. She is now a full-time staff member in programming.

Green also serves on the board of Aurora, an advocacy group for lesbians that brings together lesbian and straight women, allowing them to learn about each other and question stereotypical gender roles. As Green explained,

> In a time when lesbian/gay rights are increasingly under attack, when gay people are still denied basic civil rights and denied dignity, when touted "family values" allow vicious attacks on gay friends and neighbors, Aurora remains steadfast like a beacon (Green, personal correspondence).

Green has also been an activist for the rights of poor people, taking part in demonstrations to restore government funding for Work Readiness programs, actions that resulted in her arrest in the early 1990s. At a rally of supporters, she noted:

> I chose to be arrested because I have been poor all my life . . . because I work in a low income housing program in Duluth with women and kids who struggle constantly with poverty. I watch them jump through hoops for the system—juggle childcare, stretch a meal, improvise—make something from nothing. We're told poor people are lazy and inept. In fact the poor are forced to work long hours and be creative in ways the wealthy never dream of, while fighting overwhelming levels of depression and hopelessness because we're told that women, people of color, poor people are expendable, unimportant, throw-away people.

Whatever Green's actions, she feels a deep sense of responsibility to share, because she believes social revolution means more than reading, talking, and changing thought patterns. Rather it means doing and acting differently. Green

lives by the words of labor leader EUGENE DEBS of the late 1800s and early 1900s, who said, "While there is a lower class I am in it, while there is a criminal element I am of it, while there is a soul in prison, I am not free."

References

Green, Sadie. n.d. Personal correspondence.

———. n.d. "Essay on Class."

———. n.d. *Evalina: Years in Hiding*. Unpublished manuscript.

GREGORY, DICK

(1932–)

Comedy was Dick Gregory's weapon against racism. During the 1960s and 1970s, Gregory was the first black comedian to perform in white nightclubs in the United States, ridiculing racism. Offstage, he protested racism by organizing and participating in marches, sit-ins, and fasts. Gregory's deft ability to get media coverage for these activities helped inform and involve the public. The publicity also got him arrested countless times and riled some individuals and groups such as the Ku Klux Klan. Later, as Gregory drew attention to police brutality and government cover-up, the ranks of those offended by his message grew.

Gregory's career, outgoing personality, and political activism brought him in touch with many powerful people who were shaping or reshaping the United States. It was MARTIN LUTHER KING, JR., who warned Gregory to be careful. "I'm just afraid they're going to kill you," King said. Gregory's answer was typical, "If they do, Doc, will you preach my funeral?" (Gregory 1976, 171).

Strictly adhering to the principles of nonviolence, Gregory brought a rational presence to every event he attended. Often the line between the police and the public was an electric wire between two opposing, passionate entities. Feeling that he could be of use, he went to Watts after the first wave of riots in that city in 1965. Police and state troopers were armed, crouching behind parked cars. A crowd of men, women, and children had gathered in front of a housing project. During a lull, Gregory began walking toward the crowd, urging them to go inside. Suddenly, in Gregory's words,

A volley of about twenty shots came from the direction of the project. I heard the police behind me screaming, "Get back, Mr. Gregory!" But I kept walking toward the crowd. I decided that if the cops were going to shoot, they would have to shoot through my back.

I continued to plead with the people to get back inside. "There's a hundred cops across the street fixin' to wipe you all out. We can avoid a bloodbath. Get back inside!" Then, for the first time, I felt something warm trickling down my leg. I knew I was scared, but I didn't think I'd lost bladder control! Then I felt the burning sensation, and I realized I had been shot. I walked right up to one of the cats who had been doing the shooting and said, "All right, goddamit, brother. You had your fun. I been shot. Now get the hell out of here!"

The shock value worked. The crowd began to disperse, and, on that corner at least, we avoided a potential bloodbath (Gregory 1976, 115).

Although some black militants were outraged that Gregory had been telling blacks not to riot, one white policeman thanked Gregory. "I've got a wife and kids at home too. I want to thank you for what you did tonight. As long as I live, I'll never forget it. I'll never forget you turning your back on our guns." As he reflected on the Watts episode, Gregory wrote in *Up from Nigger*, "Freedom is worth dying for, but nothing justifies killing" (Gregory 1976, 116).

Because Gregory was a man who could not help but respond when he encountered injustice or deceit, racism was not the only thing he fought against. As he became more involved in activism, his sphere of concerns widened to include questioning the Kennedy assassination; protesting the Vietnam War; campaigning for Native American rights; and speaking out against anti-Semitism, unequal housing, and hunger. His stance against killing eventually led him to become a vegetarian.

Gregory seemed to be in the midst of all the major political events of the 1960s and 1970s. He was at a convention of specialists trying to untangle the mystery surrounding Kennedy's death when he saw Abraham Zapruder's film of the assassination. His conviction that the American people needed to see the film led to its being shown on television.

The government's apparent cover-up in the Kennedy assassination was one of many deceptions that appalled Gregory. He thought that he might change this by becoming involved in politics. In 1967, he ran for mayor of Chicago. In 1968, he ran for president of the United States.

As a presidential candidate, Gregory felt that he needed to find out the truth about what was going on in Vietnam, so he arranged a meeting in Paris with members of the North Vietnamese team who were reportedly involved in negotiating a truce. From this meeting, he discovered that there were no negotiations going on, despite the assurance from U.S. government officials that negotiations were well under way. Although Gregory lost both elections, his campaigns enabled him to publicize the Vietnamese-American negotiation deception and increase Americans' awareness of what their government was doing.

Gregory grew up in a poor family of six children. As the second oldest, he found odd jobs to help out his mother, who had been abandoned by Gregory's father. His mother taught her children pride, security, and the value of humor. When a relief truck arrived at their house, she said, "Aren't we lucky to get such service?" (Browne 1990, 182).

When he was in high school, Gregory decided that his way out of the ghetto was to become a track star. Of the 12 athletic scholarships he was offered, he chose Southern Illinois University at Carbondale. There he studied business administration and, in 1953, was named the university's outstanding athlete for his record in track.

The U.S. Army interrupted Gregory's education. While in the army, he performed comedy routines. Afterward, he did odd jobs until he broke into the field of entertainment. The break came in January 1961 when he filled in for another comedian at Chicago's Playboy Club. He was offered a contract, and a month later, *Time* magazine published a profile of Gregory.

By then, Gregory had been married for two years to Lillian. As the years went by, she not only supported Gregory in his fight for civil rights and other human rights but also frequently joined him. She often marched with him, was arrested with him, and was usually released before him so that she could care for their ten children.

As Gregory's awareness of his own health grew, he saw a connection between his lifestyle as a comedian and his unhealthy drinking and smoking habits. In 1973, he retired from comedy. Because he had used fasting as a way to protest various causes, he pursued his interest in health and fasting. He eventually developed the Slim-Safe Bahamian diet formula, a seaweed-based diet drink. In the late 1980s, he sold the rights of his formula to Cernitin America, Inc. for $100 million. He gave $1 million each to about 15 different civil rights and humanitarian organizations.

In recent years, Gregory has focused on educating blacks about the damaging effects of drugs, alcohol, and caffeine. These, he believes, are destroying the black community.

References
Browne, Ray B., ed. 1990. *Contemporary Heroes and Heroines*. Detroit, MI: Gale Research.
Gregory, Dick. 1976. *Up from Nigger*. New York: Stein & Day.

H

HALE, CLARA

(1906–1992)

S he has been called a national icon. President
Ronald Reagan, in his 1985 state of the union
message, praised Clara Hale of New York's
Harlem as "a true American hero." After she "retired" at the age of 65, "Mother
Hale," as she was affectionately known, was a nurturing symbol for more than
20 years. She founded Hale House in Harlem and dedicated her life to caring for
children of heroin and cocaine addicts. In the womb, some children of drug users
become addicted or infected with HIV, the virus that causes AIDS. At a time
when many people shunned anyone infected with HIV, Mother Hale held, fed,
and nurtured infected infants.

Clara McBride was born in Elizabeth City, North Carolina, and learned early
in life about adversity. After the family moved to Philadelphia when she was just
a small child, Clara's father was murdered. Her mother died when she was 16
years old but was a major influence in her life. As Clara once said:

> My mother taught me pride. She said: "Don't be ashamed you're black.
> God didn't make a mistake when he created you." The pride involved
> holding my head up. My mother said the person who dropped his chin
> was neither sure of himself nor sincere. She equated sincerity with a
> straight-on gaze. I never look sideways. I always look people in the eye
> (Christy 1987).

After Clara finished high school, she married Thomas Hale, and they
moved to New York City, where he began a floor-waxing business and she was
a domestic worker. The couple had two children—Lorraine and Nathan. When
the children were six and four years old, Thomas died of cancer. To support
herself and her family, Hale began to care for children, charging $2 per child
per week. In 1940, she became a licensed foster parent and over four decades
raised about 40 foster children. She adopted one of the children, Kenneth, as an
infant.

In 1969, Mother Hale was about to retire from her child-rearing duties, but
an impetuous act by her daughter changed that decision. Lorraine Hale, who
has a doctorate in child development, was driving through New York's Harlem
one day when she saw a woman sitting on a crate with a baby in her lap. Dr.
Hale feared that the woman, who was in a drug trance, would drop the baby,
so she got out of her car and told the woman to take her child to Mrs. Hale. The
drug-addicted woman left her baby with Mother Hale, who nursed the child
through withdrawal and never charged for her services. Within six months,
more than 20 drug-addicted babies had been placed in her care. Because she
was not approved or licensed for such an operation, city officials tried to close
up her home, but with the help of her daughter, Hale applied for a federal grant
to renovate a vacant city-owned brownstone. In 1975, she opened Hale House

Clara Hale, noted for her work with drug, alcohol, and AIDS-infected infants, celebrates her eighty-third birthday surrounded by children in 1988.

to take in drug-addicted children whose parents were undergoing treatment. The nonprofit Hale House is supported by private donations, including food and clothing as well as funds.

Mother Hale never had formal training but always used a hands-on approach. She cared for new arrivals by placing them in cribs in her own bedroom, rocking and soothing them when they cried out from the pain of withdrawal. When they were able to sleep peacefully, the children were moved to other rooms, where caretakers could supervise them. Throughout the years that Mother Hale operated Hale House, she frequently repeated her philosophy of child care to those who sought her advice or to audiences who invited her to speak. She simply urged that caregivers love the children. "It wasn't their fault they were born addicted. Help one another. Love each other," she counseled. In her view, she was simply doing God's work and following the best tradition of the black community. She once told a California group that, years ago, when black women were in trouble, "we would take our sisters' children. They never went into institutions" (Beyette 1990). Hale also told numerous audiences how she herself overcame adversity and lived through hardships:

I have a sign on my door: "You Can Make It." People who think they can't are just plain lazy. They don't try to make things happen. They want to be given things. Sometimes people stand in their own way. Some problems, some obstacles can be so overwhelming that a human can't handle it alone. It takes courage to admit there's nothing more you can do. But there is outside help. That help can move mountains. That help is from God. You have to let go and let God take over. That is what has given me peace. I'm at peace with myself. . . . I've done some right things (Christy 1987).

From the time Mother Hale took in the first drug-addicted baby in 1969, she and her small staff cared for approximately 1,000 children. Hale House expanded its programs to house and educate mothers who had gone through detoxification. Another home cares for mothers and infants suffering from AIDS.

Over the years, Mother Hale received many honors, among them the 1990 Salvation Army Booth Community Service Award, the organization's highest award, and the 1989 Truman Award for Public Service. She received an honorary doctorate of humane letters from John Jay College of Criminal Justice in 1985.

After Mother Hale's death, a *Washington Post* editorial likened her to "Mother Teresa of Calcutta," declaring that "Mother Hale of Harlem inspired others by selfless work on behalf of the neediest outcasts."

References

Beyette, Beverly. 1990. "Mother Hale's Solution." *Los Angeles Times*, 8 March, View section.

Christy, Marian. 1987. "Mother Hale's Love Shelter." *Boston Globe*, 27 May, Living section.

"Clara Hale Dies." 1993. *Jet*, 11 January.

Lewis, Nancy, and Lyle V. Harris. 1985. "Two Women Cited as 'American Heroes' by President." *Washington Post*, 7 February.

HARRIS, MARY

(1830–1930)

S he was born in County Cork, Ireland, and named Mary Harris, but during the last half of her long life, she was known as Mother Jones. She spent those years organizing and speaking out for the rights of working people and the poor in the United States. "I belong to a class," she once told a U.S. congressional committee, "which has been robbed, exploited, and plundered down through many long centuries. And because I belong to that class, I have an impulse to go and help break the chains" (Atkinson 1978, 15). She continued her tireless efforts until the day she died.

Harris grew up in an atmosphere of protest. Her father was forced to leave Ireland when he was named as one of the many conspirators protesting the living conditions in his county. These bands of men burned manor homes, barns, and crops and ruined the pastures of landowners who tried to enforce the collection of high rents by evicting peasants en masse. The English army, occupying Ireland at the time, cracked down on the violence by arresting known troublemakers. When Harris was two years old, her grandfather was hanged because of protest activities, and three years later, her father left on a boat for North America to avoid the same brutal end.

Harris was 11 years old when her father sent for the family and they relocated to Toronto, Canada, where she excelled in school. She studied at a new teacher's college, Toronto Normal School, but was unable to get a teaching position because she was Roman Catholic. Catholic teachers were barred from local schools, so Harris moved to the United States and found a teaching job in Michigan. There, she had to be more a disciplinarian than a mentor, so she left Michigan and moved to Chicago to use another of her talents, dressmaking.

By 1860, Harris left Chicago to resume teaching, this time in Memphis, Tennessee. There she met George Jones, an iron molder who was active in organizing workers and establishing a local chapter of the Iron Molders Union to demand improvements in the dangerous conditions of the foundry. The couple was married and had four children. Union organizing was put on hold through the Civil War years, as Memphis was occupied by Union forces, but soon thereafter, George became a paid leader in the movement.

Just as their life was beginning to take shape, a yellow fever epidemic swept through the city in 1867, taking the lives of hundreds in Memphis. Jones nursed each of her children as they were stricken, but they died one by one. George succumbed after his young ones, and his wife was left to go on alone. With some money raised by the Iron Molders Local, she returned to Chicago. There she opened a seamstress shop that catered to the needs of the wealthy in the city. At this time—the beginning of the industrial age—a few major industrialists were amassing great wealth by profiting from the long, hard labor of their underpaid and abused workers. When Jones went to her clients' homes, she saw the

opulence that marked their lives—a sharp contrast to the conditions that her neighbors and most of the people in Chicago had to endure. When the three-day Chicago fire swept through one-sixth of the city in 1871, conditions for the poor worsened considerably. Jones lost her home, her shop, and all her possessions.

Wandering among the burned-out ruins one night, she happened upon a secret meeting of the Knights of Labor, whose mission was to unite all workers in an effort to change society through education and legislation. Employers fired any workers who were members or even attended meetings of the Knights of Labor. Nevertheless, the movement appealed to Jones, and she asked to join. In short order, she became an organizer, speaker, and recruiter for the order—the only woman in such a high position of leadership. She became a familiar face to the workers and poor of Chicago as she went throughout the neighborhoods spreading the word about the Knights and the need to work together.

During the depression of the 1870s, Jones's ideas about how to bring about a better life for the underclass changed. Whereas the Knights preached persuasion over direct confrontation with the bosses, anarchists were advocating an opposite path. Chicago was a hotbed of labor activism at the time, and Jones was a part of it all. While still active in the Knights, she began to argue that strike action was justified to achieve their goal. By the time of the Haymarket riot in 1886 and the execution of the martyrs falsely accused of instigating the violence, Jones had broken from the Knights. She could not abide the fact that the leaders had distanced themselves from the men who were hanged, simply to protect the organization. Although not an anarchist herself, Jones set out from Chicago to do the work that she felt personally called to do.

In the 1890s, Jones went to the South, where she worked with coal miners and their families, who lived in extreme poverty. In West Virginia, she became a full-time union organizer—a dangerous job, because mine owners constantly threatened organizers or fired miners who joined a union. Company guards and agents from the Pinkerton Detective Agency, hired by companies to break strikes, often brutally beat strikers and organizers. Jones, even though she was 60 years old, continued with her work. She also gave away whatever money, food, and clothing she could spare to poor mining families, who soon began calling her Mother Jones.

Mother Jones helped organize the United Mine Workers (UMW) in West Virginia and was on the front lines when the workers called a strike, which was broken by the company after 12 weeks. From the late 1890s to the 1920s, Mother Jones went on to organize workers in other states. In 1903, she also led a "Crusade of the Mill Children," a march against child labor that called attention to the deformities and injuries young children suffered while working in factories, for which they were paid only $2 or $3 per week.

Eventually, Mother Jones took over many responsibilities within the UMW, always as a leader and organizer of strikes and work actions. Threats from company guards, Pinkerton men, and government agents had little effect on the tenacious woman. By her actions and bravery, she encouraged others to stand up for freedom, equality, and the rights of workers. Everything else in her life was subordinate to her work leading parades, marches, strikes, meetings, protests,

and rallies from Virginia to California and countless stops in between. Although she worked for the UMW, she also supported the Western Federation of Miners (WFM) in Colorado, where she was arrested at the age of 83 and placed in a rat-infested cell in the basement of a jail for 26 days. She was arrested many other times, including once when she was almost 90 and was working in support of the Pennsylvania steelworkers.

She was still speaking out on behalf of workers on her one hundredth birthday, and because of her selfless crusade and that of other great labor organizers of the early twentieth century, American workers eventually found some justice in the workplace.

References

Atkinson, Linda. 1978. *Mother Jones: The Most Dangerous Woman in America*. New York: Crown Publishers.

Fetherling, Dale. 1974. *Mother Jones: The Miners' Angel*. Carbondale: Southern Illinois University Press.

Foner, Philip S., ed. 1983. *Mother Jones Speaks: Collected Writings and Speeches*. New York: Monad Press.

Hawxhurst, Joan C. 1994. *Mother Jones: Labor Crusader*. Austin, TX: Steck-Vaughn.

Long, Priscilla. 1976. *Mother Jones: Woman Organizer*. Boston: South End Press.

Parton, Mary Field, ed. 1980. *The Autobiography of Mother Jones*. Chicago: Charles H. Kerr.

HAVEL, VÁCLAV

(1936–)

"What can I do, as president, not only to remain faithful to [my] notion of politics, but also to bring it to at least partial fruition?" Václav Havel asked this question in his first book published after his election as president of the Czech and Slovak Federal Republic, which was restored to a democracy following 42 years of communist rule. Havel answered his own question by stating:

As in everything else, I must start with myself. That is: in all circumstances try to be decent, just, tolerant, and understanding, and at the same time try

to resist corruption and deception. In other words, I must do my utmost to act in harmony with my conscience and my better self (Havel 1992, 7).

Havel was born in Prague, Czechoslovakia, to a bourgeois family—for generations, the Havels had been part of the educated, cultured, wealthy class. Václav and his brother Ivan came into the world at a time when Hitler was on the rise in Europe and Nazi troops would soon occupy Czechoslovakia. After World War II, communists gained control of the nation's government, and it became a Soviet-style state.

From childhood, Havel considered himself a writer, and he later became well known as a playwright and essayist—hardly the type destined to be a hero of the so-called velvet revolution in Czechoslovakia. Early in his life, however, Havel showed signs of being a philosophical dissident and a political renegade who never accepted communist beliefs. At age 15, Havel founded a small literary group of youths his age. They spent hours discussing philosophical topics, which, as his biographer explained, was a dangerous practice: "If they had been over eighteen, they could easily have ended up in a Stalinist concentration camp; they could even have been sentenced to death . . . they were supposed to be brought up strictly with Communist ideology . . . filtering out and eradicating everything they inherited that was not created by the working class and its avant-garde, the Communist Party" (Kriseová 1993, 3–4).

During the 1950s, Havel attempted to become a student at the Academy of Performing Arts but was rejected because of his bourgeois background—only members of the Communist Party were allowed to attend the academy. He enrolled instead in the Czechoslovak University of Technology. He hoped that his student status would exempt him from the draft, but he was forced to join the military in 1957. While a student at the technical school, however, he had had his work published in a noted literary magazine and was subsequently asked to address young Czech writers loyal to the communist regime. In his speech, he berated the writers for their hypocrisy in seeking truth but ignoring the past, in talking and writing about change but doing nothing to bring about real social and economic reforms. His bold speech was just the beginning of more daring protests to come.

Throughout the 1960s, Havel wrote and published essays and plays, contributing to a literature that increasingly questioned the oppression of a government that claimed to be utopian in nature. He was finally able to take classes at the Academy of Performing Arts, where he met his future wife, Olga; they married in 1964. During this time, he was also asked to write for the Theater on the Balustrade, a theater of the absurd, and became known as a successful playwright not only in Europe but also in the United States, where his plays were performed. He also continued to write articles, criticizing the government and demanding intellectual freedom in the country.

Although the Czech government under the leadership of Alexander Dubcek attempted to make some reforms and allow more freedom, party leaders in Russia considered these actions a threat. In August 1968, communist leaders sent 400,000 troops from Russia and communist-controlled Poland, Hungary, East Germany, and Bulgaria to invade Czechoslovakia, and in 1969, Dubcek was

replaced by a less liberal communist official, Gustav Husak. Against a background of increased oppression, with many Czecks losing their jobs or being intimidated, jailed, or even executed if they were deemed disloyal to the communists, Havel wrote to Husak in 1975, clearly denouncing the government's fear tactics and repression. Havel also wrote more political articles, essays, and plays at this time. In 1977, he became one of the founding members of an association of dissidents called Charter 77. They wrote a manifesto declaring that they would "devote themselves, individually and collectively, to the respecting of civil and human rights" in Czechoslovakia and throughout the world. The document contained 242 signatures.

When the manifesto was released, the communist government immediately took action against the signers, many of whom lost their jobs, driver's licenses, passports, and other official documents. Most were interrogated for hours on a daily basis. Havel, as one of several spokespeople for the Charter, was a special target for the police. For the next few years, his apartment was constantly under surveillance. He was convicted of "actions injurious to the republic" and sent to prison in 1978 for six weeks. Upon his release, he helped found the Committee for the Defense of the Unjustly Prosecuted and continued to be a spokesperson for Charter 77. He was then put under house arrest, and police set up a long-term surveillance outside, allowing no one in except his wife. By March 1979, the police had become more oppressive, and Havel wrote: "I am forbidden to leave my house even to purchase something to eat. The police officers who guard my house even told me that they did not care if I starved to death. . . . I am not breaking the laws of this country, but . . . those who ought to uphold these laws are breaking them more and more openly and conspicuously" (Kriseová 1993, 167).

In June 1979, Havel was jailed again for subversion of the republic and spent more than four years in prison, where he wrote *Letters to Olga*, eventually published in 1988. He was jailed once more in 1989. Throughout the years of Havel's imprisonment, various dissident groups, student organizations, and others held protests against the government. When Havel was released again, the communist regime was ousted, and Havel was elected to a two-year term as Czech president. In 1992, the Federation of Slovakia and Czechoslovakia separated and became two independent nations, and in 1993, Havel was elected to a five-year term as president of the Czech Republic. He has vowed to be true to his conscience and his belief that "genuine politics" is a "moral responsibility, expressed through action, to and for the whole" (Havel 1992, 6).

References

Havel, Václav. 1991. *Open Letters: Selected Writings 1965–1990*. Edited by Paul Wilson. New York: Alfred A. Knopf.

———. 1992. *Summer Meditations*. Translated by Paul Wilson. New York: Alfred A. Knopf.

Kriseová, Eda. 1993. *Václav Havel: The Authorized Biography*. Translated by Caleb Crain. New York: St. Martin's Press.

HAYSLIP, *LE LY*

(1949–)

When Le Ly Hayslip accepted an invitation to appear on a southern California Vietnamese television station in 1994, she expected to face tough questions about her life in Vietnam, which was portrayed in a 1993 movie directed by Oliver Stone. She did not, however, expect that Vietnamese Americans in the area would stage an angry protest and threaten violence against her and her mother and sister who were visiting her in the United States. Yet, Hayslip understood that the movie *Heaven and Earth* offended many Vietnamese Americans because it told how Hayslip, a Vietnamese rice farmer's daughter, was caught between the Viet Cong and the South Vietnamese forces—both sides demanding loyalty from Vietnamese peasants and quickly punishing or killing anyone who did not comply. Many Vietnamese in the United States have labeled Hayslip a communist and believe she sold out to the Viet Cong because she collaborated with them. Stone's film was based on two books written by Hayslip *(When Heaven and Earth Changed Places* and *Child of War, Woman of Peace)* that describe suffering on both sides of the Vietnam battleground and look at people as human rather than political creatures.

The youngest of six children in a close-knit Buddhist family, Phung Hayslip was born Thi Le Ly in the village of Ky La in central Vietnam. She spent only three years in school, and as a young child her life was not much different from most poor Vietnamese peasants. She was illiterate and spent most of her time tending oxen and planting rice in the paddies. By the time she was a teenager, Hayslip already knew about war because Vietnam had been at war since 1946 with France. Then the conflict was "Americanized" and peasants were told by leaders of North Vietnamese cadres that the Viet Cong should be supported because it had organized to ward off Western imperialism. As Hayslip wrote:

> That all nations had a right to determine their own destiny . . . seemed beyond dispute, since we farmers subsisted by our own hands and felt we owed nothing to anyone but god and our ancestors for the right to live as we saw fit. . . .
>
> The cadres told us that the division of Vietnam into North and South in 1954 was nothing more than a ploy by the defeated French and their Western allies, mainly the United States, to preserve what influence they could in our country . . . the Viet Cong asked, "why should outsiders divide the land and tell some people to go north and others south? If Vietnam were truly for the Vietnamese, wouldn't we choose for ourselves what kind of government our people wanted? (Hayslip with Wurts 1989, x).

In short, peasants were encouraged to support the North Vietnamese regime of Ho Chi Minh who, they were told, would bring about independence for

Vietnam by waging total war. Hayslip and other village children were recruited by both sides to be spies and saboteurs. She eventually worked with the Viet Cong, stealing food and firearms from the Republicans (South Vietnamese soldiers) and the Americans. In fact, "the Viet Cong established regular tasks for the villagers." In Hayslip's words:

> One week, our family would cook rations for them—although the Viet Cong never asked for anything special and refused to take food if it meant we would have nothing ourselves. The next week, it might be our duty to sew clothes: to repair old uniforms or make new ones—sometimes with the parachute silk taken from the captured fliers or from the wreckage of an American plane. As standing orders, young girls like me were supposed to make friends with the Republicans and steal their toothpaste, cigarettes, and other sundries that were welcomed in the jungle (Hayslip with Wurts 1989, 47).

When any peasants were caught by the South Vietnamese, as Hayslip was, they were subjected to severe punishment. At the age of 14, she was captured, imprisoned, beaten, and tortured. After two more arrests, the Viet Cong were convinced she had become a traitor and they condemned her to death, then soldiers raped her. She was, however, able to escape to nearby Da Nang where she worked as a servant. Her family was still suspect, and, after months of surveillance by the Viet Cong, Hayslip's father petitioned the Viet Cong for a pardon, which was granted in exchange for the exile of his wife and daughter. Hayslip and her mother went to Saigon, while her father stayed to "keep our land and worship the ancestors its soil protected." Although both women soon found jobs working in the household of a wealthy family, Hayslip became pregnant by her employer, and she and her mother were forced to return to Da Nang, where her son Jimmy was born in 1966. For two years she earned a living selling to the black market. She even agreed to prostitution in order to earn enough to support her family for a year.

Once she returned secretly to her village to see her father and found him battered by Americans who thought he was hiding Viet Cong. While she nursed her father's wounds, she told him she regretted leaving Ky La and wanted to stay to fight. Her father then insisted that she was not a killer and should not seek vengeance. He asked her who she could blame for all the suffering:

> If you ask the Viet Cong, they'll blame the Americans. If you ask the Americans, they'll blame the North. If you ask the North, they'll blame the South. If you ask the South, they'll blame the Viet Cong. If you ask the monks, they'll blame the Catholics, or tell you our ancestors did something terrible so brought this endless suffering on our heads. So tell me, who would you punish? (Hayslip with Wurts 1989, 200–201).

Hayslip's father advised her to go back "to fight the battle" of raising her son. A few weeks later he killed himself, but his message stayed with her and prompted her to find a more productive way to earn a living.

By 1970, she had married Ed Munro, an American civilian contractor about twice her age who was working in Da Nang. Munro wanted to adopt Jimmy, and in order to gain permission from Vietnamese authorities Hayslip had to pay numerous bribes, depleting her household allowance and some of her own savings. Her second son was born in Da Nang, and the family of four eventually left the country and settled in San Diego, California. After her husband died of emphysema in 1973, Hayslip was forced to learn to survive in an entirely different culture by herself.

In 1975, she married Dennis Hayslip, a Baptist whose religious views clashed with her Buddhist traditions. Religious conflicts as well as many other problems undermined the marriage, and the two were in the process of a divorce when Dennis was killed in a 1982 automobile accident. By this time, she had a third son, Alan. While raising her family she managed and then owned a restaurant and also sold real estate.

In 1986, Hayslip returned to Vietnam to see her surviving family members and in the next few years completed a book about her life. After publication of the book, she returned to Vietnam and visited medical clinics serving war victims. She was so affected by the poor quality of care that in 1987 she organized the nonprofit East Meets West Foundation to establish rural clinics in Vietnam and to "heal the wounds of war and break the circle of vengeance that perpetuates suffering in the name of justice around the world."

References:

Dizon, Lily. 1994. "Hostile Fire in Little Saigon." *Los Angeles Times*, 16 January.

Evans, Karen. 1989. "Le Ly Hayslip's American Life." *Los Angeles Times*, 5 February, Magazine section.

Hayslip, Le Ly, with James Hayslip. 1993. *Child of War, Woman of Peace*. New York: Doubleday.

Hayslip, Le Ly, with Jay Wurts. 1990. *When Heaven and Earth Changed Places*. New York: Penguin Books.

Kidder, Rushworth M. 1994. *Shared Values for a Troubled World: Conversations with Men and Women of Conscience*. San Francisco: Jossey-Bass.

HERDAHL, LISA

(1960–)

Because of her stand on religious freedom, Lisa Herdahl has been falsely called an "atheist," a "whore," a "devil worshiper," and worse. Her school-age children, who are baptized Lutherans and attend a Pentecostal church, have been harassed, and the family has been threatened with violence. Family members have been the focus of a name-calling campaign by a majority—including elected officials—of the primarily Baptist community of Ecru, Mississippi, a town of about 23,000 in Pontotoc County. Even the speaker of the U.S. House of Representatives, Newt Gingrich, publicly scolded Herdahl.

The Herdahl family woes began in 1993, not long after Lisa, manager of a convenience store; her husband, Darel, a mechanic; and their six children moved to northern Mississippi from Wisconsin to be near Darel's parents. After Herdahl registered five of the children (the youngest is a preschooler) at North Pontotoc Attendance Center, she visited the school one morning and was shocked to hear a student recite a Bible verse and prayer over the school intercom. Despite the fact that public schools are legally prohibited from sponsoring school prayer and Bible classes, each school-day morning, a prayer is read by a member of the school's Christ and You Club, which is partially supported by a religious group with a conservative political agenda.

Herdahl tried at first to work within the school system, lodging a complaint with the school principal and then the school board, but she met a wall of resistance: school officials and residents argued that school prayer and Bible classes had been a custom for more than 50 years in the county schools. Herdahl told school officials that she did not want her children taking part in the religious activities, which she thought belonged in the church and at home. As she has often stated, "I'm not against prayer or religion," but "I simply do not want the school telling my children how and when to pray" (Mauro 1994).

As a result of Herdahl's request, a teacher put headphones on one of the Herdahl children, who was then seven years old, as a way to muffle the prayers and Bible reading. When his classmates began taunting and teasing, the teacher had to remove the headphones. The older Herdahl children have been ostracized, and teachers have branded them "atheists" for not participating in religious activities.

Before Herdahl became involved in the church-state issue, she consulted with her family, all of whom supported her decision to speak out, which has been a courageous and difficult ordeal. During most of 1994 and 1995, the townspeople waged an abusive campaign against the Herdahls. Newspaper editorials and letters to the editor damned the family, people shunned Herdahl in stores, motorists yelled insults at her as they drove past her home, school-prayer advocates put "Religious Freedom" signs in their yards, and many townspeople publicly

demanded that she and her family leave town. Herdahl has become even stronger in her convictions, however, which stem from her family background. As she noted:

> My Dad always taught me that if I believed in something I should stand up for what I thought, no matter what anybody else thought. . . . Things that were happening at the school were affecting my children's education, and I wanted to teach my kids that standing up to something and saying, "No," even if the majority wants it, is the right thing to do (Yardley 1995).

Herdahl's husband, Darel, has stayed out of the public conflict because he does not "believe in any one religion" and thinks his "kids should have the basic knowledge of God and decide for themselves if they want to go to Sunday school or church and what church they want to go to" (Yardley 1995). Still, he does not try to convince Lisa to withdraw from the fray, and her children proudly back her.

In December 1994, Herdahl's attorney brought suit against the Pontotoc County school district to force an end to the local school's support of specific religious activities that, even though approved by the town's majority, infringe on the constitutional rights of others. In April 1995, a federal judge granted Herdahl a temporary restraining order, which prohibited school-sponsored prayers while the lawsuit is pending. The case is expected to be heard in 1996.

Herdahl has gained support from others across the United States who write to tell her to "hang tough." Several newspapers have editorialized on her behalf. *USA Today* noted that because the Herdahls "refused to conform to others' beliefs, state-sponsored voluntary prayer and religious studies have made school a nightmare" for them. The family's predicament is just an example of how a constitutional amendment legalizing school prayer "could make religious freedom a joke," the editorial stated (Mauro 1994).

According to an *Atlanta Constitution* editorial, "The best arguments against public school prayer often come not from agnostics or atheists but rather from believers who take their religion seriously. A case in point is the year-long effort of [Lisa Herdahl] . . . to make the local school system quit subjecting her children to the Southern Baptist version of prayers and Bible study" ("When Prayer Offends Believers" 1994).

As for Lisa Herdahl, her religious beliefs were not the intended focus of her stand or the lawsuit she filed:

> I didn't think it should matter if I were Baptist, Jewish, or Catholic—it's a constitutional issue, not a religious one . . . the town has made it a religious issue. I think it has made me stronger as a Christian, because there are a lot of things I have to overlook. When someone says something cruel, or talks behind my back, I want to get angry. But I remember that's not what it's about. I don't hold a grudge against them, and that surprises me. I actually feel sorry for people if that's what they believe Christianity is (Montgomery 1995).

References

Booth, William. 1995. "Fight over School Prayer Riles up Mississippi Town." *Washington Post*, 26 March.

Mauro, Tony. 1994. "Mom Sues over Prayer at School." *USA Today*, 21 December.

Montgomery, Peter. 1995. "Mississippi Mother Stands Strong." *People for the American Way News*, spring.

Reuters. 1995. "Gingrich Voucher Remark Is Called 'Nuts.'" *Washington Post*, 19 June.

"When Prayer Offends Believers" (Editorial). 1994. *Atlanta Constitution*, 28 December.

Yardley, Jim. 1995. "School Prayer Standoff." *Atlanta Constitution*, 12 February.

HIGHTOWER, JIM

(1943–)

Just before he began airing his nationally syndicated radio talk show on ABC in 1994, Jim Hightower, former Texas agricultural commissioner, announced that he would crusade against big business and government on behalf of people with little power. As Hightower noted, his program is not the type that major corporations such as Exxon and General Electric would sponsor, since it deals primarily with empowering the "little person." He also deals with environmental issues, such as the effects of toxic chemicals in products ranging from paint to paper—a topic that elicits a vast number of calls from listeners. In Hightower's view:

The notion that the environmental movement is in a slump is a Washington fixation, for people not paying attention to what's happening in the countryside. . . . Most people don't call themselves environmentalists, but they're the working stiffs who try to take their kids down to the shore for a vacation at Labor Day and find they can't go in the water. They're the people who work in the chemical plants that are taking 10 years off their lives while management does away with health plans and pensions.

They're the people who live in the suburbs . . . next to cotton fields, finding that they're getting sprayed on a regular basis and their neighbor's cat died and the kids are developing rashes. These are the most radical environmentalists that we could have in the country, but they don't put a big "E" in front of their names (Motavalli 1995).

Populist and environmental crusades are not new for Hightower. Most political pundits believe that he was forced out of his elected position, an office he held from 1982 to 1990, because he dared to challenge powerful agribusinesses and other big-money interests not only in Texas but also nationwide. In fact, he made so many political enemies among major corporations while he was in office that a high-finance campaign was launched to defeat him. He simply could not raise enough money to counteract hundreds of thousands of dollars in mudslinging and red-baiting television commercials and other misleading advertising against him.

Throughout his two terms as agricultural commissioner, Hightower became known nationally for his outspoken attacks on the overuse of pesticides in agriculture. According to Hightower, his department "promulgated the toughest pesticide regulations in the country to protect farm workers and farmers. And you would have thought that I had personally gone out and set fields on fire, the way the chemical lobby and the Farm Bureau reacted" (Dreifus 1993). State officials in the administration of Governor Bill Clements aggressively attempted, but failed, to move the regulatory authority for pesticides out of the department of agriculture.

Hightower's views were honed during his early years. He was born and grew up in the Red River Valley town of Denison, Texas, where his relatives were politically conservative "small-town businesspeople, farmers, firemen, truck drivers . . . opposed to big oil and big government." Hightower noted, however, "that if you scratch a conservative oftentimes you find a progressive human being" (Taylor 1985).

Hightower studied government at North Texas State College and international affairs at Columbia University, then went to Washington to work for the late Senator Ralph Yarborough (D-Texas). While there, he helped establish and codirect, with his longtime companion Susan DeMarco, the Agribusiness Accountability Project, a privately funded Nader-type organization set up to investigate how corporate agriculture affects farmers, farmworkers, and the nation's food supply. He wrote two books on the subject: *Hard Tomatoes, Hard Times* and *Eat Your Heart Out: How Food Profiteers Victimize the Consumer*.

In 1976, Hightower returned to Texas, where for three years he was the editor of the Austin-based *Texas Observer*, a newspaper that focused on the economic concentrations of power in the United States and the woes of the underdogs. He has consistently written or spoken out on those themes, which he believes are expressed well in a Bob Wills song: "The little bee sucks the blossom, the big bee gets the honey, little man picks the cotton, big man gets the money."

Before running for office and while he was agricultural commissioner, Hightower took part in a variety of rallies, protests, and marches in support of

environmental protection, labor, and civil rights. In 1980, for example, he fasted in support of union leader CESAR CHAVEZ, who protested the use of pesticides on table grapes. He also took part in a 1988 rally in Atlanta, Georgia, where union members and civil rights activists gathered at the end of a four-state "pilgrimage for economic justice" calling for better pay and benefits. When Hightower addressed a crowd of about 10,000, he said: "People aren't poor because they don't have jobs, but because of the low pay for the jobs they've got" ("10,000 Rally To Protest Low Wage Rate" 1988).

During the late 1980s, Hightower thought about running for the Senate seat held by Phil Gramm (who became a presidential candidate in 1995) but decided against it because he thought that it was "the right thing to do," even though that decision could prove detrimental to any future political aspirations he might have. Instead, he continued his efforts to help build a progressive movement nationwide—a coalition of rural poor, people of color, urban have-nots—that empowers the masses to take charge of their government and encourages more grassroots people to run for office.

References

Dreifus, Claudia. 1993. "Jim Hightower" (interview). *Progressive*, August.

Hightower, Jim. 1975. *Eat Your Heart Out: How Food Profiteers Victimize the Consumer*. New York: Vintage Books/Random House.

———. 1989. "'I Do Not Choose To Run': Raising Issues, Hope and Hell." *Nation*, 6 February.

Motavalli, Jim. 1995. "Jim Hightower" (interview). *E Magazine*, January/February.

Taylor, Ronald B. 1985. "Texas' New-Style Agriculture Commissioner." *Los Angeles Times*, 19 December.

"10,000 Rally To Protest Low Wage Rate." 1988. *Los Angeles Times*. 1 May.

HILL, *ANITA F.*

(1956–)

The youngest of 13 children of Irma and Albert Hill, Anita Hill grew up on a farm in Okmulgee County, Oklahoma. Her childhood "was one of a lot of hard work and not much money," as she stated in testimony before the U.S. Senate Judiciary Committee in 1991. She certainly had no way to foresee that she would be forced into a harsh public debate about the sexual harassment of women, a debate that continues to this day.

Hill's early years were filled with family affection, and she grew up in a religious atmosphere in the Baptist faith. Her elementary and secondary education in Okmulgee County was followed by undergraduate work at Oklahoma State University and graduate work at Yale Law School, where she received her law degree in 1980. She became a practicing lawyer with a Washington, D.C., law firm, and in 1981 met Clarence Thomas (now a Supreme Court justice), who asked her to work for him as special counsel in his appointed position as assistant secretary of education for civil rights and later as an adviser when Thomas became chairman of the Equal Employment Opportunity Commission (EEOC). In 1983, Hill accepted a teaching position at Oral Roberts University in Oklahoma; in 1986, she joined the faculty of the University of Oklahoma School of Law, teaching civil rights, commercial law, and contracts.

Hill's life as a relatively obscure law professor changed dramatically in the fall of 1991. The U.S. Senate Judiciary Committee had convened to determine whether, as the Constitution requires, the Senate should confirm or deny President George Bush's nominee Clarence Thomas for U.S. Supreme Court justice. The nomination gained widespread attention because, after the resignation of renowned Justice THURGOOD MARSHALL, Thomas would be the only black man on the Court. Thomas was practically assured the nomination, but rumors had been circulating that Thomas had sexually harassed Hill while they both worked for EEOC during the 1980s. When nothing was done to investigate the rumors, public protest mounted, and the committee announced that it would hold televised hearings and would call Hill to testify.

Unbeknownst to Hill and most Democratic members of the Judiciary Committee, Republican members had developed a strategy to ensure that the president's choice for the Supreme Court would be confirmed, even though they knew that Thomas was not the best-qualified candidate, as President Bush claimed. For example, when it became clear that the National Association for the Advancement of Colored People (NAACP) would not endorse Thomas, Republican strategists staged a march on Washington by friends, neighbors, and relatives from Thomas's boyhood home in Pin Point, Georgia. From then on, attention shifted from Thomas's unimpressive legal record to his background of poverty.

Law professor Anita Hill listens to Counsel Charles Ogeltree during her testimony at the confirmation hearings of Judge Clarence Thomas on 11 October 1991.

Hill's testimony, which is now a matter of public record, included calmly stated accusations against Thomas. She was then grilled for hours by members of the committee—all of them white men. As they questioned Hill about the details of her story, the TV audience could hardly mistake the antagonistic manner of some senators, who clearly gave the impression that they thought that Hill was lying or even psychologically unstable. The committee failed to call Angela Wright, a potential witness who could have corroborated Hill's testimony. Although Wright did not want to testify, she could have been subpoenaed to do so. Senator Alan Simpson, an avid Thomas supporter, said in a taped interview that he did not want the chairman to order Wright to testify because "she was going to say some highly detrimental things [about Thomas]." Simpson also declared that he "was fully ready to damage her [Wright's] character in the process" (Graves 1995). Thomas, who had been carefully coached by a Justice Department lawyer, vigorously denied all accusations, calling the hearings "a high-tech lynching" of a black man. The Senate eventually voted to seat him on the Supreme Court.

Hill has been both harshly criticized and roundly applauded for her testimony—in her words, the response has been both "heartwarming and heart-wrenching." She has been hounded by news reporters and others in the media. She has been asked on numerous occasions how she feels about speaking out and has consistently said that it would be irresponsible not to talk about the issues of sexual harassment and the inequities women face in the workplace and politics.

"I will not be satisfied anymore with living my life simply for myself," Hill told one interviewer. "Other issues are much broader than my own little world." When asked if she felt that she had betrayed a black man, contributing to the stereotype of oversexed black males, she responded: "I have to live with my conscience as a Black woman. It doesn't do us any good as Black people to hide what we believe is wrong because it may be perceived as a betrayal. It's an unfortunate and awful position for Black women to be in. It's interesting that people haven't seen the harassment of Black women as a betrayal" (Nelson 1992).

In 1994, Hill took an extended leave from the University of Oklahoma to work on two book projects—one about her 1991 testimony before the Senate Judiciary Committee, the other about race and gender issues of the 1990s. She announced in March 1995 that another book is also in the works.

References

Graves, Florence George. 1995. "Responding to Sen. Simpson." *Washington Post*, 28 January.

Hill, Anita. 1991. Statement during Senate Judiciary Committee hearing, 11 October.

———. 1995. "Race and Gender Issues of the 1990s." Keynote address, YWCA's Tribute to Women, South Bend, Indiana, 21 March.

Mayer, Jane, and Jill Abramson. 1994. *Strange Justice*. Boston: Houghton Mifflin.

Nelson, Jill. 1992. "Anita Hill: No Regrets." *Essence*, March.

HORTON, MYLES

(1905–1990)

"He's been beaten up, locked up, put upon and railed against by racists, toughs, demagogues and governors," wrote Bill Moyers in a foreword for Myles Horton's autobiography. Horton was foremost an educator—founder of the Highlander Folk School in Monteagle, Tennessee, where he developed and led a new kind of social activism. He was a champion of the

oppressed in the southern United States and other parts of the world, and for more than five decades, he helped "people to discover within themselves the courage and ability to confront reality and change it" (Horton with Kohls 1990, ix).

Horton was born in Savannah, Tennessee, to Elsie Falls Horton and Perry Horton. Before his birth, both his parents had been schoolteachers "in the days before you had to go to college" to teach, as he explained it, but later they worked at a variety of jobs from insurance sales to sharecropping. Growing up in Appalachia in an area dominated by powerful coal mining companies that exploited poverty-stricken miners, Horton recalled: "We didn't think of ourselves as working-class, or poor, we just thought of ourselves as being conventional people who didn't have any money" (Horton with Kohls 1990, 1).

Horton learned from his family the value of education—the kind of education that transforms rather than maintains the status quo—and acquired a straightforward philosophy of what is right and wrong. Although his parents were members of the Presbyterian church, his mother taught him that religion was very basic; put simply, "God is love, and therefore you love your neighbors." Later in life, Horton acted on this belief

> on another level . . . trying to serve people and building a loving world. If you believe that people are of worth, you can't treat anybody inhumanely, and that means you not only have to love and respect people, but you have to think in terms of building a society that people can profit most from, and that kind of society has to work on the principle of equality (Horton with Kohls 1990, 7).

Because there was no high school in his community, Horton left home at the age of 15 to attend school in Forkadeer River Valley, working at odd jobs in factories and sawmills to earn a living. His family, which included younger siblings, eventually moved to the area so they too could find work, and Horton was able to live at home again. In 1924, with the encouragement of his church, Horton went to Cumberland University in Lebanon, Tennessee, where he educated himself, primarily because, in his words, "I didn't have many good teachers." He spent a lot of time in the college library reading and forming his own opinions (Horton with Kohls 1990, 13).

While at the university, he was active in the student YMCA and in campaigns to break down barriers between whites and blacks, which were rigid in the South at that time, and he worked for racial justice. He also publicly supported CLARENCE DARROW, who defended the freedom to teach evolution in the famous Scopes trial. As a result, teachers and students labeled Horton a heretic. After graduating from Cumberland, Horton worked for a year as state secretary for the student YMCA and also "roamed the mountains, hitchhiked around, talked to and worked with people" in order to synthesize his ideas about changing society in nonviolent ways. "The laws of the land are supported by the use of violence; that is, the use of physical force to make people obey the law," he wrote. "If you're trying to change things, first you have to know that violence can be used against you" (Horton with Kohls 1990, 26–27).

In 1929, Horton enrolled at the Union Theological Seminary in New York, where Reinhold Niebuhr, a Christian socialist, was on the faculty and greatly influenced Horton. The following year, Horton attended the University of Chicago, studying sociology and often visiting nearby Hull House and its founder JANE ADDAMS. During those years, Horton further formulated his concepts for bringing love and social justice together and establishing a people's school where adults—especially those from poor communities who were being displaced from their land and forced into factories and mines—could learn to make their own decisions and empower themselves.

After visiting model schools in Denmark, Horton returned to Tennessee in 1932 and, along with Niebuhr and other supporters from Union Seminary, set up the Highlander Folk School in an old house that had once been a school run by suffragist Lillian Johnson. The school was integrated in spite of state laws requiring separate facilities for whites and people of color—blacks, Native Americans, and Hispanics. Included in the curriculum were classes on cultural geography and local economic and social problems and seminars on social change.

Just a few months after the school opened, Horton and the rest of his staff became involved in workshops to help exploited workers organize and establish unions. Throughout the years of the Great Depression and for decades thereafter, Horton and the school were active in numerous strikes against mines, mills, and factories.

Highlander also offered classes in music and drama, using plays and songs representing folk culture and the struggles of mountain people. A song of the civil rights movement, "We Will Overcome" (later changed to "We Shall Overcome" by folk singer PETE SEEGER, who often visited Highlander), was developed by musician and storyteller Zilphia Johnson, who worked at Highlander and married Horton in 1935. Many other folk musicians visited Highlander, as did such civil rights activists as ROSA PARKS and ELLA BAKER.

A major project at Highlander during the 1950s was the citizenship school movement, which focused on poor blacks living on Johns Island off the South Carolina coast. The project was designed to "exist outside the formal educational system . . . [and] never forget that its pupils were adults entitled to dignity and respect." The school's immediate goal was to help people gain "minimal literacy required for the voter registration test" (Berson 1994, 148).

Because of Horton's political activities, he and the school were accused of communist conspiracies and were investigated by the Federal Bureau of Investigation and hounded by segregationists, particularly James Eastland, in the U.S. Congress. After MARTIN LUTHER KING, JR., attended the twenty-fifth anniversary celebration of the school in 1957, he was immediately accused of being involved in training at a communist school. Southern states pressured Tennessee to close down Highlander, which the state eventually confiscated, auctioning off all the private property, including Horton's belongings, without ever compensating the owners.

Horton and his coworkers were able to open the school in Knoxville during the 1960s, renaming it the Highlander Research and Education Center. It was

later moved to New Market. After its reopening, the school focused on its original concern—regional economic and social problems—concentrating on empowering those in Appalachia who had been demoralized by poverty and also trying to prevent environmental degradation brought about by strip mining and toxic waste dumps. In 1973, Horton resigned from the school staff but continued to live on the property and conduct workshops. The school has influenced people from around the world who either came to Tennessee or were involved in workshops that Horton conducted in South America, Asia, Africa, and Australia.

One person who gained much from his experiences at Highlander was Brazilian educator Paulo Freire, whose poverty-stricken family life, ideas for democratic education, and advocacy of national literacy programs were similar to Horton's. Freire eventually left Brazil and went to Harvard, where his lectures and writings gained widespread attention.

In 1987, Horton and Freire met, became fast friends, and began collaborating on a book about education and social change. Horton was anxious to share his ideas, since he suffered from cancer and was concerned that he had little time left to write. Their final meeting was in 1990 in Horton's mountain home, and it was obvious that Horton was dying. Freire reflected on the sadness of death being part of life but noted that "it is wonderful that Myles may die here. Dying here is dying in the midst of life" (Horton and Freire 1990, xxxiii).

References

Adams, Frank, with Myles Horton. 1975. *Unearthing Seeds of Fire: The Idea of Highlander*. Winston-Salem, NC: John F. Blair.

Berson, Robin Kadison. 1994. *Marching to a Different Drummer: Unrecognized Heroes of American History*. Westport, CT: Greenwood Press.

Horton, Myles, and Paulo Freire. 1990. *We Make the Road by Walking: Conversations on Education and Social Change*. Philadelphia: Temple University Press.

Horton, Myles, with Judith Kohl and Herbert Kohl. 1990. *The Long Haul: An Autobiography*. New York: Doubleday.

Wigginton, Eliot, ed. 1991. *Refuse To Stand Silently By: An Oral History of Grass Roots Social Activism in America, 1921–1964*. New York: Doubleday.

J

JACKSON, JESSE

(1941–)

I am—Somebody!
I may be poor, but I am—Somebody!
I may be on welfare but I am—Somebody!
I may be uneducated but, I am—Somebody!
I may be in jail, but I am—Somebody!
I am—Somebody!
I must be, I'm God's child.
I must be respected and protected.
I am black and I am beautiful!
I am—Somebody!
SOUL POWER!!! (Jakoubek 1991, 68)

This is the trademark cheer that the Reverend Jesse Jackson delivered during his speeches in support of Operation Breadbasket, a project of the Southern Christian Leadership Conference (SCLC). As leader of this economic development arm of MARTIN LUTHER KING, JR.'S, and RALPH ABERNATHY'S SCLC in the late 1960s, he did what he has always done best: he motivated the masses. There is no lukewarm reaction to the man who has evolved to become the political leader of Democratic Party liberals and the spiritual voice of the

United States' African American population. He has come a long way from Greenville, South Carolina.

Born there to Helen Burns as a result of an affair with the deacon Noah Robinson, a married next-door neighbor, Jesse Louis Burns was forced to endure the taunts of his playmates. They called him a bastard and said that he would never amount to anything in this life. His family, including his stepfather, Charles Jackson, was very loving, however, and the young boy received plenty of support and encouragement. He also found comfort in the local Baptist church, where he first exhibited his talent as a public speaker when he was only four years old.

He was soon making a name for himself as an athlete as well. He was an excellent student and a tireless worker in all his endeavors, but football proved to be his favorite physical outlet. By the time high school ended, he had led the all-black institution to the state championship as his team's quarterback. Jackson was not unfamiliar with prejudice or the injustice of segregation prior to his graduation. He had already been inspired to lead a protest against one of his after-school employers for equal conditions. Jackson felt the full impact of being black, however, because of his success on the gridiron. He was shocked to learn that whereas the New York Giants offered him a contract to play ball for $6,000 a year, a comparable white player from a rival school in Greenville was going to get $95,000 from the same organization. Jesse turned down the offer.

He chose, instead, to attend the University of Illinois on a football scholarship. His tenure at the Chicago campus was short, however. He became disillusioned when he discovered that black players were allowed to play only lineman positions—certainly not quarterback—and that de facto segregation in the North was as pervasive as the institutional segregation of the South. When he saw television news reports in 1960 about four students from the all-black North Carolina Agricultural and Technical State College in Greensboro who were sitting in at a "whites only" lunch counter, he was inspired to transfer his studies there.

No longer a second-class citizen in the friendly confines of the southern campus, Jackson came into his own as a fraternity leader, student body president, star quarterback, top student, and leader of the local branch of the Congress of Racial Equality (CORE). In the latter role, he gained notoriety as the voice of protest for better conditions for African Americans in Greensboro. He led demonstrations that lasted months and was jailed for his activism. By the time of graduation in 1964, Jackson had chosen politics for his career. Soon after taking a job with the North Carolina governor's office, however, he had a change of heart. Realizing that his heroes were men like Martin Luther King, Jr.—activist preachers working to better the lot of their congregations—he decided to get his divinity degree. He returned to Chicago and the Theological Seminary.

Jackson continued his organizing activities there, now as a member of the SCLC. When King planned to mount a voter rights' demonstration in Selma, Alabama, Jackson decided to end his studies to join his mentor. Not content to join the ranks of followers, Jackson immediately took on a leadership role: barking out instructions to the marchers, organizing lines, and speaking to the assembled. Many of the SCLC leadership were taken aback by Jackson's aggressive style, but Ralph Abernathy saw that his natural leadership ability would be an asset as the SCLC started to concentrate activity in the North. King reluctantly agreed to give the young man an administrative position in the organization in Chicago.

Throughout their relationship, King was often suspicious of Jackson's motives. He understood Jackson's charismatic nature and driving ambition, but the two often experienced personality conflicts. King saw that Jackson could get things done, however, so he tolerated his involvement. By the spring of 1968, just a few days before King was assassinated, Jackson was openly pressing King to pay less attention to his antiwar protest and more to Operation Breadbasket. At the end of a particularly bitter meeting on 30 March, the SCLC leader told his protégé, "If you want to carve out your own niche in society, go ahead, but for God's sake don't bother me" (Jakoubek 1991, 61).

After King's death, Jackson continued for some time as the leader of Operation Breadbasket but eventually resigned from the SCLC when his relationship with the new leader, Ralph Abernathy, deteriorated. Adept at making news and "carving his own niche," he started Operation PUSH—People United to Save (later, Serve) Humanity—with the same goals as Operation Breadbasket. PUSH had obvious political goals too. With this organization as a base of power, Jackson ran against Richard Daley in the 1971 mayoral election in Chicago. Jackson lost, getting only 35 write-in votes. In 1972, at the Democratic National Convention in

Miami Beach, the tables were turned. Jackson led a group of alternative "multicultural" delegates to challenge the seating of the Illinois delegation led by Daley, then the last of the big-city bosses. The convention voted to seat Jackson's group instead.

From that point, the Reverend Jackson took his place on the world stage, setting himself as an example and a leader for his people. Always controversial, he will not be ignored, and he has always been willing to act the part of the lightning rod to further the crucial issue of equality of opportunity for all humans regardless of color, gender, and economic status.

References

Jackson, Jesse. 1988. *A Time to Speak: The Autobiography of the Reverend Jesse Jackson*. New York: Simon & Schuster.

Jakoubek, Robert. 1991. *Jesse Jackson*. New York: Chelsea House.

Otfinoski, Steven. 1989. *Jesse Jackson: A Voice for Change*. New York: Fawcett Columbine.

JONES, MOTHER

See *HARRIS, MARY*

JORDAN, BARBARA

(1936–1996)

"I've always felt that as long as you're alive, you should be doing something that makes a difference." That was how Barbara Jordan, U.S. representative from Texas, described her basic philosophy during an interview in 1992 (Zauber 1992). In spite of serious illnesses, she made a difference in each of the varied roles she played—lawyer, politician, educator, lecturer, writer—and was dedicated to upholding her strong belief in democratic principles and faith in the U.S. Constitution. A search for truth and justice for all was basic to her life's work and the message she repeatedly conveyed.

Born in Houston to Arlyne and Benjamin Jordan, Barbara was the third of three children—all girls—in the Jordan family. The household also included her grandparents, her father's father and his second wife.

Although her father, a Baptist minister and strict disciplinarian, had a great influence on her life, Jordan's grandfather, John Ed Patten, also had a major impact. Patten, who was fiercely independent and operated his own junkyard, taught her a maxim that became one of her basic creeds: "The world is not a playground, but a schoolroom. Life is not a holiday but an education. One eternal lesson for us all: to teach us how better we should love" (Jordan and Hearon 1979, 10).

Jordan and her sisters were reared in Houston's black ghetto and educated in all-black public schools. Segregation was a way of life at the time, and the Jordans, like many other blacks, had to suffer the indignities of racism and, in effect, second-class citizenship. Jordan was an excellent student and was constantly encouraged by her father and grandfather to read, to expand her vocabulary, and to develop speaking and debating skills. She went on to obtain a degree at Texas Southern University in 1956, and three years later, she earned her law degree from Boston University.

In 1960, she established a law practice in Houston and took part in voter registration and the presidential campaign of John F. Kennedy and his running mate, Texas Congressman Lyndon Johnson. The campaign sparked Jordan's interest in politics, and in 1962, she decided to run for the office of state representative. She lost that bid and tried again in 1964, suffering a second loss. That did not stop her political efforts, however, and in 1966, she was elected to the Texas State Senate, becoming the first black member in 84 years and the first black woman ever.

At the height of the civil rights movement during the mid to late 1960s, many blacks urged Jordan to become more militant in her efforts to achieve equal opportunities and rights for blacks who were locked into poverty. She refused to advocate any type of violent action. Jordan continually urged solutions to racial problems through reason, understanding, and personal responsibility.

In 1972, Jordan won election to the U.S. House of Representatives, where she served for three terms. While in Congress, Jordan was assigned to the House Judiciary Committee, which held hearings in 1974 on whether to impeach President Richard Nixon for his role in the Watergate break-in and cover-up. Each member of the committee was asked to make a statement before voting on impeachment, and when Jordan's turn came, she gave a passionate speech about the U.S. Constitution and the responsibilities of the U.S. president. She began by saying that in spite of the eloquent words at the beginning of the U.S. Constitution, she had believed for years that she was "not included in that 'We the people.' I felt somehow . . . that George Washington and Alexander Hamilton just left me out by mistake. But through the process of amendment, interpretation and court decision, I have finally been included in 'We, the people.'" Jordan proclaimed her total faith in the Constitution and said, "I am not going to sit here and be an idle spectator to the diminution, the subversion, the destruction of the Constitution" (Pearson 1996).

Jordan's deep, resonant voice captured the audience watching the Watergate hearings on television, and in 1976, Jordan's powerful speech making again was

heard nationwide at the Democratic National Convention, where she was one of the keynote speakers.

Her oratory skills were not her only assets, however. She never swerved from her quest for justice for all and from her commitment to her country. Even when she surprised most political pundits and left public life in 1978 to accept a professorship at the Lyndon Baines Johnson School of Public Affairs at the University of Texas in Austin, she urged her students to be "premier public servants" guided by a "core of principles." During the late 1970s, it was revealed that she suffered from multiple sclerosis (MS), a neurological disease that eventually forced her to use a wheelchair. In 1988, she nearly drowned after falling from her wheelchair into her backyard pool. She recovered, however, and returned to teaching, stressing devotion to constitutional principle and public service.

For the most part, Jordan stayed out of the public spotlight during the 1980s and 1990s, but she was in demand as a voice of moral authority and made several major speeches, including a keynote address at the 1992 Democratic National Convention, where she challenged delegates and the nation "to change the decaying inner cities from decay to places where hope lives" and to learn how to get along with one another. She also chaired the independent U.S. Commission on Immigration Reform, which suggested a controversial plan to set up a national computer registry of all eligible workers as a way of preventing the employment of illegal immigrants.

Besides MS, Jordan also suffered from leukemia, and her death in January 1996 was a result of pneumonia, a complication of the leukemia. After her death, numerous eulogies praised her integrity and her role as a voice of conscience for the nation. President Bill Clinton stated that "Barbara's words . . . challenged us as a nation to confront our weaknesses and live peacefully together as equals," and Governor George W. Bush noted that "Texas has lost a powerful voice of conscience" (Associated Press 1996b).

References

Associated Press. 1996b. "Ex-Rep. Barbara Jordan Dies." 17 January.

Blue, Rose, and Corinne Naden. 1992. *Barbara Jordan*. New York: Chelsea House.

Haskins, James. 1977. *Barbara Jordan*. New York: Dial Press.

Jordan, Barbara, and Shelby Hearon. 1979. *Barbara Jordan: A Self-Portrait*. New York: Doubleday.

Pearson, Richard. 1996. Obituary (Barbara Jordan). *Washington Post*, 18 January, A1.

Zauber, Karen. 1992. Interview. *NEA Today*, 9 December.

JÜGERSTÜTTER, FRANZ

(1907–1943)

Some called him deranged; others compared him to Saint Thomas More. Few who knew him during his youth ever expected that he would become a committed antiwar activist and a hero of conscience. According to Franz Jügerstütter's biographer, "It is almost an accident that we know anything at all" about this man who defied Adolf Hitler during World War II, refused to serve in the armed forces, and was imprisoned and then beheaded (Zahn 1968, 4).

Jügerstütter was born in a small Austrian village, the illegitimate son of Franz Bachmeier, a farmer who became a soldier and died in World War I. Illegitimacy was no disgrace in his village, and when his mother married Herr Jügerstütter, his stepfather immediately adopted him.

A Catholic by birth, Jügerstütter attended a village parochial school until he was 14 years old. Although a "satisfactory" student, he was known as "a little wild in his ways and in his style of living," and as a young adult he gained a reputation as a sportsman, fighter, and "lady's man" (Zahn 1968, 25). He was not especially religious as a youth but attended Catholic mass on a regular basis. It was not until 1936—about the time he married—that he experienced a dramatic religious "awakening" that changed him so much that his family, friends, and neighbors hardly knew him, and some said that he seemed "possessed by a higher power" (Zahn 1968, 38). There was speculation that the change came about after his honeymoon trip to Rome, where Jügerstütter and his bride received the pope's blessing in a public audience, although there were other theories that the "new" Jügerstütter, with his intense religiosity, had already emerged somewhat earlier.

Whatever the timing of his newfound devotion and dedication to Christianity, Jügerstütter gained a reputation for his religious practices, which included receiving Holy Communion on a daily basis, fasting every day until noon, and distributing food and other items to the poor. He became a sexton in the village church, caring for the church buildings and assisting in the services.

Even before the Nazis occupied Austria, Jügerstütter was outspoken in his opposition to Adolf Hitler's regime and its persecution of the church. When he was greeted with the common "Heil Hitler," he often responded with "Pfui Hitler!" In the spring of 1938, Austrians voted on *Anschluss*—incorporation—with Germany, which in fact had already occurred, and Jügerstütter was the only villager to cast a negative vote. This was just one of his many acts of defiance over the next six years. He was deeply disturbed when his fellow townspeople, including leaders of the Catholic Church, voluntarily cooperated with the Germans. Even when a hailstorm destroyed most crops in the village, Jügerstütter was the only farmer to refuse help from the Nazi-supported cash subsidy programs.

In spite of his anti-Nazi stance, Jügerstütter registered for the draft in April 1939 and served briefly in the military before he was able to gain a deferment, perhaps because he had a family. He determined at the time, however, that he would refuse service again if called, and he made those intentions public on numerous occasions over the next few years. He was convinced of the injustice of war and believed that army life presented too many opportunities for sin. Village priests and townspeople tried to persuade him that he would gain little by such a stand and that he should consider his family, which included three children. He would certainly face death for refusing to be drafted. Apparently, however, Jügerstütter planned to sacrifice his life to show that the Nazis were fighting an unjust war.

The most critical time in Jügerstütter's life came in March 1943, when he was ordered to report again for induction into the military. His refusal to serve led to his arrest and imprisonment. Although he did not regret his decision, Jügerstütter suffered deep despair because of his concern for his family. He feared that there would be reprisals from the Nazis or even from some of their neighbors who thought that Jügerstütter's punishment was what he deserved. In one attempt to comfort his wife, he wrote: "you should not be sad because of my present situation. . . . As long as a man has an untroubled conscience and knows that he is not really a criminal, he can live at peace even in prison" (Zahn 1968, 65).

During Jügerstütter's months of imprisonment, several chaplains as well as his court-appointed attorney, Friedrich Leo Feldmann, tried in numerous ways to persuade Jügerstütter to change his mind. Feldmann, who had no particular interest in the case at first, did everything in his power to save his client's life. He was able to gain permission from the court to allow two high-ranking military officers to meet with Jügerstütter to try to convince him of his obligation to serve the fatherland. The officers made it clear that they would have no choice but to condemn him to death if he continued to refuse to serve or at least accept some noncombatant service. "Jügerstütter rejected this offer too. As he explained it, such an agreement would only complicate matters by adding to any already immoral compromise, the sin of falsehood, through his only 'seeming' to accept service as a means of avoiding the death penalty" (Zahn 1968, 88).

On the night before Jügerstütter was executed in August 1943, he was visited by a priest, who found him

completely calm and prepared. Not a word of complaint passed his lips. On the table before him lay a document; he had only to put his signature on it and his life would be saved. When the priest called his attention to it, he smilingly pushed it aside with the explanation: "I cannot and may not take an oath in favor of a government that is fighting an unjust war" (Zahn 1968, 106–107).

Reference
Zahn, Gordon. 1968. *In Solitary Witness: The Life and Death of Franz Jügerstütter*. Boston: Beacon Press.

K

KERR, ANDY

(1955–)

Long involved in conservation organizations, Andy Kerr has worked with the Oregon Natural Resources Council (ONRC) since 1976, beginning as a grassroots organizer. He is now conservation director of the organization, a paid position, but he has gone well beyond the requirements of the job to be an outspoken champion for environmental causes, often spending much of his free time as an activist. This has ignited the wrath of some Oregonians as well as others across the United States who are opposed to environmentalists.

Born in Caswell, Oregon, Kerr is a fifth-generation Oregonian and grew up surrounded by the timber industry and its proponents. In high school, part of his education included reading timber industry materials claiming that "forests were just a crop and one could start cutting at one end of a forest and by the time they were done at the other end, start over." He said, "It was then that I figured out that their [the timber industry's] plan wasn't to replace the forest, but rather to eliminate it and have plantations instead. It was closer to a cornfield than to a forest," which is a complex ecosystem with many types of interdependent plant and animal life (Dietrich 1992, 215).

Kerr has been called the timber industry's most hated man in Oregon, Oregon's version of the anti-Christ, and a white-collar terrorist. In 1994, effigies of Kerr and fellow environmentalist Ric Bailey were hanged in Wallowa County, where Kerr and Bailey live. The effigies, which some considered a death threat, were part of a protest organized by members of the "wise-use" movement, a group that formed in Bellvue, Washington, in 1989 and is supported by representatives of major U.S. corporations and mining, cattle ranching, and timber organizations. The movement takes its name from early conservationists in the United States who urged the wise use of natural resources, but the wise-use movement of today is stridently antienvironmentalist and has organized campaigns calling for clear-cutting ancient forests and opening up federal lands (national parks and wilderness areas) for mining and energy production.

Wallowa County residents who are dependent on the timber industry for their livelihoods oppose Kerr's efforts to restrict logging in national forests and to preserve wilderness areas. Many in the sparsely settled county have expressed deep animosity toward Kerr and Bailey and have boycotted businesses in a small county mall where Bailey's office is located. An owner of a Christian bookstore in the mall said that she wanted Kerr and Bailey to leave the area. During a fall 1994 March of Dimes campaign, many residents refused to contribute to the effort simply because Kerr was involved with the fund-raising. Both Kerr and Bailey have been subjected to insults, have been barred from local business places, and have been refused services by local repair people.

The intimidation, threats, and animosity are not new to Kerr. He has characterized his work and that of the ONRC to protect the environment, particularly ancient forests that contain trees up to 1,000 years old, as "bold and innovative." Since the 1980s, the strategy at the ONRC has been to fight for the preservation

of ancient forests by garnering public support and also by seeking protective legislation on the state and national levels. In the late 1980s, the ONRC filed lawsuits against the U.S. Forest Service to stop clear-cutting in national forests. The Oregon group, along with other environmental organizations, conducted hikes and tours through forestlands, and a volunteer group known as Project Lighthawk flew public officials, reporters, and others over forests to see the vast denuded areas. As a result, clear-cutting was halted by court order for a time but was resumed after much pressure by the timber industry on Congress to pass legislation that would prevent the courts from enforcing environmental laws— legislation that was eventually found unconstitutional.

In spite of legal setbacks and personal attacks, Kerr has continued his work, seeking public support of legislation to protect Oregon's natural resources as well as recreation areas such as Crater Lake National Park, where geothermal exploitation was limited due to ONRC efforts. Kerr has also served on the board of directors of the Oregon League of Conservation Voters, a political action committee working for the environment.

In 1994, Kerr and many other environmentalists became incensed with proposed legislation to open up national forests to salvage logging. In March 1995, he committed a civil act of disobedience by refusing to leave the hall outside the Portland office of Senator Mark O. Hatfield, who is chairman of the Senate Appropriation Committee and is considered one of the most powerful members of the Senate. The Republican senator is the key to whether a number of antienvironmental laws pass. Kerr and a fellow activist demanded that Hatfield meet with them. Instead, the two men were arrested and charged with second-degree criminal trespass but were later released on their own recognizance.

References
Cockle, Richard. 1994. "Environmentalists Face Bitter Foes in Northeastern Oregon." *Oregonian*, 4 October.
Dietrich, William. 1992. *The Final Forest: The Battle for the Last Great Trees of the Pacific Northwest*. New York: Simon & Schuster.
Kerr, Andy. 1994. "ONRC'S Executive Director Outlines 100-Year Plan for State." *Oregonian*, 11 September.
Laatz, Joan. 1995. "Kerr, Fellow Activist Arrested." *Oregonian*, 28 March.
Sleeth, Peter, and Richard Cockle. 1994. "Anti-Environmentalist Feelings Hurt Wallowa County Neighbors." *Oregonian*, 21 October.

KEVORKIAN, JACK

(1929–)

"We want Dr. Kevorkian to pack up his itinerant circus and go away," editorialized the *Detroit Free Press* in December 1995. Many of Jack Kevorkian's opponents agree, but his supporters believe that he is a hero fighting for personal freedom and praise him for alleviating suffering and assisting some very sick people in their choice not to prolong their lives.

A former pathologist in Oakland County, Michigan, Kevorkian came to public attention in the early 1990s for helping terminally ill patients control their own deaths. The first, Janet Adkins of Portland, Oregon, was suffering with Alzheimer's

disease. A member of the Hemlock Society (which espouses the right of terminally ill patients to take their own lives), Adkins chose not to let the disease take its course, which would have left her physically and mentally helpless. She used a device that Kevorkian had invented to commit suicide. The device consists of three bottles: one of saline solution, the second a sedative, and the third a lethal dose of potassium chloride. Adkins was able to activate the device on her own. Kevorkian was arrested, jailed, and placed on trial for murder. He was eventually released because he had not administered the lethal injection and it is not a crime in Michigan to provide information about suicide. State legislators, however, have attempted to pass legislation that would either make assisted suicide a felony or legalize the practice of euthanasia.

Kevorkian began his quest to legalize doctor-assisted suicide in 1958 when he was a second-year resident in the Pathology Department of the University of Michigan Medical Center. That year, he went to Columbus, Ohio, and spoke to a prisoner who was going to be executed. Shortly after the meeting, the prisoner wrote to Kevorkian and mentioned that he would like to see a more humane method of execution. Also, the prisoner had a desire to help someone, somewhere, so that his life would not have been a total waste.

The incident turned out to be pivotal in Kevorkian's life. Although he stressed his neutrality on the issue of the death penalty, he insisted that there were far more humane, rational, and beneficial ways to accomplish executions. Among the benefits he advocated was saving human organs so that they could be used for research or for donation. Criminologists could even study, in a literal sense, the criminal mind during an autopsy. The Ohio prisoner's request to be an organ donor was denied, and as Kevorkian points out in his book *Prescription: Medicide*, seven other people died because they were denied the organs the condemned man wanted to donate.

In March 1993, Michigan passed a temporary law making it a felony to assist a suicide, but the law expired in late 1994. Kevorkian continued providing assistance. Since his medical license had been revoked prior to the law's passage, drugs were no longer available to him, so he started using carbon monoxide. Kevorkian was also targeted by members of the religous right, who applied the same pressure on him that they normally reserved for abortion clinics.

The most important issue raised by Kevorkian's actions is that of morality. Although some forms of euthanasia are legal in other parts of the world, it has not been addressed in the United States as a national issue. Few experts dispute that physicians can ethically halt certain types of medication or treatment to allow death to take its natural course, but Kevorkian has shaken up the establishment by taking a much more active role. Because the Michigan Supreme Court ruled in 1994 that common law allowed for the prosecution of assisted suicide, Kevorkian will be tried again. Whatever the outcome, nothing will be settled regarding the legality of physician-assisted death until the question of euthanasia is thoroughly addressed in the United States.

In Kevorkian's view, legislators should stay out of the process and allow the medical profession to help patients who want to die to escape from a terminal or agonizing illness. "I will help a suffering human being at the right time when the patient's condition warrants it, despite anything else," Kevorkian said in an interview. "That's what a doctor should do" (Morganthau with Barrett and Washington 1993).

References

Gay, Kathlyn. 1993b. *The Right To Die*. Brookfield, CT: Millbrook Press.

Kevorkian, Jack. 1991. *Prescription: Medicide*. Buffalo, NY: Prometheus Books.

Morganthau, Tom, with Todd Barrett and Frank Washington. 1993. "Dr. Kevorkian's Death Wish." *Newsweek*, 8 March.

KING, *MARTIN LUTHER, JR.*

(1929–1968)

Upon receiving the Nobel Peace Prize in 1964, Martin Luther King, Jr., said that he accepted the award "in behalf of a civil rights movement which is moving with determination and a majestic scorn for risk and danger to establish a reign of freedom and a rule of justice. . . . [T]his award . . . is profound recognition that nonviolence is the answer to the crucial political and moral question of our time—the need for man to overcome oppression and violence without resorting to violence and oppression." Those words reflected the basis for the actions of one of the most notable civil rights leaders of our time.

Born in Atlanta, Georgia, to Martin Luther and Alberta Williams King, Martin Jr. was the son and grandson of Baptist ministers. According to one of his biographers, King's father, called Daddy King, "provided young Martin with a strong role model. Daddy King was a stern disciplinarian with a volcanic temper, imposing his patriarchal authority with the aid of frequently administered corporal punishment . . . [but] throughout his life King exhibited unabashed respect and affection for his father" (Fairclough 1995, 6).

From his mother, who was a schoolteacher, King inherited patience and a love for books and reading. Young King liked books even before he learned how to read and was reading when he entered first grade. He used his aptitude to excel in school, skipping his last year of high school and passing an examination to enter Morehouse College in 1940.

King realized that he had a talent for oratory, and he debated for years about following in his father's footsteps to become a minister, but he was not sure that that would be the appropriate forum to speak on contemporary issues. For a time, he considered medicine and law, but while in his junior year at college, he majored in sociology and decided to enter the ministry. In 1948, he was ordained as a Baptist minister; that same year, he received a scholarship to study divinity at Crozer Theological Seminary in Chester, Pennsylvania.

While at Crozer, King attended a lecture by Dr. Mordecai Johnson on the life of MOHANDAS GANDHI, which inspired King to delve further into the teachings of the Indian leader. After his graduation from Crozer in 1951 with a bachelor of divinity degree, King began his doctoral studies at Boston University in Boston, Massachusetts, where he met Coretta Scott, whom he married in 1953. Almost a year later, King accepted the position as pastor of the Dexter Avenue Baptist Church in Montgomery, Alabama. The Kings' first child, Yolanda, was born in 1955, and the couple eventually had three more children: Martin III, Dexter, and Bernice.

The mid-1950s were momentous times in the civil rights movement. About six months after King was awarded his Ph.D. from Boston University in 1955, the Montgomery bus boycott began when a black passenger, ROSA PARKS, refused to

give up her seat on a public bus to a white person and move to the rear of the vehicle. King, having been elected president of the newly formed Montgomery Improvement Association that organized the boycott, led the successful 381-day protest. During that time, blacks organized car pools for transportation, which white city leaders tried to disrupt by arresting drivers on trumped-up charges or charging waiting riders with vagrancy. King was arrested and jailed for allegedly exceeding the speed limit, but this was only the first of many such incarcerations and confrontations with racists and bigots, many of whom wanted to see him maimed or dead.

In February 1956, King was indicted (along with more than 100 other blacks, including 24 other ministers) for conspiring to prevent the Montgomery bus company from operating a business. On 4 June 1956, a U.S. district court ruled that segregation on city bus lines was unconstitutional. It was a decision that was upheld by the U.S. Supreme Court in November, forcing Montgomery buses to desegregate.

Along with the bus boycott, there were attempts by black students to follow up on the landmark 1954 U.S. Supreme Court decision *(Brown v. Board of Education of Topeka)* that had paved the way for school desegregation, but many were turned away from the schools they had hoped to enter or faced hostile, hate-filled crowds of whites. Tension mounted in many parts of the South; black homes (among them the Kings') and churches were bombed. The Ku Klux Klan and other hate groups raided and harassed black communities and killed a number of blacks.

By 1957, King had called together over 60 black ministers committed to southern civil rights, and they formed the Southern Christian Leadership Conference (SCLC). King was unanimously elected president and led a prayer pilgrimage to Washington, D.C., where he delivered his first major national speech.

King's first book, *Stride toward Freedom*, was published in 1958, and during an autographing session in Harlem, New York, he was stabbed in the chest by Izola Curry. Although Curry was later found to be criminally insane, Coretta reflected that "even one of our own" could easily kill Martin, as had been the case with Gandhi; the Kings resolved to fly to India to meet with that country's proponent of nonviolence and learn his principles of *satyagraha*, or soul-force. According to Coretta, "Martin returned from India more devoted than ever to Gandhian ideals. . . . He constantly pondered how to apply them in America" (King 1993, 158, 164).

By 1960, the civil rights movement was in high gear, and sit-ins were a common tactic, beginning with the historical sit-in at a Woolworth lunch counter in Greensboro, North Carolina, on 1 February. The movement spread to movie theaters, hotels, libraries, and other public places that were segregated.

Early that year, as part of the constant surveillance and harassment of King by local, state, and federal authorities, a warrant was issued for King's arrest on charges that he did not pay his 1956 and 1958 state income taxes. In May 1960, he was acquitted of the charges by an all-white jury in Montgomery. In October, he was arrested in Atlanta during a sit-in at a department store. All the demonstrators were released except for King, who was held on a previous traffic warrant

and sentenced to four months at hard labor. However, Senator John F. Kennedy of Massachusetts intervened, and King was released on $2,000 bond.

As the decade progressed, it became even more volatile than the 1950s. The SCLC, the Student Nonviolent Coordinating Committee, and the Congress of Racial Equality jointly announced a campaign to desegregate public transportation facilities with Freedom Rides departing from Washington, D.C., and traveling to Anniston, Alabama. Along the route, buses were burned and stoned, and martial law ensued. However, by November, the U.S. Interstate Commerce Commission banned segregation on buses, trains, and other such facilities.

There were voter registration drives all across the South, and civil rights workers such as MEDGAR EVERS, Andrew Goodman, Michael Schwerner, James Chaney, and others were brutally murdered. Boycotts of segregated stores and public facilities took place, and after a mass demonstration in Birmingham, Alabama, in 1963, King was arrested and placed in solitary confinement. While there, he wrote the famous "Letter from Birmingham Jail" to fellow clergymen, in which he outlined the need for nonviolent civil disobedience and explained why blacks could not wait any longer for justice:

> This "Wait!" has almost always meant "Never." . . . We have waited for more than 340 years for our constitutional and God-given rights. . . . Perhaps it is easy for those who have never felt the stinging arrows of segregation to say, "Wait." But when you have seen vicious mobs lynch your mothers and fathers at will and drown your sisters and brothers at whim; when you have seen hate-filled policemen curse, kick, and even kill your black brothers and sisters . . . when you are humiliated day in and day out by nagging signs reading "white" and "colored"; when your first name becomes "nigger," your middle name becomes "boy" (however old you are) and your last name becomes "John," and your wife and mother are never given the respectful title "Mrs"; when you are harried by day and haunted by night . . . never quite knowing what to expect next, and are plagued with inner fears and outer resentments; when you are forever fighting a degenerating sense of "nobodiness"—then you will understand why we find it difficult to wait (Schulke and McPhee 1986, 278).

Later that year, on 28 August, King led the March on Washington, D.C., and over 250,000 marchers filled the mall from the Lincoln Memorial to the Washington Monument and heard King deliver his "I Have a Dream" speech, which to this day is played on tape and stirs listeners.

In 1964, King received *Time* magazine's Man of the Year award and the Nobel Peace Prize and witnessed the signing of the Civil Rights Act (which was subsequently amended). A year later, he met with President Lyndon Johnson at the White House to discuss voting rights, and by 1966, King was taking his civil rights efforts north, moving into a Chicago tenement to initiate the "Chicago Project." That year in Chicago was tumultuous; riots took place in the summer as Chicago began an "open city" campaign. By 1967, a strong open housing provision was incorporated in the 1968 Civil Rights Act.

There was still much more work to do—organizing a Poor People's Campaign and advocating for equal treatment and pay for black workers. In early 1968, sanitation workers went on strike in Memphis, Tennessee, and King led a march in support of the workers, which became violent. King left Memphis but returned later, on 3 April 1968, hoping to lead a peaceful demonstration. He told followers: "I may not get there with you, but I want you to know tonight that we as a people will get to the promised land." On the following day, he was assassinated, shot while he stood on the balcony of the Lorraine Hotel in Memphis. Millions mourned his death, and since then, countless words have been spoken or written in his memory. Harry Belafonte and Stanley Levison noted:

> He was incontestably one of history's preeminent black leaders. Yet he was, as well, a leader to millions of white people who learned from him that in degrading black men they diminished themselves, that in supporting black liberation they enriched themselves. . . . He wrote his own obituary to define himself in the simple terms his heart comprehended. "Tell them I tried to feed the hungry. Tell them I tried to clothe the naked. Tell them I tried to help somebody." And that is all he ever did (King 1993, 311).

References

Colaiaco, James A. 1988. *Martin Luther King, Jr: Apostle of Militant Nonviolence*. New York: St. Martin's Press.

Fairclough, Adam. 1995. *Martin Luther King, Jr.* Athens: University of Georgia Press.

King, Coretta Scott. 1993. *My Life with Martin Luther King, Jr.* Rev. ed. Original edition, 1969. New York: Henry Holt.

King, Martin Luther, Jr. 1958. *Stride toward Freedom: The Montgomery Story*. New York: Harper & Row.

———. 1963. *Strength To Love*. New York: Harper & Row.

Paterson, Lillie. 1989. *Martin Luther King, Jr., and the Freedom Movement*. New York: Facts on File.

Schulke, Flip, and Penelope O. McPhee. 1986. *King Remembered*. New York: W. W. Norton.

Williams, Juan. 1987. *Eyes on the Prize: America's Civil Rights Years, 1954–1965* (companion volume to the PBS television series). New York: Viking Penguin.

KOVIC, RON

(1946–)

Highly patriotic Ron Kovic enlisted in the marines during the Vietnam War and during his second tour of duty was severely wounded. The treatment he received when he returned to the United States so disillusioned him that he eventually became an outspoken critic of the war, and his experiences were the subject of the 1989 movie *Born on the Fourth of July*, based on his book of the same title.

Born in Massapequa, New York, Kovic took his 4 July birth date very seriously, considering it a "sign" of patriotism. During his growing-up years, Kovic listened to his father and uncle, who had fought in Korea with the U.S. Marines, when they held kitchen-table discussions about the significance of Ron's birthday and how it related to defending the nation. So early in his life, Ron decided

that his calling was the military. While in high school, he saw recruiting posters, "Marine Corps Builds Men: Body, Mind and Spirit," and knew that it was true.

After graduation, Kovic joined the marines and completed his basic training at Parris Island, a process that began with this greeting from the staff sergeant: "Awright, Ladies! My name is Staff Sergeant Joseph." He then introduced the junior drill instructor, saying: "Your souls today may belong to God, but your asses belong to the United States Marine Corps!" (Kovic 1976, 63). From that time on, Kovic was transformed from a civilian to a marine. He lost his personal identity to become a member of the Corps in September 1964.

Following basic training, Kovic was sent to Camp Lejeune in North Carolina, then on to radio school at Norfolk Marine Barracks in Virginia. He was promoted to private first class and was eager to see combat but spent his time cleaning radios, which began to irritate him when he heard about the battles in Vietnam. In order to serve his country, he requested an immediate transfer to Vietnam. Within ten days, his orders came through, and he was on his way into battle. Within three months, he was promoted to lance corporal and volunteered for "Recon," a platoon that had been surrounded and attacked, leaving only eight survivors. Volunteers were needed to rebuild the unit, and Kovic was the first to offer himself. The unit had a reputation for being studs, and he wanted to be part of that image. He was tied to the unit called Dunn's Raiders, which lived by the motto: "We came to kill. Never have so few done so foul to so many." One incident turned his stomach, however. When his tour of duty was over and he was ready to go home, some marines showed him a jar containing two fingers and an ear of enemy captives that one of them was going to try to mail home.

Once home, Kovic was assigned to a Hawk missile battalion while his friends were dying overseas. When he saw a photo in the *New York Daily News* of four "longhairs"—men obviously espousing an alternative lifestyle—burning the American flag in Central Park to protest the war, he requested transfer back to Vietnam but was turned down. It was considered insane to want to go back. After 14 more such requests, he was considered crazy enough to be returned.

In the battlefield again, Kovic was severely wounded—paralyzed from the mid-chest down when a bullet shattered his spinal cord. After months of hospitalization in the Bronx Veterans Hospital, where his treatment and that of other veterans was less than adequate—overcrowded conditions, lack of cleanliness and care, and rats crawling across his chest—he was finally released. Discharged from the marines with a bronze star and best wishes, he moved to Los Angeles. By now, he was so disgusted with the military and the U.S. government that he became an antiwar activist and a leader in the Vietnam Veterans against the War, a group that staged numerous protest marches and demonstrations.

During one demonstration outside the Wilshire Boulevard headquarters for then presidential candidate Richard Nixon, there was an ugly confrontation with the Los Angeles Police Department, and demonstrators decided to move to McArthur Park, some distance away. Kovic was caught in the middle and deliberately dumped from his wheelchair. He was called a "commie" by a police officer, who threatened to haul him to a rooftop and throw him off. Kovic, along with other protesters, was imprisoned and heaped with verbal and physical abuse while in jail. Still, Kovic continued speaking out against the war and has never recanted his change of heart from blind faith in the military to his antiwar views.

In 1995, Robert McNamara's sharply self-critical autobiography *In Retrospect: The Tragedy and Lessons of Vietnam* was published. It describes U.S. government officials' failure to educate themselves about Vietnamese history and culture and the huge costs of expanding U.S. involvement in the war. Kovic, with a *Los Angeles Times* reporter, wrote a response, stating in part:

> I have no malice toward Robert McNamara, I have nothing but forgiveness, but I want him to understand the real lessons of the Vietnam War . . . the human cost of war, for those who served and those who did not question. All the dead whose names are on the Wall in Washington, their voices have been silenced forever. But I can still speak, and I want to express to the former secretary of defense my understanding of a war that I continue to live with each day.

Kovic went on to describe the "hospital slum" he came home to and the feeling that "no one cared." He recounted his days of despair, long bouts of depression, anxiety attacks, and fear during his first two years as a paralyzed veteran. He added that he is "now happy to be alive, very thankful," but he continued:

> I want Robert S. McNamara and the other architects of that war to know what it was like when we veterans spoke out against the war, when we

were thrown out of our wheelchairs, put behind bars, put on trial, treated like non-persons, called traitors, simply for trying to stop a war that was ruining our country. . . .

[McNamara's] statement that the war was "terribly wrong" is just the beginning of a national confessional that is inevitable. The greatest gift would be that our country learned the real lessons about war. Not the "Vietnam syndrome," so that we can learn to fight another war with even more bombs, even more ruthlessness, even more viciousness. What we did in the (Persian) Gulf was an atrocity, and it was an insult to the real lessons of the Vietnam War: that war is deeply immoral, that warfare is not a way to solve our problems. That's what I would tell Robert S. McNamara. That's what I would tell the people of this country (Kovic and Scheer 1995).

References

Kovic, Ron. 1976. *Born on the Fourth of July*. New York: McGraw-Hill.

Kovic, Ron, and Robert Scheer. 1995. "McNamara Still Owes Vets a Debt." *Los Angeles Times*, 23 April, Opinion section.

Love, Robert, ed. 1993. *The Best of Rolling Stone: 25 Years of Journalism on the Edge*. New York: Doubleday.

KUHN, MARGARET

(1905–1995)

W hen Maggie Kuhn faced mandatory retirement from her job at the age of 65, she did not go peacefully from the workforce. She hated the idea of being "sent out to pasture" and decided to fight back, seeking changes in public attitudes about older people and lobbying against ageism— stereotyping and discrimination based on age. She believed that the old should not be separated from the young—a common practice in much of U.S. society— and she spent decades educating the public on the concept that old age is a triumph, not a "disease," as many are prone to believe.

Kuhn became a peace activist during U.S. involvement in the Vietnam War and joined with five other women who shared her views. As a way to bring old

and young activists together, Kuhn and her friends formed the Consultation of Older and Younger Adults for Social Change. The group soon took up other social issues such as ageism, sexism, and racial injustice, which brought public condemnation but did not deter their activities. A television producer called the group the Gray Panthers after the militant civil rights group the Black Panthers,

and the term stuck. In fact, the Gray Panthers eventually became an international organization with tens of thousands of members in six countries. Their motto has long been "age and youth in action."

Born in Buffalo, New York, Kuhn grew up in Cleveland, Ohio, and Memphis and Louisville, Tennessee. As a girl, she was interested in feminist issues, particularly the fight for women's right to vote. She graduated from the College for Women in Cleveland, and in the 1920s, while working for the YMCA, she began advocating for working women. The YMCA sent her to Columbia University to take courses in social reform.

During World War II, Kuhn worked with the United Service Organization (USO), helping women who worked in defense plants. She joined the national office of the Presbyterian Church in the 1940s and became involved in a variety of social causes over the next two decades: desegregation, affordable housing, national health care, peace, and antipoverty. She was one of only two whites who worked in the Presbyterian Church's civil rights department.

Kuhn's advocacy for seniors included public criticism of those who stereotyped seniors. She once reproached Johnny Carson for his "Aunt Blabby" skit that made fun of the elderly. She also demanded that older people be a part of the community and that mandatory retirement be abolished because, as she noted decades ago, "it is socially wasteful and often personally devastating." She declared that "an institution that forces older people out of their work roles requires perpetuation of an agist belief system. This system requires that all groups buy into the concept that old people are less able than young and ought to enjoy leisure time, even if they don't want it" (Hessel 1977, 66, 70). Successful lobbying by the Gray Panthers eventually helped raise the age limit on mandatory retirement, but the requirement itself has not yet been outlawed.

Kuhn refused to live in a housing complex for the elderly, calling such facilities "glorified playpens," a categorization that she admitted was exaggerated. In her view, even though retirement communities kept "wrinkled babies" safe, they also kept seniors "out of the way of the rest of society." Throughout her 25 years as a Gray Panther activist, she lived in her own home in Philadelphia, Pennsylvania, sharing it with younger housemates (in their twenties and thirties) who provided companionship and helped with chores in exchange for a place to live at a reasonable rent. She also encouraged others to create group homes shared by people of various ages and began the Shared Housing Resources Center.

In spite of poor health (she suffered from severe arthritis and osteoporosis), public criticism of her liberal views, and the hostile attitude of the government during the Reagan administration, she constantly fought discrimination against seniors. During a 1990 ceremony at Northern Illinois University in De Kalb, where she received an honorary doctorate, Kuhn declared, "When I turned 80, I made a solemn vow to myself that I would try to do something outrageous at least once a week. The current and immediate past administrations have given me endless opportunities to do so."

In 1990, an editorial in *Nation* explained:

What distinguishes the Gray Panthers from conventional advocacy groups for older people is their refusal to pit the interests of the old against those of the young. While well funded senior citizens' lobbying groups like the American Association of Retired Persons battle for a bigger piece of a shrinking pie, the Panthers, with their smaller numbers and minuscule budget, fight for everyone's place at the table ("Gray Power" 1990).

For years, the Gray Panthers have also advocated for living wills, so that terminally ill people can decide for themselves whether they want to prolong their lives by artificial means, and they have fought against funeral practices that exploit survivors.

During her lifetime, Kuhn traveled hundreds of thousands of miles for speaking engagements and organizing events. Two documentary films, *Aging in America* and *Maggie Kuhn: Wrinkled Radical*, detailed much of her fight for social justice. She never married but made no secret of her affair with a married man and a man 50 years her junior. As she explained, sexuality is part of life, "and to deny it in old age is to deny life itself" (Folkart 1995).

She often expressed the hope that she would die before she turned 90, and her wish was fulfilled, almost as if she had planned it that way. She expressed her desire to have her gravestone inscribed with these words: "Here lies Maggie Kuhn under the only stone she left unturned" (Folkart 1995).

References

Folkart, Burt A. 1995. Obituary (Maggie Kuhn). *Los Angeles Times*, 23 April.

"Gray Power." 1990. Editorial. *Nation*, 28 May.

Hessel, Dieter T., ed. 1977. *Maggie Kuhn on Aging*. Philadelphia: Westminster Press.

Kuhn, Maggie, with Christina Long and Laura Quinn. 1991. *No Stone Unturned: The Life and Times of Maggie Kuhn*. New York: Ballantine Books.

Shapiro, Bruce. 1995. "Corliss and Maggie." *Nation*, 29 May.

L

LING, CHAI

(1966–)

On Chai Ling's twenty-third birthday, 15 April 1989, Hu Yaobang, a former Communist Party leader in China, died, and Ling was among the students who gathered in Tiananmen Square to honor Hu with wreaths, poetry readings, and similar activities. The leader had been ousted in 1987 because he had not cracked down on pro-democracy demonstrations by students. Ling had no idea that her life would be turned upside down and that she would have to go into hiding to escape the People's Liberation Army, which placed her number 4 on the list of the country's 21 most wanted student leaders.

Ling, who is the oldest of three children, was born in the northeastern province of Shandong. Because both her parents were Communist Party members, Ling followed their example and joined the Central Communist Youth League as a teenager. The league singled her out as one of the top 100 students of the nation at the age of 16. At Beijing Normal University, she studied child psychology and helped establish the first campus café, where she was a waitress for a time. Because of her college education, Ling could easily have become part of China's elite. Instead, she chose to risk imprisonment by taking part in massive pro-democracy demonstrations in early 1989. The thought of arrest and imprisonment—the minimum sentence for those considered counterrevolutionaries in China is 17 years—was certainly frightening, but Ling felt that she had no choice. As she explained to a *Los Angeles Times* reporter in 1990:

> My generation grew up since the Cultural Revolution. And because of economic reform and the open door policy, we saw many things. We saw the inequality of the Chinese system, we saw the corruption among Chinese officials, we saw the censoring of the Chinese people. We saw all this, and we felt a responsibility. For most young people wanted to do something for their country because this type of patriotic feeling is a tradition among Chinese intellectuals. But the corruption and inequality in the system was so widespread that students felt hopeless (Finke 1990).

When Ling joined students and labor leaders for a sit-in at Tiananmen Square in April 1989, they were protesting their government's lack of response to their demands for more freedom—demands that had been made over several years. She and a few others began a hunger strike, but as the sit-in went on, she decided on 12 May to stand up and be heard. She delivered an impassioned speech, declaring that "this nation is our nation, these people are our people, this government is our government," and asked the protesters: "If we do not speak, who will? If we do not act, who will?" Her words were recorded, and tape cassettes of her speech were distributed throughout China, prompting hundreds of students, labor leaders, and Communist Party reformers to come to Tiananmen Square to participate in the protest.

Although she never intended to take command of the students, the Students' Democracy Movement elected her as their leader. During the night of 3 June,

army troops and riot police advanced on the square, and many demonstrators dispersed. In the morning, as the tanks rolled in, Ling spoke to the estimated 5,000 that stayed: "Countrymen! The darker the age, the sooner the dawn will come. The tighter the mindless fascist suppression, the sooner the true people's republic will be born."

On their television screens, the world watched with horror as the scene unfolded in Tiananmen Square. Chinese troops fired on the students, trying to provoke an attack in return, killing hundreds of unarmed demonstrators. Ling was forced to leave the square, urging students to remain passive so that they would not be killed. Many people risked execution to protect her and her husband, Feng Congde, also a student activist. The couple went into hiding for ten months, staying in individual homes and offices of various organizations. They eventually found asylum in France in April 1990. Later that year, Ling was nominated for the Nobel Peace Prize. She was invited to the United States for a five-city speaking tour in June and described the agony over the massacre in Tiananmen Square and the nightmares she suffered because of the many deaths. She also expressed deep concern for her parents, who are still living in China, and regret that she cannot care for them in the traditional Chinese way.

Ling was able to obtain asylum in the United States and complete her graduate degree at Princeton University. She now concentrates on a career advising businesses on management skills. Although she is still hailed as a heroine, Ling always credits people in China—particularly those who helped her get out of the country—as the true heroes.

References

Chin, Paula. 1990. "One Year Later, the Pasionaria of Tiananmen, Chai Ling, Implores the World Not To Forget the Bloodbath." *People Weekly*, 18 June.

Finke, Nikke. 1990. "Woman with a Country." *Los Angeles Times*, 18 June.

Martinez, Jose. 1995. "Chinese Dissident Concentrates on Her Business Career in U.S." Associated Press, 10 July.

Tempest, Rone. 1994. "Chinese Activists Trade Dreams of '89 for Careers." *Los Angeles Times*, 2 June.

LOVING, MILDRED JETER, AND
LOVING, RICHARD

(1940–) and (1934–1975)

The couple had no idea when they married in 1958 that years later they would be arguing for their constitutional right to marry whomever they chose and would be considered civil rights heroes. Certainly they never imagined that their interracial marriage would be the subject of a landmark U.S. Supreme Court decision *(Loving v. Virginia)* nine years later.

The late Richard Loving, who was white, and Mildred Jeter, who is of mixed African and Native American ancestry, grew up in rural Caroline County, Virginia, and were childhood friends and then sweethearts. When they decided to marry, they went across the state line to Washington, D.C., because there was no waiting period there. Not long after they returned to their home, they were arrested for breaking Virginia's antimiscegenation law, which made it a felony for a black person and a white person to marry, despite the fact that the couple's marriage was legal in the nation's capital. At that time, 15 other states also had antimiscegenation laws on the books.

The Lovings' arrest took place in the early hours of the morning, when the local sheriff burst into their bedroom and took them to the county jail in Bowling Green. They were jailed for five days before going before the county court. Circuit Judge Leon M. Basil sentenced them to a year in prison with the lecture that "Almighty God created the races white, black, yellow, Malay and red, and He placed them on separate continents, and but for the interference with His arrangement there would be no cause for such marriages. The fact that he separated the races shows that He did not intend for the races to mix." The judge offered to suspend the sentence on the condition that the Lovings move to Washington, D.C., and stay there for 25 years. He ruled that they could visit relatives in Virginia, but only if Mildred and Richard came separately.

Since the couple felt that they had no choice, they accepted the exile, living for several years with relatives in the District of Columbia, where all three of their children were born. One day, Mildred and Richard decided to visit Richard's mother in Virginia, and they were arrested. This time, the couple, though intensely private people, decided to take action and to challenge Virginia's antimiscegenation statutes—a challenge that would have far-reaching effects on hundreds of thousands of other interracial couples in the years ahead.

Mildred Loving wrote to then U.S. attorney general Robert F. Kennedy, asking for help. Kennedy turned the case over to Bernard S. Ocean, a young American Civil Liberties Union (ACLU) lawyer, and his assistant Phillip Hirschkop. The two appealed the Lovings' case to the Virginia Supreme Court and lost. The lawyers as well as the Lovings faced harassment, name-calling, and death

Mildred and Richard Loving

threats, especially from the Ku Klux Klan, but the couple and the ACLU lawyers pursued the case until it reached the U.S. Supreme Court in 1967. In a unanimous decision, the justices struck down as unconstitutional the Virginia law that barred interracial marriages, which effectively overturned similar laws in other states.

Although the Loving case is frequently cited in books and articles about civil rights gains, Mildred and Richard Loving never thought of themselves as pioneers who blazed legal trails. Nevertheless, their courage and determination to make their case heard helped establish the fact that a person's right to choose a mate is protected by the U.S. Constitution.

In 1975, Richard Loving was killed in an automobile accident, and Mildred Loving has continued to live quietly in the Virginia county where she grew up, with her children and grandchildren nearby. Peggy Loving Fortune, the youngest of the Loving children, who married a man of mixed racial ancestry, told a 1992 conference of interracial families that she felt that her parents had helped make life "a lot easier" for people to "be with whomever they want. I feel it's what they were put on earth for, God used them to do what they did."

References
Duke, Lynne. 1992. "25 Years after Landmark Decision, Still the Rarest of Wedding Bonds." *Washington Post*, 12 June.

Gay, Kathlyn. 1995a. *"I Am Who I Am": Speaking Out about Multiracial Identity.* New York: Franklin Watts.

Hollis, Yvette Walker. 1992. "A Legacy of Loving." *New People,* summer, special commemorative section.

Margolick, David. 1992. "A Mixed Marriage's 25th Anniversary of Legality." *New York Times,* 12 June.

M

MAATHAI, WANGARI

(1940–)

Honored as the leading environmentalist in Kenya, Africa, Wangari Maathai, a professor at the University of Nairobi (and the first woman in Kenya to earn a Ph.D.), has also been denounced as a subversive, arrested, severely beaten, and abused in numerous ways by the national government because she has dared to speak up for her convictions. The Kenyan government is headed by President Daniel arap Moi, whom critics charge has amassed a great deal of power over the courts and Parliament, some members of which have been expelled for disagreeing with presidential programs. Moi is also said to be intolerant of public dissent. According to Maathai, "People in this country are afraid to speak out. But it's the silence that hurts. That's how you create dictatorship"—by not speaking out (Press 1990).

An outspoken advocate of democracy, Maathai also heads the Green Belt Movement, a tree-planting project that has helped stop deforestation and overdevelopment in Kenya. For years, government officials have tried to silence her because of her opposition to various development schemes. In 1989, for example, Maathai opposed the government's plan, endorsed by President Moi, to build a 62-story office building in a public park, one of the few green places left in the city. As a result, she was evicted from her state-owned office, but she immediately set up headquarters for her Green Belt project in her home. Investors, which included the World Bank, withdrew their support of the office building.

Maathai founded the Green Belt Movement in Kenya in 1977 as a means of stopping the massive clearing of trees, which has contributed to the advance of the desert and soil erosion and has caused problems such as lack of firewood and food. The campaign began in Maathai's own backyard when she began talking to women about establishing and caring for tree nurseries and planting trees as a means of providing for basic needs as well as protecting the soil and water systems. She also visited schools to enlist the help of children, encourage them to go to the tree nursery for saplings, dig holes to plant them, and care for the trees during the school year. Since the movement began, more than 1,500 nurseries have been started, nearly all of them operated by women, and more than 1 million children have helped with the planting.

In 1991, Maathai was awarded the Goldman Prize, funded by the Goldman Environmental Foundation of California, which selects winners from around the world who are grassroots activists for causes ranging from tropical forest preservation to protection against hazardous-waste dumping. She was also the recipient of the Africa Prize for Leadership, the Better World Award, and many others, but that did not stop the Kenyan government from arresting Professor Maathai in January 1992 because she had attended a public meeting to support expanded democratic rights and a multiparty system of government. The meeting had been called because President Moi planned to turn the government over to a military junta to prevent democratic elections. Several who attended the meeting were arrested immediately. Maathai was arrested in her home,

which was surrounded by approximately 200 police officers, and charged with "spreading a malicious rumor."

She was released but was arrested again in March and attacked by riot police while in a park demanding the release of political prisoners. Reportedly, police clubbed her unconscious, and she was hospitalized in critical condition. Many activists worldwide were incensed and wrote to President Moi to protest his government's deplorable actions and its "blatant lack of respect for fundamental rights of freedom of speech and association." One of the protest groups, Nonviolence International, condemned the "ongoing assault on Ms. Maathai and the other women. This treatment is intolerable and we strongly urge your government to desist from such actions and uphold its pledge to bring about a free society with equal rights for all citizens" (Anyadike 1993).

Domestic and international pressure, including a cutoff of aid, finally resulted in some respite from the brutal harassment of Maathai, and President Moi reluctantly accepted a multiparty political system. In the December 1992 election, three parties opposed Moi but were unable to unseat him, although they gained seats in the national legislature. Maathai founded a political organization known as the Middle Ground Group to try to establish a common front to oppose Moi, but various factions refused to unite. She has also continued with her environmental and human rights activities, insisting that "we must educate people on their rights" (Anyadike 1993).

References

Anyadike, Obinna. 1993. "Interview with Wangari Maathai" (electronic posting). *InterPress Service*, 24 June.

Press, Robert M. 1990. "Kenyan President on Dubious Course." *Oregonian*, 30 January.

McCLOSKEY, JAMES

(1942–)

James (Jim) McCloskey calls himself "a radical disciple of Christ" and has developed an unlikely career helping free what he calls the "convicted innocent." His heroic and successful efforts for justice have resulted in freedom for people who have been sentenced to life imprisonment or death for crimes they did not commit.

The eldest of three children, McCloskey was born into what he describes as a conservative Republican family in suburban Philadelphia. His father, an elder in the Presbyterian Church, was executive vice-president of McCloskey & Company, a large family construction firm, and once served as U.S. ambassador to Ireland.

After graduating from Bucknell University, McCloskey served in the navy and saw combat in the Vietnam War. During the 1970s, he worked for a management consulting firm, and when he was in his mid-thirties, he started to attend church for the first time since high school. As a result of the minister's preaching, he began reading the New Testament and, as he explained, felt "that Christ was speaking to me." He was "feeling an emptiness" and was not gaining much satisfaction from a business career that was going well. "I didn't feel that I was doing anything really worthwhile. I've been a bachelor all my life. I wanted to do something more with my life than just feed myself," he told a news reporter (Rohrlich 1990).

At the age of 37, McCloskey gave up a prosperous lifestyle in suburban Philadelphia to "do something that had redeeming purpose." He astounded his friends, colleagues, and family when, in 1979, he enrolled in the Princeton Theological Seminary, intending to become a Protestant minister. In 1980, as part of his course of study, McCloskey elected to do fieldwork for a year at Trenton State Prison, serving as a chaplain for the most troublesome inmates. According to a news account, "He overcame his natural fears, learned to ignore the taunts of radical Black Muslims and formed close relationships with many prisoners" (Hammer 1986). One of the prisoners was an illiterate drug addict, George "Chiefie" De Los Santos, who claimed to be innocent of the murder of a Newark, New Jersey, car salesman, even though he supposedly had confessed to the crime. After numerous visits and conversations with Chiefie, McCloskey learned that the "confession" had been fabricated by a police informant. McCloskey eventually believed Chiefie's story and promised to begin an investigation that lasted two and a half years and eventually brought about Chiefie's release.

That first case prompted McCloskey to give up his plan to become a pastor in a church. He decided instead to pattern his life after men who followed Christ's teachings at great risk to themselves, challenging injustices and trying to reform the social order. He established a nonprofit agency in his own apartment near Princeton University. Called Centurion Ministries, the agency is named for the Roman soldier who, according to biblical accounts, was stationed to guard the crucified Christ and said, "Surely this one must be innocent." McCloskey's ministry is supported only by modest contributions from foundations, churches, and individuals and the pro bono services of criminal defense lawyers. Centurion Ministries functions as a free detective service for prisoners sentenced to life imprisonment or to death and whose appeals are exhausted. McCloskey, however, will not take any case unless he is convinced of the prisoner's innocence.

One such case involved Clarence Chance and Benny Powell, who had been convicted in 1975 of killing a Los Angeles County sheriff's deputy and had spent 17 years behind bars for the crime. After 4 years of painstaking research, McCloskey found evidence indicating that the two men had been framed by

overzealous Los Angeles Police Department investigators, and Chance and Powell were released. In another case, McCloskey showed that a New Jersey man who had been convicted of raping a teenage girl and sentenced to life in prison had been framed by a witness under pressure from a police detective, who had hidden evidence pointing to another person's guilt. When the New Jersey superior court judge reviewed the case, he noted that there were many aspects that "truthfully terrify me" (Rohrlich 1990).

According to McCloskey, "There are a lot of common characteristics that combine to create false convictions," such as the misconduct of police and prosecutors, "lazy investigations, poor defense lawyering. [The accused] get caught between a rock and a hard place, and they get swept away anonymously" (Pressley 1995). In some instances, a case may be built against a person to fit a theory that police have about a crime. McCloskey is also convinced that some innocent people are convicted because jurors do not really believe that a person accused of a crime is innocent until proven guilty—in short, a defendant appears guilty just because she or he has been brought to trial. McCloskey estimates that about one in ten defendants in criminal cases that go to jury trial are wrongly convicted.

Because of his single-minded dedication and his ability to distinguish between a sob story and the truth, McCloskey has won praise from numerous investigators nationwide. Since his first success in finding justice for a "convicted innocent," he has won the release of at least a dozen inmates in several states. In recent years, he has worked on behalf of former Black Panther Elmer "Geronimo" Pratt, who was convicted of the murder of a California teacher and sentenced in 1972 to life in prison. For more than two decades, Pratt's lawyers have conducted a campaign to free him, presenting new evidence that witnesses lied, that evidence was suppressed, and that the FBI had a role in framing Pratt. In 1996, McCloskey wrote an editorial for the *Los Angeles Times*, explaining:

> I have conducted an exhaustive reinvestigation of every single facet of this case for 3 1/2 years, and I have absolutely no doubt that Pratt is completely innocent of this crime. I have submitted my findings and evidence to Dist. Atty. Gil Garcetti with the request that he review the fairness of the trial and the validity of the verdict. He agreed to do so. That was in July, 1993. Now, having waited 2 1/2 years in vain for the district attorney to respond, we at Centurion Ministries are assisting Pratt in seeking justice from the courts. Soon he will file a writ of habeas corpus, presenting in detail the documented evidence that amply demonstrates not only his innocence but also the extent to which his conviction was based on false testimony knowingly presented by the prosecution (McCloskey 1996).

In his newspaper editorial, McCloskey presented evidence showing that, as he has always maintained, Pratt was in Oakland, California, when the crime for which he was convicted was committed. "All of the evidence that we have collected and documented is persuasive and more than enough to reopen this case and see that justice is served for this innocent man," McCloskey concluded, in effect, summarizing what his own life and Centurion Ministries are all about.

References

Associated Press. 1996a. "Black Panther Seeks Retrial." AP Wire Services, 27 March.

Furia, Claire. 1992. "Defender of Wrongly Jailed Draws the Eye of Hollywood." *Phildelphia Inquirer*, 9 June.

Hammer, Joshua. 1986. "Prison Samaritan Jim McCloskey Wins Freedom for an Innocent Man." *People Weekly*, 24 November.

McCloskey, James. 1996. "Reopen the Case of Geronimo Pratt." *Los Angeles Times*, 2 January.

Pressley, Sue Anne. 1995. "Speedy Justice Can Be Dead Wrong, Texas Case Shows." *Los Angeles Times*, 19 February.

Rohrlich, Ted. 1990. "Minister of Justice for the Wrongly Convicted." *Los Angeles Times Magazine*, 23 December.

McPHERSON, AIMEE SEMPLE

(1890–1944)

To some, she was a huckster, liar, and master show person; to others, she was a healer, heroic church leader, and compassionate helper. She had a flair for the dramatic and became a colorful, inspiring evangelist who brought biblical messages to life and made them relevant to Americans in the midst of the Roaring Twenties and the Great Depression. Her gospel was nondenominational and all-inclusive, and she marched to her own drummer while preaching it.

Her simple beginnings hardly hinted at the controversial personality she would become. Aimee was born in 1890 on a farm near Salford, Ontario, Canada, to James and Minnie Kennedy. Minnie had been James's housekeeper and was 35 years younger than he. Minnie had been orphaned as an adolescent and had lived with guardians, a captain of the Canadian Salvation Army and his wife. After her marriage and the birth of Aimee, she maintained close ties with the evangelical group, teaching, visiting the sick, and speaking at missions.

When Aimee was just three weeks old, her mother took her to a Salvation Army meeting and at six weeks dedicated her to Christian service. Throughout

her childhood, Aimee took part in Salvation Army activities, attending prayer meetings and street meetings, selling copies of the army's publication *The War Cry*, and learning about the army's worldwide mission. Some historians believe that Aimee was especially influenced by Evangline Booth, daughter of the Salvation Army founder, who became a preacher and presented highly dramatized sermons to her audiences in England, Canada, and other nations.

Aimee was educated at the Salford village school and the secondary school in the nearby town of Ingersoll. During her third year at Ingersoll, she attended Pentecostal meetings and experienced a religious transformation, entering a trance state that charismatic Christians believe is the working of the Holy Spirit. At the Pentecostal revival, she also met Robert Semple, an evangelist. In 1908, she gave up her schooling and married him.

The Semples traveled to London and the United States, holding meetings and working with and learning from William Durham, leader of the Pentecostals in Chicago. During her time with Durham, Aimee began speaking in tongues, presenting what Pentecostals believe are biblical messages in an unknown language that the messenger later interprets. Aimee also experienced divine healing.

In June 1910, the Semples sailed to Hong Kong, where they joined Pentecostal missionaries and hoped to establish a presence in China. Robert Semple became ill with malaria and died in August. A month later, Aimee gave birth to their child, a girl she named Roberta. Aimee spent a restless year trying to find herself, visiting with her aged father in Canada and her mother in New York, where she was working with the Salvation Army.

In New York, Aimee met Harold McPherson. They were married in 1912, and their child, Rolf, was born in 1913. Aimee became restless and moody; she believed that she was called to serve God, and one day in 1915, she took her children and went to Canada. She left her children with her parents at the family farm and went to Kirshner (then known as Berlin), where the Pentecostals were holding revival meetings. She prayed for healings, spoke in tongues, and began a ministry that would continue for the rest of her life.

Once Aimee devoted her life to religion, her marriage with McPherson was virtually over, although Harold joined his wife for some revival meetings. He and Aimee were divorced in 1921.

McPherson spread her Pentecostal Christianity far and wide, traveling the United States and abroad with her children and her mother and holding meetings in tents, concert halls, and even boxing arenas. Her first nationwide revival was held in Philadelphia in the summer of 1918, which brought her fame as a healer and evangelist and a huge following of faithful who began to call her Sister. Over the next two years, she held revivals in cities from Baltimore to San Diego. In 1921, she broke ground for the huge Angelus Temple in Los Angeles, which was dedicated in 1923. By then, she was calling her version of Christianity Foursquare Gospel, "a complete gospel for body, for soul, for spirit and eternity" (Epstein 1993, 264). Throughout her ministry in the 1920s and 1930s, Sister Aimee gained hundreds of thousands of converts and was adored by her followers, but she also had many enemies, who criticized and ridiculed her healings, trances, and dramatic sermons. One of the most controversial incidents

during this time was a disappearance, which she claimed was a kidnapping, while she was swimming off Ocean Park beach in Los Angeles. For a time, she was thought to have drowned, and a memorial service was held. She reappeared 32 days after she had been reported missing, walking into the United States from Mexico, where she said she had been held captive by two men and a woman.

The press and much of the public accused her of running off with a lover, and she was charged with "criminal conspiracy to commit acts injurious to public morals and to prevent and obstruct justice." After a lengthy trial and thousands of dollars in court costs, the case was dismissed for lack of evidence.

Sister Aimee continued her ministry at the Angelus Temple and in England and the Holy Land. In 1930, she suffered a nervous breakdown and was close to death, but within the year she was back preaching and healing. Out of loneliness, she married for a third time, but that marriage also ended in divorce a few years later.

Although Sister Aimee continued to hold revival meetings during the Great Depression of the 1930s, she also developed the Angelus Temple Commissary, an outreach based on her admonition: "Let us strive to lighten our brothers' load and dry tears of a sister; race, creed and status make no difference. We are all one in the eyes of the Lord" (Blumhofer 1993, 346). She encouraged temple volunteers to do their part to feed, clothe, and find work for tens of thousands of needy local people and transients. Meantime, Sister held at least 20 meetings—healing services, prayer meetings, and sermons—a week at the temple.

The international Foursquare ministry continued to grow as McPherson toured through the latter part of the 1930s and into the 1940s, but her grueling activities finally took their toll. In 1944, McPherson, who had long suffered from insomnia, took an overdose of sleeping pills, which was later ruled accidental, and died. She left a legacy of Foursquare churches with more than 200,000 members in the United States and a total of at least 1.5 million members in other countries.

References

Blumhofer, Edith L. 1993. *Aimee Semple McPherson: Everybody's Sister*. Grand Rapids, MI: William B. Eerdmans.

Epstein, Daniel Mark. 1993. *Sister Aimee: The Life of Aimee Semple McPherson*. New York: Harcourt Brace Jovanovich.

McVAY, KENNETH

(1941–)

"The condition upon which God hath given liberty to man is eternal vigilance; which condition if he break, servitude is at once the consequence of his crime, and the punishment of his guilt." That quote from John Philpott Curran (1750–1817) announces Kenneth McVay's home page on the World Wide Web (WWW) and states the reason for his presence on the Internet. Since 1992, McVay has devoted most of his waking hours to countering hatemongers and Holocaust deniers—neo-Nazis and other white supremacists—who spread their lies, propaganda, and vitriolic anti-Semitism worldwide via electronic means. His efforts have cost him a great deal of time and money, and he must maintain a constant vigilance in terms of safeguarding his life and the lives of his family members. McVay is well aware of how Alan Berg, a talk-show host in Denver, Colorado, was gunned down by neo-Nazis in 1984 because Berg had ridiculed their white-supremacist organization, the Aryan Nation.

McVay was born in Santa Clara Valley, California, and lived there for most of his early life, except when he served with the U.S. Marines. He married in 1961, and the McVays have three children. In 1967, the McVays moved to British Columbia, Canada, although McVay will not reveal his exact whereabouts for safety reasons. Neo-Nazis and other white supremacists often vilify and threaten McVay on the Internet.

Holding dual citizenship in the United States and Canada, McVay was once a computer salesperson but is now retired and spends all his time tracking neo-Nazis and white supremacists who post materials on countless newsgroups and home pages on the Internet. Why has McVay, a non-Jew, devoted long hours on a daily basis to such activities? He might have taken on as his "cause" any other group regularly maligned on the "Net," but as he has explained numerous times, neo-Nazi groups and Holocaust revisionists offend his humanity and make him angry because they deliberately try to hurt and destroy people. In his view, the hatemongers stand for death and destruction. During one interview, he explained: "I don't have the time or the energy to take on the whole world. Everybody has to decide sometime in their life what's important and what's not" (Betz 1995).

For McVay, "what's important" is the Holocaust revisionism he has found on the Internet. Revisionists often post outright lies, such as stating that Jews and others at the infamous Nazi concentration camps of World War II died from natural causes and were not killed by Hitler's goons. They try to appear scholarly by reinforcing their statements with partial quotes and citations from reference works. Revisionists may fool some people with this tactic, because many readers tend to believe that no one would lie about the Holocaust, so the statements must be true. If the revisionists were lying, some people might reason, the

hundreds of thousands of documents and the many survivors and families of survivors of Hitler's extermination plan would act to prove the revisionists wrong.

Unfortunately, few (including Jewish groups) in the early 1990s were counteracting lies and misrepresentations about the Holocaust on the Internet. Most scholars believed that anti-Semitic Holocaust-denial arguments were so absurd that they should not be dignified with a response and that the activities of the few neo-Nazis out there were blown out of proportion and sensationalized by the media. McVay, however, was alarmed by the fact that naive Internet surfers would begin to believe revisionists who repeated their claims over and over again. He was convinced that history could repeat itself and that another Nazi movement could become widespread. He began making trips to his local library, searching for Holocaust information and borrowing armloads of books on the subject. He not only read countless new materials but also reread many of the 300 books about World War II he had read as a teenager. He then copied relevant information into his aging computer to post on newsgroups, refuting specific revisionist claims wherever he could find them.

Because he was unemployed at the time, McVay spent up to 20 hours a day typing, which brought on carpal tunnel syndrome, forcing him to wear braces for a time. He "soon found that he had somehow amassed over 3,500 pages of information. As the flood of information increased, so did demands for the information; requests inundated McVay's electronic mailbox, and he soon found himself a defacto, full-time Holocaust researcher and librarian to the world of the Internet" (Ken McVay home page).

As his archive of materials began to swell, McVay heard via the Internet from others like himself who were concerned about neo-Nazis and their hatemongering, and these activists have helped track and refute hate material. As a result, a project called Nizkor, which in Hebrew means "we will remember," was born. To finance Nizkor, McVay kept a $300-a-week job at a convenience store and gas station but has since received help from such groups as the Committee for Racial Justice in Vancouver, British Columbia, which donated a scanner so that he would not have to input material through the computer keyboard. One business group donated equipment to replace McVay's outdated computer and hard drive.

In 1995, Nizkor was established as a nonprofit foundation in Canada and the United States. Nizkor hopes to provide educational materials to several hundred million Internet users within the next few years. Through the project, McVay and about 150 volunteers are compiling one of the world's largest resources for Holocaust materials and an information base about the activities of racists and white supremacists on the Internet, offering about one gigabyte (1 billion bytes) of data, including the transcripts of the Nuremberg trials.

In June 1995, the provincial government honored McVay with its highest award, inducting him into the Order of British Columbia. The award recognizes that McVay has served "with the greatest distinction and excellence in a field of endeavor benefiting the people of the Province of British Columbia or elsewhere."

References

"Battle on the Internet." 1994. *Maclean's*, 17 October.

Betz, Michelle. 1995. "mcvay@internet.fighter." *Jewish Western Bulletin*, 9 March (reprinted in electronic format).

"Holocaust Defender." 1994. *Toronto Globe & Mail*, 18 October.

McVay, Ken. Ken McVay home page. http://nizkor.almanac.bc.ca/~kmcvay/index.html.

MAKEBA, MIRIAM

(1932–)

She has been called "Mama Africa" and the "Empress of African Song." Indeed, as Miriam Makeba wrote: "My life, my career, every song I sing and every appearance I make, are bound up with the plight of my people" (Makeba with Hall 1987, 1). A native South African, Makeba was exiled from her home for decades but never stopped fighting for the rights of her people, and in spite of being oppressed and humiliated herself, she became an internationally acclaimed singer. She has appeared in almost every major concert hall in the United States and throughout the world.

Makeba had her first experience with oppression when she was only 18 days old. Her mother, Christina, was jailed for making beer from cornmeal—an illegal act, since blacks were not allowed to drink. Caswell Makeba, Miriam's father, was unable to pay the 18-pound fine, so his wife was sentenced to six months in jail, which meant that their daughter would be jailed along with Christina. Jailings for small offenses have long been common for blacks in South Africa.

Throughout her growing-up years in the township of Soweto, Makeba's life reflected the oppression that increasingly harsh apartheid laws had wrought on blacks and coloreds, people of mixed race, in that land. In her autobiography, she describes the lack of educational, health, and job opportunities for people of color; the harassment and intimidation; and the grinding poverty that most of her people had to endure. Yet Makeba was able to find some joy, particularly when she joined a school chorus and had her first performing experiences.

Singer Miriam Makeba performs at the Blue Angel in New York City in 1960. On and off the stage, Makeba spoke out against apartheid in South Africa.

After becoming pregnant at the age of 17, Makeba married the father of her child, but the marriage soon ended because of the increasingly severe beatings she suffered from her husband. Makeba took her infant daughter, Bonzi, and went to live with members of her large extended family in Johannesburg. There, she joined an amateur band as the female vocalist, performing for community functions. She was soon asked to sing with a professional group, the Manhattan Brothers, and in 1953, she made her first solo recording, a love song from the Xhosa, a people whose language includes delightful clicking sounds, which some have compared to the popping of champagne corks. Makeba, in fact, became known as the "click-clack girl." In the late 1950s, she performed for a documentary movie, *Come Back, Africa,* which won the Critic's Award at the Venice Film Festival in 1959. That year, Makeba left South Africa to attend the festival and then to appear in the United States on the Steve Allen television show.

From then on, Makeba continued to achieve fame for both her performances of songs with traditional African rhythms and her harsh criticism of apartheid in South Africa. The words of one of her most popular songs called for the release of African National Congress leader NELSON MANDELA, who was imprisoned for nearly 28 years and was later elected president of South Africa. Because of her political activism and public statements against apartheid, her South African passport was revoked in 1960 when she tried to return to her homeland for her mother's funeral.

Makeba lived in the United States for the next eight years, where her mentors included such stars as Marlon Brando, Sidney Poitier, and Harry Belafonte. Belafonte and Makeba won Grammy Awards for the best folk record in 1966. She performed for President John F. Kennedy and for the United Nations and made numerous concert and club appearances.

Makeba also spoke to the United Nations Special Committee on Apartheid, where she pleaded for "the UN to use its influence to open the doors of the prisons and concentration camps in South Africa, where thousands of our people—men, women, and children—are now in jail." She urged a boycott of South Africa and a stop to arms shipments, which she was certain were used against her people. Many in the UN praised her for her eloquent and impassioned speech, and she became a spokesperson for her people. She was "no longer just an African singer" but "a symbol of my repressed people. To be in such a position is to live with a great responsibility," she wrote (Makeba with Hall 1987, 112–113).

During the 1960s and 1970s, Makeba married and divorced several times. Among her husbands were jazz great Hugh Masekela and black activist Stokely Carmichael, who was president of the Student Nonviolent Coordinating Committee. When she was married to Carmichael, many of Makeba's bookings for concerts and other appearances were canceled because of the widespread belief that she was a revolutionary. After much harassment in the United States and in British Jamaica, the Carmichaels moved to Conakry, Guinea. They split up after ten years of marriage, but that was only one of many tribulations in Makeba's volatile life. She has lived through police brutality, a serious car accident, a plane crash, two bouts with cancer, an invasion of Guinea, the tragic death of her

daughter (who apparently suffered from an emotional disorder), and the hurt and longing of being exiled from her homeland.

Although Makeba lived in Guinea and was able to visit other parts of Africa on tour—one of the most famous being Paul Simon's "Graceland" tour in Harare, Zimbabwe, in 1987—she longed to return to her home in South Africa. By 1990, with President F. W. de Klerk dismantling some apartheid laws, many South Africans were able to return for visits or to stay permanently. Makeba visited for a short time in 1991, after 31 years in exile, and stayed with her brother in Soweto. Then she returned to the United States and her life as a performer.

Three days before her sixty-second birthday in March 1994, Miriam Makeba performed in Washington, D.C., appearing with a touring ensemble that included her granddaughter. Although graying and obviously no longer young, a reviewer for the *Washington Post* noted:

The moment each song began, Makeba seemed utterly rejuvenated by the music. It didn't matter whether the tune was a lovely and lilting ballad from Kenya ("Malaika"), a contemporary South African pop song rooted in folk tradition ("African Sunset") or a tragic remembrance of apartheid and oppression ("Soweto Blues")—or even whether the rhythms inspired a sensual dance or echoed the percussive Xhosa language. Suddenly Makeba seemed ageless, as radiant as her extraordinary smile and as committed as ever to furthering the hopes and aspirations of her people. Small wonder she was accorded several standing ovations (Joyce 1994).

References
Joyce, Mike. 1994. "Miriam Makeba." *Washington Post*, 1 March.
Makeba, Miriam, with James Hall. 1987. *Makeba: My Story*. New York: New American Library, Penguin.
Ottaway, David B. 1990. "Makeba, Out of Exile." *Washington Post*, 11 June.

MANDELA, *NELSON*

(1918–)

An international hero, Nelson Mandela has been a major part of the effort to dismantle apartheid in South Africa and move the nation toward a multiracial government, a cause for which he spent 27 years in prison. After his release, Mandela shared the Nobel Peace Prize in 1993 with then South African President F. W. de Klerk, and in 1994, Mandela was elected president of South Africa.

The son of a chief of the Thembu people, who are part of the Xhosa nation, Mandela was born in a small village in the district of Transkei. His mother had accepted Christianity and had her son baptized in the Methodist Church. Sent to a one-room church school when he was seven years old, Rolihlahla Nelson Dalibhunga Mandela was required to use his British name and was henceforth known as Nelson. Two years later, his father died suddenly, and he was placed under the guardianship of a cousin, the acting paramount chief and regent of the Thembu people living in Mqhekezweni, the capital of Thembuland and a Methodist mission station. While growing up in Mqhekezweni, Mandela noted that the two principal guiding forces in his life

> were chieftaincy and the Church. These two doctrines existed in uneasy harmony, although I did not then see them as antagonistic. For me, Christianity was not so much a system of beliefs as it was the powerful creed of a single man: Reverend Matyolo . . . [whose] presence embodied all that was alluring in Christianity. He was as popular and beloved as the regent, and the fact that he was the regent's superior in spiritual matters made a strong impression on me (Mandela 1994, 17).

In Mqhekezweni, Mandela also learned about governing and leadership from regular tribal meetings over which the regent presided. Everyone from farmer to warrior was given the chance to speak, although women were not allowed to participate. Mandela recalled:

> Only at the end of the meeting . . . would the regent speak . . . to sum up what had been said and form some consensus among the diverse opinions. . . .
> As a leader, I have always followed the principles I first saw demonstrated by the regent (Mandela 1994, 19).

Mandela received his secondary education at Clarkebury Boarding Institute, founded by Methodist missionaries, and then enrolled at Healdtown, another mission school, where students were taught that the "best" ideas, government, and men came from Great Britain. During his time at Healdtown, Mandela was

inspired by a Xhosa poet who came to speak, predicting that the day would come when foreigners would no longer control the nation and that the false notions of white men would be thrown off. So strong was the poet's influence that Mandela recalled, "As I left Healdtown at the end of the year, I saw myself as a

Xhosa first and an African second" (Mandela 1994, 37). In 1939, Mandela entered Fort Hare University, where he competed in soccer and cross-country running and joined the drama society. He also met students who would become his future comrades in the African National Congress (ANC), including Oliver Tambo, who later became president of the organization. In 1940, he and Tambo were suspended from school because of their participation in a student strike.

When tribal elders, according to custom, arranged marriages for both Mandela and his brother, Justice, the two felt that they could not accept their brides, and they ran off to Johannesburg. Several years later, in 1944, Mandela married Evelyn Ntoko Mase, a nurse, and the couple eventually had three children (their first child, a daughter, died in infancy), but their marriage suffered when Evelyn became increasingly involved with the Jehovah's Witnesses and their Watch Tower organization and Mandela became ever more dedicated to the struggle for freedom. "I tried to persuade her of the necessity of the struggle, while she tried to persuade me of the value of religious faith" (Mandela 1994, 179). He wrote in his autobiography:

> I cannot pinpoint a moment when I became politicized . . . I had no epiphany, no singular revelation, no moment of truth, but a steady accumulation of a thousand sights, a thousand indignities, a thousand unremembered moments, produced in me an anger, a rebelliousness, a desire to fight the system that imprisoned my people (Mandela 1994, 83).

During the 1940s, Mandela, with the help of Walter Sisulu, the head of the local ANC, found work as a law clerk in Johannesburg. He also completed his undergraduate degree and began work on a correspondence law degree at the University of the Witwatersrand. Sisulu, who believed that the ANC was the means to bring about change in South Africa, persuaded Mandela to join the organization.

After completing his degree, Mandela and Tambo opened a law office in 1952, the first black law firm in South Africa. In addition, he met and associated with people of other races, many of them connected with the South African Communist Party, which led to his and Sisulu's arrest and conviction under the Suppression of Communism Act, passed by a government dominated by the virulently anticommunist Nationalist Party. Their nine-month sentences were suspended, but Mandela became disillusioned with the lack of militancy on the part of the ANC, prompting him, Sisulu, and Tambo to join other more radical members and form the ANC Youth League. Within five years, the league took over the organization and helped write a freedom charter, calling for a democratic South Africa.

Although some believed that the charter supported a socialist order, Mandela noted that it spelled out goals that "could not be achieved without radically altering the economic and political structure of South Africa. It was not meant to be capitalist or socialist but a melding together of the people's demands to end the oppression" (Mandela 1994, 153).

In 1956, Mandela and Evelyn were divorced, and not long afterward, he met Nomzamo Winnie Madikizela, whom he immediately decided to marry. "Her spirit, her passion, her youth, her courage, her willfulness—I felt all of these things the moment I first saw her," he wrote. Madikizela, a medical social worker 16 years his junior, and Mandela married in 1958, and they had two children.

At the time of the Mandelas' marriage, Nelson and 155 other activists had been charged with treason for staging strikes and opposing apartheid laws. The activists were forced to undergo months of preparatory examinations before the formal trial began in 1959, two years and eight months after their arrests. Meantime, the South African government continued its repressive policies, passing more stringent apartheid laws to prevent Africans of color from being integrated into any part of white South Africa and rigorously enforcing a law requiring blacks to carry passes when traveling from one area to another.

On 21 March 1960, several thousand demonstrators in the small township of Sharpeville gathered to peacefully protest the pass law. The police, who were outnumbered, panicked and began firing on the unarmed crowd, killing 69 and wounding more than 400. The brutal massacre was the subject of news stories around the world, prompting outraged protests from numerous governments, including the United States and the United Nations Security Council. The massacre also convinced Mandela that demonstrations were a futile means of freeing his people.

After the treason trial, which lasted more than four years and acquitted the activists, the government became even more repressive. The ANC was outlawed, and Mandela and other ANC members set up an underground, independent organization called Umkhonto we Sizwe (Spear of the Nation) for the purpose of ending apartheid through guerrilla activities—primarily sabotage—to force the South African government to negotiate.

Mandela was able to slip out of the country illegally to obtain military training in Ethiopia and Algeria, then returned to South Africa to take charge of the new military wing of the ANC. Their sabotage efforts included bombings of power plants, rail lines, and other government facilities, making Mandela a hero among his people and the press, which dubbed him the "Black Pimpernel." Despite the use of disguises and moving frequently to evade police, he was arrested in 1962 on another charge. Mandela and seven of his ANC comrades, including Sisulu, were again placed on trial (known as the Rivonia Trial), where Mandela was allowed to present a four-hour speech in his own defense, disputing claims that the ANC and the Communist Party shared the same goals and declaring that the ANC's struggle was a nationalist cause. He ended with these words:

I have fought against white domination, and I have fought against black domination. I have cherished the ideal of a democratic and free society in

which all persons live together in harmony and with equal opportunities. It is an ideal which I hope to live for and to achieve. But if need be, it is an ideal for which I am prepared to die (Mandela 1994, 322).

Mandela and the others were sentenced to life imprisonment and shipped to Robben Island Prison off Cape Town, often compared to Alcatraz in the United States. "The Dark Years," as he called the 16 years at Robben Island, included back-breaking labor in a stone quarry, periods of solitary confinement because he dared to speak out for humane treatment and against vindictive warders, strict restrictions on letters and visits from family, less food for black prisoners, and bans on newspapers and other reading materials, plus countless indignities. Yet he and his ANC comrades used every possible opportunity to keep their dream of a free South Africa alive and to smuggle information in and out of the prison. They also staged hunger and labor slow-down strikes to better their conditions.

At the same time, there were uprisings within the country to protest apartheid, and during the 1970s, several African nations gained independence, creating pressure on South Africa. In addition, the United States and other nations imposed sanctions on South Africa in an attempt to strangle the nation's economy.

In 1982, Mandela and several other prisoners were transferred to Pollsmoor Maxiumum Security Prison near Cape Town. Compared with Robben Island, their quarters there were "luxurious," with beds, toilets, showers, and towels provided for the first time. By the mid-1980s, the South African government began to respond to worldwide condemnation of apartheid, which included "Free Mandela" campaigns as well as internal guerrilla activities.

In 1988, Mandela was hospitalized with tuberculosis. When he recovered, he was sent to Victor Verster Prison Farm, and government officials began secret negotiations with Mandela for his release. President P. W. Botha offered to free Mandela in exchange for his publicly renouncing ANC violence. Mandela refused the offer, which F. W. de Klerk, Botha's successor, repeated toward the end of 1989. Again Mandela refused, and de Klerk finally agreed to an unconditional release. Mandela was freed in 1990.

Although his release was cheered by thousands of supporters, thousands of whites protested, some of them carrying Nazi flags and shouting white-supremacist slogans and vowing to fight rather than submit to a black government. Some militant blacks protested any government based on freedom-charter principles stating that South Africa belongs to both black and white Africans.

Over the next few years, Mandela led ANC political activities supporting a multiracial government, continually seeking cooperation with de Klerk and attempting to end the violence that had escalated in the country, due in part to forces competing against the ANC. In 1994, South Africa held its first national all-race election, and the majority blacks (about 80 percent of the population) voted for the first time, electing Mandela president. Even though some liberties have been achieved, Mandela is well aware that it will take a long time to free some South Africans of prejudice and hatred and that the "true test of our devotion to freedom is just beginning" (Mandela 1994, 544).

References

"At the Gates of Freedom." 1990. *Washington Post*, 8 April, Magazine section.

Benson, Mary. 1986. *Nelson Mandela: The Man and the Movement*. New York: W. W. Norton.

Corelli, Rae. 1990. "A Symbol of Freedom." *Maclean's*, 12 February.

Hewitt, Bill. 1990. "Nelson Mandela." *People Weekly*, 26 February.

Mandela, Nelson. 1994. *Long Walk to Freedom*. Boston: Little, Brown.

Mandela, Winnie, Anne Benjamin, and Mary Benson. 1985. *Part of My Soul Went with Him*. New York: W. W. Norton.

Meer, Fatima. 1990. *Higher than Hope: The Authorized Biography of Nelson Mandela*. London: H. Hamilton, 1988. Reprint, New York: Harper & Row.

"Nelson Mandela: From Prisoner to President." 1994. *Ebony*, August (special issue).

Stengel, Richard. 1994. "The Making of a Leader." *Time*, 9 May.

MANKILLER, WILMA

(1945–)

"Especially in the context of a tribal people, no individual's life stands apart and alone from the rest. My own story has meaning only as long as it is a part of the overall story of my people. For above all else, I am a Cherokee woman" (Mankiller and Wallis 1993, 14). Long before Christopher Columbus landed on North American soil, Cherokee women were involved in the political, social, and cultural decisions of the tribe. It was only after being exposed to the European male-dominated culture that the role of women in tribes began to change—so much so that, hundreds of years later, when Mankiller ran for deputy chief of the Cherokee Nation in 1983, she received hate mail, threatening telephone calls, and death threats—all because she was a woman.

Mankiller ran in the 1983 election at the urging of Ross Swimmer, who recognized her enormous contributions in her job with the Cherokee Nation. Swimmer

was running for reelection as chief, and despite their political differences (he was a conservative Republican, she a liberal Democrat), he wanted her to be his running mate. They won the election, and Mankiller served two years as deputy chief before Swimmer decided to step down when he was asked to head the U.S. Bureau of Indian Affairs. In such an instance, according to tribal law, the deputy chief automatically becomes chief. Two years later, Mankiller was elected in her own right, chosen by her people to lead them. Reelected by a wide margin in 1991, her record has silenced critics who were once worried about her gender.

One of Mankiller's primary concerns in her role as chief is to help her people achieve economic independence and rebuild a strong sense of community. She explained:

> We operate from a bubble-up theory that's a little bit different than that of most tribes. We simply act as a resource: our people define and resolve many of their problems at the community level. They plan a project, such as a community building, and then erect it. That puts them in a position of assuming responsibility for change, and it builds pride. People develop a sense that they can indeed alter their lives and community ("People Expect Me To Be More Warlike" 1986).

Born in Oklahoma, Mankiller is one of 11 children of her Cherokee father and Dutch-Irish mother. Her family name, Mankiller, is understood as a military title of respect and great honor, similar to Captain. Her childhood in Oklahoma was a happy one. She enjoyed the connections to the community, nature, and her roots. However, shortly before Mankiller turned 11 years old, her family moved to San Francisco, California, as part of a federal relocation program. Mankiller felt the enormous pain of her ancestors, comparing the move to the Trail of Tears in 1838, when thousands of Cherokees died in a U.S. government–forced move from the southeastern United States to northeastern Oklahoma.

Much of what Mankiller gained from life in San Francisco she credits to the Indian Center, a gathering place for Native Americans of all ages. Her father's dedication to the center and to other native people was a profound influence on Mankiller:

> When he believed in something, he worked around the clock to get the job done. He was always dragging home somebody he had met, someone who was down on his luck and needed a meal and a place to stay. It was a tight fit, but we made room. My dad never gave up on people. I think my father's tenacity is a characteristic I inherited. Once I set my mind to do something, I never give up. I was raised in a household where no one ever said to me, "You can't do this because you're a woman, Indian, or poor." No one ever told me there were limitations (Mankiller and Wallis 1993, 112).

Before her eighteenth birthday, Mankiller married Hugo Olaya, a South American college student. Together they had two daughters. When Mankiller wanted more than the traditional role of wife and mother, she went back to

school and became interested in women's liberation. She watched with fascination the work that CESAR CHAVEZ was doing to help migrant workers and mourned the death of Robert Kennedy, who had shown an active compassion for the plight of Native Americans. The focus for Mankiller's spirit of activism became clear, however, when a group of Native Americans representing over 20 tribes took over Alcatraz in November 1969. As she wrote in her autobiography:

> Citing a forgotten clause in treaty agreements that said any unused federal lands must revert to Indian use, they took over the twelve-acre island to attract attention to the government's gross mistreatment of generations of native people. They did it to remind the whites that the land was ours before it was theirs (Mankiller and Wallis 1993, 163).

Mankiller went to Alcatraz several times during the occupation, but mostly she stayed at the Indian Center, which became a center for support, fund-raising, and communication during that period.

In 1975, Mankiller and her husband separated, and the following year she left San Francisco with her daughters to return to her ancestral Oklahoma. She was hired by the Cherokee Nation as economic stimulus coordinator. In addition to helping native people get training in environmental science and health, Mankiller looked for opportunities to draft grant proposals for special projects. During this time, she met and worked with Chief Ross Swimmer. In 1981, she was named the first director of the Cherokee Nation Community Development Department, which she helped found. Just two years later, she was Swimmer's running mate for the position of deputy chief.

In addition to battling social, economic, and political issues, Mankiller had to fight for her life after an accident left her with a crushed face and leg. In the hospital, Mankiller was devastated to learn that, as a result of the head-on collision, the other driver—one of her closest friends—had been killed. Only months after the accident, while still recovering, Mankiller began to suffer from systemic myasthenia gravis, a kind of muscular dystrophy that can lead to paralysis. Fortunately, an operation and drug therapy were successful. She also inherited a kidney disease from her father that caused frequent infections and hospitalizations until 1990, when her brother donated one of his kidneys to her.

In 1986, Mankiller married the man who had become her best friend, Charlie Soap. She described him as "a full-blooded, bilingual Cherokee, and probably the most well-adjusted male I have ever met" (Mankiller and Wallis 1993, 235).

In 1987, Mankiller was named *Ms.* magazine's Woman of the Year, "for compassionate skills in building economic power and self-esteem as the first woman elected Principal Chief of the Cherokee Nation, and for enriching all Americans with a new style of leadership" (Straub 1992, 359).

References
Mankiller, Wilma, and Michael Wallis. 1993. *Mankiller, A Chief and Her People*. New York: St. Martin's Press.

"People Expect Me To Be More Warlike." 1986. *U.S. News & World Report*, 17 February.

Straub, Deborah Gillan, ed. 1992. *Contemporary Heroes and Heroines, Book II*. Detroit, MI: Gale Research.

MARCANTONIO, VITO

(1902–1954)

Vito Marcantonio was a longtime advocate of working-class people and while serving in the U.S. House of Representatives for 14 years was a national spokesperson for those associated with the Communist Party. Although never a communist himself, his radical views and fierce defense of civil rights and freedom of conscience for Communist Party members subjected him to much vilification and denunciation.

According to biographer Gerald Meyer, "Nothing about Vito Marcantonio's origins presaged his later notoriety as a radical Congressman" (Meyer 1989, 7). He was born in the New York City Italian neighborhood of East Harlem to Sanario (or Samuel as his father identified himself) and Angelina Marcantonio. His father was a second-generation Italian and skilled carpenter; his mother was born in Italy and immigrated to the United States after her arranged marriage to Sanario.

While in elementary school Marcantonio "displayed marked leadership and intellectual qualities." He earned excellent grades in history and public speaking, but "showed little interest in organized sports. He had many friends, and he became a favorite of his teachers" (Meyer 1989, 9).

Because there was no high school in East Harlem, Marcantonio enrolled in De Witt Clinton High School on West 59th Street, about four miles from his home, in 1917. During his high school years, his father was killed in a streetcar accident, and his mother and grandmother were forced to take in washing and do sewing to earn income for the family and to keep him in school. It was in high school that Marcantonio first began to develop socialist views, influenced by his history teacher, Abraham Lefkowitz, an ardent socialist who believed the nation's wealth should be more fairly distributed.

Another teacher, Leonard Covello, also greatly influenced Marcantonio. Covello set up a cultural club called Circolo Italiano to encourage students to take

pride in their Italian heritage and to overcome the suspicion many families from southern Italy had about higher education (immigrant families believed education beyond the teenage years would disrupt or destroy family life). Covello also established a settlement house in Italian East Harlem, and Marcantonio became involved in this effort, committing himself for the remainder of his life to his neighborhood.

While attending law school at New York University during the early 1920s, Marcantonio was deeply affected by U.S. government unconstitutional actions against labor organizers, social reformers, and those with anarchist views. At the time, Marcantonio was a clerk with a law firm that "specialized in civil liberties and labor disputes" (Berson 1994, 220) and that had among its clients anarchists EMMA GOLDMAN and Alexander Berkman, who were deported because of their communist affiliations.

Marcantonio was shaken by the case of Nicola Sacco and Bartolomeo Vanzetti, who were arrested, tried, and convicted of killing a clerk and guard at a shoe factory. Many believed that evidence against the men was rigged because of their Italian ancestry and their anarchist views. In addition, the judge and most of the jurors were openly biased against the defendants, who were given the death penalty and executed in 1927. Ten years later, Marcantonio published a pamphlet titled *Labor's Martyrs: Haymarket, 1887, Sacco and Vanzetti, 1927*, in which he declared that "Sacco and Vanzetti were legally murdered by the State of Massachusetts. The tragedy of their untimely and cruel death is still an open wound in the hearts of many of us who remember them as shining spirits, as truly great men such as only the lowly of the earth can produce" (Meyer 1989, 14).

In 1925, Marcantonio married social worker Miriam Sanders who helped him learn the way of life outside the Italian neighborhood and to speak "proper" English. Miriam strongly supported his political activities, which began with Alderman Fiorello LaGuardia, whom Marcantonio met while still in high school. LaGuardia became the young man's mentor and father figure, guiding him throughout much of his career in politics; however, in the 1940s, LaGuardia's support cooled as Marcantonio (or Marc as he was known by many) championed the civil rights of communists.

When LaGuardia ran for the U.S. Congress in 1924, Marcantonio organized the campaign in the East Harlem district. Ten years later, LaGuardia left Congress to become mayor of New York City, and Marcantonio campaigned and won election for LaGuardia's congressional seat. Marcantonio served his home district as a member of the newly formed American Labor Party (although he was supported by both Democrats and Republicans) until 1951, with the exception of one term (1936–1938). He lost his congressional office when he vehemently opposed Mussolini and his fascist regime in Italy. People in his district thought their congressman had turned against a fellow Italian, but they later denounced Mussolini and overwhelmingly voted to return Marcantonio to office.

Throughout his years in Congress, Marcantonio focused on a variety of social justice issues. He "defended the right of the unemployed, the nonunionized, the ethnic, religious, and political minority or outcast to speak out, to assemble, to petition for redress of grievances" (Berson 1994, 222). He worked for mine safety,

civil rights legislation, antilynching laws, the abolishment of the poll tax that prevented many blacks in the South from voting, and Puerto Rican independence. Marcantonio also spoke out strongly against the House UnAmerican Activities Committee (HUAC), which became increasingly secretive and aggressive in its investigation of Americans suspected of any type of communist associations and often undermined the civil liberties of U.S. citizens. In short, he was a man of the people and for the people.

In 1939, before the United States entered World War II, Marcantonio harshly criticized U.S. policies, describing them as imperialistic and noting that war preparations would not benefit workers in factories, mines, and mills. The war, he contended, would be waged to protect

> the American dollar and the British pound for the possible extension of our imperialism in South and Central America. You are not going to forever solve the problem of unemployment in America by giving the American unemployed the job of stopping bullets and shrapnel at the front. The American workers want overalls; they do not want soldier's uniforms (Meyer 1989, 57).

Marcantonio opposed war-preparation measures in the U.S. Congress and also spoke out against the Federal Bureau of Investigation (FBI), which was collecting dossiers on U.S. citizens for the HUAC. In Marcantonio's view, the FBI was setting up a Gestapo-like system. He warned congressional members that, if they took away the rights of people they disliked and the rights of dissident minorities, they too would be "engaging in Un-American activities" (Meyer 1989, 58).

Marcantonio was virulently denounced when he voted against U.S. participation in the Korean War—the only congressional member to do so—and when he took a strong stand against Senator Joseph McCarthy's "witch-hunt" for supposedly "disloyal" Americans. His antiwar views and his actions in defense of communists cost him the 1950 congressional election. But at the time, he said it was "best to live one's life with one's conscience rather than . . . accept in silence those things which one believes to be against the interests of one's people and one's nation" (Berson 1994, 224).

In spite of his political defeat, Marcantonio continued to work for civil rights causes. He returned to private law practice and in a celebrated case defended W. E. B. DuBois, one of the founders of the National Association for the Advancement of Colored People (NAACP). The federal government charged DuBois with being a foreign agent because of his support for the Stockholm Peace Appeal, but Marcantonio's pro bono defense won DuBois's acquittal.

Marcantonio also worked on behalf of people in his district, some of whom lived in abject poverty. He helped them get food, medical care, housing, jobs, and assistance in other areas, frequently paying the costs of aid out of his own funds. He was considered a "prince" of his people and planned to run again for his former congressional seat, but he died suddenly of a heart attack in 1954. Thousands mourned his death, and one lifelong friend, Luigi Albarelli, eulogized that Marcantonio's life "was ever dedicated to lighten the load of the people who were in

need." Addressing Marcantonio, Albarelli said, "You lived fearlessly and coura-geously, with affection in your heart for the common man. You were a man of the people and the people loved you" (Meyer 1989, 183).

References:
Berson, Robin Kadison. 1994. *Marching to a Different Drummer: Unrecognized Heroes of American History*. West-port, CT: Greenwood Press.
Meyer, Gerald. 1989. *Vito Marcantonio: Radical Politician 1902–1954*. Albany: State University of New York Press.
Whitman, Alden, ed. 1985. *American Reformers*. New York: H. W. Wilson.

MARIA, MOTHER

(1891–1945)

She was named Lisa Pilenko at birth and, although she grew up within a wealthy aristocratic Russian family, she became a committed political activist and then a nun known as Mother Maria. Her life was dedicated to working with the destitute—people in the slums, prisons, hospitals, and mental asylums. And during World War II she helped Jews and other political refugees escape Hitler's Gestapo, which eventually resulted in her death at Ravensbruck concentration camp.

Born in Anapa near the Red Sea, Pilenko's family moved to Yalta when she was 13 years old. There the family found peasant riots, persecution of Jews, and revolutionary upheaval. Pilenko's father, Yuri Pilenko, became director of Nikit-ski Garden, a vast estate with homes and a school for poor boys, many of whom eagerly adopted the Bolshevik philosophy to gain power from the ruling elite. Pilenko allowed the students to take part in political activities, but this brought censure and wrath from czarist authorities, who instigated a group of thugs called the Black Hundred (similar to the Ku Klux Klan) to set fire to the school one night and beat families as they fled their homes. The Nikitski students were often attacked by the Black Hundred while police looked the other way, and Pilenko attended to badly beaten students who were left to fend for themselves.

Once when her father had to leave on business, she overheard the police chief threaten to search the school for evidence to convict Yuri Pilenko as a revolutionary. Young Pilenko warned teachers, students, and others at the school, who were able to burn any leaflets or other materials that might incriminate them. It was her first act on the side of justice.

Yuri Pilenko moved his family back to Anapa in 1906 but died soon afterward. His wife took her children to St. Petersburg so that they could be well educated in private schools. Young Pilenko became a distinguished poet and later returned to her hometown to become mayor.

Twice married, Pilenko had two children and was pregnant with a third when she had to flee Russia because of the civil war. Poverty stricken, she and her second husband, Danilo Skobtzov, settled in Paris, where Skobtzov found a part-time teaching job. Her third child, Yuri, was born, but not long afterward, her second child died of meningitis. This tragic loss changed her life. She decided to find a way to bring more meaning to her existence and to provide care and protection for people in need.

In Paris, she joined the Russian Christian Student Movement, which included intellectual and theological discussion groups and work among destitute Russian refugees, many of whom were thieves, drunks, or mentally unbalanced. When others warned her about working in the slums, she told them, "There is nothing which can frighten me. I feel these people so close to my heart that even if they do shocking things it does not frighten me. On the contrary—I would like to go to the depths of this life to see if I can help" (Smith 1965, 113).

Increasingly, she felt that this type of work was her calling and stressed its religious nature. Her bishop often talked to her about becoming a nun, but she refused to consider it if it meant giving up her relationship with her son Yuri. After receiving assurance that her son could live with her when possible, and that she would be free to work in the world, she became Mother Maria. Later that year, in 1932, she rented a large two-story house in Paris, converting part of it into a chapel and setting up a soup kitchen and shelter for destitute Russians. She slept on a cot in the basement beside the boiler.

The home became a haven for the poor, who came for soup prepared from leftover produce and other foods she bought from the local marketplace at bargain prices. It was also a place for the intellectuals of Paris to gather, and they often discussed the relation between faith and social action. Eventually, Mother Maria and her colleagues organized Orthodox Action, which raised funds to help the poor and sick. Maria used some of the funds to rent a larger place, a run-down, three-story mansion on rue de Lourmel, which allowed her to increase her outreach and serve more poor people. She also rented another house in Noisy-le-Grand, east of Paris, which became a convalescent home for the elderly and others with no funds for care after a hospital stay.

During World War II, when the Nazis occupied France, Mother Maria continued her usual work with the help of a parish priest, Father Dimitri Klepinin. It soon became clear that Jews and other political refugees were more in need of urgent help than were the local poor. Their efforts were linked to the French Resistance movement, and some members of the movement supplied food for

refugees. In 1943, the Gestapo, which had often searched the Lourmel and Noisy homes, arrested Father Klepinin and later Mother Maria, who was sent to Ravensbruck concentration camp. In spite of terrible deprivation and cruelty at the camp, she often shared scarce food with those in dire need, such as a young girl dying of tuberculosis. She also held discussions about the Russian Orthodox Church, read biblical passages to prisoners, and tried to bolster those who had become numb with despair. She accepted the fact that she would face death and was not afraid of it, and she tried to instill that acceptance in others.

Mother Maria was imprisoned for two years at Ravensbruck, and her health steadily declined. She eventually was slated for the gas chamber. Just a few days before the liberation of the camp, on the night before Easter, 31 March 1945, Mother Maria died. Her ashes, along with those of other prisoners, were scattered on a nearby slope that led to a lake.

References

Hackel, Sergei. 1981. *Pearl of Great Price: The Life of Mother Maria Skobtsova.* Crestwood, NY: St. Vladimir's Seminary Press.

Smith, S. Stratton. 1965. *The Rebel Nun.* Springfield, IL: Templegate.

MARSH, CLINTON

(1916–)

Now a retired pastor with the United Presbyterian Church, USA, Dr. Clinton Marsh was moderator of the church's General Assembly, president of Knoxville College, on the staff of the All-Africa Council of Churches, and interim president of Johnson C. Smith Seminary. In his retirement years, he founded Georgians against Violence to advocate for gun control in his state and has remained active in the Presbyterian Peace Fellowship, Concerned Black Clergy, and Open Door, an organization in Georgia that aids the homeless and those in prison.

Even though Marsh, like many other African Americans growing up in the United States during the early 1900s, lived a life of fear, harassment, and

intimidation, he was able to acquire an education and to become a member of the clergy. He began life in Wilcox County, Alabama, where he lived with his parents, a brother and sister, and his grandparents, both of whom were born into slavery on a plantation just eight miles from Marsh's birthplace. In an interview for the Open Door staff, Marsh pointed out that his life story could not be told without placing it in the context and "climate of racial hatred that has existed since the beginning of this country." In Marsh's view, the founding fathers committed what he described as something akin to "original sin," because

> they belied everything they were saying when they decided they could not tackle the institution of slavery. Here were all of these words and democratic concepts and yet, because the southern part of the country held them hostage by saying they would refuse to come into the Union unless slavery were preserved, the founders bowed the knee to Baal (an idol god). So it was the founding fathers who started this stream of sewage which is such an awful thing today (Marsh 1995).

The legacy of slavery and suppression of blacks were everyday experiences in Marsh's growing-up years. "Wilcox County was one of those places where the worst things you could hear were not as bad as the truth," he stated. "From the time I began to be aware of the nature of my surroundings, I lived in fear every day of my life. You see, I knew that any time my mother would send me to the store I would have to wonder whether I could go there and back without something terrible happening to me." Marsh recalled a time in the late 1920s when a white mob surrounded the jail and demanded the release of an imprisoned black man. The sheriff obliged, and "the mob tied the prisoner behind a pair of mules and rode them around the courthouse until the man was just a bloody pulp. The crowd stood there with their guns, shooting into the corpse as it went by. . . . Maybe you can understand why I grew up in terror" (Marsh 1995).

Because no public schools were open to blacks, Marsh, like his father before him and his siblings, was educated through Presbyterian mission schools. In his words:

> That's the only reason I was freed from the slavery of illiteracy: not because the state of Alabama willed it, but because God willed it through the Church, and many churches did this sort of thing. . . . My father went to those schools and went on to Knoxville College in Tennessee, which was run by the same church. He went back to teach in the mission school, and I was born on one of these mission school campuses (Marsh 1995).

During Marsh's years in Wilcox County, the school he attended received gifts of band instruments from a church in Iowa. One Saturday afternoon, the band presented a free concert in the Camden, Alabama, town square. After the concert, people milled around drinking sodas that a merchant had provided, and the town law officer, known as Jenkins, ordered everyone to clear the walk. Marsh's older brother, who was in the band, was talking to another band member and

did not hear Jenkins's order. His brother responded to the other band member's question with "Uh huh." The law officer hit Marsh's brother on the side of the head, knocking his glasses off, and yelled, "You say 'uh huh' to a white man? I'll teach you how to talk to a white man." According to Marsh:

> My father was in the crowd and he stepped up between them. Jenkins said, "What is it to you ol' man?" then pulled his gun out and shouted, "I'll blow your brains out." The incredible thing is that my father grabbed him by the collar! . . . I think it shocked him so that it just immobilized him. He put his gun in his holster and went on down the street.

The elder Marsh's story of confronting a white man became a legend in Wilcox County and certainly had an influence on his children, but these types of incidents instilled in young Clinton Marsh the concept of "the law" as enemy— "the law" became a pejorative term in his and other blacks' vocabulary. Yet he persevered, and with the constant encouragement of his parents, who helped steer him through the minefield of racial barriers, he was able to graduate from college.

In 1939, with the support of the National Association for the Advancement of Colored People (NAACP) and its chief legal counsel THURGOOD MARSHALL, Marsh was one of six black students who attempted to enroll at the University of Tennessee graduate school. All the students had completed the requirements and had submitted their applications in a timely manner to prevent the school from employing previously used tactics to bar blacks. When the students showed up to register, the university officials herded Marsh and the others into a boardroom and tried to convince them to leave. The students' attorney simply said, "These young gentlemen are citizens of the state of Tennessee. They pay taxes to support this University; their academic credentials are in order, and they just want to register in the school they support." However, that did nothing to convince the school officials. Marsh recalled:

> Finally a red-headed, freckled fellow, who was the business manager, lost his temper and said, "Damn it, you know we can't register these boys. It's against the law." So the attorney said, "Thank you," and we got up and left. He had evidently tipped off the newspeople because they were able to take [a] picture, which showed up on the front page of the *News Sentinel*. The next day I lost my job.

Marsh completed his graduate degree, pastored churches in the South, and became an administrator with his denomination. During the 1960s, he took part in voter registration campaigns, which was no easy task. Even though participants met in black churches to support one another and plan their strategy, "We were afraid," he admitted, pointing out that there easily could have been "massacres" of blacks prompted by the likes of a Sheriff Bull Connor of Birmingham and Sheriff Jim Clark of Selma, Alabama. Having national religious leaders there, many of them white, helped prevent killings, Marsh contended.

Although Marsh felt much anger during his life because of his struggles for justice, he noted that many whites who reached out with love toward him helped him overcome the bitterness. He continues to be a leader in denominational work and in volunteer efforts for peace and justice.

Reference
Marsh, Clinton. 1995. "A Reflection on My Life." Edited by Murphy Davis. *Hospitality*, January/February.

MARSHALL, *THURGOOD*

(1908–1993)

In the numerous eulogies after his death, Thurgood Marshall was hailed as a civil rights pioneer, an uncompromising champion of the underclass, a courageous and brilliant lawyer, a role model and real hero, an agent of change, and certainly one who worked for "Equal Justice under Law," as inscribed above the front entrance to the U.S. Supreme Court building. Even before he became the first African American appointed to the high court, Justice Marshall was well known for the series of school desegregation cases he argued that led to the overturning of *Plessy v. Ferguson*, an infamous case that allowed segregated but equal schools, a practice that the Supreme Court found unconstitutional in 1954.

Marshall was born in the Chesapeake Bay region of Baltimore, Maryland. He was named for his paternal grandfather, Thoroughgood, but by second grade he "got tired of spelling all that and shortened it" (Davis and Clark 1992, 31). Marshall grew up in a loving, protective home with his parents, Norma and William, and his maternal grandmother. He learned early that discrimination and bigoted acts were common practice in the outside world. One of his first fistfights came about because a white man called him "nigger," a racial slur that he had been told by his father never to tolerate. Although similar situations occurred throughout his life, he learned in his teens more practical ways of dealing with racism and often applied a sense of humor that he maintained into his elderly years.

Marshall credited his father with guiding him toward a legal career. William Marshall often read the Constitution, studied court cases, and spent much of his

leisure time attending Baltimore court sessions as a spectator, frequently taking Thurgood with him.

Graduating from high school at the age of 16, Marshall attended all-black Lincoln University in Chester, Pennsylvania, and met Vivian Burey. Marshall and Vivian married in 1929 when they were both 21 years old. After a 25-year marriage that biographers described as devoted and loving, Vivian died of cancer in 1955. In 1956, Marshall married Cecilia Suyat, and the couple had two sons.

Marshall began his legal practice in 1933, serving many poor black Baltimore clients who were unable to pay his fees, and he soon became known as the little

person's lawyer. He also was hired as legal counsel for the Baltimore branch of the National Association for the Advancement of Colored People (NAACP) and helped fight segregation and discrimination in the city, such as defending the rights of black citizens to boycott and picket white store owners who would not hire blacks and winning salaries for black schoolteachers that were equal to those of whites. As his pro bono and NAACP efforts became known, Marshall gained paying clients who helped keep his law practice afloat.

One of his first high-profile civil rights cases was a successful desegregation suit against the University of Maryland in 1936. After that, he decided to devote his full-time legal efforts to equal rights and accepted a position as assistant counsel at NAACP headquarters in New York City. He became chief counsel for the NAACP in 1938 and in 1939 became head of the organization's Legal Defense Fund, which was established to provide legal aid to blacks who were unable to afford the fees. Throughout the 1940s, he argued numerous civil rights cases before the U.S. Supreme Court, including successful suits to gain black voting rights and against housing discrimination. Although he did not argue the famous *Brown v. Board of Education of Topeka*, in which the Court found school segregation unconstitutional, he did lead the team of lawyers who argued four companion cases on school desegregation that were before the Court at the same time.

In 1965, President Lyndon Johnson nominated Marshall as U.S. solicitor general; two years later, he appointed him to the U.S. Supreme Court. Marshall consistently argued for civil rights, criminal justice, prisoner appeals, citizen privacy rights, and the right to abortion. He was unalterably opposed to the death penalty and often pointed out that evidence clearly showed that innocent people had been convicted and executed. Marshall retired in 1991 and turned over his papers to the Library of Congress, with instructions that the library allow public access after his death. When he died two years later, controversy erupted over the publication of some of his documents, but as noted author and columnist Juan Williams explained, Marshall "was continuing his role as the Supreme Court justice who would not let his colleagues forget about the impact of discrimination and poverty as they deliberated on the laws of this land. The release of his papers is another reminder to the justices left behind that people are watching" (Williams 1993).

References

Davis, Michael D., and Hunter R. Clark. 1992. *Thurgood Marshall: Warrior at the Bar, Rebel on the Bench*. New York: Birch Lane Press, Carol Publishing Group.

Weil, Martin, and Stephanie Griffith. 1993. "Marshall Transformed Nation in the Courts." *Washington Post*, 25 January.

Williams, Juan. 1993. "Marshall's Plan: Prod the Living." *Washington Post*, 30 May.

MASIH, IQBAL

(1983–1995)

"Loaned" by his parents to a carpet maker for indentured servitude at the age of four, Iqbal Masih of Pakistan escaped from enslavement and torture when he was ten years old, gained his freedom, and became a human rights activist. His dream was to prevent other Pakistani children from suffering the way he did, and for two years he was able to speak out against forced and brutal child labor. In April 1995, while Masih was riding his bike in front of his grandmother's home in Pakistan, he was shot and killed. Many speculate that the gunman was connected with the carpet manufacturers, but no one has been charged with the murder.

Masih was born in the village of Muridke, Pakistan. When he was 4 years old, his parents were forced to pay off a debt, and for the sum of $12, they turned him over to a carpet manufacturer, with the promise that he could return home periodically. This was not to be the case, however. Like other indentured children (an estimated 7.5 million in Pakistan), he was chained to a carpet loom and forced to work 16 hours a day. Masih and the other children received little food or pay and were often starved, beaten, and tortured. Because of malnourishment and being immobile for hours in front of a loom, Masih did not develop properly, and at the age of 12 he was about the size of a 6-year-old.

In 1992, Masih and several other children were able to escape from the factory to attend a meeting of the Bonded Labour Liberation Front (BLLF), where they learned about their rights. At the gathering, Masih gave an impromptu speech

describing the abuse he had suffered, and afterward, he refused to go back to the factory. Instead, he went to a BLLF lawyer, who wrote Masih's owner a letter declaring the boy's rights under a 1992 Pakistani law prohibiting child labor. Masih was freed, but the anti-child-labor law in Pakistan is seldom enforced, because rich and influential owners of carpet factories are protected by the local police.

Masih, who was an articulate and an eloquent speaker, was able to organize at least 2,000 other bonded children and helped gain the freedom of many. Although his life was threatened because of his activities, he continued to advocate for bonded children, and in 1994, he was invited to speak at an international labor conference in Sweden about the plight of child workers. He also visited the United States, where he was honored with the Reebok Human Rights Youth in Action Award, and he planned to use the $15,000 prize to help him in his quest to become a lawyer so that he could help free other bonded children. During the awards ceremony, Masih reportedly held up a pen and told the audience that he wanted the pen to "replace the instruments [such as carpet needles] that are used to torture young child laborers" (Walsh 1995).

During his time in the United States, he visited the Broad Meadows Middle School in Quincy, Massachusetts, and through an interpreter told about his life, explaining that he toiled from 4:00 A.M. to 7:00 or 8:00 P.M. each day. He shared his dream of having a school in his village so that children could be educated and free. Masih also told about his experiences in the "punishment" room. If his owner disapproved of his work or if he fell asleep, he was sometimes sent to the room, tied with a rope around his knees, and hung upside down. Other children were punished by having their fingers burned with boiling oil. One student, Dan Long, asked Masih whether he had ever been beaten, and Dan reported on a World Wide Web home page:

> He [Masih] said he couldn't even count how many times he was hit. He also said the owners told the carpet children that it was the Americans who ordered them to make rugs. He wondered all those years who are these Americans who make children suffer so much just for rugs. He said he was happy to finally see that Americans are not demons with horns. I was glad to see him smile at our school (Grade 7 Reflections 1994).

Another student reported:

> When he was telling his story, I could not believe that he was still alive after all the beatings he got from the factory owners. I am going to write a letter to the Prime Minister of Pakistan and to President Clinton. I think if enough adults and kids work on this slavery in Pakistan, I think we can stop it (Grade 7 Reflections 1994).

After Masih's visit, the middle-school students went into action. According to a news report, "In the days following Iqbal's visit, the school's 325 students wrote more than 600 letters: 400 to the prime minister of Pakistan, 150 to Massachusetts

Sens. John Kerry (D) and Edward Kennedy (D), and 60 to local carpet stores asking about their policies on selling rugs made by children" (Nifong 1994).

When Iqbal was shot in April 1995, the news so shocked and outraged the students that they were spurred to even further action. They began a major fundraising campaign to collect $5,000 by the end of 1995 to help build a school in Masih's village, spreading word about their efforts through E-mail to classrooms across the United States. With the help of Amnesty International, the students set up a site on the World Wide Web (WWW) called "A Bullet Can't Kill a Dream: A School for Iqbal Campaign," which allowed people worldwide to learn about and contribute to their goal. On their WWW page, the students presented drawings, photographs, articles, and poems, and the lines from one poem titled simply "Iqbal" summarizes the legacy of a brave young person: "A boy is dead/his cause is not" (Pezzula 1995).

References

ABC World News Tonight with Peter Jennings. 1994. "Person of the Week," 9 December.

Associated Press. 1995. "Pakistani March Targets Child Labor." *Boston Globe*, 26 April, National/Foreign section.

Bejder, Eva. 1995. "Students Work To Honor Slain Activist." *USA Today*, 7 June.

Grade 7 Reflections on the 2 December 1994 Visit by Human Rights Hero, Iqbal Masih of Pakistan. http://www.digitalrag.com/mirror/iqbal.html.

Nifong, Christian. 1994. "Making Human Rights Come Alive." *Christian Science Monitor*, 13 December.

Pezzula, Tara. 1995. "Iqbal." *Poems for a Lost Friend*. http://www.digitalrag.com/mirror/iqbal/Poems.

Walsh, Pamela M. 1995. "Slain Pakistani Child Crusader Honored." *Boston Globe*, 30 April.

MEIR, *GOLDA MABOVITCH MYERSON*

(1966–)

"The State of Israel! My eyes filled with tears, and my hands shook. We had done it. We had brought the Jewish state into existence—and I, Golda Mabovitch Myerson, had lived to see the day" (Meir 1975, 226). With these emotional words in her memoirs, Golda Meir pointed out her role in bringing about Israeli independence in 1948, providing a homeland for hundreds of thousands of "displaced" Jews seeking refuge during and after World War II.

Golda Mabowehz (changed to Mabovitch in the United States) was born in Kiev, Russia, into an extremely poor family. Four children in the family died when they were very young—two before they were a year old. Golda was one of three living children. The family was also terrorized whenever pogroms were

initiated against Jews. "I didn't know then, of course, what a pogrom was," Meir wrote, "but I knew it had something to do with being Jewish and with the rabble that used to surge through town, brandishing knives and huge sticks, screaming 'Christ killers' as they looked for the Jews" (Meir 1975, 13).

When Golda was about five years old, the family moved to Pinsk to live with her mother's parents while her father went to the United States to make his fortune. Her older teenage sister, Sheyna, became part of the Labor Zionists, an illegal revolutionary movement that conspired to overthrow the Russian czar and worked to establish a Jewish homeland in Palestine. Sheyna's activities caused great apprehension in Golda's home—they all could have been arrested for being subversives—but Sheyna insisted on working for the cause, which had a profound influence on Golda. She wrote: "I must have begun, when I was about six or seven, to grasp the philosophy that underlay everything that Sheyna did: the right way . . . [she] lived according to the highest principles, whatever the price" (Meir 1975, 26).

Three years later, in 1906, Golda, her two sisters, and her mother sailed for the United States to meet her father in Milwaukee, Wisconsin, where he practiced carpentry. Her mother opened a small grocery in the neighborhood where they lived, and Golda tended the shop during the early-morning hours—a task she bitterly resented—while her mother went to the market to buy produce and other items to sell in the store. When her mother suffered a miscarriage, Golda had to take on the responsibility of the store as well as household chores. Her older sister had become ill with tuberculosis and was in a hospital in Denver, Colorado.

Although she was often late to class and sometimes missed days because of her responsibilities at home, Golda completed elementary school and planned to

go on to high school, but her parents insisted that she go to work and begin look-ing for a husband. Golda rebelled and secretly made arrangements to go live in Denver with her sister, who by then was in better health and had married. For a time, Golda continued her studies but left school to get a job and be on her own. She returned to her parents' home when she was 16, went to high school in Mil-waukee, and kept in touch by mail with an artistic young man in Denver, Mor-ris Myerson, whom she married in 1917.

During her high school years, Golda joined her father in working with World War I relief programs for European Jews and in the Socialist-Zionist movement. The family often hosted visiting speakers, and their home was a gathering place for Zionists, who spent hours discussing the possibility of a homeland in Pales-tine. As a teenager, Golda also gave her first speeches on Zionism at street-cor-ner meetings, and she eventually became a member of the Zionist Party, but not until she "had firmly decided to go to Palestine." She "did not understand how one could be a Zionist and not go to settle in Palestine" (Meir 1973, 31).

In 1921, Golda and her husband immigrated to Palestine, which the League of Nations had placed under the mandate of the British, who were supposed to help improve conditions for the people and pave the way for self-government in the area. The Myersons lived and worked on a desert agricultural kibbutz called Merhavia, which Golda loved but Morris came to hate, especially after he be-came ill with malaria. They eventually moved to Jerusalem, where their two chil-dren were born, but Golda longed to go back to the kibbutz and to dedicate her life to building the Jewish homeland.

The Myersons' marriage began to falter. As Golda explained: "The tragedy was not that Morris didn't understand me, but, on the contrary, that he under-stood me only too well and felt that he couldn't make me over or change me . . . and what I was made it impossible for him to have the sort of wife he wanted and needed" (Meir 1975, 112). He did not try to stop Golda from accepting a de-manding job with the Women's Labor Council, part of the Histradrut that ad-ministered much of the economic and cultural life, with little British interference. She was virtually the only female executive at Histradrut headquarters in Tel Aviv, where she and the two children moved in 1928. Morris, who kept a cleri-cal job in Jerusalem, visited them on weekends. It was the beginning of a sepa-ration that became final ten years later, although the two never divorced and remained good friends until Morris's death in 1951.

For the rest of her life, Golda was deeply involved with and committed to the Zionist cause, traveling extensively in the United States and Europe, speaking at numerous meetings, raising funds, and carrying out her duties in the important posts she held with the World Zionist Organization before and after World War II. She worked desperately to open up Palestine to Jewish refugees fleeing the Nazis during World War II, but a so-called British white paper of 1930 (the Pass-field paper) was in force, which regulated the exact number of Jewish immi-grants allowed into Palestine each month, supposedly to prevent opposition from and armed conflict with Arabs in the region. Thousands of Jews were turned away and forced into refugee camps in other countries. In one instance, a shipload of refugees announced a hunger strike if they were not allowed to

enter Palestine, and Golda convinced more than a dozen Jewish leaders to stage a hunger strike on the refugees' behalf in Jerusalem. Two days later, the refugees entered Palestine.

The conflict with the British was not over, however. A Jewish underground self-defense force known as the *Haganah* carried out numerous activities to bring refugees into Palestine. Golda and both of the Myerson teenagers secretly belonged to this group. The British attempted to stop the immigration on 29 June 1946. On that day, known as the "Black Sabbath," tens of thousands of British soldiers and police raided Jewish kibbutzim, institutions, and homes and jailed more than 3,000 Jews. This was a turning point that strengthened the Jewish determination for independence and for the establishment of a Jewish state, in spite of the fact that Palestine had become an armed camp, with the British an occupying force. Yet, contrary to some factions in the underground and some false impressions worldwide, Golda was against violence. Her son, Menahem, described his mother's worldview as one that

> recoiled from violence. Even at home, when Sarah and I were children, the one taboo consistently and rigorously enforced was against any physical fighting. Not that my mother believed in turning the other cheek or that she was a pacifist. . . . Self-defense, in her eyes, was one of the cardinal tenets of Zionism, and she admired greatly the initiative, resourcefulness, courage and dedication of the Israel Defense Forces. It was murder, kidnapping and mindless collective punishment that she so abhorred (Meir 1983, 90).

After Israeli independence in 1948, Golda became the ambassador to Moscow in the USSR. She was labor minister from 1949 to 1956, then foreign minister for the next decade. She took the Hebrew name Meir (meaning "light-giver") in 1956 and became interim prime minister of Israel after the death of Levi Eshkol in 1969. She was elected to the position later that year, serving until 1974.

Before leaving office, she was forced to rally forces for war—an extension of Arab-Israeli conflicts that had erupted immediately after Israel achieved independence and later in 1967, with the famed Six-Day War. Egyptian and Syrian aggression began on 6 October 1973, on the Jewish holy day of Yom Kippur. Although caught off-guard with inadequate equipment, the Israel Defense Forces prevailed and won the Yom Kippur War, as it became known, but at the cost of 2,500 Israeli lives. A United Nations peacekeeping force was sent in, and a ceasefire agreement was signed by all parties on 11 November 1973.

After the war, the public mood in Israel was bleak, and people appeared to have lost faith in themselves and their government. Many protested Meir's role in not being prepared for war, and she began to feel the draining effects of her responsibilities as well as the side effects of the cancer treatments that only her family and a few close associates knew about. She resigned in 1974 and went home "for good," with the new prime minister, YITZHAK RABIN, in charge. She was not inactive, however. As Menahem Meir wrote:

Like the rest of her life, her retirement was filled with movement and content; abroad she remained in great demand as a speaker; in Israel she was turned to as a mentor and adviser. And most of all, she avidly, knowledgeably followed Sadat's peace overtures with the eagerness, curiosity and enthusiasm of someone whose own most fervent wish was perhaps now finally being fulfilled (Meir 1983, 229).

References

Mann, Peggy. 1971. *Golda: The Life of Israel's Prime Minister*. New York: Coward, McCann & Geoghegan.

Martin, Ralph G. 1988. *Golda, Golda Meir: The Romantic Years*. New York: Charles Scribner's Sons.

Meir, Golda. 1973. *A Land of Our Own: An Oral Autobiography*. Edited by Marie Syrkin. New York: G. P. Putnam's Sons.

———. 1975. *My Life*. New York: G. P. Putnam's Sons.

Meir, Menahem. 1983. *My Mother Golda Meir: A Son's Evocation of Life with Golda Meir*. New York: Arbor House.

Slater, Robert. 1981. *Golda, the Uncrowned Queen of Israel: A Pictoral Biography*. Middle Village, NY: J. David.

Syrkin, Marie. 1963. *Golda Meir: Woman with a Cause*. New York: Putnam.

MENCHU, RIGOBERTA

(1959–)

"I consider this prize not as an award to me personally, but rather as one of the greatest conquests in the struggle for peace, for human rights and for the rights of the indigenous people who . . . [for] 500 years, have been . . . the victims of genocides, repression and discrimination," said Rigoberta Menchu, a Maya Indian activist from Guatemala, when she was awarded the Nobel Peace Prize

in 1992. In awarding the prize, the Nobel committee noted, "Like many other countries in South and Central America, Guatemala has experienced great tension between the descendants of European immigrants and the native Indian population. In the 1970s and 1980s, that tension came to a head in the large-scale repression of Indian peoples. Menchu has come to play an increasingly prominent part as an advocate of native rights" (Farah 1992).

Her prize was controversial, however, because the Guatemalan government considered her a subversive, as did some ultraconservative commentators in the United States, who claimed that Menchu espoused violence and supported leftist rebels in Guatemala. Others, such as Bill Hutchison, who is director of the Marin Interfaith Task Force of Central America, praised the award by pointing out that the prize

> serves to shine a light into what has been for the past two decades one of the Western Hemisphere's black holes—Guatemala. The same violence that took the lives of Menchu's mother, father and brother during the mid-1980s, also took the lives of thousands of other Guatemalans. Using the scorched-earth and "rural pacification" tactics taught to them by U.S. military personnel, a succession of Guatemalan regimes annihilated villages, burned off croplands and drove survivors into refugee camps in southern Mexico (Hutchison 1992).

Menchu has been a consistent champion of human rights, especially indigenous rights, and of social justice, which has brought death threats from those working for dictatorial rulers in Guatemala. Most of the land and power in the country are vested in non-Indians, primarily a mixed-race group known as Ladinos who make up less than 20 percent of the 10 million Guatemalans. Military and paramilitary forces have killed tens of thousands of indigenous people, most of whom were unarmed peasants and men who refused to become part of the so-called voluntary patrols. Nevertheless, Menchu has continued to work for Mayan causes and has used her $1.2 million Nobel prize money to set up the Vincente Menchu Foundation, named for her father, to help finance human rights and development organizations in Guatemala. The U.S. office for the foundation was opened in San Francisco in May 1993.

Menchu was born in a poverty-stricken village in the department of Quiche in Guatemala. The ten children in the family, along with their parents, were migrant workers, picking cotton and coffee on large coastal plantations. Like other workers, the Menchus were treated like farm animals, working from 3:00 A.M. until dark, crowded into open sheds housing more than 500 people, without adequate food and no toilet or sanitation facilities. One of Menchu's brothers died from malnutrition at the age of two, but when her mother took time off to bury the boy, she was taxed for the burial and fired from her job. Another brother died from toxic sprays used on crops in the fields, as did one of Menchu's friends.

These inhumane conditions and the wealthy employers' prejudice toward Indians formed the basis for Menchu's later efforts to seek human rights for her

people. She was also encouraged by a few priests and nuns who, unlike most of the Catholic Church officials in the country, struggled alongside the poor and helped them organize and defend their rights and land.

Because wealthy farmers appropriated land from peasants, many Indians were displaced, forced to move to "model villages," where they were controlled by the military. In some mountain and jungle communities, people refused to leave their land and were "disappeared" or murdered outright. Nevertheless, resistance went on, and the Menchu family was at the forefront. "My father fought for our village's land rights and helped organize a national peasant's organization [United Peasant Committee]," Menchu explained during a 1988 interview while she was in the United States. "He exhausted every legal remedy in his struggles. In 1981 he and other peasant leaders occupied the Spanish Embassy in Guatemala City. The ambassador refused to turn them over to the authorities, so the police burned down the embassy" (Farnsworth 1988).

Just a few months before Menchu's father was burned alive in the embassy, he had been arrested and tortured. Her brother had also been kidnapped by the military forces. His fingers were cut off, and the skin was ripped from his head and face; then he was doused with gasoline and set afire in front of his family, who were forced to watch. Menchu's mother was also captured, raped, tortured—her body cut to pieces—and tied to a tree, where she was guarded until she died from exposure and was left to be ravaged by dogs and maggots.

These atrocities forced Menchu to flee the country in 1981. Because she worked with her parents in the peasants' union, she would certainly have met the same fate as others in her family. Indeed, another brother was killed after she left Guatemala. She noted, "Of my nine brothers and sisters, only three of us are left. It is a miracle that I am alive at all" (Farnsworth 1988).

When she was a teenager, Menchu took a job as a live-in maid in Guatemala City and began teaching herself to read and write Spanish. After she fled Guatemala, she went to live in the poorest section of Mexico City, sharing a home with other Guatemalan refugees and vowing to continue her parents' struggle for the rights of indigenous people. In Mexico, she met Venezuelan writer Elisabeth Burgon-Debray, to whom she told her story. That story was published in 1983 as *I, Rigoberta Menchu: An Indian Woman in Guatemala* and has been translated into 11 languages.

Menchu also traveled to the United Nations and around the United States, speaking to human rights groups and calling attention to the plight of Guatemalan peasants. She was appointed a member of the United Nations Working Group on Indigenous Populations and the International Indian Treaty Council.

Although peace negotiations began in Guatemala in 1991, military and right-wing death squads continued their torture and killing of anyone thought to be connected or related to armed guerrillas known as the Guatemalan National Revolutionary Union, according to reports from human rights organizations. Menchu returned to the country a number of times, especially as peace talks in Guatemala seemed to make more headway and some refugees began to return to their country in 1993.

In early 1995, Menchu initiated a campaign urging indigenous people to try

to make changes through the political system—to register and vote. The task is formidable, since only a small percentage of Indians vote, but Menchu has no intention of giving up. Her life and her work are dedicated to improving the conditions of the impoverished and repressed native population in Guatemala.

References

Bell-Villada, Gene H. 1993. "Why Dinesh D'Souza Has It in for Rigoberta Menchu." *Monthly Review*, May.

Buchsbaum, Herbert. 1993. "Extraordinary People." *Scholastic Update*, 3 December.

Farah, Douglas. 1992. "Indian from Guatemala Wins Nobel Peace Prize." *Washington Post*, 17 October.

Farnsworth, Elizabeth. 1988. "Guatemalan's Viewpoint Hope Exists Despite Little Change in Rights." *San Francisco Chronicle*, 16 November, Briefing section.

Grogan, David. 1992. "Sister Courage." *People Weekly*, 21 December.

Hutchison, Bill. 1992. "Rigoberta Menchu: A Light in Guatemala." *San Francisco Chronicle*, 3 December.

Menchu, Rigoberta. 1984. *I, Rigoberta Menchu: An Indian Woman in Guatemala*. Edited by Elisabeth Burgon-Debray. Translated by Ann Wright. New York: Verso.

MOORE, HOWARD

(1889–1993)

At the time of his death, Howard Moore was 104 years old and then the world's oldest known conscientious objector (CO), resisting both World War I and World War II.

Moore's family was of German ancestry, and he was born in Sing Sing (later called Ossining), New York, where his father, Frank, worked in a foundry. Frank Moore lost his job after a workers' strike for better pay, making it difficult to support his wife and four children. Six-year-old Howard was sent to live with relatives in Cherry Valley, near where the family owned a hops farm. Moore

described the next few years with his uncle and his uncle's family as being "full of the joy of learning." Moore not only learned about hops production and general farm life but also began to develop his views about being his own person and living according to his conscience, although he never accepted a religious doctrine. He attended a rural school and completed the eighth grade, then went to New York at the age of 14 to work for the telephone company.

Moore advanced on the job, and during his early twenties, he continued his education through avid reading and listening to soapbox orators in Madison Square Park, where he heard such speakers as MARGARET SANGER on birth control, EMMA GOLDMAN on anarchism, and many labor organizers. As he explained, "One could hear almost any philosophy, economics, or religion expounded eloquently. I became an eager listener and persistent questioner" (Moore 1993, 87). In addition, Moore visited the headquarters for the Socialist Party, where he listened to such leaders as EUGENE DEBS. He also attended various churches and synagogues where pacifist messages were delivered. Although he never joined any political group and considered himself an agnostic, he developed strong convictions about the futility and evils of violence and war.

When the United States entered World War I, Moore, who was 28 years old at the time, was automatically drafted under the Conscription Act of 1917. His letters of protest to the draft board brought only verbal abuse; he thought about evasion but instead decided to "oppose war openly and take the consequences" (Moore 1993, 95).

Moore was forced into military service, but he refused to wear a uniform and to obey officers. For that, he was thrown out a second-story window of the barracks, which was only the beginning of the brutality that Moore and other COs experienced. He, like other COs who refused to take part in combat or noncombat duties, was court-martialed, imprisoned, beaten, put in solitary confinement, chained to cell bars, and forced to stand for nine hours straight; he was seldom able to sleep or eat because of torments by sadistic prison guards. When another CO asked Moore how he survived without a belief in God, Moore replied: "My own sense of moral responsibility. To accept an authority outside oneself is to deny oneself the right to make an ultimate decision. Understanding that and the consequences to follow is to know freedom in the deepest sense" (Moore 1993, 136).

Moore and other COs were held in prison for two years after the armistice was signed. Released the day before Thanksgiving 1920, Moore returned to the family farm in Cherry Valley, where he stayed for a time. He went on to work with a manufacturing firm as an industrial engineer. During the Great Depression, he became a supervisor with the Works Progress Administration (WPA), then worked again in private industry.

When the United States entered World War II, the federal government required that men between the ages of 45 and 65 register, in case they were needed for military service. Once again, Moore publicly refused to register and sent a letter to the attorney general declaring that his opposition to war was as strong as it had been during World War I:

It is my fervent belief that the resort to force, as a means of settling differ-

ences between nations, is as stupid and immoral as it is futile. . . .

Modern total war cannot be waged without universal military conscription and all its adjunct machinery for the regimentation, enslavement, and exploitation of whole peoples.

Registration is but the first step in the process of such . . . enslavement, and I am therefore compelled by the deepest convictions of my conscience and intelligence to refuse to comply with the law requiring such registration (Moore 1993, 183).

Moore noted that he would wait on his farm for whatever action the government might take. He was ordered to report for the draft, or, in the event he did not comply, he would be required to present himself for arrest. Moore appeared for his arrest in Utica, New York, but was released. He returned to subsistence farming in Cherry Valley until his death in 1993.

References

Meyer, Ernest L. 1930. *Hey! Yellowbacks: The War Diary of a Conscientious Objector*. New York: John Day.

Moore, Howard. 1993. *Plowing My Own Furrow*. Syracuse, NY: Syracuse University Press.

Thomas, Norman. 1923. *The Conscientious Objector in America*. New York: B. W. Huebsch.

MOTHER JONES

See *HARRIS, MARY*

MOTHER MARIA

See *MARIA, MOTHER*

MOTHER TERESA

See *TERESA, MOTHER*

MURROW, *EDWARD R.*

(1908–1965)

E gbert Roscoe Murrow changed his first name to Edward while in college, and "Edward R. Murrow" eventually became the most respected name in the history of broadcast journalism. Murrow was born in rural Polecat Creek, near Greensboro, North Carolina, to a poor, hardworking, Quaker family. Although he later rejected organized religion, Murrow absorbed from his Quaker background a social conscience, a freedom to disagree with the rest of the world, and an uncompromising sense of right and wrong. All of these qualities were applied in his radio and television reporting.

When he was five years old, Murrow's family moved to the state of Washington.  At Washington State College, one of the first colleges in the nation to have its own radio station, Murrow got his first taste of broadcasting. He could not major in broadcast journalism, however, for that was a profession he would help invent years later. In his senior year, his speaking abilities helped him be elected president of the National Student Federation of America (NSFA). After graduating in 1930, he moved to New York and convinced the Columbia Broadcasting System (CBS) that the NSFA could deliver famous people to CBS for interviews. CBS subsequently gave Murrow regularly scheduled "University on the Air" features. In 1935, he became a program director for the CBS radio network.

In the 1930s, radio seldom gave firsthand news reports, and summaries of newspaper accounts read on the air were typical fare. Murrow would change broadcast journalism forever by being the right person in the right place at the right time. When the Nazis invaded Austria in 1938, Murrow happened to be in Poland. Murrow chartered a plane to fly him to Vienna. There, without any journalism background but a natural gift for it, he made live broadcasts from the occupied city—although he refrained from saying anything that would cause the Nazi censor to cut him off the air. This new kind of broadcast, an instant eyewitness report from across the world, became the norm for broadcast journalism.

For most of World War II, Murrow lived in London. There he endured countless air raids from Nazi bombers and made nightly broadcasts during the blackouts. He constantly sought out news in dangerous situations, such as flying on bombing runs over Berlin, and his coolness under fire made him a legend. His broadcasts riveted the people of the United States. When Murrow visited New York in 1941, he received a hero's welcome. He toured the country giving speeches,

but he gave most of the fees to the British War Relief and related charities.

The poet Archibald MacLeish paid Murrow tribute: "You burned the city of London in our houses and we felt the flames that burned it. You laid the dead of London at our doors and we knew that the dead were our dead. . . . [Y]ou have destroyed . . . the superstition that what is done beyond 3,000 miles of water is not really done at all" (Sperber 1986, 204).

At the end of World War II, Murrow returned to live in the United States and helped start radio journalism, then later did the same for television journalism. His popularity, his distinctive low voice, and his appealing physical appearance facilitated his transition from radio personality to television personality. His "See It Now" show began broadcasting in 1951 and was an instant success. Murrow's reputation for seeking out and telling the truth grew weekly.

Murrow's battle with Senator Joseph McCarthy has often been cited as his finest performance. McCarthy's investigation of people who were supposedly sympathetic to the ideals and goals of communism grew out of the spreading "Red scare" of the early 1950s. The senator's blacklist contained names of so-called communists, people who were friends or relatives of "communist sympathizers," or those who had made remarks that were critical of U.S. policies. Because of the general fear of being tainted by association, people on McCarthy's list were often unable to keep or find jobs. The victims could not fight back because no trials were held and no proof was needed to justify the accusations.

Murrow examined McCarthy's methods at a time when other reporters were unwilling to risk their careers on such a controversial topic. Murrow's 9 March 1954 broadcast revealed film of McCarthy ranting, accusing without proof, and bullying witnesses and opponents. Murrow commented: "The line between investigation and persecution is a very fine one, and [McCarthy] has stepped over it repeatedly. . . . We must not confuse dissent with disloyalty. We must remember always that accusation is not proof and that conviction depends upon evidence and due process of law" (Murrow 1967, 247).

CBS offered McCarthy free airtime to respond, and McCarthy did so on 6 April. He called Murrow "the leader and the cleverest of the jackal pack which is always found at the throat of anyone who dares to expose Communist traitors" (Sperber 1986, 449). In this TV appearance, McCarthy proved to be his own worst enemy, and the following weeks showed that Murrow had helped break McCarthy's reign of fear. McCarthy was eventually censured by the Senate and stripped of power.

Many of Murrow's programs caused controversy. Programs on topics such as Robert J. Oppenheimer (critical of the nuclear weapons he had helped create), apartheid in South Africa, the problems of small farmers competing against large agricultural businesses, and the link between cigarettes and cancer (Murrow himself was a chain smoker) all aroused protests. Murrow was attacked by newspapers, other broadcasters, politicians, and sponsors. He also had conflicts with Frank Stanton, the president of CBS. Stanton thought that television reporting should bring in viewers, but Murrow believed that reporting should explore controversy.

With rising complaints about his shows and declining revenues, CBS put

Murrow on the air less frequently. After a run of seven years, controversy over a program addressing statehood for the territories of Alaska and Hawaii finally caused the show's cancellation. Murrow was relegated to the role of an occasional reporter for CBS. However, he was able to make one final major contribution, "Harvest of Shame," a classic 1960 documentary on the plight of migrant workers, who, in Murrow's words, worked in the "sweat shops of the soil" (Vonier 1989, 54).

Murrow was appalled at the trivial nature of most television programs. He wanted the biggest advertisers to contribute to public-affairs programs, warning:

> If we go on as we are, then history will take its revenge. . . . This instrument can teach, it can illuminate; yes, and it can even inspire. But it can do so only to the extent that humans are determined to use it to those ends. Otherwise it is merely wires and lights in a box (Sperber 1986, 52).

In 1961, President John F. Kennedy appointed Murrow director of the U.S. Information Agency. The agency's purpose was to communicate information about the United States to the world, to inform the government about foreign opinion regarding the United States, and to arrange cultural and educational exchanges with foreign countries. Murrow's appointment boosted the morale of the department, which had been plagued by problems of identity, bureaucracy, and politics. Shortly after Kennedy's assassination, Murrow had to resign his position for health reasons. He had contracted lung cancer and died two years later.

In his lifetime, Murrow did more than 5,000 radio and television broadcasts. Decades later, journalism students still listen to his tapes, read his transcripts, and study his television programs. Journalist Theodore White said: "Murrow bequeathed a sense of conscience and importance with which neither management nor government might interfere. . . . [He] left behind a tradition that the reporting of the news . . . was to be what its correspondents and producers wanted it to be, not what management sought to make it" (Sperber 1986, xi).

References:

Levy, Elizabeth. 1975. *By-Lines: Profiles in Investigative Journalism*. New York: Four Winds Press.

Murrow, Edward R. 1967. *In Search of Light: The Broadcasts of Edward R. Murrow, 1938–1961*. Edited by Edward Bliss, Jr. New York: Alfred A. Knopf.

Sperber, A. M. 1986. *Murrow: His Life and Times*. New York: Freundlich Books.

Vonier, Sprague. 1989. *Edward R. Murrow*. Milwaukee, WI: Gareth Stevens Children's Books.

N

NADER, RALPH

(1934–)

Ralph Nader is a lawyer who has probably done more to protect consumers from defective products than anyone else in U.S. history.

Nader's parents emigrated from Lebanon in 1912 and settled in the small Connecticut town of Winsted, where they established a restaurant and bakery. The Naders were Greek Orthodox Catholics, but in Winsted, they attended a Methodist Sunday school. They were always politically outspoken, and nightly political discussions took place around the family dinner table. Nader's father, who was "perpetually angry over injustice," believed that citizens owed a debt to society that they must freely repay by working to make life better for everyone (McCarry 1972, 36).

As a quiet, studious boy, Ralph had an early interest in law. He could often be found in the town hall, listening to lawyers argue cases. His "literature" of choice

was the *Congressional Record*, the daily proceedings of Congress. At Princeton University, he blossomed as an activist. He battled conformist clothing by once going to class in a bathrobe and waged an unsuccessful campaign to prevent the campus trees from being sprayed with the pesticide DDT. While at Harvard Law School, he became interested in auto safety. Studying auto injury cases, he became convinced that driver error was unfairly emphasized and unsafe vehicle design ignored.

After attaining a law degree in 1958, Nader began a David-and-Goliath battle with the automotive industry to force safety design changes, such as adding seat belts, collapsible steering columns, and padded dashes. (The auto industry had, until that time, often demeaned such items.) Nader campaigned for safety through magazine articles, in speeches to civic groups, and in testimony before governmental bodies. His best-selling 1965 book *Unsafe at Any Speed: The Designed-In Dangers of the American Automobile* was an indictment of Detroit's emphasis on profits and styling over safety. Although Congress was already contemplating auto safety legislation, the publicity and information that Nader generated assured passage of the National Traffic and Motor Vehicle Safety Act of 1966. Until that time, the auto industry had been free from safety regulation. Nader helped change that forever.

While he was working on auto safety, Nader was subjected to harassment from General Motors (GM). The company hired a private detective to investigate Nader, and the detective apparently made harassing phone calls to Nader and hired women who attempted to lure Nader into compromising situations. Nader complained and sued GM for invasion of privacy. GM President James Roche denied the charges at first, but before a congressional subcommittee, he apologized to Nader for some of the actions. GM also paid a $425,000 settlement that Nader used to fund further political activism.

The image of one man successfully battling the world's biggest corporation—reforming the auto industry and winning a public apology and cash settlement from GM—made Nader a folk hero. Nader became a symbol for uncompromising integrity, self-sacrifice for the common good, and the power of the individual to change society.

Having won an initial victory for auto safety, Nader turned his attention to other threats. His advocacy helped in the passage of the Freedom of Information Act of 1966, the Wholesome Meat Act of 1967, and dozens of other consumer protection laws.

In 1968, Nader set up his first task force, composed of volunteer law students, to investigate the inefficiencies of the Federal Trade Commission (FTC). Its report, released in 1969, eventually triggered a major revamping of FTC headquarters and its field offices. Because of this success, thousands of idealistic students wanted to work for Nader, and Nader began hiring dedicated young people to amplify his efforts. Nader's task forces were soon turning out explosive reports. "By naming names and providing meticulous documentation, the Nader study groups made for hot copy. The spectacle of greenhorn students exposing one instance after another of government footdragging, special-interest collusion, corporate malfeasance and outright corruption made the reports all the more compelling" (Bollier 1989, 7). Journalist William Greider, then a reporter for the *Washington Post*, dubbed the investigative teams "Nader's Raiders."

Needing a more permanent base of operations, Nader launched his Center for Study of Responsive Law. At the center, young lawyers worked long hours for low pay to help correct injustices. One journalist described work at the center as "a cross between a political campaign headquarters and a college fraternity house" (Bollier 1989, 6).

Nader started dozens of other public-interest organizations on such topics as consumer health, product safety, and environmental concerns. Nader said, "I like to think of myself as a Johnny Appleseed, getting consumer groups started and letting them grow on their own" (Bollier 1989, 86).

Corporate greed and indifference angered Nader, but he said that to be a "Raider" one must control the outrage, not suppress it. "Your outrage must be considered fuel that doesn't quite surface, but must be the metabolism of your energy. But don't spill it out until you're behind that typewriter, white-hot, putting out that memo of that final product" (Peduzzi 1990, 25).

Nader gained a reputation for the passion and accuracy of his reports, reflecting his stern moral convictions and encyclopedic memory. This intensely private man, working 18-hour days, seven days a week, had no social life. Work was his life, his total passion. He shunned personal glory or comfort and lived a lifestyle of legendary frugality. Since he believed that corporations were basically ruthless and motivated by profit rather than human values, "in his own life he rejected all the things that corporations produced: he owned no machines, ate no processed foods, and shunned money" (McCarry 1972, 21). "Reporters have tended to dismiss Nader's habits as eccentricities and have been reluctant to come to grips with the values that inform them," commented one journalist.

"Here was a man who lived in a rooming house, owned no car, and kept his material wants to a minimum so he could do the work he really cared about" (Rowe 1989).

With his strident advocacy for consumers, it is no surprise that Nader has made enemies in corporate America, and even consumers were not fond of hearing that their comfortable lifestyles supported wastefulness and pollution. Nader's critics called him an egotistical, paranoid, presumptuous, arrogant, fascist Don Quixote sparring with windmills.

Less was heard from Nader in the 1980s than in the previous two decades. In the late 1980s, he was stricken with Bell's palsy. The disease paralyzed the right side of his face, making talking and eating difficult. He was forced to slow down his grueling schedule, and he kept out of the public eye until he recovered. Another factor in the decreased press coverage was the change in the political climate. President Ronald Reagan rode the crest of the backlash against governmental regulations. Forgetting that national standards had reduced a multitude of hazards to people and the environment, the Reagan administration saw regulations as excessive red tape that strangled business and hurt the economy. A 1990 British *Economist* editorial, describing the shifting political winds that Nader faced, summarized the situation in these words: "In the 1980s Mr. Nader's microscopic fault-finding was out of favour, at least on the national stage. . . . During the past ten years Mr. Nader's Darth Vader view of corporate America was shunted aside as people scrambled for the loose change dropped by Reaganism."

In the 1990s, American attitudes shifted again, and Nader was more influential than ever. "He has a large organisation, Paul Newman–like name recognition and a reputation that most politicians might commit serious crime to possess. To many, Mr. Nader is just what the *New Republic* once called him: 'Saint Ralph'" ("Spreading Saint Ralph's Gospel" 1990).

References

Bollier, David. 1989. *Citizen Action and Other Big Ideas: A History of Ralph Nader and the Modern Consumer Movement*. Washington, DC: Center for Study of Responsive Law.

McCarry, Charles. 1972. *Citizen Nader*. New York: Signet.

Peduzzi, Kelli. 1990. *Ralph Nader*. Milwaukee, WI: Gareth Stevens Children's Books.

Rowe, Jonathan. 1989. "Ralph Nader Reconsidered." *Washington Monthly*, February.

"Spreading Saint Ralph's Gospel." 1990. *Economist*, 17 November.

NASRIN, *TASLIMA*

(1962–)

Taslima Nasrin had written ten books before *Lajja*, which means "shame." Although all her books have dealt with social issues, it was the eleventh one that caused Bangladesh's Islamic fundamentalist group to call for her death. The book was written after Hindu fundamentalists destroyed an Islamic mosque in northern India. In the rioting between Hindus and Muslims that followed, many people were killed. In Bangladesh, where Muslims are the majority, Hindu homes, shops, and temples were burned. Nasrin's novel follows one Hindu family during this violent period. Banned in Bangladesh, the novel was interpreted by Muslim fundamentalists as sympathetic to Hindus. Nasrin believes that fundamentalism, regardless of the religion, is the problem:

> In this book I have accused all fundamentalists of all countries who, in the name of one religion, persecute members of another. "Shame," in fact, is shame to our country, shame to our government, shame to our society, shame to myself. For we have all deviated from our national ideal. We have all deviated from the humanism of man. . . . I believe that, like all other types of obscurantism, religious fundamentalism is evil (Nasrin 1994).

As the fever of Muslim fundamentalism was reaching its peak against Nasrin, she was interviewed by two journalists in Calcutta. One journalist wrote that Nasrin was calling for a revision of the Koran. Because the Koran is believed to be the literal word of God, this so incensed Muslim fundamentalists that "Dhaka experienced an astonishing escalation of violent protests, bombings, and clashes between Islamic militants and secularists" (Walsh 1994, 26–27). However, Nasrin insists that she never said that the Koran should be rewritten; this was corroborated by the second journalist present, who agreed that Nasrin had been misquoted.

Under pressure from Muslim fundamentalists, a Bangladeshi court issued a warrant for Nasrin, charging her with violating a code that forbids "deliberate and malicious acts intended to outrage religious feelings . . . by insulting religion or religious beliefs" (Edwards 1994). In response to the court order, the author went into hiding. After some months, Nasrin surrendered. She was released on bail and allowed to leave the country.

Nasrin's childhood memories are perhaps more violent than the unrest she has seen as an adult novelist. When she was nine, the revolt in former East Pakistan resulted in the creation of Bangladesh. "My childhood memories are full of this war and painful, bloody birth of the new nation. And since then, I have dedicated myself to the political ideal of a sovereign Bangladesh" (Nasrin 1994).

Although she wrote poetry as a child, Nasrin did not expect to be a writer. As she got older, she noticed more and more differences between the way she and

her brother were raised. Their father, a doctor, inspired Nasrin to study medicine. Her study, combined with her father's devotion to logic, made her begin to question everything around her—in particular, the exploitation, malnutrition, ignorance, and fear of many of her female patients.

Despite her work as a physician, Nasrin found time to write. For five years, she wrote columns in Bangladeshi daily newspapers that challenged Islamic fundamentalism. One aspect of her novels that fundamentalists have criticized is the ease with which Nasrin writes about sex. Although she has been accused of immorality, the author says, "I am not in favor of free sex or adultery. What I demand is freedom of sex from the clutches of male domination. The woman should have an equal right to choose her partner" (Bhattacharya 1994). Particularly abhorrent to Nasrin is the male privilege of divorcing his wife if he tires of her. Nasrin has consistently advocated civil rights for women and believes that "it is not possible to change a woman's destiny by accepting the confines of scriptures [and] . . . nothing much will be achieved by reforming scriptural tenets. I want a uniform civil code which is equally applicable to men and women" (Nasrin 1994).

In her conservative culture, Nasrin's personal life further alienated her from liberal sympathizers who share her convictions and might otherwise have come to her defense. By the age of 31, she had been married and divorced three times. Her writing is seen as sensationalistic, and the sight of her short haircut is a visible reminder that Nasrin will not be bound by tradition.

In 1991, Nasrin was awarded a significant Bengali literary prize from Calcutta. Although this was quite an honor for the author, the Bangladeshi papers mentioned it only briefly on the back page, because they were afraid of offending the literary community, which is largely male.

Despite her persecution, Nasrin said in her speech to the International Student Festival in 1994:

> I promise before you that I shall continue my fight for women's freedom, women's liberation, women's progress and development. I do not know how poetic my poetry is, how good my prose, how novel-like my novel. What I know is that I have not written just with my pen; I have wrung my heart into my words. I do not know if my words will reach the hearts of others. I know this and only this: that the dumb women of my country know that I have written for them. Dumb, mute women whose hearts break but whose lips do not form words (Nasrin 1994).

References

Baker, Deborah. 1994. "Exiled Feminist Writer Tells Her Own Story." *New York Times*, 28 August.

Bhattacharya, Pallab. 1994. "A Rushdie in Bangladesh." *World Press Review*, January.

Edwards, Frederick. 1994. "International Humanism: In Defense of Taslima Nasrin." *Humanist*, September/October.

Nasrin, Taslima. 1994. Speech given at the International Student Festival (ISFiT-94), Trondheim, Norway.

Walsh, James. 1994. "Death to the Author." *Time*, 15 August.

NORMAN, MILDRED

(1908–1981)

S eldom did the millions who met her know her real name. Mildred Norman took the name Peace Pilgrim in 1953 and used that appellation for almost three decades as she walked throughout the United States and into Mexico and Canada on a pilgrimage for peace.

Peace Pilgrim began her life on a small farm in New Jersey. She received no religious training, entering a church for the first time at age 16 to attend a wedding. However, as a high school student in Egg Harbor, New Jersey, she often questioned the nature of God and learned to practice the Golden Rule: do unto others as you would have them do unto you. During her young adulthood, she tried to subscribe to the common notion that to be successful she had to take her share of the world's goods, but she knew that this conflicted with her early childhood training to be generous and unselfish. Although she was financially successful, a turning point came when she sought a "meaningful way of life" by "walking all night through the woods." Prayer and a religious experience helped her decide to dedicate her life to service. From then on, she knew that her life work would be for peace and that it would cover the whole peace picture: peace among nations, peace among groups, peace among individuals, and the all-important inner peace.

In 1952, Peace Pilgrim made plans to begin her journey, saying, "I realized . . . that this was the proper time for a pilgrim to step forth. The war in Korea was raging and the McCarthy era was at its height. It was a time when congressional committees considered people guilty until they could prove their innocence. There was a great fear at that time and it was safest to be apathetic" (Friends of Peace Pilgrim 1991, 1, 5, 7).

She began her pilgrimage in January 1953, vowing to wander until humankind had learned the way of peace. In those early years, few knew who she

was, but she usually received food and shelter from strangers along the way. When no one took her in, she slept in wheat fields, haystacks, cemeteries, and drainage ditches, under bridges and by roadsides. Although many people thought that she subjected herself to dangerous situations, she believed that they were tests. According to one news account:

> She was arrested twice for vagrancy, but found behind bars a receptive audience for her philosophy and songs. Once a disturbed teen-age boy, set off by a thunderstorm, began to beat her, but Norman said she was able to contact "the spark of good" in him, and avoided serious harm (Japenga 1986).

By 1964, Peace Pilgrim had walked 25,000 miles alone, without funds, and with only a few personal possessions—a toothbrush, comb, ballpoint pen, and current correspondence—which she carried in the pockets of her navy blue tunic. She talked to thousands of people from all walks of life and was interviewed by radio, TV, and newspaper reporters, always presenting her vision of peace. As many who listened to her pointed out, Peace Pilgrim's message was not new. She simply restated ancient truths, urging people to aspire for inner peace and to work for world peace.

Because she was invited to speak in so many different places, Peace Pilgrim began to accept rides to various locations. She flew to Hawaii and Alaska, for example, walking in those states and speaking to small groups and the media. She also walked in ten Canadian provinces and parts of Mexico. On 7 July 1981, Peace Pilgrim was being driven to a speaking engagement in Indiana. Near the small town of Knox, the car was involved in a head-on collision, and Peace Pilgrom was killed instantly. For months after her death, friends of Peace Pilgrim compiled her words from her booklet *Steps toward Inner Peace*, her newsletters, personal correspondence, and audiotapes of her talks and interviews.

References

Friends of Peace Pilgrim, comps. 1991. *Peace Pilgrim: Her Life and Work in Her Own Words*. Santa Fe, NM: Ocean Tree Books.

Japenga, Ann. 1986. "Peace Pilgrim's Journey—'On Foot and in Faith.'" *Los Angeles Times*, 2 January.

"Peace Pilgrim." 1994. *Backpacker*, September.

O

O'NEAL, JOHN

(1940–)

Actor John O'Neal has been called "a keeper of the civil rights era's original flame" and a master of "folkeloquence." A founding member of the Free Southern Theater, O'Neal traveled throughout Mississippi and other parts of the South during the 1960s, dramatizing the struggles of blacks to achieve voting and other civil rights and to end segregation. He also was field secretary of the Student Nonviolent Coordinating Committee (SNCC).

O'Neal had never planned to be a civil rights activist. The eldest of three children, he was reared by his parents—both teachers—in Mound City, a small town in southern Illinois. The family lived in an all-black neighborhood, and O'Neal and his brother and sister attended a segregated school. When the U.S. Supreme Court ruled in 1954 that segregation in public schools was unconstitutional, O'Neal expected to enter an integrated high school. However, that did not happen, and it was not until he graduated three years later and entered Southern Illinois University at Carbondale, 60 miles north of his hometown, that he had any real contact with whites. During his years in college, O'Neal became interested in theater, and after earning his degree, he hoped to go to New York City to write and produce plays. He also learned about the fledgling civil rights movement in the South and admired the work and courage of Reverend MARTIN LUTHER KING, JR. King's words and deeds helped O'Neal develop his own religious beliefs, and the concept of nonviolence became his way of life.

Several months before his college graduation, O'Neal joined the SNCC and directed numerous nonviolent demonstrations in Cairo, Illinois, where public places such as swimming pools and roller-skating rinks were segregated and often closed down when integrated groups tried to gain admittance. At one Cairo demonstration, the SNCC group was attacked with chains, bats, clubs, and knives. After graduation, O'Neal went to work full time for the SNCC in the South. At that time, he also made another major life decision. He was eligible for the draft, but because he was opposed to war on religious grounds, he registered as a conscientious objector (CO).

While working with the SNCC, O'Neal met Gil Moses, editor of the *Mississippi Free Press*, and the two developed and initiated their plan for the Free Southern Theater (FST). The folk theater brought *In White America*, a play about blacks from slave days to the current century, to Mississippi audiences that had never seen a "real live play." That drama, in which O'Neal played a leading role, and other plays performed later helped stir blacks to become involved in political action and the civil rights movement.

Meantime, O'Neal's CO registration had been rejected by the draft board, and he was arrested by the FBI for draft evasion on the evening of a performance. During the trial in October 1965, the judge recognized O'Neal's legal right to CO status and allowed him to perform substitute nonmilitary service in a hospital.

Although the FST continued to operate, by 1980, interest in it and in the civil rights movement had dwindled, and O'Neal decided to dramatize the sad state

of both. He staged a "funeral" in the streets of New Orleans, with a marching jazz band and a coffin rolling along the streets with the words "Free Southern Theater" emblazoned on it.

O'Neal has carried on in the FST spirit as a solo performer under the name Junebug Productions. He puts together real and fictional tales of black folklore, drawing from oral histories of former slaves and their descendants, many of which were recorded during the depression by the Works Progress Administration (WPA). O'Neal chose the name Junebug for his dramatic persona, a character who tells stories, such as a coming-of-age journey based on his own life from his growing-up years to the infamous 1968 Democratic National Convention in Chicago. O'Neal, dressed in Bojangles-style clothes, performs on an almost bare stage. He travels most of the year but also teaches playwriting at Cornell University in New York. "I deal in the lessons of history, showing the patterns of mistakes in each generation of the civil rights movement. I think there'll be another broad movement someday," he told a news reporter (Hulbert 1989).

In the 1990s, O'Neal became involved in the movement to call attention to and eradicate environmental racism, a term that describes various practices in which pollutants adversely affect more people of color and the poor than mainstream Americans. O'Neal has been working with Pat Bryant of the Gulf Coast Tenants Association, a community service organization based in New Orleans, Louisiana. The tenants association has been heavily involved in efforts to stop the degradation in St. Charles Parish, which is in the heart of "cancer alley," the 85-mile stretch from Baton Rouge to New Orleans, where at least one-fourth of the nation's petrochemical industries are located. O'Neal and Bryant have helped lay the groundwork for a 1997 New Orleans festival that will focus on environmental racism, with performances created by arts organizations and community groups.

References

Hulbert, Dan. 1989. "Storyteller Brings Civil Rights History to Life through Tales of 'Junebug Jabbo Jones.'" *Atlanta Constitution*, 19 January.

Ocean, Tom. 1969. *Three Who Dared*. New York: Doubleday.

OSBORN, JOHN

(1956–)

"I do two things. I do medicine and I do conservation." That is how Dr. John Osborn of Spokane, Washington, describes himself, explaining that his efforts to preserve national forests are related to one of the principles of the American Medical Association's Code of Ethics: "A physician shall recognize a responsibility to participate in activities contributing to an improved community."

In Osborn's view, community can be as broad as the world or as scaled down as a small timber town. Although some loggers and millworkers hold Osborn in disdain because they believe that he has contributed to job losses in the timber industry, others are among his patients, and Osborn told a reporter that he cares "very much what happens both to my patients and the forests, and to the communities that depend on those forests." He is convinced that the practices of major timber companies will destroy the natural resource on which many logging families depend (Titone 1991).

The middle child of five, Osborn spent his childhood in Bellingham, Washington, and Boise, Idaho, where his father, an IBM executive, took him and his two brothers on hiking, bird-watching, and fishing trips. He often fished trout streams in northern Idaho.

While attending the College of Idaho in Caldwell, Osborn paid for his education by working for the U.S. Forest Service, cleaning up roadside debris and outhouses and fighting forest fires. During his residency at the University of Washington Medical School in Spokane, he continued to work for the Forest Service but became convinced that the agency had moved away from its original purpose to conserve U.S. forests and had betrayed its trust by allowing large timber companies to destroy public forestlands. He also became disillusioned when he returned to Idaho to find that the trout had disappeared because the streams had become polluted with sediment washed down from logging roads bulldozed through the forests and by the practice of clear-cutting (cutting down huge areas of timber).

Now a physician at the Veterans Hospital in Spokane, Washington, Osborn supervises the hospital's nursing home and also an AIDS program that he created for veterans in their twenties and thirties. In 1983, he joined an area conservation group and the following year went to Washington, D.C., to testify before a congressional committee holding hearings on wilderness issues. Today, he is executive director of the Inland Empire Public Lands Council, an organization of sports enthusiasts, environmentalists, and conservationists. The group has publicized and fought major timber companies that liquidate their own forests,

export logs, then use the profits to buy timber in national forests, which squeezes small mills out of business.

Living modestly in a bachelor apartment near the Spokane Veterans Hospital, Osborn has spent years studying what he believes is at the root of forest problems: the Northern Pacific land grant. Under that 1864 act, Congress granted the Northern Pacific Railroad 40 million acres of forestland as an incentive for the railroad to construct a rail line from Minnesota to the Pacific Ocean. The act required Northern Pacific to auction off lands if the company failed, which happened twice. During the 1890s, James J. Hill bought Northern Pacific and the forestlands the company controlled.

Another provision of the law required that lands be open to homesteaders once the rail line was completed, but that provision was never honored, Osborn contends. Much of Northern Pacific's acreage was sold to entrepreneurs, who developed major timber empires in the Northwest, including Weyerhaeuser, Plum Creek Timber, Potlatch, and Boise Cascade. In Osborn's view, Northern Pacific violated the conditions that Congress imposed when it approved the land grant, a charge that the federal government made decades ago but has been unable to prove in court. Nevertheless, Osborn and the Inland Empire Public Lands Council believe that "fraud and corruption" are the foundation of corporate timber empires, which today are trying to grab timber from national forests by pressuring for congressional action to gut environmental laws (Laszewski 1995).

Osborn has spent much of his own money, driven tens of thousands of miles to attend conservation meetings, and given countless hours for the conservation of national forestland, while maintaining his medical practice. To him, conservation work "is like caring for someone you love and trying still to be objective in your diagnosis and treatment" (Titone 1991). He continues his campaign even though he is opposed by multimillion-dollar corporations and is frequently harassed by logging groups who believe that he threatens their livelihood. He sometimes despairs when he looks at denuded timberland—common in many parts of the Northwest—but he believes that it is his duty, as a matter of conscience, to go on educating people about environmental conservation.

References

Koberstein, Paul. 1990. "Spokane Doctor Wages Own War of the Woods." *Oregonian*, 17 September.

Laszewski, Charles. 1995. "Hill's Land Deals Unlawful, Environmentalists Say." *St. Paul Pioneer Press*, 26 May.

Pryne, Eric. 1994. "Could the Federal Government Take Back 1864 Land Grant?" *Seattle Times*, 13 November.

Titone, Julie. 1991. "Suffering the Enviro-Doc." *American Forests*, September/October.

OWENS, JESSE

(1913–1980)

He loved to run. Even as a sickly boy living with his sharecropper parents in Oakville, Alabama, running was a favorite, freeing activity for James Cleveland Owens. J.C., as he was nicknamed, had almost died several times before his sixth birthday. A weak constitution, recurring boils, and extended bouts of pneumonia were the hard facts of life for this tenth and last child of Henry and Mary Owens, but his mother and father, the son of a former slave, would not give up on their son. Their care and prayers saw him through some very trying episodes.

When Owens was about nine, his mother decided that the family should move to the urban North to increase their opportunities and leave behind the grinding poverty that had been their lot since birth. An elder daughter sent word from Cleveland that she was making more money than she had ever imagined possible. Mary Owens was convinced. She sold the family cow, purchased train tickets for Ohio, and moved her brood into the eastside Cleveland ghetto.

All the members of this industrious family found work in short order, and they were soon better off financially than they had ever been. Young Jesse (a teacher had misunderstood the boy's southern pronunciation of his nickname and had written out the name, which stayed with him) even found part-time work after school when he was not sick in bed with yet another bout of pneumonia. The weakness of his lungs was still pronounced, and it seemed that he was going to be ill more often than not the rest of his life, but then Owens met Charles Riley.

Riley was the track coach at Fairmont Junior High School, and he approached Owens with the idea of training to compete in track and field. He had seen some potential in the boy as he observed him in gym classes over the years. Since Owens had to work after school, Riley agreed to meet him every day at sunrise so that he could get his training in. Owens became obsessed with the idea of becoming a great runner. The workouts eventually built up the capacity of his lungs, and soon he was much healthier. It also became apparent to Riley that his young charge might actually become the fastest runner in the world someday, if he was willing to work. The two dedicated themselves to making certain that the dream would come true.

Owens was a sensation as a runner, almost from the beginning of his career, and Riley agreed to assist the high school athletic program so that he could continue to coach the runner at that level. When the Great Depression hit, Owens was ready to quit school and end his training so that he could help support the family. His mother, working for a pittance doing laundry, would hear none of it. She told him to continue toward his goal. The work paid off, and by the time Owens enrolled at Ohio State University, he held world records in track and field.

Jesse Owens catapults himself to a new long jump record at the 1936 Olympics held in Berlin. Winning four gold medals, Owens spoke out against the racism of Hitler's Third Reich.

His tenure at Ohio State was marked by great success on the track and a few setbacks off. He had to work hard to keep up academically (books had never been his long suit), and he had to lobby to retain his amateur status when the Amateur Athletic Union (AAU) accused him of accepting $159 as a payoff in conjunction with a summer job as an Ohio legislative page. At this time, he also acknowledged that he was the father of Ruth Solomon's child, and he and Ruth were married. In spite of all these distractions, he continued to train hard and

win accolades as his greatest moment approached. In the summer of 1936, he went to Germany to compete in the eleventh Olympiad.

During those few days in Germany, a legend was made. Intense expectations and hopes were riding on the 20-year-old Owens as he stepped onto the track for his first event, the 100-meter sprint. Adolf Hitler had arranged these Olympic Games in Germany to showcase the great progress made by the Third Reich—a regime that considered anyone who was not Aryan of "inferior" stock. Jews, Gypsies, and nonwhites were treated as subhuman in their system. Months before the games, however, Owens had made it clear that he thought the U.S. team should withdraw from competition if there was discrimination against minorities.

Hitler expected to demonstrate the correctness of his view when his Aryan athletes dominated the games, but Owens knew that his job was to do his best against the other athletes assembled on the field of competition. Owens easily won the race and the hearts of the German people. Everywhere he went, he was pressed for autographs, handshakes, and conversation. When he and the German hero Luz Long competed in the long jump, urging each other on to greater distances with each round, the world was treated to a scene of pure competition between two superb athletes. Because of the humanity displayed by the two participants, it was no longer a test of Aryan against black ability; it was sport raised to epic proportions. Owens set a new record when he finally prevailed in the event, and Long was the first to congratulate him with a great bear hug.

Owens became perhaps the most famous athlete in the world after the games, in which he won a record four gold medals. In 1950, he was named the greatest athlete of the century by the Associated Press, but being a superstar had its negative side. The Federal Bureau of Investigation was busy compiling information about Americans who might be communist sympathizers, and it developed a file on Owens. Although the information gathered showed that he was assessed by many as a loyal American and goodwill ambassador for the United States, he was also characterized accurately as a womanizer and a poor money manager.

Owens made a great deal of money, much of which he gave away to charitable causes, particularly youth programs, but he failed to file tax returns or pay federal income taxes for eight years, federal offenses for which he was indicted by the Internal Revenue Service in 1965. He was fined but was not sentenced to jail because the judge took into consideration Owens's charitable work.

Owens also faced other problems. His conservative political views often brought him into conflict with more militant black leaders of the civil rights movement of the 1960s and 1970s. He publicly criticized the black athletes who attempted to boycott the 1968 Olympics in Mexico City and the black medal winners who raised their fists in defiance and protest against discrimination in the United States.

Owens continued in his later years to inspire athletes, especially black youth, to be disciplined, work hard, and strive for success. He was constantly on the road, delivering speeches and raising funds for youth and civic causes, as well

as being an unabashed supporter of U.S. patriotism. He insisted to the end of his life in 1980 that "in America, anyone can become somebody" (Baker 1986, 237).

References

Baker, William J. 1986. *Jesse Owens: An American Life*. New York: Free Press.

Gentry, Tony. 1990. *Jesse Owens: Champion Athlete*. New York: Chelsea House.

P

PAIKAN, *PAULINHO*

(1955?–)

In the late 1980s, environmentalists and ecologists from around the world attended a Forest Peoples' Gathering in Altamira, Brazil, on the Xingu River, where they heard speeches by tribal leaders, including Paulinho (Paulo) Paikan, chief of the Kayapo people of Aukre. Among the attendees was ANITA RODDICK, who hoped to find ways to preserve the rainforest and later set up a project run by the Kayapo to produce Brazil-nut oil for her global business, the Body Shop. She described Paikan as

> the most impressive of all the speakers, with a natural gift for oratory. His words sent a shiver down my spine: "We are fighting to defend the forest because the forest is what makes us, and what makes our hearts go. Because without the forest we won't be able to breathe and our hearts will stop and we will die" (Roddick 1991, 190).

For several years before the gathering in Altamira, Paikan had traveled to the "outside world" to spread his warning about the need to save the Amazon rainforest, one of the world's greatest natural resources, and the people who inhabit the area. The first time anyone from the world beyond the forest had met the Kayapo was in 1965, and since that time, lumbering and mining companies have been ravaging the forests, creating environmental devastation that could have adverse consequences worldwide. Rainforests such as those in the Amazon are vital in absorbing the human-produced chemicals that contribute to global warming and the so-called greenhouse effect. These forests also contain tremendous biological diversity and numerous plants that provide basic ingredients to produce medicines.

No one knows exactly when Paikan was born, since the Kayapo do not measure time in the same way that most people in industrialized countries do, but his preparation to become a leader began at birth when "the tribe received a 'vision' of his special destiny," according to a *Parade Magazine* feature. Paikan recalled that even as a young boy "I knew that one day I would go out into the world to learn what was coming to us" (Whittemore 1992).

Paikan was educated at a mission school in the village of Gorotire, where he went to work for a company building a highway through the Amazon jungle. His job was to make contact with indigenous people and describe the progress of the highway, but he soon realized that the road builders wanted him to mollify the Indians so that they would not protest the destruction of their land or would make deals with the timber and mining companies, allowing them to log and mine in exchange for a percentage of the production.

Paikan quit his job and tried to convince his villagers and other Kayapo that their way of life was endangered by the loggers and miners and that the Indians needed to relocate, but most Kayapo believed that the forest would never be destroyed and would be there as a source of survival just as it had always been.

Only about 150 people in Paikan's own village were willing to leave the area and settle 180 miles away on the river in Aukre.

The miners and loggers kept pushing onto Indian lands, bringing with them diseases that had never before afflicted the Kayapo. Paikan decided that he had to go beyond the village to the state capital, where he lived, dressed, and acted like the majority population and tried to convince government officials that Kayapo lands needed to be protected. He also learned to use a video camera and recorded the rainforest destruction to convince his people that his warnings were true. He went back and forth from his village to the outside world, trying to find a way to protect the future of the rainforest and his people.

In 1985, Paikan led a war party against gold prospectors, who were mining illegally near his village. The miners were driven out, but a year later, the Brazilian government was ready to dump nuclear waste on Kayapo lands. Once again, Paikan led protests, stopping the government's plan.

The livelihood and lives of indigenous people in Brazil were seriously threatened when the national government proposed to build a hydroelectric dam, which would flood up to 97,000 square miles (250,000 square kilometers) of land. The World Bank planned to finance the project with loans, but with the help of environmentalists and ecologists from around the world, Paikan and other Kayapo leaders launched a campaign to stop the dam project. They presented their case not only to World Bank officials but also to legislators in the United States and Europe. With Paikan's leadership, the Kayapo staged an international meeting at the dam site in 1988, which resulted in worldwide publicity and pressure on Brazil to halt the dam project. However, the Brazilian government charged Paikan with breaking a law that prohibited criticism of the government by "foreigners"—Indians are not legally citizens in Brazil—and Paikan faced a three-year prison term or deportation. The charges were dropped due to international pressure and protests from several hundred Kayapo leaders.

Paikan was still in danger, however, and many villagers feared for his life. In 1988, Chico Mendex, a rubber tapper and grassroots organizer who tried to prevent deforestation, was murdered by ranchers determined to take over the land. During the 1980s, more than 1,000 people—indigenous leaders, peasants, and others—were killed because of their environmental and human rights activism.

Because of his efforts, Paikan was honored by the United Nations with its Global 500 leadership award and has received other honors as well. He served on the Brazilian board of the Rainforest Foundation, established by British musician Sting to finance the marking of Kayapo reservation boundaries. He also directs a company set up in his village by the British-based Body Shop to produce Brazil-nut oil for a popular hair conditioner.

Perhaps one of the most important results of Paikan's actions is legislation enacted in 1992. The Brazilian government set aside rainforest land for indigenous people—the Kayapo and the Yanomami. The government also appears to be discouraging huge "development" projects and massive burning or cutting of forests—for the time being.

References

Roddick, Anita. 1991. *Body and Soul: Profits with Principles—The Amazing Success Story of Anita Roddick and the Body Shop.* New York: Crown Publishers.

Whittemore, Hank. 1992. "I Fight for Our Future." *Parade Magazine*, 12 April.

PALERMO, STEVE

(1950–)

A former major league umpire, Steve Palermo never thought of himself as a hero. In fact, he was more likely to receive insults—the kind commonly hurled at umpires—than accolades, but in the words of one sports writer, Palermo "is a true, honest-to-God hero. Revere the name. . . . This is a man of courage and, of course, the kind of character that carries a glorious, even mystical, wonder" (Steadman 1993). His heroism stems from an incident in 1991 when, without a moment's hesitation, he rushed to the rescue of two women being beaten and robbed. The decision he made almost cost him his life and has prevented him from continuing his successful career as an umpire.

It started out as a fairly typical night in Dallas, Texas. After umpiring a game earlier that night at Arlington Stadium, Palermo went out to dinner with his friend, former Miami Dolphin defensive lineman Terrance Mann. However, the night of 6 July 1991 turned out to be anything but routine. Shortly after 1:00 A.M., the bartender at Campisi's Egyptian Restaurant saw four men in the parking lot attempting to rob two waitresses who had just left the establishment. Palermo, Mann, and four other men rushed out to intervene. Two of the muggers took off in a car, while a third raced off on foot. Palermo and Mann chased the runner, but the men in the car returned and one fired a pistol, hitting both Palermo and his friend. The shooter was later identified as army private Kevin Bivins, who was convicted of aggravated battery and was sentenced to a 75-year prison term.

Palermo grew up in Oxford, Massachusetts, and like many young boys, he hoped for a career in baseball. At the age of 13, he began umpiring Little League games, and in his late teenage years, he was spotted by a major league scout. He began his umpiring career in 1977 at Fenway Park and became one of the best

umpires in the American League, appearing in World Series, league play-offs, and all-star games.

Palermo had been married only five months when the incident happened that would change his life. After the shooting, doctors told Palermo's wife, Debbie, and his brother Jimmy that there was little chance Palermo would walk again due to the nature of his injury. A bullet had severed his spinal cord, causing instant paralysis of his lower extremities. What the doctors did not take into account, however, was Palermo's basic nature. When doctors told Palermo that he probably would not walk again, his determination kicked into high gear. One of the hardest things he had to cope with was developing patience, a trait that did not come naturally to Palermo. Nevertheless, little by little, he regained his mobility, primarily with the aid of two walking canes, which is a lot better than any of the doctors had hoped for.

While undergoing rehabilitation, Palermo became a friend and star of sorts to young baseball fans who were hospitalized for severe injuries. One youngster, five-year-old Jonathan, was discharged early because his family had no insurance, which Palermo thought was "crazy." So he decided to help kids like Jonathan and organized a benefit auction of baseball memorabilia, raising $125,000, which was used to establish the Steve Palermo Foundation for Spinal Cord Injuries.

Many people have praised Palermo as a hero, but it is a role that he tries to dismiss. "Hero is a word I don't wear well. There were six guys who did what I did that night, and none of us went out that door trying to make our mark as heroes. What about the four guys who didn't get shot? I guess they're smart heroes" (Newman 1992).

Although he is not yet umpiring, Palermo is still active in baseball. In April 1994, he was named assistant to the chairman of the Major League Executive Council. His job is to maintain and increase the popularity of major league baseball. In 1995, Palermo began making recommendations for speeding up the game, including raising the pitcher's mound, forcing hitters to stay in the batter's box, and calling a larger strike zone. In the back of Palermo's mind is getting back on the field as an umpire. He is on the inactive list, which means that if and when he can come back, there will be a job for him on the field. If Palermo has anything to say about it, he will be there.

References

Newman, Bruce. 1992. "Pain and Progress." *Sports Illustrated*, 6 July.

"Palermo Back in Baseball." 1994. *Houston Post*, 7 April, Sports section.

Steadman, John. 1993. "In the Game of Life, Former Umpire Palermo Has Been Called Out To Inspire Others." *Baltimore Evening Sun*, 30 April, Sports section.

"An Ump on Deck." 1995. *Sports Illustrated*, 27 February.

PARKS, ROSA

(1913–)

osa Louise Parks is widely recognized as the woman who, in 1951, helped launch the modern-day civil rights movement with her quiet and dignified act of defiance: refusing to give up her seat on a bus to a white person. The driver, James E. Blake, called police to arrest Parks for not abiding by segregation laws that required blacks to move to the back of the bus when whites wanted seats in a "neutral" middle section. Parks said later that at the time she felt no fear because of her strong belief in God and faith that He would help her.

She also was inspired by her grandfather, whom she described as "a very proud man, he was never fearful—especially when it came to defending his home and family." In the early part of the 1900s, blacks were often under attack by white-supremacy groups such as the Ku Klux Klan. Parks had learned over the years that when one's mind is made up, this diminishes fear.

> When I sat down on the bus the day I was arrested, I was thinking of going home. I had made up my mind quickly about what it was that I had to do, what I felt was right to do. . . . After so many years of oppression and being a victim of the mistreatment that my people had suffered, not giving up my seat—and whatever I had to face after not giving it up—was not important. . . . All I felt was tired. Tired of being pushed around. Tired of seeing the bad treatment and disrespect of children, women, and men just because of the color of their skin (Parks with Reed 1994, 16, 17).

Parks had no idea that her courageous act would be a catalyst for a black boycott of the Montgomery, Alabama, bus service, but it was not the first time she had defied the segregated system. Eleven years before she had refused to enter a bus by the back door. As a result, the driver—the same one who later had her arrested—took her fare, forced her to get off the bus, then drove off and left her.

The first child of James and Leona McCauley, Rosa was born in Tuskegee, Alabama, on 4 February 1913. The McCauleys moved to Pine Level, Alabama, where Rosa was educated in a rural school. Later she enrolled in Montgomery Industrial School for Girls, a private school, and because there was no other high school where blacks were allowed, she went on to the Alabama State Teachers College for Negroes for her tenth and eleventh grades. Because of her mother's illness, she had to drop out of school to care for her; a younger brother, Sylvester, helped support the family. After her marriage, she eventually completed her high school education and received a diploma.

In 1932, Rosa married Raymond Parks, a self-educated man from Wedowee, Alabama (a town widely publicized in 1994 and 1995 because of a race-related conflict that resulted in a civil rights case filed by MORRIS DEES, well-known

Rosa Parks sits in the front of a city bus following the Supreme Court ruling that banned segregation on Montgomery's public transit vehicles took effect in 1956.

lawyer and head of the Southern Poverty Law Center in Montgomery). Both Rosa and Raymond were active with the Montgomery branch of the National Association for the Advancement of Colored People (NAACP)—she as a secretary and later a youth leader. Rosa also worked part time as a seamstress.

After Parks was arrested, blacks in Montgomery organized a boycott of the bus system. Although Parks's arrest motivated people to act, the Woman's Political Council under the leadership of Jo Ann Robinson (who had once been ordered out of the "whites only" section of a bus) had been planning such a protest for years. The council had just been waiting for the right moment, and members distributed thousands of leaflets calling for blacks to unite in a boycott on the day of Parks's trial. After a successful one-day boycott, the protest continued, eventually lasting for nearly 13 months and prompting the arrest of such leaders as MARTIN LUTHER KING, JR., and RALPH ABERNATHY for initiating the boycott. Their arrest and the boycott was publicized nationwide, and after a U.S. Supreme Court decision in 1956 in favor of the boycotters, the bus system was desegregated.

In 1957, Rosa and Raymond Parks moved to Detroit, Michigan, where they stayed active in civil rights efforts and took part in the civil rights march on Washington in 1963 and the Selma-to-Montgomery march in 1965. Raymond died in 1977, and ten years later, Rosa established the Rosa and Raymond Parks Institute for Self-Development to help young people develop marketable skills. Parks also continued to speak out for civil rights and justice and against bigotry and crime. She herself was the victim of crime in 1994, when a young man broke

down her door, attacked her, and stole what money she had in her home—$103. About that incident, she stated in characteristic fashion:

I pray for this young man and the conditions in our country that have made him this way. I urge people not to read too much into the attack. I regret that some people, regardless of race, are in such a mental state that they would want to harm an older person. . . . Despite the violence and crime in our society, we should not let fear overwhelm us. We must remain strong. We must not give up hope; we can overcome (Parks with Reed 1994, 37).

References
Parks, Rosa, and James Haskins. 1992. *Rosa Parks: My Story*. New York: Dial Books.
Parks, Rosa, with Gregory J. Reed. 1994. *Quiet Strength*. Grand Rapids, MI: Zondervan Publishing House.
Williams, Juan. 1987. *Eyes on the Prize: America's Civil Rights Years, 1954–1965* (companion volume to the PBS television series). New York: Viking Penguin.

PAULING, LINUS

(1901–1994)

A peace crusader and humanitarian, Linus Pauling considered himself a chemist first, but he always lived by his conscience, and in doing so he generated much public hostility as well as praise. Twice a winner of the Nobel Prize—first for chemistry and then for peace—Pauling never hesitated to question the scientific or political establishments. In fact, his avid curiosity drove him to consistently question almost everything, and he was always trying to figure out life's puzzles.

Born in Portland, Oregon, Pauling was the eldest of three children of Herman M. and Lucy Isabelle (Belle) Pauling. His father, who died when he was nine years old, was a pharmacist and set up a drugstore in Condon, Oregon. Young Pauling's interest in chemistry probably stemmed from watching his father

Peace crusader and chemist Linus Pauling lectures in his laboratory at the Linus Pauling Institute of Science and Medicine in Palo Alto, California. Linus spoke out against the U.S. nuclear weapons testing program during the 1950s and won the Nobel Prize for peace in 1962.

grind and mix powders at work, although Pauling claimed that he did not recognize this interest until he was about 12 years old.

After Herman Pauling died, the family opened a boarding house in Portland. For the next few years, Pauling began learning what he could about science by reading books, collecting and classifying insects, and starting a mineral collection. In high school, a classmate who tinkered with chemistry invited Pauling to his home to watch an experiment. Pauling later set up his own chemistry laboratory in his basement, using donated equipment and chemicals. At the same time, he had to help support the family—his mother and two younger sisters—by taking a variety of part-time jobs, from delivering milk to working in the shipyards.

Throughout his early schooling, Pauling expressed his desire to go to college, but his mother insisted that she needed his financial support and could see no reason for him to further his education. However, Pauling persisted, and in 1917, he began his college education at Oregon Agricultural College in Corvallis (now Oregon State University), where he studied chemical engineering and worked at numerous odd jobs to support himself. Because of his mother's serious illness,

he stayed out of school for his junior year and worked to support her. Among his jobs was a full-time position at the college, apparently acting as an assistant for a sophomore course in quantitative analysis.

In 1921, Pauling returned to his studies at Corvallis. In 1922, he went to the California Institute of Technology (Caltech), where he received a doctorate in chemistry and mathematical physics. He married Ava Helen Miller in 1923 and then studied for a year at the Institute for Theoretical Physics in Munich, Germany, before returning to Caltech to teach and conduct research. The Paulings' first child, Linus Jr., was born in 1925, and two other children, Peter and Linda, were born in 1931 and 1932, respectively. Their fourth child, Edward, was born in 1937.

During the early 1930s, Pauling was invited to join the staff at the Massachusetts Institute of Technology (MIT), but he accepted only a temporary appointment from 1931 to 1932 and then returned to Caltech, eventually teaching there a total of 36 years. In 1969, he went to Stanford University to teach chemistry for several years, leaving in 1973 to set up the Linus Pauling Institute of Science and Medicine in Palo Alto, California, where he conducted research on his controversial theory that massive daily doses of vitamin C could provide protection against diseases ranging from the common cold to cancer.

Beginning in the 1920s, Pauling was one of the first researchers to use electron crystallography (x-rays of a molecule's atoms) and electron diffraction (bouncing electrons off otherwise invisible structures) to determine the structure of a molecule. He is generally regarded as the founder of molecular biology and molecular medicine. He also made groundbreaking discoveries in quantum mechanics, nuclear physics, and biochemistry. This work led to the Nobel Prize for chemistry in 1954.

Pauling's research also included an examination of human hemoglobin, the protein that carries oxygen in the blood; this work led to the discovery that the disease sickle cell anemia was linked to abnormalities in the structure of hemoglobin. In addition, he did extensive research on the structure of DNA and was one of the first scientists to theorize that protein molecules are arranged in the form of a spiral staircase.

"The war years may have been the most important years of Pauling's life," according to biographer Serafini. "For one thing his interest in molecular medicine and biology escalated sharply. For another, he became deeply interested in politics for the first time in his life. . . . Ava Helen played some role—she had always been at least marginally interested in politics. She had been particularly impressed with Franklin Roosevelt when, soon after taking office in 1933, he began formulating laws to help the unemployed" (Serafini 1989, 106).

Pauling was an advocate of Roosevelt's programs, but during World War II, he became increasingly critical of government. He was adamantly opposed to the federal government's policy of interning Japanese Americans during the war years, and he was especially concerned about nuclear testing and publicly chastised the scientists who worked on the Manhattan Project to develop the atomic bomb. During the 1950s, he campaigned against the U.S. testing program and continually spoke out for world disarmament and international peace, which

brought on the wrath of such virulent anticommunists as Senator Joseph McCarthy and the U.S. House Un-American Activities Committee. He was also harassed by the U.S. State Department and the FBI for 25 years, and he fought constantly to clear his name, which was a drain on his productivity.

In 1958, he went to the United Nations to present a petition signed by more than 11,000 scientists opposing nuclear weapons testing. Five years later, the United States and the Soviet Union signed a test ban treaty. For his efforts in this regard, Pauling received the 1962 Nobel Peace Prize.

Never one to shy away from controversy, Pauling's life can best be described as one of boundless energy. He was often impatient and impulsive and had a strong desire to be the first in whatever he set out to do, qualities that enabled him to accomplish so much. One of his most controversial crusades had to do with his research on vitamin C. In his book *Vitamin C and the Common Cold* (which he wrote in just over a month), he stated his thesis that essential ascorbic acid (vitamin C) taken in large amounts and at the right time would prevent most colds from developing and would decrease the symptoms of those that had already developed. Although Pauling's studies did not prove the veracity of his claims, it has not been possible to refute them conclusively. The controversy intensified when he linked vitamin C to cancer prevention. Pauling's contention was that vitamin C helped energize the immune system. Although his wife died of stomach cancer in 1981 and he succumbed to the disease at the age of 93, Pauling claimed that he had probably staved off cancer for at least 20 years. The controversy over the beneficial effects of vitamin C still rages, as medical science examines several options regarding a cure for cancer.

Whatever the subsequent findings, Pauling's scientific work in chemistry resulted in numerous awards during his lifetime. Along with the Nobel Prizes, he was awarded the U.S. Presidential Medal for Merit in 1948, the International Lenin Peace Prize in 1972, the U.S. National Academy of Science Medal for Chemistry in 1979, and the American Chemical Society's Priestly Medal in 1984. He also wrote several science textbooks. In spite of the fact that some scientists considered him a "crackpot," many others considered him a "first-rate genius," as he was described by the well-known science author Isaac Asimov. In 1989, Asimov praised Pauling for being "a brave man who struggled for peace and against nuclear weapons even during the McCarthy period . . . a gentleman in the highest sense of the word. He has *character*" (Serafini 1989, xvi).

References

Barnes, Bart. 1994. "Two-Time Nobel Winner Linus Pauling Dies at 93." *Washington Post*, 21 August.

Hager, Thomas. 1995. *Force of Nature: The Life of Linus Pauling*. New York: Simon & Schuster.

Pauling, Linus. 1953. *No More War!* New York: Dodd, Mead.

Serafini, Anthony. 1989. *Linus Pauling: A Man and His Science*. New York: Paragon House.

PEACE PILGRIM

See *NORMAN, MILDRED*

PILENKO, *LISA*

See *MARIA, MOTHER*

PODGORSKA, *STEFANIA*

(1926–)

Although there is little published information about the life of Stefania Podgorska (now Burzminska), she was a teenage heroine during World War II, unexpectedly thrust into the role of rescuer of Jews in Poland. One of nine children born into a wealthy farm family, Podgorska left the farm in southeastern Poland not long after her father died in 1938. She went to live with an older sister in the nearby town of Przemysl. In 1939, the year World War II began, she got a job working in a grocery story operated by an elderly Jewish woman, Lea Adler Diamant, whose husband was ill. The Diamants had four sons and a daughter, and after a year working for them, Podgorska moved in with the family and became a household helper.

By 1941, the Germans occupied the town and created a ghetto surrounded by barbed wire for the Jewish population of about 20,000. The Diamants, like the other Jews, were required to wear the Jewish star for identification and were forced out of their home and business and into the ghetto. Podgorska, at the request of the Diamants, was able to get a permit to live in the apartment over their store, and she found a job as a factory worker. The Diamants were left with no means of livelihood and were soon near starvation. When Podgorska learned about their condition, she bought food and slipped it to them under the fence.

This was only the first of Podgorska's acts of courage, which were bolstered by her religious beliefs—she was and still is a devout Catholic. Both Mr. and Mrs. Diamant were deported to Auschwitz, and their son Isaac was sent to a labor camp in Lvov, where Podgorska visited and brought him food and clothing. Together they planned his escape from the camp, but Isaac was killed in the process. Meantime nearly everyone in the Jewish ghetto was murdered or deported to death camps, including two of Isaac's brothers, Joseph and Henek, who planned to commit suicide by jumping from the train before it reached Auschwitz. Their suicide attempt failed, and Joseph found his way to Podgorska's apartment, and

Henek went back to the ghetto. Podgorska and her younger sister, Helen, who lived with her, hid and cared for Joseph, who became ill. They were soon asked to hide others, but their apartment was too small to keep anyone hidden for any length of time. Podgorska had to find a larger place but had no idea where to look in the town. According to Podgorska, she prayed for guidance: "Some voice told me, 'Don't be afraid. Go a little farther. After this corner, two women are standing, women who clean the street. They are supporting themselves on their brooms. Ask them for an apartment. They will tell you'" (Fogelman 1994, 93). Just as the "voice" had predicted, she found the women, asked for their help, and located a small cottage with an attic in what was once a Jewish neighborhood.

Podgorska, who was seventeen years old, and her seven-year-old sister moved into the cottage and immediately took in Joseph and six other Jews; later they took in six more, three of them young children. In spite of grave threats to her life, Podgorska, with the help of her young sister, managed to keep her 13 charges hidden and fed for months. She was once ordered by the German secret police to vacate her cottage, but she refused, because once again she prayed for help and the inner voice told her not to leave, that everything would be all right. The Gestapo allowed her and her sister to stay in one room while two German nurses, who worked in a makeshift hospital across the street, and their soldier boyfriends lived in the other room. None of the Germans detected the Jews hidden in the attic, and after the Germans moved on, Russians liberated the town, freeing not only Podgorska and her sister but also the Jews she had saved.

Reference

Fogelman, Eva. 1994. *Conscience and Courage*. New York: Anchor Books.

R

RABIN, *YITZHAK*

(1922–1995)

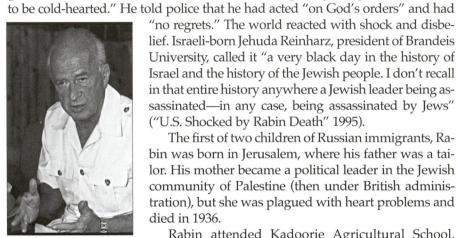

Winner of the 1994 Nobel Peace Prize, Yitzhak Rabin was assassinated on 4 November 1995, a martyr for peace. Rabin was murdered just a few minutes after he had completed an address before a huge peace rally in Tel Aviv. An Israeli law student, Yigal Amir, who was backed by an extremist group opposed to negotiations with Palestinians to bring peace to the Middle East, gunned him down. As Amir said, "I did this to stop the peace process. We need to be cold-hearted." He told police that he had acted "on God's orders" and had "no regrets." The world reacted with shock and disbelief. Israeli-born Jehuda Reinharz, president of Brandeis University, called it "a very black day in the history of Israel and the history of the Jewish people. I don't recall in that entire history anywhere a Jewish leader being assassinated—in any case, being assassinated by Jews" ("U.S. Shocked by Rabin Death" 1995).

The first of two children of Russian immigrants, Rabin was born in Jerusalem, where his father was a tailor. His mother became a political leader in the Jewish community of Palestine (then under British administration), but she was plagued with heart problems and died in 1936.

Rabin attended Kadoorie Agricultural School, graduating at the top of his class. He hoped to continue his education, but he was "compelled to resort to the gun," receiving military training instead. As he explained in his 1994 acceptance speech for the Nobel Prize:

> At an age when most youngsters are struggling to unravel the secrets of mathematics and the mysteries of the Bible; at an age when first love blooms; at the tender age of sixteen, I was handed a rifle so that I could defend myself. That was not my dream. I wanted to be a water engineer. . . . I thought being a water engineer was an important profession in the parched Middle East. I still think so today (Israel Information Service 1994).

In 1948, Rabin became a full-time soldier, one of the first to join the Palmach, a unit of the Jewish defense force fighting for an independent Jewish state. His unit successfully defended a roadway that ran through Arab territory between Tel Aviv and Jerusalem. Rabin rose quickly in the Israeli army, becoming a major general at 32 years of age and chief of staff 10 years later. A tough, uncompromising military man, he led Israel to victory in the June 1967 Six-Day War against Egypt, Jordan, and Syria. In January 1968, Rabin retired from the army and became ambassador to the United States, serving until 1973, when he returned to Jerusalem to run for a Labor Party seat in the Knesset, the Israeli parliament. In 1974, he won the election for prime minister over his longtime rival

Shimon Peres but was forced to resign in 1977 because of a minor scandal over a U.S. bank account that he and his wife, Leah, had established, which is prohibited by Israeli law.

From 1984 to 1988, Rabin was defense minister. During the 1988 Palestinian *intifada*, or uprising, against Israeli rule in the occupied territories of the West Bank and Gaza, Rabin called for a "break their bones" policy toward Palestinians, ordering Israeli soldiers to use clubs to break protesters' bones rather than shoot them. The policy was popular in Israel but brought condemnation from around the world. Rabin slowly pulled away from that policy and began to look for political alternatives to the four decades of war with neighboring Arabs. Although a revered war hero, he became a soldier for peace. When he was elected prime minister again in 1992, he said:

> No longer are we necessarily a people that dwells alone, and no longer is it true that the whole world is against us. We must overcome the sense of isolation that has held us in its thrall for almost half a century. We must join the international movement toward peace, reconciliation and cooperation that is spreading over the entire globe these days—lest we be the last to remain, all alone, in the station (Frankel 1995).

Rabin and Peres put aside their rivalry and began to work together to improve relationships with the United States and to set up negotiations with the Palestinians and other Arabs. In 1993, with the guidance of both men, Israel and Palestine reached an agreement that granted political autonomy to Palestine and started the process of withdrawing the military from the Gaza Strip, Jericho, and much of the West Bank.

On 13 September 1993, Prime Minister Rabin and Palestine Liberation Organization (PLO) Chairman Yasir Arafat signed the Israeli-Palestinian Declaration of Principles in a ceremony on the White House lawn. During this historic occasion, the two men shook hands. In 1994, Rabin signed the Treaty of Peace between Israel and Jordan, and that same year, he, Foreign Minister Shimon Peres, and Arafat shared the Nobel Prize. On 28 September 1995, he was at the White House once again to sign the Israeli-Palestinian Interim Agreement on the West Bank and the Gaza Strip.

While at the Peace Now rally in Tel Aviv on 4 November, Rabin spoke to a crowd of 100,000, thanking them for their "stand against violence and for peace." He also said:

> I am proud of the fact that representatives of the countries with whom we are living in peace are present with us here, and will continue to be here: Egypt, Jordan, and Morocco, which opened the road to peace for us. I want to thank the President of Egypt, the King of Jordan, and the King of Morocco, represented here today, for their partnership with us in our march towards peace.
> . . . I want to say bluntly, that we have found a partner for peace among the Palestinians as well: the PLO, which was an enemy, and has ceased to

engage in terrorism. Without partners for peace, there can be no peace. We will demand that they do their part for peace, just as we will do our part for peace, in order to solve the most complicated, prolonged, and emotionally charged aspect of the Israeli-Arab conflict: the Palestinian-Israeli conflict.

. . . This rally must send a message to the Israeli people, to the Jewish people around the world, to the many people in the Arab world, and indeed to the entire world, that the Israeli people want peace, support peace. For this, I thank you (Rabin 1995).

Rabin joined in the "Song of Peace" before leaving the stage and walking toward his car, where the assassin waited, piercing Rabin with several bullets. Dozens of leaders and officials of Western nations and of the Arab world came to Jerusalem to attend the funeral of Prime Minister Rabin, who was described as "one of the most important, courageous men in Israel." When U.S. President Bill Clinton paid homage to Rabin, he noted: "It falls to all of us who love peace and all of us who loved him to carry on the struggle for which he gave life and for which he gave his life."

References

Frankel, Glenn. 1995. "The Ultimate Israeli—A Soldier Who Yearned for Peace." *Washington Post*, 5 November.

Israel Information Service. 1994. Electronic posting of Rabin's acceptance speech. December.

McGrath, Peter. 1995. "An Indispensable Man." *Newsweek*, 13 November.

Rabin, Yitzhak. 1979. *The Rabin Memoirs*. Boston: Little, Brown.

———. 1995. "Yitzhak Rabin's Last Speech." Electronic posting http://www.ariga.com/index.htm. 4 November.

Slater, Robert. 1993. *Rabin of Israel*. New York: St. Martin's Press.

"U.S. Shocked by Rabin Death." 1995. Associated Press. 4 November.

RANDOLPH, ASA PHILIP

(1889–1979)

From the 1920s through the 1960s, A. Philip Randolph was a tireless activist for the rights of black workers, often risking his personal safety and life to help obtain equal job opportunities for blacks. As a labor leader, he is best known for founding the Brotherhood of Sleeping Car Porters in 1925, a union that later became affiliated with the American Federation of Labor (AFL). Within the AFL, he was so persistent in his fight against racial discrimination that AFL President George Meany once demanded to know, "Who the hell appointed you as the guardian of all the Negroes in America?" At the peak of the civil rights movement, he led the 1963 March on Washington for Jobs and Freedom (Whitman 1985).

The second son of Reverend James Randolph and Elizabeth (Robinson) Randolph, Asa was born in Crescent City, Florida, and grew up in Jacksonville, Florida, where the family moved in 1891. Randolph was educated at a local primary school and at an industrial school operated by the African Methodist Episcopal church. He later went to Florida's first high school for blacks, the Cookman Institute, where he graduated as the class valedictorian.

Unable to afford college, Randolph worked at menial jobs and honed his speaking skills (which he had learned from his father) in black churches and theaters in and around Jacksonville. He left for New York City in 1911, hoping to begin a career in the theater, and settled in Harlem. In 1912, he began taking classes at the City College of New York, where he was first exposed to socialism and the concept of labor organizations. To support himself, he worked wherever he could find a job and was frequently fired for trying to organize black workers.

Randolph married a wealthy widow, Lucille Campbell, in 1914, and she introduced him to Chandler Owen, who became his best friend. The two joined the Socialist Party and in 1917 began a monthly magazine called *The Hotel Messenger*, which supported organized black workers in the Headwaiters' and Sidewaiters' Society. Later known as simply *The Messenger*, the magazine became an advocacy publication for socialism and trade unions, particularly the Industrial Workers of the World (IWW). Editorials in *The Messenger* encouraged blacks to forcefully resist attacks by white mobs that wanted to destroy black participation in labor unions, but it also called for cooperation between black and white workers.

When Randolph organized the sleeping-car porters in 1925, many thought that he was crazy to fight a company worth millions of dollars when Randolph himself seldom had change in his pockets. At the time, the Pullman Company was the largest single employer of blacks in the United States, and porters worked 400 hours a month, earning $67.50. Membership in the Brotherhood of

Sleeping Car Porters increased rapidly over the next year but declined during the depression of the 1930s. However, by 1937, the union won the right to make an agreement with a U.S. corporation and created a contract that reduced work hours to 240 a month and raised wages.

In 1940, Randolph worked with other black leaders in efforts to convince President Franklin D. Roosevelt to integrate the armed forces and defense industries, which were gearing up as U.S. involvement in World War II became imminent. Roosevelt refused, and Randolph announced that he would organize thousands of blacks for a protest march in Washington, D.C. In his view, Washington leaders would never give the Negro civil rights until they saw tens of thousands of blacks demonstrating on the White House lawn. Although Roosevelt did not integrate the military, he signed Executive Order 8802 in 1941, which prohibited discrimination in defense industries and established the Fair Employment Practices Committee, which was supposed to investigate discrimination complaints and correct grievances. As a result, Randolph called off the march on Washington, which met with criticism from some blacks who felt that the nation needed to see a show of black power.

Randolph continued his fight for equal rights for blacks and in 1943 was named adviser to the Congress of Racial Equality (CORE), advocating nonviolent protests of racial injustices. By 1945, the segregated practices in the military had changed little, and black soldiers were often harassed even as they prepared to fight in World War II. Just before the end of the war, President Roosevelt died, and Harry Truman became president. In 1947, Truman called for a peacetime draft, and Randolph saw an opportunity to pressure Truman to issue an executive order to end segregation in the military. When Truman refused, Randolph and an associate began a civil disobedience campaign, urging young black men not to register for the draft. Randolph was willing to go to jail for his convictions, declaring that basic human rights governed his actions. In 1948, Truman began the process of desegregating the military.

Throughout the 1950s and 1960s, Randolph continued his work for equal employment opportunities for blacks. In 1955, he was elected to the AFL-CIO's executive council and helped set up a civil rights committee. In 1957, he became vice-president of the AFL. His other activities on behalf of black workers included organizing more than 200,000 people to go to Washington, D.C., for the 1963 March for Jobs and Freedom. He also took part in "freedom rides" to fight segregation in the South.

Over the years, Randolph received numerous honors and awards for his efforts. Even during his seventies and eighties, he was active in civil rights struggles. Although he was often criticized by more militant blacks for being old-fashioned, he consistently advised young people to get an education and to work in a positive, peaceful manner for reforms. He died just a few weeks after his ninetieth birthday in May 1979.

References
Anderson, Jervis. 1973. *A. Philip Randolph: A Biographical Portrait*. New York: Harcourt Brace Jovanovich.

Drexel, John, ed. 1991. *The Facts on File Encyclopedia of the 20th Century*. New York: Facts on File.

Hanley, Sally. 1989. *A. Philip Randolph Labor Leader*. New York: Chelsea House.

Harris, William. 1977. *Keeping the Faith: A. Philip Randolph, Milton P. Webster, and the Brotherhood of Sleeping Car Porters, 1925–1937*. Champaign: University of Illinois Press.

Whitman, Alden, ed. 1985. *American Reformers*. New York: H. W. Wilson.

RANKIN, JEANNETTE

(1880–1973)

As one of the few women in the U.S. Congress during the early 1900s and the first to campaign for a congressional seat, Jeannette Rankin had to face and overcome numerous obstacles. Her most courageous efforts, however, came about because of her sense of conscience, which was so strong that she dared to stand up as the only congressional member to vote against U.S. involvement in World War I.

Born on a ranch in Missoula, Montana, Rankin was the oldest of seven children in the affluent family of John and Olive Rankin. While growing up, she learned to do many of the ranching chores, from chopping wood to caring for the horses, although the family lived most of the time in their large home in town, where she attended school. She was bored with school but loved to read and often talked with her father about the ideas she discovered in books. She also accompanied her father, one of the town's leaders, when he met with other influential men and discussed politics and business.

During her teenage years, Rankin longed to find a satisfying career. After obtaining her degree from the University of Montana, she taught for a year—one of the few professions open to women at the time—but had no desire to make it her life's work. Nor did she have any plans for marriage and raising a family. While visiting her only brother, who was attending Harvard Law School in Boston, Rankin observed for the first time the terrible living conditions of the urban poor and began to read about reformers such as JANE ADDAMS. Inspired to

work for social change, she became a social worker in Spokane, Washington, for a time. In 1910, she joined the women's suffrage movement and took part in the campaign to pass a state law giving women the right to vote—only four other states had passed such laws at the time.

Her successful work with the suffrage campaign prompted Rankin to run for the U.S. House of Representatives in 1916—the first woman to campaign for a seat in the U.S. Congress. With the support of her family—particularly her brother, who helped manage and finance her campaign—she traveled across

Montana talking to people on street corners, at mines, and in their homes and meeting houses. She supported an amendment to the U.S. Constitution that would allow women nationwide the right to vote, and she called attention to the needs of children. Another major issue was keeping the United States out of World War I, which had begun in Europe in 1914.

After winning election to Congress in November 1916, Rankin continued to speak out in opposition to the war, a view that many Americans shared. In 1918, President Woodrow Wilson, who had won office on the promise to keep the United States out of the war, was forced to ask Congress to vote for a war resolution. Before the House voted, Rankin was subjected to a great deal of pressure and abuse; some representatives called her a coward and a traitor for not supporting the war, but the House leader told members, "it takes neither moral nor physical courage to declare a war for others to fight." Rankin said that she wanted to stand by her country, but she could not vote for war. Later, when asked about her nay vote, she had no regrets, saying, "I felt that the first time the first woman in Congress had a chance to say no to war, she should say it" (Davidson 1994, 45–46).

Primarily because of her antiwar stance, Rankin lost her second bid for Congress in 1918, but she continued to work for peace causes and cofounded the Women's International League for Peace and Freedom in 1919. She lobbied congressional members in support of an antiwar amendment to the U.S. Constitution. After moving to a Georgia farm in 1923, she formed a Georgia Peace Society, and between 1929 and 1939, she was a paid lobbyist for the National Council for the Prevention of War. In 1939, at the age of 59, Rankin once again ran for Congress and won the election, but once again her antiwar vote in 1941 against U.S. participation in World War II subjected her to hatred, abuse, and threats of violence from much of the American public.

After World War II, Rankin traveled worldwide, making a number of journeys to India, where she studied the way of life of the common people and learned as much as she could about MOHANDAS GANDHI and his absolute pacifist views, which she shared. She also lived simply, with few material goods, preferring to use funds from an inheritance left by her brother to work for peace and

women's rights. When the United States entered the war in Korea and later the war in Vietnam, Rankin spoke out, and in her eighties and nineties she participated in protest marches, granted newspaper and magazine interviews, and took part in radio and television shows to plead for world disarmament. She worked for the cause almost to the time of her death in 1973, a month before her ninety-third birthday.

References

Berson, Robin Kadison. 1994. *Marching to a Different Drummer: Unrecognized Heroes of American History*. Westport, CT: Greenwood Press.

Davidson, Sue. 1994. *A Heart in Politics: Jeannette Rankin and Patsy T. Mink*. Seattle, WA: Seal Press.

Frappollo, Elizabeth. 1972. "At 91, Jeannette Rankin Is the Feminists' New Heroine." *Life*, 3 March.

ROBESON, PAUL

(1898–1976)

"No man has more completely embodied the dynamics of the twentieth century than did Paul Robeson, both in his enormous gifts and in his travails born of his race and philosophy," wrote the editors of *Freedomways*, a quarterly magazine of black writing. Yet Paul Robeson's achievements as a great football player, concert singer, actor, and orator were literally abolished from U.S. history during the 1950s, and he was drummed out of the country by political leaders who disagreed with Robeson's fight to prevent the oppression of people of color at home and colonialism abroad. Not until the past few decades have the accomplishments of Robeson been revived and widely publicized; they are yet to be fully appreciated in the United States.

Robeson was the youngest child of an escaped slave who later became a minister. Following his father's teachings, Robeson learned early in life that personal integrity was the basis for developing one's full potential. Through his adolescent and college years, he honed his convictions to seek freedom and to fight racial discrimination and physical violence against oppressed people.

Robeson earned a scholarship to Rutgers University, where, in 1915, he was the only black on campus and only the third person of African ancestry to enroll since its founding in 1766. He was often the object of racist attacks, particularly when he competed for a place on the varsity football team. On several occasions during scrimmages, white ballplayers smashed him in the nose, deliberately dislocated his shoulder, and broke the bones in one hand—in short, brutally attacking him. After he made the varsity team, he faced similar racist aggression from opposing squads. Even when he felt that he could take no more, he remembered his early teachings:

> My father . . . had impressed upon me that when I was out on a football field or in a classroom or anywhere else, I wasn't just there on my own. I was the representative of a lot of Negro boys who wanted to play football, who wanted to go to college . . . I had to show that I could take whatever they [whites] handed out. . . . This was part of our struggle (*Freedomways* editors 1978, 20).

Robeson eventually was honored as a two-time Walter Camp All-America football player.

Robeson earned a law degree at Columbia Law School but decided that the profession would be too narrow a forum to protest the discrimination and inequality in the United States and worldwide. During the 1920s, he developed as an artist and established a stage career, winning the best-acting award for his role as Othello. While performing in Europe, his political views and philosophy took shape. He became convinced that the principles of socialism could help humankind achieve a higher stage of life.

In Europe, he saw that the struggles of working-class people in fascist-led countries were similar to those of black Americans and strongly supported antifascist forces who fought in the Spanish Civil War, which began in 1936. When he returned to the United States, he spoke out against fascism on many occasions, but this ran counter to the policies of the U.S. State Department and prompted the agency to harass Robeson for at least 20 years.

Robeson continued to speak out, however. "He was the first American artist to refuse to sing before a segregated audience. He spoke out against lynching, segregated theatres and eating places a generation before the beginning of what is referred to as the Black Revolution," wrote Hunter College professor John Henrik Clarke (*Freedomways* editors 1978, 191).

After World War II, Robeson challenged President Harry Truman to stop the lynchings and other brutalities against black Americans that were common occurrences at the time, but Truman refused. Even so, Robeson continued to demand equality for blacks and to urge them to fight for a free world at home as well as abroad. He also championed working people and nonconformist labor unions and was called a communist, which he denied when called before the House Un-American Activities Committee. When Robeson gave an outdoor benefit concert at Peekskill, New York, in 1949, a mob attacked concertgoers, most of whom were unionists and their families, while police stood by and watched.

Still Robeson continued to crusade and tour. For such "audacity," the federal government revoked Robeson's passport in 1950; it was not reinstated until 1958, after a worldwide protest and a U.S. Supreme Court ruling in his favor.

During the early 1950s—when U.S. forces were fighting in Korea and U.S. Senator Joseph McCarthy of Wisconsin was conducting a nationwide campaign against communism and those he labeled communists—Robeson said in a lecture in October 1953:

> No one has yet explained to my satisfaction what business a black lad from a Mississippi or Georgia sharecropping farm has in Asia shooting down the yellow or brown son of an impoverished rice-farmer. Mr. [President Dwight] Eisenhower or Senator McCarthy would have us believe that this is necessary to "save" the so-called "free world" from "communism." But the man who keeps that Negro sharecropper from earning more than a few hundred dollars a year is not a Communist—it's the landlord. And the man who prevents his son from attending school with white children is not a Communist—it's . . . the U.S. delegation to the United Nations (*Freedomways* editors 1978, 227).

Because he spoke out and acted on his convictions, Robeson was vilified throughout the United States. His concerts were canceled and he could not travel abroad for performances. U.S. officials hoped to destroy him with economic deprivation, but he refused to give up. Instead, he continued to lecture and give concerts until 1961, when he became too ill to perform. In a tribute to him 28 January 1976, U.S. Representative John Conyers said:

> Paul Robeson stands as a monument to the capacity of the human spirit to achieve excellence in the face of adversity. His talent and courage fused to manifest personal greatness despite the conditions under which he lived. Mr. Robeson gave of himself, whether on the concert stage or the picket line. He sang, struggled, suffered and died for the cause of human dignity (*Freedomways* editors 1978, 274).

References

Fast, Howard. 1951. *Peekskill: USA; a Personal Experience.* New York: Civil Rights Congress.

Foner, Philip S., ed. 1978. *Paul Robeson Speaks.* New York: Brunner/Mazel.

Freedomways editors. 1978. *Paul Robeson: The Great Forerunner.* New York: Dodd, Mead.

Hamilton, Virginia. 1971. *Paul Robeson: The Life and Times of a Free Black Man.* New York: Harper & Row.

Robeson, Paul. 1971. *Here I Stand.* New York: Othello Associates, 1958. Reprint, Boston: Beacon Press.

ROBINSON, JACKIE

(1919–1972)

Elected to the Baseball Hall of Fame in 1962, Jackie Robinson was one of the greatest players ever to step onto the baseball diamond, but John Roosevelt Robinson had had no plans to play professional baseball after he graduated from the University of California, Los Angeles. Until he paved the way, black men were barred from competing in the major leagues.

Robinson intended to be a social worker to help poor kids. He knew what it was like to grow up as an underprivileged youngster—first in Cairo, Georgia, where he was born, and later when his mother moved the family to California, hoping to find a better life. His father had left the family when he was born, and his mother did whatever work she could to make ends meet. She was also his spiritual guide and inspiration, constantly reminding him about the biblical injunction to turn the other cheek when insulted or attacked, particularly when they faced a rough life in Pasadena. African Americans were still outcasts in the 1920s and 1930s, and Jackie and his brother experienced the pain of discrimination often and got into more than one fight over a racial slur, even though their mother continued to admonish them not to retaliate. The family was also plagued with incidents of cross burning and rock throwing. To find some relief from the realities of the white world, Robinson spent a lot of time on the athletic field.

Robinson spent some time as a professional footbal player, as star halfback for the Bruins. When the United States entered World War II, Robinson joined the army. In 1944, while in Texas, Robinson exhibited the kind of strength that later helped advance the rights of black ballplayers. He was ordered to move to the back of a military bus, but he refused, knowing that he faced a court-martial. He was later exonerated and was honorably discharged from the army.

The years of constant practice and great natural talent did not go unnoticed. One of his friends suggested that Robinson try out for the Kansas City Monarchs of the Negro Baseball League—the home club of the legendary Satchel Paige. In 1945, Robinson joined the team, and he was soon one of its star players. Unbeknownst to him, he was being scouted by the general manager of the Brooklyn Dodgers, Branch Rickey. For years, Rickey had been searching for the right man to sign to the Dodger organization so that the de facto prohibition against blacks in major league baseball could be broken. Rickey thought that Robinson had the courage it would take not to respond to the taunts, names, and derision that would be directed at him because of his race. Robinson agreed to the challenge.

Robinson spent the 1946 season on the Dodgers' minor league team in Montreal. There were numerous incidents of bigotry that he quietly endured, but the overall result of his year in Canada was positive. Robinson led the league in

hitting and fielding, and the team took the pennant. Rickey was pleased with the results of his experiment, so Robinson was added to the Dodger roster for the 1947 season.

His presence angered many players, sportswriters, and fans who believed that blacks should continue to play in their own league, but Rickey and Robinson were committed to making the transition to integrated play. With great courage and endurance, Robinson remained quiet and determined. There were many times when he had to bite his lip and "turn the other cheek," and he had to stay calm and cool even when he received death threats through the mail. Robinson always honored Rickey's admonition and his own desire to succeed. With the support of the Dodger organization, his wife, Rachel, and many white players, including his teammate Pee Wee Reese, he somehow got through that first year by letting his talent speak for him. His many contributions helped lead the Dodgers to the pennant, and he was named Rookie of the Year.

After that first year, the crack in the door was widened when more players of color were signed. Had it not been for the courage and strength of Robinson and his willingness to be the point man for his people, the baseball color barrier would have remained in place much longer.

Robinson retired from baseball in 1956 and started a business career, but he also continued his civil rights activities, working with the National Association for the Advancement of Colored People (NAACP) and similar organizations. From 1966 to 1968, he served as the New York governor's special assistant for community affairs.

During a multimedia exhibit—"Jackie Robinson: An American Journey"— that toured the United States, Robinson's teammate and good friend Carl Erskine noted: "What Jack did opened a lot of minds in the world. And he was strong enough to open them in a broader sense than just baseball. When people come to this [exhibit] they'll get a lot more than baseball. It's the kind of thing that helps you learn how to handle life" (Dawidoff 1987, 73).

References

Allen, Maury. 1987. *Jackie Robinson: A Life Remembered.* New York: Franklin Watts.

Dawidoff, Nichols. 1987. "Recalling Jackie Robinson; Carl Erskine Visits an Exhibition Celebrating His Teammate." *Sports Illustrated*, 28 September.

Tygiel, Jules. 1983. *Baseball's Great Experiment: Jackie Robinson and His Legacy.* New York: Oxford University Press.

ROCKWOOD, *LAWRENCE*

(1959–)

"If Captain Rockwood is a dangerous man, we shall live in peace ever after. He's the least dangerous man you'll ever encounter." These were the words of former U.S. Attorney General Ramsey Clark in the defense of Captain Lawrence Rockwood at his 1995 court-martial hearing, during which a prosecuting counsel accused Rockwood of being a "misdirected and dangerous officer who thumbed his nose at the fabric of the army, endangering himself and others" (Riehm 1995).

During the fall of 1994, Rockwood's unit had been part of the U.S. intervention in Haiti to return President Jean-Bertrand Aristide to power in the country. Rockwood, a counterintelligence officer with the U.S. Army's 10th Mountain Division, had worked in the Joint Intelligence Center, where he read numerous reports of human rights abuses by Haiti's police and army. He had information that prison conditions were appalling and that people were being tortured and executed. One U.S. State Department report and a U.S. special forces investigation revealed that in one instance a prisoner had been chained to the wall for so long that the skin on his back had rotted away. When Rockwood asked his superior officers to take action, he was told not to believe half of what he read or heard, so he filed a complaint with the inspector general of his division.

Rockwood charged his immediate commanders "with criminal negligence for allowing gross human rights violations, including murder, to continue unabated," according to Peace Media Service, which had a reporter at the Rockwood court-martial. No action was taken, so out of frustration, Rockwood made an unauthorized investigation of the national penitentiary and found emaciated prisoners, some packed 20 to a cell. In the prison infirmary, there was one cot for every three prisoners, with some lying on the dirty floor. Rockwood asked the prison warden to notify U.S. authorities, but when a U.S. Army major arrived, he arrested Rockwood and took him to a military hospital for a psychiatric examination, which revealed no mental disorders. At his court-martial, Rockwood faced several charges, among them leaving his post without authorization and conduct unbecoming an officer.

What brought a 15-year career army man to the point of insubordination? Rockwood's father, a World War II veteran, had taken his son to visit Dachau, one of the Nazis' notorious death camps. At the camp, his father had pointed out that blind obedience to authority was one reason that the concentration camps had existed. Rockwood was also inspired by several soldiers whom he thought represented the ideal officer with high moral values. One was Chief Warrant Officer Hugh Thompson, a helicopter pilot during the Vietnam War. At the time of the My Lai massacre in March 1968, Thompson ordered his gunner to fire on U.S. forces attacking Vietnamese villagers in an attempt to prevent

atrocities. As a result of Thompson's actions, the U.S. military awarded him a medal for valor. Religious beliefs also motivated Rockwood. He was raised as a Catholic and attended seminary as a teenager. He later turned to Buddhism and is known as an idealist among his friends and colleagues.

Although the army wanted to settle Rockwood's case out of court with a reprimand, Rockwood opted for a court-martial, to make his grievances known to the public. During his court-martial, army prosecutors claimed that Rockwood was overly concerned about prison conditions, since as many human rights were violated on the streets of Haiti as in its prisons. Defense attorneys, who were financed by Amnesty International, countered that the My Lai massacre and the Nuremberg principles set down after World War II dictate that conscience should take precedence over military orders when lives are at stake and that Rockwood's superior officers had failed to comply with the rationale for being in Haiti, which was to stop gross human rights abuses.

As Rockwood expected, he was found guilty of disobedience and other charges against him. Although he was not sentenced to prison, he was dismissed from the army and stripped of his veteran's benefits. He has received support nationwide, and a *Los Angeles Times* editorial declared that one of the army's first priorities

should have been to remedy the hideous human rights abuses in Haiti's prisons. Indeed, to let those abuses go on when U.S. forces were in a position to stop them mocked the aims of the intervention. If the Rockwood case now forces the military—and its civilian bosses—to better prepare for dealing with human rights abuses in future interventions it will have served a valuable purpose ("The Real Lesson" 1995).

References

"The Real Lesson of the Rockwood Case." 1995. Editorial. *Los Angeles Times*, 16 May.

Riehm, Rebecca. 1995. "US Army Officer on Trial for Defending Haitian Human Rights." Peace Media Service electronic conference posting (peacemedia.news), 10 May.

Risen, James. 1995. "Dismissal of Army Captain Raises U.S. Policy Questions." *Los Angeles Times*, 15 May.

RODDICK, ANITA

(1943–)

She has been through lawsuits, has been the subject of negative stories in newspapers, and has been criticized by shareholders because of decreasing profits in 1992 and 1993 for her British-based Body Shop enterprise, which is now a line of toiletry products with more than 1,000 franchises around the world. Anita Roddick has survived her critics, however, and she continues to espouse social and environmental causes, particularly human rights and sustainable use of the world's resources. In a 1994 speech before a conference in Mexico on free trade, she declared

> I've heard much about increased rates of growth in trade, but little about stronger communities of healthier children. I have heard much about the march of progress, but little about the people and cultures who are being trampled underfoot.
>
> I am no loony do-gooder, traipsing the world hugging trees and staring into crystals. I'm a trader. I love buying and selling. . . . I've established England's most effective and successful international retailing company. . . . I support expanded trade. . . . But I am concerned about quality in trade, not just quantity.
>
> I have been part of a . . . business movement . . . that has tried to put idealism back on the agenda. We want a new paradigm, a whole new framework, for seeing and understanding [that] business can and must be a force for positive social change. It must not only avoid hideous evil—it must actively do good. . . . [It] is now entering centre stage. It is faster, it is more creative, it is more wealthy than governments. However if it comes with no moral sympathy, or honourable code of behaviour, God help us all (Roddick 1994).

A social activist most of her life, Roddick has a sense of outrage about numerous issues. Her social conscience was awakened during childhood. "When I was eleven years old, I was given a book on the Holocaust. It hit a nerve, and my concern has been there ever since," she said (Pope 1993).

Born in Littlehampton, Sussex, England, and named Anita Lucia Perella, she was the third of four children of Italian immigrants. She attended a Catholic school and later Newton Park College of Education at Bath, studying to be a teacher. She has always loved adventure, however, and she began traveling, working in Paris for a while, then for the United Nations in Geneva, Switzerland. She went by ship to other parts of the world, including Australia and South Africa, and then back to England, where she met Gordon Roddick, a Scotsman who had also been a world traveler. The two married and had two children, but

when the girls were still very young (six and four), Gordon left to fulfill a life-long dream of riding horseback from Buenos Aires to New York City. His wife did not object, since she has "always admired people who follow their beliefs and passions," she told a reporter (Pope 1993).

To support herself, Roddick began her business in 1976 as a cosmetics shop in Brighton, where she sold "natural" products. Within a year, she had opened a second store. After her husband returned home, they decided to franchise, setting up 138 shops by 1984. As her business continued to grow, Roddick began to use it to promote social and environmental change, supporting groups such as Amnesty International, Cultural Survival, and Greenpeace. In 1987, her company began a Trade-Not-Aid program, in which the basic philosophy is to help small communities around the world develop the resources they need for survival. Trade-Not-Aid projects have helped indigenous people in the tropics develop and market sustainable forest products; worked with such leaders as PAULINHO PAIKAN in Brazil to protect rain-forest resources and the homelands of Amazon tribes; prompted Pueblo Indians in New Mexico to produce blue corn for various Body Shop soaps and creams; and encouraged the development of various enterprises in Europe, Canada, and the United States that put economically depressed people to work and aid the homeless.

Roddick preaches corporate social and environmental responsibility, requiring her company to audit itself to determine whether it is living up to such standards, which can be summed up in a slogan posted on shop walls: "Reinvent, reach, risk, refuse, resist, and reuse." Recycling is a major part of the production and marketing processes, as is the effort to return a part of each franchise's profits to the community in which it is located.

Although much of the business world has scoffed at Roddick's approach and philosophy, she continues to speak out for and live by honorable business practices and to emphasize that business can combine altruism with profit making. She believes that "companies should not be evaluated solely on their annual report and accounts. If I bought stocks and shares . . . along with the profit and loss sheets, I would want to know about the profit and loss for the environment, or the community or the Third World. . . . I don't understand why companies are not routinely checked like that." Accumulating personal wealth is not part of Roddick's or her husband's way of life. In her autobiography, she states:

> We believe it would be obscene to die rich and we intend to ensure that we die poor by giving away all our personal wealth, through a foundation of some kind. . . . I believe we impoverish ourselves by our tendency to undervalue all the other riches that come from our life experiences—the ones that can't be bought. . . . More significant than money, I think, is the substantial time that Gordon and I devote to social and environmental matters (Roddick 1991, 255).

References
Conlin, Jennifer. 1994. "Survival of the Fittest." *Working Woman*, February.

Elmer-Dewitt, Philip. 1993. "Anita the Agitator." *Time*, 25 January.

Pope, Brock. 1993. "Anita Roddick." *People*, 10 May.

Roddick, Anita. 1991. *Body and Soul: Profits with Principles—The Amazing Success Story of Anita Roddick and the Body Shop*. New York: Crown Publishers.

———. 1994. "Corporate Responsibility." *Vital Speeches*, 15 January.

ROMERO, *OSCAR*

(1917–1980)

"**M**ay God have mercy on the assassins," were the last words of Archbishop Oscar Arnulo Romero (Chua-Eoan 1987). On 24 March 1980, the Roman Catholic archbishop of El Salvador became a martyr to the cause of human rights and social justice for the poor. He was shot and killed while saying mass at a small chapel in the Hospital of Divine Providence in San Salvador. Romero had reportedly been targeted because of his calls for peace in the worn-

torn country, where far-right military death squads and opposing Marxist guerrilla forces ravaged the country, murdering tens of thousands.

Born in a village near the city of San Miguel, Romero spent his childhood and early adult life in that remote mountainous region. At the age of 23, he began seminary school in San Miguel and later studied in San Salvador and Rome, Italy. He served as a San Miguel parish priest for a time and then became auxiliary bishop in Santiago de Maria in 1975. Government pressure resulted in the removal of Archbishop Chavez y Gonzalez, a champion of poor peasants who were repressed and abused by the military, and the conservative and cautious Romero replaced him.

By 1977, after the election of General Carlos Humberto Romero (no relation to the archbishop), political violence escalated. The military rulers engaged in a

brutal campaign against Jesuit priests and their sympathizers, who helped organize peasants for land reform and social justice. Jesuits were being forced out of the country or tortured and killed. When Father Rutilio Grande (a friend of Romero's) and a young boy and old man were killed in March 1977, Archbishop Romero was deeply affected. In fact, he underwent a "radical change," as one Jesuit priest, Father Jon Sobrino, put it:

> [Romero] was fifty nine years old at the time, an age at which people's psychological and mental structure, their understanding of the faith, their spirituality, and their Christian commitment have typically hardened. Furthermore, he had just been named an archbishop—the highest level of responsibility in the institutional church. . . . He had known the cajolery of the powerful. . . . They would build him a magnificent bishop's palace, they told him, and they hoped he would reverse the line taken by his predecessor. . . . But Archbishop Romero . . . refused the beautiful palace and went to live in Divine Providence Hospital, in a little room next to the sacristy. Thus not only were the powers cheated of their hopes for a nice, pliable ecclesiastical puppet, but the new archbishop was actually going to oppose them somehow. In store for him, of course, if he did so, was the wrath of the mighty—the oligarchy, the government, the political parties, the army, the security forces, and later, the majority of his brother bishops, various Vatican offices, and even the U.S. government (Sobrino 1990, 6–7).

Savadoran government officials were threatened by the liberation theology of Jesuit priests, and a month after the murder of Father Grande, two professors (priests) with the University of Central America were arrested and deported, followed by the deportation of three U.S. priests. Over the next few months, the violence became even more severe; many people were arrested and never seen again or killed outright. From the pulpit, Romero began to attack the military and listed the names of those arrested by the government in the archdiocese newspaper.

In October 1979, junior army officers in El Salvador staged a bloodless coup, ending the oligarchic dictatorship. The new ruling junta consisted of Catholic intellectuals, who claimed that Romero was a communist, and the military. Although some land reform schemes were implemented, repression and violation of human rights went on.

The military government was supported by the U.S. government, and in early March 1980, Romero wrote to President Jimmy Carter regarding an announcement that the United States would send economic and military support to El Salvador. The letter was among 12,000 declassified documents dealing with Salvadoran human rights issues that were released in 1993 after prodding by a United Nations Truth Commission Report on El Salvador. In part, the letter expressed Romero's concern

> that the government of the United States is studying a form of abetting the army of El Salvador by sending military teams to "train three Salvadoran

battalions in logistics, communications and intelligence." If this information is correct, the contribution, instead of promoting greater justice and peace in El Salvador, will without doubt sharpen the injustice and repression against the organizations of the people which repeatedly have been struggling to gain respect for their most fundamental human rights.

The present junta government and above all the armed forces and security forces unfortunately have not demonstrated their capacity to resolve, in political and structural practice, the grave national problems. In general, they have only reverted to repressive violence producing a total of deaths and injuries much greater than in the recent military regimes whose systematic violation of human rights was denounced by the international committee on human rights (Jones 1994).

Two weeks before Romero was murdered, he summed up for a Mexican newspaper reporter his thoughts about threats on his life: "If they kill me, I shall arise in the Salvadoran people. I say so without meaning to boast, with the greatest humility. . . . Let my death, if it is accepted by God, be for the liberation of my people and as a witness of hope in the future" (Brockman 1982, 223).

References

Brockman, James R. 1982. *The Word Remains: A Life of Oscar Romero*. Maryknoll, NY: Orbis Books.

Chua-Eoan, Howard G. 1987. "Grave Encounters." *Time*, 7 December.

Jones, Arthur. 1994. "El Salvador Revisited." *National Catholic Reporter*, 23 September, special supplement.

Sobrino, Jon. 1990. *Archbishop Romero: Memories and Reflections*. Translated by Robert R. Barr. Maryknoll, NY: Orbis Books.

ROOSEVELT, ELEANOR

(1884–1962)

First Lady Eleanor Roosevelt has been a model for numerous women in public office ever since her husband Franklin D. Roosevelt was president of the United States. A strong advocate for many social causes, she was often criticized and ridiculed, but she did not hesitate to speak out for what she believed was right and to champion human rights throughout the world.

Born to high society, her father's brother was Theodore Roosevelt, who would be president. Her mother was a Hall, another powerful family with deep roots in the founding history of the United States. Although born with a silver spoon in her mouth, Roosevelt soon found that it left a bitter taste.

Her mother Anna was reserved and proper and showed little affection. She was disappointed that her daughter was so plain looking and often called her unflattering names. Roosevelt was forced to wear a brace to correct a spinal cur-

vature and later wires on her teeth to adjust an obvious overbite. As a result, the girl became self-conscious and extraordinarily shy.

Roosevelt's father, Elliott, was quite the opposite of his wife. He doted on his daughter, whom he called "Little Nell," and considered her very talented and a gift to cherish. Unfortunately, Elliott had his own demons to fight. Never very successful in school or in life, and not required to work for a living because of his family wealth, his self-perception was one of inadequacy too. His solution was to go on safari all over the globe and consume a great deal of alcohol.

Elliott's drinking kept him away from his family (by legal order and prescribed treatment for alcoholism), and Roosevelt missed him terribly. Her mother, in poor health during most of the separation, finally succumbed to an infection when her daughter was just eight. Roosevelt and her brothers were sent to live with their strict maternal grandmother because their father was still unable to take care of himself.

On those rare occasions when Elliott would take his daughter for a fun day in the park or to the zoo, she could not have been happier. More often than not, however, her father would fail to arrive for their dates. The reason was almost always alcohol abuse. One day he did remember to pick up his daughter but stopped by a club for a "short one." Forced to wait in the outer cloakroom while he dallied inside, Roosevelt was left for six hours as her father drank himself into a stupor. The disease finally killed Elliott in 1894. Roosevelt, now an orphan, was just ten years old.

Her life continued rather uneventfully through her fifteenth year under the guardianship of her grandmother. That year, she was sent to one of the finest

finishing schools in Europe, Allenwood, outside of London. There, Roosevelt finally found some real acceptance. She was respected for her wit, intelligence, and elegant demeanor and was enjoyed by staff and students alike. During her three-year stay at Allenwood, she found success and happiness. She was also exposed, for the first time, to the ideas of social liberalism and activist reform—ideas that were quite foreign to her family but were to guide Roosevelt for the rest of her life.

When she returned to the United States for her "coming out" in 1902, Roosevelt was officially presented to New York society. The parties she was obliged to attend were also attended by some of the most desirable bachelors. One of them was 21-year-old Franklin Delano Roosevelt, a distant cousin. In short order, the couple was married, and Roosevelt took her place as a dutiful wife. In the early 1900s, this meant that she was in charge of the household management, her husband's happiness, and child rearing. Franklin, for his part, was free to pursue his career goals. In this case, he coveted the power of political office.

Between 1906 and 1916, the Roosevelts had six children, principally because they did not know how to practice birth control. She had never been anxious to be a mother, and she finally stopped the process by moving into a separate bedroom. According to some accounts, this was fine with Franklin, who had married his wife for her intellectual skills and because she would be an asset for his career. He had taken to visiting other young women early on in their marriage, and Roosevelt seemed to accept that theirs would be an unusual relationship. When she discovered that he was having an affair with her social secretary, she offered him his freedom, but Franklin refused, since divorce would have ruined his political career. During this period, Roosevelt apparently "began a long process of introspection and change" (Cook 1992, 230). She and Franklin agreed to stay married for the children and to keep their effective intellectual team together, and Roosevelt began a phase of her life in which shyness and self-doubt could be put aside.

When World War I broke out, Roosevelt began to shed the psychic shackles that had kept her in the background for the first 30 years of her life. She expressed her opinions on a variety of issues, which proved invaluable to her husband, who needed an honest assessment of his political actions from someone he trusted. She also moved outside of his influence. Championing many causes that supported a democratizing of the United States, she built a reputation of her own as one who could humanize government.

By the time Franklin D. Roosevelt was elected to the White House, his wife had become his most valued asset. When he could not travel easily because of the polio that had left him wheelchair-bound, she became his eyes and ears. When he could not publicly advocate a particular liberal political position, his partner would take the lead on the issue. She overcame her shyness through speech classes and practice and communicated whenever she could on the radio and via her newspaper column "My Day." The New Deal was Franklin, but the new vision for the country was just as much, if not more, Eleanor. She would dress in fatigues to visit the troops or don coveralls and a hard hat to inspect conditions down in a mine. She championed numerous social causes, including civil

rights, full employment, and an improved quality of life for all citizens.

She was more than ready to retire when President Roosevelt died, but the world would not let her rest. She continued to represent the United States as an official ambassador wherever her presence might be of help. She had a broad vision of the world, but it stemmed from interest in and compassion for the individual first. As she explained: "My interest or sympathy or indignation is not aroused by an abstract cause but by the plight of a single person whom I have seen with my own eyes . . . my feeling of obligation to do something has stemmed from one individual and then widened and become applied to a broader area" (Hareven 1968, 265–266).

When President Truman had to appoint a representative to the newly established United Nations, Roosevelt was his choice. She proved to be an excellent representative and chaired the important Commission on Human Rights. The "Declaration on Human Rights" that her committee wrote was later incorporated into the constitutions of many emerging countries.

References

Cook, Blanche Wiesen. 1992. *Eleanor Roosevelt.* Vol. 1, *1884–1933.* New York: Viking Press.

Hareven, Tamara K. 1968. *Eleanor Roosevelt: An American Conscience.* Chicago: Quadrangle Books.

Hoff-Wilson, Joan, and Marjorie Lightman, eds. 1984. *Without Precedent: The Life and Career of Eleanor Roosevelt.* Bloomington: Indiana University Press.

Lash, Joseph P. 1972. *Eleanor: The Years Alone.* New York: W. W. Norton.

———. 1982. *Love, Eleanor: Eleanor Roosevelt and Her Friends.* New York: Doubleday.

———. 1984. *A World of Love: Eleanor Roosevelt and Her Friends, 1943–1962.* New York: Doubleday.

Roosevelt, Eleanor. 1949. *This I Remember.* New York: Harper & Brothers.

———. 1958. *On My Own.* New York: Harper & Brothers.

Witney, Sharon. 1982. *Eleanor Roosevelt.* New York: Franklin Watts.

ROTBLAT, JOSEPH

(1908–)

A physicist who helped develop the atomic bomb, Joseph Rotblat renounced such activity in the late 1940s. As a matter of conscience, he has spent more than 50 years dedicated to ridding the world of nuclear weapons through an organization that he cofounded with ALBERT EINSTEIN and British philosopher BERTRAND RUSSELL, known as the Pugwash Conferences on Science and World Affairs. It was named for a fishing village in western Nova Scotia, Canada, where the group first met in 1957. For his efforts to "put the atomic bomb genie back in the bottle," Rotblat and the organization won the Nobel Peace Prize in 1995.

Rotblat was born in Warsaw, Poland, the fifth of seven children in a prosperous Jewish family. After World War I, however, the family paper business failed, and everyone had to fight for survival. Young Rotblat worked as an electrician, laying cable during the day and studying at night. He became interested in electromagnetic theory and the atom, which at the time was being intensely studied by Europe's greatest physicists. In 1932, he earned his master's degree in the field of atomic physics. While a student, he met Tola Gryn, whom he married a few years later.

Rotblat accepted a research position with the Radiological Laboratory of Warsaw and was expected to direct the laboratory someday. In early 1939, as German war threats spread across Europe, he received a fellowship from the Polish government to continue his research in Liverpool, England, with noted physicist James Chadwick. Since the grant was barely enough to support him, Rotblat had to leave his wife in Warsaw. For several months, he conducted experiments in Liverpool; Chadwick was impressed and offered him another fellowship. He went home for the summer to make arrangements for Tola to join him in Liverpool.

During 1939, Rotblat was working on theories about the chain reaction of uranium fission and realized:

of course, there could be an explosion because of the enormous amount of energy produced in a short time. This occurred to me, but I did not think I should follow it up. My job was to do research, and not think about how it was to be applied. But people living in Poland were thinking about the political situation. We knew that sooner or later the Germans would attack. It was only a matter of time. We trusted that Britain and France would come to our rescue. I thought that if the Germans had such a new device, it would be quite terrible for our side (Landau 1996).

Rotblat left for Liverpool again in August 1939, expecting his wife to join him soon, but on 1 September, the Germans attacked Poland, and Tola was not

allowed to leave. Rotblat was unable to make contact with his wife until early 1940, when he arranged for her to travel through Belgium. When that country also fell to the Germans, he tried to arrange passage through Denmark and Italy, but those efforts failed also. Then Rotblat lost contact with his wife, and he learned later that she had died.

As the Nazis overran European countries, Rotblat became convinced that the danger of the Nazi regime was so great that "one had to put aside one's moral scruples regarding the bomb." With Chadwick's blessings, a team of researchers in Liverpool began experiments to determine whether it was theoretically possible to build an atomic bomb. Meanwhile, in the United States, President Franklin Roosevelt ordered scientists to develop an atomic weapon before the Germans were able to do so. In 1942, Roosevelt and British Prime Minister Winston Churchill agreed to combine their countries' efforts and work together on atomic research, which would be conducted in the United States, eventually under a program called the Manhattan Project. It became a massive effort of academia, government, and industry to produce the world's first nuclear weapon at a top-secret Los Alamos laboratory in New Mexico.

Rotblat did not join the first group of British scientists on the project because the United States insisted that only British citizens be allowed to immigrate. Hoping that he could return to his homeland at the end of the war, Rotblat chose not to become a British citizen. The project was so urgent that the citizenship requirement was waived, and Rotblat joined the group of scientists in early 1944.

Early on at Los Alamos, Rotblat learned that U.S. intelligence reports revealed that the Germans had no atomic bomb program and that the Manhattan Project was actually designed to subdue the USSR. He was "terribly shocked" by this revelation. In his words: "I felt there was no need to make a bomb. The only reason I started in 1939 was to stop Hitler using it against us." Rotblat asked to leave the project soon afterward. He was under surveillance by FBI agents, who threatened him with arrest for spying if he told his fellow scientists why he was leaving. He was the only scientist to leave the Manhattan Project, and for 20 years, he was barred from entering the United States (Montalbano 1995).

Forced to remain silent about the Manhattan Project, Rotblat returned to Great Britain and became a citizen, accepting a position as acting director of the Liverpool laboratory where he had worked with Chadwick. When the United States dropped bombs on the Japanese cities of Hiroshima and Nagasaki in August 1945, killing more than 100,000 people and injuring as many, Rotblat was devastated. "The whole idea of making the bomb by us was that it should not be used," he explained (Montalbano 1995).

After that, Rotblat began to speak out, lecturing throughout England and attempting to convince other physicists "of the need for a moratorium on nuclear weapons. He also became executive vice president of a new British group, the Atomic Scientists Association (ASA), whose purpose was to help shape British policy regarding nuclear energy and to educate the public" (Landau 1996).

Throughout the latter part of the 1940s and early 1950s, Rotblat focused on medical applications of nuclear physics and became an authority on radiation hazards. About this time, the nuclear arms race was in full swing, with the

United States producing thousands of such weapons. The Soviets, British, French, and Chinese built up their nuclear arms as well. However, many people worldwide began to realize that radiation from nuclear explosions threatened public health and lives, and numerous groups organized to stop the arms race.

In 1955, Bertrand Russell suggested to Rotblat and Einstein that eminent scientists gather to discuss nuclear disarmament. Canadian industrialist Cyrus Eaton offered to pay expenses for the international meeting in his hometown of Pugwash, Nova Scotia. The conference convened two years later, in 1957, and among the 22 distinguished participants were "three Nobel laureates, the vice president of the Soviet Academy of Sciences, a former director-general of the World Health Organization, as well as the editor of the *Bulletin of the Atomic Scientists*." Because of East-West frictions, "it required a great deal of civic courage to come," Rotblat noted. "Anyone in the West who came to such a meeting, who talked peace with the Russians, was condemned as a Communist dupe" (Landau 1996).

The scientists issued a well-received report on the hazards of radiation and decided to continue to hold conferences to discuss not only arms control but also the social responsibility of scientists. "The first conference proved that scientists have a common purpose which can transcend national frontiers without violating basic loyalties," Rotblat wrote (Montalbano 1995). For 14 years, Rotblat was secretary-general of the Pugwash conferences, and in 1988, he was elected president of the organization.

When Rotblat and the group were awarded the Nobel Peace Prize in 1995, they were cited by the Nobel committee for their efforts to "diminish the part played by nuclear arms in international politics and in the longer run to eliminate such arms." The committee also noted that Pugwash has played a major role in making scientists "take responsibility for their inventions."

References

Barbash, Fred. 1995. "Anti-Bomb Physicist Wins Peace Prize." *Washington Post*, 14 October.

Landau, Susan. 1996. "Joseph Rotblat: The Road Less Traveled." *Bulletin of the Atomic Scientists*, January–February.

Montalbano, William D. 1995. "Anti-Nuclear Scientists Win Nobel for Peace." *Los Angeles Times*, 14 October.

Rotblat, Joseph. 1972. *Scientists in the Quest for Peace*. Cambridge, MA: MIT Press.

RUSHDIE, SALMAN

(1947–)

On 14 February 1989, a *fatwa,* or religious decree, was issued by the Ayatollah Ruholla Khomeini, Iran's spiritual leader, against Salman Rushdie, a novelist and Indian-born British citizen. The ayatollah declared that Rushdie's work *The Satanic Verses* blasphemed the Islamic religion. Rushdie denied the allegations. His book is a collection of satirical stories filled with allegory, depicting the struggle between good and evil. According to Rushdie, it shows in part "how religion, which is after all one of the great codifications of good human beings have invented, can become a force for evil. How it can eat its children. Which is certainly how I think about the Khomeini revolution" (Grove 1989).

Khomeini called for the assassination of Rushdie and offered a $1 million bounty for anyone who killed him; the death sentence was not lifted even after Khomeini died in late 1989. Iranian government officials demanded that Britain condemn the book or break off all political ties. When Britain refused, Iran demanded that England withdraw its small diplomatic corps from the capital, Teheran, and that Iran's two diplomats in London return home. As an expression of support for Britain and to protest the death threat and terrorist attempt to squelch free speech, 11 European nations called their diplomats home from Iran.

Thereafter, an international uproar and controversy surrounded Rushdie and his book. Numerous news articles and editorials harshly condemned Rushdie for his so-called blasphemous account of the birth of religion. Some critics described him as arrogant yet resentful, cocky and rude, and even cowardly because he sought British police protection and did not suffer the brutalities that have befallen countless writers and other dissidents in totalitarian countries. Others criticized him for his self-centered attitude and for not empathizing with those whose lives were in jeopardy because of his book.

Because of Iranian threats, numerous bookstores and other establishments in Britain and the United States decided not to offer Rushdie's book for sale, and Pearson PLC, the British parent company of Rushdie's publisher Viking Penguin, announced that it did not intend to issue a paperback of *The Satanic Verses.* One company executive declared that "commonsense is more important than principles. Some principles have to be fought to the death, but I am quite clear this isn't one of them." The president of Viking Penguin used classic doublespeak to explain his "general intentionality to proceed with a carte blanche approach to walk away from any situation when it seems clear to us we should do so" (Trueheart 1990). In contrast, some Western commentators were highly supportive of Rushdie and berated those who would not stand up for free speech. For Rushdie, not publishing the paperback was the same as suppressing his work.

In early July 1991, an Italian translator of Rushdie's book was attacked and wounded, and nine days later, a Japanese translator was stabbed to death. Another attack in 1993 was also linked to Rushdie—Norwegian publisher William Nygaard was shot and wounded. However, police closed the case in 1995 because they could not find conclusive evidence that the attack on the publisher was part of the Iranian threat on Rushdie.

Rushdie was born in Bombay, India, into an upper-class Muslim family. He once told the *Washington Post* that he "grew up in a literary tradition" and was introduced to the "Arabian Nights" as a child, "in which it was clearly understood that stories were untrue—where horses flew and so did carpets. And in spite of that blatant untruth, they reached for a deeper truth. So I grew up in a world in which it was understood that fiction was a lie—and the paradox was that the lie told the truth" (Grove 1989).

He attended a British-type school, and when he was 13 years old, his affluent parents sent him to England to the Rugby School, where he was subjected to racist attitudes because of his dark skin and immigrant status. Majoring in Islamic studies, Rushdie attended Cambridge University and later worked as an advertising copywriter. His first novel, *Grimus*, was published when he was 27, and the next work, *Midnight's Children*, was highly acclaimed and brought him celebrity status, which he used to espouse his political views and to loudly condemn (some say exaggerate) the racial prejudice he found in British society.

He has been married and divorced twice and has a son, Zafar, from his first marriage. *Haroun and the Sea of Stories*, a children's fable published in 1993, is dedicated to Zafar and describes the adventures of a storyteller who loses his ability to spin tales and is saved by the heroic feats of his son.

The author is still under a death edict from Iran, and the price on his head has been increased to $2 million. Until his second marriage broke up, he and his wife and her son lived for more than a year in secrecy and under police protection in England. Although Rushdie is still guarded by police, he began to appear at the end of 1992 to attend parties and plays, to appear on television and at news conferences, and to attend public events connected with the publication of his recent books, such as *East, West* (1994).

International publicity over Rushdie has diminished somewhat over the years, but he is still a controversial figure. A 1993 editorial in the *Washington Post* admonished that his case cannot be brushed aside:

> Though more famous than most, he [Rushdie] stands for countless lesser-known dissidents who have been violently suppressed or killed for writings that threaten authorities. Prominent among Mr. Rushdie's supporters are a group of Iranian intellectuals in exile; his predicament is theirs. If a man can be condemned to death for words in a book—and, furthermore, if the outlaw regime of one country can be allowed to order a terrorist attack on a man in another, just because it hates his views—civilized governments cannot wink at the outrage ("Learning from Mr. Rushdie" 1993).

References

Grove, Lloyd. 1989. "Rushdie and Wiggins' Uncommon Bond." *Washington Post*, 7 March.

"Learning from Mr. Rushdie." 1993. Editorial. *Washington Post*, 14 February.

Trueheart, Charles. 1990. "Publisher in the Fray." *Washington Post*, 20 March.

RUSSELL, *BERTRAND*

(1872–1970)

A philosopher by profession, Bertrand Russell also made major contributions in the areas of mathematics, education, peace, and social justice. Russell's political activism was inspired by a quest for human rationality and a compassion for people. He described his motivation in his eloquently written autobiography:

> Three passions, simple but overwhelmingly strong, have governed my life: the longing for love, the search for knowledge, and unbearable pity for the suffering of mankind. . . .
>
> Love and knowledge, so far as they were possible, led upward toward the heavens. But always pity brought me back to earth. Echoes of cries of pain reverberate in my heart (Russell 1967–1969, 1:3–4).

Russell was born into a politically active, aristocratic English family, but when he was 2, his mother died from diphtheria and, at 3, his father succumbed to acute bronchitis. He and his brother were raised by his puritanically religious but politically liberal grandmother. By the time he was 18, he had abandoned all belief in Christianity, although he retained his grandmother's liberal politics, fearlessness, and contempt for convention.

He displayed an early aptitude for mathematics but was later drawn to philosophy to find knowledge "that could be accepted as certainly true" and because of a "desire to find some satisfaction for religious impulses" (Moorehead 1993, 52). He subjected everything to intellectual skepticism, abandoning beliefs that could not withstand his rigorous questioning. As his early religious faith eroded under this scrutiny, he felt apprehension, but eventually, he calmly

accepted agnosticism and a belief that humanity must make the best of living in an indifferent universe.

He was educated at Trinity College (part of Cambridge University in England) and later lectured there as a professor. He worked with Trinity professor Alfred Whitehead to publish (between 1910 and 1913) the three-volume *Principia Mathematica*, which profoundly affected contemporary mathematics and philosophy.

World War I changed Russell's life. To someone with such highly esteemed logic and rationality, war seemed completely irrational and unreasonable. He viewed the war as a lunatic enterprise, and he believed that victory for either side would be a disaster. He became one of the most influential opponents of the war. "His activities, first in the Union for Democratic Control (UDC) and then in the No-Conscription Fellowship (NCF) alienated him from many of his Cambridge colleagues, cost him his post at Trinity, and revealed his talents as a public speaker and popular writer" (Ryan 1988, 55).

In 1916, he wrote a pamphlet protesting the sentencing of a conscientious objector to hard labor. As a result, he was fined, and Trinity College removed him from his lectureship. The British government placed Russell under surveillance and refused to issue him a passport when Harvard offered him a post in the United States. In 1918, after writing an article that supposedly dishonored the U.S. military, Russell was jailed for six months for "insulting an ally." Even many of Russell's foes agreed that the sentence was completely disproportionate to the offense.

After the war, he became even more critical of the Soviets than he was of the Americans. At first, news of the Bolshevik revolution in Russia delighted Russell. He thought, as many liberals did at the time, that socialism was an advanced society in the making. In 1920, after spending five weeks in Russia, he changed his mind. He was horrified at the human cost of the revolution and became an unwavering critic of the Soviet regime.

Over the course of his long life, Russell modified his outspoken views to meet changing circumstances. After Adolf Hitler invaded Poland and seemed to threaten the entire world, Russell altered his view of war and publicly announced his support for World War II. Although he defended democracy for the first time, he upheld the spirit of democracy rather than any institutional form of it.

For much of his life, he earned his living by lecturing on philosophy and by writing. His popular articles tackled a diversity of social controversies, such as a world government, human rights, civil disobedience, religion, politics, racism, education, and nuclear weapons. In 1929, his most notorious book, *Marriage and Morals*, defended premarital sex, open marriage, sex education in schools, and public support for birth control. The book shocked many, and a decade later, it was partially responsible for his losing a lectureship in New York City.

After the birth of his two children (with Dora, the second of his four wives), he became interested in the problems of education. In 1927, he and Dora became

owners, managers, and the primary teaching staff of an experimental school for young children. Russell left the school in 1932, however, when their marriage soured. Although he and Dora believed in open marriage and tolerated each other's affairs, their marriage collapsed after he fell in love with another woman and Dora twice gave birth to children fathered by a long-term lover.

Russell's "immoral" reputation sometimes hindered his academic career. Between 1938 and 1944, Russell served as visiting professor of philosophy at a number of U.S. universities. One appointment, at the College of the City of New York, was finally rescinded by court order because of protest and a lawsuit against him as an "enemy" of religion and morality.

Although hated by many conservatives, Russell also attained high praise. In 1949, he was awarded the Order of Merit, Britain's most prestigious civilian award. In 1950, he won the Nobel Prize in literature for his no longer quite so shocking *Marriage and Morals*, published two decades earlier. Since Russell relished being a gadfly, this temporary apogee of respectability made him feel "slightly uneasy, fearing that this might mean the onset of blind orthodoxy" (Russell 1967–1969, 2:26).

He continued to spark controversy, however, and he was especially vigorous in his condemnation of nuclear weapons. "From 1945 until his death in 1970, Russell thought, wrote and campaigned endlessly in the hope of bringing sanity and order to world politics and persuading his fellow creatures to turn away from the impending nuclear catastrophe" (Ryan 1988, 172). He was a central figure in the campaign against British nuclear weapons. He founded several anti-war organizations, such as the Campaign for Nuclear Disarmament in 1958, the Committee of 100 in 1960, and the Bertrand Russell Peace Foundation in 1963.

With Jean-Paul Sartre, he organized the Vietnam War Crimes Tribunal in Stockholm, Sweden, in 1967. The tribunal condemned American "brutality" against the people of Vietnam. As a further outlet for his political views, he participated in the 1964 organization of the Who Killed Kennedy Committee, which questioned the Warren Commission's conclusions. He had little trust of government and thought that Kennedy had been assassinated as part of a conspiracy involving U.S. government agencies.

Throughout his life, Russell scorned popularity with either the political right or left. He criticized both communists and capitalists in Britain, the United States, and the Soviet Union, and he was, in turn, denounced by them all. A fearless champion of free thought and speech, Russell remained politically active and wrote extensively until his death at the age of 97.

References

Moorehead, Caroline. 1993. *Bertrand Russell: A Life*. New York: Viking Press.

Russell, Bertrand. 1967–1969. *The Autobiography of Bertrand Russell*. 3 vols. Boston: Little, Brown.

Ryan, Alan. 1988. *Bertrand Russell: A Political Life*. New York: Hill and Wang.

S

SADAT, *ANWAR EL-*

(1918–1981)

He has been called an elusive figure—sometimes described as a villain, sometimes as a hero. Anwar el-Sadat, president of Egypt and Nobel Peace Prize recipient, was known for his authoritarianism but also for his compassionate nature. In short, he was a multifaceted person, but former U.S. President JIMMY CARTER knew him as a friend and wrote, "When I first met Anwar Sadat early in 1977 I recognized him as a rare figure on the world's political stage. . . . In my own determined search for peace with justice in the Middle East, I found him always to be like a breath of fresh air" (Sadat 1984, Foreword).

Sadat was one of 13 children of Mohammed el-Sadat, a military clerk who had eight wives, six of whom he divorced because they produced no children.

Anwar's mother was Mohammed's seventh wife and was of Sudanese and Egyptian heritage; she was known as Sit-el-Barien—"the lady of the two sides." She bore 4 children, including Anwar. Under Islamic rules, a man can have four wives simultaneously, so Mohammed married again, and his eighth wife bore 9 children.

Sadat grew up in the agrarian village of Mit Abul-Kum, about 70 miles north of Cairo. He received an elementary education at a religious school, where he was required to memorize the Koran in order to graduate. His schooling helped instill beliefs and practices that earned him a reputation as a devout Muslim. He went to high school in Cairo and then the Royal Military Academy, graduating in 1938 as a second lieutenant—"a dashing young soldier determined to liberate his country from the British oppressors," as his daughter described him (Sadat 1985, 8).

During his high school and military school years, he developed a strong desire to become part of the revolution to free Egypt from the corrupt reign of King Farouk, who was supported by the British. The British had occupied Egypt in 1882, and during World War I, Egypt became a British protectorate. It became an independent kingdom in 1922, although the British kept military forces in the country. Most of the British troops withdrew in 1936, except for those who stayed to guard the Suez Canal Zone.

In 1940, Sadat married Ekbal Madi and took her to live in his father's home in a suburb of Cairo; Sadat, as a soldier, was stationed at a nearby military base. After the couple's first child, Rokaya, was born in 1941, Sadat became involved in a liberation movement. He was arrested for his alleged part in a plan to help a liberation leader escape the country but was cleared the next day. He was arrested again in 1942 as a suspected spy working for the Germans. Because Sadat and other revolutionaries naively believed that helping the Germans would be a way to get the British out of Egypt, Sadat had accepted a shortwave radio from

the Germans and agreed to send information to Axis forces. Police arrested Sadat, and his family destroyed the radio, before any communication took place.

There was no evidence to convict Sadat, but Egypt was under martial law, and he was imprisoned without court review until 1944, when family members helped him escape. For the next year, he worked as a laborer and was able to send money to Cairo to help support his family.

When the Germans appeared near defeat and martial law was lifted in 1945, Sadat returned to Cairo. In 1946, he was arrested once more for his alleged involvement in a plot to assassinate Egyptian Minister Amin Osman, known for his close ties with the British. Sadat was imprisoned until after his trial in mid-1948, when he was found not guilty and released.

During his time in jail, Sadat met a young visitor, Jihan Raouf, a cousin of a fellow prisoner. Sadat decided to marry Jihan. Although Islamic law allowed him more than one wife, Ekbal and Anwar divorced in early 1949, and Sadat's second marriage took place a few months later. According to some reports, Jihan later urged her husband to promote reform of the family code to provide more rights for women.

In 1952, Sadat took part in a military coup, organized by a revolutionary group known as the Free Officers and led by Gamal Abdel Nasser. The coup forced King Farouk to flee to Europe. Egypt became a republic in 1953 and Nasser its president in 1954; four years later, he was elected president of a new nation formed by Syria and Egypt called the United Arab Republic.

Sadat held several government posts during the latter half of the 1950s and in the 1960s. During that time, Egypt seized the Suez Canal, and the country was attacked by Israel, Britain, and France; a cease-fire was eventually arranged by the United Nations. In 1967, Egypt believed that Israel was ready to attack and, along with Syria and Jordan, built up troops along the Israeli border in the Sinai desert. In the famed Six-Day War, Israel destroyed the Arab forces.

When Nasser died in 1970, Sadat became president. Many thought that he would maintain the ties with the Soviet Union that Nasser had established, but he reversed those policies in 1972. Like Nasser, Sadat at first took a strong stand against Israel and coordinated a 1973 attack on Israel by Arab states. Known as the Yom Kippur War, it resulted in a standoff but was proclaimed a psychological victory for Egyptians.

Sadat began to rethink Egyptian involvement in the Arab-Israeli conflict, and in February 1977, he accepted an invitation from President Carter to discuss the conflict and began in earnest to search for solutions. He decided that he "wanted to prove to the whole world" that he was a "man of peace" and began to formulate a peace initiative, thinking, "Why shouldn't I go to the Israelis directly? Why shouldn't I stand before the Knesset and address the Israelis themselves as well as the whole world, putting forward the Arab cause and stating its dimensions?" (Sadat 1984, 104–105). Sadat did just that on 19 November 1977, becoming the first Arab leader to visit the Jewish state, which helped initiate the peace process.

In 1978, Sadat and Israeli Prime Minister Menachem Begin met with President Carter at the Camp David retreat near Washington, D.C., and worked out

a peace agreement known as the Camp David Accords. It included a provision to end the Israeli occupation of the West Bank and the Gaza Strip, which had been taken over by Israel in the Six-Day War. For these efforts, Sadat and Begin shared the 1978 Nobel Peace Prize. Sadat donated his share of the prize money to his home village for modernization projects.

Sadat and Egypt were "bitterly attacked in the Arab world for concluding the Camp David agreement with Israel." As Sadat wrote:

> The sad truth is that those who attacked us so vehemently did so even before the . . . accords were known. They attacked an agreement they knew nothing about, even though it could have led to the realization of our Arab goals. They did so simply because we dared to negotiate with the Israeli enemy (Sadat 1984, 108).

Following the accords, there was great unrest in Egypt because of economic problems, as well as unrest among Islamic fundamentalists, who opposed the influx of Western ideas. Sadat instituted a crackdown on extremist groups in the fall of 1981, but in October, while he was reviewing an annual parade, Sadat was assassinated by religious fanatics who jumped from a truck and opened fire on the reviewing stand, killing the president and several other officials. Five members of the Islamic Jihad, an extremist Muslim organization, were arrested and condemned to death, and 17 others were imprisoned for Sadat's assassination.

References

Drexel, John, ed. 1991. *The Facts on File Encyclopedia of the 20th Century.* New York: Facts on File.

Lippman, Thomas W. 1989. *Egypt after Nasser: Sadat, Peace and the Mirage of Prosperity.* New York: Paragon House.

Sadat, Anwar. 1957. *Revolt on the Nile.* New York: John Day.

———. 1977. *In Search of Identity.* New York: Harper & Row.

———. 1984. *Those I Have Known.* New York: Continuum.

Sadat, Camelia. 1985. *My Father and I.* New York: Macmillan.

SAKHAROV, *ANDREI*

(1921–1989)

"Everything Andrei Dmitrievich did was dictated by his conscience, by his deep-rooted humanitarian convictions," said part of the official obituary published and broadcast during and after Sakharov's funeral on 18 December 1989 (he had died on 14 December). A brilliant physicist, Sakharov helped develop the Soviet hydrogen bomb (H-bomb) in the late 1940s and 1950s but later became a champion of nuclear disarmament and a human rights activist. As a result, he was exiled from his privileged position within Soviet government circles to the closed city of Gorky.

Born in Moscow, Sakharov was the first of two children—his younger brother, Goergy, was born in 1925. He was also part of a fairly large extended family of uncles, aunts, and grandparents. While Andrei was growing up, four Sakharov families shared a communal apartment building. Sakharov's father, a physics instructor and author, sometimes took his son to his university laboratory to show him experiments, "dazzling 'miracles,'" Sakharov wrote in his *Memoirs*, "but miracles I could understand. I soon began performing my own experiments at home" (Sakharov 1990, 12). His father encouraged his efforts and instilled in him the desire to find fulfillment in his work. As Sakharov noted, his father "passed on to his children his own firm conviction that work done conscientiously, professionally, and with zeal is work well done" (Sakharov 1990, 16).

In 1938, Sakharov enrolled in the physics department of Moscow University. After the outbreak of World War II in 1939, the Soviet Union and Germany maintained a secret alliance, but Germans attacked the Soviets in 1941, and air raids on Moscow threatened to destroy the university, which was moved for safety to Ashkhabad. Sakharov graduated in 1942 and was given the opportunity to stay on as a graduate student in physics, but he felt that "it would be wrong to continue studying when I could be making a contribution to the war effort." Sakharov was employed at a munitions plant, working 11-hour shifts, the standard for the nation; the workers received only a small portion of porridge mixed with powdered eggs and weak tea for lunch. After a few months, he began work in a central laboratory, where he became an expert on magnetic quality-control methods. He also met Klavdia Vikhireva (Klava), a laboratory assistant, whom he married in 1943. The couple had three children.

During the 1940s, Sakharov completed his graduate work in theoretical physics and taught undergraduate classes in nuclear physics, relativity, and electricity. In 1946 and 1947, he was asked to join FIAN (Physics Institute of the Academy of Sciences) in Moscow, but he refused. In 1948, he was told that the Communist Party Central Committee and its Council of Ministers had created a "special research group" and that Sakharov was to be part of it. In 1950, Sakharov was assigned to a secret city called the Installation, not far from

Moscow, where he and others developing atomic and thermonuclear weapons worked and lived. For 20 years he was involved in top-secret work on thermonuclear weapons and related research, but he became increasingly concerned about the biological effects of nuclear bomb tests and the buildup of nuclear arms as a deterrence to all-out nuclear warfare.

"The years 1965–1967 were a turning point in my life," Sakharov wrote. Although he was still heavily involved in scientific work at the Installation, he began to question the antiballistic missile (ABM) systems being developed by both the Soviet Union and the United States, which would, as Sakharov put it, "in somewhat simplified terms, increase the minimum number of nuclear weapons needed for mutual assured destruction." Sakharov realized that the work he and his colleagues were doing could easily lead to the "utter insanity of thermonuclear warfare" (Sakharov 1990, 267–268). In 1968, he began to write and speak out against nuclear proliferation and the policies of the Soviet Union, particularly its abuses of human rights. He wrote an essay titled "Reflections on Progress, Peaceful Co-Existence and Intellectual Freedom" in which he alerted readers

> to the grave perils threatening the human race—thermonuclear extinction, ecological catastrophe, famine, and uncontrolled population explosion, alienation, and dogmatic distortion of our conception of reality. I argued for *convergence*, for a rapprochement of the socialist and capitalist systems that could eliminate or substantially reduce these dangers, which has increased many times over by the division of the world into opposing camps. Economic, social, and ideological convergence should bring about a scientifically governed, democratic, pluralistic society free of intolerance and dogmatism, a humanitarian society which would care for the Earth and its future, and would embody the positive features of both systems (Sakharov 1990, 282).

Copies of Sakharov's essay circulated throughout Moscow and the Soviet Central Committee, and translations were published in a Dutch newspaper and in the *New York Times*. Other publications around the world soon reprinted "Reflections," and by 1969, over 18 million copies of Sakharov's essay were in print.

Sakharov was not allowed to return to the Installation, and after his wife died of cancer in 1968, he went back to the university to teach. In 1970, he helped found the Human Rights Committee, a voluntary group set up to study human rights violations and problems in the USSR. During this time, he met Elena (Lusia) Bonner, who had served as a nurse's aide on the battlefield during World War II; after her discharge, she had worked for years to help political prisoners in the USSR. The two married in 1972.

Because of his efforts on behalf of human rights, Sakharov received the Nobel Peace Prize in 1975. After the Soviets invaded Afghanistan in December 1979, Sakharov spoke out against the hostilities and the increased role of KGB agents in the execution of captured Afghan guerrillas and those who helped them. In 1980, the Soviet government banished the Sakharovs to Gorky, a city that was

closed to foreigners. While in Gorky, the Sakharovs were continually harassed by KGB agents. Their apartment was searached on numerous occasions, and manuscript pages for his memoirs as well as letters, diaries, and other documents were stolen. Sakharov continued to write and occasionally managed to release statements to the outside press regarding the persecution of dissidents in the USSR. He also staged two hunger strikes in protest of the treatment of dissidents.

In 1987, Soviet leader Mikhail Gorbachev ordered the release of the Sakharovs, and in the spirit of glasnost (openness) initiated by Gorbachev, Sakharov was praised for his courage and moral convictions. Sakharov was elected to the new Congress of People's Deputies in 1989 and continued to press for reforms in the Soviet government. At the end of the year, he suffered a heart attack and died.

Reference
Sakharov, Andrei. 1990. *Memoirs.* New York: Alfred A. Knopf.

SANGER, *MARGARET HIGGINS*

(1879–1966)

Margaret Sanger was probably the single most influential person in the fight for a woman's right to choose if and when to bear chldren. Concerned first about the health of women and later about world population, she defied the public's moral and religious views to give women the freedom to choose. She also challenged the Comstock Act of 1873, which labeled contraceptive information as obscene or pornographic and prohibited such material from being sent through the mail.

The two main reasons for Sanger's passion about the need for birth control were her mother's poor health and premature death and her encounters with poor working women in her job as a public-health nurse in New York City. Sanger believed that poor health and early death were often the result of too many pregnancies. Her mother, Anne, had borne 11 children (out of 18 pregnancies) and had died when she was only 48 years old. This inspired Sanger to become a doctor, but the family could not afford the expense of medical school.

From her father, Sanger undoubtedly got the energy to stand up for unpopular causes. Michael Higgins was ahead of his time, believing in socialism,

women's rights, and free education. "Few respected his principled advocacy of the rights of labor and other advanced social causes of the day. Yet, as success in business eluded him, he seems to have depended all the more for self-esteem on his political convictions" (Chesler 1992, 24). One connection that did not escape Sanger's attention was her father's identification with Robert Ingersoll, an atheist and strong advocate for women's rights and artificial contraception.

After her mother died, Sanger studied nursing but did not begin practicing right away. Instead, she married William Sanger, and they moved to the country because she was showing early signs of tuberculosis. She and her husband had three children before moving back to New York City, where the couple took an active interest in socialism. Upon their return to New York, Sanger's job as a public-health nurse

brought her into contact with thousands of women who were old and tired at thirty or thirty-five and who plunged into panic and despair at the thought of a fifth or sixth pregnancy. Many resorted to self-induced abortions, which often led to their deaths; others chose suicide. Still others died in childbirth, their bodies weakened by too many previous pregnancies. Observing the poverty, misery, and hopelessness of her clients, Sanger came to the conclusion that most of it was the result of unchecked childbirth. Since no one—not the socialists, not even the feminists—seemed interested in addressing this particular problem, she decided to take action on her own (Straub 1992, 448).

The crusader for family planning first faced up to ignorance. Neither Sanger nor most doctors in the early 1900s knew much about preventing pregnancy. She traveled to France, where there was more openness on the subject. Upon Sanger's return to the United States, she began to publish a magazine called *Woman Rebel*. The slogan of the publication was "No gods; no masters!" Interestingly, although she advocated the need for birth control, a term she coined, she was careful to obey the Comstock law. She did not disseminate birth control information but argued for women's right to such information. Despite Sanger's attention to the letter of the law, the New York Post Office banned the publication, until finally the U.S. Post Office brought charges against her.

Sanger left the United States before her trial because she did not feel that she had time to prepare a defense and because she believed that the law was not fair. She went back to Europe, where she did more research on birth control. When she returned a year or two later, Sanger was seen as a hero. The charges against her were dropped, in part because a number of prominent English liberals had written to President Wilson, asking him to intercede in Sanger's behalf.

Sanger did not consider herself victorious, however. The Comstock law had not been changed, and women still did not have access to the information they

needed to prevent conception. Sanger believed that birth control should be practiced when either spouse had an infectious disease; when the wife suffered from an illness that might be adversely affected by pregnancy; when parents were at risk of having abnormal children; when the couple were adolescents; when the couple could not afford the expense of another child; when the mother had recently given birth; and when a couple had just married, so they could have at least a year to adjust to married life.

Her next step—along with her sister, who was also a nurse—was to set up a clinic in Brooklyn, New York. This was also against the law in New York, where birth control information was prohibited—even between doctors and their patients. The law also prevented doctors from treating venereal diseases unless the patient was male. The clinic was shut down after 9 days. Sanger and her sister served 39 days in jail for the offense. Their appeal, however, finally changed the law. In 1918, the U.S. Court of Appeals ruled that doctors could advise on matters of birth control and treat any disease, including venereal ones.

Sanger continued to fight legislation blocking contraceptive use and to increase awareness of birth control by creating the American Birth Control League in 1921, which was the forerunner of Planned Parenthood Federation of America. In addition, she helped organize major conferences, such as the First National Birth Control Conference in 1921 and the International Birth Control Conference in 1925.

She also traveled extensively. Among the countries she visited were China, India, Vietnam, and Japan—all facing the serious implications of overpopulation. In 1922, "her appearance in Japan sparked intense interest from the moment she arrived and [she] was denied an entry visa, because Japanese representatives on the Washington Naval Conference, who were returning home on the same ship with her, ostensibly questioned whether their government ought to admit a woman whose right to free speech had been suppressed in her own country" (Chesler 1992, 246).

In 1935, Sanger started the *Journal of Contraception* (now called *Human Fertility*). In 1937, the American Medical Association, which had been very conservative, finally recommended that medical schools teach birth control. Even the Catholic Church relented and declared that abstinence was an acceptable means of preventing pregnancy. Later, the church would even go so far as to condone the rhythm method.

Sanger received many honors in her life, including an American Woman's Association award in 1931 and the Town Hall award in 1936 for the "most conspicuous contribution to the enlargement and enrichment of life" (Straub 1992, 589). Sanger continued to write, speak, raise money, and make public appearances to help advance the cause of family planning for as long as her health permitted. The impact of her life's work touched people all over the world. In one of her last visits with her granddaughter, Sanger told her that "she hoped she would be remembered for helping women, because women are the strength of the future. They take care of culture and tradition and preserve what is good" (Chesler 1992, 468).

References

Chesler, Ellen. 1992. *Woman of Valor: Margaret Sanger and the Birth Control Movement in America*. New York: Simon & Schuster.

Rothe, Ann, ed. 1945. *Current Biography: Who's News and Why 1944*. New York: H. W. Wilson.

Straub, Deborah Gillan, ed. 1992. *Contemporary Heroes and Heroines, Book II*. Detroit, MI: Gale Research.

SARO-WIWA, KEN

(1941–1995)

A Nigerian author, playwright, and environmentalist, Ken Saro-Wiwa was a candidate for the Nobel Peace Prize, winner of Sweden's prestigious Right Livelihood Award in 1994, and 1995 recipient of the U.S. Goldman Prize for his grassroots environmental work. In his own land, however, he was convicted without trial for murder and executed by Nigeria's military regime, which claimed that the writer and activist had taken part in a riot that killed four people. However, dozens of international human rights and environmental groups, including Amnesty International and Human Rights Watch, declared that Saro-Wiwa was a prisoner of conscience, and he became a martyr to the cause of protecting the Ogoni people and their lands and resources, which had been exploited by Royal Dutch Shell Oil and other major multinational oil interests.

A journalist who has covered human rights violations in Africa and has himself been harassed and beaten because of his efforts to expose dictatorial rule and abuses wrote in the *Christian Science Monitor*:

> We've heard a great deal about how the 1990s were supposed to be the decade of democracy for Africa. But for those of us working toward democracy in the region, this decade has also witnessed the brutal suppression of freedom of expression on the continent. . . . Ken Saro-Wiwa . . . and eight associates were hanged by the government of Gen. Sani Abacha. A military-appointed judge found them guilty . . . but it was clear to most observers that the murder charges were a thinly disguised excuse for

cracking down on Saro-Wiwa's efforts on behalf of minority rights (Owuor 1995).

Just days before Saro-Wiwa was hanged, William Schulz, executive director of Amnesty International USA, warned about the perils in Africa, pointing out that in 1990:

Nigeria, the largest and—other than South Africa—most developed country on the continent, appeared to have a bright economic future. In 1993, Gen. Sani Abacha came to power following the nullification of democratic elections, which resulted in the apparent victory of Chief Moshood Abiola. Over the next two years, General Abacha banned all political activity, suspended fundamental constitutional rights, cracked down on press freedoms, and arrested Chief Abiola.

Ethnic fighting broke out in Rivers state, the principal site of oil production and protests by local minority groups, including the Ogoni community, over the fact that the extractors of oil were ruining the environment. There is good reason to believe the Nigerian government fomented the ethnic violence, in addition to being one of the worst aggressors.

What is certain is that Abacha arranged for the arrest of Ken Saro-Wiwa and other Ogoni protest leaders, charged them with murder, and sentenced most of them to death. Though they are civilians, Saro-Wiwa and his co-defendants were tried before a military tribunal appointed by Abacha. They were denied the most elementary forms of due process (Schulz 1995).

Immediately following the announcement of the execution of Saro-Wiwa and the others, there was an international outcry and condemnation of Nigeria's military regime. Diplomats were withdrawn from Nigeria, and such African leaders as NELSON MANDELA and DESMOND TUTU expressed their outrage. Mandela called General Abacha's government a "barbaric, arrogant, military dictatorship" and urged Nigerians to resist and challenge their leaders.

Nigeria was suspended from the membership of the 52-nation commonwealth organization, and ambassadors from Britain, Canada, the United States, and about 15 other countries were recalled. The United States also banned sales of military supplies and services to Nigeria, and some international leaders have called for a worldwide ban on purchases of Nigerian oil. The World Bank announced that it would withhold a $100 million loan for development of a liquefied gas project in Nigeria. Nevertheless, Nigerian officials remained defiant and declared that other countries had no business meddling in Nigerian affairs. They maintained that Saro-Wiwa had been head of a militant and violent group that had committed murder.

Born at Bori, Rivers State, Kenule Beeson Saro-Wiwa was part of a large family and a member of the Ogoni, an ethnic group of about 500,000. Saro-Wiwa was a brilliant student and received a government scholarship to attend Government College in Umuahia in southeastern Nigeria and later Nigeria's University of

Ibadan, from which he graduated in 1965. He then taught high school and later university classes in Lagos and in eastern Nigeria.

Saro-Wiwa married and had children, and for a time he was a government official—appointed administrator of Bonny, an oil port, and then a cabinet member of the Rivers State. He left the government in 1973 and began a business as well as pursuing his writing career, earning a good income that allowed him to educate one son at Eton. He published more than 20 works, including poetry, plays, short stories, children's books, and novels. Many of his writings satirized the government and the affluent. He also wrote for various newspapers, exposing corruption in government and business.

In 1990, Saro-Wiwa helped organize the Movement for the Survival of the Ogoni People (MOSOP), a nonviolent grassroots group. The organization has protested the environmental and economic devastation caused by at least three decades of international oil exploration in the Niger River delta. MOSOP also advocates self-determination for Ogonis.

In 1992, after his son at Eton died during a rugby game, Saro-Wiwa put aside writing and devoted nearly all his time to the Ogoni struggle. He appeared before the United Nations to speak and show a film about oil pollution in Ogoniland. He also provided information for such environmental groups as Greenpeace and Friends of the Earth and for the advocacy network of the British-based Body Shop, which took up the Ogoni cause with documentary reports and videos showing the oil companies' role in environmental devastation. Saro-Wiwa was obviously a thorn in the side of the oil companies and of Nigeria's military rulers, who arrested him five times between 1992 and 1994. During that time, MOSOP split into opposing factions, with Saro-Wiwa heading one of them. When the opposition group held a meeting in May 1994, a mob attacked and brutally killed four people. Although Saro-Wiwa was not present, he was arrested and mercilessly beaten, then dragged off to jail. He was held for eight months in leg irons without being charged and with no access to a doctor or legal counsel. He was alleged to have incited the mob attack, and two prosecution witnesses were bribed to testify against Saro-Wiwa, according to their signed affidavits.

When he appeared before a military tribunal in October 1995, Saro-Wiwa declared his innocence, saying:

> I am a man of peace, of ideas. Appalled by the denigrating poverty of my people who live on a richly endowed land, distressed by their political marginalization and economic strangulation, angered by the devastation of their land, their ultimate heritage, anxious to preserve their right to life and to a decent living, and determined to usher to this country as a whole a fair and just democratic system which protects everyone and every ethnic group and gives us all a valid claim to human civilization, I have devoted my intellectual and material resources, my very life, to a cause in which I have total belief and from which I cannot be blackmailed or intimidated . . . [neither] imprisonment nor death can stop our ultimate victory.
>
> Shell [Oil Company] . . . has ducked this particular trial, but its day will surely come and the lessons learnt here may prove useful to it for there is

no doubt in my mind that the ecological war that the Company has waged in the Delta will be called to question sooner than later and the crimes of . . . the Company's dirty wars against the Ogoni people will also be punished.

On trial also is the Nigerian nation, its present rulers and those who assist them. Any nation which can do to the weak and disadvantaged what the Nigerian nation has done to the Ogoni loses a claim to independence and to freedom from outside influence. . . . The military do not act alone. They are supported by a gaggle of politicians, lawyers, judges, academics and businessmen, all of them hiding under the claim that they are only doing their duty. . . .

In my innocence of the false charges I face here, in my utter conviction, I call upon the Ogoni people, the peoples of the Niger delta, and the oppressed ethnic minorities of Nigeria to stand up now and fight fearlessly and peacefully for their rights (Saro-Wiwa 1995).

In spite of international condemnation, Royal Dutch Shell, the United States' Chevron Corporation, and several other European and U.S. petroleum companies have remained virtually silent about Saro-Wiwa's execution, claiming that their operations have nothing to do with political problems in Nigeria. Shell declared that it will continue with its planned liquefied natural gas project in southeast Nigeria. Still, there are many human rights and environmental advocates who continue their efforts to bring justice to the Ogoni and democracy to the Nigerian people. As another of Saro-Wiwa's sons in England stated:

I know that my father's life work and legacy will be cherished and remembered.

I hope that in particular his call for a non-violent and peaceful approach to the problems in Nigeria will be respected. . . . My father cared passionately for, and respected the diversity of life on this planet. Peaceful coexistence and the creation of a just and fair society were his guiding principles. In his grim struggle to defend these, he eschewed a comfortable and safe existence and in the end gave his life for his beliefs.

My father achieved more in his lifetime than most men could ever aspire to. He knew as his good friend Wole Soyinka wrote, "the man dies who stays silent in the face of evil."

As he himself said . . . as he faced his executioners, "you can kill the man, but you can't kill his ideas" (Wiwa 1995).

References

CNN. 1995. "Saro-Wiwa Was One of Nigeria's Most Effective Critics." Electronic posting, 11 November. http://www-cgi.cnn.com/WORLD/9511/nigeria/index2.html.

Daniels, Anthony. 1995. "A Good Man in Africa: The Nigerian Dictatorship Is Fighting Back against the

Weapon It Fears More than Anger." *National Review*, 10 July.

Drogin, Bob. 1995. "Mandela To Seek Oil Embargo against Nigeria Military Regime." *Los Angeles Times*, 16 November.

Human Rights Watch. 1995. "Human Rights Watch Condemns Royal Dutch Shell's Failure To Speak Out against Human Rights Abuses in Nigeria." Press release, 16 November.

Owuor, George. 1995. "Africa's Democrats Need Help." *Christian Science Monitor*, 21 November.

Saro-Wiwa, Ken. 1992. *Genocide in Nigeria: The Ogoni Tragedy*. Port Harcourt, Nigeria: Saros.

———. 1995. Statement before the military tribunal. Electronic posting. http://www.the-body-shop.com/kenalert.html.

Schulz, Willam F. 1995. "The US Ignores Africa at Its Own Peril." *Christian Science Monitor*, 6 November.

SCHINDLER, OSKAR

(1908–1974)

Schindler's story was virtually unknown to the world until Thomas Keneally wrote a factually based but fictional version of his life, which was published in 1982. *Schindler's List* became an international best-seller. However, in 1993, it was indelibly stamped on the worldwide consciousness when Steven Spielberg transformed the story into an award-winning movie. Unlike in Spielberg's *Jurassic Park*, which depicted prehistoric monsters cloned from fossilized DNA, "the wartime monsters in *Schindler's List* . . . are more evil and emerge from within the human heart," as one reviewer noted. "These monsters lived not only in Nazi Germany . . . they are older than King Herod's slaughter of the Innocents, as local as the massacre of Native Americans, as contemporary as the ethnic cleansing in Bosnia" (Stucky 1994).

The unlikely hero who battled the monsters was tall, handsome, gregarious, generous, affable, charming, and flamboyant. Schindler was also a hedonistic, alcoholic philanderer, a con artist, a black marketeer, and a Nazi spy. Yet this "scoundrel savior," at great personal risk, saved approximately 1,200 Jews from Nazi extermination.

Schindler was born to a Catholic family in Zwittau, Austria, which became part of Czechoslovakia after World War I. His father owned a farm machinery plant, and while working in the family business (until it went bankrupt in 1935), Schindler honed his sales skills. Because of his suave salesmanship and business contacts, he got a job as a sales manager. He later joined the Nazi Party because it was good for business. After Germany invaded Czechoslovakia, Schindler's shrewdness and ability to charm information out of people attracted the Nazi's Abwehr (military counter-intelligence service). The Abwehr recruited Schindler to spy for industrial and military information. In the wake of the German invasion of Poland, Schindler went to Cracow in late 1939. There, in part as cover for his intelligence-gathering operation, he took over a previously Jewish-owned firm that manufactured and distributed enamel kitchenware products.

In the beginning, he exploited cheap Jewish labor to make his fortune. However, witnessing Nazi atrocities against Jews finally prompted him to start helping them. He established his own enamel works in Zablocie, outside Cracow, in which he employed mainly Jewish workers. He treated them humanely and protected them from deportation.

In 1942, the Nazis liquidated Cracow's Jewish ghetto. Jews who were fit enough for slave labor were sent to the Plaszow labor camp under the sadistic commandant Amon Goeth; the rest were shot or gassed. In 1943, Schindler used his good connections with high German officials to set up a (more humane) branch of the Plaszow camp in his own factory compound for some 900 Jewish workers, although many were actually unfit and unqualified for the production needs. Schindler convinced the Nazis that the Jews he recruited for his factories were necessary for the German war effort.

In 1944, with the approach of the Russian army, Schindler was granted permission to reestablish his firm as an armaments production company farther from the front and to take with him the Jewish workers from Zablocie. He also managed to obtain hundreds more Jewish "workers" from other labor camps, such as Auschwitz and Goleszow. These workers were named on his famous "list," which actually went through several editions. The list enumerated Schindler's "workers" with each person's name, prisoner number, date of birth, and job classification. Many of the "skilled" workers were too old, too young, too feeble, or too unskilled to actually produce much work. To cover for the ineptitude of his factory, Schindler bought products on the black market and resold them as if he had manufactured them.

Accused of black market profiteering, among lesser charges, Schindler was arrested several times by the SS (the Nazi Party's paramilitary corps). He was always released, however, through the intervention of his many high connections.

When the Nazi regime collapsed in 1945, Schindler's workers were freed, but he was in danger of being captured and executed as a Nazi war criminal. In an act that summarized Schindler's impact, grateful former workers gave Schindler a ring with an engraved quotation from the Talmud: "Whoever saves one life, saves the world entire." Then they helped Schindler escape to Switzerland.

In 1949, he moved to Argentina with both his wife and his German mistress and bought a farm, where he bred nutria (large South American beaverlike rodents considered valuable for their skins). After the farm failed in 1957, he moved back to Germany, abandoning both his wife and his mistress. There he endured more bankruptcies and alcoholism.

Schindler visited Jerusalem, Israel, in 1962, and the *Schindlerjuden* (Schindler's Jews) received him as a hero. With their financial support, he was able to live in Frankfurt, Germany, until his death in 1974. He was buried in a Catholic cemetery in Jerusalem. By 1993, when *Schindler's List* was filmed, about 6,000 survivors and descendants were still alive because of the efforts of one highly flawed hero.

Many have wondered why such a man risked so much to save so many. Years after the war, Schindler commented that because he believed that the Jews were being destroyed, "there was no choice. . . . If you saw a dog going to be crushed under a car, wouldn't you help him?" (Miller 1993). The full psychology of this man, filled with many contradictions, will always be an enigma, but the horror of the Holocaust awakened a dormant decency—a conscience—in him at a time when the number of people acting against evil were in scarce supply.

References

Keneally, Thomas. 1982. *Schindler's List*. New York: Touchstone.

Miller, Mark. 1993. "The Real Schindler." *Newsweek*, 20 December.

Paldiel, Mordecai. 1990. "Schindler, Oskar." *Encyclopedia of the Holocaust*. Edited by Israel Gutman. New York: Macmillan.

Schickel, Richard. 1993. "Heart of Darkness." *Time*, 13 December.

Stucky, Mark D. 1994. "Put Schindler's on Your To-Do List." *Integra*, February.

SCHNEIDERMAN, *ROSE*

(1882–1972)

Known for her efforts to gain trade union membership for women and to secure their right to vote, Rose Schneiderman knew firsthand the problems and depravations that many working women suffered as the 1900s began. Throughout most of her adult life, Schneiderman, at the risk of her own health and safety, spent grueling hours organizing women and fighting for humane solutions to labor problems. This tiny woman, less than five feet in height, stood tall on behalf of those forced to work in frightful, dehumanizing sweatshops.

In 1890, when she was 8 years old, Schneiderman immigrated with her family to the United States from Saven, Russian Poland. The family settled in New York City, and two years later, Schneiderman's father died, leaving a pregnant wife and three children. Deborah Schneiderman, Rose's mother, tried to support her family as a seamstress and by taking in borders, but she soon found that she could not care for four children and maintain her job. She was forced to place Rose, the eldest, and her two brothers in separate Jewish orphanages for almost a year. Schneiderman's mother was able to reunite the family, but earning a livelihood was so difficult that Schneiderman had to quit school after the ninth grade and go to work at the age of 13 as a department store clerk. She worked 64 hours a week for $2.16, a wage that rose to $2.66 after three years.

Seeking better pay, she found a job with a cap maker but had to provide her own sewing machine and thread, and from the $6 a week she earned, she had to pay for the electricity the machine used. Conditions in the factory where she worked were similar to those in most industries of the time—unsanitary, poorly lighted, and generally unsafe. Yet she managed to put in a full workday and still go to night school.

When she was 20, Schneiderman spent a year in Montreal, Canada, where she and the rest of her family stayed with relatives. From a neighboring family, who were socialists, she learned about socialism and trade unions, and in 1903, after returning to New York, she was spurred to help organize a trade union for women, who had no representation in the all-male unions. At the time, factories were increasing their demands on workers and cutting wages, and as Schneiderman noted in later years: "We girls needed an organization. The men had organized already and had gained some advantages, but the bosses lost nothing, as they took it out on us" (Foner 1979, 280).

With the help of friends, Schneiderman signed up enough women to qualify for a charter membership in the Cloth and Cap Makers Union, and the local quickly grew so that it commanded enough strength to negotiate a half day of work on Saturdays. Schneiderman was elected a delegate to the national Central Labor Union and by the following year was on the executive board, the first woman to hold such a high position in the cap makers union.

Schneiderman joined the Women's Trade Union League (WTUL) in 1906, although she was at first suspicious of the group. It was dominated by upper-middle-class and wealthy reformers and unionists who were not factory workers and believed that their purpose was to educate working women about the importance of unions. However, Schneiderman became a dedicated member after the WTUL helped her organize a 13-week strike against the cap makers in 1905. This was a dangerous activity at the time, because women were often arrested, jailed, and abused by the police and the courts. From that time on, she pursued her life's work as a union organizer and eloquent spokesperson for the women's labor movement, although this was often a discouraging as well as a dangerous job. Organizing meant, in her words, "hours and hours of standing on corners in all sorts of weather to distribute handbills . . . calling an endless number of meetings and never knowing whether anyone will show up. On top of all this, you never have a life of your own, for there is no limit to the time you can put on this job." She had deep faith in the trade union movement and believed "with every cell in [her] body" that urging women "to organize was absolutely right for them" (Schneiderman with Goldthwaite 1967, 111).

In 1907, the WTUL provided her a grant so that she could attend the Rand School of Social Science, where her studies enabled her to become an even more effective organizer and field-worker. Her work was partly responsible for spontaneous strikes called in late 1909 among shirtwaist workers—some 20,000 women joined the walkout, creating a work stoppage that lasted until February 1910.

Although many of the workers' demands were met, the Triangle Shirtwaist Company in Greenwich Village refused to go along with improvements in unsafe factory conditions, such as well-maintained fire escapes and open staircases. The company, which was located on the eighth and ninth floors of a ten-story building, locked most doors to prevent union organizers from coming in and to keep workers on the job. On 25 March 1911, a fire was started by a careless smoker and spread through the company, killing 146 young women who were incinerated or jumped to their deaths when they were unable to use the only fire escape available—it collapsed with the weight of hundreds trying to flee the fire—or to escape by the two small passenger elevators. Ladders on fire trucks could reach only to the seventh floor.

The needless tragedy of the Triangle fire brought immediate, outraged protests from across the nation. At a civic meeting after the fire, hundreds of people from all walks of life gathered for a memorial service, and civic leaders called for "industrial improvements." Schneiderman got up to speak about the realities of working conditions:

> The old Inquisition had its rack and its thumbscrews and its instruments of torture with iron teeth. We know what these things are today: the iron teeth are our necessities, the thumbscrews are the high-powered and swift machinery close to which we must work, and the rack is here in the fire-trap structures that will destroy us the minute they catch fire.
>
> This is not the first time girls have been burned alive in this city. Every week I must learn of the untimely death of one of my sister workers. Every

year thousands of us are maimed. The life of men and women is so cheap and property is so sacred! . . .

We have tried you, citizens! We are trying you now . . . every time the workers come out in the only way they know to protest against conditions which are unbearable, the strong hand of the law is allowed to press down heavily upon us. . . .

Public officials have only words of warning for us—warning that we must be intensely orderly and must be intensely peaceable. . . . The strong hand of the law beats us back when we rise—back into the conditions that make life unbearable. . . . It is up to the working people to save themselves. And the only way is through a strong working-class movement (Stein 1962, 144–145).

Schneiderman also worked for reform legislation and women's suffrage, speaking at countless rallies, often at makeshift sites because of the violent opposition to women gaining the right to vote. Once, Schneiderman spoke against a New York State senator who opposed suffrage for women because he feared that if women had the right to vote they would lose their femininity. Schneiderman pointed out the absurdity of such reasoning by describing how women had to work in foundries stripped to the waist because of the intense heat, a condition the senator had never censured. Schneiderman reminded him that he had never been critical of the way women had to work in hot, steaming laundries for 13 and 14 hours a day. How, she challenged, could a woman lose more of her beauty and charm by voting than by working under sweatbox conditions?

During her more than 50 years of efforts in behalf of labor, Schneiderman organized the International Ladies' Garment Workers Union and helped organize laundry workers. She served as vice-president of the national WTUL and then as its president from 1926 until 1950, when the organization disbanded. In the 1930s, President Franklin D. Roosevelt appointed her to the Labor Advisory Board of the National Recovery Act, which prompted some of her critics to brand her a communist. In 1937, she became secretary of the New York Department of Labor, serving until 1943. Schneiderman officially retired in the mid-1950s and began writing a book about the struggles of the labor movement when she was in her eighties. Summing up that work in the final chapter of *All for One*, she wrote:

Working women today have not the faintest inkling of what the conditions were before the terrific increase in trade-union organization, nor do they begin to realize what their predecessors went through in order to change those conditions.

Broken skulls, arrests, jail sentences, hunger—nothing stopped them (Schneiderman with Goldthwaite 1967, 260).

Indeed, nothing stopped Schneiderman until 1967, when failing health forced her to enter the Jewish Home and Hospital for the Aged in New York. She died there at the age of 90.

References

Berson, Robin Kadison. 1994. *Marching to a Different Drummer: Unrecognized Heroes of American History*. Westport, CT: Greenwood Press.

Copeland, Edith. 1971. *Notable American Women*. Vol. 1. New York: Belknap Press.

Foner, Philip S. 1979. *Women and the American Labor Movement: From Colonial Times to the Eve of World War I*. New York: Free Press/Macmillan.

Schneiderman, Rose, with Lucy Goldthwaite. 1967. *All for One*. New York: Paul S. Eriksson.

Stein, Leon. 1962. *The Triangle Fire*. New York: J. B. Lippincott.

Whitman, Alden, ed. 1985. *American Reformers*. New York: H. W. Wilson.

SCHWEITZER, ALBERT

(1875–1965)

Albert Schweitzer could have been famous for any one of his multiple careers as theologian, philosopher, doctor, and even organist. Yet all these were overshadowed by his legendary humanitarianism.

Schweitzer was born in Alsace, which belonged alternately to Germany and France and consequently received cultural influences from both. The son of a Lutheran pastor, young Schweitzer demonstrated an early gift for playing the organ and an early compassion for other people. When he saw poorer classmates without warm coats or gloves, he refused to wear his own. His love for animals prevented him from enjoying fishing because he could not bear to cause pain to either the fish or the worm.

As he studied music, theology, and philosophy at the University of Strasbourg, he remained acutely aware of human suffering in the world and how comparatively blessed his own life was. One day during his twenty-first year, Schweitzer vowed not to pursue his own interests until he was 30 years old, and then he determined to devote himself "to the direct service of humanity" (Schweitzer 1933, 103). His deep mystical faith nourished all his actions, and he

felt that he must live his convictions and not just intellectually write about them. Schweitzer achieved a doctorate in philosophy and a licentiate in theology by the age of 26. He was a curate of a church and then a faculty member of the University of Strasbourg.

Beginning as a series of lectures at Strasbourg, *The Quest of the Historical Jesus* became Schweitzer's best-known book—and the work that branded him a heretic among conservatives. His passionate faith never wavered, however, even when challenged by his own highly critical mind. Although other scholars criticized many of his conclusions, his book was a quest for the truth about Jesus—no matter what the consequences.

In his two-volume *The Philosophy of Civilization*, Schweitzer described his own philosophy of "reverence for life." He formulated what he had felt since childhood: all life, no matter how seemingly insignificant, was sacred. Once life was taken, it could never be restored. Thus, to achieve a truly civilized world, people must maintain and further life rather than damage or destroy it.

Schweitzer always remembered his pledge made at age 21 to devote himself to furthering life, but as he neared 30, his attempts at charitable work left him unsatisfied. Then, by chance, he stumbled across an article about the medical needs of people in Africa's Upper Congo. The article related the ravages of pain and disease they suffered because of the lack of doctors willing to serve under primitive conditions. Instantly, Schweitzer knew that his "search was over" in his quest for a life's work (Schweitzer 1933, 107).

His decision to become a missionary doctor baffled and horrified his family, friends, and colleagues, who tried to persuade him to abandon the plan. Even the Paris Evangelical Missionary Society was reluctant to accept him for medical service, and did so only under the conditions that he would not preach his "liberal gospel" to the natives and that he would raise all hospital operational funds himself. In spite of the obstacles and arguments, Schweitzer persisted, declaring, "God calls me" (Bentley 1992, 125).

In 1906, he enrolled in medical school to prepare himself for a new career. His future wife, Hélène Bresslau, studied nursing so that she could work with him. In 1913, after receiving his medical degree, Schweitzer and his wife traveled to Lambaréné, a tiny French Protestant mission in French Equatorial Africa (now Gabon). There, they discovered conditions worse than they had imagined. Schweitzer initially set up his clinic in an old chicken coop with the meager supplies he and Hélène had brought with them. In the following months, Schweitzer supervised the construction of a larger four-room hospital, doing much of the manual labor himself. Other buildings eventually followed.

World War I interrupted Schweitzer's work in 1914. Local French colonial authorities considered the German-born Schweitzers enemy aliens and put them under house arrest. Friends intervened and got them released temporarily, but

in November 1917, the Schweitzers were taken to France as prisoners of war. After living for four and a half years in tropical heat, the Schweitzers were incarcerated in a chilly army barracks without winter clothing. In less than a month, both were suffering from dysentery, and Hélène contracted tuberculosis. It would take Albert nearly two years to fully recover from the effects of internment; Hélène would remain permanently disabled.

In July 1918, a prisoner-of-war exchange brought their release, and they returned to Strasbourg, where Schweitzer resumed his old position of curate and did some hospital work. During that time, his daughter, Rhena, was born, and he began writing and lecturing again. In addition, he raised funds for his hospital in Lambaréné.

The German postwar economic collapse made construction inexpensive in that country, and the Schweitzers built a home in a mountainous region of the Black Forest. In those days, clear mountain air was thought to be essential for those with tuberculosis. Leaving Hélène to care for Rhena and herself, Schweitzer returned to Lambaréné in 1924. In his absence, the hospital and house had mostly collapsed, and the jungle had reclaimed the land, so he began the task of rebuilding. In 1925, two nurses and two more doctors arrived to help.

By the early 1930s, Schweitzer was showered with honors during his fundraising trips to Europe. Although such adulation made him uncomfortable, he was grateful for the donations it attracted.

In 1939, because of the rise of the Nazis in Europe, Hélène came to live temporarily in Lambaréné. The years during World War II were very difficult. Much of Schweitzer's European staff was called back home for military service, leaving an elderly Schweitzer with an even greater workload. Medicines and bandages became so scarce that patients with less than life-threatening conditions had to be turned away.

After the war, life slowly returned to normal, and Schweitzer began receiving more worldwide attention and funds. In 1947, *Life* magazine called him "The Greatest Man in the World." In 1952, he received the Nobel Peace Prize.

Toward the end of his life, some of the adulation was replaced by criticism. Visiting physicians, who came and went while Schweitzer stayed, called the conditions at Schweitzer's hospital "unsanitary." Other critics condemned his paternalistic treatment of black Africans (only whites held positions of responsibility in his hospital, for example). Although he may have had a paternalistic attitude toward native Africans, he restored the health of about 60,000 of them.

In later life he addressed the problems of world peace, condemning the stockpiling of nuclear weapons and warning of health perils caused by radioactive fallout from nuclear tests. His 1958 Oslo radio broadcasts were published as *Peace or Atomic War?* He continued practicing surgery at his hospital until he was nearly 85. At 90, he died and was buried beside Hélène (who had died in 1957) in a simple grave at his Lambaréné hospital complex.

References
Bentley, James. 1992. *Albert Schweitzer: The Enigma*. New York: HarperCollins.

Brabazon, James. 1975. *Albert Schweitzer: A Biography*. New York: G. P. Putnam's Sons.

Schweitzer, Albert. 1933. *Out of My Life and Thought*. Translated by Charles T. Campion. New York: Henry Holt.

Straub, Deborah Gillan, ed. 1992. *Contemporary Heroes and Heroines, Book II*. Detroit, MI: Gale Research.

SEEGER, PETE

(1919–)

In 1994, during the Kennedy Center honors, Pete Seeger received a medal from the White House for his contributions to music and social change. That was a far cry from the days when Senator Joseph McCarthy ordered Seeger to appear before the House Un-American Activities Committee. Seeger and many others were accused of being communists because their views appeared to be outside of what was considered "acceptable" and patriotic. When Seeger refused to answer committee questions, claiming First Amendment rights, he was charged and convicted of contempt, but the conviction was overturned in 1962.

Born in New York City, Seeger comes from a long line of protesters and social activists. His ancestors were abolitionists during the Civil War. His father, a music professor, became a socialist and conscientious objector during World War I and gave up his teaching job to become a composer of protest songs and a traveling musician.

Seeger began playing the banjo while in prep school in Connecticut, which he attended on a scholarship. At that time, his mother was giving violin lessons to two brothers, and during a discussion with their family, Seeger brashly offered his philosophical view of life, saying, "The only way you can be honest in this world is to be a hermit. The world is so hypocritical that the more you have to do with it, the more you'll get embroiled in hypocrisy" (Wigginton 1991, 201). The students' family responded by telling Seeger, in effect, that he was copping out—that he wanted to be pure himself and let the rest of the world go to hell. Seeger decided that the family was right and ever since has been involved in causes to bring about positive changes for humankind.

Following prep school, Seeger enrolled in Harvard but dropped out after his second year. He was disgusted by what he felt was hypocrisy and cynicism on the part of the professors. When he asked one of his sociology professors why he used long, complicated words on a regular basis, the professor replied in all se-

riousness that it was necessary in order to impress people. For Seeger, that was a turning point. After he left Harvard, he made an attempt at journalism, but when that did not succeed, he committed himself to social change through his folk music, which has been motivated for more than half a century by "a vision of radical transformation through the communal experience of song; of socialism grounded in the rhythms of the workplace, neighborhood and church rather than the insular discourse of the academy. If such optimism is hard to imagine today, all the more reason to contemplate it" ("Isn't This a Time" 1994).

In 1941, Seeger formed the Almanac Singers (which featured Woodie Guthrie). However, his first real taste of stardom came when he joined the Weavers, who recorded hits such as "If I Had a Hammer" and "Goodnight Irene." Ironically, the Weavers' greatest public acceptance came when Seeger was under investigation by the House Un-American Activities Committee. The pressure got to the group, and the Weavers disbanded in 1952. Since that time, Seeger has been a solo artist, performing in such diverse venues as tiny coffeehouses and Carnegie Hall.

Seeger has also been an active environmentalist, as is his wife, Toshi, who worked for 25 years on the Hudson River Revival Festival, which has now been turned over to younger volunteers. In 1968, he and others built a sailboat, the *Clearwater*, which sails the Hudson River during the summer and is used to raise funds and to educate people about the need to clean up the river, its banks, and the surrounding area. His motto has been: "think globally, act locally." In other words, clean up your own small corner of the world, since it is just as important as any other spot, and many individual actions can make a difference.

Although the river cleanup project has been successful over the years, Seeger is not as optimistic as he once was. He feels that we are slowly poisoning ourselves by the chemicals in our food, air, and water—a situation that we will not understand until it becomes irreversible. He believes (as do an increasing number of people) that the best way to reverse the negative trends is to question why things are happening the way they are and to educate ourselves enough to change them.

References

Drexel, John, ed. 1991. *The Facts on File Encyclopedia of the 20th Century*. New York: Facts on File.

Harris, Scott. 1994. "Pete Seeger: Folk Music's Granddad Plays It Green." *E Magazine*, November/December.

"Isn't This a Time?" 1994. Editorial. *Nation*, 26 December.

Seeger, Pete. 1973. *Henscratches and Flyspecks: How To Read Melodies from Songbooks in Twelve Confusing Lessons.* New York: G. P. Putnam's Sons.

Wigginton, Eliot, ed. 1991. *Refuse To Stand Silently By: An Oral History of Grass Roots Social Activism in America, 1921–1964.* New York: Doubleday.

SEGREST, MAB

(1949–)

T he middle child in a white southern family, Mab Segrest was born in Tuskegee, Alabama, at a time when whites in the South were steeped in the fear of integration and had been resisting it with increasing intensity ever since the end of World War II. Segrest was a teenager when Alabama's Governor George Wallace declared that he would defend segregation forever in his state and refused to integrate schools, actions that were overruled by federal courts. She can also recall the Ku Klux Klan bombing of a church in Birmingham that killed four black girls; the white racist attacks on demonstrators in the civil rights march from Selma to Montgomery; and the deaths of such civil rights activists as Jimmy Lee Jackson, James Reeb, and Viola Luizo. One of Segrest's own family—a 67-year-old cousin, Marvin Segrest—shot and killed Sammy Younge, a young black man, because he used a "whites only" bathroom at a segregated bus terminal.

From such a background, Segrest went on work as an activist against racism. One deciding factor was an incident in 1965, when black students at Tuskegee Institute attempted to integrate churches. Students who tried to enter Segrest's church were locked out. As she explained in her autobiography:

the irony was not lost on me as I looked out from the choir loft at the stained glass windows, the one nearest the back, portraying a fair-haired Jesus knocking at the door. "Knock, and it shall be opened," I knew the verses by heart, "Seek, and you shall find." I had been raised in the Tuskegee Methodist Church by people who loved and nurtured me. Along

with my parents, they had taught me all the values I knew. "Love thy neighbor as thyself," we had studied in Sunday School. . . . Like most adolescents, I was an idealist, and this rupture between my teachers' lessons and their behavior shook me profoundly. If we could decide who could not come into our church, then it was just a building that belonged to us, not God. It took me years to articulate my disquiet (Segrest 1994, 25).

Segrest left Alabama in 1971 to study at Duke University in Durham, North Carolina, where she first "came out" as a lesbian. In the late 1970s, she joined a lesbian collective, editing the *Feminary*, which questioned what it meant to be a lesbian in the South. "The query brought us face to face with a potent mixture: the racism of a former slave system, the capitalism that generated it and the misogyny and homophobia that also held it in place," Segrest wrote. She "could not accept a 'sisterhood' as segregated as that of my Alabama girlhood, where it had been enforced by police dogs, fire hoses, firebombs, and the deaths of children" (Segrest 1994, 41).

After earning her doctorate in English, Segrest continued to live and work in Durham and became a lesbian activist. She helped organize the first Gay Pride March in North Carolina after a gay man was beaten to death. In November 1979, Klansmen and neo-Nazis massacred five members of the Communist Workers Party, who had organized a march against the exploitation and repression of workers, especially underpaid millworkers. The murderers were acquitted, which Segrest and many others believe contributed to increased violence by hate groups in the South and other parts of the United States.

In 1983, Segrest joined North Carolinians against Racist and Religious Violence (NCARRV), where she was one of only a few outwardly gay people in a predominantly black antiracist and anti-Klan organization that included some members who were homophobic and challenged her right to be her own person. It was within the NCARRV, however, that Segrest learned to build not only coalitions but also relationships. "I figured I was doing work on racism and anti-Semitism because it was the right thing to do, and once I laid out the case about homophobia, the people I was working with would do the same for me and mine. I was not disappointed. . . . Our work carried a lot of risk, but the risk gave us occasions to develop substantial trust" (Segrest 1994, 49).

For six years, Segrest coordinated the work of the NCARRV to counteract such hatemongers as Glenn Miller, head of the Carolina Knights of the Ku Klux Klan (which later became the White Patriot Party), with close ties to neo-Nazi groups; the Christian Identity group, which broadcasts and publishes hate messages denigrating Jews and people of color while claiming the "superiority" of Aryans (whites); and those connected with the Posse Comitatus, a virulent antigovernment, white-supremacist organization. Several murders in North Carolina have been linked to these hate groups, and Segrest and her coworkers often fear that they too will be killed by neo-Nazis or Klansmen, who consider someone like Segrest a race traitor. Yet Segrest has never regretted her efforts. She cautions, however, that the ugliness and hatred she "uncovered in North Carolina in the 1980s will be our legacy into the next century, unless we intervene.

The racism, the homophobia, the hatred of Jews and women, the greed acceler-
ate, and they sicken us all. . . . There is a lot to be done, but how we go about it
is also important. Because all we have ever had is each other" (Segrest 1994, 180).

Reference
Segrest, Mab. 1994. *Memoir of a Race Traitor*. Boston:
South End Press.

SILKWOOD, KAREN GAY

(1946–1974)

On 13 November 1974, Karen Silkwood paid the
ultimate price for questioning the procedures
and policies of one of the key companies in the
U.S. atomic energy industry. That night, she was on her way to a meeting with
New York Times reporter David Burnham and two other men, who were expecting her to deliver a manila envelope full of evidence that would implicate her
employer, Kerr-McGee, in myriad health and safety violations. Silkwood left a
union meeting in Crescent, Oklahoma, to drive to the rendezvous in Oklahoma
City. Ten minutes later, she was killed when her vehicle went over an embank-
ment after skidding 300 feet off the highway. The state police ruled that she had
fallen asleep at the wheel, and a small amount of alcohol and tranquilizer was
discovered in her bloodstream during the subsequent autopsy. However, a private investigator who later examined the crash scene and her automobile found
a dent in the rear bumper of the Honda, which still held residue of rubber and
metal. This was consistent with a scenario that he was drawing from interviews
and other physical evidence: Silkwood had been followed that night by person
or persons unknown and hit from behind at high speed, causing the fatal wreck.
Only the manila envelope was missing from the car when Drew Stephens—one
of the men who had been waiting for her in Oklahoma City—arrived at the accident scene hours later. No one has ever been indicted for the murder of Silkwood, and it is likely that no one will ever know what really happened to this
ordinary woman who found herself in an extraordinary situation.

Nothing in her early life indicated that Silkwood's name would become a ral-
lying call for the anti–nuclear power movement around the world. Silkwood

grew up in Texas and spent a year in Lamar College in Beaumont, studying to be a medical technician. She dropped out to get married and subsequently had three children. Her marriage ended, and she gave custody of her children to her ex-husband. She then found a job working for Kerr-McGee at its nuclear fuel-rod manufacturing site.

In a matter of months, she was involved in the Oil, Chemical and Atomic Workers (OCAW) strike. Although she was not a union activist, Silkwood believed that she was duty-bound to support the strike and to join the picket line. The union demanded higher wages and better training and safety policies for workers. After two months, the strike had accomplished little, and strikers returned to work under a contract dictated by Kerr-McGee. The union had been defeated, but the strike had been an eye-opener for Silkwood. She had taken a stand against the company, had lived on part-time wages, and had seen OCAW members give in to company pressure. Nevertheless, her ties remained strong with the union.

There was real concern among the union representatives that Kerr-McGee was negligent in training its employees (turnover was very high at the time) in the proper techniques for handling plutonium, one of the most lethal substances on earth. There were allegations that monitoring was lax and that radioactive material had even been discovered in the employees' cafeteria.

After meeting with national union representatives in Washington, D.C., Silkwood agreed to keep a notebook on the company's activities and to attempt to get documentation that fuel rods were being manipulated illegally to meet standards. Her colleagues agreed that she became obsessed with the cause. A week and a half before her death, Silkwood discovered that she was contaminated with plutonium. She checked her house and found that radiation was measurable in her refrigerator. As a result, she was convinced that she would die from radioactive particle exposure. Kerr-McGee accused her of stealing plutonium.

As a result of the Silkwood affair, the public no longer trusts industry spokespeople when they say that they have a model operation and that atomic energy is the answer to our future energy needs. Too many Chernobyls, Three Mile Islands, and Kerr-McGees have come to light. Silkwood's efforts and her untimely demise must be credited with beginning this turn in the public attitude. Silkwood was eventually cleared of the charge of plutonium theft, her heirs were awarded huge punitive damages, and the Atomic Energy Commission found that the Kerr-McGee plant had violated safety regulations.

Reference
Rashke, Richard. 1981. *The Killing of Karen Silkwood*. Boston: Houghton Mifflin.

SIMONS, *DONALD L.*

(1945–)

Many Americans have resisted the draft and chosen conscientious objector (CO) status during U.S. involvement in various wars. They have been praised for their heroic efforts by some and damned and punished for not "doing their duty" by others. Donald Simons was subjected to the same kind of treatment during the Vietnam era, when he declared himself a CO, was denied that status, and refused to be inducted into the U.S. Army. Simons was part of a mass movement for social change that took place during the 1960s and 1970s, and he joined the ranks of hundreds of thousands of COs, peace activists, and others who opposed the war in Vietnam.

Born 29 September 1945 in Morgantown, West Virginia, Simons was reared in a middle-class family that included an older brother and parents whom he described as traditionalists and political moderates. Simons's father was a university professor who had been a pilot in the Naval Reserves, and his mother was a homemaker and hospital volunteer. In a book about his experiences as a war resister, he noted that his parents "hedged on the issue of the war," but during his early years, he had received religious training in a Baptist church. There, the emphasis was

> on love and compassion for others. Life was a gift we were to nurture in harmony with all God's creations. The opposite was war, prime example of the sin of pride. . . . Love was the goal of life. . . .
>
> I could not understand . . . why this view seemed to be held by a minority in a town where it was taught to so many. Why was everyone else choosing war? I did not know, but it did make me feel lonely. Either there was something right with me—I had gotten the message—or there was something wrong with them (Simons 1992, 43).

Simons's self-examination to assure his own sincerity as a CO began after he entered graduate school in 1967 at West Virginia University. He continually analyzed his motives for wanting to resist the draft, trying to reach an honest conclusion about the sincerity of his beliefs. At the time, the war in Vietnam was escalating, and many draft deferments, such as those for married men without children and graduate school students, were canceled. He received notice that he was classified I-A. After several postponements, he was eventually ordered to report for induction in 1969 and formally filed for CO status.

Although Simons did not belong to one of the traditional "peace churches" or pacifist congregations, he knew that the U.S. Supreme Court had found that "those who lived by some 'guiding principle' that prevented them from participating in war could qualify for conscientious objector status." That was difficult

to achieve, however, since the local or state draft board determined the worthiness of a claim.

Even though it was illegal for a board to refuse CO status without clear evidence that the request was insincere, Simons's claim was rejected. He therefore had to report for induction or face the consequences, but obeying the induction order meant going against the biblical command "thou shalt not kill." As Simons wrote: "Our governments contend thou shalt kill under certain political circumstances. One had better follow the government's line or there was the threat of prosecution and prison. For most, that threat canceled the moral choice" (Simons 1992, 68).

Simons went through the induction process, but noted: "I did not believe what the government was doing was right, anymore than I believed that blind loyalty was a good enough reason to allow oneself to be inducted into an organization that killed people. Indeed if there was loyalty to be had, it was me to my conscience" (Simons 1992, 78–79). When Simons was ordered to submit to military service, he said, "I refuse." At that moment, he became a felon. Some weeks later, he was arrested at the university bookstore, where he held a part-time job while finishing up his graduate work, but he was released on bail.

With legal counsel, Simons appealed his case to the Selective Service State Appeal Board but was once again denied CO status and classified I-A. During this same period, there were numerous antiwar demonstrations across the United States, and one demonstration at Kent State University in Ohio resulted in the death of four people, killed by national guardsmen who fired into the crowd.

Simons pondered whether to leave the country, as thousands of potential draftees had already done, and seek refuge in Canada or Sweden, which would not extradite offenders of the draft law. However, he still had some faith in the judicial system and felt that his trial would make a statement of opposition to violence and war. During Simons's trial, the judge allowed no evidence or discussion of his CO claim, and a jury found him guilty of refusing induction. The judge allowed him to go free on bond until his sentencing. Only then did Simons decide to go to Canada. "Some would argue that only by going to prison would my statement be complete . . . but my case did not have the national prominence of a David Harris, an early noncooperator who turned in his draft card and served a prison term" (Simons 1992, 126). Simons's parents had supported him throughout his trial. His father had become disillusioned with the courts and selective service system. Simons left for Canada and never saw his father again; the elder Simons died six months later.

In Toronto, Simons sought the help of the Toronto Anti-Draft Programme, set up to aid U.S. immigrants who refused to fight against Vietnam. The organization provided counselors who assisted with housing, advised on immigration procedures, and provided legal and medical help through professionals on the staff. Simons spent five years in exile and suffered bouts of anxiety and deep depression, although he eventually was able to gain some peace and a feeling of security with regular employment and a modest lifestyle in downtown Toronto. After President Jimmy Carter granted amnesty to draft resisters on 21 January 1977, Simons's indictment was dismissed and the bench warrant for his arrest

following his nonappearance for sentencing was withdrawn. He returned to the United States, settling on the West Coast. He continues to advise young people to listen to their hearts and refuse to kill if they believe that it is wrong. "If you do not listen to the wisdom of your heart, you may suffer for the rest of your days. However, if you are true to yourself and reject the weapons thrust into your hands, you may suffer in the short run, but you will forever be at peace" (Simons 1992, 166).

References

Gioglio, Gerald R. 1989. *Days of Decision: An Oral History of Conscientious Objectors in the Military during the Vietnam War*. Trenton, NJ: Broken Rifle Press.

Kupferberg, Tuli, and Robert Bashlow. 1967. *1001 Ways To Beat the Draft*. New York: Grove Press.

Simons, Donald L. 1992. *I Refuse: Memories of a Vietnam War Objector*. Trenton, NJ: Broken Rifle Press.

Zaroulis, Nancy, and Gerald Sullivan. 1985. *Who Spoke Up? American Protest against the War in Vietnam 1963–1975*. New York: Henry Holt.

SNYDER, MITCH

(1943–1990)

Many people believe that Mitch Snyder was little better than a common thief or at best a grandstanding self-server. A cursory overview of his past might lead one to conclude that these critics are at least partially correct, but he also became a champion of the homeless.

Snyder's father abandoned the family when Snyder was nine years old. Used to living a comfortable middle-class life, the family was suddenly dropped into poverty and emotional hell. From early adolescence, Snyder was in and out of trouble with the law. He spent some time in juvenile hall for petty crimes and left school at fifteen.

Adult education brought Snyder a diploma and a wife. By 1969, the couple had two children, and Snyder had a great job. The trauma associated with his

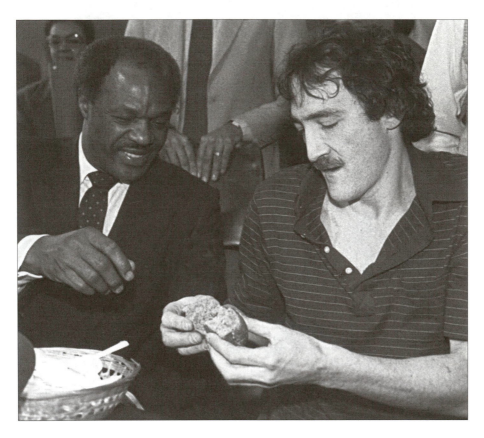

Homeless advocate Mitch Snyder breaks his 33-day hunger strike and shares bread with Mayor Marion Barry of Washington, D.C., at a press conference in 1986. The purpose of the press conference was to announce a deal with the Reagan administration to establish an 800-bed homeless shelter in the capital.

difficult early life is probably an important reason that he was not satisfied with this situation. One day, he woke up and made the radical decision to take to the road, alone, "looking for myself," as he said.

Snyder got as far as California. He was a passenger in a stolen car that was stopped by the police, and although Snyder always claimed that he had no reason to believe the car was stolen, he was charged with grand theft. He was sentenced to three years in prison.

The prison where Snyder was sent was also where the radicals DANIEL AND PHILIP BERRIGAN were incarcerated. From these two he learned the philosophy of anarchism and the tactics of nonviolent protest and confrontation. His first fast, while still a prisoner, lasted 33 days and was initiated to protest many issues, including prison conditions and the Vietnam War. The success of that action was a revelation to Snyder. He became convinced of the power he had to make a difference by putting his life on the line.

Upon his release from prison, Snyder did not return to his family or to any-thing like a normal life. He believed anyone who worked for money was guilty of prostitution. He joined the Community for Creative Non-Violence and helped that grassroots organization run homeless shelter programs in Washington, D.C.

In 1976, Snyder was in the Washington, D.C., area and solicited help from the leaders of more than 1,000 churches, synagogues, and mosques. He asked them to provide space or other services for the homeless, but only one person re-sponded positively.

To publicize the plight of the homeless, who were a hidden problem of the 1970s and early 1980s, he and others in the group mounted controversial stunts, such as carrying around the frozen body of a homeless man. Fasting was one tac-tic that was particularly effective in focusing Americans' attention on the grow-ing problem of poverty. Snyder often fasted to get the government to accede to one of his demands in behalf of the invisible ones who had no voice.

Snyder tried once in the 1970s to reconcile with his wife but failed. He became romantically involved with Carol Fennelly, who ran the nation's largest home-less shelter in Washington, D.C., and they were companions for 13 years. By the early 1990s, he was increasingly despondent and announced plans to leave his work with the homeless and retreat to a Trappist monastery. On 5 July 1990, he was found hanged in his room at the Community for Creative Non-Violence. He had committed suicide. Although some claim that his motive was his failed ro-mance, others believe that he killed himself because he was so discouraged with the country's apathetic response to the homeless. Today, few doubt that his sac-rifices were instrumental in making homelessness a national issue.

References

Ayers, Tiffany. 1990. "Mitch Snyder, Homeless Advo-cate, Mourned." *National Catholic Reporter*, 27 July.

Bethell, Tom. 1990. "Mitch Snyder, RIP." *National Re-view*, 6 August.

"Died, Mitch Snyder." 1990. *Time*, 16 July.

McCarthy, Colman. 1990. "Mitch Snyder." *Nation*, 30 July.

Ocean, Charles E. 1990. "Mitch Snyder Saved Many Lives but Finally Took His Own." *People Weekly*, 23 July.

SUGIHARA, *CHIUNE*

(1900–1986)

He has been called the "Japanese Schindler," but the efforts of Chiune "Sempo" Sugihara to save thousands of Polish Jews, many of whom escaped to the United States, were unknown to the vast majority of Americans until the early 1990s. Survivors of the Holocaust have described Sugihara as a true hero, a samurai, who gives for the sake of humanity and receives no gain for himself. He was called "a lighthouse in a sea of darkness."

In January 1995, Sugihara's widow, Yukiko, toured the United States to be reunited with some of the people she and her husband had helped save. She pointed out through an interpreter at a news conference in San Francisco, California, that her husband had listened to his conscience and to Polish Jews who needed visas to escape from the Nazis. At the beginning of World War II, all routes from Poland had been cut off except through Lithuania and the Soviet Union, where refugees could sail from the eastern port of Vladivostok to Japan and, from there, travel to China or North America.

Sugihara's efforts began in late 1939, when he became the Japanese consul general in Kovno (now Kaunas), the Lithuanian capital. At the time, Lithuania was still a free nation, and the Japanese government wanted Sugihara, a Russian-language teacher, to report on relations between Soviets and Germans; such information would aid the Japanese in their plan to join Germany and Italy against the Allies. However, Sugihara, with the help of Yukiko, played a much different role.

Thousands of Polish Jews had fled to Lithuania, but by June 1940, the Russians had annexed Lithuania. Since the Jews were not Russian or Lithuanian citizens, they knew that they would have to leave the country, but that meant obtaining visas through the consulate offices, which the Russians planned to close. In the weeks before the official closing, hundreds of Jews lined up daily at the Lithuanian consulate seeking help. A Dutch diplomat provided visas to Curaçao and Suriname, but to get there, people would have to pass through Russia and Japan. Sugihara was the only one with the authority to provide the necessary Japanese transit visas.

Three times, Sugihara sent cables asking permission from the Japanese government to grant the visas, but each time, permission was forcefully denied. Japan did not want to risk offending Germany, with which it would soon be allied. When the Russians ordered the consular offices to close, Sugihara requested an extension—to keep the office open until the end of August 1940. Then Sugihara decided to defy his government and write visas for the Jews gathered outside at the consulate gates. As Yukiko explained during her 1995 visit to the United States: "Every morning, I would stand by the window with my husband and see this ocean of faces, eyes filled with desperation and hope, and I could

not let that go unanswered. He couldn't stand by and watch this inhuman thing happen—that's why he chose humanity over his career" (Magagnini 1994). She and her husband also worried about their family—they had three small children, the oldest only five—and they had no idea what the consequences of their actions would be.

For a month, Sugihara interviewed applicants and wrote visas, as many as 300 a day, from early in the morning until late at night. Yukiko sometimes massaged her husband's hands so that he could keep working. Even when the consulate was closed, the Sugiharas continued to write visas in their hotel room and signed documents after they boarded a train that took them out of Kovno. Jews who were issued visas traveled by train to Siberia and from there to Japan, where there was no retaliation, in spite of the government's orders not to issue visas. Refugees then went to a Jewish ghetto in Shanghai, China. Since a single visa was issued for an entire family, an estimated 8,000 to 10,000 Jews may have escaped by this route, according to Hillel Levine, director of the Center for Judaic Studies at Boston University, who spent the summer of 1994 researching in Japan and is writing a book about Sugihara. When the Nazis occupied Lithuania in 1941, Lithuanians fought on the German side, and most of the Jewish community in Lithuania was exterminated.

During the remaining years of World War II, Sugihara and his family were assigned to diplomatic posts first in Germany and then in Czechoslovakia and Romania. When the Soviets captured Bucharest, the Sugiharas were sent to a prisoner-of-war camp, where they were held until 1947. After being released, the Sugiharas returned to Japan, but Chiune was fired from the Foreign Ministry for "recklessly ignoring instructions" from the government. Many of his former colleagues shunned him, and for decades he was considered a disgrace to his country. To earn a living, he worked as a part-time translator and interpreter (he spoke six languages), as a lightbulb salesman, and finally as an executive with a Japanese import-export firm. A year before his death, Sugihara was recognized by Israel as "Righteous among the Nations," the nation's highest honor, and a tree was planted in his honor near Jerusalem.

In the early 1990s, when Japan began to seek ways to improve relations with Israel and with what is now the independent state of Lithuania, the Japanese changed their public attitude. Sugihara is now included in textbooks as a courageous humanitarian, and his name has been restored to Foreign Ministry documents. Yukiko's book *6,000 Visas for Life*, published in Japan in 1992, has helped create awareness of Sugihara's heroic efforts. In 1994, a group of Americans traveled to Japan to honor Sugihara and spread the word about his deeds. Among the group were Holocaust survivors and members of the San Francisco–based Holocaust Oral History Project. The group also included about two dozen U.S. veterans of Japanese ancestry who won fame fighting Nazis in Europe and rescued Jews sent on a forced death march from the infamous Dachau concentration camp. Some of the veterans recalled with sadness and perhaps some bitterness that their own families—American citizens—had been held in U.S. internment camps during World War II. A photo exhibit titled "Unlikely Liberators" and featuring Sugihara, the 522d unit of Japanese-American soldiers at

Dachau, and the people of Japanese descent in U.S. internment camps toured the United States in 1995.

References

Lindelof, Bill. 1995. "Japanese Couple Saved Jews in WWII." *Sacramento Bee*, 23 January.

Magagnini, Stephen. 1994. "Belated Honors Sought for 'Samurai Schindler' of WWII." *Sacramento Bee*, 11 September.

Nickerson, Colin. 1993. "Japan Rehabilitates Diplomat Who Saved 6,000 Jews." *Seattle Times*, 3 January.

Shioya, Tara. 1994. "Tribute to Japanese 'Schindler.'" *San Francisco Chronicle*, 18 August.

Silver, Eric. 1992. *The Book of the Just: The Unsung Heroes Who Rescued Jews from Hitler*. New York: Grove Press.

Watanabe, Teresa. 1994. "Japanese Consul Who Saved Thousands of Polish Jews." *San Francisco Chronicle*, 21 March.

T

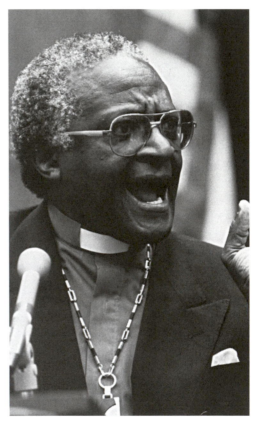

TALL, JOANN

(1953–)

I n 1993, JoAnn Tall, an Oglala Lakota (Sioux), was among the winners of the international Goldman Environmental Prize, an annual award presented to an individual on each continent for grassroots achievement. Tall's award stemmed from her successful opposition to nuclear weapons testing and the dumping of toxic waste on the Pine Ridge Reservation in South Dakota, one of the poorest areas in the United States. Her opposition frequently brought harassment from waste-disposal companies and sometimes harsh criticism from Lakota leaders and elders.

Tall, who lives on the Pine Ridge Reservation, began her fight for social and environmental justice for Native Americans in the late 1980s, when Amcor, a subsidiary of O&G, a waste-disposal firm in Connecticut, promised jobs and cash payments to the Lakotas in exchange for permission to dump trash on their reservation. Tall formed a group called the Native Resource Coalition (NRC) to protest the dumping.

In June 1990, Tall was informed that Amcor was entertaining tribal leaders at a luncheon at the Hilton in Rapid City, South Dakota. She "crashed the meeting," as she put it, and began to ask Amcor representatives questions about the proposed waste-disposal operation. Although a tribal councilwoman accused her of being disrespectful, Tall was not deterred. She told the tribal leaders that they were being "bought" with the big meal and other enticements, similar to the way Native Americans had been bribed years ago with whiskey to give up their land. Tall urged tribal leaders to take responsibility for protecting tribal rights and to do their own research.

Not long after the meeting, Lakota leaders learned that many other Native American groups were being enticed by waste-disposal companies, and they broke off negotiations with Amcor, refusing to accept an agreement that required them to waive their sovereign rights. The waste-disposal company then turned to the neighboring Rosebud Reservation, sending a representative from another subsidiary of the company. Like the Pine Ridge dealings, negotiations with the Rosebud tribal council were conducted behind closed doors. In spite of objections from many of the 600 residents of the Rosebud Reservation, in late 1990, the tribal council signed a contract with the waste-disposal company to develop a 5,760-acre regional landfill in exchange for jobs. The proposed site would accept hazardous and solid waste from such major cities as Minneapolis and Denver, as well as other urban areas in the region.

Before the landfill was developed, a citizens' meeting was held, which Tall attended. She told the group that she had come from Pine Ridge to let them know that the same company had brought them the same kind of proposal. Tall explained:

> They told us their dump was the only solution. They told us it was perfectly safe. They told us everything they are telling you, and they almost

got it through our council. But so far we have been able to stop them. I wanted to come and tell you that, because you can stop them here if you want to.

Tall also explained that the waste-disposal company "will try to divide you . . . . They will tell you you will be fined. They told us that. But we weren't fined" (Schneider 1991).

Residents of the Rosebud Reservation formed a coalition group similar to the one at Pine Ridge, and Tall coached the group on how to do their own research. Although the coalition and Rosebud tribal leaders were divided on the waste-disposal deal, the proposal was defeated. When it was brought up again in 1992, it was turned down once more.

Tall's activism has also included an organized protest in 1992 to maintain the integrity of KILI, an independent radio station founded in 1979 by the American Indian Movement to keep alive the traditions and language of the Oglala Lakota. According to Tall, who is an original KILI board member, another purpose of the station is to broadcast information that the tribal council, which is supported by the federal Bureau of Indian Affairs, might want suppressed. For months, beginning in May 1992, the protest group camped out in teepees, blockading the entrance to the radio station and demanding the resignation of KILI's white manager, whom the group claimed had reduced traditional Lakota broadcasts and introduced public-affairs programming that supported various development projects on the reservation. An article published in the *Los Angeles Times* explained:

> One of KILI's early objectives was to give voice to the reservation's "treaty people," who hold that the Lakotas' 1851 and 1868 treaties with the U.S. government—which granted the Lakota far more land and sovereignty than they now enjoy—are sacred documents that must be honored. Treaty people tend to have contempt for those who cooperate with the U.S. government, such as tribal council members and employees. They also resist development schemes that involve sacrificing either land or sovereignty. The debate between the treaty people and those who say their first priority is bringing jobs and income to this desperately poor reservation— where unemployment tops 80%—is the fundamental political struggle here (Baum 1992).

Tall will no doubt continue to participate in the struggle to preserve the Lakota way. As she pointed out during the KILI blockade, "Every spring when the thunder comes back we would have a ceremony to put an eagle feather on top of the station's tower. For the first time this year, lightning hit the tower" (Baum 1992).

References
Baum, Dan. 1992. "Protest Broadcasts Displeasure with KILI Radio." *Los Angeles Times*, 31 August.

Gay, Kathlyn. 1994. *Pollution and the Powerless: The Environmental Justice Movement.* New York: Franklin Watts.

Koenenn, Connie. 1993. "Awards for Aid at the Grass Roots." *Los Angeles Times*, 19 April.

Schneider, Paul. 1991. "Other People's Trash." *Audubon*, July/August.

TARBELL, IDA M.

(1857–1944)

"They will get you in the end," friends and family members warned Ida Tarbell in the early 1900s, when she began investigating and reporting on the monopolistic practices of Standard Oil Company and its president, John D. Rockefeller. It was a time of great debate about the formation of trusts in the United States—the mergers of small businesses into one huge corporation—which some said stifled competition and raised prices, benefiting only the company officials. Indeed, Tarbell's two-year investigation of Standard Oil revealed

illegal price-fixing and corruption within the company, and her book *The History of Standard Oil*, published in 1904, brought on the wrath of Rockefeller and U.S. President Theodore Roosevelt, who called Tarbell's reporting "muckraking."

During her childhood, Tarbell was no stranger to Standard Oil practices. Born in Erie County, Pennsylvania, Tarbell was the daughter of teachers, Franklin Sumner and Esther Ann McCullough Tarbell. Although her father tried to settle and build a home in Iowa, bank closings across the United States forced him to return to Pennsylvania. There, in the northwestern part of the state, oil had been discovered, so the Tarbell family settled in Rouseville, an oil town, and Franklin started an oil tank business. At the age of 13, Ida and her family moved to Titusville, another town whose economy depended on oil. The South Improvement Company—a combination of companies that later became

Standard Oil—soon stifled growth of the town by controlling most of the business, including railroad transport. Rates for local producers doubled, but South Improvement paid low freight costs for the transport of oil. At the time, Tarbell did not understand exactly how the monopoly was affecting her father's and others' small businesses, but "she perceived that privilege, at least the version of it accorded to owners of expanding oil companies, badly upset her world" (Kochersberger 1994, xxix).

During high school, Tarbell was interested in scientific study and was introduced in her later teenage years to the emerging women's rights movement, a crusade that convinced her that she needed to continue her education in order to be independent. However, years later, Tarbell was highly critical of feminists, whom she thought were divisive. She did not believe that it was necessary for women to have the right to vote.

In 1880, Tarbell graduated from Allegheny College in Meadville, Pennsylvania, and taught science classes and languages for two years at the Poland Union Seminary in Poland, Ohio. Not long afterward, at the urging of a family friend who was the editor of *The Chautauquan*, Tarbell went to work for the magazine. The publication had grown out of the Chautauqua movement, named for a group of Methodists who gathered at Lake Chautauqua every summer for religious study and later espoused lifetime learning through the Chautauqua Literary and Scientific Circle.

After seven years with *The Chautauquan*, performing numerous editorial duties and writing some articles, Tarbell quit her job in 1890 and moved to Paris, where she began writing features about Paris and French revolutionaries for U.S. newspapers and magazines. It was in France that she honed her skills and dedicated herself to writing honestly, basing her material on facts she had uncovered rather than being an advocate for some particular issue or group.

In 1894, she accepted a full-time writing position with *McClure's Magazine* in the United States and eventually became associate editor. In 1900, she began writing the series of articles for *McClure's* that exposed the Standard Oil monopoly and the deliberate way Rockefeller tried to destroy competition. In one article, she described how Rockefeller had coerced owners of refineries in Cleveland, Ohio, who had suffered for several years because of the preferential rates that railroad companies gave to the South Improvement Company. Tarbell explained how Rockefeller went to the owners

one by one and explained the South Improvement Company. "You see," he told them, "this scheme is bound to work. It means an absolute control by us of the oil business. There is no chance for anyone outside. But we are going to give everybody a chance to come in. You are to turn over your refinery to my appraisers, and I will give you Standard Oil Company stock or cash, as you prefer, for the value we put upon it. I advise you to take the stock. It will be for your good." Certain refiners objected. They did not want to sell. They did want to keep and manage their business. . . . It was useless to resist . . . they would certainly be crushed (Kochersberger 1994, 83–84).

Indeed, as Tarbell wrote, independent companies were soon out of business, sometimes being paid only half of what their firms were worth. Standard Oil held a monopoly on the oil business in Cleveland.

Tarbell was widely criticized not only by Standard Oil executives but also by other wealthy business officials for her magazine articles. However, newspaper and magazine editors and other writers and reporters called her work admirable, and later biographers applauded her efforts to show that big business was unethical. She built her case and made "a formidable indictment," showing "that almost every step the Standard Oil Company had taken toward trust and monopoly had necessarily trampled a competitor to death, and had been accomplished by fraud, deceit, special privilege, gross illegality, bribery, coercion, corruption, intimidation, espionage, or outright terror" (Lyon 1963, 213).

Tarbell's investigative reporting was a major factor in the U.S. attorney general's decision to bring charges against Standard Oil in 1906. The company was convicted of conspiracy to control interstate commerce in oil. Standard Oil appealed, but in 1911, the U.S. Supreme Court upheld the conviction, which broke the monopoly.

Throughout the rest of her writing career, Tarbell continued to expose fraudulent business practices and the unhealthy and unsafe conditions under which many people had to work. She also wrote favorably about some corporations and produced a number of biographies about executives. Her magazine writing continued as well, and after World War I, she went to Europe to observe firsthand and write about the devastation of the war. Her horror of war prompted her to write a number of articles, later compiled in a book: *Peacemakers—Blessed and Otherwise*.

In 1935, although she was terribly debilitated by Parkinson's disease, which caused her hands and body to shake, she began her autobiography, published in 1939 by Macmillan. She continued to work in spite of ill health and planned to write another book, *Life after Eighty*, but she was unable to complete the work and died in 1944.

References

Brady, Kathleen. 1984. *Ida Tarbell: Portrait of a Muckraker*. New York: G. P. Putnam's Sons.

James, Edward T. 1936. *Notable American Women, 1607–1950*. Cambridge, MA: Harvard University Press.

Kochersberger, Robert C., Jr., ed. 1994. *More than a Muckraker: Ida Tarbell's Lifetime in Journalism*. Knoxville: University of Tennessee Press.

Lyon, Peter. 1963. *Success Story: The Life and Times of S. S. McClure*. New York: Charles Scribner's Sons.

Whitelaw, Nancy. 1994. *They Wrote Their Own Headlines: American Women Journalists*. Greensboro, NC: Morgan Reynolds.

TEN BOOM, *CORRIE*

(1892–1983)

C orrie ten Boom is known for the relentless and legendary aid she gave to Jews during World War II. She spent all of the years of her life until the beginning of the war in the house of her father, which at times served as a refuge for the persecuted.

She had been raised in a loving environment in the small home near the Queen of Holland's palace in Amsterdam. While her father could advertise that his jewelry was a favorite of the monarch, the family had very little wealth. Money was always short, but the family was able to live happily because of a Christian faith that sustained their every hour. Ten Boom formed a habit of never undertaking an important action without praying on the subject first. This attitude came from her father, who had also taught the family that their Jewish neighbors were to be respected and honored because of the position they had been given by their Lord.

When the Nazis overran her country in just five days in 1940, her family's faith, courage, and commitment to their Jewish friends were sorely tested. It quickly became obvious that the German soldiers were targeting the Jews for discrimination and eventually death. Ten Boom, with the help of her family, found ways to aid their friends.

At the beginning of the occupation, ten Boom was 48 years old and was frequently ill, but her energy and organizing ability became legendary. She helped to set up an underground network that first helped Jews escape from her homeland and eventually evolved to provide sanctuary from the occupying forces. For nine tense months in 1943 her own small family home was refuge to hundreds of people who required a meal and a couple of nights' stay out of harm's way.

Many people thought the family was foolish, endangering their lives to protect those who were not their "own." Ten Boom answered this one day by saying, ". . . don't you believe that the Lord will protect us with His angels? Even if He should allow us to be found, aren't we saving God's ancient people, the Jews?" When the knock finally came upon the door of their family home, ten Boom could barely move from her bed. She had gone there a few days before to fight off a case of pleurisy, but the German soldiers could not have cared less. She, her sister Betsie, and her father were all taken into custody and sent to a prison, betrayed by neighbors who lived down the street.

Ten Boom's father was too old and too weak to withstand the captivity. He died within ten days of being jailed. The middle-aged ten Boom was placed in solitary confinement because of her disease, and it was during those four months in the dark, dank cell that she found the courage to go on against the forces of Nazi Germany. She reaffirmed her strong faith in Jesus during those lonely hours, and the proof of the power it brought her was seen as soon as she was

taken to be interrogated. The "judge," a Nazi officer, showed her some papers that had been found in the house, which incriminated her family as well as many others who had been lending support to the Jews in Holland. Ten Boom's reaction was to begin talking about her faith and the possibilities of salvation for those who accepted the Lord. The officer was incredulous and sent her away to resume the interrogation the next day. On the morrow, the once cold Nazi confessed to her that he had been unable to sleep the night before as he thought about what she had said. Over the next several days the two talked and prayed, and the German officer eventually destroyed the evidence so none of those mentioned would receive punishment.

Months later, ten Boom and her sister were transferred to a concentration camp where they were reunited. They worked hard to help the other inmates maintain hope in the living hell that was their new home, and they were even able to hold two secret Bible study classes every day. Late in December 1944, Betsie succumbed to the conditions of her confinement. She died just four days before the New Year 1945. On that day ten Boom was released and vowed to honor the memory of her sister who helped her to keep going in prison and showed her how important it was to tell the world about their Lord. If He was there in the darkness of the death camp, He was there for anyone who could be shown how to reach Him.

For the next three decades ten Boom traveled throughout the world to bring that message, in the form of her own parables, to those who might not have heard. On one occasion right after the war in 1947, she spoke at a church in Munich, Germany, where she had gone to deliver "the message that God forgives." After her talk, a man, whom she recognized as one of her former guards in the Nazi concentration camp, approached her. "It was the first time since my release that I had been face to face with one of my captors and my blood seemed to freeze," she recalled. The guard told her he had changed his ways and that God had forgiven him for all the horrible things he had done at the camp; he had come to ask her forgiveness, but ten Boom could hardly move or speak.

> It could not have been many seconds that he stood there, hand held out, but to me it seemed hours as I wrestled with the most difficult thing I had ever had to do. For I had to do it. The message that God forgives has a prior condition—that we forgive those who have injured us. . . .
>
> I knew it not only as a commandment of God, but as a daily experience. Since the end of the war I had had a home in Holland for victims of Nazi brutality. Those who were able to forgive their former enemies were able also to return to the outside world and rebuild their lives, no matter what the physical scars. Those who nursed their bitterness remained invalids. It was as simple and as horrible as that (Peale 1972, 23–24).

After wrestling with her feelings and reminding herself that "forgiveness is an act of will," ten Boom was able to shake the hand of her former persecutor, receiving what she described as a "healing warmth." Since that time, her story of forgiveness has been told repeatedly in sermons.

Ten Boom kept writing, speaking, traveling, and ministering with good humor and a loving heart. She was especially effective ministering to convicts in prison, never showing any fear for her own well-being. In 1978, she suffered a debilitating stroke that took her powers of speech. Even then she was able to keep communicating for months, sending signed messages to her helpers about praying for less fortunate people. Since her death, her books and other writings, which include *The Hiding Place* (1971), *Tramp for the Lord* (1974), *Corrie ten Boom's Prison Letters* (1975), *In My Father's House: The Years before the Hiding Place* (1976), and *Clippings from My Notebook* (1982), have been an inspiration to countless readers.

References:

Carlson, Carole C. 1983. *Corrie ten Boom*. Old Tappan, NJ: Fleming H. Revell.

Peale, Norman Vincent, ed. 1972. *The Guideposts Pocket Book of Inspiration*. Carmel, NY: Guideposts Associates.

SerVaas, Cory. 1987. "A Time for Forgiveness." *Saturday Evening Post*, November.

ten Boom, Corrie. 1977. *He Sets the Captives Free*. Old Tappan, NJ: Fleming H. Revell.

TENZIN GYATSO

See *DALAI LAMA*

TERESA, MOTHER

(1910–)

Agnes Gonxha Bojaxhia was born into a happy family in Skopje, Albania, in 1910. Her father was a political activist who may have been murdered for his views when Bojaxhia was only nine years old. His passing left the once prosperous family with nothing but the roof over their heads. Shaken by

As a symbol of peace, Mother Teresa and Robert Morgan release a dove in front of 20,000 people at Varsity Stadium in 1982.

the new state of affairs, Bojaxhia's mother sought comfort in her religion. She had always taken her religion seriously, and she had been diligent about teaching her children the importance of their Catholic faith, but now she combined that belief with a stubborn will to see her family through this crisis. In short order, she created a successful clothing company to support her brood.

The young girl who was to become Mother Teresa was duly affected by this trait in her mother. Hardship, adversity, and poverty could be overcome, she learned, and this helped her decide on a path for her own life's work. A sharp child who was especially adept at writing, Bojaxhia had many options in life, but

by the time she reached her eighteenth birthday, her mind was set: she would help the poor as a missionary in India. Since the only way to accomplish this was by becoming a nun, she was soon on her way to Dublin and the novitiate of the Sisters of Loreto.

Six weeks later, Bojaxhia was sent to Darjeeling in India for further training. By the next year, she was a novice, choosing the name Sister Teresa on 23 May 1929. Finally, in 1937, Sister Teresa took her final vows, and she was assigned to be principal of St. Mary's School for the poor in Calcutta. She enjoyed teaching and her life behind the walls of the Loreto Convent, in the locus of economic, political, and social crisis that was Calcutta. The sisters there were protected from the violence and upheaval of the 1943 famine, the bombings during World War II, and the "day of great killing" in 1946, when over 4,000 people died in a fight between Hindus and Muslims.

During this last event, Sister Teresa had to leave the safety of the convent to find food for her 300 students. Normal life was so disrupted in the city that few supplies were available anywhere. Soldiers warned her to get off the streets, which were piled high with the bodies of murdered men, women, and children, but Sister Teresa refused to put her personal security over the needs of her charges. Convinced that this feisty nun would not heed their orders, the soldiers eventually helped the sister find some staples and trucked them back to the convent.

It was soon after this incident that Sister Teresa received what she refers to as the "call within a call." On 10 September 1946, she knew what God had planned for the remainder of her existence on earth. She asked the archbishop for permission to accomplish the Lord's order: leave her respected position as principal and the security of the convent to go out into the poorest, most wretched slums of Calcutta to personally minister to the people there. By the next year, she was given permission to leave the order, but she was to retain her standing as a nun. Overjoyed with the news, but practical as always, Sister Teresa quickly learned all she could about nursing the ill. Just before Christmas in 1948, she went into the poorest slum of Calcutta.

Dressed in a thin white sari edged in blue (the common dress of the poor in Bengali), sandals, and a simple black cross, she established a school by teaching a few children in an open place in the slum using a stick and mud as chalk and a blackboard. There was so much misery to overcome in the narrow alleyways of the slum that a weaker person would certainly have walked away. Sister Teresa's faith was all-encompassing, however, and she continued undaunted. She has often spoken of seeing the poor in a spiritual perspective:

> We must acknowledge the dignity of the poor, respect them, esteem them, love them, serve them. . . . We owe a debt of gratitude to the poor. . . . Often I think they are the ones to whom we owe our greatest gratitude. They teach us by their faith, their resignation, their patience in suffering. . . . To serve well our poor, we must understand them; to understand their poverty, we must experience it. Working for them, we come to identify ourselves with them. Our sisters must feel as they feel, feel their poverty

before God, know what it is to live without security, depending on God for the morrow (Le Joly 1985, 220–221).

Many other women joined Sister Teresa's crusade, and people began to donate goods, services, and space so that she could continue her work. After a one-year trial period, the archbishop reviewed the work of the remarkable woman and the preliminary constitution of the group she was forming. Sister Teresa vowed to seek out the poorest and most desperate, the lost and the dying all over the world, and care for them.

She received recognition for her order, the Missionaries of Charity, in 1950, and it has grown to over 300 "Motherhouses" in dozens of countries throughout the world. Sister Teresa became Mother Teresa. She has frequently stated that she and her sisters "are not social workers, we are religious. We are women dedicated to God, of our own free will, consecrated to his service. In our lives God comes first. We live in poverty; we leave the world. We are not of the world, though we remain in the world" (Le Joly 1985, 284).

Mother Teresa has received numerous awards, among them the Pope John XXIII Peace Prize (1971), John F. Kennedy International Award (1971), Albert Schweitzer International Prize (1975), and Nobel Peace Prize (1979). She continues to minister to the most wretched on earth and attempts to visit all her devotees at least once every two years. This pace is maintained even though she suffers from a debilitating heart condition.

References

Egan, Eileen. 1986. *Such a Vision of the Street: Mother Teresa, the Spirit and the Work*. New York: Doubleday.

Le Joly, Edward. 1985. *Mother Teresa of Calcutta: A Biography*. San Francisco: Harper & Row.

Porter, David. 1986. *Mother Teresa, the Early Years*. Grand Rapids, MI: William B. Eerdmans.

Spink, Kathryn. 1981. *The Miracle of Love: Mother Teresa of Calcutta, Her Missionaries of Charity, and Her Co-Workers*. San Francisco: Harper & Row.

Teresa, Mother. 1987. *Heart of Joy*. Ann Arbor, MI: Servant Books.

Teresa, Mother, Jose Luis Gonzalez-Balado, and Janet N. Playfoot. 1985. *My Life for the Poor*. San Francisco: Harper & Row.

TIMERMAN, *JACOBO*

(1923–)

In April 1977, Jacobo Timerman was arrested by an extremist faction of the Argentine army. Although no charges were ever filed, Timerman spent 30 months in captivity and was interrogated about his participation in Zionist organizations and in what was perceived as an international Jewish conspiracy to control the world—a myth formulated years ago and widely circulated by Nazis during World War II.

Timerman was born in the Ukrainian town of Bar. In 1928, he and his family moved to Argentina, where he eventually married and had three children. A journalist, he founded two weekly newsmagazines and was a prominent news commentator during the 1960s in Argentina.

During the 1970s, Timerman used his newspaper *La Opinion* to publish editorials that were highly critical of the Argentine government and its anti-Semitic policies and repressive tactics against leftist guerrillas. "On many occasions the military expressed their admiration for my open confrontations with the leftist terrorists, whom I accused in my newspaper and named, using no euphemisms," Timerman wrote. "But they subsequently found it hard to fathom why, with the same vociferousness, I likewise accused those who used terrorist methods to liquidate left-wing guerrillas. They questioned my motives in fighting against military allies, the right-wing terrorists, and none of my replies provided them with any satisfaction. They invariably felt that the tactic of repression was of greater importance than the ideology behind the process" (Timerman 1981, 138).

From 1973 to 1976, there were four Perónist presidents, among them General Juan Domingo Perón and his wife, Isabel. Violence enveloped Argentina, and, as Timerman wrote:

> [it] erupted on all fronts, completing a development that had begun in 1964 with the appearance of the first guerrillas trained in Cuba. . . . Coexisting in Argentina were: rural and urban Trotskyite guerrillas; right-wing Perónist death squads; armed terrorist groups of the large labor unions, used for handling union matters; paramilitary army groups, dedicated to avenging the murder of their men; para-police groups of both the Left and the Right vying for supremacy within the organization of federal and provincial police forces; and terrorist groups of Catholic rightists organized by cabals who opposed Pope John XXIII's proposals to reconcile the liberal leftist Catholic priests seeking to apply—generally with anarchistic zeal— the ideological thesis of rapprochement between the Church and the poor (Timerman 1981, 13).

Thousands of Argentines died or disappeared in this climate, and Timerman concluded that the country was headed toward an inevitable push toward occupation by military power. Although he was warned to leave the country to save his life, he and other political journalists working for *La Opinion* formed a group dedicated to publishing information about violent government repression. In retaliation, the Argentine government tried to shut down *La Opinion* with bomb assaults at Timerman's home and office and the kidnapping and disappearance of one of the paper's journalists. In more subtle ways, the government also initiated advertising sanctions. Argentina's economy was almost 70 percent government controlled, and advertising from various government agencies made up a large portion of the needed revenue to maintain the newspaper's financial solvency. When government advertising was pulled, *La Opinion* turned to its readers, increasing the price until it became the most expensive newspaper in the country. However, it remained independent of public or private advertising, unlike the other papers. When these measures failed to stop the paper, the government intervened by confiscating it.

During his time in prison, which Timerman recounted in a highly praised memoir *Prisoner without a Name, Cell without a Number*, he was repeatedly tortured, beaten, and locked in isolation in an attempt to get him to denounce his loyalty to Argentina. In spite of a ruling by Argentina's Supreme Court that there were no judicial grounds to confine him, the government refused to release Timerman until 1979. In September of that year, he was stripped of his citizenship and expelled from Argentina to Israel, where he still holds citizenship. Timerman often credits the administration of President Jimmy Carter for doing more than any other group to call attention to human rights abuses in Argentina, thus helping to save his life and the lives of hundreds of other innocent people.

The facts about his case eventually became public in 1988, when General Carlos Suarez Mason admitted ordering Timerman's arrest and taking part in the Argentine military government's efforts to quell internal dissent. General Mason, who fled to the United States in 1983 after a civilian government in Argentina took control of the military, was eventually extradited back to Argentina, where he faced trial on 39 murder charges (Morain 1988).

In January 1984, Timerman returned to Argentina. In August of that year, he became deputy managing editor of *La Razon*, an afternoon daily, which Timerman said would be "a paper for democracy, stressing pluralism, peace, open-mindedness and freedom of expression" (Andersen 1984).

References
Andersen, Martin. 1984. "Timerman Joins Buenos Aires Daily." *Washington Post*, 16 August.
Morain, Dan. 1988. "Ex-General Ordered Argentine Writer's Arrest." *Los Angeles Times*, 8 May.
Timerman, Jacobo. 1981. *Prisoner without a Name, Cell without a Number*. Translated by Toby Talbot. New York: Alfred A. Knopf.

TROCMÉ, *ANDRÉ*

(1943–1971)

He was called the "soul of Le Chambon," a small town in southern France. During the Nazi occupation of France in World War II, André Trocmé was the inspiration for his parishioners, who helped thousands of Jews escape death camps, even though Nazis and their French government allies, who had set up headquarters in Vichy, had facilities nearby.

A descendant of French Huguenots—Protestants who were persecuted in primarily Catholic France—on his father's side and Germans on his mother's side, Trocmé was born in Saint-Quentin in northeastern France. His affluent family hired private tutors to educate their children at home, and during his childhood, Trocmé was isolated from "ordinary" people, primarily because his father insisted on a provincial lifestyle and strict upbringing. According to biographer Philip Hallie, an experience in Trocmé's sheltered childhood probably shaped his later resolve to work on behalf of others. One day, the boy was confronted in his walled yard where he played with his brother by a "bony, pale man" who had pushed open the garden gate. The man "looked at the two upper-class boys for what seemed to be a long time, in silence. Then he started shaking his head, and a glance of bitter but detached pity came into his eyes as he said, '*Tas de cons*' ('Bastards'). Then he left closing the gate behind him" (Hallie 1979, 50). The image of the pale man stayed with Trocmé, and he vowed to work for the poor.

While he was still a teenager, Trocmé and his family left their hometown, which was occupied by Germans during World War I and was cut off from receiving food supplies. They went to Belgium, where, as refugees, they had to search and beg for food among the poor. At the end of World War I, the family moved to Paris, and Trocmé studied theology at the University of Paris and joined the Fellowship of Reconciliation, an international pacifist organization. He won a scholarship to study at the Union Theological Seminary in New York, where he met and later married Magda Grilli of Florence, Italy. Both were committed to nonviolence and fighting social injustice and poverty.

When the couple returned to Europe, Trocmé accepted a parish among the poor in the industrial cities of northern France, and then among poverty-stricken miners living near the Belgian border. In 1934, the Trocmés and their four children went to Le Chambon, a tightly knit village that had been a refuge for Protestants seeking protection from French authorities during the 1600s; during the 1900s, it had become a tourist town because of its proximity to the mountains. In the Le Chambon parish, Trocmé, with the help of a friend from his university days and Magda, set up Cévenol School, which prepared teenagers for trades and crafts but also taught the concepts of nonviolence.

After World War II broke out in Europe, the northern and western parts of France were occupied once again by Germans. Southern France, where Le

Chambon was located, was an unoccupied or free zone. The country was controlled by the Vichy government and Marshal Petain, who followed the example of Hitler's Nazis and generated virulent propaganda against Jews, communists, and others who were considered enemies of the state.

Between 1940 and 1944, Pastor Trocmé and Magda set the example and led the entire village in an effort to house, clothe, feed, and hide between 2,500 and 5,000 Jews fleeing from Nazi atrocities in Europe. The village became a "city of refuge," and although Vichy and German officials tried countless times to intimidate Trocmé and his parishioners, Trocmé insisted, "We do not know what a Jew is. We know only men" (Hallie 1979, 103). He was also urged by religious leaders not to hide or help Jewish refugees because of the danger to the villagers, but Trocmé firmly believed that the identity of refugees must be concealed, and he and his wife helped make counterfeit identification and ration cards, an act that presented a moral dilemma, since they believed that duplicity was wrong. Saving lives was more important, however, and in many cases, deceit was the only way Jews could escape certain death.

This was only the beginning of many other lifesaving acts and deeds of conscience performed by the Trocmés and Le Chambon villagers. Trocmé was once arrested and sent to a prison camp, and although he was offered his freedom if he would sign a loyalty oath to the Vichy government, he refused. He was released more than a month later on the order of a high official, but no one is certain who the official was or why the order was given. The Trocmés, along with most of the villagers, continued their work. At great personal risk, they sheltered refugees, who were whisked from the village to mountain hideouts when the Vichy police, closely supervised by the Nazi Gestapo, came to search homes. One of Trocmé's cousins, who taught and sheltered Jewish boys in a dormitory-like building called the House of the Rocks, was arrested by the Gestapo. He and the boys were sent to the Majdanek camp, where they were all put to death in the gas chambers.

After the war, Trocmé preached against retaliation, exhorting the villagers and others to forgive rather than kill their enemies, a sermon that was seldom heeded. He broadened his ministry and became the European secretary of the Fellowship of Reconciliation, spreading the concept of nonviolence in Europe and the United States. He also solicited funds and people to work for Cévenol School. In 1971, the Israeli government planned to honor Trocmé by awarding him the Medal of Righteousness, but he suffered a stroke and died before the ceremony was held. His widow received the medal on his behalf.

References

Hallie, Philip. 1979. *Lest Innocent Blood Be Shed*. New York: Harper & Row.

Silver, Eric. 1992. *The Book of the Just: The Unsung Heroes Who Rescued Jews from Hitler*. New York: Grove Press.

TULA, MARIA TERESA

(1951–)

"**I** grew up in a very poor family and never had big dreams like the ones I have now. I never imagined that I would travel all over the world, come to the United States, and have a book published about my life." Those words of Maria Teresa Tula conclude her story, *Hear My Testimony*, which illustrates not only her incredible stamina and endurance of terrible poverty, torture, and imprisonment but also the courage of many women in El Salvador working for human rights through CO-MADRES, the Committee of Mothers and Relatives of Political Prisoners, Disappeared and Assassinated, established with the aid of priests and nuns of the Christian Base Communities.

During her early years, Tula was cared for primarily by her grandmother. Her mother had left her father after learning that he was living with another woman. Tula was able to attend school in Izalco for a short time, but when her grandmother moved to San Salvador, Tula had to work in the market selling bread and eggs to help support the family. Her grandmother died when Tula was about 14 years old, and she went to Santa Anna to live with her mother, who had remarried and had other children. Tula's life in her stepfamily was miserable. Her stepfather abused her mother, and an older stepbrother often beat Tula just because he was a man and thought that he could control her—until Tula turned on him one day and defended herself.

When Tula was 16, her first child, a daughter, was born. Tula's mother would not allow her to live with the baby's father and his family, and she never saw him again. She later met and married Rafael Canales Guevara, who was a construction worker and later worked as a blacksmith in a sugar refinery. The two lived happily for a time and had two more children, but they were always struggling to provide for their family, with Tula taking in ironing to earn the equivalent of $2 for eight or nine hours of labor.

Tula's first experience with the political system and the brutally repressive government came about in 1978, when her husband helped organize a strike to demand better working conditions for the exploited workers at the sugar mill. Guevara was arrested with other labor leaders, accused of being a terrorist, tortured, and held as a political prisoner. Tula had to search to discover her husband's whereabouts—most prisoners were detained without trial or any word to their families or friends. After finding out where her husband was jailed, Tula visited frequently, and during one of her visits, she met Alicia Nerio de Blandino, cofounder of CO-MADRES, who was looking for her son, a student accused of terrorism. De Blandino invited Tula to join their group.

In 1978, Tula became part of CO-MADRES and learned about many women whose children had been taken away—accused of terrorist activities—and would probably never return. Some women recovered only their children's

mutilated bodies. In spite of their terrible hardships and threats to their own lives, CO-MADRES women worked to try to change the inequities of Salvadoran society and to bring to light the repression that was so prevalent. After Tula joined CO-MADRES, she took part in demonstrations designed to call international attention to the conditions in El Salvador. As Tula explained: "In 1979 and 1980, there was a lot going on. There were student movements, labor movements, and all kinds of human rights organizations springing up to publicize human rights violations. During this time, many people had to leave El Salvador and go into exile in other countries" (Tula 1994, 79).

Murder and slaughter were regular occurrences. Some members of CO-MADRES were captured by death squads and brutally tortured or murdered. One member, who was secretary of the Electrical Workers Union, was found mutilated—her breasts cut off, part of her genitals cut off and stuffed into her nose, her tongue pulled out, and her eyes burned with acid. "You can't imagine how terrible it is to find someone like that, especially someone you admired and cared for," Tula wrote (1994, 80).

Guevara was released from jail, but not long afterward, he was forcefully taken from his home and was later found murdered. Tula was pregnant at the time, and after her husband's death, she too was captured. For days she was imprisoned, beaten, half-starved, raped, and eventually dumped bloody and battered in a park. She continued to work for CO-MADRES, but in 1983, she decided that she and her family would be killed if she did not leave the country. She went to Mexico and worked in a CO-MADRES office there and also traveled in Canada for several months, talking to Canadian officials about the atrocities in El Salvador. CO-MADRES members, including Tula, also traveled to the United States and Europe to set up chapters of the organization and raise funds to counteract human rights abuses. The group was the first recipient of the Robert F. Kennedy Human Rights Award in 1984.

When Tula returned to El Salvador, she was again taken by the death squad. In 1986, she spent months in a women's prison, where her son was born. Because of international pressure, Tula was eventually released and went to the United States with two of her children, hoping to find political asylum, but the U.S. State Department denied her request. She was ordered to leave the country but was able to obtain temporary residency.

Tula has been invited to speak in many communities across the country and has given her testimony, but as she wrote, "Telling my story in the United States is difficult." People cannot believe the horrible abuse she has suffered, and many have questioned her truthfulness. They tell her, "it is only the communists that administer this kind of torture." Even journalists have made her story seem questionable by using phrases such as "alleged" or "according to Tula." Although she is often discouraged in her efforts, Tula wrote: "I guess I just keep talking because . . . the U.S. public needs to know. They have to hear people who are from what is called the 'Third World' talk about the kinds of human rights abuses we suffer. These abuses are not just about torture and killing. There are many other kinds of human rights abuses . . . like the lack of education . . . [no] access to basic education . . . insufficient nutrition and substandard or no housing" (Tula 1994,

176–177). Still, Tula keeps hoping and working for a future with justice in El Salvador.

References

Barry, Tom. 1987. *Roots of Rebellion: Land and Hunger in Central America*. Boston: South End Press.

Berryman, Phillip. 1984. *The Religious Roots of Rebellion: Christians in Central American Revolution*. Maryknoll, NY: Orbis Books.

Diskin, Martin, and Kenneth Sharpe. 1985. *The Impact of U.S. Policy in El Salvador 1979–1985*. Berkeley, CA: Institute of International Studies.

Parkman, Patricia. 1988. *Nonviolent Insurrection in El Salvador*. Tucson: University of Arizona Press.

Tula, Maria Teresa. 1994. *Hear My Testimony: Maria Teresa Tula, Human Rights Activist of El Salvador*. Translated and edited by Lynn Stephen. Boston: South End Press.

TUTU, DESMOND

(1931–)

After South African Bishop Desmond Tutu received the Nobel Peace Prize in 1984, he spoke to a group of jubilant supporters in Johannesburg, saying the award "is for you, who down the ages have said we seek to change this evil system [white oppression of blacks] peacefully. The world recognises that we are agents of peace, of reconciliation, of love, of justice, of caring, of compassion. I have the great honour of receiving this award on your behalf. It is our prize. It is not Desmond Tutu's prize" (Du Boulay 1988, 17). In spite of many attempts to discredit him, Tutu has long been a fearless critic of South Africa's racism and a spokesman for black South Africans.

Tutu was the third of four children of Zachariah and Aletha Tutu, who gave all their children European as well as African names, a custom among those of Christian background. At the time of Tutu's birth, his father was headmaster of

Methodist Primary School in western Transvaal, and his mother was a domestic servant. Although Tutu described his childhood as happy, he pointed out years later that the racial discrimination he and other blacks experienced in South Africa resulted in a kind of brainwashing, in which there is "an acquiescence in your oppression and exploitation. You come to believe what others have determined about you, filling you with self-disgust, self-contempt and self-hatred, ac-

cepting a negative self-image . . . and you need a lot of grace to have that demon of self-hatred exorcised, when you accept that only white races really matter and you allow the white person to set your standards and provide your role models" (Du Boulay 1988, 22).

When his father was transferred to a school in Ventersdorp, Tutu attended classes there for about four years. Then, when he was 12, the family moved again to Krugersdorp, where they "lived in a typically crowded house . . . three rooms . . . there was no electricity, no sewage, and the dirt street in front of the house had rocky outcrops" (Du Boulay 1988, 26). About this time, the family, who had always been devoutly religious, joined the Anglican Church. Desmond began high school in 1945, attending a government secondary school near Sophiatown. He was forced to drop out of school at age 14, because he became ill with tuberculosis and was sent to a sanitarium for 20 months of treatment. At the hospital, he developed what would be a lifelong friendship with Father Trevor Huddleston, then an Anglican parish priest who later became an archbishop. Father Huddleston visited Tutu often, bringing books to read and sharing conversations. Tutu credits Huddleston with being one of the greatest influences on his life.

By the time Tutu was ready to attend college, numerous laws had been passed to enforce the apartheid system, including a law against mixed marriages; the Population Registration Act, which required every individual to be classified by race; and the Groups Areas Act, which required separate living and trading areas for each classified group of people. Thousands of nonwhite South Africans were uprooted from their homes and removed to their allocated areas. In spite of all the restrictions and racial prejudice in and out of the classroom, Tutu obtained a teaching certificate in 1954 from the Bantu Normal College and taught high school for several years, quickly becoming known as a successful and inspiring teacher. Apartheid laws became even more stringent, however, and education for blacks was restricted to studying language and religion and taking part in manual labor. Teachers in Bantu schools lost all professional status, tenure, and appropriate salaries.

In 1955, Tutu married Leah Shenxane. They eventually had four children, the youngest of whom was born in Great Britain.

Because of the restrictive apartheid laws, Tutu felt compelled to leave teaching, a profession he thoroughly enjoyed. When he began training for the priesthood, he admitted that he was not motivated by "very high, noble, reasons for

going to theological college," but he was actively involved in the church and was a dedicated Christian. He excelled at St. Peter's College, run by the Fathers of the Community of Resurrection, whom he credited with his spiritual development. In 1960, he was ordained deacon, and the following year was ordained priest.

Even though many black protests had taken place in the previous decade, Tutu was not political in his thinking at the time. Rather, he was engrossed in being a good priest and serving his parishioners. In 1962, church officials arranged for Tutu to study at King's College, University of London, where he earned a master's degree. He and his family lived in Great Britain until 1966. When they returned to South Africa, Tutu struggled with once again having to face restrictions in the apartheid society and often asked friends to pray that he would not become bitter and hateful. One helpful aspect was the fact that he was assigned to a teaching post at a seminary in Alice, near Port Elizabeth, where staff and students refused to live by apartheid rules, ignoring regulations about where people should live, eat, and bathe.

While at Alice, Tutu slowly began to "experience politics and religion as being indivisible" (Du Boulay 1988, 74). By 1968, the black consciousness movement had emerged, and although Tutu sympathized with radical students and their views about racial justice, he advocated cooperation and harmony rather than confrontation. Still, he often spoke out against apartheid and went to the defense of students at Fort Hare University who went on strike to protest government-controlled racist education. When the students were surrounded by police with dogs, guns, and tear gas, Tutu defied police and demanded to be with the students as their chaplain.

During the 1970s, Tutu held five different positions, including lecturer at the University of Botswana, Lesotho, and Swaziland in Roma, Lesotho, and a post in London with the Theological Education Fund, whose aim was to improve theological education in the so-called younger churches of Africa, Asia, and Latin America. In 1974, he returned to Johannesburg as Anglican dean of the diocese, where he had a platform to present his views on reconciliation and peaceful dismantling of the apartheid system, warning that there could be tragic consequences if whites did not listen to the anguished cries of blacks for justice. After much personal anguish, he left the country again in 1976 to become bishop of Lesotho.

From 1978 to 1984, he was general secretary of the South African Council of Churches (SACC), leading a struggle against apartheid—a struggle that was undermined by a government front organization called the Christian League, which was paid to campaign against the SACC. During this time, his passport was seized several times, causing immediate international condemnation. Every time he wanted to travel, he was forced to request permission, which was usually refused. In 1984, he was awarded the Nobel Peace Prize, but white South Africans, including government officials, ignored or roundly criticized Tutu's honor. That same year, Tutu was elected bishop of Johannesburg, and he often spoke out about the ever-increasing restrictions on blacks and castigated other national leaders for their lack of support for reforms in South Africa. In one speech, after U.S. President Ronald Reagan had refused to consider sanctions

against South Africa, Tutu accused Reagan as well as Britain's Margaret Thatcher and West Germany's Helmut Kohl of saying to blacks that they were, in effect, "utterly dispensable." He denounced Reagan's speech against sanctions as "nauseating" and declared that "America and the West can go to hell" (Du Boulay 1988, 252). His words brought criticism, and although he apologized for his "salty language," he defended his right to speak out forcefully and with anger about the pain that blacks felt.

In 1986, Tutu was elected to the highest seat in the Anglican Church of South Africa—archbishop of Cape Town. He has continued his activism and strong, unequivocal stand for justice, no matter what the cause. For example, he has supported a woman's right to an abortion in cases of rape or incest or when medical evidence suggests that a pregnancy endangers the physical or mental health of the mother. In addition, he has supported the right of homosexuals to serve in the clergy. In short, he is opposed to injustice wherever it occurs. When NELSON MANDELA was elected president of South Africa in 1994, Tutu became an important adviser, although not a part of Mandela's cabinet. In 1996, Tutu announced his retirement from the Archdiocese of Cape Town to teach at Emory University's Chandler School of Theology in Atlanta, Georgia, during the 1996–1997 academic year.

References

"Archbishop Desmond Tutu To Teach at Emory University." 1995. *Jet*, 27 November.

Du Boulay, Shirley. 1988. *Tutu: Voice of the Voiceless*. Grand Rapids, MI: William B. Eerdmans.

Scheer, Ron. 1994. "Archbishop Desmond Tutu: Peacemaker in a Diverse Nation." *Christian Science Monitor*, 26 October.

"Tutu Supports Gay Priests." 1995. *Cape Times*, 2 December.

W

WAITE, TERRY

(1939–)

"I think that you can imagine after 1,763 days in chains it's an overwhelming experience to come back and receive your greetings" (Waite 1993, 359). These were Terry Waite's words in an extemporaneous speech to a British audience after his release in November 1991 from captivity in the underground prisons of Beirut, Lebanon—nearly four years of it in solitary confinement. Waite, a lay official of the Church of England, had volunteered to negotiate with an Iran-connected group known as the Islamic Jihad, which had kidnapped and was holding Americans and other westerners hostage in Beirut. As a result, he himself had been taken captive.

In his homecoming speech and also in his book *Taken on Trust*, published in 1993, Waite recalled a poignant moment in his captivity. One day, "out of the blue," after years of complete isolation, a guard came in with a postcard that showed a stained-glass window in Bedford, England, depicting the imprisonment of seventeenth-century preacher John Bunyan. Waite said:

I looked at that card and I thought, My word, Bunyan, you're a lucky fellow. You've got a window out of which you can look, see the sky, and here I am in a dark room; you've got pen and ink, you can write and I've got nothing; and you've got your own clothes and a table and a chair. I turned the card over and there was a message from someone whom I didn't know simply saying, We remember, we shall not forget, we shall continue to pray for you and to work for all people who are detained around the world (Waite 1993, 360).

Early in his life, Waite certainly had no way of knowing that he would become one of those detainees or would be a negotiator on behalf of political prisoners. The eldest of three children, Terence Hardy Waite grew up in Styal, south of Manchester, England, where his father was a policeman. When Waite was 13, the family moved to Thelwall, and Waite enrolled in Stockton Heath, five or six miles away, where his formal religious education began. He earned a degree in theology at an Anglican college in London but decided that he did not want to become an Anglican priest, although he seriously considered it. Instead, Waite wrote in his autobiography, "I recognized within myself a desire to assist those who were less fortunate than I," and he opted to work with the Church Army, a society of the Church of England devoted to social and mission work (Waite 1993, 119). In 1964, he married Helen Frances Watters, and the couple eventually had four children.

Waite became the first Anglican lay adviser to the archbishop of Uganda. Then, in the early 1970s, he accepted a position with the Roman Catholic Church, coordinating an educational program for the Society of Catholic Medical Missionaries, which involved visiting medical missions throughout the world. After several years with the missions, the family returned to England, and Waite

worked with the British Council of Churches for a time. In 1980, he became an envoy for the Anglican Archbishop of Canterbury Robert Runcie. Although some of the British press and others have criticized Waite over the years, calling him a "deluded and willful egotist" working for his own glory, he became a hostage mediator in a somewhat accidental manner.

In 1981, he was sent as the archbishop's representative to negotiate with Iranian officials for the release of three Anglican missionaries who had been arrested on spy charges. As a result of Waite's efforts, they were freed. In 1985, he made

four trips to Libya to help free British hostages held by Libyan radicals, who were retaliating because Britain had broken off diplomatic relations with Libya. Eventually, Waite negotiated with Colonel Muammar Gadhafi and helped gain the release of the British workers.

In 1985 and 1986, Waite worked to gain the release of American and British hostages held in Beirut and was credited with freeing Benjamin Weir in September 1985; Father Lawrence Martin Jenco in July 1986; and David Jacobsen, administrator of the American University Hospital in Beirut. Waite returned again to Lebanon in January 1987, hoping to have another round of talks with the Shiite captors for the release of other Western hostages. A few months earlier, media around the world had begun to publish and broadcast stories linking the hostage releases to secret arms deals undertaken by a network of cohorts under the direction of U.S. Lieutenant Colonel Oliver North, a member of the National Security Council staff in the Reagan administration. The notorious arms-for-hostages deal was part of what became known internationally as the Iran-contra scandal, because the money from arms sales to Iran was illegally diverted to help rebels in Nicaragua.

Without his knowledge, Waite was a cover for U.S. attempts to free the hostages in exchange for arms. North had met with Waite more than a dozen times to learn what he could about the Muslim captors with whom Waite had had contact. U.S. officials had tried desperately to achieve that contact, but had failed. According to a British documentary released in 1991, in a taped meeting with Waite after his release from captivity, North freely admitted that the U.S. government had used the churchman.

It had never occurred to Waite that he was being duped. He truly believed that he could help with the hostage negotiations and thought that it was the right thing to do. He "felt sick, disappointed," that he had been used. However, Waite expressed no animosity toward North, even though his association with the colonel prompted his Beirut captors to beat him severely and to stage a mock execution to extract information about North (Robinson 1993).

Waite's book clearly shows how his ordeal in captivity was a major test of his faith and his ability to live by his principles. Waite had one opportunity to attempt an escape but opted against it. In that instance, he had an urgent need to use the bathroom and had to plead with his guard for permission. When the

guard finally allowed the "privilege," Waite found a gun with a silencer on top of the cistern, apparently left there by the guard. He debated whether to take and use it, but recalled that he had consistently argued with his captors against the use of violence. "I do not want to live by the gun," he wrote (Waite 1993, 90).

References
Andrés, Phillips. 1991. "Clouds of Doubt." *Maclean's*, 2 December.
Frankel, Glenn. 1991. "'1,763 Days in Chains.'" *Washington Post*, 20 November.
Hewitt, Bill, Vicke Bane, Dirk Mathison, and Terry Smith. 1991. "At Long Last, Freedom!" *People Weekly*, 2 December.
Lardner, George, Jr., and Nora Boustany. 1991. "Waite Worked Closely with North on Hostages." *Washington Post*, 19 November.
Robinson, Eugene. 1993. "A Page Out of a Hostage's Life." *Washington Post*, 23 September.
Waite, Terry. 1993. *Taken on Trust*. New York: Harcourt Brace.

WALESA, LECH

(1943–)

L ech Walesa rose from the abject poverty that was the lot of the masses of Polish people to become his nation's first freely elected president since World War II. The modern history of Poland is one of occupation and exploitation by its more powerful imperialistic neighbors: Prussia, Germany, Russia, and the Soviet Union. Few in the world would have bet that a shipyard worker from the industrial city of Gdansk would, in short order, lead a grassroots labor movement that could cause the peaceful overthrow of a communist regime that had been entrenched for over 40 years.

Walesa was born in 1943 when the German army still occupied Poland. His father died early in his life after release from a Nazi concentration camp. Relations

with his strict stepfather were strained. He did, however, find some comfort in his mother's loving attention, and she saw to it that her children had as "normal" a childhood as possible in a land that was controlled after the end of the war by the Soviet army and the despot Joseph Stalin.

Farmers like the Walesas had few belongings and little food to eat most days. Prospects for bettering their conditions were not very promising either, as the oppressive government cared little for its citizenry. In 1959, 16-year-old Walesa struck out on his own for a neighboring town to attend trade school, where he hoped to develop a skill that would someday help him find a decent-paying job in one of the shipyards along the Baltic Sea. After two years at the school, a stint in the army, and a try at work back in his hometown, he finally got employment in 1965 as an electrician in the Lenin Shipyard in Gdansk.

Although he did earn a better wage than was possible on the farm, Walesa saw immediately that working conditions for laborers were less than ideal. Long hours, few breaks, and exposure to the elements in all types of weather were the rule. This had been the status quo for many years, maintained with the aid of trade unions sanctioned by the government.

Walesa knew that life for the common Pole was one of misery and powerlessness. He soon committed himself to doing something about this. As he pointed out, "It is a Walesa family trait to be driven—toward either good or evil." He once thought about becoming a priest, but he became a union militant instead, "never pausing to think what it might cost" (Walesa 1992, 47). He and others watched the 1968 student protests for intellectual freedom in nearby Czechoslovakia with intense interest, and they began to speak out to their worker comrades in support of the insurgents. When the Polish government raised prices on staple goods in 1970 without raising workers' wages, the time was right for Walesa to organize a protest movement of his own.

As a member of the strike committee, he led the shipyard workers on a work stoppage action, which eventually led to confrontations with the police. Several workers were wounded or killed in the ensuing battles. The first secretary of the Polish communists was forced to resign, and Walesa was among those called in to speak to the newly installed leader, Edward Gierek. Gierek made many promises to improve conditions so that the men would agree to return to the production lines. Soon it became obvious that little had changed, and nothing was likely to change in the future. Wages had risen, but hours were lengthened. Goods were now on the shelves, but people had to stand hours in line to buy even basic necessities. Life was still miserable.

In 1976, Walesa stood up in a union meeting and denounced that organization for helping to keep its members powerless. In this speech, he also criticized the government for failing to keep its promises to the workers and the nation, and his remarks resonated with the audience. By putting himself on the line in this way, becoming a leader and a spokesman, he also drew the attention of the authorities. Rabble-rousing, especially by one of the organizers of the 1970 strike, would not be tolerated. Walesa was fired.

The unrest of the people was becoming apparent, however. Many were coming to the conclusion that a life without freedom and choices was a life not worth

living. The government squelched such talk wherever it could, and those who were interested in organizing for change were forced to meet in secret.

The Baltic Committee for Free and Independent Trade Unions, of which Walesa was a founding member, began to organize in this way. Soon the 35-year-old activist was being followed by the police, harassed and jailed for days without charges, and fired from other jobs. For over a year, Walesa tolerated the abuse because he knew that he was slowly building the support he needed from the people.

The government was aware of the threat he represented to its power, and as the anniversary of the 1970 riots neared, officials decided to arrest Walesa to keep him out of the public view. Colleagues spirited their leader away in the trunk of a car as the police arrived to arrest him. The next day, 14 August 1980, he was at the gates of the Lenin Shipyard, giving a fiery speech to the assembled workers. He called for a sit-down strike and urged the people to express their demands to the authorities. The strike was a remarkable success. Food shortages and price increases had created a climate of dissatisfaction throughout Polish society. The people had finally had enough. With Walesa in the lead, unafraid for his own safety, they were inspired to bring the government to its knees.

Strikes were taking place all over the nation, the Soviet Union was threatening to invade, and the Polish leader Gierek was losing control. Finally, the deputy prime minister was dispatched to the shipyard, where 10,000 strikers were in position. The government negotiator met with Walesa, who presented the workers' 21 demands. Over many hours, the two men reached a compromise. Although they did not obtain everything they wanted, the main points were achieved. Free trade unions were the most important issue, and it was on this new right that Walesa built the first independent labor organization inside the communist bloc. It was named Solidarnosc (Solidarity).

Walesa traveled throughout the world trying to gain the support of international workers for his movement at home. The notoriety was helpful for the cause, but the Polish government reacted forcefully. The new leader, General Jaruzelski, declared martial law just a year after Solidarity was formed. Walesa was arrested and placed in solitary confinement. The union was declared illegal once more in 1982, and to defuse a tense situation, Walesa was released from custody.

Throughout his activist years, Walesa's family—wife Danka and their eight children—has been a constant support and inspiration. Although many asked him why he had such a large family when he was constantly harassed, always in danger of imprisonment and possible assassination, he simply noted that he was a "man of faith."

Offered the Nobel Peace Prize in 1983, Walesa decided not to leave his country for fear that he would be kept out by the authorities. When asked if the prize would change his life, Walesa said, "I'm as ready to receive prizes as I am to be thrown into prison, not that I'm ungrateful for this honor; it's just that neither the one nor the other could ever divert me from the course I've set myself (Walesa 1987, 286).

For the next five years, Walesa remained in the background as the country was ruled with an iron fist. Protesters were dealt with ruthlessly; often they were

found dead. The people no longer had hope. Conditions were worse than they had been for decades. Finally, in 1989, the government found itself without any hope either. Not knowing how to save the country from the economic, social, and psychic malaise that now held Poland in its grip, General Jaruzelski called on Walesa to help him turn things around. The result of their discussions was the reinstatement of Solidarity and the scheduling of free general elections. On 9 December 1990, Walesa was elected president of his country, and as he noted in his autobiography, he "would not perform miracles," but he would begin reforms. "One struggle was ending; another was just beginning" (Walesa 1992, 286).

References

Walesa, Lech. 1987. *A Way of Hope: An Autobiography.* New York: Henry Holt.

————. 1992. *The Struggle and the Triumph: An Autobiography.* New York: Arcade Publishing.

WALLENBERG, RAOUL

(1912–?)

Called "one of the greatest moral figures of our century," Raoul Wallenberg mysteriously disappeared while working to save Hungarian Jews being deported to Nazi death camps during World War II. It is known that he was arrested by the Soviets, who reported that he died in 1947; however, later reports said that he was seen alive in a Soviet prison camp.

Born to a wealthy and distinguished banking family in Sweden, Wallenberg hardly seemed destined to become a heroic figure. Three months before Wallenberg's birth, his father died of cancer, and he was reared by his mother, Maj, and paternal grandfather. His grandfather expected and planned for his grandson to be a leader in global affairs. At the age of 18, Wallenberg was sent to the United States to study architecture at the University of Michigan in Ann Arbor. During this time, he kept up an extensive correspondence with his grandfather and mother, who remarried. While completing his studies, Wallenberg traveled the United States and also parts of Mexico. After earning his diploma, Wallenberg

worked for about six months for a Swedish company in Cape Town, South Africa, traveling and selling building materials throughout the country.

In the latter 1930s, Wallenberg began a career in banking, working first as a trainee in a Haifa bank owned by a friend of his grandfather. While in Haifa, Wallenberg stayed in a boardinghouse, where he met young Jews who had fled Germany and the horrors of Nazi persecution. Their stories had a profound effect on Wallenberg and perhaps helped prompt his heroic actions some years later.

After his grandfather died in 1937, Wallenberg spent a number of years in other enterprises. At the time World War II began, he was the director and part owner of an import-export company established by Kálmán Lauer, a Jewish refugee from Hungary who had settled in neutral Sweden. Wallenberg's negotiating skill, his knowledge of several languages, and his personal charm helped him in European business dealings in Nazi-occupied countries as well as in Hungary, an ally of Germany. He and Lauer became close friends, and when Wallenberg was in Europe on business, he checked on the well-being of Lauer's family members still living in Hungary.

During his travels in Europe, Wallenberg repeatedly heard stories of Nazi atrocities, but like many other people worldwide, he did not really comprehend the horrors. In fact, the Allies and neutral governments concealed reports that the Nazis had murdered hundreds of thousands of Jews since the beginning of the war and had been carrying out Hitler's "final solution"—a systematic plan to exterminate European Jews. Belatedly, in January 1944, U.S. President Franklin Roosevelt set up the War Refugee Board to help rescue European Jews from certain death.

By the spring of 1944, the board decided to set up a rescue operation within Hungary, but because the United States was at war with Hungary, no U.S. representative could go to Budapest as a diplomat. Instead, with financial support from the United States, the Swedish government expanded its diplomatic representation at its embassy in Budapest, and Wallenberg was selected to be a special attaché for humanitarian causes. Wallenberg, who was, in effect, an American agent with Swedish diplomatic credentials, arrived in Budapest in July 1944 and immediately began to issue reports about the brutalities against Jews. They were rounded up by Adolf Eichmann and starved or beaten to death or packed like sardines into freight cars without food or water and sent to death camps or gas chambers. Testimony at the Eichmann trial in 1961 revealed that during a two-month period, between 15 May and 17 July 1944, about 600,000 Jews were deported from Hungary.

Wallenberg used every means at his disposal in rescue efforts. He bribed Hungarian and Nazi officials to prevent rampages against Jews in ghettos and to gain visas for Jews to leave the country. In some cases, he arranged to have Jews disguised in uniforms of the Arrow Cross, storm troopers of the Hungarian fascist party, who entered internment camps and freed Jews on the pretense that they were being deported. He hired Jews to work for the Swedish legation, eventually employing up to 400 people who were exempt from anti-Jewish laws.

At the legation, Wallenberg supervised the allocation of Swedish passports for Jewish families, which saved them from deportation. Wallenberg's efforts

influenced other neutral countries to increase the number of protective passes and the speed with which they issued them. Special housing was set up for Jews waiting for emigration, and many Jews were secretly brought to the buildings, which included a hospital and food distribution center. After the war, records showed that nearly 50,000 Jews had been rescued through these efforts, and more than half of the rescues were attributed to Wallenberg and his staff.

Although it appeared for a time in mid-1944 that deportation of Hungarian Jews had slowed or come to a halt, the situation changed in the fall, when a new government with the support of Arrow Crossmen took over, and Eichmann once again set out to murder Jews. In December 1944, Wallenberg reported that about 40,000 Jews were "seized in their homes or in the street" and were "forced to march on foot to Germany. It is a distance of 240 kilometers. The weather has been cold and rainy ever since these death marches began. They have had to sleep under rain shelters and in the open. Most have only been given something to eat and drink three or four times. Many have died" (Wallenberg 1995, 265).

Wallenberg continued to work feverishly in his rescue operations, which were often countered by Arrow Crossmen, who randomly attacked, tortured, and executed between 10,000 and 15,000 Jews during December 1944 and January 1945. In January, Wallenberg learned of a plan to massacre all the Jews who had been rounded up in Budapest ghettos. He was able to get a message to the commander of the Arrow Crossmen, threatening him with prosecution as a war criminal if the massacre was carried out. The commander called off the massacre just two days before the Russian army captured Budapest, saving the lives of about 120,000 Jews.

Although Wallenberg's mission seemed to be accomplished, he was arrested by the Soviet military on 17 January 1945 and accused of spying for the Germans. He was apparently imprisoned at Lubyanka Prison in Moscow, according to accounts from fellow inmates after their release. The Soviets denied knowing his whereabouts until 1947, when they announced that Wallenberg had died of a heart attack. However, evidence that has surfaced over the years suggests that Wallenberg was alive and continued to be held prisoner for years after his announced death. Indeed, several books on Wallenberg published in the 1970s and 1980s supported this theory and also helped bring to light the deeds of an individual who had been virtually an unknown hero of the Holocaust.

References

Anger, Per. 1981. *With Raoul Wallenberg in Budapest*. New York: Schocken Books.

Bierman, John. 1981. *Righteous Gentile: The Story of Raoul Wallenberg, Missing Hero of the Holocaust*. New York: Viking Press.

Marton, Kati. 1995. "The Liquidation of Raoul Wallenberg." *Washington Post*, 22 January.

Wallenberg, Raoul. 1995. *Letters and Dispatches 1924–1944*. Translated by Kjersti Board. New York: Arcade Publishing.

Warren, Spencer. 1990. "Wallenberg—A Major Test of Glasnost." *Christian Science Monitor*, 22 May.

Werbell, Frederick E., and Thurston Clarke. 1982. *Lost Hero: The Mystery of Raoul Wallenberg*. New York: McGraw-Hill.

WALSH, MARIE

(1946–)

As a successful securities broker and mother of eight, Marie Walsh had no idea in the 1970s that she would become an activist and work for the benefit of millions of women with silicone-related diseases. Founder and president of a California-based support and information group for women who have suffered severe illness due to silicone-gel breast implants, Walsh has been instrumental in helping women file successful lawsuits against manufacturers of such implants for their negligence in informing the public of the known dangers of the devices and for damages incurred because of them.

Throughout the 1970s, she was pursuing a promising business career but began to experience debilitating health problems and was forced to leave her job and accept permanent social security disability payments as a means of survival. Divorced at the time, Marie later married Jim Walsh, a former running back for the Seattle Seahawks and coach at Stanford University. He, along with the rest of the family, has been a constant support in Walsh's efforts to inform the public and other women about silicone implant safety, although both Marie and Jim admit that Marie's crusade has been a strain on their personal relationship.

The crusade grew out of Walsh's own plight. In 1969, she had undergone implant surgery to correct a deformity—she had a small left breast and a large right breast, causing humiliation and discomfort as she grew up. In 1979, her implants were replaced because of problems with hardening—a common occurrence—and about two years later, she began to suffer from rashes, night sweats, abdominal pains, aching muscles, and hair loss. She did not connect these problems with the breast implants because she had been told that there was no possible health danger from the silicone devices. Even after another surgery in 1984 to remove and replace ruptured implants, neither the doctors nor Walsh

recognized the relationship between her deteriorating health and the silicone that had seeped into her body. Walsh filed a lawsuit against the manufacturer of the ruptured breast implant and was awarded an $80,000 settlement in 1990.

By the mid-1980s, Walsh had begun to suspect that her breast implants might be the cause of her many debilitating health problems, and she researched medical studies, reports from the U.S. Food and Drug Administration, congressional hearings, and any other information she could find on silicone-gel implants. She was outraged to learn that manufacturers such as Dow Corning had suppressed information regarding the health dangers of silicone for years, a fact that was later revealed in court cases. She filed another lawsuit, this time suing her attorneys, whom she claimed had wrongfully withheld information. Her $80,000 settlement for ruptured implants had been based on the condition that documents about the case be sealed, which effectively kept Walsh and thousands of other women uninformed about the potential dangers of silicone-gel implants. Her case against her lawyers was settled in 1993 for an undisclosed amount.

For more than six years, Walsh sought treatment for her problems, but not until 1991 did she find a rheumatologist in Westminister, California, who advised permanent removal of the breast implants. Although her health improved somewhat after the implants were removed, much of the silicone from the devices remained in her body, which she and some medical experts say has resulted in tumors and continued debilitation. Nevertheless, Walsh was determined to turn her misery into something worthwhile, and she became an avowed activist. With the help of another implant victim, Marsha Chambers, Walsh started a nationwide nonprofit support group, the Breast Implant Information Foundation (known as BIFF), which was initiated in the dining room of Walsh's home in Laguna Hills, California. Based on a quote from MOTHER TERESA—"We must do small things for one another with great love"—Walsh has written newsletters and answered calls from thousands of women across the United States and throughout the world. Most of the callers are women who are ill with immune-system diseases, cancer, and other serious ailments related to implants.

Walsh also appeared before a panel of medical experts at a congressional hearing in late 1991. Rather than read a prepared speech, she described her painful ordeal and courageously presented a color photo showing the gruesome effects of her breast surgery. With her testimony at the federal hearing, appearances on radio and TV talk shows, and interviews with news reporters, Walsh has inspired thousands of other women to overcome their reticence to speak out about an embarrassing subject and to join the campaign to persuade the federal government to remove silicone-gel breast implants from the market.

Walsh and others who suffer from silicone-related diseases have been criticized by many in the medical community, particularly plastic surgeons, who point to studies concluding that there is no evidence linking silicone-gel implants to disease. However, many of those studies were paid for by manufacturers or conducted by consultants with vested interests in silicone devices.

Even with these obstacles and in spite of extreme pain, additional surgeries, chemotherapy, and the emotional strain caused by the death of both her parents, Walsh and volunteers who work with her have been able to research and inform

women about those in the medical community who can help them. In 1992, Walsh donated funds won from her lawsuit for an independent study conducted by the School of Medicine at the University of California, Davis. Published in 1995, the study concluded that women with silicone-gel breast implants—even some with intact implants—had elevated levels of serum silicon, the breakdown product of silicone. The study is expected to counter the continued arguments from manufacturers that silicone is biologically inert and will not break down in the body.

To date, although Walsh is literally dying from health complications due to the silicon levels in her body, she and volunteers continue to advise women on where to find legal experts and to share information on breast implant litigation cases. Because of BIFF's efforts and those of similar groups across the United States, a class-action suit involving an estimated 280,000 claims against silicone-gel implant manufacturers Dow Chemical/Dow Corning and Bristol Myers Squibb was settled, and funds were expected to be dispersed sometime in 1995. Additional claims outside the class-action agreement will also be paid by the manufacturers.

References

Berkman, Leslie. 1992. "O.C. Woman's Implant Ordeal Sparks Crusade." *Los Angeles Times*, 12 January.

Gay, Kathlyn. 1993a. *Breast Implants: Making Safe Choices.* New York: Macmillan, Silver Burdett Press.

Peterson, Susan. 1993. "Now Lawyers Face Suits over Implant Cases." *Orange County Register*, 20 May, Focus on Health section.

Teuber, Suzanne S., Robert L. Saunders, Georges M. Halpern, Robert F. Brucker, Victor Conte, Brian D. Goldman, Ed E. Winger, W. Graham Wood, and M. Eric Gershwin. 1995. "Elevated Serum Silicon Levels in Women with Silicone Gel Breast Implants." *Biological Trace Element Research*, March.

WAMWERE, KOIGI WA

(1949–)

A native of Kenya, Africa, and a graduate of Cornell University in the United States, Koigi wa Wamwere served as a member of Kenya parliament from 1978 to 1982. In 1988, he was forced to seek political asylum in Norway because of his outspoken criticism of the dictatorial regime of President Daniel arap Moi and human rights abuses in Kenya. Worldwide, he is held in high esteem and is often compared with such activists for human rights as NELSON MANDELA and STEVEN BIKO.

When he returned to Africa in the early 1990s, he was imprisoned a number of times for his opposition to the oppressive government. In one incident, he was charged with treason, but the charge was later dropped. After his release, he became involved for a time with the Released Political Prisoners group, a nonviolent organization. He then founded the National Democratic Human Rights Organization in Kenya.

In November 1993, Wamwere, his brother Charles, cousin James Maigwa, and local attorney G. G. Mjuguna Ngengi were arrested on unsubstantiated charges of participating in an armed raid of a police station in order to foment an insurrection. According to Amnesty International (AI), the men were arrested "solely on the basis of their non-violent opposition to the government." AI learned that the raid may have been fabricated, because postmortem reports showed that the men killed in the incident had died before the raid supposedly began. Wamwere was in Nairobi at the time of the raid, staying at the house of Gibson Kamau Kuria, a prominent human rights lawyer and former prisoner of conscience. The police made no attempt to investigate his alibi, AI stated. Wamwere and his codefendants went on trial in April 1994, which AI declared was

> part of a pattern of harassment of human rights activists, opposition figures and journalists, and especially those who, like Koigi wa Wamwere, have been attempting to investigate or report incidents of political violence in the Rift Valley and other parts of Kenya. Government violence has been alleged in the ethnic-based violence which has killed around 15,000 people and displaced more than 300,000 since it began in December 1991 (Amnesty International 1994).

Regular observers from human rights and legal organizations attended the trial and were convinced that the four men did not receive a fair trial under national or international standards. As Wamwere wrote to one observer:

> We are 100% innocent of the charges for which we are being tried in this court. This trial has been most unfair and we expect no justice at the end of

it. The real problem in this trial is President Moi. He is afraid that I might contest presidency in 1997, so we must be destroyed now. Moi also wants to use this trial and the judiciary in general to effect his diabolical policy of ethnic cleansing against Kikuyu people who live in Rift Valley. In destroying us, Moi's chosen instrument is Mr. William Tuiyot, the trial magistrate in this court. Knowing this, we have more than five times asked Mr. Tuiyot to disqualify himself but he has refused to do so. And to be able to convict us, Mr. Tuiyot has been heard to say that he will ignore all defence evidence including our alibis which the investigating officer refused to investigate (Wamwere).

In October 1995, Wamwere, his brother, and Ngengi were convicted of two counts of robbery and sentenced to eight years in prison (four on each count), to be served concurrently, along with 12 strokes of the cane. Wamwere's cousin was acquitted. The convictions brought protests from international legal observers, who concluded that the trial was not only unfair but also political in nature and "procedurally flawed."

International efforts continue to free Wamwere and other political prisoners in Kenya. In fact, U.S. Senator Nancy Kassebaum of Kansas, who sits on the Senate Foreign Relations Committee and the Africa subcommittee, sent a letter on Wamwere's behalf to President Moi and the Kenyan ambassador to the United States, who responded that Kenya's judicial affairs were no business of the United States. Aid to the country, much of which comes from the United States, has been suspended for some time and may not be forthcoming in the near future if human rights abuses continue. That aid is desperately needed, since 11 million of Kenya's 26 million people are unemployed, and the country's infrastructure is falling apart.

References

Amnesty International. 1994. Summary document. Electronic posting, 13 November. http://www.spidergraphics.com/khrai.html.

Wamwere, Koigi wa. n.d. Letter to David Sullivan. Electronic posting. http://www.spidergraphics.com/khrdsletr.html.

WHITE, *RYAN*

(1972–1990)

Although he lived only 18 years, Ryan White's quiet dignity made a tremendous impact on Americans' perception of acquired immune deficiency syndrome (AIDS) and the virus that leads to the disease. Born a hemophiliac—without the platelets that cause blood to clot—White knew that his life could be short. Even a small cut might cause him to bleed to death, and he had to receive a blood-clotting agent on a regular basis to combat his deficiency. In 1984, White learned that some of the blood product had been contaminated; as a result, he had contracted AIDS.

White's tragic plight first became known to the public in 1985, when word of his disease spread in his hometown of Kokomo, Indiana. White then became a  double victim, as his classmates at Western Middle School shunned and harassed him, and a parent group launched hysterical and bigoted protests that resulted in White's being barred from school. Even when health authorities assured the parent group and school officials that AIDS could not be spread through casual contact, White was not allowed to return to classes. He was able to keep up with his schoolwork via a computer-telephone system. White and his mother, Jeanne, were determined to fight this violation of White's civil rights, and they began a yearlong legal battle that ended with White being able to return to eighth-grade classes—to jeers and harassment from some students and parent groups. Some parents kept their children out of school. The battle with fearful and prejudiced parents continued, and few townspeople offered any public support for White. Jeanne decided to move with him and his sister, Andrea, to Cicero, Indiana, where he attended Hamilton Heights High School. In stark contrast to his reception in Kokomo, White was warmly welcomed at Hamilton, partly because students at the school had decided that they wanted to support White and take on his cause as a challenge; they learned how AIDS is transmitted, and their fears, for the most part, were alleviated.

White also did more than his share to educate the public about AIDS. He appeared on national TV talk shows and testified at congressional hearings and before a presidential AIDS commission. One of his most effective appearances was in a PBS special "I Have AIDS—A Teenager's Story." During the special, he talked about his disease with elementary students.

One of the points White often stressed during public appearances was the fact that he "came face to face with death at 13 years old," as he put it, but decided

he wanted "to live a normal life." That was difficult to do, since his life became the subject of an ABC TV movie, *The Ryan White Story*, and a feature in *People* magazine and many other publications.

Nevertheless, White was able to go on with his classes, obtain a driver's license, and get a job at a skateboard store. He was a popular student, and although he was a year behind because of being barred from school in Kokomo, he hoped to graduate from high school. White suffered an AIDS-related pulmonary infection in late March 1990 and died on 9 April.

Just a few days before White's death, President George Bush had visited Indianapolis and had planted a tree in White's honor in a downtown park. When he learned of White's death, the president noted, "All Americans are impressed by his courage, strength and his ability to continue fighting." Among the many other tributes to White was one from Woodrow A. Myers, Jr., the Indiana state health commissioner who had supported the Whites during their legal battle. Myers said of White: "Through his eloquence, he showed all of us our true colors and showed all of us we had picked the wrong enemy. We should have been fighting all along against the disease rather than the people who had it" (Pearson 1990).

References
"Beloved Pariah." 1990. *U.S. News & World Report*, 23 April.
Friedman, Jack. 1988. "The Quiet Victories of Ryan White." *People Weekly*, 30 May.
"The 'Miracle' of Ryan White." 1990. *Time*, 23 April.
Pearson, Richard. 1990. "AIDS Patient Ryan White Dies." *Washington Post*, 9 April.
SerVaas, Cory. 1988. "The Happier Days for Ryan White." *Saturday Evening Post*, March.
Valk, Elizabeth P. 1990. "People's Report on AIDS Victim Ryan White." *People Weekly*, 23 April.
White, Ryan, and Ann M. Cunningham. 1991. *Ryan White: My Own Story*. New York: Dial Press.

WIESEL, *ELIE*

(1928–)

In 1986, the Nobel Peace Prize was awarded to Elie Wiesel, a Holocaust survivor and well-known author of more than 30 books that contain a message for all humankind. As the Norwegian Nobel Committee noted in its citation: "[Wiesel's] message is one of peace, atonement and human dignity. His belief that the forces fighting evil in the world can be victorious is a hard won belief. His message is based on his own personal experience of total humiliation and of the utter contempt for humanity shown in Hitler's death camps. The message is in the form of a testimony, repeated and deepened through the works of a great author." Those works include his first book, *Night*, published in France in 1958, which describes the Nazi death camp horrors and the death of family members, and numerous other books of nonfiction and fiction such as *Twilight* (1988) and *The Forgotten* (1992).

Accepting the Nobel prize, Wiesel referred to his parents and a younger sister who had perished in the death camps when he said: "I sense their presence. I always do—and at this moment more than ever. . . . This honor belongs to all the survivors and their children and, through us, to the Jewish people with whose destiny I have always identified." Wiesel, a professor at Boston University, helped coin the word *Holocaust* with his writings in the late 1950s and vowed that the peace prize would inspire him to continue to speak out against all forms of repression and to be a witness for the dead. As he stated in his acceptance speech for the peace prize:

> We must always take sides. Neutrality helps the oppressor, never the victim. Silence encourages the tormentor, never the tormented.
>
> When human lives are endangered, when human dignity is in jeopardy, national borders and sensitivities become irrelevant. Whenever men or women are persecuted because of their race, religion or political views, that place must, at that moment, become the center of the universe. I have tried to fight those who would forget. Because if we forget, we are guilty, we are accomplices. If we forget, then they will be killed a second time (Schmetzer 1986).

Indeed, Wiesel has been tireless and determined in his efforts to see that the public does not forget the millions who were brutalized and murdered in Nazi concentration camps during World War II. Since the end of the war, Wiesel has become "the ordained Rememberer, the thorn of conscience in the side of our collective forgetfulness," as Daphne Merkin, book reviewer for the *Washington Post*, put it.

Born in the town of Sighet in Transylvania, Wiesel was 15 years old when he and his family were taken by the Nazis and deported to Auschwitz, where his

Nobel Peace Prize winner Elie Wiesel (right), along with President Bill Clinton (center) and the U.S. Holocaust Council chairman Harvey M. Meyerhoff (left), lights the eternal flame outside the Holocaust Museum during dedication cere-monies in Washington, D.C., on 22 April 1993.

mother and a younger sister died in the gas chamber. Wiesel and his father were sent to Buchenwald, another notorious death camp, where his father starved to death. Liberated from the camp in 1945, Wiesel moved to Paris, adopting the French language and living in the city for a decade. He worked as a journalist and traveled to Israel and the United States on assignment. Eventually, he moved to the United States and made his home in New York City with his wife, Marion, and their son, Shlomo Elisha. In 1976, he became professor in the humanities at Boston University.

Several days after accepting the Nobel prize, Wiesel traveled to the former Soviet Union (now the Russian Federation) to appear at opening ceremonies for the Solomon Mikhoels Cultural Center, named for a Jewish actor and director whose theater had been shut down, as were countless synagogues, libraries, and schools, during the Stalin era. Wiesel likened the center to the "start of a marvelous dream," a breakthrough in official attitudes toward Soviet Jews, although there have been numerous anti-Semitic incidents since then in Moscow and elsewhere in the Russian Federation.

Wiesel was the first chairman of the council in charge of building the U.S. Holocaust Memorial Museum, dedicated in 1993. Today, he is not only a literary voice for the millions who died in the Holocaust but also a popular speaker on the lecture circuit. He has personally taken his message to powerful political leaders. During President Ronald Reagan's term, for example, Wiesel tried to

dissuade Reagan from going to Bitburg, Germany, to lay a wreath at a Nazi graveyard, but Reagan ignored the advice. Wiesel also made his voice heard when addressing President Bill Clinton, begging him to help stop the bloodshed in the former Yugoslavia—now Bosnia.

Although carrying a message of conscience is an obsession and sometimes a burden for Wiesel, he also believes that it is a privilege. In his words, "It is a burden when people don't listen. But you have to go on. Here and there, there is always one who understands, one whose life changes. I am both humble and ambitiously arrogant. I cannot do much. I am one man. But I still hope that there will be one here and there that will be moved and changed. That's enough for me" (Leavy 1986).

References

Leavy, Jane. 1986. "The Restless Witness." *Washington Post*, 15 October.

Schmetzer, Uli. 1986. "Wiesel Accepts Nobel Prize." *Washington Post*, 11 December.

Schuman, Michael. 1994. *Elie Wiesel: Voice from the Holocaust*. Hillside, NJ: Enslow Publishers.

Wiesel, Elie. 1960. *Night*. Translated by Stella Rodway. Les Editions de Minuit, 1958. Reprint, New York: Bantam Books/Doubleday.

———. 1970. *One Generation After*. New York: Random House.

——— 1978. *A Jew Today*. New York: Random House.

———. 1988. *Twilight*. New York: Summit Books.

———. 1990. *From the Kingdom of Memory: Reminiscences*. New York: Summit Books.

WILLIAMS, BETTY

See *CORRIGAN, MAIREAD, AND WILLIAMS, BETTY*

WU, HARRY

(1937–)

"They can destroy me, but not defeat me," Harry Wu, a native of China, said when he returned to the United States in August 1995 after two months of imprisonment in his homeland, where he had been arrested and jailed for alleged spying. A naturalized U.S. citizen, Wu has been a human rights activist ever since coming to the United States in 1985 and has spoken out about abuses that Amnesty International (AI) declared are "systematic and widespread" in China. In a March 1995 report, AI noted:

> The Chinese government continues to suppress dissenting opinions and maintains political control over the legal system, resulting in an arbitrary and sometimes abusive judicial regime. The lack of accountability of the government and the Chinese Communist Party (CCP) means that abuses by officials often go unchecked . . . the most common types of abuses [include] arbitrary detention, torture and ill-treatment of prisoners, severe restrictions on freedom of expression and association and violations specific to women.

According to AI and prisoner reports, people held in detention centers, prisons, and labor camps are tortured by a variety of methods, which include:

> beatings using electric batons; rubber truncheons on hands and feet; long periods in handcuffs and/or leg irons, often tightened so as to cause pain; restriction of food to starvation levels; and long periods in solitary confinement. Furthermore, corrupt authorities . . . have extorted large sums of money from families of detainees for the state's provision of "daily supplies" and "medical expenses" (Amnesty International 1995).

The third of eight children, Wu Hongda, as he was named, was born into a wealthy banking family in Shanghai. He was baptized as a Catholic and was educated at an elite Jesuit boys' school. When the communists gained power, Wu's father, like many other Chinese, believed that he should help rebuild the nation after the devastation of World War II, so the family remained in China, and Wu studied at the Beijing Geology Institute during the 1950s. While a student, Wu was an outspoken critic of the Communist Party. That criticism, plus his family's capitalist background, led to his being branded a counterrevolutionary and his arrest at the age of 23. In 1960, he was imprisoned and spent the next 19 years being shuffled from one Chinese forced labor camp to another. The *laogai*, as the camp system is called, is designed to "reform" those who do not abide by the communist regime.

In these camps, Wu saw fellow prisoners die of disease and starvation. He became "a beast," as he called himself, because he had to fight, lie, and steal for food. He sometimes had to catch and eat snakes and frogs or eat grass and insects to stay alive. "At one point he was reduced to fending off a fellow prisoner for the right to the food stored in a rat's burrow," according to one report. "The experience forged a consuming, almost reckless, determination to shed light on the inner workings of a Chinese regime that had nearly smothered him" ("Back to the Gulag" 1995).

When Wu was released from the prison labor camp, he taught geology and was granted permission to attend the University of California at Berkeley as a visiting scholar, but he had to wait more than four years to get a passport. When he was able to leave for the United States he had, in his words:

> barely scraped together enough money for my air ticket by selling my possessions and borrowing from friends. I arrived in San Francisco with $40 in my pocket. During my first weeks in the United States, I worked day and night, even sleeping on the desk in my university office so that I could stay awake to work the late shift in a Berkeley doughnut shop (Wu with Wakeman n.d.).

During his first year in the United States, Wu found that many books about China written in English lacked information about the *laogai*. He became determined to call attention to China's human rights abuses and to show how the prison system helped keep the Communist Party in power. He founded the Laogai Research Foundation, which is "dedicated to compiling factual information about life within the Laogai," with these goals:

> To conduct continuing research into the Laogai and the human rights abuses perpetrated there.
> To serve as a clearinghouse for information about Chinese forced labor products, maintaining an extensive computer database on individual Laogai camps and their products.
> To educate the public about the Laogai.
> To provide speakers and visual materials to groups interested in learning more about the Laogai (Laogai Home Page).

In 1991, Wu married Ching-lee, a woman from Taiwan, with whom he "found deep personal happiness." Four months after their marriage, he and his wife (who insisted that she accompany him) went back to China with a CBS camera crew to film secret prison facilities where goods were produced under slave conditions and sold to international markets. "Even though I had wanted to forget the suffering of the past after arriving in the United States and had wanted to heal the wounds in my heart . . . I could not forget what I had experienced or those who still suffered inside the camps," Wu wrote. "If I didn't undertake this task, I asked, who would?" (Wu with Wakeman 1994).

Since his trip in 1991, Wu has returned to China two more times to expose its prison system. Because of his efforts, the U.S. Customs Service has been able to enforce the ban on imported goods produced by prisoners. It was no surprise when he was arrested in 1994 while attempting to show how the Chinese government repressed its citizens.

Describing his trial and release to *U.S. News & World Report*, Wu said:

> The trial took less than four hours. Everything was prearranged; I was quite sure they were going to deport me. When I came back to the detention place, they had already prepared my belongings, my wedding ring, my camera, my video, my clothes, my jacket; we left right away for the airport. One of the senior police officials came to me and said, "I know you have some American money. We want to borrow $800." "For what?" I said. "Do I have to pay for my own deportation?" He said I had probably. missed the China Airlines flight and would have to fly on a foreign airline, and he didn't have the American dollars to pay for a ticket. But when we arrived in Shanghai, the Chinese plane was still waiting and they put me on board. Before they closed the door, I shouted to the officer, "Hey, where's my money?" But he said it was too late—so they took my money! ("The Trials of Harry Wu" 1995).

When Wu was able to return to his home in Milpitas, California, just north of San Jose, he expressed his delight and appreciation for his own liberty but worry about his parents and fellow Chinese. He is driven by "survivors' guilt." That guilt, in the opinion of journalist Richard Cohen, "is his animating emotion. He cannot abide doing nothing while others languish in prison camps." Wu also makes Americans and many others uncomfortable because

> most of us prefer not to think about forced labor (or even how people live in the ghetto) . . . we also sometimes resent those who insist that we pay attention to such matters. Moreover, in the government—any government, really—individuals like Wu are detested. They gum up the works. China is a major market, a billion consumers. Who is Wu to endanger this business? (Cohen 1995).

The answer may be that he is a man motivated not just by guilt but also by what many would presume to be a conscience. He will do doubt continue his one-man crusade. In an interview for *People Weekly*, he stated, "I cannot turn my back on my former inmates or my suffering country. I won't give up. No way" (Sanz 1995).

References
Amnesty International. 1995. "China Human Rights Fact Sheet." March.

"Back to the Gulag." 1995. *Columbia Journalism Review*, September–October.

Cohen, Richard. 1995. "Harry Wu." *Washington Post*, 11 July.

Laogai home page. http://www.christusrex.org/www1/sdc/laogai.html.

Sanz, Cynthia. 1995. "Rebel with a Cause: Human-Rights Gadfly Harry Wu Vows He Won't Stop Blasting China's Abuses." *People Weekly*, 11 September.

Sciolino, Elaine. 1995. "Harry Wu: China's Prisons Forged Zeal of U.S. Crusader." *New York Times*, 10 July.

"The Trials of Harry Wu." 1995. *U.S. News & World Report*, 11 September.

Wu, Harry, with Carolyn Wakeman. 1994. *Bitter Winds: A Memoir of My Years in China's Gulag*. New York: John Wiley and Sons.

Y

YASUI, _MINORU_

(1916–1986)

"If a citizen believes that the sovereign state is committing an illegal act, it is incumbent upon that citizen to take measures to rectify such error. . . . If we believe in America, if we believe in equality and democracy, if we believe in law and justice, then each of us, when we see or believe errors are being made, has an obligation to make every effort to correct them" (Tateishi 1984, 70–71). That was Minoru Yasui's statement of belief when, as an American-born citizen, he was required along with all other people of Japanese ancestry on the West Coast to abide by a curfew in preparation for internment in U.S. concentration camps during World War II; it was an ideal that remained with him until his death.

Yasui was born in Hood River, Oregon, one of six boys and three girls in the family of Masuo and Shidzuyo Yasui, both of whom came from the same village in Japan. Masuo hoped to become a lawyer, but racist and nativist attitudes in the United States, which had produced discriminatory laws against the Japanese and earlier the Chinese, barred Masuo from citizenship and from a legal profession. So a few years before Minoru's birth, Masuo opened a small store in partnership with an older brother. The Yasui Brothers Company helped Japanese immigrant families with capital to establish themselves on farms, and as a result the company held shares of about 1,000 acres of farmlands and orchards and owned several farms outright. As the enterprises prospered, Masuo became a prominent member of his community and the founder of the Japanese Methodist Church in Hood River.

Yasui's mother, a former teacher in Japan, encouraged all of her children to obtain a good education and to maintain their Japanese heritage. The children attended both public schools and a Japanese-language school. In 1933, Yasui entered the University of Oregon, where he joined the Reserve Officers Training Corps (ROTC) and received his commission as a second lieutenant in 1937. He earned his law degree at the university, the first _Nisei_ (an American-born citizen whose parents were born in Japan) to graduate from the law school and the first ever _Nisei_ lawyer in Oregon. No one would hire him, however, and he finally found a job with the Japanese consulate in Chicago, where his work was primarily clerical.

When the Japanese bombed Pearl Harbor on 7 December 1941, the lives of Yasui and his family along with most other Americans of Japanese ancestry began to fall apart. Yasui resigned his job at the consulate and at the urging of his father enlisted in the army. In mid-January 1942, he was ordered to report for duty at Camp Vancouver, Washington; however, when he went to the railroad station, the agent refused to sell him a ticket because of his Japanese ancestry. As Yasui reported,

> Despite my showing him travel orders from the U.S. Army, I could not persuade him to issue me a railroad ticket. I finally had to make an appointment

to see one of the attorneys in the general counsel's office for the Union Pacific Railroad in Chicago to obtain authorization for me to buy a ticket to report for active duty with the U.S. Army. I had to point out the Fourteenth Amendment to the Constitution of the United States to persuade the lawyer that I was a citizen of the United States, on the basis of my birth certificate alone (Tateishi 1984, 65–66).

Yasui was able to comply with orders and report at Camp Vancouver, but he was not accepted for active duty. Although he attempted eight more times to serve, he was told each time to leave and in late 1944, without explanation, received an official discharge.

In the meantime, his family was undergoing a terrible crisis—his father had been arrested by the FBI as a probable "enemy alien" and sent to an internment camp set up by the U.S. Justice Department. As a lawyer, Yasui hoped to help his father at his hearing in Fort Missoula, Montana, but the federal government only allowed him to attend as a private citizen. According to Yasui, "the proceedings were a complete farce." To "prove" that his father had subversive intentions, officials cited the family's visit to Japan, their extensive landholdings, and a medal given to Masuo by the Japanese emperor for improving relations between Japan and the United States. The final blow, however, came in the form of children's drawings of the Panama Canal produced as school assignments but "submitted as evidence that he was plotting to blow up the Panama Canal. In a total perversion of the assumption of innocence, the official challenged Masuo" to prove he had no such intention. "Unable to prove what he hadn't intended, Masuo Yasui was classified as disloyal and interned until 1945" (Berson 1994, 329).

Shortly after his father's internment, Yasui decided to offer himself as a test case in response to President Franklin Roosevelt's Executive Order 9066 to require a curfew for German and Italian enemy aliens and *all* people of Japanese ancestry. The latter requirement, Yasui believed, was unconstitutional because it was based on ancestry and infringed on his right as a citizen. He challenged the law, even though he later condemned young men of Japanese ancestry who refused to submit to the draft. In his view, the military draft "offered Japanese Americans the chance to fulfill their obligations of citizenship alongside those of other races" (Irons 1983, 87).

When he openly defied the curfew order, he invited arrest but was released on bail in March 1942. He also refused to obey a military order for Americans of Japanese ancestry to report for evacuation from Oregon. He was eventually escorted by the military to the North Portland Livestock Pavilion, where several thousand Japanese Americans were held in quarters designed for horses and cows and "surrounded by eight-foot-high, barbed wire fences with watchtowers on the corners. There were also searchlights, sentries, and .30-caliber, water-cooled machine guns" (Tateishi 1984, 73). Yasui and others were eventually shipped to Minidoka Relocation Center—a guarded detention camp with barbed wire—in a remote section west of Pocatello, Idaho.

In June 1942, Yasui was brought back to Portland, Oregon, to stand trial for violating the curfew law. He was tried before Judge Lager Fee, who in his decision

claimed that Yasui was not a citizen because he had worked for the Japanese consulate and that certain characteristics of anyone of Japanese ancestry predisposed them to subversion. Yasui's military oath while in the Army Reserves, registration with the State Department before working for the consulate, and his acceptance by the Bar of Oregon were disregarded. He was sentenced to a year in solitary confinement.

Yasui's case was appealed to the U.S. Supreme Court, which sided with the military and the general view that Japanese Americans were a threat even though none of the tens of thousands (two-thirds of whom were American citizens) deported from the West Coast of the United States had ever been charged with any kind of treasonable act. The High Court upheld Yasui's conviction, but restored his citizenship and sent the case back to a lower court, where Yasui's sentence was reduced to the time already spent—nine months—in solitary. He was released and taken to the Minidoka camp where he volunteered for the infantry but was rejected.

After a year, Yasui was released from the concentration camp and spent some time in Chicago, then went to Denver to live. Because he had not had an active law practice for five years, he had to pass the Colorado Bar examinations, which he did in 1945, standing first in test results of all the applicants. Although he was told he would not be admitted to the bar because of his criminal conviction, his case was heard by the Colorado Supreme Court, which granted him the right to practice law in Colorado.

Yasui set up his law practice, married, and beginning in the 1950s was active in efforts to seek reparations for people of Japanese ancestry who had lost property and had been illegally confined for up to four years. Not until the 1980s did the U.S. government begin an investigation into the relocation program and the injustices perpetrated against loyal Japanese Americans who were victims of racism and war hysteria. Finally, in 1988, the U.S. Congress passed the Redress Act, and the federal government formally apologized for its violations of the constitutional rights of Japanese American citizens, awarding $20,000 to each person illegally interred.

Unfortunately, Yasui did not live to reap that small reward. He died two years earlier, still waiting to hear that he had been wronged. In spite of his long and seemingly unfruitful efforts for justice, Yasui never became embittered to the point of fighting back with violence. In fact, several years before his death, he said that if the U.S. government once again deprived masses of citizens of their civil liberties, he would not hesitate to passively resist the U.S. government.

References:

Berson, Robin Kadison. 1994. *Marching to a Different Drummer: Unrecognized Heroes of American History*. Westport, CT: Greenwood Press.

Irons, Peter. 1983. *Justice at War: The Story of the Japanese American Internment Cases*. New York: Oxford University Press.

Tuteishi, John. 1984. *And Justice for All: An Oral History of the Japanese American Detention Camps*. New York: Random House.

Z

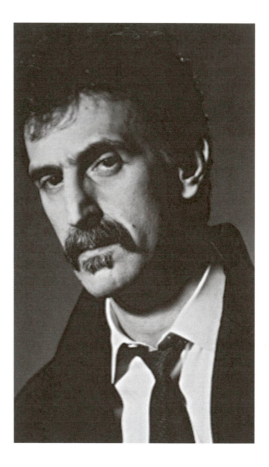

ZAPPA, *FRANK VINCENT*

(1941–1993)

An eclectic composer whose satirical lyrics mocked much of the U.S. establishment as well as the so-called hippies of the 1950s and 1960s, Frank Zappa was both vilified and praised for his activism against censorship in the recording industry. He was a relentless advocate of First Amendment rights yet "was attacked in print, on a personal level, for years" by people he had never met "who appeared to be trying to punish" him because he wrote about taboo topics or insulted icons. According to Zappa, one Colorado newspaper called him a "degenerate" and a "menace to society" (Zappa with Occhiogrosso 1989, 221).

Born in Baltimore to Sicilian immigrants, Zappa was the oldest of four children. His father was a meteorologist at the Edgewood, Maryland, arsenal, where poison gas was produced. His father made extra money for the family by vol-

unteering for chemical (and maybe biological) warfare testing, called patch tests, for which the army paid $10. Military officials would not say what was on the patch, and a volunteer had to agree not to tamper with it in any way.

During his childhood, Zappa suffered from asthma, sinus problems, and ear infections, and the family moved to Florida in the hope that the climate would be beneficial for him. After Zappa's health improved, the family returned to Maryland, where he got sick again. The family moved to California and eventually settled in Lancaster, where Zappa attended Antelope Valley High School.

Around the age of 12, Zappa got interested in the drums. In fact, his first gigs were as a drummer in garage bands. However, he was eventually fired as a drummer because he played the cymbals too much. At about the same time, he became interested in rhythm and blues, as well as the complete works of Edgard Varese and the music of Igor Stravinsky. Later in his teens, he picked up a guitar and stayed with it, eventually forming a band called the Blackouts.

The band never really took off, and after failing in filmmaking, college, and a marriage, Zappa moved to Los Angeles. He became guitarist for a group called the Soul Giants, which eventually became the Mothers of Invention. In the mid-1960s, there was an era of rich experimentation in rock music. The Mothers of Invention were among the leaders in theatrical and satirical montages. "Freak Out" was their first recording, later described as "rock's first experimental music masterpiece . . . with an anarchist aggression that is far more defiantly celebratory than arty," according to the *Rolling Stone Record Guide*. The record had only moderate success commercially, but Paul McCartney once said that it was an inspiration for the Beatles' Sgt. Pepper album. More albums were produced by the group, but none were commercial successes. By 1970, the band had broken up, and Zappa went on to produce music in his own manner.

In the 1970s, Zappa had minor hits with "Don't Eat the Yellow Snow," "Dancin' Fool," and "Valley Girl." In later interviews, he proclaimed that "Valley Girl" had been a joke, pointing out that the American public loves celebrating the infantile. In fact, there were many parts of American culture that Zappa found disgusting, among them drugs, hippies, corporate record companies, fundamental Christianity, and the public school system. Although many Americans considered Zappa weird, outrageous, and certainly controversial, his private life was fairly conventional. When he died, he had been married for over 25 years, and he and his wife, Gail, had four children. The couple co-owned a record and merchandising company, and Zappa was an astute businessman, calling himself a "devout capitalist" (Feldman 1993).

By the late 1980s, Zappa had taken on the U.S. Congress and the Parent's Music Resource Center (PMRC), which was demanding that the recording industry place warning labels on records that they deemed offensive. In Zappa's view, the PMRC was practicing censorship in the guise of protecting young children. Speaking at a congressional hearing on 19 September 1985, he pointed out that proposed legislation requiring the labels was an ill-conceived piece of nonsense that would fail to give any real benefits to children. He contended that if children were vulnerable, the parents should support music appreciation programs in schools. He lost the labeling battle but continued to speak out about what he believed was a conspiratorial and repressive government.

Zappa's political interests were also international. His work was admired by many in Soviet-dominated countries, and he was a hero to students in Czechoslovakia, where his song "Plastic People" was a favorite of those working underground for democracy. One of his fans was Czechoslovakian President VÁCLAV HAVEL, himself an advocate of free speech and a champion of human rights. Havel named Zappa the country's special ambassador to the West on trade culture and tourism, but the appointment was derailed by Secretary of State James Baker, whose wife was a member of PMRC. Zappa was left with the impression that some retribution was involved.

Because of his belief that people should have a voice in their government and stand up for their rights, Zappa was an adamant supporter of voter registration drives. He set up voter registration booths or tables in lobbies where he played concerts, providing opportunities for people to register before or after concerts and during intermissions. In a profile for the *Los Angeles Times*, Daniel Schorr recalled that Zappa "wanted to use music to lead young people to an interest in politics," and he once asked Schorr to "join him onstage to urge 'the kids' to register and vote. . . . He wanted to foster a peaceful youth revolution to take over a government he saw as corrupt" (Schorr 1993).

Zappa's activism was somewhat curtailed in the early 1990s when he was diagnosed with prostate cancer. One of the plans that had to be canceled was a presidential bid in 1992. He wanted to run, but it would have been too hard to run a political campaign and battle cancer at the same time. Therefore, he limited his activities to composing at home on his computer (in addition to regular musical instruments) and making master tapes from some of his older recordings.

His body finally gave in to cancer on 6 December 1993. One of the tributes accorded to him was a comet named in his memory.

References

Feldman, Paul. 1993. "Frank Zappa, Iconoclast of Rock, Dies at 52." *Los Angeles Times*, 6 December.

Schorr, Daniel. 1993. "Frank Zappa: A Maverick Pied Piper." *Los Angeles Times*, 7 December.

Zappa, Frank, with Peter Occhiogrosso. 1989. *The Real Frank Zappa Book*. New York: Poseidon Press.

ZORICH, CHRIS

(1969–)

He is a Chicago Bears defensive tackle who graduated from the University of Notre Dame, and in many ways, Chris Zorich is an unlikely hero. His humanitarian efforts stem from a belief in doing whatever he can to help those in need, in spite of a background that could have made him bitter and unwilling to share with others.

Zorich grew up in Chicago in a poor neighborhood. His parents were racially mixed—his mother was white, and his father was black—but his father disappeared not long after Zora Zorich became pregnant. Growing up in the neighborhood, he had a difficult time on the streets. By his own estimates, he was mugged "about 100 times, give or take one or two." Mainly, he was harassed or attacked by older black boys, who made fun of his mixed racial parentage. "We received hate mail, had bricks tossed through our window. It was rough," he declared (Johnson et al. 1995). Gang members also targeted him because he refused to join them. The worst, however, was when he was beaten up by a sixteen-year-old girl. Although he was only seven years old at the time, it was a traumatic experience.

Things started to change for Zorich when he joined the football team at Chicago Vocational High School. According to coach John Potocki, Zorich was the meanest and toughest football player he had ever seen. That was high praise,

since another alumnus of Chicago Vocational High was Hall of Fame linebacker Dick Butkus (also of the Chicago Bears). Potocki credits Zorich's background as the reason he turned out to be so tough as a football player. As Potocki once said: "There's a bit of hate in Chris from people picking on him" (Looney 1990).

With such a tough image, it is sometimes difficult to believe that there would be much to like about Zorich. However, hate and bitterness have never consumed Zorich's life and have all but disappeared. He attributes his humanitarian qualities to his mother, who taught him to share whatever little they had. While he was growing up in Chicago, his mom, disabled and unable to work because of diabetic complications, had a monthly income of $200. Of that, $140 went for rent. Zorich and his mother would go to a local church to wait in line for holiday food baskets, or they would stand in welfare lines to receive cheese and powdered milk. As a result, he said, "I swore that I'd never make anyone stand in line for food" (Johnson et al. 1995).

His mother, who died in 1991, also taught him to be the best he could be at whatever he did. When he worked for five summers as a janitor for a church, for example, it was important to him to do the job well, mopping the floor several time to make the place sparkling clean.

In a 1990 interview, Zorich said that his "goal in life is to be a great person—like my mother. She has nothing, but she has everything. I don't want people to remember me as a good noseguard. I want them to remember me, eventually, as a wonderful husband, a wonderful father, and as somebody who would always help. I think the main thing is, if you can't be honest with yourself, then you can't be a decent human being" (Looney 1990).

His mother suffered a heart attack on the day after the Orange Bowl game, 1 January 1991, when Chris was named most valuable player. He returned from the game to find his mother dead in her apartment.

It is a minor miracle that Zorich wound up at Notre Dame. Academically, there was no way he should have been admitted. Whereas the average SAT score for entering freshmen is 1220, Zorich managed a score of only 740. However, one of the forms he had to fill out when he applied asked about his family. "Well, it's only my mom and she is the best thing that ever happened," he wrote. He managed to impress admissions director Kevin Rooney, who said that "you can develop a sense of a person by looking into his eyes" (Looney 1990).

After a very successful football career at Notre Dame—he was a three-time all-American—Zorich was drafted in the second round of the pro football draft by the Chicago Bears in 1991. Although he spent the first two years on the bench under coach Mike Ditka, by 1993 his role was redefined under the new Bears coach Dave Wannstedt. Since then, his career has gone into high gear, and he has become a leader both on and off the field.

Among his off-field endeavors was the establishment of the Zora Zorich Scholarship Fund at Notre Dame in honor of his mother. Additionally, during the holiday season, he delivers toys and food baskets to folks in his old neighborhood. Although he has been honored many times for all his local contributions, he does not do it for the awards. He now has the financial means to give back to the community, and he does that simply because he believes that it is right.

As for the future, a *Chicago* magazine report noted:

Zorich is looking beyond football. He talks about one day adopting children—a biracial girl and two boys, one black and one white. And working with Father John Smyth, the executive director of Maryville Academy in Des Plaines, he's exploring the possibility of opening his own orphanage. . . . Smyth recites an endless litany of Zorich's many virtues: "I don't think there's a phony bone in his whole body. And the kids all love him. They think Chris Zorich is their brother" (Johnson et al. 1995).

Zorich is quick to deflect such praise. "I'm not saying I'm going to change the world or even find a cure for the common cold," he says. "I just want to help others. I know that's what my mom would want me to do" (Johnson et al. 1995).

References

Johnson, Geoffrey, Dale Eastman, and Gretchen Reynolds. 1995. "Seven Who Made a Difference." *Chicago*, January.

Looney, Douglas S. 1990. "Hard Man, Soft Heart: Notre Dame's Chris Zorich Is Mean on the Football Field, but He Is a Gentle Soul Elsewhere." *Sports Illustrated*, 1 October.

O'Malley, Kathy. 1995. "Gentle Giant Bears Lineman Chris Zorich Honored at Gold and Silver Ball." *Chicago Tribune*, 4 October, Tempo section.

Womer, Kelly. 1995. "Zorich Gives Mom Credit for His Spirit of Sharing." *Chicago Tribune*, 7 November.

APPENDIX

UNIVERSAL DECLARATION OF HUMAN RIGHTS

PREAMBLE

WHEREAS recognition of the inherent dignity and of the equal and inalienable rights of all members of the human family is the foundation of freedom, justice and peace in the world,

WHEREAS disregard and contempt for human rights have resulted in barbarous acts which have outraged the conscience of mankind, and the advent of a world in which human beings shall enjoy freedom of speech and belief and freedom from fear and want has been proclaimed as the highest aspiration of the common people,

WHEREAS it is essential, if man is not to be compelled to have recourse, as a last resort, to rebellion against tyranny and oppression, that human rights should be protected by the rule of law,

WHEREAS it is essential to promote the development of friendly relations between nations,

WHEREAS the peoples of the United Nations have in the Charter reaffirmed their faith in fundamental human rights, in the dignity and worth of the human person and in the equal rights of men and women and have determined to promote social progress and better standards of life in larger freedom,

WHEREAS Member States have pledged themselves to achieve, in co-operation with the United Nations, the promotion of universal respect for and observance of human rights and fundamental freedoms,

WHEREAS a common understanding of these rights and freedoms is of the greatest importance for the full realization of this pledge,

Now, Therefore,

The General Assembly

proclaims

This Universal Declaration of Human Rights

A s a common standard of achievement for all peoples and all nations, to the end that every individual and every organ of society, keeping this Declaration constantly in mind, shall strive by teaching and education to promote respect for these rights and freedoms and by progressive measures, national and international, to secure their universal and effective recognition and observance, both among the peoples of Member States themselves and among the peoples of territories under their jurisdiction.

ARTICLE 1 All human beings are born free and equal in dignity and rights. They are endowed with reason and conscience and should act towards one another in a spirit of brotherhood.

ARTICLE 2 Everyone is entitled to all the rights and freedoms set forth in this Declaration, without distinction of any kind, such as race, colour, sex, language, religion, political or other opinion, national or social origin, property, birth or other status.
Furthermore, no distinction shall be made on the basis of the political, jurisdictional or international status of the country or territory to which a person belongs, whether it be independent, trust, nonselfgoverning or under any other limitation of sovereignty.

ARTICLE 3 Everyone has the right to life, liberty and security of person.

ARTICLE 4 No one shall be held in slavery or servitude; slavery and the slave trade shall be prohibited in all their forms.

ARTICLE 5 No one shall be subjected to torture or to cruel, inhuman or degrading treatment or punishment.

ARTICLE 6 Everyone has the right to recognition everywhere as a person before the law.

ARTICLE 7 All are equal before the law and are entitled without any discrimination to equal protection of the law. All are entitled to equal protection against any discrimination in violation of this Declaration and against any incitement to such discrimination.

ARTICLE 8 Everyone has the right to an effective remedy by the competent national tribunals for acts violating the fundamental rights granted him by the constitution or by law.

ARTICLE 9 No one shall be subjected to arbitrary arrest, detention or exile.

ARTICLE 10 Everyone is entitled in full equality to a fair and public hearing by an independent and impartial tribunal, in the determination of his rights and obligations and of any criminal charge against him.

ARTICLE 11 (1) Everyone charged with a penal offence has the right to be presumed innocent until proved guilty according to law in a public trial at which he has had all the guarantees necessary for his defence.

(2) No one shall be held guilty of any penal offence on account of any act or omission which did not constitute a penal offence, under national or international law, at the time when it was committed. Nor shall a heavier penalty be imposed than the one that was applicable at the time the penal offence was committed.

ARTICLE 12 No one shall be subjected to arbitrary interference with his privacy, family, home or correspondence, nor to attacks upon his honour and reputation. Everyone has the right to the protection of the law against such interference or attacks.

ARTICLE 13 (1) Everyone has the right to freedom of movement and residence within the borders of each State.

(2) Everyone has the right to leave any country, including his own, and to return to his country.

ARTICLE 14 (1) Everyone has the right to seek and to enjoy in other countries asylum from persecution.

(2) This right may not be invoked in the case of prosecutions genuinely arising from non-political crimes or from acts contrary to the purposes and principles of the United Nations.

ARTICLE 15 (1) Everyone has the right to a nationality.

(2) No one shall be arbitrarily deprived of his nationality nor denied the right to change his nationality.

ARTICLE 16 (1) Men and women of full age, without any limitation due to race, nationality or religion, have the right to marry and to found a family. They are entitled to equal rights at a marriage, during marriage and at its dissolution.

(2) Marriage shall be entered into only with the free and full consent of the intending spouses.

(3) The family is the natural and fundamental group unit of society and is entitled to protection by society and the State.

ARTICLE 17 (1) Everyone has the right to own property alone as well as in association with others.

(2) No one shall be arbitrarily deprived of his property.

ARTICLE 18 Everyone has the right to freedom of thought, conscience and religion; this right includes freedom to change his religion or belief, and freedom, either alone or in community with others and in public or private, to manifest his religion or belief in teaching, practice, worship and observance.

ARTICLE 19 Everyone has the right to freedom of opinion and expression; this right includes freedom to hold opinions without interference and to seek, receive and impart information and ideas through any media and regardless of frontiers.

ARTICLE 20 (1) Everyone has the right to freedom of peaceful assembly and association.
(2) No one may be compelled to belong to an association.

ARTICLE 21 (1) Everyone has the right to take part in the government of his country, directly or through freely chosen representatives.
(2) Everyone has the right of equal access to public service in his country.
(3) The will of the people shall be the basis of the authority of the government; this will shall be expressed in periodic and genuine elections which shall be by universal and equal suffrage and shall be held by secret vote or by equivalent free voting procedures.

ARTICLE 22 Everyone, as a member of society, has the right to social security and is entitled to realization, through national effort and international co-operation and in accordance with the organization and resources of each State, of the economic, social and cultural rights indispensable for his dignity and the free development of his personality.

ARTICLE 23 (1) Everyone has the right to work, to free choice of employment, to just and favourable conditions of work and to protection against unemployment.
(2) Everyone, without any discrimination, has the right to equal pay for equal work.
(3) Everyone who works has the right to just and favourable remuneration ensuring for himself and his family an existence worthy of human dignity, and supplemented, if necessary, by other means of social protection.
(4) Everyone has the right to form and to join trade unions for the protection of his interests.

ARTICLE 24 Everyone has the right to rest and leisure, including reasonable limitation of working hours and periodic holidays with pay.

ARTICLE 25 (1) Everyone has the right to a standard of living adequate for the health and well-being of himself and of his family, including food, clothing, housing, and medical care and necessary social services, and the right to security in the event of unemployment, sickness, disability, widowhood, old age, or other lack of livelihood in circumstances beyond his control.

(2) Motherhood and childhood are entitled to special care and assistance. All children, whether born in or out of wedlock, shall enjoy the same social protection.

ARTICLE 26 (1) Everyone has the right to education. Education shall be free, at least in the elementary and fundamental stages. Elementary education shall be compulsory. Technical and professional education shall be made generally available and higher education shall be equally accessible to all on the basis of merit.

(2) Education shall be directed to the full development of the human personality and to the strengthening of respect for human rights and fundamental freedoms. It shall promote understanding, tolerance and friendship among all nations, racial or religious groups, and shall further the activities of the United Nations for the maintenance of peace.

(3) Parents have a prior right to choose the kind of education that shall be given to their children.

ARTICLE 27 (1) Everyone has the right freely to participate in the cultural life of the community, to enjoy the arts and to share in scientific advancement and its benefits.

(2) Everyone has the right to the protection of the moral and material interests resulting from any scientific, literary or artistic production of which he is the author.

ARTICLE 28 Everyone is entitled to a social and international order in which the rights and freedoms set forth in this Declaration can be fully realized.

ARTICLE 29 (1) Everyone has duties to the community in which alone the free and full development of his personality is possible.

(2) In the exercise of his rights and freedoms, everyone shall be subject only to such limitations as are determined by law solely for the purpose of securing due recognition and respect for the rights and freedoms of others and of meeting the just requirements of morality, public order and the general welfare in a democratic society.

(3) These rights and freedoms may in no case be exercised contrary to the purposes and principles of the United Nations.

ARTICLE 30 Nothing in this Declaration may be interpreted as implying for any State, group or person any right to engage in any activity or to perform any act aimed at the destruction of any of the rights and freedoms set forth herein.

BIBLIOGRAPHY

"ABC World News Tonight with Peter Jennings." 1994. "Person of the Week," 9 December.

Abernathy, Ralph David. 1989. *And the Walls Came Tumbling Down: An Autobiography*. New York: Harper & Row.

Adams, Frank, with Myles Horton. 1975. *Unearthing Seeds of Fire: The Idea of Highlander*. Winston-Salem, NC: John F. Blair.

Addams, Jane. 1990. *Twenty Years at Hull House*. Urbana: University of Illinois Press.

Allen, Maury. 1987. *Jackie Robinson: A Life Remembered*. New York: Franklin Watts.

Amnesty International. 1994. Summary document. Electronic posting, 13 November. http://www.spider-graphics.com/khrai.html.

———. 1995. "China Human Rights Fact Sheet." March.

Andersen, Martin. 1984. "Timerman Joins Buenos Aires Daily." *Washington Post*, 16 August.

Anderson, Christopher. 1990. *Citizen Jane: The Turbulent Life of Jane Fonda*. New York: Henry Holt.

Anderson, Jervis. 1973. *A. Philip Randolph: A Biographical Portrait*. New York: Harcourt Brace Jovanovich.

Andres, Phillips. 1991. "Clouds of Doubt." *Maclean's*, 2 December.

Anger, Per. 1981. *With Raoul Wallenberg in Budapest*. New York: Schocken Books.

Anyadike, Obinna. 1993. "Interview with Wangari Maathai" (electronic posting). *InterPress Service*, 24 June.

Aquino, Corazon Cojuangco. 1986–1989. *Speeches of President Corazon C. Aquino*. Manila: Republic of the Philippines.

"Archbishop Desmond Tutu To Teach at Emory University." 1995. *Jet*, 27 November.

Ashe, Arthur. 1993. *Days of Grace*. New York: Alfred A. Knopf.

Ashe, Geoffrey. 1968. *Gandhi*. New York: Stein & Day.

Associated Press. 1991. "Burma Denounces Pleas on Suu Kui." *Boston Globe*, 27 December.

———. 1992. "Bald Mountain Activist Won't Be Ousted." *Oregonian*, 31 July.

———. 1993. "Burma Extends Opposition Leader's House Arrest." *Boston Globe*, 21 July, National/Foreign section.

———. 1995. "Pakistani March Targets Child Labor." *Boston Globe*, 26 April, National/Foreign section.

———. 1996a. "Black Panther Seeks Retrial." AP Wire Services, 27 March.

———. 1996b. "Ex-Rep. Barbara Jordan Dies." 17 January.

"At the Gates of Freedom." 1990. *Washington Post*, 8 April, Magazine section.

Atkinson, Linda. 1978. *Mother Jones: The Most Dangerous Woman in America*. New York: Crown Publishers.

Auerbach, Jerold S. 1990. *Rabbis and Lawyers: The Journey from Torah to Constitution*. Bloomington: Indiana University Press.

Ayers, Tiffany. 1990. "Mitch Snyder, Homeless Advocate, Mourned." *National Catholic Reporter*, 27 July.

"Back to the Gulag." 1995. *Columbia Journalism Review*, September/October.

Bains, Rae. 1982. *Clara Barton, Angel of the Battlefield*. Mahwah, NJ: Troll Associates.

Baker, Deborah. 1994. "Exiled Feminist Writer Tells Her Own Story." *New York Times*, 28 August.

Baker, William J. 1986. *Jesse Owens: An American Life*. New York: Free Press.

Balch, Emily Greene. 1972. *Beyond Nationalism: The Social Thought of Emily Greene Balch*. New York: Twayne Publishers.

Barbash, Fred. 1995. "Anti-Bomb Physicist Wins Peace Prize." *Washington Post*, 14 October.

Barnard, Jeff. 1994. "Forest Activist Battles To Save the Biggest Trees." *Seattle Times*, 6 November.

Barnes, Bart. 1994. "Two-Time Nobel Winner Linus Pauling Dies at 93." *Washington Post*, 21 August.

Barnett, Ida B. Wells. 1970. *Crusade for Justice: The Autobiography of Ida B. Wells*. Chicago: University of Chicago Press.

Barnett, Victoria. 1993. *For the Soul of the People*. New York: Oxford University Press.

Barry, Tom. 1987. *Roots of Rebellion: Land and Hunger in Central America*. Boston: South End Press.

Barton, Clara. 1907. *The Story of My Childhood*. New York: Baker & Taylor.

Barton, William Eleazar. 1969. *The Life of Clara Barton, Founder of the American Red Cross*. New York: AMS Press.

"Battle on the Internet." 1994. *Maclean's*, 17 October.

Baum, Dan. 1992. "Protest Broadcasts Displeasure with KILI Radio." *Los Angeles Times*, 31 August.

Becklund, Laurie. 1985. "Sanctuary Movement Leaders Assailed." *Los Angeles Times*, 16 November, sec. 1.

Bejder, Eva. 1995. "Students Work To Honor Slain Activist." *USA Today*, 7 June.

Bell, Derrick. 1994. *Confronting Authority: Reflections of an Ardent Protester*. Boston: Beacon Press.

Bell-Villada, Gene H. 1993. "Why Dinesh D'Souza Has It in for Rigoberta Menchu." *Monthly Review*, May.

"Beloved Pariah." 1990. *U.S. News & World Report*, 23 April.

Benson, Mary. 1986. *Nelson Mandela: The Man and the Movement*. New York: W. W. Norton.

Bentley, James. 1992. *Albert Schweitzer: The Enigma*. New York: HarperCollins.

Berkman, Leslie. 1992. "O.C. Woman's Implant Ordeal Sparks Crusade." *Los Angeles Times*, 12 January.

Berrigan, Daniel. 1973. *Prison Poems*. Greensboro, NC: Unicorn Press.
———. 1987. *To Dwell in Peace*. New York: Harper & Row.

Berryman, Phillip. 1984. *The Religious Roots of Rebellion: Christians in Central American Revolution*. Maryknoll, NY: Orbis Books.

Berson, Robin Kadison. 1994. *Marching to a Different Drummer: Unrecognized Heroes of American History*. Westport, CT: Greenwood Press.

Bethell, Tom. 1990. "Mitch Snyder, RIP." *National Review*, 6 August.

Bethge, Eberhard, Renate Bethge, and Christian Gremmels. 1987. *Dietrich Bonhoeffer: A Life in Pictures*. Philadelphia: Augsburg Fortress.

Betz, Michelle. 1995. "mcvay@internet.fighter." *Jewish Western Bulletin*, 9 March (reprinted in electronic format).

Beyette, Beverly. 1990. "Mother Hale's Solution." *Los Angeles Times*, 8 March, View section.

Bhattacharya, Pallab. 1994. "A Rushdie in Bangladesh." *World Press Review*, January.

Bibb, Porter, 1993. *It Ain't as Easy as It Looks: Ted Turner's Amazing Story*. New York: Crown Publishers.

Bierman, John. 1981. *Righteous Gentile: The Story of Raoul Wallenberg, Missing Hero of the Holocaust*. New York: Viking Press.

"Billing the Victim." 1994. *Time*, 2 May.

Bilski, Andrew. 1990. "A God-King in Exile." *Maclean's*, 15 October.

Blue, Rose, and Corinne Naden. 1992. *Barbara Jordan*. New York: Chelsea House.

Blumhofer, Edith L. 1993. *Aimee Semple McPherson: Everybody's Sister*. Grand Rapids, MI: William B. Eerdmans.

Bollier, David. 1989. *Citizen Action and Other Big Ideas: A History of Ralph Nader and the Modern Consumer Movement*. Washington, DC: Center for Study of Responsive Law.

Bonhoeffer, Dietrich. 1995. *Love Letters from Cell 92*. Nashville, TN: Abingdon Press.

Boo, Katherine. 1992. "Universal Soldier: What Paula Coughlin Can Teach American Women." *Washington Monthly*, September.

Booth, William. 1995. "Fight over School Prayer Riles up Mississippi Town." *Washington Post*, 26 March.

Bosanquet, Mary. 1968. The Life and Death of Dietrich Bonhoeffer. New York: Harper & Row.

Boylston, Helen Dore. 1955. *Clara Barton, Founder of the American Red Cross*. New York: Random House.

Brabazon, James. 1975. *Albert Schweitzer: A Biography*. New York: G. P. Putnam's Sons.

Brady, Kathleen. 1984. *Ida Tarbell: Portrait of a Muckraker*. New York: G. P. Putnam's Sons.

Brandt, Willy. 1976. *People and Politics: The Years 1960–1973*. Translated by Maxwell Brownjohn. Boston: Little, Brown.

———. 1992. *My Life in Politics*. New York: Viking Press.

Brandt, Willy, as told to Leo Lania. 1960. *My Road to Berlin*. Garden City, NY: Doubleday.

Broadway, Bill. 1995. "The Theology and Martyrdom of Dietrich Bonhoeffer." *Washington Post*, 8 April.

Brockman, James R. 1982. *The Word Remains: A Life of Oscar Romero*. Maryknoll, NY: Orbis Books.

Brodeur, Paul. 1993. "Legacy." *New Yorker*, 7 June.

Brooks, Paul. 1972. *The House of Life: Rachel Carson at Work*. Boston: Houghton Mifflin.

Brown, Judith M. 1989. *Gandhi: Prisoner of Hope*. New Haven, CT: Yale University Press.

Browne, Ray B., ed. 1990. *Contemporary Heroes and Heroines*. Detroit, MI: Gale Research.

Buchsbaum, Herbert. 1993. "Extraordinary People." *Scholastic Update*, 3 December.

Buck, Pearl S. 1960. *My Several Worlds*. New York: Pocket Books.

Buck, Pearl S., with Theodore F. Harris. 1966. *For Spacious Skies: Journey in Dialogue*. New York: John Day.

Buckley, Stephen. 1992. "Berrigan Released while Appealing Contempt Term." *Washington Post*, 28 March.

Bucky, Peter A. 1992. *The Private Albert Einstein*. Kansas City, KS: Andrews & McMeel.

"Burma's Captives." 1994. Editorial. *Boston Globe*, 18 July.

"Burma's Long Walk to Freedom." 1995. Editorial. *Boston Globe*, 11 July.

Bush, Malcolm. 1993. "Jane Addams: No Easy Heroine." *Free Inquiry*, fall.

Carlson, Carole C. 1983. *Corrie ten Boom*. Old Tappan, NJ: Fleming H. Revell.

Carter, Jimmy. 1982. *Keeping Faith: Memoirs of a President*. New York: Bantam Books.

Carver, George Washington, and Gary R. Kremer. 1987. *George Washington Carver in His Own Words*. Columbia: University of Missouri Press.

Chalberg, John. 1991. *Emma Goldman: American Individualist*. New York: HarperCollins.

Chandler, David L. 1991. "Nobel Goes to Burmese Dissident." *Boston Globe*, 15 October, National/Foreign section.

Chesler, Ellen. 1992. *Woman of Valor: Margaret Sanger and the Birth Control Movement in America*. New York: Simon & Schuster.

Chestnut, J. L., Jr. 1990. *Black in Selma: The Uncommon Life of J. L. Chestnut*. New York: Farrar, Straus & Giroux.

Chiang, Harriet. 1989. "Verdicts Upheld in Sanctuary Smuggling Case." *San Francisco Chronicle*, 31 March, A6.

The Children's Voice. 1984–1995. Bimonthly newsletter of the National Coalition To End Racism in America's Child Care System.

Chin, Paula. 1990. "One Year Later, the Pasionaria of Tiananmen, Chai Ling, Implores the World Not To Forget the Bloodbath." *People Weekly*, 18 June.

Christy, Marian. 1987. "Mother Hale's Love Shelter." *Boston Globe*, 27 May, Living seciton.

Chua-Eoan, Howard G. 1987. "Grave Encounters." *Time*, 7 December.

"Clara Hale Dies." 1993. *Jet*, 11 January.

Clark, Ronald W. 1971. *Einstein: The Life and Times*. New York: World Publishing.

Coccia, Carol. 1995. Personal correspondence, March.

CNN. 1995. "Saro-Wiwa Was One of Nigeria's Most Effective Critics." Electronic posting, 11 November. http://www-cgi.cnn.com/WORLD/9511/nigeria/index2.html.

CNN News transcript of "Newsmaker Sunday." 1992. Remarks by Navy Lt. Paula Coughlin, 28 June.

Cockle, Richard. 1994. "Environmentalists Face Bitter Foes in Northeastern Oregon." *Oregonian*, 4 October.

Cohen, Richard. 1995. "Harry Wu." *Washington Post*, 11 July.

Colaiaco, James A. 1988. *Martin Luther King, Jr.: Apostle of Militant Nonviolence*. New York: St. Martin's Press.

Collier, Gene. 1992. "Pride and Petulance." *Sporting News*, 28 December.

Collins, Sheila D. 1986. "The New Underground Railroad." *Monthly Review*, May.

Conlin, Jennifer, 1994. "Survival of the Fittest." *Working Woman*, February.

Cook, Blanche Wiesen. 1992. *Eleanor Roosevelt*. Vol. 1, *1884–1933*. New York: Viking Press.

Copeland, Edith. 1971. *Notable American Women*. Vol. 1. New York: Belknap Press.

Corelli, Rae. 1990. "A Symbol of Freedom." *Maclean's*, 12 February.

Coté, Charlotte. 1988. *Olympia Brown: The Battle for Equality*. Racine, WI: Mother Courage Press.

Crisostomo, Isabelo T. 1987. *Cory: Profile of a President*. Boston: Branden Publishing Company.

Crittenden, Ann. 1988. *Sanctuary: A Story of American Conscience and the Law in Collision*. New York: Weidenfeld & Nicolson.

Currie, Harold W. 1976. *Eugene V. Debs*. Boston: Twayne Publishers.

Dalai Lama. 1977. *My Land and My People*. New York: Potala Corporation.

———. 1995. "The Dalai Lama on Compassion." Electronic posting from an article in *Asian Age*, 1 January.

Daly, Christopher B. 1992. "Black Law Professor Fights Harvard." *Washington Post*, 2 July.

Daniels, Anthony. 1995. "A Good Man in Africa: The Nigerian Dictatorship Is Fighting Back against the Weapon It Fears More than Anger." *National Review*, 10 July.

Darrow, Clarence. 1932. *The Story of My Life*. New York: Charles Scribner's Sons.

Davidson, Bill. 1990. *Jane Fonda: An Intimate Biography*. New York: Dutton.

Davidson, Miriam. 1988. *Convictions of the Heart: Jim Corbett and the Sanctuary Movement*. Tucson: University of Arizona Press.

Davidson, Sue. 1994. *A Heart in Politics: Jeannette Rankin and Patsy T. Mink*. Seattle, WA: Seal Press.

Davis, Allen Freeman. 1973. *American Heroine: The Life and Legend of Jane Addams*. New York: Oxford University Press.

Davis, Michael D., and Hunter R. Clark. 1992. *Thurgood Marshall: Warrior at the Bar, Rebel on the Bench*. New York: Birch Lane Press, Carol Publishing Group.

Dawidoff, Nichols. 1987. "Recalling Jackie Robinson; Carl Erskine Visits an Exhibition Celebrating His Teammate." *Sports Illustrated*, 28 September.

Debs, Eugene. 1948. *Writings and Speeches of Eugene V. Debs*. New York: Hermitage Press.

Dees, Morris, and Steve Fiffer. 1991. *A Season for Justice: The Life and Times of Civil Rights Lawyer Morris Dees*. New York: Macmillan.

———. 1993. *Hate on Trial: The Case against America's Most Dangerous Neo-Nazi*. New York: Villard Books/Random House.

Dell'Apa, Frank. 1994. "Flood Recalls His Breakthrough." *Boston Globe*, 7 August, Sports section.

Dellinger, David. 1993. *From Yale to Jail: The Life of a Moral Dissenter*. New York: Pantheon Books.

"Deporting Dissent." 1986. *Nation*, 19 April.

Deutsch, Richard. 1977. *Mairead Corrigan, Betty Williams*. Woodbury, NY: Barron's.

"Died, Mitch Snyder." 1990. *Time*, 16 July.

Dietrich, William. 1992. *The Final Forest: The Battle for the Last Great Trees of the Pacific Northwest*. New York: Simon & Schuster.

Diskin, Martin, and Kenneth Sharpe. 1985. *The Impact of U.S. Policy in El Salvador 1979–1985*. Berkeley, CA: Institute of International Studies.

Dizon, Lily. 1993. "Hosannas for Slain Activist." *Los Angeles Times*, 4 September.

———. 1994. "Holistic Fire in Little Saigon." *Los Angeles Times*, 16 January.

Dreifus, Claudia. 1993. "Jim Hightower" (interview). *Progressive*, August.

———. 1994. "The Widow Gets Her Verdict." *New York Times Magazine*, 27 November.

Drexel, John, ed. 1991. *The Facts on File Encyclopedia of the 20th Century*. New York: Facts on File.

Drinnon, Richard. 1961. *Rebel in Paradise: A Biography of Emma Goldman*. Chicago: University of Chicago Press.

Drogin, Bob. 1995. "Mandela To Seek Oil Embargo against Nigeria Military Regime." *Los Angeles Times*, 16 November.

Du Boulay, Shirley. 1988. *Tutu: Voice of the Voiceless*. Grand Rapids, MI: William B. Eerdmans.

Duke, Lynne, 1992. "25 Years after Landmark Decision, Still the Rarest of Wedding Bonds." *Washington Post*, 12 June.

Durbin, Kathie. 1990. "Lou Gold." *Oregonian*, 20 September.

Easterbrook, Gregg. 1994. "Averting a Death Foretold." *Newsweek*, 28 November.

Editors of *Freedomways*. 1965. *Paul Robeson: The Great Forerunner*. New York: Dodd, Mead.

Editors of *World Almanac*. 1990. *World Almanac Biographical Dictionary*. New York: Pharos Books.

Edwards, Audrey, and Gary Wohl. 1977. *Muhammad Ali: The People's Champ*. Toronto, Canada: Little, Brown.

Edwards, Frederick. 1994. "International Humanism: In Defense of Taslima Nasrin." *Humanist*, September/October.

Egan, Eileen. 1986. *Such a Vision of the Street: Mother Teresa, the Spirit and the Work*. New York: Doubleday.

Einstein, Albert. 1954. *Ideas and Opinions*. New York: Bonanza Books.

Ellsberg, Robert, ed. 1988. *By Little and by Little: The Selected Writings of Dorothy Day*. New York: Alfred A. Knopf.

Elmer-Dewitt, Philip. 1993. "Anita the Agitator." *Time*, 25 January.

Epstein, Daniel Mark. 1993. *Sister Aimee: The Life of Aimee Semple McPherson*. New York: Harcourt Brace Jovanovich.

European Bureau for Conscientious Objection (Peace Media Service). 1995. "War Heroes Who Refused To Kill." Electronic posting, 1 June.

Evans, Karen. 1989. "Le Ly Hayslip's American Life." *Los Angeles Times,* 5 February, Magazine section.

Fairclough, Adam. 1995. *Martin Luther King, Jr.* Athens: University of Georgia Press.

Falk, Candace. 1990. *Love, Anarchy, and Emma Goldman*. New Brunswick, NJ: Rutgers University Press.

Farah, Douglas. 1992. "Indian from Guatemala Wins Nobel Peace Prize." *Washington Post*, 17 October.

Farber, David. 1988. *Chicago '68*. Chicago: University of Chicago Press.

Farnsworth, Elizabeth. 1988. "Guatemalan's Viewpoint Hope Exists Despite Little Change in Rights." *San Francisco Chronicle*, 16 November, Briefing section.

Fast, Howard. 1951. *Peekskill: USA; a Personal Experience*. New York: Civil Rights Congress.

Feldman, Jay, 1993. "Roberto Clemente Went To Bat for All Latino Ballplayers." *Smithsonian*, September.

Feldman, Paul. 1993. "Frank Zappa, Iconoclast of Rock, Dies at 52." *Los Angeles Times*, 6 December.

Fetherling, Dale. 1974. *Mother Jones: The Miners' Angel*. Carbondale: Southern Illinois University Press.

Finke, Nikke. 1990. "Woman with a Country." *Los Angeles Times*, 18 June.

Fischer, Louis. 1950. *The Life of Mahatma Gandhi*. New York: Harper & Brothers.

———. 1954. *Gandhi: His Life and Message for the World*. New York: Signet Key Books.

Flood, Curt. 1970. *The Way It Is*. New York: Trident Press.

Fogelman, Eva. 1994. *Conscience and Courage*. New York: Anchor Books.

Folkart, Burt A. 1995. Obituary (Maggie Kuhn). *Los Angeles Times*, 23 April.

Foner, Philip S. 1979. *Women and the American Labor Movement: From Colonial Times to the Eve of World War I*. New York: Free Press/Macmillan.

Foner, Philip S., ed. 1978. *Paul Robeson Speaks*. New York: Brunner/Mazel.

———. 1983. *Mother Jones Speaks: Collected Writings and Speeches*. New York: Monad Press.

Ford, Betty, with Chris Chase. 1978. *The Times of My Life*. New York: Harper & Row.

———. 1987. *A Glad Awakening*. Garden City, NY: Doubleday.

Forman, James. 1985. *The Making of Black Revolutionaries*. Washington, DC: Open Hand Publishers.

Fossey, Dian. 1983. *Gorillas in the Mist*. Boston: Houghton Mifflin.

Frankel, Glenn. 1991. "'1,763 Days in Chains.'" *Washington Post*, 20 November.

———. 1995. "The Ultimate Israeli—A Soldier Who Yearned for Peace." *Washington Post*, 5 November.

Frappollo, Elizabeth. 1972. "At 91, Jeannette Rankin Is the Feminists' New Heroine." *Life*, 3 March.

Free Burma. 1995. "Daw Aung San Suu Kyi's Address at Beijing Forum." Electronic Conference on EcoNet, 31 August.

Freedomways editors. 1978. *Paul Robeson: The Great Forerunner*. New York: Dodd, Mead.

Freeman, Orville. 1968. *Letter to Dr. Ralph Abernathy on the Poor People's Campaign.* Washington, DC: U.S. Department of Agriculture, 14 June.

Freeman, Patricia. 1988. "Black and White and Heard All Over, Johnny Clegg and Savuka Cross South Africa's Color Barriers." *People Weekly*, 24 October.

Friedman, Jack. 1988. "The Quiet Victories of Ryan White." *People Weekly*, 30 May.

Friends of Peace Pilgrim, comps. 1991. *Peace Pilgrim: Her Life and Work in Her Own Words.* Santa Fe, NM: Ocean Tree Books.

Furia, Claire. 1992. "Defender of Wrongly Jailed Draws the Eye of Hollywood." *Philadelphia Inquirer*, 9 June.

Gandhi, Mohandas K. 1957. *An Autobiography: The Story of My Experiments with Truth.* Translated by Mahadev Desai. Boston: Beacon Press.

Gay, Kathlyn. 1987. *The Rainbow Effect: Interracial Families.* New York: Franklin Watts.

———. 1993a. *Breast Implants: Making Safe Choices.* New York: Macmillan, Silver Burdett Press.

———. 1993b. *The Right To Die.* Brookfield, CT: Millbrook Press.

———. 1994. *Pollution and the Powerless: The Environmental Justice Movement.* New York: Franklin Watts.

———. 1995a. *"I Am Who I Am": Speaking Out about Multiracial Identity.* New York: Franklin Watts.

———. 1995b. *Rights and Respect: What You Need To Know about Gender Bias and Sexual Harassment.* Brookfield, CT: Millbrook Press.

Gay, Martin, and Kathlyn Gay. 1996. *The Importance of Emma Goldman.* San Diego, CA: Lucent Books.

Gentry, Tony. 1990. *Jesse Owens: Champion Athlete.* New York: Chelsea House.

Gerard, Warren. 1980. "The Agony and Ecstasy of Terry Fox." *Maclean's*, 15 September.

Gibbs, Nancy. 1989. "Norway's Radical Daughter: Gro Harlem Brundtland. . . ." *Time*, 25 September.

Giddings, Paula. 1984. *When and Where I Enter: The Impact of Black Women on Race and Sex in America.* New York: William Morrow.

Ginger, Ray. 1949. *The Bending Cross: A Biography of Eugene Victor Debs.* New Brunswick, NJ: Rutgers University Press.

Gioglio, Gerald R. 1989. *Days of Decision: An Oral History of Conscientious Objectors in the Military during the Vietnam War.* Trenton, NJ: Broken Rifle Press.

Gold, Lou. 1990. "A Call from the Forest." *Orion*, winter.

Goldman, Emma. 1969. *Anarchism and Other Essays.* 1910. Reprint, New York: Dover.

———. 1970. *Living My Life.* 1931. Reprint, New York: Dover.

Gordon, Nicholas. 1993. *Murders in the Mist: Who Killed Dian Fossey.* London: Hodder and Stoughton.

Grade 7 Reflections on the 2 December 1994 Visit by Human Rights Hero, Iqbal Masih of Pakistan. http://www.digitalrag.com/mirror/iqbal.html.

Graves, Florence George. 1995. "Responding to Sen. Simpson." *Washington Post*, 28 January.

"Gray Power." 1990. Editorial. *Nation*, 28 May.

Green, Martin. 1993. *Gandhi: Voice of a New Age Revolution.* New York: Continuum.

Green, Martin, ed. 1987. *Gandhi in India: In His Own Words.* London: University Press of New England.

Green, Sadie. n.d. Personal correspondence.

———. n.d. "Essay on Class."

———. n.d. *Evalina: Years in Hiding.* Unpublished manuscript.

Gregory, Dick. 1976. *Up from Nigger.* New York: Stein & Day.

"Gro Harlem Brundtland" (interview). 1990. *UNESCO Courier*, September.

Grogan, David. 1992. "Sister Courage." *People Weekly*, 21 December.

Grove, Lloyd. 1989. "Rushdie and Wiggins' Uncommon Bond." *Washington Post*, 7 March.

"Growing with Brundtland." 1993. *Economist*, 4 September.

Gullas, Cecilia K. 1987. *Corazon Aquino: The Miracle of a President*. New York: Cultural House.

Gupte, Pranay. 1992. *Mother India: A Political Biography of Indira Gandhi*. New York: Charles Scribner's Sons.

Hackel, Sergei. 1981. *Pearl of Great Price: The Life of Mother Maria Skobtsova*. Crestwood, NY: St. Vladimir's Seminary Press.

Hager, Thomas. 1995. *Force of Nature: The Life of Linus Pauling*. New York: Simon & Schuster.

Hallie, Philip. 1979. *Lest Innocent Blood Be Shed*. New York: Harper & Row.

Hamilton, Leni. 1988. *Clara Barton*. New York: Chelsea House.

Hamilton, Virginia. 1971. *Paul Robeson: The Life and Times of a Free Black Man*. New York: Harper & Row.

Hammer, Joshua. 1986. "Prison Samaritan Jim McCloskey Wins Freedom for an Innocent Man." *People Weekly*, 24 November.

Hanley, Sally. 1989. *A. Philip Randolph Labor Leader*. New York: Chelsea House.

Hano, Arnold. 1977. *Muhammad Ali the Champion*. New York: G. P. Putnam's Sons.

Hareven, Tamara K. 1968. *Eleanor Roosevelt: An American Conscience*. Chicago: Quadrangle Books.

Harris, Frank III. 1989. "'Freedom Summer' Born in Violence." *St. Louis Post Dispatch*, 20 June.

Harris, Scott. 1994. "Pete Seeger: Folk Music's Granddad Plays It Green." *E Magazine*, November/December.

Harris, Theodore. 1969. *Pearl S. Buck: A Biography*. New York: John Day.

Harris, William. 1977. *Keeping the Faith: A. Philip Randolph, Milton P. Webster, and the Brotherhood of Sleeping Car Porters, 1925–1937*. Champaign: University of Illinois Press.

Haskins, James. 1977. *Barbara Jordan*. New York: Dial Press.

Haskins, Jim. 1974. *Ralph Bunche: A Most Reluctant Hero*. New York: Hawthorn Books.

Hauser, Thomas. 1991. *Muhammad Ali: His Life and Times*. New York: Simon & Schuster.

Havel, Václav. 1991. *Open Letters: Selected Writings 1965–1990*. Edited by Paul Wilson. New York: Alfred A. Knopf.

———. 1992. *Summer Meditations*. Translated by Paul Wilson. New York: Alfred A. Knopf.

Hawxhurst, Joan C. 1994. *Mother Jones: Labor Crusader*. Austin, TX: Steck-Vaughn.

Hayes, Harold T. P. 1990. *The Dark Romance of Dian Fossey*. New York: Simon & Schuster.

Hayslip, Le Ly, with James Hayslip. 1993. *Child of War, Woman of Peace*. New York: Doubleday.

Hayslip, Le Ly, with Jay Wurts. 1990. *When Heaven and Earth Changed Places: A Vietnamese Woman's Journey from War to Peace*. New York: Penguin Books.

Hearst, Margo Ruark, ed. 1993. *Interracial Identity: Celebration, Conflict, or Choice?* Chicago: Biracial Family Network.

Height, Dorothy I., and Jacqueline Trescott. 1994. "Remembering Mary McLeod Bethune." *Essence*, February.

Hellman, Peter. 1981. *Avenue of the Righteous*. New York: Bantam Books.

Hentoff, Nat. 1987. *American Heroes: In and out of School.* New York: Delacorte.

Hessel, Dieter T., ed. 1977. *Maggie Kuhn on Aging.* Philadelphia: Westminster Press.

Hewitt, Bill. 1990. "Nelson Mandela." *People Weekly,* 26 February.

Hewitt, Bill, Vicke Bane, Dirk Mathison, and Terry Smith. 1991. "At Long Last, Freedom!" *People Weekly,* 2 December.

Hightower, Jim. 1975. *Eat Your Heart Out: How Food Profiteers Victimize the Consumer.* New York: Vintage Books/Random House.

———. 1989. "'I Do Not Choose To Run': Raising Issues, Hope and Hell." *Nation,* 6 February.

Hill, Anita. 1991. Statement during Senate Judiciary Committee hearing, 11 October.

———. 1995. "Race and Gender Issues of the 1990s." Keynote address, YWCA's Tribute to Women, South Bend, Indiana, 21 March.

Hochman, Steve. 1990. "South Africa's Clegg Has a Song of Change." *Los Angeles Times,* 23 May.

Hoff-Wilson, Joan, and Marjorie Lightman, eds. 1984. *Without Precedent: The Life and Career of Eleanor Roosevelt.* Bloomington: Indiana University Press.

Hoffman, Banesh. 1972. *Albert Einstein: Creator and Rebel.* New York: New American Library.

Hollis, Yvette Walker. 1992. "A Legacy of Loving." *New People,* summer, special commemorative section.

"Holocaust Defender." 1994. *Toronto Globe & Mail,* 18 October.

Holt, Rackham. 1944. *George Washington Carver: An American Biography.* Garden City, NY: Doubleday, Doran and Company.

———. 1964. *Mary McLeod Bethune: A Biography.* Garden City, NY: Doubleday.

Horton, Myles, and Paulo Freire. 1990. *We Make the Road by Walking: Conversations on Education and Social Change.* Philadelphia: Temple University Press.

Horton, Myles, with Judith Kohl and Herbert Kohl. 1990. *The Long Haul: An Autobiography.* New York: Doubleday.

Hulbert, Dan. 1989. "Storyteller Brings Civil Rights History to Life through Tales of 'Junebug Jabbo Jones.'" *Atlanta Constitution,* 19 January.

Human Rights Watch. 1995. "Human Rights Watch Condemns Royal Dutch Shell's Failure To Speak Out against Human Rights Abuses in Nigeria." Press release, 16 November.

Hutcheon, Stephen. 1995. "The World Can Learn from Us, Says Suu Kyi." *Sydney Morning Herald,* 1 September.

Hutchison, Bill. 1992. "Rigoberta Menchu: A Light in Guatemala." *San Francisco Chronicle,* 3 December.

Huzinec, Mary, Maria Speidel, Rochelle Jones, and Sarah Skolnik. 1993. "Man of Grace and Glory." *People Weekly,* 22 February.

Hynes, H. Patricia. 1989. *The Recurring Silent Spring.* New York: Pergamon Press.

"Isn't This a Time?" 1994. Editorial. *Nation,* 26 December.

Irons, Peter. 1983. *Justice at War: The Story of the Japanese American Internment Cases.* New York: Oxford University Press.

Israel Information Service. 1994. Electronic posting of Rabin's acceptance speech. December.

"Isn't This a Time?" 1994. Editorial. *Nation,* 26 December.

Jackson, James O. 1992. "A Bold Peacemaker: Willy Brandt: 1913–1992." *Time,* 19 October.

Jackson, Jesse. 1988. *A Time To Speak: The Autobiography of the Reverend Jesse Jackson.* New York: Simon & Schuster.

Jakoubek, Robert. 1991. *Jesse Jackson*. New York: Chelsea House.

James, Edward T. 1936. *Notable American Women, 1607–1950*. Cambridge, MA: Harvard University Press.

Japenga, Ann. 1986. "Peace Pilgrim's Journey—'On Foot and in Faith.'" *Los Angeles Times*, 2 January.

Jayakar, Pupul. 1992. *Indira Gandhi: An Intimate Biography*. New York: Pantheon Books.

Jenkins, Sally. 1992. "Another Battle Joined." *Sports Illustrated*, 20 April.

Johnson, Geoffrey, Dale Eastman, and Gretchen Reynolds. 1995. "Seven Who Made a Difference." *Chicago*, January.

Jones, Arthur. 1994. "El Salvador Revisited." *National Catholic Reporter*, 23 September, special supplement.

Jordan, Barbara, and Shelby Hearon. 1979. *Barbara Jordan: A Self-Portrait*. New York: Doubleday.

Jordan, Mary. 1992. "Black Harvard Law Professor Files Discrimination Complaint against School." *Washington Post*, 3 March.

Joyce, Mike. 1994. "Miriam Makeba." *Washington Post*, 1 March.

Katz, William Loren. 1986. *Black Indians: A Hidden Heritage*. New York: Atheneum.

Kaufman, Burton I. 1993. *The Presidency of James Earl Carter, Jr.* Lawrence: University Press of Kansas.

Kelly, Geffrey B., and F. Burton Nelson, eds. 1990. *A Testament to Freedom: The Essential Writings of Dietrich Bonhoeffer*. San Francisco: Harper San Francisco.

Keneally, Thomas. 1982. *Schindler's List*. New York: Touchstone.

Kerr, Andy. 1994. "ONRC's Executive Director Outlines 100-Year Plan for State." *Oregonian*, 11 September.

Kevorkian, Jack. 1991. *Prescription: Medicide*. Buffalo, NY: Prometheus Books.

Kidder, Rushworth M. 1994. *Shared Values for a Troubled World: Conversations with Men and Women of Conscience*. San Francisco: Jossey-Bass.

King, Coretta Scott. 1993. *My Life with Martin Luther King, Jr.* Rev. ed. Original edition, 1969. New York: Henry Holt.

King, Martin Luther, Jr. 1958. *Stride toward Freedom: The Montgomery Story*. New York: Harper & Row.

———. 1963. *Strength To Love*. New York: Harper & Row.

Knoll, Erwin. 1994. "'Put Away Your Flags.'" *Progressive*, April.

Koberstein, Paul. 1990. "Spokane Doctor Wages Own War of the Woods." *Oregonian*, 17 September.

Kochersberger, Robert C., Jr., ed. 1994. *More than a Muckraker: Ida Tarbell's Lifetime in Journalism*. Knoxville: University of Tennessee Press.

Koenenn, Connie. 1993. "Awards for Aid at the Grass Roots." *Los Angeles Times*, 19 April.

Komisar, Lucy. 1987. *Corazon Aquino: The Story of a Revolution*. New York: G. Braziller.

Kovic, Ron. 1976. *Born on the Fourth of July*. New York: McGraw-Hill.

Kovic, Ron, and Robert Scheer. 1995. "McNamara Still Owes Vets a Debt." *Los Angeles Times*, 23 April, Opinion section.

Kraft, Scott. 1989. "Slain Apartheid Foe Mourned in Protest March." *Los Angeles Times*, 7 May.

Kriseová, Eda. 1993. *Václav Havel: The Authorized Biography*. Translated by Caleb Crain. New York: St. Martin's Press.

Kuhn, Maggie, with Christina Long and Laura Quinn. 1991. *No Stone Unturned: The Life and Times of Maggie Kuhn*. New York: Ballantine Books.

Kupferberg, Tuli, and Robert Bashlow. 1967. *1001 Ways To Beat the Draft*. New York: Grove Press.

Kutzner, Patricia L. 1991. *World Hunger*. Santa Barbara, CA: ABC-CLIO.

Laatz, Joan. 1995. "Kerr, Fellow Activist Arrested." *Oregonian*, 28 March.

Landau, Susan. 1996. "Joseph Rotblat: The Road Less Traveled." *Bulletin of the Atomic Scientists*, January/February.

Laogai home page. http://www.christusrex.org/www1/sdc/laogai.html.

Lardner, George, Jr., and Nora Boustany. 1991. "Waite Worked Closely with North on Hostages." *Washington Post*, 19 November.

Lash, Joseph P. 1972. *Eleanor: The Years Alone*. New York: W. W. Norton.

———. 1982. *Love, Eleanor: Eleanor Roosevelt and Her Friends*. New York: Doubleday.

———. 1984. *A World of Love: Eleanor Roosevelt and Her Friends, 1943–1962*. New York: Doubleday.

Laszewski, Charles. 1995. "Hill's Land Deals Unlawful, Environmentalists Say." *St. Paul Pioneer Press*, 26 May.

Le Joly, Edward. 1985. *Mother Teresa of Calcutta: A Biography*. San Francisco: Harper & Row.

"Learning from Mr. Rushdie." 1993. Editorial. *Washington Post*, 14 February.

Leavy, Jane. 1986. "The Restless Witness." *Washington Post*, 15 October.

Lerner, Gerda. 1973. *Black Women in White America: A Documentary History*. New York: Vintage Books.

Lerner, Max. 1994. *Nine Scorpions in a Bottle: Great Judges, Great Cases of the Supreme Court*. New York: Arcade Publishing.

Levy, Elizabeth. 1975. *By-Lines: Profiles in Investigative Journalism*. New York: Four Winds Press.

Levy, Jacque E. 1975. *Cesar Chavez*. New York: W. W. Norton.

Lewis, Nancy, and Lyle V. Harris. 1995. "Two Women Cited as 'American Heroes' by President." *Washington Post*, 7 February.

Lewis, Randy. 1993. "Clegg Faces Up to the Pain of Life." *Los Angeles Times*, 12 August.

Lewis, Robert, ed. 1993. *The Best of Rolling Stone: 25 Years of Journalism on the Edge*. New York: Doubleday.

Lindelof, Bill. 1995. "Japanese Couple Saved Jews in WWII." *Sacramento Bee*, 23 January.

Linn, James Weber. 1968. *Jane Addams: A Biography*. New York: Greenwood Press.

Lippman, Thomas W. 1989. *Egypt after Nasser: Sadat, Peace and the Mirage of Prosperity*. New York: Paragon House.

Lipscomb, Elizabeth Johnsonton, ed. 1994. *The Several Worlds of Pearl S. Buck: Essays Presented at a Centennial Symposium, Randolph-Macon Woman's College, March 26–28, 1992*. Westport, CT: Greenwood Press.

Lockwood, Lee. 1993. "Still Radical after All These Years." *Mother Jones*, September/October.

Long, Priscilla. 1976. *Mother Jones: Woman Organizer*. Boston: South End Press.

Looney, Douglas S. 1990. "Hard Man, Soft Heart: Notre Dame's Chris Zorich Is Mean on the Football Field, but He Is a Gentle Soul Elsewhere." *Sports Illustrated*, 1 October.

Love, Robert, ed. 1993. *The Best of Rolling Stone: 25 Years of Journalism on the Edge*. New York: Doubleday.

Lyon, Peter. 1963. *Success Story: The Life and Times of S. S. McClure*. New York: Charles Scribner's Sons.

McCallum, John D. 1975. *The Encyclopedia of World Boxing Champions*. Radnor, PA: Chilton Book Company.

McCarry, Charles. 1972. *Citizen Nader*. New York: Signet.

McCarthy, Colman. 1990. "Mitch Snyder." *Nation*, 30 July.

McCarthy, Tim. 1993. "Light of Day Shines Yet at Catholic Worker." *National Catholic Reporter*, 21 May.

McCloskey, James. 1996. "Reopen the Case of Geronimo Pratt." *Los Angeles Times*, 2 January.

McGrath, Peter. 1995. "An Indispensable Man." *Newsweek*, 13 November.

McMurry, Linda O. 1981. *George Washington Carver, Scientist and Symbol*. New York: Oxford University Press.

McNulty, Timothy. 1994. "Jail Time Still Doesn't Deter Philip Berrigan." *Chicago Tribune*, 20 June.

McQuilken, Robert. 1983. "Making a Legend Indelible." *Runner's World*, April.

McVay, Ken. Ken McVay home page. http://nizkor.almanac.bc.ca/kmcvay/index.html.

Magagnini, Stephen. 1994. "Belated Honors Sought for 'Samurai Schindler' of WWII." *Sacramento Bee*, 11 September.

Mailer, Norman. 1975. *The Fight*. Boston: Little, Brown.

Makeba, Miriam, with James Hall. 1987. *Makeba: My Story*. New York: New American Library, Penguin.

Malhotra, Inder. 1989. *Indira Gandhi: A Personal and Political Biography*. Boston: Northeastern University Press.

Malone, Kenny. 1944. "Do You Want To Lose Your Voice?" *The Searchlight*, 20 January.

Mandela, Nelson. 1994. *Long Walk to Freedom*. Boston: Little, Brown.

Mandela, Winnie, Anne Benjamin, and Mary Benson. 1985. *Part of My Soul Went with Him*. New York: W. W. Norton.

Mankiller, Wilma, and Michael Wallis. 1993. *Mankiller, a Chief and Her People*. New York: St. Martin's Press.

Mann, Peggy. 1971. *Golda: The Life of Israel's Prime Minister*. New York: Coward, McCann & Geoghegan.

Manning, Anita. 1995. "Rachel Carson's Letters Speak Volumes of Love and Nature." *USA Today*, 22 March.

Margolick, David. 1992. "A Mixed Marriage's 25th Anniversary of Legality." *New York Times*, 12 June.

Marsh, Clinton. 1995. "A Reflection on My Life." Edited by Murphy Davis. *Hospitality*, January/February.

Martin, Ralph G. 1988. *Golda, Golda Meir: The Romantic Years*. New York: Charles Scribner's Sons.

Martinez, Jose. 1995. "Chinese Dissident Concentrates on Her Business Career in U.S." Associated Press, 10 July.

Marton, Kati. 1995. "The Liquidation of Raoul Wallenberg." *Washington Post*, 22 January.

Mathews, Jay, 1989. "The Dalai Lama's Call for Kindness." *Washington Post*, 6 October.

Mauro, Tony. 1994. "Mom Sues over Prayer at School." *USA Today*, 21 December.

May, Eric Charles. 1990. "19 Arrested Protesting Gulf Action." *Washington Post*, 31 December.

Mayer, Jane, and Jill Abramson. 1994. *Strange Justice*. Boston: Houghton Mifflin.

Meer, Fatima. 1990. *Higher than Hope: The Authorized Biography of Nelson Mandela*. London: H. Hamilton, 1988. Reprint, New York: Harper & Row.

Meir, Golda. 1973. *A Land of Our Own: An Oral Autobiography*. Edited by Marie Syrkin. New York: G. P. Putnam's Sons.

————. 1975. *My Life*. New York: G. P. Putnam's Sons.

Meir, Menahem. 1983. *My Mother Golda Meir: A Son's Evocation of Life with Golda Meir*. New York: Arbor House.

Menchu, Rigoberta. 1984. *I, Rigoberta Menchu: An Indian Woman in Guatemala*. Edited by Elisabeth Burgon-Debray and translated by Ann Wright. New York: Verso.

Meyer, Ernest L. 1930. *Hey! Yellowbacks: The War Diary of a Conscientious Objector*. New York: John Day.

Meyer, Gerald. 1989. *Vito Marcantonio: Radical Politician 1902–1954*. Albany: State University of New York Press.

Miller, Mark. 1993. "The Real Schindler." *Newsweek*, 20 December.

"The 'Miracle' of Ryan White." 1990. *Time*, 23 April.

Moffett, George. 1995. "Tibet's 'God-King' Tours US in Stoic Quest for Self-Rule." *Christian Science Monitor*, 13 September.

Montalbano, William D. 1995. "Anti-Nuclear Scientists Win Nobel for Peace." *Los Angeles Times*, 14 October.

Montgomery, Peter. 1995. "Mississippi Mother Stands Strong." *People for the American Way News*, spring.

Moore, Howard. 1993. *Plowing My Own Furrow*. Syracuse, NY: Syracuse University Press.

Moore, Kenny. 1992. "The Eternal Example." *Sports Illustrated*, 21 December.

Moorehead, Caroline. 1993. *Bertrand Russell: A Life*. New York: Viking Press.

Moraes, Dom. 1980. *Indira Gandhi*. Boston: Little Brown.

Morain, Dan. 1988. "Ex-General Ordered Argentine Writer's Arrest." *Los Angeles Times*, 8 May.

Morais, Fernando. 1990. *Olga*. Translated by Ellen Watson. New York: Grove Weidenfeld.

Motavalli, Jim. 1995. "Jim Hightower" (interview). *E Magazine*, January/February.

Mowat, Farley. 1987. *Woman in the Mists: The Story of Dian Fossey and the Mountain Gorillas of Africa*. New York: Warner Books.

Moyniham, Marua. 1989. "Tibet's Agony: Nobel Prize, Ignoble Story." *New Republic*, 20 November.

Murrow, Edward R. 1967. *In Search of Light: The Broadcasts of Edward R. Murrow, 1938–1961*. Edited by Edward Bliss, Jr. New York: Alfred A. Knopf.

Musick, Phil. 1974. *Who Was Roberto: A Biography of Roberto Clemente*. New York: Doubleday.

Nadel, Laurie. 1987. *Corazon Aquino: Journey to Power*. New York: Julian Messner.

Nasrin, Taslima. 1994. Speech given at the International Student Festival (ISFIT-94), Trondheim, Norway.

National Baseball Hall of Fame Staff and Gerald Aastor. 1990. *The Baseball Hall of Fame Fiftieth Anniversary Book*. Englewood Cliffs, NJ: Prentice-Hall.

Nelson, Jill. 1992. "Anita Hill: No Regrets." *Essence*, March.

"Nelson Mandela: From Prisoner to President." 1994. *Ebony*, August (special issue).

"The New Face of America." 1993. *Time*, fall (special issue).

Newman, Bruce. 1992. "Pain and Progress." *Sports Illustrated*, 6 July.

Nickerson, Colin. 1993. "Japan Rehabilitates Diplomat Who Saved 6,000 Jews." *Seattle Times*, 3 January.

Nickson, Liz. 1988. "The Dalai Lama." *Life*, June.

Nifong, Christian. 1994. "Making Human Rights Come Alive." *Christian Science Monitor*, 13 December.

No Collective, ed. 1992. *Voices of Identity, Rage and Deliverance: An Anthology of Writings by People of Mixed Descent*. Oakland, CA: No Press.

O'Brien, Jim. 1994. *Remember Roberto: Clemente Recalled by Teammates, Friends and Fans.* Pittsburgh: J. P. O'Brien.

Ocean, Charles E. 1990. "Mitch Snyder Saved Many Lives but Finally Took His Own." *People Weekly*, 23 July.

Ocean, Tom. 1969. *Three Who Dared.* New York: Doubleday.

O'Malley, Kathy. 1995. "Gentle Giant Bears Lineman Chris Zorich Honored at Gold and Silver Ball." *Chicago Tribune*, 4 October, Tempo section.

Otfinoski, Steven. 1989. *Jesse Jackson: A Voice for Change.* New York: Fawcett Columbine.

Ottaway, David B. 1990. "Makeba, Out of Exile." *Washington Post*, 11 June.

Owuor, George. 1995. "Africa's Democrats Need Help." *Christian Science Monitor*, 21 November.

Pacheco, Ferdie. 1992. *Muhammad Ali: A View from the Corner.* New York: Birch Lane Press, Carol Publishing Group.

Paldiel, Mordecai. 1990. "Schindler, Oskar." *Encyclopedia of the Holocaust.* Edited by Israel Gutman. New York: Macmillan.

"Palermo Back in Baseball." 1994. *Houston Post*, 7 April, Sports section.

Parkman, Patricia. 1988. *Nonviolent Insurrection in El Salvador.* Tucson: University of Arizona Press.

Parks, Rosa, and James Haskins. 1992. *Rosa Parks: My Story.* New York: Dial Books.

Parks, Rosa, with Gregory J. Reed. 1994. *Quiet Strength.* Grand Rapids, MI: Zondervan Publishing House.

Parton, Mary Field, ed. 1980. *The Autobiography of Mother Jones.* Chicago: Charles H. Kerr.

Paterson, Lillie. 1989. *Martin Luther King, Jr., and the Freedom Movement.* New York: Facts on File.

Pauling, Linus. 1953. *No More War!* New York: Dodd, Mead.

"Peace Pilgrim." 1994. *Backpacker*, September.

Peale, Norman Vincent, ed. 1972. *The Guideposts Pocket Book of Inspiration.* Carmel, NY: Guideposts Associates.

Peare, Owen. 1951. *Mary McLeod Bethune.* New York: Vanguard Press.

Pearson, Richard. 1990. "AIDS Patient Ryan White Dies." *Washington Post*, 9 April.
———. 1996. Obituary (Barbara Jordan). *Washington Post*, 18 January, A1.

Peavy, Linda, and Ursula Smith. 1983. *Women Who Changed Things.* New York: Charles Scribner's Sons.

Peduzzi, Kelli. 1990. *Ralph Nader.* Milwaukee, WI: Gareth Stevens Children's Books.

"People Expect Me To Be More Warlike." 1986. *U.S. News & World Report*, 17 February.

Peterson, Susan. 1993. "Now Lawyers Face Suits over Implant Cases." *Orange County Register*, 20 May, Focus on Health section.

Pezzula, Tara. 1995. "Iqbal." *Poems for a Lost Friend.* http://www.digitalrag.com/mirror/iqbal/Poems.

Pope, Brock. 1993. "Anita Roddick." *People Weekly.* 10 May.

Porter, David. 1986. *Mother Teresa, the Early Years.* Grand Rapids, MI: William B. Eerdmans.

"Portraits of Leadership: Great African Americans in the Struggle for Freedom." 1994. *Black Collegian*, January/February.

Press, Robert M. 1990. "Kenyan President on Dubious Course." *Oregonian*, 30 January.

Pressley, Sue Anne. 1995. "Speedy Justice Can Be Dead Wrong, Texas Case Shows." *Los Angeles Times*, 19 February.

Pryne, Eric. 1994. "Could the Federal Government Take Back 1864 Land Grant?" *Seattle Times*, 13 November.

Rabin, Yitzhak. 1979. *The Rabin Memoirs*. Boston: Little, Brown.

———. 1995. "Yitzhak Rabin's Last Speech." Electronic posting. http//www.arlga. com/index.htm. 4 November

Randall, Mercedes M. 1964. *Improper Bostonian: Emily Greene Balch*. New York: Twayne Publishers.

Rashke, Richard. 1981. *The Killing of Karen Silkwood*. Boston: Houghton Mifflin.

Rasmussen, Larry, and Renate Bethge. 1989. *Dietrich Bonhoeffer: His Significance for North Americans*. Philadelphia: Augsburg Fortress.

"The Real Lesson of the Rockwood Case." 1995. Editorial. *Los Angeles Times*, 16 May.

Reardon, Patrick T. 1990. "Protestant Pastor Bonhoeffer's Life Has Tough Message for All." *Chicago Tribune*, 24 November.

Reed, Susan. 1989. "Arthur Ashe Remembers the Forgotten Men of Sport—America's Early Black Athletes" (interview). *People Weekly*, 6 March.

———. 1995. "Survivors in the Mist: Threats to Last Surviving Mountain Gorillas in Rwanda." *People Weekly*, 6 March.

Reuters. 1990. "Activists Dump Dye in White House Fountain." *Los Angeles Times*, 31 December.

———. 1995. "Gingrich Voucher Remark Is Called 'Nuts.'" *Washington Post*, 19 June.

Riehm, Rebecca. 1995. "US Army Officer on Trial for Defending Haitian Human Rights." Peace Media Service electronic conference posting (peacemedia.news), 10 May.

Risen, James. 1995. "Dismissal of Army Captain Raises U.S. Policy Questions." *Los Angeles Times*, 15 May.

"The Road from Rio." 1993. *Technology Review*, April.

Robertson, Edwin. 1988. *Shame and Sacrifice: The Life and Martyrdom of Dietrich Bonhoeffer*. New York: Macmillan.

Robeson, Paul. 1971. *Here I Stand*. New York: Othello Associates, 1958. Reprint, Boston: Beacon Press.

Robinson, Eugene. 1993. "A Page Out of a Hostage's Life." *Washington Post*, 23 September.

Roddick, Anita. 1991. *Body and Soul: Profits with Principles—The Amazing Success Story of Anita Roddick and the Body Shop*. New York: Crown Publishers.

———. 1994. "Corporate Responsibility." *Vital Speeches*, 15 January.

Rodriquez, Consuelo. 1991. *Cesar Chavez*. New York: Chelsea House.

Rogers, Teresa. 1992. *George Washington Carver: Nature's Trailblazer*. Frederick, MD: Twenty-First Century Books.

Rohrlich, Ted. 1990. "Minister of Justice for the Wrongly Convicted." *Los Angeles Times Magazine*, 23 December.

Rolland, Romain. 1924. *Mahatma Gandhi: The Man Who Became One with the Universal Being*. New York: Century.

Roosevelt, Eleanor. 1949. *This I Remember*. New York: Harper & Brothers.

———. 1958. *On My Own*. New York: Harper & Brothers.

Root, Maria P. P., ed. 1992. *Racially Mixed People in America*. Newbury Park, CA: Sage Publications.

Rosellini, Lynn. 1990. "The Days of a Holy Man." *U.S. News & World Report*, 29 October.

Ross, Ishbel. 1956. *Angel of the Battlefield: The Life of Clara Barton*. New York: Harper & Brothers.

Rotblat, Joseph. 1972. *Scientists in the Quest for Peace*. Cambridge, MA: MIT Press.

Rothe, Ann, ed. 1945. *Current Biography: Who's News and Why 1944*. New York: H. W. Wilson.

Rowe, Jonathan. 1989. "Ralph Nader Reconsidered." *Washington Monthly*, February.

Russell, Bertrand. 1967–1969. *The Autobiography of Bertrand Russell*. 3 vols. Boston: Little, Brown.

Ryan, Alan. 1988. *Bertrand Russell: A Political Life*. New York: Hill and Wang.

Sadat, Anwar. 1957. *Revolt on the Nile*. New York: John Day.

———. 1977. *In Search of Identity*. New York: Harper & Row.

———. 1984. *Those I Have Known*. New York: Continuum.

Sadat, Camelia. 1985. *My Father and I*. New York: Macmillan.

Sakharov, Andrei. 1990. *Memoirs*. New York: Alfred A. Knopf.

Sanz, Cynthia. 1994. "A League of His Own: Roberto Clemente Jr. Builds on His Father's Legacy with an Ambitious Inner-City Baseball Program." *People Weekly*, 6 June.

———. 1995. "Rebel with a Cause: Human-Rights Gadfly Harry Wu Vows He Won't Stop Blasting China's Abuses." *People Weekly*, 11 September.

Saro-Wiwa, Ken. 1992. *Genocide in Nigeria: The Ogoni Tragedy*. Port Harcourt, Nigeria: Saros.

———. 1995. Statement before the military tribunal. Electronic posting. 12 November. http://www.the-body-shop.com/kenalert.html.

Sawaya, Francesca. 1994. "Domesticity, Cultivation, and Vocation in Jane Addams and Sarah Orne Jewett." *Nineteenth-Century Literature*, March.

Sayer, Jamie. 1985. *Einstein in America*. New York: Crown Publishers.

Scariano, Margaret. 1987. *The Picture Life of Corazon Aquino*. New York: Franklin Watts.

Scheer, Ron. 1994. "Archbishop Desmond Tutu: Peacemaker in a Diverse Nation." *Christian Science Monitor*, 26 October.

Scheibal, Steve. 1995. "Foundation To Continue Work of Amy Biehl." *Los Angeles Times*, 19 March.

Schickel, Richard. 1993. "Heart of Darkness." *Time*, 13 December.

Schlesinger, Arthur M., Jr. 1990. "The Difference Willy Brandt Has Made. *New Leader*, 29 October.

Schmetzer, Uli. 1986. "Wiesel Accepts Nobel Prize." *Washington Post*, 11 December.

Schneider, Paul. 1991. "Other People's Trash." *Audubon*, July/August.

Schneiderman, Rose, with Lucy Goldthwaite. 1967. *All for One*. New York: Paul S. Eriksson.

Schorr, Daniel. 1993. "Frank Zappa: A Maverick Pied Piper." *Los Angeles Times*, 7 December.

Schroeder, Steven. 1994. "Toward a Higher Identity: An Interview with Mairead Corrigan Maguire." *Christian Century*, 20 April.

Schulke, Flip, and Penelope O. McPhee. 1986. *King Remembered*. New York: W. W. Norton.

Schulz, William F. 1995. "The US Ignores Africa at Its Own Peril." *Christian Science Monitor*, 6 November.

Schuman, Michael. 1994. *Elie Wiesel: Voice from the Holocaust*. Hillside, NJ: Enslow Publishers.

Schuyler, Ed, Jr. 1992. "Muhammad Ali Turns 50." *South Bend Tribune*, 12 January.

Schweitzer, Albert. 1933. *Out of My Life and Thought*. Translated by Charles T. Campion. New York: Henry Holt.

Sciolino, Elaine. 1995. "Harry Wu: China's Prisons Forged Zeal of U.S. Crusader." *New York Times*, 10 July.

Seeger, Pete. 1973. *Henscratches and Flyspecks: How To Read Melodies from Songbooks in Twelve Confusing Lessons*. New York: G. P. Putnam's Sons.

Segrest, Mab. 1994. *Memoir of a Race Traitor*. Boston: South End Press.

Serafini, Anthony. 1989. *Linus Pauling: A Man and His Science*. New York: Paragon House.

SerVass, Cory. 1987. "A Time for Forgiveness." *Saturday Evening Post*, November.

———. 1988. "The Happier Days for Ryan White." *Saturday Evening Post*, March.

Shapiro, Bruce. 1995. "Corliss and Maggie." *Nation*, 29 May.

Shioya, Tara. 1994. "Tribute to Japanese 'Schindler.'" *San Francisco Chronicle*, 18 August.

Shulman, Alix. 1972. *Red Emma Speaks: Selected Writings and Speeches by Emma Goldman*. New York: Random House.

Sicherman, Barbara, and Carol Hurd Green, eds. 1980. *Notable American Women: The Modern Period*. Cambridge, MA: Belknap Press.

Siegel, Beatrice. 1988. *Cory: Corazon Aquino and the Philippines*. New York: Dutton.

Silver, Eric. 1992. *The Book of the Just: The Unsung Heroes Who Rescued Jews from Hitler*. New York: Grove Press.

Simons, Donald L. 1992. *I Refuse: Memories of a Vietnam War Objector*. Trenton, NJ: Broken Rifle Press.

Slater, Robert. 1981. *Golda, the Uncrowned Queen of Israel: A Pictoral Biography*. Middle Village, NY: J. David.

———. 1993. *Rabin of Israel*. New York: St. Martin's Press.

Sleeth, Peter, and Richard Cockle. 1994. "Anti-Environmentalist Feelings Hurt Wallowa County Neighbors." *Oregonian*, 21 October.

Smith, Gary. 1988. "Peace Warriors. *Washington Post Magazine*, 5 June, W22.

Smith, Jessie Carney. 1992. *Notable Black American Women*. Detroit, MI: Gale Research.

Smith, S. Stratton. 1965. *The Rebel Nun*. Springfield, IL: Templegate.

Sobrino, Jon. 1990. *Archbishop Romero: Memories and Reflections*. Translated by Robert R. Barr. Maryknoll, NY: Orbis Books.

Solomon, Martha. 1987. *Emma Goldman*. Boston: Twayne, Macmillan.

Soosaipillai, Miruni. 1993. "Dear Amy . . . My Unstoppable Friend, Slain in South Africa." *Washington Post*, 5 September.

Spayde, Jon. 1995. "100 Visionaries." *Utne Reader*, January-February.

Sperber, A. M. 1986. *Murrow: His Life and Times*. New York: Freundlich Books.

Spilken, Aron. 1983. *Escape*. New York: New American Library.

Spink, Kathryn. 1981. *The Miracle of Love: Mother Teresa of Calcutta, Her Missionaries of Charity, and Her Co-Workers*. San Francisco: Harper & Row.

"Spreading Saint Ralph's Gospel." 1990. *Economist*, 17 November.

Steadman, John. 1993. "In the Game of Life, Former Umpire Palermo Has Been Called Out To Inspire Others. *Baltimore Evening Sun*, 30 April, Sports section.

Stein, Leon. 1962. *The Triangle Fire*. New York: J. B. Lippincott.

Stengel, Richard. 1994. "The Making of a Leader." *Time*, 9 May.

Sterling, Nora B. 1983. *Pearl Buck, a Woman in Conflict*. Piscataway, NJ: New Century Publishers.

Straub, Deborah Gillan, ed. 1992. *Contemporary Heroes and Heroines, Book II*. Detroit, MI: Gale Research.

Strauss, Valerie. 1992. "'A Simple Buddhist Monk.'" *Washington Post*, 30 April.

Strum, Philippa. 1993. *Brandeis: Beyond Progressivism*. Lawrence: University Press of Kansas.

Stucky, Mark D. 1994. "Put Schindler's on Your To-Do List." *Integra*, February.

Suitts, Steve. 1990. "Liberating Selma." *Philadelphia Inquirer*, 29 July, Features View.

Syrkin, Marie. 1963. *Golda Meir: Woman with a Cause*. New York: Putnam.

Taylor, Ronald. 1975. *Chavez and the Farm Workers*. Boston: Beacon Press.

Taylor, Ronald B. 1985. "Texas' New-Style Africulture Commissioner." *Los Angeles Times*, 19 December.

Tempest, Rone. 1994. "Chinese Activists Trade Dreams of '89 for Careers." *Los Angeles Times*, 2 June.

Teresa, Mother. 1987. *Heart of Joy*. Ann Arbor, MI: Servant Books.

Teresa, Mother, Jose Luis Gonzalez-Balado, and Janet N. Playfoot. 1985. *My Life for the Poor*. San Francisco: Harper & Row.

ten Boom, Corrie. 1977. *He Sets the Captives Free*. Old Tappan, NJ: Fleming H. Ravell.

Teuber, Suzanne S., Robert L. Saunders, Georges M. Halpern, Robert F. Brucker, Victor Conte, Brian D. Goldman, Ed E. Winger, W. Graham Wood, and M. Eric Gershwin. 1995. "Elevated Serum Silicon Levels in Women with Silicone Gel Breast Implants." *Biological Trace Element Research*, March.

Thomas, Norman. 1923. *The Conscientious Objector in America*. New York: B. W. Huebsch.

Thomas, R. L., dir. 1982. "The Terry Fox Story." Home Box Office.

Thompson, Mildred I. 1990. *Ida B. Wells-Barnett: An Exploratory Study of an American Black Woman, 1893–1930*. Brooklyn, NY: Carlson Publishing.

Tierney, Kevin. 1979. *Darrow: A Biography*. New York: Thomas Y. Crowell.

Timerman, Jacobo. 1981. *Prisoner without a Name, Cell without a Number*. Translated by Toby Talbot. New York: Alfred A. Knopf.

Tims, Margaret. 1961. *Jane Addams of Hull House, 1860–1935*. New York: Macmillan.

Titone, Julie. 1991. "Suffering the Enviro-Doc." *American Forests,* September/October.

"The Trials of Harry Wu." 1995. *U.S. News & World Report*, 11 September.

Trueheart, Charles. 1990. "Publisher in the Fray." *Washington Post*, 20 March.

Truman, Margaret. 1976. *Women of Courage*. New York: William Morrow.

Tula, Maria Teresa. 1994. *Hear My Testimony: Maria Teresa Tula, Human Rights Activist of El Salvador*. Translated and edited by Lynn Stephen. Boston: South End Press.

"Tutu Supports Gay Priests." 1995. *Cape Times*, 2 December.

Tuteishi, John. 1984. And Justice for All: An Oral History of the Japanese American Detention Camps. New York: Random House.

"Two in South Africa Charged in Killing." 1993. *Washington Post*, 27 August.

Tygiel, Jules. 1983. *Baseball's Great Experiment: Jackie Robinson and His Legacy*. New York: Oxford University Press.

Uglow, Jennifer S., comp. and ed. 1989. *The Continuum Dictionary of Women's Biography*. New York: Continuum.

"An Ump on Deck." 1995. *Sports Illustrated*, 27 February.

Urofsky, Melvin I. 1981. *Louis D. Brandeis and the Progressive Tradition*. Boston: Little, Brown.

Urquhart, Brian. 1993. *Ralph Bunche: An American Life*. New York: W. W. Norton.

Valk, Elizabeth P. 1990. "People's Report on AIDS Victim Ryan White." *People Weekly*, 23 April.

Vollers, Maryanne. 1995. *Ghosts of Mississippi: The Murder of Medgar Evers, the Trials of Byron De La Beckwith, and the Haunting of the New South*. Boston: Little, Brown.

Vonier, Sprague. 1989. *Edward R. Murrow*. Milwaukee, WI: Gareth Stevens Children's Books.

Wackerman, Daniel T. 1995. "Mind's Eye" (interview). *America*, 18 March.

Waite, Terry. 1993. *Taken on Trust*. New York: Harcourt Brace.

Walesa, Lech. 1987. *A Way of Hope: An Autobiography*. New York: Henry Holt.

———. 1992. *The Struggle and the Triumph: An Autobiography*. New York: Arcade Publishing.

Wallace, Bruce, 1995. "High above It All: How War Brought Peace to Rwanda's Gorillas." *Maclean's*, 6 February.

Wallenberg, Raoul. 1995. *Letters and Dispatches 1924–1944*. Translated by Kjersti Board. New York: Arcade Publishing.

Waller, Douglas. 1994. "Tailhook's 'Lightning Rod.'" *Newsweek*, 28 February.

Walsh, James. 1994. "Death to the Author." *Time*, 15 August.

Walsh, Pamela M. 1995. "Slain Pakistani Child Crusader Honored." *Boston Globe*, 30 April.

Warren, Spencer. 1990. "Wallenberg—A Major Test of Glasnost." *Christian Science Monitor*, 22 May.

Watanabe, Teresa. 1994. "Japanese Consul Who Saved Thousands of Polish Jews." *San Francisco Chronicle*, 21 March.

Watkins, T. H. 1990. "The Laughing Prophet of Bald Mountain." *Orion*, winter.

Weil, Martin, and Stephanie Griffith. 1993. "Marshall Transformed Nation in the Courts." *Washington Post*, 25 January.

Wells, Ida B. 1970. *Crusade for Justice: The Autobiography of Ida B. Wells*. Edited by Alfreda M. Duster. Chicago: University of Chicago Press.

Werbell, Frederick E., and Thurston Clarke. 1982. *Lost Hero: The Mystery of Raoul Wallenberg*. New York: McGraw-Hill.

"When Prayer Offends Believers." 1994. Editorial. *Atlanta Constitution*, 28 December.

White, Ryan, and Ann M. Cunningham. 1991. *Ryan White: My Own Story*. New York: Dial Press.

Whitelaw, Nancy. 1994. *They Wrote Their Own Headlines: American Women Journalists*. Greensboro, NC: Morgan Reynolds.

Whiteside, Larry. 1994. "Flood's Gates Opened It Up." *Boston Globe*, 8 November, Sports section.

Whitman, Alden, ed. 1985. *American Reformers*. New York: H. W. Wilson.

Whittemore, Hank. 1992. "'I Fight for Our Future.'" *Parade Magazine*, 12 April.

Wiesel, Elie. 1960. *Night*. Translated by Stella Rodway. Les Editions de Minuit, 1958. Reprint, New York: Bantam Books/Doubleday.

———. 1970. *One Generation After*. New York: Random House.

———. 1978. *A Jew Today*. New York: Random House.

———. 1988. *Twilight*. New York: Summit Books.

———. 1990. *From the Kingdom of Memory: Reminiscences*. New York: Summit Books.

Wigginton, Eliot, ed. 1991. *Refuse To Stand Silently By: An Oral History of Grass Roots Social Activism in America, 1921–1964*. New York: Doubleday.

Wiley, Jean. 1990. "On the Front Lines." *Essence*, February.

Will, George F. 1993. "A Baseball Lesson in Freedom." *Washington Post*, 21 November.

Williams, Juan. 1987. *Eyes on the Prize: America's Civil Rights Years, 1954–1965* (companion volume to the PBS television series). New York: Viking Penguin.

———. 1993. "Marshall's Plan: Prod the Living." *Washington Post*, 30 May.

Wind, Renate. 1992. *Dietrich Bonhoeffer: A Spoke in the Wheel*. Grand Rapids, MI: William B. Eerdmans.

Witney, Sharon. 1982. *Eleanor Roosevelt*. New York: Franklin Watts.

Womer, Kelly. 1995. "Zorich Gives Mom Credit for His Spirit of Sharing." *Chicago Tribune*, 7 November.

Woods, Donald. 1987. *Biko*. New York: Henry Holt.

Wooten, Jim. 1995. "Meddler, Moralist or Peacemaker?" *New York Times Magazine*, 29 January.

Wright, Lawrence. 1993. *Saints and Sinners*. New York: Alfred A. Knopf.

Wu, Harry, with Carolyn Wakeman. 1994. *Bitter Winds: A Memoir of My Years in China's Gulag*. New York: John Wiley and Sons.

Wulf, Steve. 1994. "Roberto Clemente." *Sports Illustrated*, 19 September.

Yardley, Jim. 1995. "School Prayer Standoff." *Atlanta Constitution*, 12 February.

Zahn, Gordon. 1968. *In Solitary Witness: The Life and Death of Franz Jügerstütter*. Boston: Beacon Press.

Zappa, Frank, with Peter Occhiogrosso. 1989. *The Real Frank Zappa Book*. New York: Poseidon Press.

Zaroulis, Nancy, and Gerald Sullivan. 1985. *Who Spoke Up? American Protest against the War in Vietnam 1963–1975*. New York: Henry Holt.

Zauber, Karen. 1992. Interview. *NEA Today*, 9 December.

INDEX